FREE SPEECH AND CENSORSHIP

Recent Titles in
Documentary and Reference Guides

Substance Abuse in America: A Documentary and Reference Guide
James A. Swartz

The Iraq War: A Documentary and Reference Guide
Thomas R. Mockaitis

Animal Rights and Welfare: A Documentary and Reference Guide
Lawrence W. Baker

Water Rights and the Environment in the United States: A Documentary and Reference Guide
John R. Burch Jr.

Endangered Species: A Documentary and Reference Guide
Edward P. Weber

9/11 and the War on Terror: A Documentary and Reference Guide
Paul J. Springer

Vaccination and Its Critics: A Documentary and Reference Guide
Lisa Rosner

Arab-Israeli Conflict: A Documentary and Reference Guide
Priscilla Roberts

Modern Slavery: A Documentary and Reference Guide
Laura J. Lederer

Poverty in the United States: A Documentary and Reference Guide
John R. Burch Jr.

Afghanistan War: A Documentary and Reference Guide
Ryan Wadle

Modern Genocide: A Documentary and Reference Guide
Paul R. Bartrop

Cyber Warfare: A Documentary and Reference Guide
Paul J. Springer

Attacks on the American Press: A Documentary and Reference Guide
Jessica Roberts and Adam Maksl

FREE SPEECH AND CENSORSHIP

A Documentary and Reference Guide

Cari Lee Skogberg Eastman

Documentary and Reference Guides

GREENWOOD

An Imprint of ABC-CLIO, LLC
Santa Barbara, California • Denver, Colorado

Library of Congress Cataloging-in-Publication Data

Names: Eastman, Cari Lee Skogberg, 1974- author.
Title: Free speech and censorship : a documentary and reference guide / Cari Lee Skogberg Eastman.
Description: Santa Barbara : Greenwood, An Imprint of ABC-CLIO, LLC, [2022] | Series: Documentary and reference guides | Includes bibliographical references and index.
Identifiers: LCCN 2021032130 (print) | LCCN 2021032131 (ebook) | ISBN 9781440865381 (hardcover) | ISBN 9781440865398 (ebook)
Subjects: LCSH: Freedom of speech—United States—History. | Censorship—United States—History. | Freedom of speech—United States—Public opinion. | United States—Politics and government.
Classification: LCC KF4772 .E33 2022 (print) | LCC KF4772 (ebook) | DDC 342.7308/53—dc23
LC record available at https://lccn.loc.gov/2021032130
LC ebook record available at https://lccn.loc.gov/2021032131

ISBN: 978-1-4408-6538-1 (print)
978-1-4408-6539-8 (ebook)

26 25 24 23 22 1 2 3 4 5

This book is also available as an eBook.

Greenwood
An Imprint of ABC-CLIO, LLC

ABC-CLIO, LLC
147 Castilian Drive
Santa Barbara, California 93117
www.abc-clio.com

This book is printed on acid-free paper ∞

Manufactured in the United States of America

CONTENTS

READER'S GUIDE TO RELATED DOCUMENTS

Free Speech and the Threat of Communism

Free Speech and Hollywood/Music Industry/the Arts

Free Speech Restrictions during War, Revolt, or National Security Threats

Free Speech and Political Protest/Government Limitations on Free Speech

Free Speech and Students

Freedom of the Press

Statement in Support of Freedom of the Press from Eighty Organizations "Committed to the First Amendment" (2017)

"Truth and Democracy" by Senator Jeff Flake of Arizona (2018)

Government Regulation of Communication/Government Transparency

Message from President Roosevelt to Congress Recommending Creation of a Federal Communications Commission (1934)

President Roosevelt Establishes the Office of Censorship (1941)

President Johnson's Statement upon Signing the Freedom of Information Act (1966)

Congressional Hearing on "Violent Video Games: What Parents Need to Know" (1993)

Cyberporn and Children: The Scope of the Problem, the State of the Technology, and the Need for Congressional Action (1996)

Ashcroft v. Free Speech Coalition Supreme Court Decision (2002)

Testimony of James E. Hansen on Science Censorship to Committee on Oversight and Government Reform (2007)

President Obama Calls for Increased Openness and Transparency in Government (2009)

The Committee to Protect Journalists Calls Trump "a Threat to Press Freedom" (2016)

Summary of "Allow States and Victims to Fight Online Sex Trafficking Act of 2017" (2018)

Statement in Support of Freedom of the Press from Eighty Organizations "Committed to the First Amendment" (2017)

Unprotected Speech: Obscenity/Indecency/Pornography

Anthony Comstock's "Vampire Literature" (1891)

Supreme Court's Majority Decision in *Roth v. United States* (1957)

Morality in Media Co-founder Condemns the Final Report of the Commission on Obscenity and Pornography (1970)

Supreme Court Majority Opinion in *Miller v. California* (1973)

Excerpts from *New York v. Ferber* Supreme Court Ruling (1982)

Cyberporn and Children: The Scope of the Problem, the State of the Technology, and the Need for Congressional Action (1996)

Ashcroft v. Free Speech Coalition Supreme Court Decision (2002)

Summary of "Allow States and Victims to Fight Online Sex Trafficking Act of 2017" (2018)

Unprotected Speech: Fighting Words and True Threats

Supreme Court's Majority Opinion in *Chaplinsky v. New Hampshire* (1942)

Syllabus from Supreme Court Case *Elonis v. United States* (2015)

Unprotected Speech: Incitement

Supreme Court's Majority Opinion in *Brandenburg v. Ohio* (1969)

Political Communication Regulations

Supreme Court ruling in *Citizens United v. Federal Election Commission* (2010)

PREFACE

"All tyranny needs to gain a foothold is for people of good conscience to remain silent."—Thomas Jefferson

When Thomas Jefferson and other founding fathers proposed a series of amendments to the U.S. Constitution, they argued the need to guarantee certain specific personal freedoms was so great that they were willing to stake ratification of the Constitution itself on the inclusion of these protections. Their relentless desire to ensure the preservation of individual rights and to prevent federal abuse of power eventually took the form of the Bill of Rights, the first ten amendments to the Constitution.

It is no coincidence that the first of those ten amendments listed and clarified five fundamental rights and freedoms that the founding fathers felt were critical to preventing government overreach and preserving personal liberty: freedom of speech, freedom of the press, freedom of religion, freedom of assembly, and the right to petition the government for redress of grievances. These five rights and freedoms have been employed as liberators of ideas, instigators of riots, and engines of social movements. Their influence has profoundly shaped the character of the United States and set apart its governance as a unique vanguard of liberties. Today, they continue to distinguish and define a nation that has treasured, pondered, disputed, and fiercely protected them for over two centuries.

Among these five freedoms, freedom of speech and freedom of the press have historically proven themselves as bulwarks of democracy. The ability of citizens to criticize their government has historically provided a means of accountability for use or abuse of power and has allowed the free flow of ideas from which growth and progress have occurred. However, the nature of this free expression has also been the source of great conflict because the founders also recognized that free speech was not absolute. Defining the boundaries of free speech has been a continual process. In fact, the nation's collective understanding of the First Amendment has evolved over the course of more than 200 years of tensions between the power of the word and the power of the government. These clashes have defined the circumstances and extent to which speech can be rightfully expressed—and rightfully limited.

Because historical context is so critical to the determination of when expression can or should be censored, such interpretation is continually evolving. Vibrant and passionate debates about First Amendment limitations once inspired by the dissemination of birth control information now address issues such as kneeling during the national anthem, removing books from public libraries, and disseminating false or hateful information through social media platforms. By exploring diverse examples of both censorship victories and triumphs of free expression, readers will better understand how contemporary understanding of the First Amendment came to be. Such examples also enable readers to more clearly see how decisions about First Amendment freedoms have shaped and strengthened democracy in the United States.

Starting with the Bill of Rights itself, chapter 1 presents foundational documents used by a young nation as it defined the breadth and depth of free expression under the First Amendment. Also highlighted are some of the first challenges to those freedoms. Obscenity and immorality were targeted through legislation and the influence of moral crusaders, and civil liberties were suspended during the Civil War. Some of the most severe antiwar and antigovernment speech restrictions were enacted during World War I, when dissenters faced fines, imprisonment, deportation, or even death. In spite of this, courageous antiwar activists and feminists continued to fight for the right to speak freely and promote their political beliefs. Soon after, the Supreme Court issued landmark decisions and arguments in its first two free speech cases, both involving seditious speech. Please note that the Court opinions handed down in this chapter (as well as subsequent chapters) are excerpts, not the opinions in their entirety.

Chapter 2 provides a look at the tumultuous era from the end of World War I to 1950. This period of American history was marked by deterioration of civil liberties on one hand and more expansive free speech rights on the other. This period begins and ends with marked challenges to free political expression, particularly communism, during the country's two Red Scares. Expression was also restricted in Hollywood, which engaged in self-censorship to avoid the growing threat of government regulation. During a period of calm between the wars, the Supreme Court clarified the reach of the First Amendment in cases involving public safety, seditious behavior, and flag salutations. Modern communication policy was also established during this time through the Communications Act of 1934. As the United States entered World War II, however, the nation's tolerance for divergent views diminished. Even as President Roosevelt defended the value of free speech, he encouraged the media to self-censor during the war for the overall safety and well-being of the country.

Selections in chapter 3 represent a country wrestling with numerous political and social challenges during the 1950s and 1960s. The Supreme Court further clarified its First Amendment interpretations and definitions of obscenity, and a presidential commission was formed to study the effects of pornography on society. A pivotal free speech case involving criticism of public officials resulted in a win for civil rights advocates and the free press. Additional Supreme Court decisions upheld the First Amendment rights of students while at school and defined the limits of hate speech and broadcasting of indecent speech. Advocates for greater government transparency won access to the workings of the government through passage of the Freedom of Information Act. Finally, free speech considerations became a central focus during the Vietnam War, when antiwar protests engulfed college campuses across the country.

Chapter 4 examines a number of controversies and court cases challenging the limits of free speech and freedom of the press in schools and society, including those related to library censorship, flag burning, and the ability of public figures to sue for libel. Additionally, legislators and citizens alike debated free speech considerations in government funding for the arts and the production of violent video games, pornography, and online content.

Many of the documents featured in chapter 5 involve questions of government control over speech and distribution of information in the wake of the terrorist attacks of September 11, 2001—especially after the passage of the PATRIOT Act, which gave federal authorities heightened powers of surveillance over America's communication infrastructure. This period also included revelations of government interference in the release of scientific information, renewed battles over book censorship, increased scrutiny of the boundaries of free speech on college campuses, and a momentous Supreme Court ruling (*Citizens United v. FEC*) that reclassified corporate political spending as free speech.

Chapter 6 addresses many of the challenges to free speech and the free press that emerged during the years of Donald Trump's candidacy and presidency. Featured documents illuminate how attacks on the media, the growing influence of "fake news," and responses to national controversies such as the Black Lives Matter movement affected public trust in media and its capacity to carry out its role as a watchdog for the public trust. Other primary sources explore the enormous societal impact of social media and the consequences of Big Tech's content restrictions and mismanagement of user data.

The documents selected for this book offer insights into some of the most noteworthy, interesting, and formative catalysts for America's evolving understanding of free speech and censorship issues since the nation's founding. They provide an important starting point from which to gain a better understanding of the confluence of governmental, media, and cultural factors that have shaped our collective understanding of freedom of speech and expression for nearly 250 years—and which will shape the nation's response to First Amendment issues in the decades to come.

ACKNOWLEDGMENTS

Abundant thanks to all whose guidance and expertise helped shape this book. Your collaborative contributions are invaluable. To my tremendous editors Kevin Hillstrom and Robin Tutt, thank you for your critical feedback and perseverance through all the challenges that arose during a global pandemic. Special thanks to Kevin for his tremendous, unwavering support and sharp insight. Every writer should be so lucky to work with such an exceptional editor. Many thanks to the brilliant minds who offered vital critiques throughout the writing process, including Professor Stewart Hoover, Professor Robert E. Trager, Professor Peter Schotten, Dr. Curtis Coats, and Dave Skogberg. I am so grateful for the legal expertise shared by Alex Hagen, Esq., Ali Schellpfeffer, Esq., Taneeza Islam, Esq., and multiple scholars from the University of Colorado Law School. Librarians, you are my heroes! Special thanks to the incredible professionals at the Library of Congress, the National Archives, the University of Colorado, Augustana University, and Walker Public Library for assisting in my search for elusive documents. I owe a debt of gratitude to Jordan Beck whose timely assistance was invaluable and whose intellect is second to none. Proofreaders deserve great credit for catching mistakes my eyes did not see; thank you, Dave, for scanning so many pages for errors. To my parents, your unwavering support is a gift beyond measure. Finally, heartfelt thanks to my husband and daughters for encouraging me from start to finish and reminding me of the endless possibilities on every blank page.

INTRODUCTION*

"To learn who rules over you, simply find out who you are not allowed to criticize."—Voltaire

For citizens of democratic societies, the right to criticize government officials, make political statements, or express personal opinions in public may seem inherent. Ideally, all would have the opportunity for such expression; freedom of opinion and expression are specifically included in the 1948 United Nations International Declaration of Human Rights.

A glance at international headlines, however, serves a jarring reminder that millions of people around the globe live in censored societies in which they are denied the right to speak freely. Many have risked and lost their lives in efforts to procure that right for themselves and their fellow citizens. Within months of this book going to press, reports surfaced of extrajudicial killings of peaceful protesters by Myanmar's police and military. U.S. intelligence reports implicated the Saudi government in the killing of journalist Jamal Khashoggi, exposing that country's tight control over dissent and free speech. And citizens who circumvent strict censorship laws in countries like China and North Korea remain at risk of imprisonment or death.

In contrast, citizens of the United States of America enjoy some of the broadest speech freedoms in the world. The First Amendment of the Constitution provides protections for hate speech, public disruption, and other types of controversial expression not permitted even in many fellow democracies. This protection of the free interchange of ideas has long been considered essential to the advancement of human knowledge and the preservation of a well-functioning democratic government.

Yet freedom of speech and of the press in the United States are not without limitations. Particularly since the early twentieth century, the country has wrestled with complex issues involving the limits and boundaries of free speech. Many such questions have been answered by the courts, whose determinations have literally set the stage for entire chapters of U.S. history. For example, rulings supporting suppression

* Primary documents have been reproduced in their original form.

of antigovernment sentiment during both World Wars were used after those conflicts ended to justify anti-Communist sentiment and policies, thus squelching the voices of prominent social leaders of the time. Conversely, a Supreme Court decision restricting the ability of government officials to sue for libel (*NY Times v. Sullivan)* paved the way for citizen voices to inspire social change through the civil rights movement. Similarly, events in the aftermath of the Supreme Court's Pentagon Papers decision (*New York Times Co. v. United States*) reinforced the necessity of a free press to expose government deception and abuses of power.

Although determining the limits of free expression is often messy, continuous judicial evaluation of its boundaries has actually strengthened its democratic role. Justices have argued in cases like *Terminiello v. Chicago* that the ability to speak freely, even when such speech is unpopular or invites dispute, is what sets the United States apart from totalitarian regimes. In fact, they argue, some of the country's most significant social changes have been accomplished precisely because free expression produced conditions of disturbance or unrest.

But what happens when speaking freely results in direct harm to others? Should First Amendment protections be restricted when the perpetuation of falsehoods causes great societal unrest? And what about issues involving the private sector that are not technically First Amendment issues, but greatly affect the spirit of free expression? The Supreme Court has weighed in on some of these issues, but as society evolves, new questions are continually raised regarding the breadth and limitations of free expression.

Advances in technology have presented particularly nuanced free expression considerations. Among the most notable and stark examples is debate over the degree to which free speech can be limited or censored on new media platforms as they develop. Debates over the permissibility of indecent language on the radio have evolved to controversy over the limitations of free speech on social media. For example, when President Donald Trump was suspended and later banned from Facebook, Twitter, and other platforms for violating those companies' policies, many decried the actions as a violation of free speech. Other observers, however, pointed out that while the actions of the Big Tech companies may arguably violate the spirit of free speech, they do not technically violate the First Amendment, which protects citizens from *government* overreach and restrictions, not that of private organizations or actors (in this case, companies whose users agree to follow terms of use on those private platforms). In spite of this important legal point, a growing number of bipartisan critics argue that Big Tech companies wield such great power and influence that their ability to censor content at will has become a threat to democracy. The larger, unresolved question has become whether government regulation of Big Tech is necessary to ensure First Amendment protections for all.

The influence of "cancel culture" in the United States has also led to calls for changes in First Amendment interpretations. "Canceling," rejecting, or withdrawing support from individuals, groups, or other entities whose statements or actions are considered offensive has resulted in lost jobs, isolation, social stigmatization, and other severe repercussions for those targeted. While the act of protesting or criticizing others' ideas is timeless, holding individuals *publicly* accountable for their speech has been greatly facilitated by the internet and the subsequent introduction of social media. "Cancel culture" conflicts often result in self-censorship, thus damaging the spirit of free expression. Like the Big Tech issue, "cancel culture" involves responses of private entities to offensive expression and is thus not technically a First Amendment issue. However, how might widespread self-censorship affect the health of the free expression the First Amendment was designed to protect?

Finally, what happens when dissemination of falsehoods, protected by the First Amendment, leads to violence? One of the country's greatest free speech tests to date, classified as an act of domestic terrorism by the FBI, occurred on January 6, 2021 when a mob of angry protesters attacked the U.S. Capitol. This attempt to disrupt certification of the 2020 presidential election was seen as a direct reaction to President Trump's repeated false claims that the election had been stolen. Trump's allegations of fraud, although disproven in multiple courts, were widely perpetuated through media and social media, causing anger and distrust among his supporters. Even as this book goes to press, the United States remains deeply divided between those who believe the election was fair and those who believe it was fraudulent.

The role and culpability of tech companies whose platforms permit the wide dissemination of false information has also raised free speech concerns. Twitter and other social media companies responded to public demands for greater oversight by temporarily or permanently suspending the accounts of users who violate their terms of agreement (including the former president). The move prompted outcries of censorship from those who felt free speech was under attack. Thus, while private companies have a legal right to create policies and user agreements that specify what is allowed on a platform, does their near ubiquitous presence in American society place them under greater obligation to protect even false, misleading, or harmful speech?

The manner in which such questions are addressed will be determined not only by the judiciary and legislative branches of the U.S. government but particularly by citizens who speak out in defense of their right to free expression. The health of the First Amendment, and of democracy itself, depends on informed participation by those who the Constitution was designed to protect. As Benjamin Franklin once stated, "Whoever would overthrow the liberty of a nation must begin by subduing the freeness of speech." Exploration of the complex history of free speech under the First Amendment—and the historical and cultural influences that have shaped the nation's perceptions of it over time—not only promotes greater appreciation for free speech in its various forms but also fosters a greater understanding of the constitutional limits of those precious freedoms.

1

CENSORSHIP AND SUPPRESSION OF SPEECH IN EARLY AMERICA (1776–1920)

- ***Document 1:*** First Amendment of the Constitution, in the Bill of Rights
- ***Date:*** Amendments ratified on December 15, 1791
- ***Where:*** Drafted in New York City at Federal Hall, ratified by two-thirds majority vote of the states
- ***Significance:*** In December 1791, Congress ratified the Bill of Rights, the collective name for the first ten amendments to the U.S. Constitution. These amendments to the original document were meant to protect individual rights and define fundamental civil liberties of U.S. citizens so as to guard against the misuse or abuse of federal powers. The First Amendment of the Constitution, in the Bill of Rights states that the federal government may not establish an official religion or interfere in religious practice, nor may it prohibit free speech, freedom of the press, the right to peacefully assemble, and the right to petition the government.

DOCUMENT

The Preamble to The Bill of Rights

Congress of the United States

begun and held at the City of New York, on
Wednesday the fourth of March, one thousand seven hundred and eighty nine.

THE Conventions of a number of the States, having at the time of their adopting the Constitution, expressed a desire, in order to prevent misconstruction or abuse of its powers, that further declaratory and restrictive clauses should be added: And as extending the ground of public confidence in the Government, will best ensure the beneficent ends of its institution.

RESOLVED by the Senate and House of Representatives of the United States of America, in Congress assembled, two thirds of both Houses concurring, that the following Articles be proposed to the Legislatures of the several States, as amendments to the Constitution of the United States, all, or any of which Articles, when ratified by three fourths of the said Legislatures, to be valid to all intents and purposes, as part of the said Constitution; viz.

ARTICLES in addition to, and Amendment of the Constitution of the United States of America, proposed by Congress, and ratified by the Legislatures of the several States, pursuant to the fifth Article of the original Constitution.

The Bill of Rights

Amendment I

Congress shall make no law respecting an establishment of religion, or prohibiting the free exercise thereof; or abridging the freedom of speech, or of the press; or the right of the people peaceably to assemble, and to petition the Government for a redress of grievances.

SOURCE: The U.S. Bill of Rights. From the Library of Congress. https://www.archives.gov/founding-docs/bill-of-rights-transcript

ANALYSIS

The Bill of Rights is revered as a foundational element of the participatory democratic system of government of the United States. Drafted by the founding fathers who feared potential government overreach and abuse of power, the bill's ten sections place strong emphasis on personal liberties and some of the country's most coveted individual rights and freedoms.

Initial support for a Bill of Rights, however, was not universal among key leaders working to formulate a new government. Framers of the Constitution had worked for months to carefully design an effective framework for a new government—a constitutional federal republic characterized by representation from each of the states and a balance of federal powers among three major branches. These leaders were mindful of the revolution that had just been fought to escape the suppression of rights by centralized British powers. Federalists such as James Madison, Alexander Hamilton, and John Jay favored a strong central government that would unite the states and offer a central authority to ensure state compliance with federal laws. This group felt individual rights were guaranteed through the Constitution itself and the democratic process inherent within it. They argued that adding an immediate addendum to the Constitution would undermine the strength of the original document.

Anti-Federalists such as Thomas Jefferson, however, feared that too much power had been granted to the federal government at the expense of the states and individuals. Anti-Federalists insisted that without specific guidelines prohibiting the government from forcing its will on the people, basic civil liberties necessary for a healthy, involved society and well-functioning government could be suppressed by authorities. A guarantee of specific rights inherent to all U.S. citizens, they argued, would embolden individuals to have faith in their government and increase the likelihood of democratic civic participation.

After much debate, the Federalists conceded that in order to gain the states' support for ratification of the Constitution, a series of amendments listing individual freedoms would need to be drafted. Thus, immediately after the Constitution was ratified on June 21, 1788, discussion began on how to craft an addendum to the original governing document that would specifically outline such freedoms. James Madison, author of the Bill of Rights, introduced the document in 1789. Madison's proposal initiated passionate debate, scrutiny, and compromise in Congress and in the states. It took nearly three years before the final draft of the Bill of Rights was ratified on December 15, 1791.

Of all the individual freedoms outlined in the Bill of Rights, five of the most cherished and distinguishing liberties of U.S. citizens are found in the First Amendment. The Amendment explicitly states that the government may not establish an official religion or prevent citizens from practicing their chosen religions, nor may it reduce citizens' freedom of speech, of the press, of peaceful assembly, and of the right to petition the government in order to resolve an issue.

The inclusion of the right to free expression in the very first amendment was not a coincidence. By ensuring the ability of citizens to express themselves without fear of retribution, the founders were prioritizing a form of rational decision-making resulting from exposure to varied opinions and voices. These specific provisions ensuring freedom of speech and of the press reinforce the notion that the best way to engage citizens and allow a more tolerant and representative government is through a marketplace of ideas in which numerous views and opinions can be offered without fear of government reprisal. Even unpopular viewpoints and hate speech are tolerated (unless they are intended to or likely to incite unlawful action), because the founders felt that intelligent, truthful counter-speech and discourse were the best types of rebuttals against false claims. First Amendment freedom of expression emphasizes the power of persuasion, not regulation.

Freedom of expression, as outlined in the Bill of Rights, protects not only the right of citizens to say what they wish to say about their laws and governments, but it also prevents minority voices from being lost or overshadowed. The First Amendment safeguards the right to be heard and to hear the views of others. This principle has formed a critical aspect of American identity. A 2015 Pew Research Center survey found the United States to be the world's most supportive country of free expression, even when such expression is offensive (Wike 2016).

Indeed, the ability to criticize laws and leaders, to protest policies, and speak out against perceived injustices is a precious and coveted right that is lacking in many parts of the world. Russia, Saudi Arabia, China, North Korea, and Syria are examples of countries in which protesters have been imprisoned or even sentenced to death for criticizing government policies and actions. Such censorship extends to journalists in many parts of the world as well, and is often integrated into official policy to stifle dissention and prevent access to information that could reveal abuses of power.

Born from a history of repressive English monarchical rule that squelched free speech, the basis and strength of the participatory democracy in the United States are rooted in First Amendment freedoms of expression. For more than 200 years, protecting the right of minority ideas and opinions to be heard has prevented those in authority from stifling alternative voices. It was the hope of the founding fathers that the power of robust debate and the ability to speak freely would bolster accountability, create a more informed and active citizenry, and support the fundamental ideals of the Constitution so the new government of the United States would belong not to a ruling elite, but to "We the people."

FURTHER READING

Amar, Akhil Reed. *The Bill of Rights: Creation and Reconstruction*. New Haven, CT: Yale University Press, 1998.

Anastaplo, George. *Reflections on Freedom of Speech and the First Amendment*. Lexington, KY: University Press of Kentucky, 2007.

Blasi, Vincent. "The Checking Value in First Amendment Theory." *American Bar Foundation Research Journal* 2, no. 3 (1977): 521–649.

Emerson, Thomas I. "Toward a General Theory of the First Amendment." *Yale Law School Legal Scholarship Repository*. (1963). Faculty Scholarship Series. 2796.

Farber, Daniel A. *The First Amendment*. Foundation Press, 2019.

Heyman, Steven. *Free Speech and Human Dignity*. New Haven, CT; London: Yale University Press, 2008.

- ***Document 2:*** Sedition Act of 1798
- ***Date:*** Written November 13, 1797, approved by President John Adams in 1798
- ***Where:*** Philadelphia, Pennsylvania
- ***Significance:*** The Sedition Act of 1798, part of the Alien and Sedition Acts, outlined legal punishments for anyone who actively opposed existing U.S. laws or who expressed through writing or speaking any criticism of the president or Congress that could be construed as malicious. This act was one of the first direct affronts on the freedom of speech as outlined in the First Amendment of the Constitution. The passage of the Sedition Act and subsequent prosecution of those found guilty of violating it prompted heated debate about the meaning and reach of the First Amendment, particularly freedom of the press.

DOCUMENT

Fifth Congress of the United States

At the Second Session,

Begun and held at the city of Philadelphia, in the state of Pennsylvania, on Monday, the thirteenth of November, one thousand seven hundred and ninety-seven.

AN ACT IN ADDITION TO THE ACT, ENTITLED "AN ACT FOR THE PUNISHMENT OF CERTAIN CRIMES AGAINST THE UNITED STATES."

SECTION 1. Be it enacted by the Senate and House of Representatives of the United States of America, in Congress assembled, That if any persons shall unlawfully combine or conspire together, with intent to oppose any measure or measures of the government of the United States, which are or shall be directed by proper authority, or to impede the operation of any law of the United States, or to intimidate or prevent any person holding a place or office in or under the government of the United States, from undertaking, performing or executing his trust or duty, and if any person or persons, with intent as aforesaid, shall counsel, advise or attempt to procure any insurrection, riot, unlawful assembly, or combination, whether such conspiracy, threatening, counsel, advice, or attempt shall have the proposed effect or not, he or they shall be deemed guilty of a high misdemeanor, and on conviction, before any court of the United States having jurisdiction thereof, shall be punished by a fine not exceeding five thousand dollars, and by imprisonment during a term not less than six months nor exceeding five years; and further, at the discretion of the court may be holden to find sureties for his good behaviour in such sum, and for such time, as the said court may direct.

SEC. 2. And be it further enacted, That if any person shall write, print, utter or publish, or shall cause or procure to be written, printed, uttered or published, or shall knowingly and willingly assist or aid in writing, printing, uttering or publishing any false, scandalous and malicious writing or writings against the government of the United States, or either house of the Congress of the United States, or the President of the United States, with intent to defame the said government, or either house of the said Congress, or the said President, or to bring them, or either of them, into contempt or disrepute; or to excite against them, or either or any of them, the hatred of the good people of the United States, or to stir up sedition within the United States, or to excite any unlawful combinations therein, for opposing or resisting any law of the United States, or any act of the President of the United States, done in pursuance of any such law, or of the powers in him vested by the constitution of the United States, or to resist, oppose, or defeat any such law or act, or to aid, encourage or abet any hostile designs of any foreign nation against the United States, their people or government, then such person, being thereof convicted before any court of the United States having jurisdiction thereof, shall be punished by a fine not exceeding two thousand dollars, and by imprisonment not exceeding two years.

SEC. 3. And be it further enacted and declared, That if any person shall be prosecuted under this act, for the writing or publishing any libel aforesaid, it shall be lawful for the defendant, upon the trial of the cause, to give in evidence in his defence, the truth of the matter contained in publication charged as a libel. And the jury who shall try the cause, shall have a right to determine the law and the fact, under the direction of the court, as in other cases.

SEC. 4. And be it further enacted, That this act shall continue and be in force until the third day of March, one thousand eight hundred and one, and no longer: Provided, that the expiration of the act shall not prevent or defeat a prosecution and punishment of any offence against the law, during the time it shall be in force.

Jonathan Dayton, Speaker of the House of Representatives.
Theodore Sedgwick, President of the Senate pro tempore.

I Certify that this Act did originate in the Senate.
Attest, Sam. A. Otis, Secretary

APPROVED, July 14, 1798
John Adams
President of the United States.

SOURCE: Alien and Sedition Acts of 1798; 1798; Enrolled Acts and Resolutions of Congress, 1789–2011; General Records of the United States Government, Record Group 11; National Archives Building, Washington, DC. [Online Version, https://www.docsteach.org/documents/document/alien-sedition-acts, April 20, 2019]

ANALYSIS

The Alien and Sedition Acts of 1798 were a series of four laws that limited immigrant rights and freedom of speech. These laws were passed during a time of strained relations and heightened tensions between the United States and revolutionary France. The first three acts, known as the Alien Acts, aimed to limit the rights of immigrants and protect the United States from what was perceived to be dangerous foreign influence and prevent support of a possible French invasion. The fourth act, known as the Sedition Act, made unlawful any speech or written material that could be construed as malevolent toward the U.S. president or Congress. The curtailing of free expression under the Sedition Act directly violated guarantees of freedom of speech and freedom of the press as outlined in the First Amendment, which had been ratified just seven years prior.

The Alien and Sedition Acts were written by Alexander Hamilton and Federalists in Congress who feared that any rebellious actions toward the U.S. government could substantially weaken it. The laws were crafted at a time when the United States was engaged in a "quasi-war" with France. Federalists, in particular, were watching with a wary eye the outcomes of the French Revolution and were fearful that critics of the U.S. government might incite violence or provoke sympathies toward the French should the French decide to invade U.S. territory. Thus, the Federalist-controlled Congress passed the Alien and Sedition Acts in an attempt to limit the threat of foreign powers, namely France, and to prevent malicious attacks or attempts to undermine the U.S. government.

Members of the Republican Party (also called the Democratic-Republican Party or the Jeffersonian-Republican Party), on the other hand, viewed the French Revolution more as a positive outgrowth of the American Revolution than as a threat, and were openly critical of what they considered tyrannical Federalist policies. They adamantly opposed the Alien Acts' restriction of immigrant rights as well as limits on free speech and freedom of the press for the entire populace. Republican leaders such as Thomas Jefferson and James Madison viewed the legislation as an effort to suppress criticism of governmental leaders and policies and limit fundamental individual freedoms.

Passage of the Alien and Sedition Acts sparked national debate, and Republican editors of newspapers used the press to protest the Sedition Act's new libel laws. The Federalist government, in turn, attempted to quell dissent by prosecuting these editors to the maximum degree possible by imposing fines and prison time. In total, at least twenty-five individuals were arrested, including Benjamin Franklin's grandson, and seventeen were indicted under the Sedition Act of 1798. Most found guilty of violating the law were Republican newspaper editors who were outspoken in their opposition to President Adams and his administration. The uproar raised by these prosecutions led to the country's first lengthy debate about what freedom of the press under the First Amendment entailed and what limits could lawfully be placed upon that freedom.

Within months of the passage of the Alien and Sedition Acts, the Virginia and Kentucky legislatures each passed resolutions condemning the acts and declaring that the government had no right to exercise powers not specifically granted to it by the Constitution. The Virginia Resolution, initially drafted by James Madison but whose authorship was not revealed until much later, argued that the prohibitions of freedom of speech and the press were specifically forbidden by the Constitution's First Amendment and that all should be alarmed by the effort to curtail the right to freely communicate and criticize the government, the "only effectual guardian of every other right."

The Kentucky Resolution, whose initial authorship by Thomas Jefferson remained unknown to all but a few for many years, stated similar opposition to federal overreach of power and declared that states have the right to nullify federal laws when those laws are unconstitutional. A second set of Kentucky Resolutions was passed in 1799. It is not clear who authored this second set, but the language used was similar to Jefferson's original resolution calling on states to nullify unauthorized acts by the federal government.

The Virginia and Kentucky Resolutions were written with an intent to convince other states to pass similar resolutions and challenge federal powers. Although no other state opted to do so, these original resolutions created unity within the Republican Party and sparked widespread debate about the extent of federal powers and the relationship of those powers to the Constitution.

The unpopularity of the Alien and Sedition Acts was said to have contributed to Republican Thomas Jefferson's victory over Adams in the presidential election of 1800 and the election of a Republican-majority to Congress. All but one of the Alien Acts were allowed to expire after two years. The Sedition Act expired on March 3, 1801, the last day of John Adams' term. Thus, the controversy over the constitutionality of the acts was never examined by the Supreme Court, but rather was settled with the election of a new president and shift in the makeup of Congress. It was not until the twentieth century that significant cases involving freedom of speech and freedom of the press were examined and decided by the Supreme Court.

FURTHER READING

Belt, Gordon T. "Sedition Act of 1798." The Freedom Forum Institute. 2011. https://www.freedomforuminstitute.org/wp-content/uploads/2016/10/Sedition_Act_cases.pdf

Bird, Wendell. "The Sedition Act and the Assault on Freedoms of Press and Speech: The Sitting Supreme Court Justices and the Trials." *Press and Speech under Assault* (2016): 248–329.

Halperin, Terri Diane. *The Alien and Sedition Acts of 1798: When a Congressional Majority Assaulted Immigrants and Civil Liberties*. Baltimore: Johns Hopkins University Press, 2016.

Jenkins, David, "The Sedition Act of 1798 and the Incorporation of Seditious Libel into First Amendment Jurisprudence." *The American Journal of Legal History* no. 45 (2001): 154–213.

Watkins, William J. *Reclaiming the American Revolution: The Kentucky and Virginia Resolutions and Their Legacy*. New York: Palgrave Macmillan, 2008.

- ***Document 3:*** President Lincoln's Letter on Habeas Corpus to Erastus Corning
- ***Date:*** June 12, 1863
- ***Where:*** Washington, DC
- ***Significance:*** In 1863, a group of Democrats from New York adopted resolutions criticizing President Lincoln's restriction of civil liberties during the first two years of the Civil War as unconstitutional. These resolutions were sent to Lincoln by moderator Erastus Corning. In his response to Corning and the group, President Lincoln outlines his position on civil liberties in the midst of rebellion and argues the Constitution permits executive action to curtail such freedoms when public safety requires their suspension.

DOCUMENT

Executive Mansion Washington

1863
Hon: Erastus Corning & others

Gentlemen,

Your letter of May 19th inclosing the resolutions of a public meeting held at Albany, N. Y. on the 16th of the same month, was received several days ago—

The resolutions, as I understand them, are resolvable into two propositions—first, the expression of a purpose to sustain the cause of the Union, to secure peace through victory, and to support the administration in every constitutional, and lawful measure to suppress the rebellion; and secondly, a declaration of censure upon the administration for supposed unconstitutional action such as the making of military arrests. And, from the two propositions a third is deduced, which is, that the gentlemen composing the meeting are resolved on doing their part to maintain our common government and country, despite the folly or wickedness, as they may conceive, of any administration. This position is eminently patriotic, and as such, I thank the meeting, and congratulate the nation for it. My own purpose is the same; so that the meeting and myself have a common object, and can have no difference, except in the choice of means or measures, for effecting that object.

And here I ought to close this paper, and would close it, if there were no apprehension that more injurious consequences, than any merely personal to myself, might follow the censures systematically cast upon me for doing what, in my view of duty, I could not forbear. The resolutions promise to support me in every constitutional and lawful measure to suppress the rebellion; and I have not knowingly employed, nor shall knowingly employ, any other. But the meeting, by their resolutions, assert and argue, that certain military arrests and proceedings following them, for which I am ultimately responsible, are unconstitutional. I think they are not. The resolutions quote from the constitution, the definition of treason; and also the limiting safe-guards and guarantees therein provided for the citizen, on trials for treason, and on his being held to answer for capital or otherwise infamous crimes; and, in criminal prosecutions, his right to a speedy and public trial by an impartial Jury. They proceed to resolve "That these safe-guards of the rights of the citizen against the pretentions of arbitrary power, were intended more especially for his protection in times of civil commotion." And, apparently, to demonstrate the proposition, the resolutions proceed "They were secured substantially to the English people, after years of protracted civil war, and were adopted into our constitution at the close of the revolution." Would not the demonstration have been better, if it could have been truly said that these safeguards had been adopted, and applied during the civil wars and during our revolution, instead of after the one, and at the close of the other? I too am devotedly for them after civil war, and before civil war, and at all times "except when, in cases of Rebellion or Invasion, the public safety may require" their suspension— . . . Let us consider the real case with which we are dealing, and apply to it the parts of the Constitution plainly made for such cases.

Prior to my installation here it had been inculcated that any State had a lawful right to secede from the National Union; and that it would be expedient to exercise the right whenever the devotees of the doctrine should fail to elect a President to their own liking. I was elected contrary to their liking; and accordingly, so far as it was legally possible, they had taken Seven States out of the Union, had seized many of the United States Forts, and had fired upon the United States' Flag, all before I was inaugerated; and, of course, before I had done any official act whatever. The rebellion, thus began soon ran into the present civil war; and, in certain respects, it began on very unequal terms between the parties. The insurgents had been preparing for it more than thirty years, while the government had taken no steps to resist them. The former had carefully considered all the means which could be turned to their account. It undoubtedly was a well pondered reliance with them that in their own unrestricted effort to destroy Union, Constitution, and Law, all together, the government would, in great degree, be restrained by the same Constitution and Law, from arresting their progress. Their sympathizers pervaded all departments of the government, and nearly all communities of the people. From this material, under cover of "Liberty of speech", "Liberty of the press" and "Habeas Corpus", they hoped to keep on foot amongst us a most efficient corps of spies, informers, Supplyers, and aiders and abettors of their cause in a thousand ways. They knew that in times such as they were inaugurating, by the Constitution itself, the "Habeas Corpus" might be suspended; but they also knew they had friends who would make a question as to who was to suspend it; meanwhile their spies and others might remain at large to help on their cause. Or if, as has happened, the Executive should suspend the writ, without ruinous waste of time, instances of arresting innocent persons might occur, as are always likely to occur in such cases; and then a clamor could be raised in regard to this, which might be, at least, of some service to the insurgent cause. It needed no very keen perception to discover this part of the enemies' programme, so soon as by open hostilities their machinery was fairly put in motion. Yet, thoroughly imbued with a reverence for the guarantied rights of individuals, I was slow to adopt the strong measures, which by degrees I have been forced to regard as being within the exceptions of the Constitution and as indispensable to the public Safety. Nothing is better known to history than that Courts of justice are utterly incompetent to such cases. Civil Courts are organized chiefly for trials of individuals, or, at most, a few individuals acting in concert; and this in quiet times, and on charges of crimes well defined in the law. Even in times of peace, bands of horse-thieves and robbers frequently grow too numerous and powerful for the ordinary Courts of justice. But what comparison, in numbers, have such bands ever borne to the insurgent sympathizers even in many of the loyal States? Again, a jury too frequently have at least one member, more ready to hang the panel than to hang the traitor. And yet again, he who dissuades one man from volunteering or induces one soldier to desert weakens the Union cause as much as he who kills a Union Soldier in battle. Yet this dissuasion, or inducement may be so conducted as to be no defined crime of which any civil court would take cognizance.

Ours is a case of Rebellion—so called by the resolutions before me—in fact, a clear, flagrant, and gigantic case of Rebellion; and the provision of the Constitution that "The privilege of the writ of Habeas Corpus shall not be suspended, unless when in cases of Rebellion or Invasion, the public safety may require it," is the provision which specially applies to our present case. This provision plainly attests the understanding of those who made the Constitution, that ordinary Courts of justice are inadequate to "Cases of Rebellion"—attests their purpose that, in such cases, men may be held in custody whom the Courts, acting on ordinary rules, would discharge. Habeas Corpus does not discharge men who are proved to be guilty of defined crime; and its suspension is allowed by the Constitution on purpose that men may be arrested and held, who can not be proved to be guilty of defined crime, "when, in cases of Rebellion or Invasion, the public Safety may require it." This is precisely our present case, a case of Rebellion, wherein the public safety does require the suspension. Indeed, arrests by process of courts, and arrests in cases of rebellion, do not proceed altogether upon the same basis. The former is directed at the small percentage of ordinary and continuous perpetration of crime; while the latter is directed at sudden and extensive uprisings against the government, which, at most, will succeed or fail, in no great length of time. In the latter case, arrests are made, not so much for what has been done, as for what probably would be done. The latter is more for the preventive, and less for the vindictive, than the former—In such cases the purposes of men are much more easily understood than in cases of ordinary crime. The man who stands by and says nothing, when the peril of his government is discussed, can not be misunderstood. If not hindered, he is sure to help the enemy. Much more, if he talks ambiguously—talks for his country with "buts" and "ifs" and "ands". Of how little value the constitutional provision I have quoted will be rendered, if arrests shall never be made until defined crimes shall have been committed, may be illustrated by a few notable examples. General John C. Breckinridge, General Robert E. Lee, General Joseph E. Johnston, General John B. Magruder, General William B. Preston, General Simon B. Buckner, and Commodore Franklin Buchanan, now occupying the very highest places in the rebel war service, were all within the power of the government since the rebellion began, and were nearly as well known to be traitors then as now. Unquestionably if we had seized and held them, the insurgent cause would be much weaker. But no one of them had then committed any crime defined in the law. Every one of them, if arrested, would have been discharged on Habeas Corpus, were the writ allowed to operate. In view of these and similar cases, I think the time not unlikely to come when I shall be blamed for having made too few arrests rather than too many. . . .

I understand the meeting, whose resolutions I am considering, to be in favor of suppressing the rebellion by military force—by armies. Long experience has shown that armies can not be maintained unless desertion shall be punished by the severe penalty of death. The case requires, and the law and the Constitution, sanction this punishment. Must I shoot a simple-minded soldier boy who deserts, while I must not touch a hair of a wily agitator who induces him to desert? This is none the less injurious when effected by getting a father, or brother, or friend, into a public meeting, and there working upon his feelings, till he is persuaded to write the soldier boy that he is fighting in a bad cause, for a wicked administration of a contemptible government, too weak to arrest and punish him if he shall desert. I think that in such a case, to silence the agitator, and save the boy, is not only constitutional, but, withal, a great mercy. and a great merit.

If I be wrong on this question of constitutional power, my error lies in believing that certain proceedings are constitutional when, in cases of Rebellion or Invasion, the public safety requires them, which would not be constitutional when, in absence of rebellion or invasion, the public Safety does not require them;—in other words, that the constitution is not, in its application, in all respects the same, in cases of Rebellion or Invasion, involving the public safety, as it is in times of profound peace and public security. The constitution itself makes the distinction; and I can no more be persuaded that the government can constitutionally take no strong measures in time of rebellion, because it can be shown that the same could not be lawfully taken in time of peace, than I can be persuaded that a particular drug is not good medicine for a sick man, because it can be shown to not be good food for a well one. Nor am

I able to appreciate the danger, apprehended by the meeting, that the American People will, by means of military arrests during the rebellion, lose the right of public discussion, the liberty of speech and the press, the law of evidence, trial by jury, and Habeas Corpus, throughout the indefinite peaceful future which I trust lies before them, any more than I am able to believe that a man could contract so strong an appetite for emetics during temporary illness as to persist in feeding upon them through the remainder of his healthful life. . .

SOURCE: Lincoln, Abraham. *Abraham Lincoln papers: Series 1. General Correspondence. 1833–1916: Abraham Lincoln to Erastus Corning and Others, June 1863 Copy No. 1 of Lincoln's Reply to Resolutions Concerning Military Arrests and Suspension of Habeas Corpus*. June 1863. Manuscript/Mixed Material. https://www.loc.gov/item/mal2401700/.

ANALYSIS

When Abraham Lincoln took the oath of office as president of the United States on March 4, 1861, he faced the most serious challenge to date in the young nation's history. Seven southern states had already seceded from the Union over the election of Lincoln and their fears that he would limit or abolish slavery. Just one month after Lincoln's inauguration, on April 12, Confederate firing upon Union-controlled Fort Sumter in Charleston Bay, South Carolina, marked the start of the Civil War. Seeing an already unstable country further breaking apart and fearing for the stability of the government, on April 27, 1861, Lincoln ordered General Winfield Scott to suspend the writ of habeas corpus between Philadelphia and Washington if public safety required it. In doing so, he hoped to establish greater Union control in a rebellious state; preserve transportation, communication, and troop movement between Maryland and Washington; and squelch efforts of Confederate sympathizers to impede the efforts of Northern troops.

Lincoln's decision to suspend the writ of habeas corpus permitted the military to make arrests without filing specific charges against the accused. His proclamation was met with resistance from numerous sources, including Supreme Court chief justice Roger Taney, trial judge for John Merryman, who was arrested by federal troops in Maryland for aiding Confederates. When the judge ordered delivery of a writ of habeas corpus requiring the arresting general and Merryman to appear on May 28, the general refused. Thereafter, Judge Taney ruled that only Congress, not the president, has the power to suspend the writ because the provision for the writ appears in the article of the Constitution dealing

DID YOU KNOW?

The writ of habeas corpus is a procedure aimed at challenging the legality of an individual's detention or imprisonment. When issued a writ of habeas corpus, the custodian of a detained individual must bring that person before a court of law and explain the reasons for confinement. If those reasons are not found to be valid, the subject must be released. This protection against false imprisonment dates back to the Magna Carta in 1215 and originally was seen as a protection against the king's "divine right" to imprison his subjects. The procedure evolved, however, as a right of the English king to demand accountability from constables and others acting under his authority to ensure they were not abusing their power.

The legal protections offered through a writ of habeas corpus were brought to the United States and observed first in colonial courts, later through state governments and finally in the U.S. Constitution, which simply stated that "The privilege of the Writ of Habeas Corpus shall not be suspended, unless when in Cases of Rebellion or Invasion the public Safety may require it" (U.S. Constitution, art. 1 sec. 9).

with legislative, not executive powers. Lincoln did not respond to Taney's ruling; instead, he spoke publicly of his obligation to exercise such powers in order to end the rebellion in the South, and he later expanded the suspension of the writ to additional Union-held areas.

Lincoln addressed Congress in July 1861 and acknowledged the controversy over whether the executive or legislative branch of government is vested with the power to suspend the writ of habeas corpus. He further suggested that Congress should take up the matter. However, Congress was slow to act. Thus, Lincoln issued a more drastic proclamation in the fall of 1862, not only suspending the writ of habeas corpus to those imprisoned by military authorities but also imposing martial law until the end of the war. Anyone who discouraged a volunteer from enlisting, provided aid to Confederates, or engaged in any other disloyal practice (a phrase that could have included any number of offences or interpretations of disloyalty) was subject to arrest. Finally, on March 3, 1863, Congress passed an act that gave Lincoln discretionary power to suspend the writ of habeas corpus as long as the rebellion was ongoing. By this time, Lincoln's suspensions and proclamations had been in place for nearly two years.

In spite of this Congressionally approved legitimacy, Lincoln's decisions were met with great resistance by those who felt he had overstepped his presidential authority and, in doing so, had discarded fundamental civil liberties. In May 1863, Democrats in New York passed resolutions denouncing Lincoln's infringement of personal freedoms, specifically in regard to the arrest and detention of prominent Ohio politician Clement Vallandigham. The former congressman was a member of an antiwar branch of the Democratic Party called the Peace Democrats. Vallandigham was arrested for delivering a speech in which he openly criticized the administration for prosecution of the war and specifically encouraged people to disobey General Burnside's order number 38 that prohibited any declaration of sympathy for the enemy. The New York Democrats purported that Vallandigham's arrest abrogated basic freedoms such as the right to assemble and express opinions critical of the government, the right to free speech, freedom of the press, trial by jury, and other privileges guaranteed by law.

The resolutions passed in New York were forwarded to President Lincoln by Erastus Corning, a businessman and politician who had moderated the Democratic meeting. Lincoln's response to Corning (and others) is considered one of his most influential writings, both because it was well crafted and so widely read. In addition to sending his response to Corning, Lincoln sent copies to key political figures as well as the influential *New York Tribune*. The letter was also reprinted in newspapers across the country and circulated widely in pamphlet form.

In his letter, Lincoln carefully and skillfully states that although the committee's resolutions assert that certain military arrests and proceedings are unconstitutional, he sees it as his duty under the Constitution to enact them in order to safeguard the public and contain the rebellion. Lincoln defends his position that civil liberties are protected during peacetime but must sometimes (as in this case) be suspended or lost during a time of war, invasion, or rebellion when public safety requires it. He reiterates he was "slow to adopt the strong measures" but sees them as "within the exceptions of the Constitution and as indispensable to the public Safety."

Lincoln views his actions as necessary to prevent much greater harm to the nation. He defends the affront on civil liberties by asserting that "he who dissuades one man from volunteering or induces one soldier to desert weakens the Union cause as much as he who kills a Union Soldier in battle." In one of the letter's most famous lines, Lincoln points out desertion is a crime punishable by death and says, "Must I shoot a simple-minded soldier boy who deserts, while I must not touch a hair of a wily agitator who induces him to desert?" He continues, "[T]o silence the agitator, and save the boy, is not only constitutional, but, withal, a great mercy. [A]nd a great merit."

Lincoln also uses the argument in his letter that suspension of the writ of habeas corpus is justified because civil courts are inadequate to handle cases of rebellion, and the conflict at hand is "a clear, flagrant, and gigantic case of Rebellion." To make his point, he lists numerous prominent military leaders from the South and argues, "Unquestionably if we had seized and held them, the insurgent cause would be much weaker."

Lincoln's letter to Corning was well received and widely praised by influential politicians and leaders. It seemed to offer reassurance to Unionists who were skeptical of the growing powers of the executive branch. They commended Lincoln for his wisdom, clarity, and strong arguments outlining the need for such drastic measures during a time of war. Even Corning and Democrat writers of the original proclamation acknowledged receipt of Lincoln's letter and offered that indeed Lincoln, in his arguments, had purported to work within the Constitution to undertake such powers. Nevertheless, they warned against the danger of arbitrary power turning into absolute sovereignty, under which liberty would perish.

FURTHER READING

Dueholm, James. "Lincoln's Suspension of the Writ of Habeas Corpus: An Historical and Constitutional Analysis." *Journal of the Abraham Lincoln Association* 29, no. 2 (Summer 2008): 47–66. http://hdl.handle.net/2027/spo.2629860.0029.205

Hesseltine, William B., and J. G. Randall. "Constitutional Problems under Lincoln." *Journal of Southern History* 17, no. 2 (1951): 266. doi:10.2307/2198288

"Mr. Lincoln and New York: Erastus Corning (1794–1872)." The Lehrman Institute. n.d. http://www.mrlincolnandnewyork.org/new-yorkers/erastus-corning-1794-1872/

Williams, Frank J. "Abraham Lincoln, Civil Liberties and the Corning Letter," *Roger Williams University Law Review* 5, no. 2 (2000): 319–339. http://docs.rwu.edu/rwu_LR/vol5/iss2/1

- ***Document 4:*** Anthony Comstock's "Vampire Literature"
- ***Date:*** August 1, 1891
- ***Where:*** *The North American Review*
- ***Significance:*** Free speech and morality in the eighteenth-century United States were profoundly influenced by the work of Anthony Comstock, who engaged in a personal crusade to rid society of indecency. He successfully lobbied Congress to pass the 1873 Comstock

Law, which made it a crime to possess, sell, advertise, publish, or distribute obscene or indecent materials, including materials that could be used to promote contraception or abortion. He also oversaw the prosecution of hundreds of individuals for publishing or disseminating what was deemed indecent or obscene literature. In this article, Comstock describes the impact of his censorship efforts on publishers and vendors and warns that dissemination of sinful material will lead to destruction of the nation's free institutions and the downfall of its youth.

DOCUMENT

. . . The first thing after an author has written a book of questionable character is to secure some reputable publisher or bookseller to handle and push it. The next step towards the realization of his desire for fame and gain is to have the book roundly attacked because of its lustful tendencies, by the daily and weekly papers and periodicals. The New York Society for the Suppression of Vice long ago learned that to attack a book or paper, and not carry through the prosecution to success in the courts, was to secure a quasi-indorsement by the courts and a large amount of free advertising for the offensive matter. Our plan has always been to discover the author and publisher, and secretly strike a blow at the fountain head by seizing the publication and plates and arresting the publisher and author.

The care taken by the society in the preparation of cases may be illustrated by the results for the past three years. During 1888, of 103 cases brought to trial 101 were convicted. In 1889, out of 127 cases brought to trial 125 were convicted; while during 1890 we had 155 convictions out of 156 cases. This record speaks well for our district attorneys, as well as for the preparation of these cases.

Again, this society has always aimed to reach authors and publishers, and not merely venders. This is illustrated by the fact that out of 227 different books published in this country, the stereotypes and electroplates, woodcuts and steel and copper plate engravings for printing and illustrating 225 have been seized and destroyed; while the plates for the other two books were destroyed by the publisher for fear we would secure them and prosecute him.

It is both lamentable and disheartening, just as the New York Society for the Suppression of Vice has practically suppressed the grosser books and pictures which for years have cursed this country, that we should have an epidemic of lewdness through the channels of light literature. There is at present a strong competition among writers and publishers of cheap books and papers to see which one can excel the others in unclean stories.

The object and ambition of many writers seem to be to show how they can evade the law and yet publish stories of a suggestive and criminal character. The basest representatives of profligacy and unhallowed living are made the subjects for leading characters in many novels published at the present day. Many newsstands are no longer either safe or respectable places for children and youth to visit or purchase books at. Many of the publications are of such a character that they are sufficient when seen in the hands of any girl to blast her good name and reputation. . . .

Better that our youth be taken by their parents into the sinks of iniquity and dens of vice, and their finer sensibilities shocked by the realities of crime, than that their fancies shall be taught fantastic scenes from these sensational and vivid descriptions of the purlieus of sin and shame.

Our newspapers are constantly filled with accounts of the victims of "dime novels" or "blood-and-thunder" story papers. To show something of the enormous amount of this kind of criminal literature, we may cite the fact that six tons' weight of books and plates was seized by this society in a single office of one of these criminal story-paper publishers. . .

Many a boy or youth has been led to commit crimes which have brought him to the penitentiary or the State's prison, from the infection or seduction of this class of crime-breeding publications.

There is still another class of books which are to-day appearing in great numbers, comparatively speaking, which reflect no honor on those who make them a source of personal profit and gain. Many publishers seem to have searched the archives of foreign libraries for erotic books, classics, standard literature, suppressed editions of notoriously vile writers of old, and these are translated, or obscene selections taken from them, and bound up in cheap sensational shape, and placed in indiscriminate circulation with a wanton desire to make money from the sale thereof, utterly regardless of the degrading effect of the matter thus reduced from literary purposes to sensational circulation.

Garbage smells none the less rank and offensive because deposited in a marble fount or a gold or silver urn. So these foul stories and unclean tales of ancient writers find no justification in the moral world simply because clothed in smooth verse or choice rhetoric. Decaying matter breeds disease, whether confined in costly receptacles or ash-barrels. So this wretched tainted matter, stolen from ancient writers, which is made to appeal to the depraved taste, is equally deadly in its polluting effects; indeed, it is in some respects worse, for coarse words shock and disgust, while the smooth flow of genius and talent thus prostituted more easily deludes and captivates the fancy and engages attention. . .

Our country is making mighty strides towards affluence and prosperity. Mighty responsibilities are keeping pace with every step in advance made by this nation. Unless the restraining forces of religion and morality keep ahead of all other considerations, the ship of state will soon be dashed to pieces upon the boulders and quicksands of immorality.

Save our youth from this fetid blast of corruption which is being sent out by the fiery greed of thoughtless, reckless, or criminal authors and publishers. Authors and publishers need to call a halt upon themselves, ere they further curse the youth of this free land and undermine our free institutions.

SOURCE: Comstock, Anthony. "Vampire Literature." *North American Review* 153, no. 417 (1891): 160–71. http://www.jstor.org/stable/25102226.

ANALYSIS

Late-nineteenth-century America was a period of dramatic change for the young country. In addition to the advancement of citizen participation and women's suffrage, the post-Civil War era was marked by urbanization, industrialization, and unprecedented levels of immigration. Civil War veterans, rural workers, and immigrants seeking work and opportunity made their way to large urban centers like New York City where many encountered easy access to gambling, alcohol, prostitution, and sexually explicit literature. The city was also a hub for proponents of feminism, sexual freedom, and expanded religious freedoms.

While numerous civic and religious leaders fought back against moral temptations and radical new ideas of the time, none was so well known as Anthony Comstock. Born in 1844 to a devoutly religious family in Connecticut, Comstock grew up with a definitive moral code that drove his efforts to abolish obscenity and immorality from public life and led to his notoriety as one of the most influential moral crusaders of the late nineteenth and early twentieth centuries.

From a young age, Comstock was shaped by his devout religious upbringing. As a young Civil War soldier, Comstock wrote about how he loathed his own sinful actions as well as those of his comrades (Blanchard & Semonche 2006). He felt his calling was to preserve society's purity, particularly among the nation's youth.

After the war, Comstock settled in New York City. He was disgusted by the immoral debauchery he witnessed there and vowed to fight back against the obscenities and moral temptations that surrounded him. He began his first successful crusade by insisting police enforce the closure of saloons on Sundays.

Successful in this endeavor, he focused next on the circulation of what he considered sexually explicit materials. Comstock partnered with the New York YMCA to attempt to limit the availability of sexually explicit literature, initially through the arrest and conviction of store employees who sold the materials. The YMCA was pleased with his efforts and eventually created a separate organization for him to lead called the Committee for the Suppression of Vice.

As the head of this group (later known as the New York Society for the Suppression of Vice, the New England Society for the Suppression of Vice, and finally the New England Watch and Ward Society), Comstock sought "the enforcement of laws for the suppression of the trade in, and circulation of obscene literature and illustrations, advertisements, and articles of indecent of immoral use" (Gilfoyle 1992, 187). He lobbied Washington for more stringent laws, and in 1873, Congress passed what became known as the Comstock Act. This law forbade individuals from selling, lending, giving away, publishing, mailing, or possessing any printed materials or other items considered immoral or obscene, including drugs or information intended to prevent conception or cause abortion. A later amendment emphasized the illegality of mailing such materials and appointed Comstock to a newly created position of special agent in the U.S. Postal Service. In this role, Comstock confiscated illegal materials sent through mail and arrested individuals involved in their distribution. He often obtained arrests and convictions by purchasing prohibited items himself or by using a false name and ordering such materials through mail.

Penalties were severe for individuals found guilty of violating the Comstock Act. Those caught mailing indecent materials, for example, were subject to fines of $100–$2,000 and/or hard labor of one to ten years for each offense. During his forty-two years as a special agent of the U.S. Post Office, Comstock is said to have prosecuted more than 3,600 defendants and destroyed more than 160 tons of obscene literature.

One of the most problematic aspects of the Comstock Act was that it did not provide a specific definition of what made something indecent, immoral, or obscene. That was left to the scrutiny of Comstock himself, who took great liberties in his interpretations. In addition to dime store novels and sexually suggestive reading materials that he felt were particularly harmful for youth, Comstock sought the arrest of those circulating any type of printed material mentioning or discussing birth control, family planning, abortion, and sex education. He also felt that certain literature intended for adults, including medical articles and works considered classics, overstepped the bounds of decency. Comstock argued that if circulated among the general public, these would only arouse the senses and provoke sinful ideas.

For a period of time, Comstockery (as strict censorship of obscene materials or immoral behavior came to be known) flourished, as evidenced by legal and societal crackdowns on material considered inappropriate. The publishing industry largely self-censored rather than face fines or jail sentences for exposing children to immoral literature, thus encouraging authors to avoid controversial topics and characters. Simultaneously, various states passed censorship laws of their own, called "little Comstock laws" (Graham 1970). The phrase "banned in Boston" described the efforts of the Boston Watch and Ward Society to mirror Comstock's efforts. Ironically, publishers began to promote certain books as "banned in Boston" (such as Walt Whitman's *Leaves of* Grass) because this label increased their popularity.

Eventually, public support for censorship efforts faded as society grew more accepting of new, progressive ideas and as Comstock made broader and bolder attempts to rid society of what he considered filth. Previous efforts to educate the masses about topics such as family planning and sexuality had been met with disdain from civic and public leaders who protested what they considered a degradation of morals and societal values and a challenge to a woman's accepted place in society. Comstock's zeal for prosecuting distributors of vice pitted him against a rising number of advocates for women and families who argued that discussion, consumption, and dissemination of information related to such topics should be permissible. Groups such as the Free Love Movement argued the Comstock Act encouraged sexual repression; general critics pointed to restrictions of free speech and freedom of the press; and contraception advocates decried the violation of basic freedoms to discuss, promote, and ensure the health of women. The writings of birth control advocate Margaret Sanger, for example, put her squarely at odds with Comstock. When Margaret fled the country to avoid arrest, her husband served jail time for distributing her work. Although convicted, he found considerable public support in decrying Comstock's law as unjust.

DID YOU KNOW?

This idea that media have the power to "inject" messages into the minds of an audience and cause a specific reaction was largely accepted in Comstock's time. The assumption gained popularity in the 1930s after a fictional "War of the Worlds" radio broadcast resulted in mass hysteria among some listeners who believed aliens were actually invading earth. This theory, called the "Magic Bullet Theory" (also called the "Hypodermic Needle Theory," the Transmission-Belt Model," and "Hypodermic Syringe Model") assumes that media have the power to uniformly "inject" powerful ideas and thoughts into the minds of passive, susceptible audiences. It does not take into consideration the power of critical thinking, individuality of media consumers, or other important factors that affect responses to media messages. Eventually, this theory was dismissed in favor of more contextual approaches that also consider the power of human agency in terms of how a message is received.

When Comstock attacked visual and literary arts enjoyed by the upper classes, his support diminished further. He targeted art he felt violated the moral sensibilities of society, including a 1906 promotional pamphlet for the Art Students' League in New York City that contained studies of nude figures. Although his public backing waned, he unabashedly pursued his battle against obscenity until his death in 1915 from pneumonia.

Anthony Comstock is regarded as one of the most influential moral crusaders of the late eighteenth century. He pushed restrictive laws through Congress and used his government positions to effectively halt production of material deemed offensive, obscene, or indecent. It took decades for many provisions of the Comstock Act to be repealed or amended. By the 1930s, courts had ruled that drugs, including contraceptives, could be sent through the mail and that free speech prohibits laws restricting discussion of contraceptives or family planning. The 1973 Supreme Court case *Miller v. California* established guidelines more clearly defining obscenity, and a 1983 Supreme Court decision declared the Comstock law did not meet the necessary standards for lawful government regulation of commercial speech or advertisements.

Nonetheless, Comstock's strict interpretations of decency/indecency effectively set the foundation for critical arguments supporting censorship laws over the next century; many modern legal challenges to pornography and other perceived obscenities are rooted in the same types of arguments and justifications as those used to pass the original Comstock Act.

DID YOU KNOW?

Comstock's legacy reached far beyond his attempts to abolish the circulation of obscene print materials. His successful efforts to censor publications and materials related to family planning publications were sustained for decades. Certain laws limiting distribution of/access to birth control remained in effect until 1965 when the Supreme Court decided in *Griswold v. Connecticut* that married couples have a "fundamental" right to privacy that includes the right to use contraception. That right would later be extended to unmarried couples in the 1972 Supreme Court ruling for *Eisenstadt v. Baird*.

FURTHER READING

Beisel, Nicola. *Imperiled Innocents: Anthony Comstock and Family Reproduction in Victorian America*. Princeton, NJ: Princeton University Press, 1997.

Blanchard, Margaret A., and John E. Semonche. "Anthony Comstock and His Adversaries: The Mixed Legacy of This Battle for Free Speech." *Communication Law and Policy* 11, no. 3 (2006): 317–365. doi:10.1207/s15326926clp1103_2

Comstock, Anthony. *Frauds Exposed, or, How the People Are Deceived and Robbed, and Youth Corrupted Being a Full Exposure of Various Schemes Operated Through the Mails*. New York: J.H. Brown, 1880. http://archive.org/stream/cu31924030319325#page/n7/mode/2up

Giesberg, Judith. *Sex and the Civil War: Soldiers, Pornography, and the Making of American Morality*. Chapel Hill, NC: University of North Carolina Press, 2017.

Horowitz, Helen Lefkowitz. "Victoria Woodhull, Anthony Comstock, and Conflict over Sex in the United States in the 1870s." *Journal of American History* 87, no. 2 (2000): 403–434. doi:10.2307/2568758

Weingarten, Karen. "The Inadvertent Alliance of Anthony Comstock and Margaret Sanger: Abortion, Freedom, and Class in Modern America." *Feminist Formations* 22, no. 2 (2010): 42–59.

Werbel, Amy. *Lust on Trial: Censorship and the Rise of American Obscenity in the Age of Anthony Comstock*. New York; Chichester, West Sussex: Columbia University Press, 2018.

- ***Document 5:*** Espionage Act of 1917
- ***Date:*** June 15, 1917
- ***Where:*** U.S. Congress
- ***Significance:*** The Espionage Act, passed shortly after the United States entered World War I, was designed to prevent disclosure of national defense secrets by criminalizing the sharing of information or other actions that could potentially benefit enemy forces or that would hinder domestic war efforts. Those found guilty of committing such crimes could be punished with steep fines, imprisonment, or death. The act was so broad in its language and interpretations that it effectively limited antiwar protests and dissent. Opponents argued that First Amendment freedoms were being crushed, but courts later ruled that dangers during wartime generally justified the restrictions.

DOCUMENT

Title I.

Espionage

SECTION 1. That (a) whoever, for the purpose of obtaining information respecting the national defense with intent or reason to believe that the information to be obtained is to be used to the injury of the United States, or to the advantage of any foreign nation, goes upon, enters, flies over, or otherwise obtains information concerning any vessel, aircraft, work of defense, navy yard, naval station, submarine base, coaling station, fort, battery, torpedo station, dockyard, canal, railroad, arsenal, camp, factory, mine, telegraph, telephone, wireless, or signal station, building, office, or other place connected with the national defense, owned or constructed, or in progress of construction by the United States or under the control of the United States, or of any of its officers or agents, or within the exclusive jurisdiction of the United States, or any place in which any vessel, aircraft, arms, munitions, or other materials or instruments for use in time of war are being made, prepared, repaired, or stored, under any contract or agreement with the United States, or with any person on behalf of the United States, or otherwise on behalf of the United States, or any prohibited place within the meaning of section six of this title; or (b) whoever for the purpose aforesaid, and with like intent or reason to believe, copies, takes, makes, or obtains, or attempts, or induces or aids another to copy, take, make, or obtain, any sketch, photograph, photographic negative, blue print, plan, map, model, instrument, appliance, document, writing, or note of anything connected with the national defense; or (c) whoever, for the purpose aforesaid, receives or obtains or agrees or attempts or induces or aids another to receive or obtain from any person, or from any source whatever, any document, writing, code book, signal book, sketch, photograph, photographic negative, blue print, plan, map, model, instrument, appliance, or note, of anything connected with the national defense, knowing or having reason to believe, at the time he receives or obtains, or agrees or attempts or induces or aids another to receive or obtain it, that it has been or will be obtained, taken, made, or disposed of by any person contrary to the provisions of this title; or (d) whoever, lawfully or unlawfully having possession of, access to, control over, or being intrusted with any document, writing, code book, signal book, sketch, photograph, photographic negative, blue print, plan, map, model, instrument, appliance, or note relating to the national defense, willfully communicates or transmits or attempts to communicate or transmit the same to any person not entitled to receive it, or willfully retains the same and fails to deliver it on demand to the officer or employee of the United States entitled to receive it; or (e) whoever, being intrusted with or having lawful possession of control of any document, writing, code book, signal book, sketch, photograph, photographic negative, blue print, plan, map, model, note or information, relating to the national defense, through gross negligence permits the same to be removed from its proper place of custody or delivered to anyone in violation of his trust, or to be lost, stolen, abstracted, or destroyed, shall be punished by a fine of not more than $10,000, or by imprisonment for not more than two years, or both.

SEC. 2. (a) Whoever, with intent or reason to believe that it is to be used to the injury of the United States or to the advantage of a foreign nation, communicates, delivers, or transmits, or attempts to, or aids or induces another to, communicate, deliver, or transmit, to any foreign government, or to any faction or party or military or naval force within a foreign country, whether recognized or unrecognized by the United States, or to any representative, officer, agent, employee, subject, or citizen thereof, either directly or indirectly, any document, writing, code book, signal book, sketch, photograph, photographic negative, blue print, plan, map, model, note, instrument, appliance, or information relating to the national defense, shall be punished by imprisonment for not more than twenty years: *Provided,* That whoever shall violate the provisions of subsection (a) of this section in time of war shall be punished by death or by imprisonment for not more than thirty years; and (b) whoever, in time of war, with intent that the same shall be communicated to the enemy, shall collect, record, publish, or communicate, or attempt to elicit any information with respect to the movement, numbers, description, condition, or disposition of any of the armed forces, ships, aircraft, or war materials of the United States, or with respect to the plans or conduct, or supposed plans or conduct of any naval or military operations, or with respect to any works or measures undertaken for or connected with, or intended for the fortification or defense of any place, or any other information relating to the public defense, which might be useful to the enemy, shall be punished by death or by imprisonment for not more than thirty years.

SEC. 3. Whoever, when the United States is at war, shall willfully make or convey false reports or false statements with intent to interfere with the operation or success of the military or naval forces of the United States or to promote the success of its enemies and whoever, when the United States is at war, shall willfully cause or attempt to cause insubordination, disloyalty, mutiny, or refusal of duty, in the military or naval forces of the United States, or shall willfully obstruct the recruiting or enlistment service of the United States, to the injury of the service or of the United States, shall be punished by a fine of not more than $10,000 or imprisonment for not more than twenty years, or both.

SEC. 4. If two or more persons conspire to violate the provisions of sections two or three of this title, and one or more of such persons does any act to effect the object of the conspiracy, each of the parties to such conspiracy shall be punished as in said sections provided in the case of the doing of the act the accomplishment of which is the object of such conspiracy. Except as above provided conspiracies to commit offenses under this title shall be punished as provided by section thirty-seven of the Act to codify, revise and amend the penal laws of the United States approved March fourth, nineteen hundred and nine.

SEC. 5. Whoever harbors or conceals any person who he knows, or has reasonable grounds to believe or suspect, has committed, or is about to commit, an offense under this title shall be punished by a fine of not more than $10,000 or by imprisonment for not more than two years, or both.

SEC. 6. The President in time of war or in case of national emergency may by proclamation designate any place other than those set forth in subsection (a) of section one hereof in which anything for the use of the Army or Navy is being prepared or constructed or stored as a prohibited place for the purposes of this title: *Provided,* That he shall determine that information with respect thereto would be prejudicial to the national defense.

SEC. 7. Nothing contained in this title shall be deemed to limit the jurisdiction of the general courts-martial, military commissions, or naval courts-martial under sections thirteen hundred and forty-two, thirteen hundred and forty-three, and sixteen hundred and twenty-four of the Revised Statutes as amended.

SEC. 8. The provisions of this title shall extend to all Territories, possessions, and places subject to the jurisdiction of the United States whether or not contiguous thereto, and offenses under this title when committed upon the high seas or elsewhere within the admiralty and maritime jurisdiction of the United States and outside the territorial limits thereof shall be punishable hereunder.

SEC. 9. The Act entitled "An Act to prevent the disclosure of national defense secrets," approved March third, nineteen hundred and eleven, is hereby repealed.

SOURCE: Library of Congress. Sixty-fifth Congress. Found at https://www.loc.gov/item/llsl-v40/

- ***Document:*** Sedition Act of 1918 (Amendment to 1917 Espionage Act)
- ***Date:*** May 16, 1918
- ***Where:*** Congress

- ***Significance:*** The Sedition Act of 1918 was actually a series of amendments to the original 1917 Espionage Act. These revisions included new restrictions on written or verbal commentary critical of the war effort. Any criticism of the military or negative comments about the role of the U.S. in the war could result in prosecution, resulting in fines up to $10,000 and prison sentences up to 20 years. Under the Sedition Act, it also became illegal to display the flag of an enemy country during wartime, and the legislation gave the postmaster general the right to refuse to mail any material suspected of criticizing the government's war efforts or violating other provisions of the Act. The Sedition Act was designed to silence opposition to the war and suppress any encouragement or support of enemy countries. Critics decried the Sedition Act as a ruthless attack on First Amendment guarantees of freedom of speech and freedom of the press.

DOCUMENT

Be it enacted by the Senate and House of Representatives of the United States of America in Congress assembled, That section three of title one of the Act entitled "An Act to punish acts of interference with the foreign relations, the neutrality, and the foreign commerce of the United States, to punish espionage, and better to enforce the criminal laws of the United States, and for other purposes," approved June fifteenth, nineteen hundred and seventeen, be, and the same is hereby, amended so as to read as follows:

> **Sec. 3.** Whoever, when the United States is at war, shall willfully make or convey false reports or false statements with intent to interfere with the operation or success of the military or naval forces of the United States, or to promote the success of its enemies, or shall willfully make or convey false reports or false statements, or say or do anything except by way of bona fide and not disloyal advice to an investor or investors, with intent to obstruct the sale by the United States of bonds or other securities of the United States or the making of loans by or to the United States, and whoever when the United States is at war, shall willfully cause or attempt to cause, or incite or attempt to incite, insubordination, disloyalty, mutiny, or refusal of duty, in the military or naval forces of the United States, or shall willfully obstruct or attempt to obstruct the recruiting or enlistment services of the United States, and whoever, when the United States is at war, shall willfully utter, print, write or publish any disloyal, profane, scurrilous, or abusive language about the form of government of the United States or the Constitution of the United States, or the military or naval forces of the United States, or the flag of the United States, or the uniform of the Army or

Navy of the United States into contempt, scorn, contumely, or disrepute, or shall willfully utter, print, write, or publish any language intended to incite, provoke, or encourage resistance to the United States, or to promote the cause of its enemies, or shall willfully display the flag of any foreign enemy, or shall willfully by utterance, writing, printing, publication, or language spoken, urge, incite, or advocate any curtailment of production in this country of any thing or things, product or products, necessary or essential to the prosecution of the war in which the United States may be engaged, with intent by such curtailment to cripple or hinder the United States in the prosecution of war, and whoever shall willfully advocate, teach, defend, or suggest the doing of any of the acts or things in this section enumerated, and whoever shall by word or act support or favor the cause of any country with which the United States is at war or by word or act oppose the cause of the United States therein, shall be punished by a fine of not more than $10,000 or the imprisonment for not more than twenty years, or both: Provided, That any employee or official of the United States Government who commits any disloyal act or utters any unpatriotic or disloyal language, or who, in an abusive and violent manner criticizes the Army or Navy or the flag of the United States shall be at once dismissed from the service. . . .

Sec. 4. When the United States is at war, the Postmaster General may, upon evidence satisfactory to him that any person or concern is using the mails in violation of any of the provisions of this Act, instruct the postmaster at any post office at which mail is received addressed to such person or concern to return to the postmaster at the office at which they were originally mailed all letters or other matter so addressed, with the words 'Mail to this address undeliverable under Espionage Act' plainly written or stamped upon the outside thereof, and all such letters or other matter so returned to such postmasters shall be by them returned to the senders thereof under such regulations as the Postmaster General may prescribe.

SOURCE: Library of Congress. Found at https://www.loc.gov/law/help/statutes-at-large/65th-congress/session-2/c65s2ch75.pdf

ANALYSIS

As the United States slowly healed from physical and emotional fractures in the decades following the Civil War, there was little desire to engage in any manner of additional conflict. This sentiment remained strong even as fighting erupted among major European powers in 1914. However, as the war overseas progressed, America found itself embroiled in the turmoil. Germany's unrestricted submarine warfare sunk the British ship *Lusitania* as well as U.S. merchant ships in British coastal waters, claiming the lives of more than 150 U.S. citizens. Additionally, the interception of the Zimmermann Telegram revealed German efforts to form an alliance with Mexico in exchange for help repossessing territory lost during the Mexican-American War. President Woodrow Wilson decided the United States could no longer remain isolationist, and the country entered World War I on April 6, 1917.

Just two months after U.S. entry into WWI, Congress passed the Espionage Act at the urging of President Woodrow Wilson. Prior to passage of the Espionage Act of 1917, criticism of policy and opposition to governmental actions were protected under the First Amendment. However, under the act, criticism was restricted or censored during wartime with the justification that such attitudes could impede U.S. military efforts to defeat Germany. The act prohibited the exchange of information related to national security, particularly if such information might be used to aid foreign governments or in any way harm the United States. It also prohibited disloyalty or interference with military efforts, including recruitment and enlistment in the draft or sharing any information potentially beneficial to the enemy.

Although the primary aim of the Espionage Act was to ensure the nation's safety by identifying and punishing acts of disloyalty that could hamper the war effort, the language of the legislation was so vague that many previously protected forms of opposition or resistance to the war could now be interpreted as criminal. The result was a crackdown on various forms of dissent and antiwar expression.

These restrictions were further extended with passage of the Sedition Act on May 16, 1918. This legislation amended Section 3 of the 1917 Espionage Act, further restricting freedom of speech and freedom of the press in regard to antiwar sentiment. More specifically, this act made illegal any form of profanity, unpatriotic, or disloyal language toward the military, the draft, the government, Constitution, the U.S. flag, or military uniforms during the war. The act prohibited individuals from flying the flag of an enemy country and also granted Postmaster General Albert S. Burleson permission to censor the mailing of any publication or materials that expressed antiwar sentiment (or materials that in any way violated the Espionage or Sedition Acts). This gave Burleson tremendous influence in determining which reading materials would be circulated during the war. Advertisements, stories, or editorials critical of the war were not tolerated; even attempting to send items in violation of these acts was punishable by five years in prison, a $5,000 fine, or both. Burleson refused to circulate numerous newspapers, especially pacifist, Socialist, or immigrant (specifically, German-language) publications. The ensuing loss of revenue caused some newspapers to fold and required others to practice strict self-censorship in war-related matters.

Although interpretation of seditious speech or expression was broad under the Sedition Act and punishment for violations was harsh, President Woodrow Wilson and members of the administration defended censorship, particularly of the press, as necessary to preserve national security and prevent public disorder during wartime. Critics of the law cried foul, insisting the intention of the law was to stifle dissent. Furthermore, they argued, the act directly violated First Amendment protections that guarded against legislation "abridging the freedom of speech, or of the press." The *New York Times* and other major U.S. newspapers decried the act as unconstitutional, arguing that in addition to limiting free speech, it restricted their abilities to accurately and thoroughly report on critical war-related news.

Support for both the Espionage and Sedition Acts among President Wilson and U.S. legislators was due in part to a fear that certain groups of immigrants, particularly Germans, pacifists, or individuals with Socialist sympathies may not remain loyal to the United States and its wartime goals. Even prior to entrance into the war, in 1915, President Wilson spoke out about disloyal immigrants debasing U.S.

politics and destroying industries. Officials hoped to sever the strong emotional ties binding recent immigrants to their home countries and to replace European identities with patriotism and support for the U.S. cause. To that end, they passed legislation designed to stamp out protests and criticism that would undermine U.S. war efforts. Any opposition to U.S. involvement in the war was considered an example of disloyalty. Peace activist Jane Addams, for example, lost public support for her reform work when she spoke out against the conflict. Socialist leader Eugene Debs and some members of the Industrial Workers of the World (IWW) were jailed for spoken and written criticism of both the draft and the war in general. Communist leaders in the United States during this time were also eyed with great suspicion, reflecting an anti-Communist sentiment that led to the country's first Red Scare.

Over 2,000 cases were prosecuted under the Sedition Act of 1918, and roughly one thousand individuals were convicted. The Sedition Act was repealed by Congress in 1921, but provisions of the original Espionage Act of 1917 remain in place today and are still being utilized. While no one was prosecuted under the Espionage Act during WWI, it was used in 1951 to try Julius and Ethel Rosenberg, U.S. citizens accused of spying for the Soviet Union. Both were found guilty, and in 1953, they became the first Americans sentenced to death under the Espionage Act. Few have been charged under the act since then, but recent years have seen a resurgence in cases. In 2013, Edward Snowden was charged with violation of the Espionage Act for unauthorized communication of national defense information and leaking classified Intelligence information. Julian Assange, who published the information from Snowden through WikiLeaks, was indicted on seventeen counts of violating the Espionage Act.

These indictments, in addition to the outcomes of numerous Espionage Act prosecutions brought under the Trump administration, could have long-lasting implications for the press and particularly for investigative journalism. Court rulings will shape the role, function, and reach of a free press tasked with protecting the national interest while providing citizens accurate and reliable information about government activity.

FURTHER READING

Forte, David F. "Righting a Wrong: Woodrow Wilson, Warren G. Harding, and the Espionage Act Persecutions." *Case Western Reserve Law Review* 68, no. 4 (2018): 1097–151.

Hodges, Adam J. "The Espionage and Sedition Acts in World War I: Using Wartime Loyalty Laws for Revenge and Profit," *Journal of American History* 100, no. 3 (2013): 863–64.

Hyde, Charles Cheney. "The Espionage Act." *American Journal of International Law* 12, no. 1 (1918): 142–46.

Scheiber, Harry N. *The Wilson Administration and Civil Liberties, 1917–1921*. Ithaca, NY: Cornell University Press, 1960.

Stone, Geoffrey R. *Perilous Times: Free Speech in Wartime from the Sedition Act of 1798 to the War on Terrorism*. New York: W. W. Norton & Company, 2004.

- ***Document 6:*** *New York Times* Article "Emma Goldman and A. Berkman behind the Bars"
- ***Date:*** June 16, 1917

- ***Where:*** *New York Times*, page 1
- ***Significance:*** This front-page article in the *New York Times* highlights the immense contributions made by Emma Goldman to antiwar efforts and the fight for freedom of speech and the determination of authorities to silence this critic who was seen as a threat to the political establishment. Goldman's unwavering defense of First Amendment freedom of expression at a time when it was under attack made her one of the most influential figures of the early twentieth century.

DOCUMENT

Emma Goldman and A. Berkman Behind the Bars (June 16, 1917) New York Times

Anarchist Headquarters Raided and Leaders Held for Anti-Draft Conspiracy.
Many Documents Seized
Card Index of Reds in the United States Simplifies Secret Service Men's Work.
Rioters Menace Soldiers
Some 200 Without Registration Cards Detained at Anti-Conscription Gatherings in This City.

Emma Goldman and Alexander Berkman, the two most notorious anarchists in the United States, who for weeks have been conducting a campaign against all the aspirations and activities of this Government, particularly against our part in the war and army conscription, in the course of which they have at times almost preached sedition, were arrested by Federal agents yesterday afternoon in the anarchist headquarters at 20 East 125th Street.

For several weeks Secret Service agents have kept close watch on Emma Goldman and Berkman. . . . Yesterday that evidence [of sedition] was forthcoming when the Government came into possession of copies of the anarchist publications known as Mother Earth, which is owned by Emma Goldman, and The Blast, the editor and proprietor of which is Berkman. . . .

SLACKER ARRESTED ALSO.

The raiding party which left the Federal Building at 4:10 P. M. under command of Marshal McCarthy included Assistant United States District Attorney E. M. Stanton, Lieutenant Barnitz, Deputy Marshals Doran, Hearne, and Meade, and Detectives Murphy and Kiely of the Police Department. A few minutes before 5 o'clock the

Government automobiles arrived at 20 East 125th Street. In the publication office of the anarchist papers Marshal McCarthy and his aids found Miss Goldman, a Miss Fitzgerald, Walker Merchant, Carl Newlander, and a young man named Bales, who was subsequently arrested when it was discovered that although of draft age he had failed to register on June 5.

"I have a warrant for your arrest," Marshal McCarthy said to Emma Goldman.

"I am not surprised, yet I would like to know what the warrant is based on," the woman said.

Marshal McCarthy answered by producing a copy of Mother Earth containing an article on the so-called No-Conscription League signed "Emma Goldman."

"Did you write that?" asked the Marshal.

Miss Goldman replied that she had written the article, and in answer to another question said she stood for everything in Mother Earth, because, she added, she was the sole owner of the publication.

Lieutenant Barnitz asked her if she knew where Berkman was, and she told him that Berkman was upstairs in another room. A few minutes later the man who in 1892 tried to murder H. C. Frick and subsequently served fourteen years in the penitentiary for his crime, appeared. He was taken completely by surprise and did not appear nearly so brave or defiant as his woman companion.

The young man, Bales, was busy in a corner of the room wrapping copies of the Blast and Mother Earth and addressing them when the officers entered. Mr. Stanton walked over and touched him on the shoulder. Bales looked up.

"How old are you?" Mr. Stanton demanded.

"Who, me?"

"Yes, you."

"I don't care to make any statement at this time," young Bales answered.

"Where is your registration card?"

"I have no registration card."

A moment later Bales was under arrest and in the custody of a detective.

Miss Fitzgerald, who gave her address as the Hotel Brevoort, seemed completely upset. "I can't understand it at all," she said to a reporter, "for they (Berkman and Goldman) are fine and beautiful characters, and are hundreds of years ahead of their time."

A big crowd quickly gathered in front of the anarchist headquarters and the reserves from the East 126th Street Police Station were summoned to keep order.

ARRAYED IN ROYAL PURPLE.

Marshal McCarthy told the prisoners to get ready for a quick trip to the Federal Building. Miss Goldman asked if she could have time to put on a more presentable gown. Permission was given, and she disappeared upstairs, to return a few minutes later dressed in royal purple.

In the meantime the Marshals and the police were busy searching the room. All the papers of every kind were seized, including some of George Bernard Shaw's works. The Shaw books, however, were later ordered to be left on the shelves, together with other works not of an anarchistic character. The entire unmailed editions of Mother Earth and The Blast were seized.

The issue of The Blast on which the arrest of Berkman was based is, in the opinion of the Federal officials, one of the vilest things ever sent through the United States mails, for several hundred copies were mailed before the paper was brought to the attention of the authorities.

The outside cover to the issue shows an American carrying on his back a fat man in uniform, who is labeled "American militarism." Nearby stands a Russian peasant. Russia asks the American who is carrying the man in uniform. "What's the idea!" And the American answers, "Democracy," whereupon the Russian remarks, "Well, you know how I got mine."

The article for the writing of which Berkman was arrested is captioned "Registration."

It follows another article, captioned "To the Youth of America," in which the men of the country are urged to refuse to go to war against Germany.

BERKMAN'S OFFENDING ARTICLE.

The article on registration, which is the one specifically referred to in the complaint reads:

Registration is the first step of conscription.

The war shouters and their prostitute press, bent on snaring you into the army, tell you that registration has nothing to do with conscription.

They lie.

Without registration, conscription is impossible.

Conscription is the abdication of your rights as a citizen. Conscription is the cemetery where every vestige of your liberty is to be buried. Registration is its undertaker.

No man with red blood in his veins can be forced to fight against his will.

But you cannot successfully oppose conscription if you approve of, or submit, to registration.

Every beginning is hard. But if the Government can induce you to register it will have little difficulty in putting over conscription.

By registering you willfully supply the Government with the information it needs to make conscription effective.

Registration means placing in the hands of the authorities the despotic power of the machinery of passports which made darkest Russia what it was before the revolution.

There are thousands, perhaps hundreds of thousands of young men in this country who have never voted and who have never paid taxes, and who, legally speaking, have no official existence. Their registration means nothing short of suicide in a majority of cases.

Failure to register is punishable by imprisonment. Refusal to be conscripted may be punishable by death.

To register is to acknowledge the right of the Government to conscript.

The consistent conscientious objector to human slaughter will neither register nor be conscripted.

ALEXANDER BERKMAN

Miss Goldman's Proclamation

The article in Mother Earth, which is mentioned in the Barnitz complaint is quite long. That part which counsels defiance of the Selective Draft law reads:

> The No-Conscription League has been formed for the purpose of encouraging conscientious objectors to affirm their liberty of conscience, and to translate their objection to human slaughter by refusing to participate in the killing of their fellowmen. The No-Conscription League is to be the voice of protest against war, and against the coercion of conscientious objectors to participate in the war. Our platform may be summarized as follows:
>
> > We oppose conscription because we are internationalists, anti-militarists, and opposed to all wars waged by capitalistic Governments.
> >
> > We will fight for what we choose to fight for; we will never fight simply because we are ordered to fight.
> >
> > We believe that the militarization of America is an evil that far outweighs in its anti-social and anti-libertarian effects any good that may come from America's participation in the war.
> >
> > We will resist conscription by every means in our power, and we will sustain those who, for similar reasons, refuse to be conscripted. . . .

SOURCE: "Emma Goldman and A. Berkman Behind the Bars." *New York Times*, June 16, 1917.

ANALYSIS

Emma Goldman was an outspoken immigrant and political activist whose unapologetic anarchist and feminist views were seen as a threat by the U.S. political establishment. Although she was born to a Jewish family in what is now Lithuania, anti-Semitic sentiment later drove the family to settle in Russia. Goldman spent her teenage years between Russia and her grandmother's home in Germany. At the age of sixteen, Goldman immigrated with her sister to the United States, partly to escape an arranged marriage and her father's view that women needed no education. Goldman settled in Rochester, New York, where she worked in a garment factory. The grueling labor for sparse pay sparked in her a deep sense of injustice and discouragement. In 1886, the violent Haymarket Affair in Chicago and the resulting backlash toward immigrants and anarchists who were blamed for the incident moved a distressed Goldman to action. She began to study and adopt anarchist ideas and principals. At the same time, she became a vocal advocate of workers' rights and improved labor conditions, making her an integral part of a burgeoning labor movement. She moved to New York in 1889 at age twenty to participate more fully in both the anarchist and labor movements.

In New York City, Goldman was well known for delivering impassioned speeches and lectures that advocated for workers' and women's rights as well as anarchist ideals such as the need for liberty from repressive institutions. She criticized emphasis on wealth and the deep monetary and social divides between the rich and poor. She believed liberty, autonomy, and freedom of expression for all people required universal freedom from oppressive government structures. Freedom of speech became a primary topic of her lectures, and she worked with the Free Speech League to encourage others to speak out against injustices. By 1909, she was delivering lectures across the United States. In many cities, police and other officials who saw her as a threat to the social order did their best to stop her teaching by physically disrupting her lectures or placing her under arrest. Goldman fought back by publishing articles exposing their tactics and warning of the dangers of First Amendment suppression.

Goldman's fiery speeches at times incited protests, which further angered authorities. She was also eyed with suspicion because of the ideas promoted in *Mother Earth* magazine, which she founded and edited with partner Alexander Berkman. Her anarchist views and insistence on individual freedoms were unpopular with leaders who feared her teaching would incite rebellion and destabilize the government. As Goldman's notoriety grew and her popularity increased, resistance to her message among the wealthy and powerful grew as well. Anarchists in the early twentieth century were blamed for creating economic and political instability, and as a leading advocate of anarchy, Goldman became a popular target for political leaders and the media. Soon the public image of Goldman changed from that of a free-thinking advocate for improved social conditions to that of a violent and dangerous political radical. Her personal history to some degree bolstered this image. In 1892, she was arrested for conspiring with Berkman to kill industrialist Henry Clay Frick. Berkman was sentenced to twenty-two years in jail, but Goldman was not convicted for lack of evidence that she was part of the assassination plot. Then, in 1901, President William McKinley was assassinated by anarchist Leon Czolgosz, who said he was inspired by Goldman. Some insisted that she must have had something to do with the murder. She denied any connection to Czolgosz, and investigators never found evidence associating her with the crime, but her reputation remained damaged.

Goldman's arrests and growing unpopularity with authorities did not dampen her resolve to speak freely about issues to which she was passionately devoted. However, with the outbreak of World War I and subsequent U.S. involvement in the war, Goldman shifted her focus toward opposition to U.S. involvement in the war and the censorship of speech critical of the country's military involvement. To object, she organized antiwar protest meetings, argued against registration and the draft, and organized the No-Conscription League.

Ultimately, it was Goldman's opposition to the war rather than her support for feminist thought or labor rights that resulted in her final arrest and conviction. Under new wartime restrictions outlined in the Espionage and Sedition Acts, any interference with the war effort, including impeding conscription, was a crime. In 1917, police raided Goldman's office, collected papers and manuscripts of *Mother Earth*, and charged her under the Espionage Act for conspiracy against registration for the draft. By this time, she was a well-known figure, and news of her arrest earned a place on the front page of the *New York Times*. At her trial Goldman gave an eloquent testimony, stating, "We say that if America has entered the war to make the world safe for democracy, she must first make democracy safe in America. How else is the world to take America seriously, when democracy at home is daily being outraged, free speech suppressed, peaceable assemblies broken up by overbearing and brutal gangsters in uniform; when free press is curtailed and every independent opinion gagged." (Goldman 1917). In spite of her bold defense she was found guilty, fined $10,000, and sentenced to two years in prison. By the time she was released in 1919, the United States was caught up in an anti-Communist Red Scare. Goldman was declared to be a subversive alien, and after the courts rejected her citizenship claims, she was deported back to Russia. Goldman was prohibited from ever living again in the United States but spent the remainder of her life traveling and lecturing, mostly through Europe and Canada.

Goldman's legacy is multidimensional. She was a hero to many for her willingness to speak out against social injustices, including mistreatment of workers and lack of access to reproductive rights and information. Her political activism and bullish refusal to submit to what she felt was an unjust system made her the object of hatred by many others, particularly those in positions of authority. Although she was forcibly deported because of her outspoken views, her contributions to the history of free speech in the United States are seminal. It was Goldman's work that inspired American Civil Liberties Union founder Roger Baldwin to consider the meaning and value of freedom and dedicate his life to its protection. Additionally, Goldman's writings have inspired countless others to advocate for human rights and free speech. Her legacy exposes a period of U.S. history fraught with assaults on the First Amendment, but Goldman's story also contributes to a great lineage of thinkers, speakers, and writers, who, inspired by this courageous woman, vigorously defended and protected the freedom of expression for which she valiantly fought.

FURTHER READING

Falk, Candace. "Emma Goldman." *Jewish Women: A Comprehensive Historical Encyclopedia*. Jewish Women's Archive. February 27, 2009.

Goldman, Emma. *Living My Life*. New York: Dover, 1970.

Goldman, Emma, Candace Falk, Barry Pateman, and Jessica Moran. *Emma Goldman, Vol. 1: A Documentary History of the American Years*. Volume 1: Made for America, 1890–1901. Champaign, IL: University of Illinois Press, 2016.

Goldman, Emma, Candace Falk, Barry Pateman, Jessica M. Moran, Susan Wengraf, and Robert Cohen, eds. *Emma Goldman, Vol. 2: A Documentary History of the American Years*. Volume 2: Making Speech Free, 1902–1909. Urbana; Chicago: University of Illinois Press, 2008.

Lynskey, Bill. "'I Shall Speak in Philadelphia': Emma Goldman and the Free Speech League." *Pennsylvania Magazine of History and Biography* 133, no. 2 (2009): 167–202. www.jstor.org/stable/40543455

- ***Document 7:*** Justice Holmes Presents the "Clear and Present Danger" Rule in *Schenck v. United States*
- ***Date:*** Decided March 3, 1919

- ***Where:*** Supreme Court of the United States
- ***Significance:*** The *Schenck* case was the first major free speech case examined by the U.S. Supreme Court. In a major test of the First Amendment, defendant Charles Schenck challenged the constitutionality of the 1917 Espionage Act, arguing that his right to protest the draft was protected under the free speech clause. In a unanimous court ruling on the case Justice Oliver Wendell Holmes established the "clear and present danger" rule, indicating that the First Amendment does not protect free speech when such speech, in certain contexts, is used in a way that will result in substantive evil. Holmes's "clear and present danger" formula became a critical framework used in legal interpretations of free speech constitutionality and limitations on free speech in the United States until 1969.

DOCUMENT

Mr. Justice HOLMES delivered the opinion of the Court.

This is an indictment in three counts. The first charges a conspiracy to violate the Espionage Act of June 15, 1917 by causing and attempting to cause insubordination, &c., in the military and naval forces of the United States, and to obstruct the recruiting and enlistment service of the United States, when the United States was at war with the German Empire, to-wit, that the defendant wilfully conspired to have printed and circulated to men who had been called and accepted for military service under the Act of May 18, 1917, a document set forth and alleged to be calculated to cause such insubordination and obstruction. The count alleges overt acts in pursuance of the conspiracy, ending in the distribution of the document set forth. The second count alleges a conspiracy to commit an offense against the United States, to-wit, to use the mails for the transmission of matter declared to be non-mailable by title 12, 2, of the Act of June 15, 1917) to-wit, the above mentioned document, with an averment of the same overt acts. The third count charges an unlawful use of the mails for the transmission of the same matter and otherwise as above. The defendants were found guilty on all the counts. They set up the First Amendment to the Constitution forbidding Congress to make any law abridging the freedom of speech, or of the press, and bringing the case here on that ground have argued some other points also of which we must dispose.

It is argued that the evidence, if admissible, was not sufficient to prove that the defendant Schenck was concerned in sending the documents. According to the testimony Schenck said he was general secretary of the Socialist Party and had charge of the Socialist headquarters from which the documents were sent. He identified a book found there as the minutes of the Executive Committee of the party. The book showed a resolution of August 13, 1917, that 15,000 leaflets should be printed on the other side of one of them in use, to be mailed to men who had passed exemption boards, and for distribution. Schenck personally attended to the printing. On August 20 the general secretary's report said 'Obtained new leaflets from printer and started work addressing envelopes' &c.; and there was a resolve that Comrade Schenck be allowed $125 for sending leaflets through the mail. He said that he had about fifteen or sixteen thousand printed. There were files of the circular in question in the inner office which he said were printed on the other side of the one sided circular and were there for distribution. Other copies were proved to have been sent through the mails to drafted men. Without going into confirmatory details that were proved, no reasonable man could doubt that the defendant Schenck was largely instrumental in sending the circulars about. As to the defendant Baer there was evidence that she was a member of the Executive Board and that the minutes of its transactions were hers. The argument as to the sufficiency of the evidence that the defendants conspired to send the documents only impairs the seriousness of the real defence.

It is objected that the documentary evidence was not admissible because obtained upon a search warrant, valid so far as appears. The contrary is established. *Adams v. New York*, *Weeks v. United States*. The search warrant did not issue against the defendant but against the Socialist headquarters at 1326 Arch street and it would seem that the documents technically were not even in the defendants' possession. See *Johnson v. United States*. Notwithstanding some protest in argument the notion that evidence even directly proceeding from the defendant in a criminal proceeding is excluded in all cases by the Fifth Amendment is plainly unsound. *Holt v. United States*.

The document in question upon its first printed side recited the first section of the Thirteenth Amendment, said that the idea embodied in it was violated by the conscription act and that a conscript is little better than a convict. In impassioned language it intimated that conscription was despotism in its worst form and a monstrous wrong against humanity in the interest of Wall Street's chosen few. It said, 'Do not submit to intimidation,' but in form at least confined itself to peaceful measures such as a petition for the repeal of the act. The other and later printed side of the sheet was headed 'Assert Your Rights.' It stated reasons for alleging that any one violated the Constitution when he refused to recognize 'your right to assert your opposition to the draft,' and went on, 'If you do not assert and support your rights, you are helping to deny or disparage rights which it is the solemn duty of all citizens and residents of the United States to retain.' It described the arguments on the other side as coming from cunning politicians and a mercenary capitalist press, and even silent consent to the conscription law as helping to support an infamous conspiracy. It denied the power to send our citizens away to foreign shores to shoot up the people of other lands, and added that words could not express the condemnation such cold-blooded ruthlessness deserves, &c., &c., winding up, 'You must do your share to maintain, support and uphold the rights of the people of this country.' Of course the document would not have been sent unless it had been intended to have some effect, and we do not see what effect it could be expected to have upon persons subject to the draft except to influence them to obstruct the carrying of it out. The defendants do not deny that the jury might find against them on this point.

But it is said, suppose that that was the tendency of this circular, it is protected by the First Amendment to the Constitution. Two of the strongest expressions are said to be quoted respectively from well-known public men. It well may be that the prohibition of laws abridging the freedom of speech is not confined to previous restraints, although to prevent them may have been the main purpose, as intimated in *Patterson v. Colorado.* We admit that in many places and in ordinary times the defendants in saying all that was said in the circular would have been within their constitutional rights. But the character of every act depends upon the circumstances in which it is done. *Aikens v. Wisconsin.* The most stringent protection of free speech would not protect a man in falsely shouting fire in a theatre and causing a panic. It does not even protect a man from an injunction against uttering words that may have all the effect of force. *Gompers v. Buck's Stove & Range Co.* The question in every case is whether the words used are used in such circumstances and are of such a nature as to create a clear and present danger that they will bring about the substantive evils that Congress has a right to prevent. It is a question of proximity and degree. When a nation is at war many things that might be said in time of peace are such a hindrance to its effort that their utterance will not be endured so long as men fight and that no Court could regard them as protected by any constitutional right. It seems to be admitted that if an actual obstruction of the recruiting service were proved, liability for words that produced that effect might be enforced. The statute of 1917 in section 4 punishes conspiracies to obstruct as well as actual obstruction. If the act, (speaking, or circulating a paper,) its tendency and the intent with which it is done are the same, we perceive no ground for saying that success alone warrants making the act a crime. *Goldman v. United States.* Indeed that case might be said to dispose of the present contention if the precedent covers all *media concludendi.* But as the right to free speech was not referred to specially, we have thought fit to add a few words.

It was not argued that a conspiracy to obstruct the draft was not within the words of the Act of 1917. The words are 'obstruct the recruiting or enlistment service,' and it might be suggested that they refer only to making it hard to get volunteers. Recruiting heretofore usually having been accomplished by getting volunteers the word is apt to call up that method only in our minds. But recruiting is gaining fresh supplies for the forces, as well by draft as otherwise. It is put as an alternative to enlistment or voluntary enrollment in this act. The fact that the Act of 1917 was enlarged by the amending Act of May 16, 1918, of course, does not affect the present indictment and would not, even if the former act had been repealed.

Judgments affirmed.

SOURCE: Schenck v. United States, 249 U.S. 47 (1918). https://caselaw.findlaw.com/us-supreme-court/249/47.html

ANALYSIS

When President Woodrow Wilson ran for reelection in 1916, he depicted himself as the antiwar candidate. However, less than six months later, at President Wilson's urging, the United States entered World War I. Although Wilson was aware that many of his countrymen opposed involvement in Europe's conflict, he felt the country must respond to aggressive German attacks on merchant and passenger ships that had claimed the lives of U.S. civilians.

The German attacks provoked a change in public opinion regarding U.S. neutrality. Nevertheless, certain groups remained steadfast in their opposition to the conflict and U.S. involvement in it. Socialists, anarchists, pacifists, Marxists, and religious groups opposed to violence were among many factions voicing antiwar sentiment. In an effort to control public dialog and subdue the influence of these groups, Congress passed the Espionage Act on June 15, 1917. This controversial act prohibited citizens from impeding U.S. military progress during the war, aiding the enemy in any way, and impeding or otherwise interfering with the draft.

The Socialist Party during this time was unapologetic in its opposition to the war, and particularly to the draft. General Secretary of the Party Charles T. Schenck prepared and distributed approximately 15,000 leaflets arguing against conscription and encouraging men of military age to resist the draft. The leaflet urged readers, "Do not submit to intimidation" and "Exercise your right of free speech, peaceful assembly, and petitioning the government for a redress of grievances." Readers were further encouraged to assert their rights and petition to repeal the Conscription Act.

Authorities arrested Schenck and fellow Socialist Elizabeth Baer, saying that by distributing the leaflets and thus hampering recruiting efforts they had violated the Espionage Act. The charges were serious; both faced up to $10,000 in fines and as many as twenty years in prison. Although there was little evidence the leaflets had in fact been widely distributed at the time of the arrest—eight of the eleven men called to testify had not even received them—a federal court jury convicted both and sentenced them to six months and ninety days in prison, respectively.

Schenck and Baer appealed the decision to the Supreme Court, saying the contents of the leaflet were protected under the First Amendment. Only weeks later, a similar case was brought before the Supreme Court. Eugene Debs, a Socialist who spoke out against the war and conscription, was also charged with impeding draft recruitment and indicted under the Espionage Act. Rulings for both cases were handed down within a week of each other in March 1919. Although the outcomes were similar, the court ruled first on *Schenck*, making it the better-known and more widely cited case. Most importantly, arguments and examples used to justify the *Schenck* ruling have been regarded as critical parameters of First Amendment constitutionality ever since.

In presenting the court's unanimous ruling in the *Schenck* case, Justice Oliver Wendell Holmes emphasized that the Constitutional right to free speech is not absolute; its permissibility depends both on the intent of the message and the circumstances of the time. The court's decision established that the intent of the document prepared and distributed by Schenck and Baer was to impede the draft during wartime, and this intent alone—regardless of the actual consequences—was enough to be a violation of the Espionage Act.

Holmes then offered the well-known analogy that "The most stringent protection of free speech would not protect a man in falsely shouting fire in a theatre and causing a panic." Subsequent scholars have noted the weight of this argument in the *Schenck* case is debatable, as no apparent panic was caused by the distribution of the leaflet (in fact, no apparent action resulted at all). Nevertheless, the leaflet questioned the validity of the draft, and its intent was to obstruct conscription efforts. Therefore, such intent *could* have had a powerful effect on those to which it was distributed. In the court's reasoning, that possibility affirmed the *need* to suppress such speech. Holmes's "fire in a crowded theatre" analogy became a well-established paradigm of First Amendment limitations.

According to the court, free expression of ideas crosses a line when those ideas are likely to inspire illegal or dangerous actions. The *Schenck* case was the Supreme Court's first major attempt to distinguish how and when this line is crossed. Holmes argued that free speech is not protected by the First Amendment when it presents a "clear and present danger" to society that could bring about "substantive evils that Congress has a right to prevent." Notably, Holmes explained that an individual's' right to speak freely can be curtailed when special circumstances warrant such a restriction. The court felt speaking freely against conscription during ordinary times has a different effect than it does during wartime. During peacetime, such expression would be protected under the First Amendment, but the same expression in the context of war could result in incitement to action that would be a clear danger to society. In this case, men refusing to fight on behalf of their country would place the entire country in danger. This, felt Holmes, was an example of a circumstance in which free speech cannot be permitted because of the *likelihood* that such speech could generate widespread harm or inspire others to violate the law.

The impact of the *Schenck* case on freedom of speech in the United States was tremendous. The ruling established that the Espionage Act did not violate the First Amendment, setting the stage for the conviction of many additional individuals charged with violating the act for publicly protesting the war. Additionally, Holmes's "clear and present danger" guideline became a sort of legal test by which many subsequent First Amendment cases would be measured. Although Holmes would later change course and vigorously defend First Amendment freedoms and the free trade of ideas in *Abrams v. United States* and subsequent cases, this ruling made its mark on history by conveying that the circumstances in which words are expressed and the nature of the words must be considered when determining their character. Under those considerations, if the character or tendency of a message lends itself to creating a clear and present danger, such words are not protected under the First Amendment.

FURTHER READING

Eastland, Terry, ed. *Freedom of Expression in the Supreme Court: The Defining Cases*. Lanham, MD: Rowman & Littlefield Publishers, 2000.

Kendrick, Leslie. "Free Speech and Guilty Minds." *Columbia Law Review* 114, no. 5 (2014): 1255–95.

Levinson, Michael R. "Clear and Present Danger during World War I." *Litigation* 35, no. 4 (2009): 47–54.

Lynskey, Bill. "Reinventing the First Amendment in Wartime Philadelphia." *Pennsylvania Magazine of History and Biography* 131, no. 1 (2007): 33–80.

Ragan, Fred D. "Justice Oliver Wendell Holmes, Jr., Zechariah Chafee, Jr., and the Clear and Present Danger Test for Free Speech: The First Year, 1919." *Journal of American History* 58, no. 1 (1971): 24–45.

- ***Document 8:*** Zechariah Chafee Jr.'s "Freedom of Speech in War Time"
- ***Date:*** June 1919
- ***Where:*** *Harvard Law Review*
- ***Significance:*** Zechariah Chafee became nationally known as an outspoken defender of free speech in the United States during World War I, largely because of his opposition to legislation that criminalized criticism of, or interference with, U.S. involvement in the war. Chafee's advocacy for free speech rights was a response to the U.S. government's most restrictive laws concerning freedom of expression in over one hundred years. Chafee is considered one of the nation's first and most influential First Amendment Scholars. His writings were later referenced by Supreme Court justices as they decided landmark free speech cases.

DOCUMENT

. . . Clearly, the problem of the limits of freedom of speech in war time is no academic question. On the one side, thoughtful men and journals are asking how scores of citizens can be imprisoned under this constitution only for their disapproval of the war as irreligious, unwise, or unjust. On the other, federal and state officials point to the great activities of German agents in our midst and to the unprecedented extension of the business of war over the whole nation, so that in the familiar remark of Ludendorff, wars are no longer won by armies in the field, but by the morale of the whole people. The widespread Liberty Bond campaigns, and the shipyards, munition factories, government offices, training camps, in all parts of the country, are felt to make the entire United States a theater of war, in which attacks upon our cause are as dangerous and unjustified as if made among the soldiers in the rear trenches. The government regards it as inconceivable that the Constitution should cripple its efforts to maintain public safety. Abstaining from countercharges of disloyalty and tyranny, let us recognize the issue as a conflict between two vital principles, and endeavor to find the basis of reconciliation between order and freedom.

. . . We can, of course, be sure that certain forms of utterance, which have always been crimes or torts at common law, are not within the scope of the free speech clauses. The courts in construing such clauses have, for the most part, done little more than place obvious cases on this or that side of the line. They tell us, for instance, that libel and slander are actionable, or even punishable, that indecent books are criminal, that it is contempt to interfere with pending judicial proceedings, and that a permit can be required for street meetings; and on the other hand, that some criticism of the government must be allowed, that a temperate examination of a judge's opinion is not contempt, and that honest discussion of the merits of a painting causes no liability for damages. But when we ask where the line actually runs and how they know on which side of it a given utterance belongs, we find no answer in their opinions. Justice Holmes in his Espionage Act decisions had a magnificent opportunity to make articulate for us that major premise, under which judges ought to classify words as inside or outside the scope of the First Amendment. He, we hoped, would concentrate his great abilities on fixing the line. Instead, like the other judges, he has told us that certain plainly unlawful utterances are, to be sure, unlawful.

> The First Amendment. . obviously was not 'intended to give immunity for every possible use of language . . . We venture to believe that neither Hamilton nor Madison, nor any other competent person then or later, ever supposed that to make criminal the counselling of a murder . . . would be an unconstitutional interference with free speech.
>
> The most stringent protection of free speech would not protect a man in falsely shouting fire in a theatre and causing a panic.
>
> (*Schenck v. United States*, 249 U.S. 47, 39 Sup. Ct. Rep. 247 (1919))

How about the man who gets up in a theater between the acts and informs the audience honestly but perhaps mistakenly that the fire exits are too few or locked? He is a much closer parallel to Schenck or Debs. How about James Russell Lowell when he counseled, not murder, but the cessation of murder, his name for war? The question whether such perplexing cases are within the First Amendment or not cannot be solved by the multiplication of obvious examples, but only by the development of a rational principle to mark the limits of constitutional protection . . .

. . . The real issue in every free-speech controversy is this—whether the state can punish all words which have some tendency, however remote, to bring about acts in violation of law, or only words which directly incite to acts in violation of law. If words do not become criminal until they have an immediate tendency to produce a breach of the peace, there is no need for a law of sedition, since the ordinary standards of criminal solicitation and attempt apply. Under those standards the words must bring the speaker's unlawful intention reasonably near to success. Such a limited power to punish utterances rarely satisfies the zealous in times of excitement like a war. They realize that all condemnation of the war or of conscription may conceivably lead to active resistance or insubordination. Is it not better to kill the serpent in the egg? All writings that have a tendency to hinder the war must be suppressed.

Such has always been the argument of the opponents of free speech. And the most powerful weapon in their hand, since the abolition of the censorship, is this doctrine of indirect causation, under which words can be punished for a supposed bad tendency long before there is any probability that they will break out into unlawful acts. Closely related to it is the doctrine of constructive intent, which regards the intent of the defendant to cause violence as immaterial so long as he intended to write the words, or else presumes the violent intent from the bad tendency of the words on the ground that a man is presumed to intend the consequences of his acts . . .

The censor is the most dangerous of all the enemies of liberty of the press, and cannot exist in this country unless made necessary by extraordinary perils . . .

It is now clear that the First Amendment fixes limits upon the power of Congress to restrict speech either by a censorship or by a criminal statute, and if the Espionage Act exceeds those limits it is unconstitutional. It is sometimes argued that the Constitution gives Congress the power to declare war, raise armies, and support a navy, that one provision of the Constitution cannot be used to break down another provision, and consequently freedom of speech cannot be invoked to break down the war power. I would reply that the First Amendment is just as much a part of the Constitution as the war clauses, and that it is equally accurate to say that the war clauses cannot be invoked to break down freedom of speech. The truth is that all provisions of the Constitution must be construed together so as to limit each other. In war as in peace, this process of mutual adjustment must include the Bill of Rights. There are those who believe that the Bill of Rights can be set aside in war time at the uncontrolled will of the government. The first ten amendments were drafted by men who had just been through a war. Two of these amendments expressly apply in war. A majority of the Supreme Court declared the war power of Congress to be restricted by the Bill of Rights in *Ex parte Milligan*, which cannot be lightly brushed aside, whether or not the majority went too far in thinking that the Fifth Amendment would have prevented Congress from exercising the war power under the particular circumstances of that case. If the First Amendment is to mean anything, it must restrict powers which are expressly granted by the Constitution to Congress, since Congress has no other powers. It must apply to those activities of government which are most liable to interfere with free discussion, namely, the postal service and the conduct of war.

The true meaning of freedom of speech seems to be this. One of the most important purposes of society and government is the discovery and spread of truth on subjects of general concern. This is possible only through absolutely unlimited discussion, for, as Bagehot points out, once force is thrown into the argument, it becomes a matter of chance whether it is thrown on the false side or the true, and truth loses all its natural advantage in the contest. Nevertheless, there are other purposes of government, such as order, the training of the young, protection against external aggression. Unlimited discussion sometimes interferes with these purposes, which must then be balanced against freedom of speech, but freedom of speech ought to weigh very heavily in the scale. The First Amendment gives binding force to this principle of political wisdom.

Or to put the matter another way, it is useless to define free speech by talk about rights. The agitator asserts his constitutional right to speak, the government asserts its constitutional right to wage war. The result is a deadlock. Each side takes the position of the man who was arrested for swinging his arms and hitting another in the nose, and asked the judge if he did not have a right to swing his arms in a free country. "Your right to swing your arms ends just where the other man's nose begins." To find the boundary line of any right, we must get behind rules of law to human facts. In our problem, we must regard the desires and needs of the individual human being who wants to speak and those of the great group of human beings among whom he speaks. That is, in technical language, there are individual interests and social interests, which must be balanced against each other, if they conflict, in order to determine which interest shall be sacrificed under the circumstances and which shall be protected and become the foundation of a legal right. It must never be forgotten that the balancing cannot be properly done unless all the interests involved are adequately ascertained, and the great evil of all this talk about rights is that each side is so busy denying the other's claim to rights that it entirely overlooks the human desires and needs behind that claim . . .

The First Amendment protects two kinds of interests in free speech. There is an individual interest, the need of many men to express their opinions on matters vital to them if life is to be worth living, and a social interest in the attainment of truth, so that 'the country may not only adopt the wisest course of action but carry it out in the wisest way. This social interest is especially important in war time. Even after war has been declared there is bound to be a confused mixture of good and bad arguments in its support, and a wide difference of opinion as to its objects. Truth can be sifted out from falsehood only if the government is vigorously and constantly cross-examined, so that the fundamental issues of the struggle may be clearly defined, and the war may not be diverted to improper ends, or conducted with an undue sacrifice of life and liberty, or prolonged after its just purposes are accomplished. Legal proceedings prove that an opponent makes the best cross- examiner. Consequently it is a disastrous mistake to limit criticism to those who favor the war. Men bitterly hostile to it may point out evils in its management like the secret treaties, which its supporters have been too busy to unearth. The history of the last five years shows how the objects of a war may change completely during its progress, and it is well that those objects should be steadily reformulated under the influence of open discussion not only by those who demand a military victory but by pacifists who take a different view of the national welfare. Further argument for the existence of this social interest becomes unnecessary if we recall the national value of the opposition in former wars.

The great trouble with most judicial construction of the Espionage Act is that this social interest has been ignored and free speech has been regarded as merely an individual interest, which must readily give way like other personal desires the moment it interferes with the social interest in national safety . . .

. . . Action in proportion to the emergency was justified, but we have censored and punished speech which was very far from direct and dangerous interference with the conduct of the war . . . It may be questioned, too, how much has actually been gained. Men have been imprisoned, but their words have not ceased to spread . . .

. . . In our efforts to silence those who advocated peace without victory we prevented at the very start that vigorous threshing out of fundamentals which might to-day have saved us from a victory without peace.

SOURCE: Chafee, Zechariah. "Freedom of Speech in War Time." *Harvard Law Review* 32, no. 8 (1919): 932–73.

ANALYSIS

Zechariah Chafee Jr. was a professor at Harvard University Law School who studied and championed preservation of the First Amendment. Chaffee is best known for vigorously advocating protection of free speech, even during wartime. He was a vocal critic of the Espionage and Sedition Acts and the way they were interpreted by federal prosecutors, who used the measures to try to squelch opposition to World War I. Chafee was the first prominent scholar to study varying interpretations of the First Amendment and the constitutionality of federal laws that restricted freedom of expression.

Chafee's primary arguments for free expression stemmed from restrictions imposed under the Espionage Act of 1917 and the Sedition Act of 1918. These acts, passed under the Wilson administration, were the most constraining to free speech since the passage of the Alien and Sedition Acts over a century earlier. Chafee wrote numerous works defending freedom of speech as essential to a healthy democracy, even when such expression is critical of the government.

During World War I, the Espionage and Sedition Acts were used to stifle the voices of those who vocally opposed the war. Outspoken critics of the war were arrested, labeled as political radicals, and charged with crimes related to impeding the progress of the United States during WWI. Even speaking out against the draft was grounds for arrest and prosecution. Chafee argued that the interpretation of the Espionage and Sedition laws to justify arrests and convictions of wartime dissenters in the name of national security was unconstitutional. He contended national security and national defense were not adequate reasons to limit free speech, especially when such speech does not directly interfere with the war or the country's participation in it. On the contrary, he viewed political agitation and dissention as natural and necessary elements of a democracy. Chafee felt the "discovery and spread of truth on subjects of general concern" was essential to a well-functioning society and government. Truth, he said, can only be ascertained through cross-examination and dialogue that includes criticism—even criticism of the government.

To illustrate the far-reaching implications of censorship of ideas and truthful dialogue, Chafee cited the case of *United States v. Rose Pastor Stokes*. The judge in this case ruled that antiwar opinions should be restricted not only among audiences with men of fighting age in attendance but also in areas where mothers, sisters, and sweethearts may hear them because the troops' success depended upon the enthusiasm and support of such figures. In highlighting this case, Chafee pointed out that restricting all oppositional voices does not allow honest public discussion to take place. Few will speak up and voice concerns if they are fearful that their antigovernment or antiwar opinions could be construed as inciting illegal acts or causing insubordination.

Chafee also considered problematic the way in which the two acts were interpreted to punish speech thought to potentially (not directly) incite rebellion or result in illegal action. He emphasized the dangers of applying a doctrine of indirect causation or of justifying censorship laws through the lens of constructive intent. Free speech should be protected, Chafee said, unless it *directly* results in criminal action or directly threatens public safety. Probability or intent of causing harm is not enough to warrant its restriction. He explained that because free speech serves both an individual and a societal interest, the determination of what makes speech unlawful requires finding the balance between public safety and the search for truth. Society as a whole, he felt, benefits from the acquisition of truthful information. Therefore, members of society must be able to speak and write freely so multiple perspectives can be heard and considered. Free speech should only be restricted when public safety is truly endangered, not when such speech simply produces a possibility that public safety could be compromised. He noted "the First Amendment forbids the punishment of words merely for their injurious tendencies."

Furthermore, Chafee pointed out that the use of language, even if it is antiwar language, is not a crime in itself just as an intention to commit a crime is not the same as actually committing a crime. As an example, Chafee states in Freedom of Speech in War Time that a man cannot be charged for murder when he shoots from forty miles away, even if he discharges the gun with the intention of killing. Likewise, he cited Judge Learned Hand in the case *Masses Publishing Co. v. Patten* arguing that suppression of speech should be based on its likelihood to cause injury to others, not on the substance or decency of the speech itself. Chafee argued that nothing in the 1917 Espionage Act makes speech criminal unless it actually incites others to overt acts or promotes false statements.

Chafee's theories and writings were largely unpopular at the time he penned them. His vigorous defense of the right to free speech, even among individuals considered political radicals, prompted a wary government response; J. Edgar Hoover's FBI monitored Chafee's writing and activities for decades. While Chafee was unsuccessful in altering judicial opinions and restrictive interpretations of the Espionage and Sedition Laws during World War I, his writings were later reconsidered and his ideas embraced by scholars and members of the judiciary alike, including Justice Oliver Wendell Holmes. Numerous arguments made by Chafee defending freedom of expression were later adopted by members of the Supreme Court in landmark decisions on free speech cases.

FURTHER READING

Irons, Peter H. "'Fighting Fair": Zechariah Chafee, Jr., the Department of Justice, and the 'Trial at the Harvard Club.'" *Harvard Law Review* 94, no. 6 (1981): 1205–36. doi:10.2307/1340754

Smith, Donald L. *Zechariah Chafee, Jr., Defender of Liberty and Law*. Cambridge, MA: Harvard University Press, 1986.

Wertheimer, John, and Zechariah Chafee. "Freedom of Speech: Zechariah Chafee and Free-Speech History." *Reviews in American History* 22, no. 2 (1994): 365–77. doi:10.2307/2702912

Wilson, Lynne. Review of *Zechariah Chafee, Jr., Defender of Liberty and Law*, by Donald L. Smith. *Seattle University Law Review* 11, no. 2 (1988): 387.

2

DEBATING THE EXTENT OF FREE SPEECH RIGHTS (1920–1950)

- ***Document 9:*** "A Case against the Reds" by U.S. Attorney General A. Mitchell Palmer
- ***Date:*** First published in February 1920
- ***Where:*** *The Forum*, v. 63, pp. 173–180
- ***Significance:*** By 1919, a war-weary U.S. populace faced numerous challenges: an economic recession, labor unrest, bombings, and the spread of Communist ideology following the Russian Revolution of 1917. This combination of factors stoked widespread fear and gave rise to an ultra-patriotic movement backed by those determined to root out Socialists, anarchists, Communists, and other radicals blamed for the political and civil unrest. During this first Red Scare in the United States, U.S. Attorney General A. Mitchell Palmer led the effort to implement a peacetime sedition act, casting aside civil liberties in the name of making the country safe from Communist threat. Thousands of arrests were made on the basis of political speech and writing, and hundreds of "undesirable aliens" were deported without trial.

DOCUMENT

SOURCE: "The Cheerful GIver—Or, Do Your Christmas Shopping Early." It is by Edwin Marcus and was printed in *The New York Times* on December 21, 1919

By request of The Forum, Attorney-General Palmer presents herewith his explanation of the Government's reason for deporting the "Reds." The plans for fomenting a nation-wide revolution in this country, prepared by Trotsky in Moscow, are in the files of the Attorney-General's office. It is upon these proofs that the Attorney-General has decided upon a vigorous system of arrest and deportation of radical aliens, which he says he will pursue until the United States is purged of Bolshevism. In this article, the Attorney-General sets forth his legal authority for wholesale arrests and deportation, revealing the entire program of the Department of Justice against Radicalism.

In this brief review of the work which the Department of Justice has undertaken to tear out the radical seeds that have entangled American ideas in their poisonous theories, I desire not merely to explain what the real menace of communism is, but also to tell how we have been compelled to clean up the country almost unaided by any virile legislation. Though I have not been embarrassed by political opposition, I have been materially delayed because the present sweeping processes of arrests and deportation of seditious aliens should have been vigorously pushed by Congress last spring. The failure of this is a matter of record in the Congressional files.

The anxiety of that period in our responsibility, when Congress, ignoring the seriousness of these vast organizations that were plotting to overthrow the Government, failed to act, has passed. The time came when it was obviously hopeless to expect the hearty cooperation of Congress . . . to stamp out these seditious societies in their open defiance of law by various forms of propaganda.

Like a prairie-fire, the blaze of revolution was sweeping over every American institution of law and order a year ago. It was eating its way into the homes of the American workman, its sharp tongues of revolutionary heat were licking the alters of the churches, leaping into the belfry of the school bell, crawling into the sacred corners of American homes, seeking to replace marriage vows with libertine laws, burning up the foundations of society.

Robbery, not war, is the ideal of communism. This has been demonstrated in Russia, Germany, and in America. As a foe, the anarchist is fearless of his own life, for his creed is a fanaticism that admits no respect of any other creed. Obviously it is the creed of any criminal mind, which reasons always from motives impossible to clean thought. Crime is the degenerate factor in society.

Upon these two basic certainties, first that the "Reds" were criminal aliens, and secondly that the American Government must prevent crime, it was decided that there could be no nice distinctions drawn between the theoretical ideals of the radicals and their actual violations of our national laws. An assassin may have brilliant intellectuality, he may be able to excuse his murder or robbery with fine oratory, but any theory which excuses crime is not wanted in America. This is no place for the criminal to flourish, nor will he do so, so long as the rights of common citizenship can be exerted to prevent him . . .

My information showed that communism in this country was an organization of thousands of aliens, who were direct allies of Trotsky. Aliens of the same misshapen caste of mind and indecencies of character, and it showed that they were making the same glittering promises of lawlessness, of criminal autocracy to Americans that they had made to the Russian peasants. How the Department of Justice discovered upwards of 60,000 of these organized agitators of the Trotsky doctrine in the United

States is the confidential information upon which the Government is now sweeping the nation clean of such alien filth . . . .

Merely as a part of this review, to make it complete, it must be shown how the Department of Justice proceeds to cause deportations today. For the moment we must go back to my report to the Senate of the United States on November 4th, 1919, in response to the Senate Resolution of October 14, 1919, which is as follows:

> Resolved, that the Attorney-General of the United States is requested to advise and inform the Senate whether or not the Department of Justice has taken the legal proceedings, and if not, why not, and if so, to what extent, for the arrest and punishment of the various persons within the United States, who, during recent days and weeks, and for a considerable time, continuously previous thereto, it is alleged, have attempted to bring about the forcible overthrow of the Government of the United States; who, it is alleged have preached anarchy and perdition, and who it is alleged have advised the defiance of law and authority, both by the printing and circulation of printed newspapers, books, pamphlets, circulars, stickers, and dodgers, and also by spoken word; and who, in like manner it is alleged, have advised and openly advocated the unlawful obstruction of industry and the unlawful and violent destruction of property, in the pursuance of a deliberate plan and purpose to destroy existing property rights and to impede and obstruct the conduct of business essential to the prosperity and life of the community.
>
> Also the Attorney-General is requested to advise and inform the Senate whether or not the Department of Justice has taken legal proceedings for the arrest and deportation of aliens, who, it is alleged, have, within the United States, permitted the acts aforesaid, and if not, why not, and if so, to what extent . . .

One of the chief incentives for the present activity of the Department of Justice against the "Reds" has been the hope that American citizens will themselves become voluntary agents for us, in a vast organization for mutual defense against the sinister agitation of men and women aliens, who appear to be either in the pay or under the criminal spell of Trotsky and Lenin.

Temporary failure to seize the alien criminals in this country who are directly responsible for spreading the unclean doctrines of Bolshevism here only increased the determination to get rid of them. Obviously, their offenses were related to our immigration laws, and it was finally decided to act upon that principle . . .

Although this law is entirely under the jurisdiction of the Department of Labor, it seemed to be the only means at my disposal of attacking the radical movement. To further this plan, as Congress had seen fit to refuse appropriations to the Department of Labor which might have enabled it to act vigorously against the "Reds," I offered to cooperate with the immigration officials to the fullest extent. My appropriation became available July 19, 1919. I then organized what is known as the Radical Division.

Briefly this is a circumstantial statement of the present activities of the Department of Justice, cooperating with the Department of Labor, against the "Reds." They require no defense, nor can I accept as true the counter claims of the "Reds" themselves, who, apparently indifferent to their disgrace, violent in their threats against the United States Government, until they are out of sight and sound of it, betray the characterless ideas and purposes that Trotsky has impressed upon the criminal classes which constitute communism.

Behind, and underneath, my own determination to drive from our midst the agents of Bolshevism with increasing vigor and with greater speed, until there are no more of them left among us, so long as I have the responsible duty of the task, I have discovered the hysterical methods of these revolutionary humans with increasing amazement and suspicion. In the confused information that sometimes reaches the people, they are compelled to ask questions which involve the reasons for my acts against the "Reds." I have been asked, for instance, to what extent deportation will check radicalism in this country. Why not ask what will become of the United States Government if these alien radicals are permitted to carry out the principles of the Communist Party as embodied in its so-called laws, aims, and regulations?

There wouldn't be any such thing left. In place of the United States Government we should have the horror and terrorism of Bolshevik tyranny such as is destroying Russia now. Every scrap of radical literature demands the overthrow of our existing government. All of it demands obedience to the instincts of criminal minds, that is, to the lower appetites, material and moral. The whole purpose of communism appears to be a mass formation of the criminals of the world to overthrow the decencies of private life, to usurp property that they have not earned, to disrupt the present order of life regardless of health, sex, or religious rights. By a literature that promises the wildest dreams of such low aspirations, that can occur to only the criminal minds, communism distorts our social law . . .

It has been impossible in so short a space to review the entire menace of the internal revolution in this country as I know it, but this may serve to arouse the American citizen to its reality, its danger, and the great need of united effort to stamp it out, under our feet, if needs be. It is being done. The Department of Justice will pursue the attack of these "Reds" upon the Government of the United States with vigilance, and no alien advocating the overthrow of existing law and order in this country shall escape arrest and prompt deportation.

It is my belief that while they have stirred discontent in our midst, while they have infected our social ideas with the disease of their own minds and unclean morals, we can get rid of them! And not until we have done so shall we have removed the menace of Bolshevism for good.

SOURCE: Palmer, A. Mitchell. "A Case against the Reds." *The Forum.* February 1920, v. 63, pp. 173–80.

ANALYSIS

The end of World War I brought hope for a more peaceful, stable America. The country's attention shifted from foreign intervention to domestic concerns and promotion of safety and stability at home. However, isolating the country from foreign influence proved more difficult than expected. After Vladimir Lenin rose to power following the 1917 Russian Revolution, he established the world's first Communist government and called on proletarians around the world to rise up against capitalist rule. As Bolshevik ideology spread beyond Russian borders, a deep-seated fear of communism began to take root among the American public.

Additionally, postwar recession created frustration and uncertainty for U.S. workers who had lost wartime contracts and among soldiers returning to a nation that hailed them as heroes but offered few jobs. Among the employed, anger grew over long workdays with meager pay. Strikes, race riots, and bombings throughout 1919 created anxiety and fear. These combined frustrations created the backdrop for the first Red Scare in the United States.

When a general strike was called in February by unions in Seattle, newspapers framed the strike as an effort by Reds and Bolsheviks to test U.S. waters for revolution. Although the Seattle strike was called off, fear of Bolshevism spread during the spring of 1919 when mail bombs were sent to thirty-six prominent Americans, including Supreme Court Justice Oliver W. Holmes, Judge K.M. Landis, John D. Rockefeller, and J.P. Morgan. Although no one was killed, these assassination attempts exacerbated public anxieties. Despite the fact that police were unable to trace the origin of these bombs, numerous newspapers and public officials blamed "Reds" and anarchists, with some calling for drastic action to crush rebel activities. Public disquietude was made greater by May Day riots in New York City, Cleveland, and Boston.

Just when fear and anger against radicals seemed to reach its height, another bomb scare set off nationwide panic. On June 2, eight bombs exploded within an hour of each other in eight American cities, one damaging the home of Attorney General A. Mitchell Palmer. This was the first coordinated terrorist attack on American soil. The general public, bolstered by media reports warning of the dangerous "Red threat" and foreign-born Socialists, assumed the bombs were the work of Bolshevik revolutionaries. Palmer reinforced this idea by directly blaming the bombings on radicals trying to overtake the government. His assertions were unfounded, but the country was in no mood for moderation or tolerance. Citizens supported any measures designed to stop the terrorizing influence of radicals.

Then, in the fall of 1919, another series of walkouts occurred, contributing to what became the largest strike wave in U.S. history. Strikers demanded improved pay and better working conditions, but the public was unwilling to distinguish between legitimate concerns and labor radicalism. Instead of sympathy, members of the Industrial Workers of the World (IWW, or Wobblies), the United Mine Workers Union, and the Steel Workers' Union were treated with disdain. The country watched anxiously, and chaos followed when Boston police struck in early September, steelworkers struck nationwide in late September, and coal workers struck in November. Emotions ran high; on November 11 in Centralia, Washington, a clash between IWW demonstrators and American Legion members led to a lynching and five additional deaths.

Ultimately, underlying the national tension was widespread unease, stoked by politicians and the press, that Communist radicals (especially, immigrants) were planning a violent government overthrow. Self-proclaimed Bolsheviks were in fact involved in the U.S. labor movement, but their overall numbers were small. Nevertheless, media and politicians outdid one another promoting hysteria over the purported efforts of subversives to overthrow democracy. These assertions stoked ultranationalist fervor and pitted groups like the American Legion, American Defense Society, and National Security League against all those considered a threat—particularly, Bolsheviks (Reds), Socialists, anarchists, Germans, and immigrants in general.

In this way, public opinion was skewed to believe that radicalism lay at the core of the unrest, and a fear- gripped nation willingly gave up personal liberties in exchange for safety from communism. Soon, any dissenting opinion was viewed as traceable to the Reds. Few spoke up for the First Amendment right of individuals to express their beliefs for fear of either being labeled a Red themselves or for fear of violating the Espionage and Sedition Acts, which criminalized criticism of the government.

Therefore, when Attorney General Palmer announced a crackdown on Socialists and anarchists, using the Espionage and Sedition Acts to reinforce his claims of disloyalty, he faced little resistance. Between November 1919 and January 1920, Palmer directed a series of raids in the homes and headquarters of suspected radicals across the nation and arrested over 3,000 individuals—not because of what they had done, but because of what they purportedly believed in. Many who were targeted were badly beaten during the raids and then abused or tortured while in government custody. Incredibly, most were imprisoned in spite of little or no evidence of wrongdoing. Some did not even speak English or know why they were being arrested. Meanwhile, newspapers announced that the Department of Justice under J. Edgar Hoover had compiled a list of 60,000 additional radicals yet to be apprehended.

The public initially treated Palmer as a hero. After the first November raid, he deported 249 radicals, including well-known Socialist Emma Goldman. This was the first U.S. mass deportation of political dissidents of the twentieth century. Palmer issued 1,600 total deportation orders over the next year and succeeded in expelling over 550 dissidents, but nearly 70 percent of the orders were later overturned when Labor Secretary Louis F. Post pointed out the raids were generally conducted without warrants and due process was largely ignored. In fact, the violence and illegality of Palmer's January 1920 raids led to the establishment of the American Civil Liberties Union. Presidents Harding and Roosevelt would eventually pardon most remaining prisoners who had been detained by Palmer and sentenced under the Espionage Act.

Eventually, the public tired of Palmer's constant warnings of Communist threats. Soon after his prediction of a 1920 May Day revolution proved completely without merit, Palmer's reign of terror ended as the nation turned its attention to baseball, radio, prohibition, and women's right to vote. In the end, Palmer's perpetuation of a cultural war against Communism led to his downfall, but his success in equating dissention with treason during the first Red Scare had a profound effect on free speech in the United States for many years thereafter.

FURTHER READING

Finan, Christopher M. *From the Palmer Raids to the Patriot Act: A History of the Fight for Free Speech in America*. Boston, MA: Beacon Press, 2008.

Guariglia, Matthew. "Wrench in the Deportation Machine: Louis F. Post's Objection to Mechanized Red Scare Bureaucracy." *Journal of American Ethnic History* 38, no. 1 (2018): 62–77.

Murray, Robert K. *Red Scare: A Study in National Hysteria, 1919–1920*. Westport, CT: Greenwood Press, 1980.

Shepley, Nick. *The Palmer Raids and the Red Scare: 1918–1920: Justice and Liberty for All*. 2nd ed. Explaining Modern History, 3. Luton: Andrews UK, 2011.

Watson, Bruce. "Crackdown!" *Smithsonian* 32, no. 11 (2002): 50.

- ***Document 10:*** *Gitlow v. New York*: Public Safety and the Fourteenth Amendment
- ***Date:*** Decided on June 8, 1925

- ***Where:*** Supreme Court of the United States
- ***Significance:*** This Supreme Court ruling made explicit that freedom of expression is not absolute if it intends or is likely to harm public safety or welfare and that states have a right to act in a reasonable manner to suppress such expression before actual acts of violence or harm occur. However, equally important was the court's partial reversal of a prior decision indicating that only the federal government is subject to the Bill of Rights. *Gitlow v. New York* opened the door for greater individual rights by initiating the incorporation doctrine—the understanding that under the Fourteenth Amendment's Due Process Clause certain Constitutional provisions, including freedom of expression as outlined in the Bill of rights, apply to both the state and federal governments.

DOCUMENT

OCTOBER TERM, 1924.
Opinion of the Court. 268 U.S.
GITLOW v. PEOPLE OF NEW YORK.
. . . MR. JUSTICE SANFORD delivered the opinion of the Court.

. . . For present purposes we may and do assume that freedom of speech and of the press—which are protected by the First Amendment from abridgment by Congress—are among the fundamental personal rights and "liberties" protected by the due process clause of the Fourteenth Amendment from impairment by the States. We do not regard the incidental statement in *Prudential Ins. Co. v. Cheek*, that the Fourteenth Amendment imposes no restrictions on the States concerning freedom of speech, as determinative of this question.

It is a fundamental principle, long established, that the freedom of speech and of the press which is secured by the Constitution, does not confer an absolute right to speak or publish, without responsibility, whatever one may choose, or an unrestricted and unbridled license that gives immunity for every possible use of language and prevents the punishment of those who abuse this freedom.

That a State in the exercise of its police power may punish those who abuse this freedom by utterances inimical to the public welfare, tending to corrupt public morals, incite to crime, or disturb the public peace, is not open to question . . . .

And, for yet more imperative reasons, a State may punish utterances endangering the foundations of organized government and threatening its overthrow by unlawful means. These imperil its own existence as a constitutional State. Freedom of speech and press . . . does not protect disturbances to the public peace or the attempt to subvert the government. It does not protect publications or teachings which tend to subvert or imperil the government or to impede or hinder it in the performance of its governmental duties. It does not protect publications prompting the overthrow of government by force; the punishment of those who publish articles which tend to destroy organized society being essential to the security of freedom and the stability of the State. And a State may penalize utterances which openly advocate the overthrow of the representative and constitutional form of government of the United States and the several States, by violence or other unlawful means. In short this freedom does not deprive a State of the primary and essential right of self preservation; which, so long as human governments endure, they cannot be denied . . . .

. . . That utterances inciting to the overthrow of organized government by unlawful means, present a sufficient danger of substantive evil to bring their punishment within the range of legislative discretion, is clear. Such utterances, by their very nature, involve danger to the public peace and to the security of the State. They threaten breaches of the peace and ultimate revolution. And the immediate danger is none the less real and substantial, because the effect of a given utterance cannot be accurately foreseen. The State cannot reasonably be required to measure the danger from every such utterance in the nice balance of a jeweler's scale. A single revolutionary spark may kindle a fire that, smouldering for a time, may burst into a sweeping and destructive conflagration. It cannot be said that the State is acting arbitrarily or unreasonably when in the exercise of its judgment as to the measures necessary to protect the public peace and safety, it seeks to extinguish the spark without waiting until it has enkindled the flame or blazed into the conflagration. It cannot reasonably be required to defer the adoption of measures for its own peace and safety until the revolutionary utterances lead to actual disturbances of the public peace or imminent and immediate danger of its own destruction. . . .

SOURCE: Sanford, Edward Terry, and Supreme Court of the United States. *U.S. Reports: Gitlow v. New York*, 268 U.S. 652 (1924). Periodical. https://www.loc.gov/item/usrep268652/

ANALYSIS

When Communist Party member Benjamin Gitlow published a revolutionary manifesto in 1919 advocating mass strikes and violent overthrow of the government, the United States was at the height of its first Red Scare. Officials and citizens alike viewed Communists with distrust, fearing they would rise up in response to Vladimir Lenin's call for an international proletariat revolution The manifesto added to those fears. Gitlow was convicted of criminal anarchy under a New York state law, and his conviction was upheld by the state appellate court. Gitlow argued that the statute under which he had been charged and convicted was unconstitutional because it prohibited his First Amendment rights to speak and publish freely. He also argued that no violence had resulted from the publication and distribution of the manifesto, thus making his conviction invalid.

Gitlow's case came before the Supreme Court in 1923 as the American Civil Liberties Union's first major Supreme Court case, and in 1925, the court issued its decision to uphold the prior rulings. The majority of the justices determined the New York statute under which Gitlow was convicted *was* indeed constitutional because freedom of speech under the First Amendment is not absolute. Justice Sanford argued that states, in addition to the federal government, can restrict free speech when such speech presents a reasonable probability of danger or violence to the general public. In justifying this notion, the court rejected Holmes's "clear and present danger" test (*Schenck v. US*) in favor of the "bad tendency" test, which asserted that it was not necessary for a state to wait for actual incitement or criminal action to occur; an utterance or written instruction that demanded or expected such action was enough to make it criminal in nature. Thus, even though no action had resulted from Gitlow's manifesto, the court said the state of New York could not be expected to wait until revolutionary action occurred before acting to protect its people and ensure stability within its borders. Instead, the state had a right to take reasonable action to "suppress the threatened danger in its incipiency."

This outcome was noteworthy for two primary reasons: first, it outlined when, how, and why certain instances of free speech can be legally suppressed. In this case, expression that simply advocates violence without necessarily resulting in violence can still be prohibited if it creates a reasonable fear of danger to the public. Abstract doctrine, academic discussion, or expression that is too insignificant to have an impact, the court held, is protected as long as no threat of incitement of violence is presented. However, when expression is likely to spark a reaction posing a greater danger to the general public, it is reasonable for the state to extinguish such a spark before it can ignite destructive behavior that threatens general peace and safety. This rationale would change greatly by the 1930s as subsequent court rulings gradually expanded on the power and reach of First Amendment freedoms and offered greater protections for them.

Second, the *Gitlow v. New York* decision affirmed that states as well as the federal government are bound by the same Constitutional standards in the negotiation and regulation of certain First Amendment freedoms. In an 1833 ruling *Barron v. Baltimore*, the Supreme Court had determined that the Bill of Rights did not expressly state that such rights should apply to state governments and, therefore, these rights and freedoms applied to the federal government only. This decision affirmed the power of the states to govern themselves according to their individual constitutions. However, in *Gitlow v. New York*, the court amended its view, arguing that although the Bill of Rights was intended to limit the power of the federal government, the due process Clause of the Fourteenth Amendment incorporated certain elements of certain amendments in the Bill of Rights (in this case, freedom of speech), making these rights and freedoms also applicable to the states. With this selective incorporation of rights, the Supreme Court began a process that would drastically expand personal freedoms by prohibiting states from suppressing what the court considered fundamental rights. This incorporation doctrine was utilized for the next four decades, gradually including other civil freedoms under the due process Clause such as freedom of the press and the right of assembly and petition. By the late 1960s, most of the civil liberties outlined in the Bill of Rights had been incorporated and applied to states.

The court's ruling in *Gitlow v. New York*, however, was not unanimous. Justices Oliver Wendell Holmes and Louis Brandeis disagreed, penning an eloquent defense of free speech in their dissent. They maintained that the clear and present danger test, had it been applied to this case, would have made obvious the fact that the small group of radicals who might agree with the publishers of the manifesto presented no real danger of overthrowing the government. Additionally, the justices argued, every idea has merit and should be given the chance to be accepted or rejected by the greater population. They explained, "Every idea is an incitement. It offers itself for belief and if believed it is acted on unless some other belief outweighs it or some failure of energy stifles the movement at its birth." Although their dissent did not change the outcome of this case, their argument for the right to submit expression to the marketplace of ideas would influence the court as it navigated and altered its understanding of First Amendment freedoms in subsequent cases.

FURTHER READING

Bartholomew, Paul C. "The Gitlow Doctrine Down to Date." *American Bar Association Journal* 50, no. 2 (1964): 139–41.

Bartholomew, Paul C. "The Gitlow Doctrine Down to Date, II." *American Bar Association Journal* 54, no. 8 (1968): 785–87.

Lendler, Marc. *Gitlow v. New York: Every Idea an Incitement.* Lawrence, KS: University Press of Kansas, 2012.

Lendler, Marc. "The Time to Kill a Snake: Gitlow v. New York and the Bad-Tendency Doctrine." *Journal of Supreme Court History* 36, no. 1 (2011): 11–29.

West's Encyclopedia of American Law, edition 2. S.v. "Incorporation Doctrine." https://legal-dictionary.thefreedictionary.com/Incorporation+Doctrine

---

- ***Document 11:*** Supreme Court Concurring Opinion in *Whitney v. California*
- ***Date:*** Decided on May 16, 1927
- ***Where:*** Supreme Court of the United States
- ***Significance:*** In this 1927 decision, the Supreme Court once again upheld a conviction for seditious behavior based on the rationale that laws punishing or prohibiting expression with inherent "bad tendencies" do not violate First Amendment freedoms. Although the ruling was unanimous, Justices Brandeis and Holmes issued a separate concurrence, disagreeing with the basic premise of the decision and strongly advocating for the uninhibited exchange of ideas that eventually led to a much more liberal Supreme Court interpretation of First Amendment free speech protections.

DOCUMENT

Whitney v. California.

MR. JUSTICE SANFORD delivered the opinion of the Court.
MR. JUSTICE BRANDEIS, concurring.

Miss Whitney was convicted of the felony of assisting in organizing, in the year 1919, the Communist Labor Party of California, of being a member of it, and of assembling with it. These acts are held to constitute a crime, because the party was formed to teach criminal syndicalism. The statute which made these acts a crime restricted the right of free speech and of assembly theretofore existing. The claim is that the statute, as applied, denied to Miss Whitney the liberty guaranteed by the Fourteenth Amendment.

The felony which the statute created is a crime very unlike the old felony of conspiracy or the old misdemeanor of unlawful assembly. The mere act of assisting in forming a society for teaching syndicalism, of becoming a member of it, or of assembling with others for that purpose is given the dynamic quality of crime. There is guilt although the society may not contemplate immediate promulgation of the doctrine. Thus the accused is to be punished, not for contempt, incitement or conspiracy, but for a step in preparation, which, if it threatens the public order at all, does so only remotely. The novelty in the prohibition introduced is that the statute aims, not at the practice of criminal syndicalism, nor even directly at the preaching of it, but at association with those who propose to preach it.

Despite arguments to the contrary which had seemed to me persuasive, it is settled that the due process clause of the Fourteenth Amendment applies to matters of substantive law as well as to matters of procedure. Thus all fundamental rights comprised within the term liberty are protected by the Federal Constitution from invasion by the States. The right of free speech, the right to teach and the right of assembly are, of course, fundamental rights. These may not be denied or abridged. But, although the rights of free speech and assembly are fundamental, they are not in their nature absolute. Their exercise is subject to restriction, if the particular restriction proposed is required in order to protect the State from destruction or from serious injury, political, economic or moral. That the necessity which is essential to a valid restriction does not exist unless speech would produce, or is intended to produce, a clear and imminent danger of some substantive evil which the State constitutionally may seek to prevent has been settled. . . .

This Court has not yet fixed the standard by which to determine when a danger shall be deemed clear; how remote the danger may be and yet be deemed present; and what degree of evil shall be deemed sufficiently substantial to justify resort to abridgement of free speech and assembly as the means of protection. To reach sound conclusions on these matters, we must bear in mind why a State is, ordinarily, denied the power to prohibit dissemination of social, economic and political doctrine which a vast majority of its citizens believes to be false and fraught with evil consequence.

Those who won our independence believed that the final end of the State was to make men free to develop their faculties; and that in its government the deliberative forces should prevail over the arbitrary. They valued liberty both as an end and as a means. They believed liberty to be the secret of happiness and courage to be the secret of liberty. They believed that freedom to think as you will and to speak as you think are means indispensable to the discovery and spread of political truth; that without free speech and assembly discussion would be futile; that with them, discussion affords ordinarily adequate protection against the dissemination of noxious doctrine; that the greatest menace to freedom is an inert people; that public discussion is a political duty; and that this should be a fundamental principle of the American government. They recognized the risks to which all human institutions are subject. But they knew that order cannot be secured merely through fear of punishment for its infraction; that it is hazardous to discourage thought, hope and imagination; that fear breeds repression; that repression breeds hate; that hate menaces stable government; that the path of safety lies in the opportunity to discuss freely supposed grievances and proposed remedies; and that the fitting remedy for evil counsels is good ones. Believing in the power of reason as applied through public discussion, they eschewed silence coerced by law—the argument of force in its worst form. Recognizing the occasional tyrannies of governing majorities, they amended the Constitution so that free speech and assembly should be guaranteed.

Fear of serious injury cannot alone justify suppression of free speech and assembly. Men feared witches and burnt women. It is the function of speech to free men from the bondage of irrational fears. To justify suppression of free speech there must be reasonable ground to fear that serious evil will result if free speech is practiced. There must be reasonable ground to believe that the danger apprehended is imminent. There must be reasonable ground to believe that the evil to be prevented is a serious one. . . . The wide difference between advocacy and incitement, between preparation and attempt, between assembling and conspiracy, must be borne in mind. In order to support a finding of clear and present danger it must be shown either that immediate serious violence was to be expected or was advocated, or that the past conduct furnished reason to believe that such advocacy was then contemplated.

Those who won our independence by revolution were not cowards. They did not fear political change. They did not exalt order at the cost of liberty. To courageous, self-reliant men, with confidence in the power of free and fearless reasoning applied through the processes of popular government, no danger flowing from speech can be deemed clear and present, unless the incidence of the evil apprehended is so imminent that it may befall before there is opportunity for full discussion. If there be time to expose through discussion the falsehood and fallacies, to avert the evil by the processes of education, the remedy to be applied is more speech, not enforced silence. Only an emergency can justify repression. Such must be the rule if authority is to be reconciled with freedom. Such, in my opinion, is the command of the Constitution. It is therefore always open to Americans to challenge a law abridging free speech and assembly by showing that there was no emergency justifying it. . . .

MR. JUSTICE HOLMES joins in this opinion.

SOURCE: Sanford, Edward Terry, and Supreme Court of the United States. *U.S. Reports: Whitney v. California*, 274 U.S. 357. 1926. Periodical. https://www.loc.gov/item/usrep274357/

ANALYSIS

The contribution of the *Whitney v. California* case to a more progressive understanding of free speech in the United States is unique in two distinct ways. First, it is considered a landmark First Amendment case even though Ms. Whitney's guilty verdict for a criminal syndicalism charge was upheld by a unanimous Supreme Court. Second, the famous concurrence written by Justice Brandeis and supported by Justice

Holmes reads much like a dissent due to its repeated insistence on the importance of free expression. In it, Brandeis insists that a well-functioning democracy depends on the ability of its citizens to express opinions without fear of recourse, and he argues that only the most extreme instances of imminent danger justify the suppression of free speech.

The Brandeis/Holmes concurrence in *Whitney v. California* has been called "one of the most impressive vindications of the moral and political function of freedom of speech which has ever been uttered" (*New Republic* 1927) and "arguably the most important essay ever written, on or off the bench, on the meaning of the first amendment" (Blasi 1988). In spite of the irony that Anita Whitney did not benefit from this vigorous defense of free expression, the reasoning laid out in the Brandeis concurrence served as an important catalyst in the court's eventual shift toward greater protection of First Amendment speech and press freedoms.

Charlotte Anita Whitney was a well-educated aristocrat who dedicated her life to political and social activism. Because Whitney believed that change must come about through democratic and legal means, she worked through numerous progressive organizations to improve life for those most affected by injustice and discrimination. She was a leader in multiple state and national suffrage movements and public welfare leagues and was an instrumental player in numerous state and local organizations lobbying for major social changes. By 1914, she had become a member of the Oakland Socialist Party, and in 1919, when the Left Wing of that Party split off to form the Communist Labor Party of California, she supported and participated in this group. Whitney was highly esteemed for her social efforts, but in the midst of the nation's first Red Scare, her new affiliation with the Communist Party was considered by some to be radical and dangerous.

Whitney was largely a victim of the circumstances of her time, which included suspicion of groups with which she was loosely associated. The tumultuous post-WWI era in the United States was marked by untenable conditions for millions of workers, the growth of powerful labor unions, and a rising fear of a domestic Communist revolution like that of Russia. This unrest, combined with nationwide bombings and strikes in 1919, evoked widespread disdain for foreigners, Socialists, Communists, and members of the Industrial Workers of the World (IWW), also called Wobblies.

Wobblies, considered unpatriotic radicals, drew ire from Americans unable to recognize that the group's demands grew out of poverty and insufferable working conditions tied to a growing class division. Although some advocated violence and engaged in illegal activities, Wobblies in general were targets of vigilantes and state-supported violence that included beatings, tarring and feathering, and even lynching. Whitney was revolted by the violence and sympathetic to the Wobblies' fight against powerful forces trying to suppress their voices.

While this unrest was brewing, California passed a criminal syndicalism law in 1919 that made it illegal to advocate for strikes or industrial sabotage or to form an organization to discuss such actions. Any spoken or written word or conduct that advocated, taught, or supported criminal syndicalism also became illegal.

In 1919, Whitney was arrested and charged with violating the criminal syndicalism law as a member of the Communist Labor Party (CLP). During her trial, the prosecuting attorney tried to establish a link between Whitney's association with CLP and IWW doctrine that advocated violence, even though Whitney was never a member of the IWW. Whitney's attorney argued that the IWW had nothing to do with Whitney's political party nor with the charges against her, but anti-Communist, anti-Wobbly sentiment overshadowed this fact. Ultimately, Whitney's conviction for violating California's criminal syndicalism law was based upon the prosecutor's insistence that as an active member of the CLP Whitney supported and sympathized with treasonous ideologies and crimes of the IWW, even though there was zero evidence that Whitney had ever advocated or participated in violent or criminal behavior related to IWW or any other organization.

Similar to the rulings in *Adams v. United States* and *Gitlow v. New York*, the Supreme Court used the "bad tendency" standard to uphold Whitney's conviction. In their concurring opinion, however, Justices Brandeis and Holmes argued against the notion that Whitney was guilty by association with the IWW and its aims. Brandeis carefully distinguished between advocacy and incitement, preparation and attempt, and insisted that the clear and present danger test should have been used to discern whether or not the measure applied to Whitney.

However, Whitney's fate lay in the nature of her defense. Whitney's lawyers argued the way the California law was applied to her violated the Constitution, but they never argued in trial court that Whitney's actions did not produce "clear and present danger of serious evil." Because higher courts normally do not overturn convictions for reasons not originally presented in lower courts, Brandeis said he felt bound to uphold the original conviction. Thus, the two concurring justices voted to uphold the conviction not because they agreed with the majority's reasoning, but largely because consideration of Whitney's innocence could not be based on an argument that had not already been made.

Nonetheless, Brandeis used his concurring opinion to forcefully and eloquently defend the necessity of protecting First Amendment freedoms of expression. Heavily influenced by Judge Learned Hand and legal scholar Zechariah Chafee Jr., Brandeis penned an impassioned defense of free expression and its critical role in a democracy. He pointed to revolutionaries who fought for the country's freedom who had "confidence in the power of free and fearless reasoning through the processes of popular government." Brandeis argued that the remedy for false speech is more speech. He insisted that harmful effects of such speech can be avoided through education and discussion, not forced silence.

Brandeis went on to argue that a simple likelihood of violence or destruction of property does not warrant suppression of speech or assembly. In order for such suppression to be justified, the resulting harm must be clear, *imminent* (not merely present), and substantial enough to cause serious injury to the state.

Although the Brandeis/Holmes concurrence did not directly help Whitney, it successfully laid groundwork for much more liberal interpretations of the importance of free speech and other First Amendment freedoms. *Whitney v. California* was eventually overturned by *Brandenburg v. Ohio* in 1969.

FURTHER READING

Blasi, Vincent. "The First Amendment and the Ideal of Civic Courage: The Brandeis Opinion in Whitney v. California." *William & Mary Law Review* 29, no. 4 (1988): 653–97.

Byron, Elizabeth Todd. "A Progressive Mind: Louis D. Brandeis and the Origins of Free Speech." *Touro Law Review* 33, no. 1 (2017): 195–210.

Collins, Ronald K.L., and David M. Skover. *Curious Concurrence: Justice Brandeis's Vote in Whitney v California*. Chicago: University of Chicago, 2006.
Murray, Billie. "The Reality of Meeting Hate Speech with 'More Speech.'" *Diverse: Issues in Higher Education* 35 (19): 40. https://diverseeducation.com/article/126918/
Strum, Philippa. *Speaking Freely: Whitney v. California and American Speech Law*. Lawrence, KS: University Press of Kansas, 2015.

- ***Document 12:*** Motion Picture Production Code (The Hays Code)
- ***Date:*** Published March 31, 1930
- ***Where:*** Adopted by Association of Motion Picture Producers Inc. at Hollywood, California. Ratified by the Board of Directors of Motion Picture Producers and Distributors of America Inc.
- ***Significance:*** The Motion Picture Production Code (also known as the Hays Code) was an attempt by motion picture studios to self-regulate the content of Hollywood films in order to avoid federal government censorship. Dominated by strict moral and ethical guidelines including prohibition of controversial moral or social issues, the code and subsequent variations of it heavily influenced or regulated the content of almost all movies made in the United States between 1930 and 1965.

DOCUMENT

(The Code as Published in Pamphlet Form, March 31, 1930)

A CODE TO MAINTAIN SOCIAL AND COMMUNITY VALUES IN THE PRODUCTION OF SILENT, SYNCHRONIZED AND TALKING MOTION PICTURES

Adopted by Association of Motion Picture Producers, Inc., at Hollywood, Calif., and ratified by the Board of Directors of Motion Picture Producers and Distributors of America, Inc., March 31, 1930.

Reasons for the New Code

The advent of sound on the motion picture screen brought new problems of self-discipline and regulation to the motion picture industry. Sound unlocked a vast amount of dramatic material which for the first time could be effectively presented on the screen. It brought the dramatist to Hollywood, to supplement the work of the scenario writer. It brought stars from the legitimate stage and the variety stage to the talking motion picture screen. It brought spoken dialogue, which had to be adapted to the requirements of film presentation. It brought new "extras," many of whom were given spoken lines.

To meet this new situation it became necessary to reaffirm the standards under which silent films had been produced since 1922, and to revise, amplify and add to those principles in the light of responsible opinion, so that all engaged in the making of sound pictures might have a commonly understandable and commonly acceptable guide in the maintenance of social and community values in pictures.

The task undertaken by the Motion Picture Producers and Distributors of America, cooperating with educators, dramatists, church authorities and leaders in the field of child education and social welfare work, has now resulted in the adoption of a new Code by the Association of Motion Picture Producers.

The new Code has been accepted and subscribed to individually by such prominent producers in the motion picture industry as: Art Cinema Corporation (United Artists); Christie Film Company, Inc.; Columbia Pictures Corporation; Cecil B. de Mille Productions, Inc.; Educational Studios, Inc.; First National Pictures, Inc.; Fox Film Corporation; Gloria Productions, Inc.; Samuel Goldwyn, Inc.; Inspiration Pictures, Inc.; Harold Lloyd Corporation; Metro-Goldwyn-Mayer Studios, Inc.; Paramount Famous Lasky Corporation; Pathé Studios, Inc.; RKO Productions, Inc.; Hal Roach Studios, Inc.; Mack Sennett Studio; Tiffany Productions, Inc.; Universal Pictures Corporation; and Warner Bros. Pictures, Inc.

Principles Underlying the Code

1. Motion picture producers recognize the high trust and confidence which have been placed in them by the people of the world, and they recognize their responsibility to the public because of this trust.
2. Theatrical motion pictures (that is, pictures intended for the theatre as distinct from pictures intended for churches, schools, lecture halls, educational movements, social reform movements, etc.) are primarily to be regarded as entertainment. Mankind has always regarded the importance of entertainment and its value in rebuilding the bodies and souls of human beings.
3. It is recognized that there is entertainment which tends to improve the race, (or at least to re-create and rebuild human beings exhausted with the realities of life) and entertainment which tends to harm human beings, or to lower their standards of life and living.
4. Motion pictures are an important form of art expression. Art enters intimately into the lives of human beings. The art of motion pictures has the same object as the other arts—the presentation of human thought, emotion, and experience, in terms of an appeal to the soul through the senses.
5. In consequence of the foregoing facts the following general principles are adopted:

No picture shall be produced which will lower the moral standards of those who see it. Hence the sympathy of the audience should never be thrown to the side of crime, wrongdoing, evil or sin.
Correct standards of life shall be presented on the screen, subject only to necessary dramatic contrasts.
Law, natural or human, should not be ridiculed, nor shall sympathy be created for its violation.

Particular Applications

Crimes Against the Law

These shall never be presented in such a way as to throw sympathy with the crime as against law and justice or to inspire others with a desire for imitation.

1. *Murder*
   a. The technique of murder must be presented in a way that will not inspire imitation.
   b. Brutal killings are not to be presented in detail.
   c. Revenge in modern times shall not be justified.
2. *Methods of Crime* should not be explicitly presented.
   a. Theft, robbery, safe-cracking, and dynamiting of trains, mines, buildings, etc., should not be detailed in method.
   b. Arson must be subject to the same safeguards.
   c. The use of firearms should be restricted to essentials.
   d. Methods of smuggling should not be presented.
3. *Illegal drug traffic* must never be presented.
4. *The use of liquor* in American life, when not required by the plot or for proper characterization, will not be shown.

SEX

The sanctity of the institution of marriage and the home shall be upheld. Pictures shall not infer that low forms of sex relationship are the accepted or common thing.

1. *Adultery*, sometimes necessary plot material, must not be explicitly treated, or justified, or presented attractively.
2. *Scenes of Passion*, should not be introduced when not essential to the plot. In general, excessive passion should so be treated that these scenes do not stimulate the lower and baser element.
3. *Seduction or Rape*
   a. They should never be more than suggested, and only when essential for the plot, and even then never shown by explicit method.
   b. They are never the proper subject for comedy.

4. *Sex perversion* or any inference to it is forbidden.
5. *White-slavery* shall not be treated.
6. *Miscegenation* is forbidden.
7. *Sex hygiene* and venereal diseases are not subjects for motion pictures.
8. Scenes of *actual child birth*, in fact or in silhouette, are never to be presented.
9. *Children's sex organs* are never to be exposed.

VULGARITY

The treatment of low, disgusting, unpleasant, though not necessarily evil subjects, should be subject always to the dictates of good taste and a regard for the sensibilities of the audience.

OBSCENITY

Obscenity in word, gesture, reference, song, joke, or by suggestion, is forbidden.

DANCES

Dances which emphasize indecent movements are to be regarded as obscene.

PROFANITY

Pointed profanity or vulgar expressions, however used, are forbidden.

COSTUME

1. *Complete nudity* is never permitted. This includes nudity in fact or in silhouette, or any lecherous or licentious notice thereof by other characters in the picture.
2. *Dancing costumes* intended to permit undue exposure or indecent movements in the dance are forbidden.

RELIGION

1. No film or episode may throw ridicule on any religious faith.
2. Ministers of religion in their character as such, should not be used as comic characters or as villains.
3. Ceremonies of any definite religion should be carefully and respectfully handled.

NATIONAL FEELINGS

1. The use of the Flag shall be consistently respectful.
2. The history, institutions, prominent people and citizenry of other nations shall be represented fairly.

TITLES

Salacious, indecent, or obscene titles shall not be used.

REPELLENT SUBJECTS

The following subjects must be treated within the careful limits of good taste:

1. Actual hangings, or electrocutions as legal punishments for crime.
2. Third Degree methods.
3. Brutality and possible gruesomeness.
4. Branding of people or animals.
5. Apparent cruelty to children or animals.
6. Surgical operations.

Uniform Interpretation of the Code

That there may be no doubt about a uniform interpretation of the code by the different producers, machinery has been set up that makes available for every producer the knowledge and experience of the entire industry, aided by the cooperation available from socially-minded groups and public leaders in the selection of the material for screen use and in the treatments of such material.

SOURCE: MPPDA Digital Archive. "Record #1255: Pamphlet." Flinders University. https://mppda.flinders.edu.au/records/1255

ANALYSIS

The "Roaring Twenties" was a period of tremendous social change in the United States. By the end of this postwar decade, the economy was booming, social standards had relaxed significantly (particularly for women), and consumers who now had extra money for social pleasures began to spend it on new forms of entertainment including home radios, jazz music, and tickets to movie theaters.

Movies in particular were wildly popular, and film production became a huge money-generating enterprise. By 1930, an average of ninety million Americans attended movie theaters each week (Black 1989). Throughout the decade there had been complaints among religious and social groups that the subject matter and content of many films was unsuitable, and by the mid- to late 1920s, religious leaders were demanding federal regulation of movies. Many testified in Washington against obscenity, sexuality, and moral degradation flaunted in films, with one reformer calling movies a "threat to world civilization" (ibid).

It wasn't that producers and directors were caught off guard by such protests. Early on, they were well aware of the complaints and took steps to try to regulate the industry. In 1922, the Motion Picture Producers and Distributors of America hired Will H. Hays as its president and charged him with taming Hollywood enough to appease the public. Hays initiated a series of voluntary restrictions in 1924 that did prevent some objectionable material from being made into movies, but because he favored allowing industry self-regulation, many studios simply ignored the recommendations. By 1927 Hays formed the Studio Relations Committee (SRC) that published the "Don'ts and Be Carefuls"—key points for what should and should not be included in movies. Nudity, profanity, and drugs were prohibited, and studios were warned to be wise in how they addressed violence, sexuality, and criminal behavior. This effort, too, was largely unsuccessful, as studios often interpreted the guidelines loosely and continued producing edgy content popular with the masses.

By 1930, leaders within the Catholic Church gathered to discuss what could be done to hold Hollywood accountable and make films more respectable. The result of these discussions was a new code echoing the group's belief that movies had a moral responsibility to teach right living and values to which the masses should aspire. They believed films should clearly show the wrongs of evil and the benefits of good and stated "no picture should lower the moral standards of those who see it."

These Catholic leaders presented their new code to Hays, urging him to adopt the document in order to avoid various forms of economic and social pushback from disenchanted Catholics and Protestants alike. Under mounting pressure from religious groups as well as state and local protesters who threatened to push for government censorship, Hays accepted the code and, in March 1930, convinced the industry to voluntarily accept and adopt it. Although the document was written by Father Daniel Lord, it became popularly known as the Hays Code.

For the first four years, known as the Pre-Code era, the Hays Code went largely unheeded. Producers faced with financial ruin during the economic downturn of the early 1930s largely disregarded the rules and tried to woo back audiences with even more sensational films. However, by 1933, religious, political, and social pressures were threatening to upend Hollywood's voluntary self-censoring system. A Catholic organization called the Legion of Decency threatened large boycotts. New possibilities for regulation arose from the Roosevelt administration. And a best-selling book based on results of the *Payne Studies* suggested to the American public that movies had a tremendous, often damaging, influence on children.

Hays knew he must act quickly to avoid disaster. In 1934 he created an enforcement agency, the Production Code Administration (PCA) and hired Catholic leader Joseph Breen as the director. Under the PCA, Hollywood films now required a Code Seal signifying that all code guidelines were met and approval was granted for release. Any studio-affiliated theater that dared show a film without a Code Seal was fined $25,000.

Under Breen's direction, the PCA decided censorship was best enacted prior to production, so all scripts had to be submitted and approved before filming could begin. Breen and his staff scrutinized the scripts meticulously and with fervor, demanding not only the elimination of foul language and complete changing of immoral plots but also the lengthening of hemlines—even for cartoon characters like Betty Boop. Above all, the PCA demanded that movies serve as a moral standard and guide for viewers. Producers were prohibited from addressing moral or social issues, sexual themes, or political commentary. Those who did were often forced to accept restructured scripts or face outright rejection. Without PCA approval, movies were basically doomed; according to estimates by the MPPDA, 98 percent of all films in American theaters in 1938 had a Code Seal.

Some producers embraced the seal when it led to increased revenue, but those who wished to fight back against its restrictions had little recourse. Major studios owned most theater chains, making it nearly impossible to find a theater that would accept a film without the seal. Additionally, free speech was not a valid argument. The Supreme Court had ruled in 1915 in *Mutual Film Corp. v. Industrial Commission of Ohio* that state and federal free speech protections did not apply to movies. This decision was not reversed until 1952.

After WWII, however, studios became more willing to buck the system and address controversial social issues. Westerns; film noir; foreign films; and movies dealing with racism, alcoholism, and other social problems challenged the authority of the PCA. With Breen's retirement in 1954 came an era of looser regulation under the direction of Geoffrey Shurlock who saw value in modernizing the principal aims of the code. While still the primary regulatory agency, the PCA's power diminished throughout the late 1950s and 1960s. In 1968, the PCA was replaced by the Classification and Rating Administration (CARA), the ratings system still used today. Although its influence died with the advent of CARA, the PCA had a monumental impact on the content of roughly three decades of Hollywood films.

FURTHER READING

Black, Gregory. "Hollywood Censored: The Production Code Administration and the Hollywood Film Industry, 1930–1940." *Film History* 3, no. 3 (1989): 167–89.

Doherty, Thomas Patrick. *Hollywood's Censor: Joseph I. Breen and the Production Code Administration*. New York: Columbia University Press, 2009.

Doherty, Thomas Patrick. *Pre-code Hollywood: Sex, Immorality, and Insurrection in American Cinema, 1930–1934*. New York: Columbia University Press, 1999.

Hunt, Kristin. "The End of American Film Censorship." *JSTOR Daily Newsletter*. February 28, 2018. https://daily.jstor.org/end-american-film-censorship/

Shurlock, Geoffrey. "The Motion Picture Production Code." *Annals of the American Academy of Political and Social Science* 254, no. 1 (November 1947): 140–46.

- ***Document 13:*** Message from President Roosevelt to Congress Recommending Creation of a Federal Communications Commission
- ***Date:*** February 26, 1934
- ***Where:*** Washington, DC
- ***Significance:*** At the request of President Franklin D. Roosevelt, Congress passed the Communications Act of 1934, which became the foundation for modern U.S. communication policy. This legislation established the Federal Communications Commission (FCC), charged with regulating U.S. radio and wire communication. It was later amended to include new technologies such as cable, satellite, and Internet communication.

DOCUMENT

February 26, 1934

To the Congress:

I have long felt that for the sake of clarity and effectiveness the relationship of the Federal Government to certain services known as utilities should be divided into three fields—transportation, power and communications. The problems of transportation are vested in the Interstate Commerce Commission, and the problems of power, its development, transmission and distribution, in the Federal Power Commission.

In the field of communications, however, there is today no single Government agency charged with broad authority.

The Congress has vested certain authority over certain forms of communications in the Interstate Commerce Commission and there is in addition the agency known as the Federal Radio Commission.

I recommend that the Congress create a new agency to be known as the Federal Communications Commission, such agency to be vested with the authority now lying in the Federal Radio Commission and with such authority over communications as now lies with the Interstate Commerce Commission—the services affected to be all of those which rely on wires, cables or radio as a medium of transmission.

It is my thought that a new Commission such as I suggest might well be organized this year by transferring the present authority of the Radio Commission and the Interstate Commerce Commission for the control of communications. The new body should, in addition, be given full power to investigate and study the business of existing companies and make recommendations to the Congress for additional legislation at the next session.

Franklin D. Roosevelt

SOURCE: Franklin D. Roosevelt. "A Recommendation for the Creation of the Federal Communications Commission." The Public Papers and Addresses of Franklin D. Roosevelt, Vol. 3. New York: Random House, 1938, 107.

ANALYSIS

The Communications Act was passed by Congress in 1934 to establish one centralized federal body that would regulate communications technologies in the United States. This fundamental act provided an important framework for federal oversight of both the development and regulation of new and existing media technologies.

During the 1920s, the birth and popularity of radio broadcasting led to chaos on the airwaves as numerous stations, owned by for-profit and nonprofit entities alike, competed for a limited number of available frequencies. To oversee the rapidly growing radio broadcast industry and address interference issues, Congress passed the Radio Act of 1927. The legislation also created the Federal Radio Commission (FRC), a regulatory body charged with reallocating existing bandwidths and determining distribution of frequencies. The FRC favored commercial broadcasters such as *CBS* and *NBC* over nonprofits, leading to the development of radio primarily as a commercial enterprise.

By the mid-1930s, however, President Franklin D. Roosevelt recognized the need for a single federal authority that would govern not only radio but the growth and development of other communications systems as well. He urged Congress to consolidate the authority of the Radio Commission and the Interstate Commerce Commission into one body that would govern all communication relying on wires, cables, or radio. In 1934, Congress passed the Communications Act, which formally established a legal system of governance and regulation of wired and wireless communications (at that time, telephone, telegraph, and radio).

At the heart of the new legislation was the creation of the Federal Communications Commission (FCC), a federal body established not only to replace the FRC but to regulate *all* electronic communication. Section one of the act states that the FCC's mission is "to make available, so far as possible, to all the people of the United States, without discrimination on the basis of race, color, religion, national origin, or sex, a rapid, efficient, Nationwide, and world-wide wire and radio communication service with adequate facilities at reasonable charges, for the purpose of the national defense, for the purpose of promoting safety of life and property through the use of wire and radio communication. . . ." The FCC did not hold the authority to regulate general program content, but it was granted power to ban indecency or obscenity over the airwaves.

Under the 1934 Communications Act, telephone services were considered common carriers, necessary providers of public access to communication through telephone networks. A decade earlier, with government approval, the American Telephone and Telegraph (AT&T) company had become the primary provider of nationwide telephone services. The 1934 act formally recognized this monopoly as an essential provider of phone service for the nation.

As previously mentioned, the Communications Act was built upon existing regulations for radio. Although the act was passed during the Great Depression, that era was also the Golden Age of Radio. At a time when families had little disposable income, radios provided both free entertainment and important news. Recognizing the central role radio played in the homes and businesses across the country, the act expanded upon regulation of frequencies in the 1927 Radio Act and now gave control of these frequencies to the license holders. Radio was not viewed as a common carrier like telephone companies; thus broadcasters or their parent companies were free to choose their own program content. However, the 1934 act did recognize that the airwaves were public property and that radio served an important public purpose. Thus, the act required broadcasters to provide general public interest programming and offer debate and discussion of controversial issues. This requirement led to the FCC's establishment of the fairness doctrine in 1949, which required broadcasters to address controversial topics on the air in a fair and balanced way and to give political candidates equal air time to discuss their views.

Broadcasters were considered speakers under the Communications Act of 1934, and as such they were understood to have free speech rights under the First Amendment. However, the extent of these rights was not as great as those enjoyed by the print media. Due to the limited number of bandwidths available through which alternative opinions might be heard, the act required broadcast media to serve the public interest by presenting multiple viewpoints of controversial topics.

Aside from telephone and radio, the 1934 act addressed many additional aspects of communication in the United States, making it the foundation of contemporary U.S. communications policy. The legislation included regulations related to distribution of frequencies, determination of rates and fees, rules for programming, establishment of public interest programming, terms of government use of communications systems, marketplace competition, access for individuals with disabilities, customer privacy, rules for content and delivery of commercials, and governance of nearly all other features of the communications and broadcasting industry.

Now in place for almost nine decades, the original 1934 Communications Act has been amended numerous times to address new and emerging technologies such as satellite, cable, and internet communications and to address issues of control over content. The largest overhaul of the original 1934 Communications Act came about through passage of the Telecommunications Act of 1996. This legislation encouraged competition in the communications marketplace through deregulation or weakening of many existing policies. The Telecommunications Act also introduced stricter standards related to family and children's programming, including three mandatory hours of educational programming per week and the introduction of a ratings code for programs. Some producers protested inclusion of the ratings code, alleging it was a form of censorship.

Additional changes to the 1934 act include the Communications Assistance for Law Enforcement Act, the USA PATRIOT Act, and numerous other amendments concerning personal privacy and access for people with disabilities. More recently, the FCC has faced challenges related to internet neutrality, First Amendment freedoms vs. content regulation, enforcement measures against robocalls, and limited broadband or telephone connectivity among specific populations for purposes of telehealth, education, and business activity (particularly during the COVID-19 pandemic). While important changes have been made, the 1934 Communications Act established a framework of freedoms and restrictions that continues to guide contemporary mass communication.

FURTHER READING

Caterina, Brian. "Communications Act of 1934," The First Amendment Encyclopedia. Middle Tennessee State University, 2009. https://mtsu.edu/first-amendment/article/1044/communications-act-of-1934

Federal Communications Commission. *The Communications Act of 1934*. June 19, 1934. https://www.nsa.gov/Portals/70/documents/news-features/declassified-documents/friedman-documents/reports-research/folder_047/41786769082578.pdf

Hazlett, Thomas. "The Rationality of U.S. Regulation of the Broadcast Spectrum in the 1934 Communications Act." *Review of Industrial Organization* 45, no. 3 (2014): 203–20.

Lyons, Daniel A. "State Net Neutrality." *University of Pittsburgh Law Review* 80, no. 4 (2019): 905–52.

McChesney, Robert W. "Media and Democracy: The Emergency of Commercial Broadcasting in the United States, 1927–1935." *OAH Magazine of History* 6, no. 4 (1992): 34–40. doi:10.1093/maghis/6.4.34

- ***Document 14:*** Letter from Ten-Year-Old William Gobitas* to the Minersville School Board
- ***Date:*** November 5, 1935

- ***Where:*** Minersville, Pennsylvania
- ***Significance:*** Ten-year-old Billy Gobitas and his twelve-year-old sister Lillian were expelled from their Minersville, Pennsylvania, school for refusing to participate in a mandatory flag salute. In this letter, Billy explains to his local school directors that he will not salute the flag because doing so in his religion is considered idolatry. The conflict and ensuing legal battles related to the expulsion of the Gobitas children set off a national controversy, including two differing Supreme Court decisions, about the power of states to infringe upon First Amendment rights.

---

*Because the name Gobitas was incorrectly spelled by a court clerk, formal documentation of the Supreme Court case is thus listed as *Minersville School District v. Gobitis*. However, the correct spelling Gobitas is used in this analysis and description of the family and incident.

DOCUMENT

Minersville, PA
Nov. 5, 1935

Our School Directors
Dear Sirs

I do not salute the flag because I have promised to do the will of God. That means that I must not worship anything out of harmony with God's law. In the twentieth chapter of Exodus it is stated, "Thou shalt not make unto thee any graven image, nor bow down to them, nor serve them for I the Lord thy God am a jealous God visiting the iniquity of the fathers upon the children unto the third and fourth generation of them that hate me. I am a true follower of Christ. I do not salute the flag not because I do not love my country but I love my country and I love God more and I must obey His commandments.

Your pupil,
Billy Gobitas

SOURCE: *Letter, Billy Gobitas to Minersville, Pennsylvania, school directors, explaining why the young Jehovah's Witness refused to salute the American flag, 5 November.* November 5, 1935. Manuscript/Mixed Material. https://www.loc.gov/item/mcc.016/.

- ***Document:*** Justice Stone's Dissent in *Minersville School District v. Gobitis*

- ***Date:*** June 3, 1940
- ***Where:*** U.S. Supreme Court
- ***Significance:*** Although the Supreme Court in this case ruled against the right of the Gobitas children to refrain from participating in the flag salute, Justice Stone's singular dissent became the foundation of the Supreme Court's reversal of this ruling three years later in *West Virginia State Board of Education v. Barnette.* Stone's impassioned dissent established that the very liberty guaranteed by the Constitution prohibits authorities from compelling individuals to believe or say a certain thing.

DOCUMENT

MR. JUSTICE STONE, dissenting:

I think the judgment below should be affirmed.

Two youths, now fifteen and sixteen years of age, are by the judgment of this Court held liable to expulsion from the public schools and to denial of all publicly supported educational privileges because of their refusal to yield to the compulsion of a law which commands their participation in a school ceremony contrary to their religious convictions. They and their father are citizens, and have not exhibited by any action or statement of opinion, any disloyalty to the Government of the United States. They are ready and willing to obey all its laws which do not conflict with what they sincerely believe to be the higher commandments of God. It is not doubted that these convictions are religious, that they are genuine, or that the refusal to yield to the compulsion of the law is in good faith, and with all sincerity. It would be a denial of their faith, as well as the teachings of most religions, to say that children of their age could not have religious convictions.

The law which is thus sustained is unique in the history of Anglo-American legislation. It does more than suppress freedom of speech, and more than prohibit the free exercise of religion, which concededly are forbidden by the First Amendment and are violations of the liberty guaranteed by the Fourteenth. For, by this law, the state seeks to coerce these children to express a sentiment which, as they interpret it, they do not entertain, and which violates their deepest religious convictions. It is not denied that such compulsion is a prohibited infringement of personal liberty, freedom of speech and religion, guaranteed by the Bill of Rights, except insofar as it may be justified and supported as a proper exercise of the state's power over public education. Since the state, in competition with parents, may, through teaching in the public schools, indoctrinate the minds of the young, it is said that, in aid of its undertaking to inspire loyalty and devotion to constituted authority and the flag which symbolizes it, it may coerce the pupil to make affirmation contrary to his belief and in violation of his religious faith. And, finally, it is said that, since the

Minersville School Board and others are of the opinion that the country will be better served by conformity than by the observance of religious liberty which the Constitution prescribes, the courts are not free to pass judgment on the Board's choice.

Concededly the constitutional guaranties of personal liberty are not always absolutes. Government has a right to survive and powers conferred upon it are not necessarily set at naught by the express prohibitions of the Bill of Rights. It may make war and raise armies. To that end, it may compel citizens to give military service and subject them to military training despite their religious objections. It may suppress religious practices dangerous to morals, and presumably those also which are inimical to public safety, health and good order. But it is a long step, and one which I am unable to take, to the position that government may, as a supposed educational measure and as a means of disciplining the young, compel public affirmations which violate their religious conscience. . . .

History teaches us that there have been but few infringements of personal liberty by the state which have not been justified, as they are here, in the name of righteousness and the public good, and few which have not been directed, as they are now, at politically helpless minorities. The framers were not unaware that, under the system which they created, most governmental curtailments of personal liberty would have the support of a legislative judgment that the public interest would be better served by its curtailment than by its constitutional protection. I cannot conceive that, in prescribing, as limitations upon the powers of government, the freedom of the mind and spirit secured by the explicit guaranties of freedom of speech and religion, they intended or rightly could have left any latitude for a legislative judgment that the compulsory expression of belief which violates religious convictions would better serve the public interest than their protection. The Constitution may well elicit expressions of loyalty to it and to the government which it created, but it does not command such expressions or otherwise give any indication that compulsory expressions of loyalty play any such part in our scheme of government as to override the constitutional protection of freedom of speech and religion. . . .

The Constitution expresses more than the conviction of the people that democratic processes must be preserved at all costs. It is also an expression of faith and a command that freedom of mind and spirit must be preserved, which government must obey if it is to adhere to that justice and moderation without which no free government can exist.

For this reason, it would seem that legislation which operates to repress the religious freedom of small minorities, which is admittedly within the scope of the protection of the Bill of Rights, must at least be subject to the same judicial scrutiny as legislation which we have recently held to infringe the constitutional liberty of religious and racial minorities.

With such scrutiny I cannot say that the inconveniences which may attend some sensible adjustment of school discipline in order that the religious convictions of these children may be spared presents a problem so momentous or pressing as to outweigh the freedom from compulsory violation of religious faith which has been thought worthy of constitutional protection.

SOURCE: *Minersville School District v. Gobitis*, 310 U.S. 586 (1940). https://supreme.justia.com/cases/federal/us/310/586/

ANALYSIS

The flag movement in the United States began in earnest in the 1880s, with essay contests and patriotic observances intended to teach respect for the flag, particularly among schoolchildren. In 1892, on the 400th anniversary of Columbus's discovery of America, the United States initiated a public school observance of the flag that included both a salute and recitation of the Pledge of Allegiance. This observance, intended to encourage patriotism among youth, became popular in schools throughout the United States.

By the 1920s, a period of heightened "Americanism" in the country, the American Legion was teaching flag respect and etiquette by hosting national flag conventions and was lobbying for a mandatory pledge of allegiance in public schools. Isolated instances of resistance to the flag pledge had begun to arise from members of religious groups such as the Mennonites and the Elijah Voice Society (EVS), the original Jehovah's Witnesses. However, these cases were few and far between, and because of public support for patriotic acts, lack of legal support, and religious sentiments opposing court intervention, such cases usually did not move beyond local or district courts.

By 1935, the flag salute was mandatory in nine states and instruction in flag etiquette was required in twenty-four. It was at this time that ten-year-old William Gobitas and his sister Lillian were expelled from their elementary school in Minersville, Pennsylvania, for refusing to salute the flag. The Gobitas family members were Jehovah's Witnesses who believed saluting or pledging allegiance to anything other than God was a form of idolatry. When the school district expelled the Gobitas children for defiant behavior, their father filed a lawsuit in federal court asking that they be readmitted.

Rulings in the federal district court in 1937 and federal appeals court in 1938 sided with the Gobitas family. Judge Albert Maris wrote "To permit public officers to determine whether the views of individuals sincerely held and their acts sincerely undertaken on religious grounds are in fact based on convictions religious in character would be to sound the death knell of religious liberty."

However, the school district appealed to the U.S. Supreme Court, which handed down its decision in 1940 that states and localities could indeed mandate flag salutes and the Pledge of Allegiance. Justice Felix Frankfurter, writing for the 8–1 majority court, stated "National unity is the basis of national security" and argued that such observances as the Pledge of Allegiance are necessary to bind men together in common loyalty. He further stated that religious beliefs do not "relieve the citizen from the discharge of political responsibilities." In essence, national unity was given greater importance than individual liberty.

Justice Harlan Fiske Stone, the lone dissenter, argued the decision violated students' First Amendment rights of free speech and free exercise of religion. He stated the government should not implement measures requiring children to recite affirmations or express sentiments contrary to their religious convictions. His passionate dissent insisted, "The very essence of the liberty which they guaranty is the freedom of the individual from compulsion as to what he shall think and what he shall say, at least where the compulsion is to bear false witness to his religion."

Backlash from the *Gobitis* decision was swift. Although numerous prominent newspapers and political leaders raised cries of injustice, the most drastic effects of the ruling fell upon the Jehovah's Witnesses. With domestic peace threatened by WWI and patriotism on the rise throughout the country, many considered the Witnesses' refusal to salute the flag disloyal. A wave of violence against Witnesses ensued, including mob attacks, physical assaults, hazings, boycotts, and property destruction—sometimes instigated by public officials. Subsequent to the ruling, the Pledge of Allegiance was made mandatory in thirty-one states and over 2,000 Witness children who refused to recite it were expelled from public schools. Many were sent away to state reformatories where they suffered abuse. Numerous states charged their parents with child neglect and noncompliance with educational acts. They were tried in criminal courts where they faced fines, imprisonment, and loss of custody of their children.

By 1942, three justices stated they believed the court had incorrectly decided the *Gobitis* case. Just one year later, the Supreme Court agreed to hear a similar case involving Jehovah's Witness children expelled from school for refusing to salute the flag. On Flag Day, June 14, 1943, a six-justice majority (with two new justices) reversed its earlier decision and declared in *West Virginia State Board of Education v. Barnette* that schools could not require children to participate in flag salutes or pledges if doing so conflicted with their religious beliefs.

Reversal of a Supreme Court decision in such a short time is rare, but the reversal in the *Barnette* opinion reflected the importance and urgency of First Amendment protections in question. The majority opinion, based largely on Justice Stone's previous dissent in *Gobitis v. Minersville School District* was penned by Justice Robert Houghwout Jackson. In it, Jackson established that national symbols, even when intended to promote unity, do not hold greater value than the freedoms protected in the Constitution. Likewise, no level of government can force unity or unanimity of opinions on its people, because to do so would be to destroy the integrity of fundamental values of the First Amendment.

Jackson wrote public education should "not strangle the free mind at its source [or] teach youth to discount important principles of our government as mere platitudes" but rather should grant them the opportunity and freedom to make informed decisions. In his most-quoted passage, Jackson wrote "If there is any fixed star in our constitutional constellation, it is that no official, high or petty, can prescribe what shall be orthodox in matters of politics, nationalism, religion, or other matters of opinion[,] or force citizens to confess by word their faith therein." Ultimately, patriotism is not best developed or reflected in mandated practices, but through recognition that the First Amendment protects the beliefs and expression of all who are citizens under the same U.S. flag.

FURTHER READING

Abrams, Douglas E. "Justice Jackson and the Second Flag-Salute Case: Reason and Passion in Opinion-Writing." *Journal of Supreme Court History* 36, no. 1 (2011): 30–47.

C-SPAN. "Jehovah's Witnesses on Mandatory Flag Salute." Part of 1940s Supreme Court Cases on Flag Salute in Schools. Hosted by Robert H. Jackson Center. October 17, 2018. https://www.c-span.org/video/?452868-3/jehovahs-witnesses-mandatory-flag-salute

Henderson, Jennifer Jacobs. "Conditional Liberty: The Flag Salute before Gobitis and Barnette." *Journal of Church and State* 47, no. 4 (2005): 747–67.

Irons, Peter H. *The Courage of Their Convictions: Sixteen Americans Who Fought Their Way to the Supreme Court*. New York: Free Press, 1988.

Langer, Emily. "Touched off a Legal Battle with Refusal to Salute Flag in School." *Washington Post*. September 8, 2014. https://www.washingtonpost.com/national/lillian-gobitas-klose-who-touched-off-legal-battle-with-refusal-to-salute-the-flag-dies/2014/09/08/34c9ee46–3764–11e4-bdfb-de4104544a37_story.html

West Virginia State Board of Education v. Barnette, 319 U.S. 624 (1943). https://supreme.justia.com/cases/federal/us/319/624/#tab-opinion-1937809

- ***Document 15:*** Alien Registration Act of 1940
- ***Date:*** June 28, 1940
- ***Where:*** U.S. Congress—Washington, DC
- ***Significance:*** The Alien Registration Act of 1940, also known as the Smith Act, required all noncitizens ages fourteen and older in the United States to submit registration papers to the federal government. It also imposed criminal penalties upon anyone who advocated, through words or actions, overthrow of the U.S. government. While initially celebrated as an effort to squelch pro-German advocacy, the law was used after WWII to target Communists in the United States.

DOCUMENT

An Act

To prohibit certain subversive activities; to amend certain provisions of law with respect to the admission and deportation of aliens; to require the fingerprinting and registration of aliens; and for other purposes.

Be it enacted by the Senate and House of Representatives of the United States of America in Congress assembled,

TITLE I

SECTION 1. (a) It shall be unlawful for any person, with intent to interfere with, impair, or influence the loyalty, morale, or discipline of the military or naval forces of the United States-

(1) to advise, counsel, urge, or in any manner cause insubordination, disloyalty, mutiny, or refusal of duty by any member of the military or naval forces of the United States; or

(2) to distribute any written or printed matter which advises, counsels, or urges insubordination, disloyalty, mutiny, or refusal of duty by any member of the military or naval forces of the United States.

(b) For the purposes of this section, the term "military or naval forces of the United States" includes the Army of the United States . . . the Navy, Marine Corps, Coast Guard, Naval Reserve, and Marine Corps Reserve of the United States; and, when any merchant vessel is commissioned in the Navy or is in the service of the Army or the Navy, includes the master, officers, and crew of such vessel.

SEC. 2. (a) It shall be unlawful for any person-

(1) to knowingly or willfully advocate, abet, advise, or teach the duty, necessity, desirability, or propriety of overthrowing or destroying any government in the United States by force or violence, or by the assassination of any officer of any such government;

(2) with the intent to cause the overthrow or destruction of any government in the United States, to print, publish, edit, issue, circulate, sell, distribute, or publicly display any written or printed matter advocating, advising, or teaching the duty, necessity, desirability, or propriety of overthrowing or destroying any government in the United States by force or violence;

(3) to organize or help to organize any society, group, or assembly of persons who teach, advocate, or encourage the overthrow or destruction of any government in the United States by force or violence; or to be or become a member of, or affiliate with, any such society, group, or assembly of persons, knowing the purposes thereof. . . .

SEC. 3. It shall be unlawful for any person to attempt to commit, or to conspire to commit, any of the acts prohibited by the provisions of this title.

SEC. 4. Any written or printed matter of the character described in section 1 or section 2 of this Act, which is intended for use in violation of this Act, may be taken from any house or other place in which it may be found, or from any person in whose possession it may be, under a search warrant issued pursuant to the provisions of title XI of the Act entitled "An Act to punish acts of interference with the foreign relations, the neutrality and the foreign commerce of the United States, to punish espionage, and better to enforce the criminal laws of the United States, and for other purposes", approved June 15, 1917.

SEC. 5. (a) Any person who violates any of the provisions of this title shall, upon conviction thereof, be fined not more than $10,000 or imprisoned for not more than ten years, or both.

(b) No person convicted of violating any of the provisions of this title shall, during the five years next following his conviction, be eligible for employment by the United States, or by any department or agency thereof (including any corporation the stock of which is wholly owned by the United States). . . .

SEC. 23. (a) The first paragraph of section 1 of the Act entitled "An Act to exclude and expel from the United States aliens who are members of the anarchistic and similar classes", approved October 16, 1918, as amended, is amended to read as follows:

"That any alien who, at any time, shall be or shall have been a member of any one of the following classes shall be excluded from admission into the United States:"

(b) Section 2 of such Act of October 16, 1918, as amended, is amended to read as follows:

SEC. 2. Any alien who was at the time of entering the United States, or has been at any time thereafter, a member of any one of the classes of aliens enumerated in section 1 of this Act, shall, upon the warrant of the Attorney General, be taken into custody and deported in the manner provided in the Immigration Act of February 5, 1917. The provisions of this section shall be applicable to the classes of aliens mentioned in this Act, irrespective of the time of their entry into the United States."

TITLE III

SEC. 30. No visa shall hereafter be issued to any alien seeking to enter the United States unless said alien has been registered and fingerprinted in duplicate. One copy of the registration and fingerprint record shall be retained by the consul. The second copy shall be attached to the alien's visa and shall be taken up by the examining immigrant inspector at the port of arrival of the alien in the United States and forwarded to the Department of Justice, at Washington, District of Columbia. . . .

TITLE IV

SEC. 40. If any provision of this Act, or the application thereof to any person or circumstance, is held invalid, the remainder of the Act, and the application of such provision to other persons or circumstances, shall not be affected thereby.

SEC. 41, This Act may be cited as the "Alien Registration Act, 1940".

Approved, June 28, 1940.

SOURCE: Library of Congress. *An Act to prohibit certain subversive activities; to amend certain provisions of law with respect to the admission and deportation of aliens; to require the fingerprinting and registration of aliens; and for other purposes.* 54 Stat. 670, 18 USC. §2385 https://www.loc.gov/law/help/statutes-at-large/76th-congress/session-3/c76s3ch439.pdf

ANALYSIS

The Alien Registration Act of 1940 (also named the Smith Act after its author, Representative Howard W. Smith of Virginia) restricted civil liberties in the name of preserving security and unity. This federal anti-sedition law, the first in the country passed during peacetime, made it a crime to advocate violent or forcible overthrow or destruction of the U.S. government through word or action, or to be a member of any group advocating for such.

In addition, the Smith Act contained a provision requiring registration and fingerprints of noncitizens in the United States over the age of fourteen. With World War II already underway and a threat of involvement looming, American leaders wanted a record of foreign individuals within its borders to help protect against internal threats.

Although provisions of the Smith Act stifled basic civil liberties, the law was enthusiastically supported by the majority of the population at a time when most were willing to limit personal freedoms in exchange for purported enhancements to national security. Most Americans thought little of the provision requiring aliens to register with the government because they were unaffected by it. Politicians promoted the idea of the legislation, framing it as a friendly gesture. A *New York Times* article from August 1940 reads, "No alien who accepts the American form of government and respects American laws has anything to fear from the new set-up which puts the Immigration Service under the Department of Justice, and which will probably provide for the registration of the 3,500,000 unnaturalized foreigners in this country" (p. 14). Just four months after the Smith Act was passed, 4,741,971 individuals were registered. In spite of the alleged friendliness of the act, information from the registration was later used to identify and take into custody nearly 3,000 noncitizens from Axis countries.

The anti-sedition portion of the legislation also failed to draw much public outcry, even though it, too, was an affront to free expression. Politicians promoted the need to restrict subversive activities during a time when war was once again on the horizon and national unity was paramount. The legislation seemed sensible to loyal Americans who watched with trepidation as Nazism and Fascism gained hold in Europe. Later, as the United States was drawn into WWII, the general mindset of Americans was that the country could not afford to allow dissidents to organize and promote an antigovernment agenda.

In reality, the Smith Act was rarely invoked during WWII; when it was, it was usually to stifle the voices and activities of Socialists, Nazi supporters, or extreme right critics of the Roosevelt administration. After WWII, however, the government used the Smith Act as justification for the prosecution of Communists—an ironic turn of events considering that during WWII, the United States and the Soviet Union fought as allies against Nazi Germany, and U.S. Communists enjoyed a relatively positive relationship with the Roosevelt Administration. The about-face was even more surprising to American Communists who had originally supported passage of the Smith Act, believing it would be used against competing Trotskyists.

Postwar years were marked by an emphasis on national security, even at the expense of civil liberties. Renewed tensions with the Soviet Union sparked the Cold

War, and anti-Communist rhetoric fueled by Senator Joseph McCarthy renewed fears among the U.S. population that Communists planned to overthrow the government. In addition to supporting the Smith Act, many state legislatures passed similar laws of their own targeting Communist activity. Although political scientists have since observed that low membership numbers indicated little need for anti-Communist or anti-subversion state legislation, most states enthusiastically passed such laws with public support and used those laws to convict Communist Party members.

In 1949, a series of trials for eleven Communist leaders began in New York. General Secretary of the Communist Party Eugene Dennis and ten other Communist leaders were convicted under the Smith Act, even though there was no evidence that Dennis had ever encouraged fellow members of the party to participate in violence. The trials drew massive publicity and widespread support for prosecution.

Appeals from these trials reached the Supreme Court two years later. It was not until 1951, in *Dennis v. United States*, that the Supreme Court considered for the first time the legitimacy of convictions made under the Smith Act. Regarded as the most important First Amendment case of the 1950s, the court's ruling in *Dennis* upheld the constitutionality of the law. Justices reached their decision using an interpretation of the clear and present danger test and citing national security interests. In the majority opinion, the justices wrote, "Certainly an attempt to overthrow the Government by force, even though doomed from the outset because of inadequate numbers or power of the revolutionists, is a sufficient evil for Congress to prevent."

Six years later, however, the Supreme Court would reinterpret language of the Smith Act in a way that proved to be a turning point for use of the law to prosecute Communists. In the court's 1957 ruling for *Yates v. United States*, Justice Harlan defined advocacy as actual incitement of an individual to action, not simply furthering abstract doctrines or beliefs. This interpretation offered protection for those who had been accused of advocating for Communism simply by being members of the Communist Party. The *Yates* decision placed the burden on the government to provide evidence that defendants directly inspired or engaged in concrete action with the intent to violently overthrow the government. A 1961 Supreme Court case, *Noto v. United States*, also upheld this interpretation that violation of the Smith Act requires proof of action against the government. Justices again held that abstract teaching of violence is constitutionally protected speech and does not violate the law.

The burden of proof of actual incitement inherent in the *Yates* decision made the Smith Act nearly unenforceable as a mechanism to target members of dissident political groups. While there were a handful of prosecutions after *Yates*, that decision effectively ended the targeting of Communists under the Smith Act.

FURTHER READING

Belknap, Michal R. *Cold War Political Justice: The Smith Act, the Communist Party, and American Civil Liberties*. Westport, CT: Greenwood Press, 1977. http://gem.greenwood.com/marc/resolver.aspx?b=BCW/&p=PSI

Bruce, Erik. "Dangerous World, Dangerous Liberties: Aspects of the Smith Act Prosecutions." *American Communist History* 13, no. 1 (2014): 25–38.

Pahl, Thomas L. "G-String Conspiracy, Political Reprisal or Armed Revolt?" *Labor History* 8, no. 1 (1967): 30–51.
Wirin, A.L., and Samuel Rosenwein. "The Smith Act Score." *Nation* 180, no. 9 (1955): 177–80.
Wirin, A.L., and Sam Rosenwein. "II. Suppression by Law: The Smith Act Prosecutions." *Nation* 177, no. 24 (1953): 485–90.

- ***Document 16:*** President Roosevelt's Letter to the American Society of Newspaper Editors
- ***Date:*** April 16, 1941
- ***Where:*** Sent to the American Society of Newspaper Editors
- ***Significance:*** As the United States inched its way toward involvement in WWII, newspaper editors grew wary of legislation still on the books that could make government censorship legal and permissible. Roosevelt responded to their fears with a letter declaring that freedom of speech and freedom of the press were alive and well in the United States and would continue to be protected under his leadership.

DOCUMENT

April 16, 1941

The assurance I would bring to the American Society of Newspaper Editors, if it were possible for me to greet them in person, would be that free speech and a free press are still in the possession of the people of the United States.

Free speech is in undisputed possession of publishers and editors, of reporters and Washington correspondents; still in the possession of magazines, of motion pictures, and of radio; still in the possession of all the means of intelligence, comment, and criticism. So far as I am concerned it will remain there for that is where it belongs.

It is important that it should remain there, for suppression of opinion and censorship of news are among the mortal weapons that dictatorships direct against their own peoples and direct against the world. As far as I am concerned there will be no Government control of news unless it be of vital military information.

Like all of our liberties, liberty of speech and of the press is not a mere phrase, a mere form of words, a constitutional abstraction. It has a living meaning—whatever the press itself gives it. Government juridical process can afford a negative protection against interference with freedom of speech, but its care, its nurture, and its use are responsibilities of the press itself, which has never prized it so much as it should prize it now.

How that freedom should be used, what contributions it should make to national defense, national interest, and national morale, are questions for publishers and editors themselves to decide.

It would be a shameful abuse of patriotism to suggest that opinion should be stifled in its service. United national sentiment, which all of us should desire, bears no resemblance to a totalitarian regimentation of opinion and treatment of news.

I cannot better close this message to the American Society of Newspaper Editors than with a final assurance that those who disagree with what is being done, and with the manner in which it is being done, are free to use their freedom of speech.

SOURCE: Franklin D. Roosevelt. "A Letter to the American Society of Newspaper Editors on Free Speech and a Free Press." The Public Papers and Addresses of Franklin D. Roosevelt, 1941 Volume, Book 1. New York: Harper & Brothers, 1950, 120.

ANALYSIS

President Roosevelt's January 1941 State of the Union address was delivered to a country just barely emerging from the poverty and hardship of the depression years and determined not to become embroiled in conflicts erupting around the globe. Roosevelt had run for reelection on the premise that U.S. soldiers would not be sent to fight in a foreign war unless attacked. However, he was also faced with the reality that the rise of totalitarianism in Europe and Asia presented a major threat to the safety and stability of America. Nazis and Fascists had already overtaken most of Europe and parts of Africa with frightening speed, and Great Britain, the last surviving European power, was under attack and badly in need of assistance. Additionally, just a few months prior, Germany, Italy, and Japan had signed the Tripartite Pact forming the Axis powers who pledged support to one another in order to establish "a new order of things."

Although Roosevelt was not eager to enter into the conflict raging in Europe, he knew Allied forces desperately needed help to win the war against antidemocratic forces. He used the 1941 State of the Union Address—also known as his "Four Freedoms" speech—to convey the severity of the situation to the American people and to underscore how the United States would be affected if Axis powers were successful. In a world order ruled by tyrants focused on expanding their empires, he said, the American way of life, woven together by beloved rights and freedoms, would be unimaginable.

More importantly, Roosevelt went one step further by eloquently framing these rights and freedoms as "human rights" that should apply not only to U.S. citizens but also to people around the world. "Freedom," he said, "means the supremacy of human rights everywhere." He contrasted totalitarian governments' disdain for individualism and free thought with the cultural identity of the American people, steeped in rights and freedoms. Those freedoms, he argued, are worth fighting for beyond U.S. borders to ensure that they are kept strong within U.S. borders. In this way, Roosevelt was able to gently convince an otherwise isolationist populace to support whatever efforts may be necessary to defeat the Axis powers, because America's future was also at stake.

The immediate result of Roosevelt's "Four Freedoms" speech was general support for the administration's foreign policy, particularly the Lend-Lease Act, which supplied Allied powers with much-needed military equipment and allowed the United States to remain only indirectly involved in the war. The speech also prepared Americans for the prospect of further sacrifice and strengthened the notion that personal rights and freedoms, pillars of American cultural identity, were indeed worthy of defense not only in the United States but around the world. Artist Norman Rockwell was so inspired that he painted four drawings based on the four freedoms of which Roosevelt spoke. These drawings were later used in a war bond campaign that raised $132 million for the war effort. The content and ideas in Roosevelt's "Four Freedoms" speech also formed the basis of the Atlantic Charter developed together with Winston Churchill in 1941 and the eventual establishment of the United Nations.

When Japanese forces bombed Pearl Harbor in December 1941, there was no doubt that the United States would now be directly involved in the war. However, Roosevelt's "Four Freedoms" speech had established a national resolve to not only defeat an enemy, but more importantly, to defend an ideal.

Roosevelt's "Four Freedoms" speech created a sense of unity and purpose among the American people to further a larger agenda just as his "Fireside Chats" radio broadcasts had done in earlier terms. These direct addresses to American families created a feeling of rapport and trust between citizens and their president. Knowing the important role media played in communicating his agenda, Roosevelt also carefully cultivated good relationships with the press, hosting an unprecedented 998 press conferences during his twelve years in office.

In spite of the president's efforts to forge congenial relationships with newsmakers, isolationist publishers such as Robert R. McCormick of the *Chicago Tribune* severely criticized his policies. Roosevelt also faced scrutiny from editors and publishers who feared a formal declaration of war might unleash government censorship of press freedoms. Responding to such concerns, Roosevelt wrote a letter to the American Society of Newspaper Editors in 1941, assuring the press that he had no intention of the government controlling news except in regard to vital military information. He emphasized that free speech and a free press were indeed critical, protected elements of the American democratic system that would remain in the hands of news agencies and the American people, undisturbed by the government.

Just weeks later at the American Society of Newspaper Editors annual meeting, Columbia University School of Journalism dean Carl W. Ackerman responded to President Roosevelt's letter. Ackerman credited the president's personal message and affirmation of press freedom as a "victory" and testament to the ongoing vigilance of the press in preserving its voice and power. However, he warned of laws still on the books such as the Espionage Act of 1917 that could be invoked at any time to squelch press freedom and power. He pointed out that foreign news feeds at the time were largely censored and thus encouraged colleagues to fight for the continuance of free and open news lines in America. Ackerman argued the president's power and prestige greatly impacted public opinion. He warned if Roosevelt were to use his influence to criticize the publishing of opposing views and discount the public's confidence in the press, the integrity of the profession and its contribution to democracy would be irrevocably harmed. Freedom of the press was so important, Ackerman argued, that "Without the freedom to print no form of liberty is worth a postage stamp."

FURTHER READING

Ackerman, Carl W. "How Free Is the American Press." *Vital Speeches of the Day* 7, no. 17 (April 18, 1941): 541. http://web.a.ebscohost.com.siouxlandlib.idm.oclc.org/ehost/pdfviewer/pdfviewer?vid=7&sid=176936ac-bbf2-4a04-83c0-a628015c96b3%40sessionmgr4006

Borgwardt, Elizabeth. "FDR's Four Freedoms as a Human Rights Instrument." *OAH Magazine of History* 22, no. 2 (2008): 8–13.

Engel, Jeffrey A. *The Four Freedoms: Franklin D. Roosevelt and the Evolution of an American Idea*. New York: Oxford University Press, 2016.

Roosevelt, Franklin D. "Annual Message to Congress on the State of the Union." January 6, 1941. Online by Gerhard Peters and John T. Woolley, The American Presidency Project https://www.presidency.ucsb.edu/node/209473

Stewart, Brent G. "A Convenient Relationship: FDR and the Press." *20th Century Political Historian*, posted January 17, 2012. https://brentgstewart.com/2012/01/17/a-convenient-relationship-fdr-and-the-press/

Tarkington, Booth, Will Durant, Carlos Bulosan, and Stephen Vincent Benét. "Four Freedoms." *Saturday Evening Post* 245, no. 2 (1973): 133–41.

- ***Document 17:*** President Roosevelt Establishes the Office of Censorship
- ***Date:*** December 19, 1941
- ***Where:*** Issued by President Franklin D. Roosevelt, Washington, DC
- ***Significance:*** Using his authority under the First War Powers Act of 1941, President Roosevelt established the country's first Office of Censorship to ensure classified information did not reach enemy hands. Also restricted was any type of information that might be used by enemy forces to their advantage. Remarkably, media professionals throughout the United States diligently and voluntarily followed the "Code of Censorship" throughout U.S. involvement in the war.

DOCUMENT

December 19, 1941

Statement:

All Americans abhor censorship, just as they abhor war. But the experience of this and of all other Nations has demonstrated that some degree of censorship is essential in wartime, and we are at war.

The important thing now is that such forms of censorship as are necessary shall be administered effectively and in harmony with the best interests of our free institutions.

It is necessary to the national security that military information which might be of aid to the enemy be scrupulously withheld at the source.

It is necessary that a watch be set upon our borders, so that no such information may reach the enemy, inadvertently or otherwise, through the medium of the mails, radio, or cable transmission, or by any other means.

It is necessary that prohibitions against the domestic publication of some types of information, contained in long-existing statutes, be rigidly enforced.

Finally, the Government has called upon a patriotic press and radio to abstain voluntarily from the dissemination of detailed information of certain kinds, such as reports of the movements of vessels and troops. The response has indicated a universal desire to cooperate.

In order that all of these parallel and requisite undertakings may be coordinated and carried forward in accordance with a single uniform policy, I have appointed Byron Price, Executive News Editor of the Associated Press, to be Director of Censorship, responsible directly to the President. He has been granted a leave of absence by the Associated Press and will take over the post assigned him within the coming week, or sooner.

Executive Order:

> By virtue of the authority vested in me by the Constitution and the statutes of the United States, and particularly by section 303, Title III of the Act of December 18, 1941, Public Law 354, 77th Congress, 1st session, and deeming that the public safety demands it, I hereby order as follows:

1. There is hereby established the Office of Censorship, at the head of which shall be a Director of Censorship. The Director of Censorship shall cause to be censored, in his absolute discretion, communications by mail, cable, radio, or other means of transmission passing between the United States and any foreign country or which may be carried by any vessel or other means of transportation touching at any port, place, or Territory of the United States and bound to or from any foreign country, in accordance with such rules and regulations as the President shall from time to time prescribe. The establishment of rules and regulations in addition to the provisions of this Order shall not be a condition to the exercise of the powers herein granted or the censorship by this Order directed. The scope of this Order shall include all foreign countries except such as may hereafter be expressly excluded by regulation.
2. There is hereby created a Censorship Policy Board, which shall consist of the Vice President of the United States, the Secretary of the Treasury, the Secretary of War, the Attorney General, the Postmaster General, the Secretary of the Navy, the Director of the Office of Government Reports, and the Director of the Office of Facts and Figures. The Postmaster General shall act as Chairman of the Board. The Censorship Policy Board shall advise the Director of Censorship with respect to policy and the coordination and integration of the censorship herein directed.
3. The Director of Censorship shall establish a Censorship Operating Board, which shall consist of representatives of such departments

and agencies of the Government as the Director shall specify. Each representative shall be designated by the head of the department or agency which he represents. The Censorship Operating Board shall, under the supervision of the Director perform such duties with respect to operations as the Director shall determine.

4. The Director of Censorship is authorized to take all such measures as may be necessary or expedient to administer the powers hereby conferred, and, in addition to the utilization of existing personnel of any department or agency available therefor, to employ, or authorize the employment of, such additional personnel as he may deem requisite.
5. As used in this Order the term "United States" shall be construed to include the Territories and possessions of the United States, including the Philippine Islands.

SOURCE: Franklin D. Roosevelt. "The President Issues a Statement and Establishes the Office of Censorship. Executive Order No. 8985." The Public Papers and Addresses of Franklin D. Roosevelt, 1941 Volume, Book 1. New York: Harper & Brothers, 1950, 574.

ANALYSIS

One of the most extraordinary examples of censorship in the United States began with the 1941 entry of U.S. forces into WWII and lasted until the end of the war in late 1945. The success of federal efforts to restrict and filter news during this time was significant in and of itself, but even more remarkable was the fact that broadcasters and journalists participated in censorship requests voluntarily.

When Japanese forces bombed Pearl Harbor on December 7, 1941, the United States found itself directly entangled in another raging worldwide conflict it had hoped to avoid. Although Americans did not enter the war by choice, scenes of horrific destruction and suffering in Europe strengthened national resolve to defeat the Axis powers and end the conflict. Less than two weeks after declaring war on Japan, Congress passed the First War Powers Act, an emergency measure that expanded federal powers in order to assist and facilitate the war effort.

President Roosevelt immediately used his newly expanded powers under the First War Powers Act to establish the Office of Censorship through Executive Order 8985. He chose Byron Price, executive news editor of the *Associated Press*, as director. Price accepted the position with two conditions: that wartime news censorship would be voluntary and that he would work directly for Roosevelt. Price balanced the need to restrict information for the sake of the war effort with the need to protect and preserve freedom of expression. His leadership style invited trust among other media professionals who willingly followed his recommendations for the sake of the country's safety.

Under Price, the Office of Censorship was in charge of monitoring all international communication, including news reports, private mail, and telegrams. War correspondents working overseas were impacted, as their reports were censored in advance of publication, but domestic broadcasters and journalists were affected as well. Most Americans at that time relied on radio, newspapers, or newsreels at movie theaters for information, so stories reported through these media branches were carefully examined before being given approval for release.

The primary objective of the Office of Censorship was to prevent public dissemination of any type of information that could possibly aid or encourage the enemy. To achieve that end, the office issued a "Censorship Code" as a guide for determining information acceptable for public distribution. Editors and publishers from around the United States who served as informal liaisons or "missionaries" scrutinized articles and approved news broadcasts before they were shared with the general public. Censorship of international mail and telegrams, in contrast, was mandatory. At its peak, the Office of Censorship employed over 10,000 civil service employees to inspect and assess the content of international mail.

Unlike the Office of War Information, created nearly a year later to control and shape the narrative of the war to the American public, the Office of Censorship did not engage in propaganda activities. Instead, it focused on monitoring stories directly affecting the war effort. However, because the war effort touched nearly every aspect of American life, the Censorship Office's reach was extensive. Radio stations stopped taking music requests and giving interviews that were not preapproved for fear that spies or sympathizers could use the stations to send unwanted messages. Journalists, acting out of loyalty and patriotic duty, withheld any information they suspected could undermine American war efforts.

Even the weather was a subject of censorship during the war. The Office of Censorship feared weather data could be used advantageously by the enemy to plan an attack. Thus, weather bureau information was limited to newspapers and telephone because radio broadcasts could be too easily intercepted. The weather-related news that *was* permitted was greatly restricted. For example, newspapers could only publish routine forecasts within a small geographical area, sky conditions and exact temperatures were prohibited, no mention could be made of heavy snow, and weather reports were almost completely restricted in the western United States. Even a deadly 1942 tornado outbreak that killed 153 people received no radio coverage.

With very few exceptions, media throughout the United States honored the Censorship Code throughout the duration of U.S. involvement in WWII. Only one radio broadcaster ever intentionally violated the code, and the few print journalists who breached it received swift condemnation. Ironically, that list included First Lady Eleanor Roosevelt. She was issued a reprimand for including remarks about weather conditions in a column she had written about official travels she and the president had made to another part of the country.

The most serious breach of the Censorship Code during WWII was likely that of Andrew Jackson May, a U.S. representative from Kentucky. After visiting Hawaii on a fact-finding trip, May divulged during a press conference that Japanese attacks on U.S. submarines had been unsuccessful because the depth charges the attackers used were too shallow. The reporters present assumed that because May was a U.S. Congressman and the head of the Military Affairs Committee, his information must be printable. After the Congressman's comments appeared in U.S. and foreign newspapers, nineteen U.S. submarines were destroyed by depth charges dropped from Japanese ships and aircraft, and more than 1,500 U.S. lives were lost.

Roosevelt's creation of the Office of Censorship gave him the power to control messaging about any official duties related to the war. Trips to Crimea and Iran to meet with Churchill and Stalin, for example, were not disclosed until after they had taken place. However, Roosevelt also used press acquiescence to hide from the general public the severity of his deteriorating health (he had been warned he would likely not endure another term) and to conceal knowledge of his affair with Lucy Rutherford.

While widespread voluntary media censorship efforts during WWII did prevent dissemination of some information to the public, the United States still maintained a more unrestricted flow of information and freer press than any other nation involved in WWII. By encouraging necessary restrictions while continuing to advocate for the importance of free expression, Price's Office of Censorship helped the United States emerge from WWII victorious in the battle and in its commitment to the First Amendment.

FURTHER READING

Mock, James R., George Creel, Neville Miller, Zechariah Chafee, Jr., Ralph Casey, and Arthur Krock. "The Limits of Censorship: A Symposium." *Public Opinion Quarterly* 6, no. 1 (1942): 3–26. doi:10.1086/265530

Price, Byron. "Governmental Censorship in War-Time." *American Political Science Review* 36, no. 5 (1942): 837–49. doi:10.2307/1949286

Roeder, George H. *Censored War: American Visual Experience during World War II*. Yale University Press, 1995.

Summers, Robert Edward. *Wartime Censorship of Press and Radio*. New York: Wilson, 1942.

Sweeney, Michael S. *Secrets of Victory: The Office of Censorship and the American Press and Radio in World War II*. Chapel Hill, NC: University of North Carolina Press, 2003.

- ***Document 18:*** Supreme Court's Majority Opinion in *Chaplinsky v. New Hampshire*
- ***Date:*** Decided on March 9, 1942
- ***Where:*** United States Supreme Court
- ***Significance:*** This landmark Supreme Court case upheld the legitimacy of a state statute prohibiting offensive speech and name-calling in public and offered a two-tiered theory of the First Amendment defining what constitutes protected versus unprotected speech. This ruling established "fighting words" as unprotected by the First Amendment, in addition to speech that is lewd, obscene, profane, or libelous. Since this 1942 decision, the Supreme Court has greatly expanded upon its original categorization of legally permissible speech, now covering much of what was previously unlawful expression.

DOCUMENT

MR. JUSTICE MURPHY delivered the opinion of the Court.

Appellant, a member of the sect known as Jehovah's Witnesses, was convicted in the municipal court of Rochester, New Hampshire, for violation of Chapter 378, § 2, of the Public Laws of New Hampshire:

> "No person shall address any offensive, derisive or annoying word to any other person who is lawfully in any street or other public place, nor call him by any offensive or derisive name, nor make any noise or exclamation in his presence and hearing with intent to deride, offend or annoy him, or to prevent him from pursuing his lawful business or occupation."

The complaint charged that appellant, "with force and arms, in a certain public place in said city of Rochester, to wit, on the public sidewalk on the easterly side of Wakefield Street, near unto the entrance of the City Hall, did unlawfully repeat, the words following, addressed to the complainant, that is to say, 'You are a God damned racketeer' and 'a damned Fascist and the whole government of Rochester are Fascists or agents of Fascists,' the same being offensive, derisive and annoying words and names."

Upon appeal there was a trial de novo of appellant before a jury in the Superior Court. He was found guilty and the judgment of conviction was affirmed by the Supreme Court of the State.

By motions and exceptions, appellant raised the questions that the statute was invalid under the Fourteenth Amendment of the Constitution of the United States, in that it placed an unreasonable restraint on freedom of speech, freedom of the press, and freedom of worship, and because it was vague and indefinite. These contentions were overruled and the case comes here on appeal.

There is no substantial dispute over the facts. . . .

It is now clear that "Freedom of speech and freedom of the press, which are protected by the First Amendment from infringement by Congress, are among the fundamental personal rights and liberties which are protected by the Fourteenth Amendment from invasion by state action." Freedom of worship is similarly sheltered.

Appellant assails the statute as a violation of all three freedoms, speech, press and worship, but only an attack on the basis of free speech is warranted. The spoken, not the written, word is involved. And we cannot conceive that cursing a public officer is the exercise of religion in any sense of the term. But even if the activities of the appellant which preceded the incident could be viewed as religious in character, and therefore entitled to the protection of the Fourteenth Amendment, they would not cloak him with immunity from the legal consequences for concomitant acts committed in violation of a valid criminal statute. We turn, therefore, to an examination of the statute itself.

Allowing the broadest scope to the language and purpose of the Fourteenth Amendment, it is well understood that the right of free speech is not absolute at all times and under all circumstances. There are certain well-defined and narrowly limited classes of speech, the prevention and punishment of which have never been thought to raise any Constitutional problem. These include the lewd and obscene, the profane, the libelous, and the insulting or "fighting" words—those which by their very utterance inflict injury or tend to incite an immediate breach of the peace. It has been well observed that such utterances are no essential part of any exposition of ideas, and are of such slight social value as a step to truth that any benefit that may be derived from them is clearly outweighed by the social interest in order and morality. "Resort to epithets or personal abuse is not in any proper sense communication of information or opinion safeguarded by the Constitution, and its punishment as a criminal act would raise no question under that instrument. . . ."

On the authority of its earlier decisions, the state court declared that the statute's purpose was to preserve the public peace, no words being "forbidden except such as have a direct tendency to cause acts of violence by the persons to whom, individually, the remark is addressed." It was further said: "The word 'offensive' is not to be defined in terms of what a particular addressee thinks. . . . The test is what men of common intelligence would understand would be words likely to cause an average addressee to fight. . . . The English language has a number of words and expressions which by general consent are 'fighting words' when said without a disarming smile. . . . Such words, as ordinary men know, are likely to cause a fight. So are threatening, profane or obscene revilings. Derisive and annoying words can be taken as coming within the purview of the statute as heretofore interpreted only when they have this characteristic of plainly tending to excite the addressee to a breach of the peace. . . . The statute, as construed, does no more than prohibit the face-to-face words plainly likely to cause a breach of the peace by the addressee, words whose speaking constitutes a breach of the peace by the speaker—including 'classical fighting words', words in current use less 'classical' but equally likely to cause violence, and other disorderly words, including profanity, obscenity and threats."

We are unable to say that the limited scope of the statute as thus construed contravenes the Constitutional right of free expression. It is a statute narrowly drawn and limited to define and punish specific conduct lying within the domain of state power, the use in a public place of words likely to cause a breach of the peace. This conclusion necessarily disposes of appellant's contention that the statute is so vague and indefinite as to render a conviction thereunder a violation of due process. A statute punishing verbal acts, carefully drawn so as not unduly to impair liberty of expression, is not too vague for a criminal law.

Nor can we say that the application of the statute to the facts disclosed by the record substantially or unreasonably impinges upon the privilege of free speech. Argument is unnecessary to demonstrate that the appellations "damned racketeer" and "damned Fascist" are epithets likely to provoke the average person to retaliation, and thereby cause a breach of the peace. . . .

Our function is fulfilled by a determination that the challenged statute, on its face and as applied, does not contravene the Fourteenth Amendment.

Affirmed.

SOURCE: Murphy, Frank, and Supreme Court Of The United States. *U.S. Reports: Chaplinsky v. New Hampshire, 315 U.S. 568* (1941). Periodical. https://www.loc.gov/item/usrep315568/.

ANALYSIS

Walter Chaplinsky was living in Rochester, New Hampshire, when he was arrested for breaching a state law prohibiting offensive speech and name-calling in public. Chaplinsky, a Jehovah's Witness, had been handing out literature on the streets of Rochester and exclaiming to those around him that organized religion was a "racket." Eventually the crowd became agitated and a nearby officer proceeded to escort Chaplinsky to the local station. On the way, the two encountered the city marshal who had warned Chaplinsky earlier that day about the restlessness of the crowd. At that point, Chaplinsky addressed the marshal by saying, "You are a God damned racketeer" and "a damned Fascist and the whole government of Rochester are Fascists or agents of Fascists."

Chaplinsky was convicted by the municipal court of Rochester of Section 2 of the state statute prohibiting "offensive, derisive, or annoying" words or exclamations or preventing another individual in a public space from "pursuing his lawful business or occupation." He was then found guilty by a New Hampshire Superior Court, and his conviction was affirmed by the state supreme court.

Chaplinsky appealed to the U.S. Supreme Court, stating the statute was so vague and indefinite that it violated his due process under the Fourteenth Amendment and thus placed an unreasonable restraint on his ability to engage in free speech.

In a unanimous ruling, the U.S. Supreme Court upheld Chaplinsky's conviction, declaring the New Hampshire statute did not violate his First and Fourteenth Amendment rights and reaffirming that freedom of speech is not absolute. The court based its decision on a two-tier theory of the First Amendment that distinguished protected from unprotected speech.

Speech intended to be harmful or instigate a breach of the peace, according to the justices, exceeds the limits of First Amendment protection. Justice Murphy specified for the court that "There are certain well-defined and narrowly limited classes of speech, the prevention and punishment of which has never been thought to raise any Constitutional problem. These include the lewd and obscene, the profane, the libelous, and the insulting or "fighting" words—those which by their very utterance inflict injury or tend to incite an immediate breach of the peace." He went on to explain that words of low value or expressions with little to offer in terms of exposition of ideas or "social value as a step to truth" are not fully protected under the First Amendment. The court held that society's interest in maintaining order and morality outweighs what little benefit, if any, this type of speech might offer.

When defining the new unprotected category of "fighting words," the justices also specified that the opinion of the receiver does not determine whether or not speech is "offensive." Rather, offensive speech is "what men of common intelligence would understand would be words likely to cause an average addressee to fight . . ."

The *Chaplinsky* decision introduced the two-tiered theory and the conception of "fighting words" to future free speech cases. However, some scholars have argued that categorical exclusion of certain language from First Amendment protection is dangerous because it is made according to the sensibilities of judges who could be persuaded that many types of speech are offensive to one group or another. Notably, no subsequent Supreme Court decisions have upheld a conviction based solely on "fighting words" directed at public officials, and many of the major tenants of the *Chaplinsky* decision have changed over time.

Eventually, the Supreme Court narrowed its definition of unprotected "fighting words" to direct, face-to-face personal insults likely to incite a violent response, although some lower courts still rely on the original *Chaplinsky* doctrine. Additionally, the Supreme Court has since reallocated much of what was considered offensive or lower-tier speech into the protected, free speech realm. As seen in rulings for *Cohen v. California* and *Miller v. California*, profanity and some obscenity are now likely to be considered protected under the First Amendment, as are verbal insults to public officials unless such insults are accompanied by threats or other unlawful conduct.

Changing social circumstances and emerging technologies have also created new challenges for application of the principles established in *Chaplinsky*. As public awareness of hate crimes has risen, many have argued that hate speech should be included in the definition of "fighting words," but such speech has generally been interpreted by subsequent courts as personal opinion and thus has retained its status as constitutionally protected speech. The Supreme Court affirmed in *Brandenburg v. Ohio* (1969) that even hateful or horrifying expression is protected unless its purpose is to incite imminent violence.

The changing nature of communication in a digital age has also forced a reexamination of how the *Chaplinsky* doctrines should be applied to online speech that lacks physical and temporal boundaries. Insults or inflammatory words or images made over an app such as Snapchat lack permanence and are unlikely to cause imminent violence or breach of the peace because of physical distance between senders and receivers. However, when combined with context, age, maturity, and other social factors, this manner of communication also holds the potential to cause great harm in ways the justices in *Chaplinsky* could not have anticipated.

Finally, public protests have also created tension between the public and law enforcement officials who must determine when the utterance of "fighting words" crosses the line from civil disobedience to unlawful behavior. Under the *Chaplinsky* doctrine, angry protesters hurling insults at one another or at police would be protected under the First Amendment. During the *Black Lives Matter* protests of 2020, however, numerous examples of clashes with counter-protesters or police forced a reexamination of how the use of fighting words can or should be treated by authorities who must often make snap decisions in changing contexts (i.e., a peaceful protest turning violent). It will be the work of modern courts to determine how the two-tiered approach to the First Amendment will apply to evolving civil challenges and unrest.

FURTHER READING

Barton, Ashley. "Oh Snap: Whether Snapchat Images Qualify as Fighting Words under Chaplinsky v. New Hampshire and How to Address American's Evolving Means of Communication." *Wake Forest Law Review* 52 (2017): 1287.

Caine, Burton. "The Trouble with Fighting Words: Chaplinsky v. New Hampshire Is a Threat to First Amendment Values and Should Be Overruled." *Marquette Law Review* 88 (2004): 441.

Herbeck, Dale. "Chaplinsky v. New Hampshire." In *Free Speech on Trial: Communication Perspectives on Landmark Supreme Court Decisions*. Tuscaloosa, AL: University of Alabama Press, 2003.
Hudson, David L., Jr. "Can Anti-Profanity Laws and the Fighting Words Doctrine Be Squared with the First Amendment?" *ABA Journal* 104, no. 4 (2018): 1.
Samples, John. "Fighting Words and Free Speech." CATO Institute. June 25, 2018. https://www.cato.org/blog/fighting-words-free-speech

---

- ***Document 19:*** President Truman's Veto of the Internal Security Act (McCarran Act)
- ***Date:*** September 1950
- ***Where:*** Capitol Hill, Washington, DC
- ***Significance:*** Passage of the McCarran Act in Congress in 1950 set the stage for the nation's second Red Scare, an era of deep distrust of Communists and suspected Communist sympathizers. President Truman vetoed the act, insisting it stifled freedom of expression and claiming it "makes a mockery of the Bill of Rights." Nevertheless, Congress overrode his veto, initiating more than a decade of anti-Communist fervor in the United States.

DOCUMENT

September 22, 1950
(81st Congress, 2nd Session, *House Doc.* No. 708)

To *the House of Representatives*:

I return herewith, without my approval, H.R. 9490, the proposed Internal Security Act of 1950.

I am taking this action only after the most serious study and reflection and after consultation with the security and intelligence agencies of the Government. The Department of Justice, the Department of Defense, the Central Intelligence Agency, and the Department of State have all advised me that the bill would seriously damage the security and the intelligence operations for which they are responsible. They have strongly expressed the hope that the bill would not become law.

This is an omnibus bill containing many different legislative proposals with only one thing in common: they are all represented to be "anti-Communist." But when the many complicated pieces of the bill are analyzed in detail, a startling result appears.

H.R. 9490 would not hurt the Communists. Instead, it would help them.

It has been claimed over and over again that this is an "anti-Communist" bill—a "Communist control" bill. But in actual operation the bill would have results exactly the opposite of those intended.

It would actually weaken our existing internal security measures and would seriously hamper the Federal Bureau of Investigation and our other security agencies.

It would help the communists in their efforts to create dissension and confusion within our borders.

It would help the communist propagandists throughout the world who are trying to undermine freedom by discrediting as hypocrisy the efforts of the United States on behalf of freedom.

Specifically, some of the principal objections to the bill are as follows:

1. It would aid potential enemies by requiring the publication of a complete list of vital defense plants, laboratories, and other installations.
2. It would require the Department of Justice and its Federal Bureau of Investigation to waste immense amounts of time and energy attempting to carry out its unworkable registration provisions.
3. It would deprive us of the great assistance of many aliens in intelligence matters.
4. It would antagonize friendly governments.
5. It would put the Government of the United States in the thought control business.
6. It would make it easier for subversive aliens to become naturalized as United States citizens.
7. It would give Government officials vast powers to harass all of our citizens in the exercise of their right of free speech.

Legislation with these consequences is not necessary to meet the real dangers which communism presents to our free society. Those dangers are serious, and must be met. But this bill would hinder us, not help us, in meeting them. Fortunately, we already have on the books strong laws which give us most of the protection we need from the real dangers of treason, espionage, sabotage, and actions looking to the overthrow of our Government by force and violence. Most of the provisions of this bill have no relation to these real dangers. . . .

There is no more fundamental axiom of American freedom than the familiar statement: In a free country we punish men for the crimes they commit but never for the opinions they have. And the reason this is so fundamental to freedom is not, as many suppose, that it protects the few unorthodox from suppression by the majority. To permit freedom of expression is primarily for the benefit of the majority, because it protects criticism, and criticism leads to progress.

We can and we will prevent espionage, sabotage, or other actions endangering our national security. But we would betray our finest traditions if we attempted, as this bill would attempt, to curb the simple expression of opinion. This we should never do, no matter how distasteful the opinion may be to the vast majority of our people. The course proposed by this bill would delight the Communists, for it would make a mockery of the Bill of Rights and of our claims to stand for freedom in the world. . . .

Our position in the vanguard of freedom rests largely on our demonstration that the free expression of opinion, coupled with government by popular consent, leads to national strength and human advancement. Let us not, in cowering and foolish fear, throw away the ideals which are the fundamental basis of our free society. . . .

This is a time when we must marshal all our resources and all the moral strength of our free system in self-defense against the threat of Communist aggression. We will fail in this, and we will destroy all that we seek to preserve, if we sacrifice the liberties of our citizens in a misguided attempt to achieve national security.

There is no reason why we should fail. Our country has been through dangerous times before, without losing our liberties to external attack or internal hysteria. Each of us, in Government and out, has a share in guarding our liberties. Each of us must search his own conscience to find whether he is doing all that can be done to preserve and strengthen them.

No considerations of expediency can justify the enactment of such a bill as this, a bill which would so greatly weaken our liberties and give aid and comfort to those who would destroy us. I have, therefore, no alternative but to return this bill without my approval, and I earnestly request the Congress to reconsider its action.

HARRY S. TRUMAN.

SOURCE: Harry S. Truman. "Veto of the Internal Security Bill." Public Papers of the Presidents of the United States: Harry S. Truman, 1950. Washington, DC: Government Printing Office, 1965, 645.

ANALYSIS

Although the United States and the Soviet Union had fought together during WWII to defeat the Axis powers, the alliance was a tenuous one. As long as the war raged, the two countries cooperated to defeat the totalitarian regimes, but the end of the war revived U.S. concerns about Communist influence and aggression. These fears were exacerbated by postwar Soviet expansion into the Balkans and the rise of Communist powers in Asia. Concerns also rose as the "Comintern" which had dissolved in 1943, was reestablished in 1947 as the "Cominform" (Communist Information Bureau) with headquarters in Belgrade.

As anxiety about Communist expansion grew during the postwar years, so did fears of the spread of Communism closer to home. In 1945, a Communist spy ring was discovered in Canada. That same year, the U.S. House Un-American Activities Committee began to investigate suspected Communist-front organizations in the United States. The Smith Act of 1940, originally intended to identify and prosecute pro-German supporters, was also employed during postwar years to prosecute Communist Party leaders in the United States. Even members of Hollywood were singled out for supposed Communist ties.

An appetite for anti-subversive legislation was growing in Congress. In 1948, a series of hearings was held in Washington, DC, involving two self-proclaimed members of Communist espionage rings. Elizabeth Bentley and Whitaker Chambers testified that prominent U.S. government officials, including former State Department official Alger Hiss, were members of the Communist Party. When asked about the hearings, President Truman dismissed them as "red herring," used by the committees "to keep from doing what they ought to do." He stated, "No information has been revealed by these committees' investigations that has not long since been presented to a Federal grand jury." He added that in addition to irreparably harming the accused, the public hearings were undermining the public's confidence in the government and impairing the morale of federal employees.

Nevertheless, fear continued to grow that Communists were infiltrating basic American institutions, including the government. In June 1950, Communist forces from North Korea crossed the 38th parallel and attacked the Democratic People's Republic of Korea. For President Truman and Western nations, this attack signified more than a local land or power grab; it was a demonstration of Communist intentions to fight for worldwide supremacy. Within a month, U.S. troops were sent as part of a United Nations force to aid South Korean forces in a war aimed more at defeating international Communism than simply battling the North Korean forces. The conflict in Korea marked the start of the Cold War.

By September 1950, U.S. anti-Communist fervor had come to a boiling point. Americans were both wary of another military campaign so soon after WWII and simultaneously frightened by accusations that Communists had infiltrated domestic businesses, the entertainment industry, and the government. The resulting public anxiety paved the way for passage of anti-subversive legislation that promised greater security but eroded personal freedoms.

The most controversial and well known of these new laws was the Internal Security Act of 1950, penned by and named after Senator Pat McCarran of Nevada. The McCarran Act required Communists to register and provide personal information to the Justice Department, and it criminalized any effort to support or promote totalitarianism in the United States. Title II of the act also granted broad emergency powers to the president to detain anyone who "probably will engage in, or probably will conspire with others to engage in, acts of espionage or sabotage," effectively legalizing the establishment of concentration camps.

Although Congress enthusiastically passed the McCarran Act, President Harry Truman immediately vetoed it, pointing out constitutional concerns raised by numerous provisions in the act and arguing that the bill would "make a mockery of the Bill of Rights and of our claims to stand for freedom in the world." In examining components of the bill, he said, Instead of striking blows at communism, they would strike blows at our own liberties and at our position in the forefront of those working for freedom in the world." Truman was adamant that passage of this bill, while intended to suppress Communist activity, would actually further it by making the United States seem hypocritical in promoting freedom while suppressing it at home. Among his concerns was that the legislation would put the U.S. government in the business of thought control. He also stressed that existing laws already offered strong protections against treason, espionage, sabotage, and potential overthrow of government. Truman repeatedly admonished the idea that the nation would be better protected through suppression of opinion, belief, or assembly. "We need not fear the expression of ideas—we do need to fear their suppression," he stated. "Our position in the vanguard of freedom rests largely on our demonstration that the free expression of opinion, coupled with government by popular consent, leads to national strength and human advancement. Let us not, in cowering and foolish fear, throw away the ideals which are the fundamental basis of our free society."

In spite of Truman's bold efforts to kill the legislation, both houses of Congress overwhelmingly overrode his veto that same day with an 89 percent majority vote. Congressional anti-Communist crusades ensued, destroying numerous lives and careers throughout the 1950s and into the early 1960s.

Eventually, the courts overturned major provisions of the McCarran Act. Over the next two decades, various sections of the act were repealed by Congress or deemed unconstitutional by the Supreme Court. The remainder of the act was fully repealed in 1993.

FURTHER READING

"Internal Security—Earlier Moves to Control Subversion." *Congressional Digest* 33, no. 5 (May 1, 1954): 132. http://web.a.ebscohost.com.siouxlandlib.idm.oclc.org/ehost/pdfviewer/pdfviewer?vid=3&sid=c0efa7fa-6864-4f93-a894-2498a59a283b%40sessionmgr4008

Gruberg, Martin, and Dennis Miles. "McCarran Internal Security Act of 1950 (1950)," The First Amendment Encyclopedia, Middle Tennessee State University. https://mtsu.edu/first-amendment/article/1047/mccarran-internal-security-act-of-1950

McCarran, Patrick A. "The Internal Security Act of 1950." *University of Pittsburgh Law Review* 12, no. 4 (1951): 481.

Patenaude, Marc. *The McCarran Internal Security Act 1950–2005; Balancing Internal Security and Civil Liberties*. Saarbrücken: VDM Verlag Dr. Müller, 2008.

Ybarra, Michael J. *Washington Gone Crazy: Senator Pat McCarran and the Great American Communist Hunt*. Steerforth Press, 2005.

- ***Document 20:*** Senator McCarthy's "Enemies from Within" Speech
- ***Date:*** February 9, 1950
- ***Where:*** Delivered in Wheeling, West Virginia
- ***Significance:*** This speech by Senator Joseph McCarthy, alleging Communist infiltration into the State Department, ushered in the country's second Red Scare. With this speech, McCarthy seized upon national fears of Communist aggression and over the next four years used his power to accuse thousands of individuals in government and civil society of being Communist Party members, sympathizers, or spies. His tactics silenced critics and resulted in First Amendment violations and drastic suppression of free speech from 1950 to 1954.

DOCUMENT

. . . Five years after a world war has been won, men's hearts should anticipate a long peace, and men's minds should be free from the heavy weight that comes with war. But this is not such a period—for this is not a period of peace. This is a time of the "cold war." This is a time when all the world is split into two vast, increasingly hostile armed camps—a time of a great armaments race. . . .

Today we are engaged in a final, all-out battle between communistic atheism and Christianity. The modern champions of communism have selected this as the time. And, ladies and gentlemen, the chips are down—they are truly down. . . .

Six years ago, at the time of the first conference to map out the peace—Dumbarton Oaks—there was within the Soviet orbit 180,000,000 people. Lined up on the anti-totalitarian side there were in the world at that time roughly 1,625,000,000 people. Today, only 6 years later, there are 800,000,000 people under the absolute domination of Soviet Russia—an increase of over 400 percent. On our side, the figure has shrunk to around 500,000,000. In other words, in less than 6 years the odds have changed from 9 to 1 in our favor to 8 to 5 against us. This indicates the swiftness of the tempo of Communist victories and American defeats in the cold war. As one of our outstanding historical figures once said, "When a great democracy is destroyed, it will not be because of enemies from without, but rather because of enemies from within." . . .

The reason why we find ourselves in a position of impotency is not because our only powerful potential enemy has sent men to invade our shores, but rather because of the traitorous actions of those who have been treated so well by this Nation. It has not been the less fortunate or members of minority groups who have been selling this Nation out, but rather those who have had all the benefits that the wealthiest nation on earth has had to offer—the finest homes, the finest college education, and the finest jobs in Government we can give.

This is glaringly true in the State Department. There the bright young men who are born with silver spoons in their mouths are the ones who have been worst. . . .

. . . In my opinion the State Department, which is one of the most important government departments, is thoroughly infested with Communists.

I have in my hand 57 cases of individuals who would appear to be either card carrying members or certainly loyal to the Communist Party, but who nevertheless are still helping to shape our foreign policy. . . .

. . . I know that you are saying to yourself, "Well, why doesn't the Congress do something about it?" Actually, ladies and gentlemen, one of the important reasons for the graft, the corruption, the dishonesty, the disloyalty, the treason in high Government positions—one of the most important reasons why this continues is a lack of moral uprising on the part of the 140,000,000 American people. In the light of history, however, this is not hard to explain.

It is the result of an emotional hang-over and a temporary moral lapse which follows every war. It is the apathy to evil which people who have been subjected to the tremendous evils of war feel. As the people of the world see mass murder, the destruction of defenseless and innocent people, and all of the crime and lack of morals which go with war, they become numb and apathetic. It has always been thus after war.

However, the morals of our people have not been destroyed. They still exist. This cloak of numbness and apathy has only needed a spark to rekindle them. Happily, this spark has finally been supplied. . . .

As you know, very recently the Secretary of State proclaimed his loyalty to a man guilty of what has always been considered as the most abominable of all crimes—of being a traitor to the people who gave him a position of great trust. The Secretary of State in attempting to justify his continued devotion to the man who sold out the Christian world to the atheistic world, referred to Christ's Sermon on the Mount as a justification and reason therefore, and the reaction of the American people to this would have made the heart of Abraham Lincoln happy.

When this pompous diplomat in striped pants, with a phony British accent, proclaimed to the American people that Christ on the Mount endorsed communism, high treason, and betrayal of a sacred trust, the blasphemy was so great that it awakened the dormant indignation of the American people.

He has lighted the spark which is resulting in a moral uprising and will end only when the whole sorry mess of twisted, warped thinkers are swept from the national scene so that we may have a new birth of national honesty and decency in government.

SOURCE: *Congressional Record*, 81st Congress, 2nd Sess., 1954–1957.

- ***Document:*** Excerpts from the Declaration of Conscience Speech Given by Senator Margaret Chase Smith
- ***Date:*** June 1, 1950
- ***Where:*** Washington, DC
- ***Significance:*** This speech by Maine senator Margaret Chase Smith was given in response to the suppression of First Amendment freedoms resulting from McCarthy's anti-Communist crusade. Senator Smith criticizes Democratic leadership and calls for Republicans to discontinue supporting smear campaigns and Congressional abuses of power. Smith contends that Congress should act according to American principles and support free speech, including unpopular opinions and independent thought.

Mr. President:

I would like to speak briefly and simply about a serious national condition. It is a national feeling of fear and frustration that could result in national suicide and the end of everything that we Americans hold dear. It is a condition that comes from the lack of effective leadership in either the Legislative Branch or the Executive Branch of our Government. . . .

I speak as briefly as possible because too much harm has already been done with irresponsible words of bitterness and selfish political opportunism. I speak as briefly as possible because the issue is too great to be obscured by eloquence. I speak simply and briefly in the hope that my words will be taken to heart.

I speak as a Republican. I speak as a woman. I speak as a United States Senator. I speak as an American.

The United States Senate has long enjoyed worldwide respect as the greatest deliberative body in the world. But recently that deliberative character has too often been debased to the level of a forum of hate and character assassination sheltered by the shield of congressional immunity.

It is ironical that we Senators can in debate in the Senate directly or indirectly, by any form of words, impute to any American who is not a Senator any conduct or motive unworthy or unbecoming an American—and without that non-Senator American having any legal redress against us—yet if we say the same thing in the Senate about our colleagues we can be stopped on the grounds of being out of order.

It is strange that we can verbally attack anyone else without restraint and with full protection and yet we hold ourselves above the same type of criticism here on the Senate Floor. Surely the United States Senate is big enough to take self-criticism and self-appraisal. Surely we should be able to take the same kind of character attacks that we "dish out" to outsiders.

I think that it is high time for the United States Senate and its members to do some soul-searching—for us to weigh our consciences—on the manner in which we are performing our duty to the people of America—on the manner in which we are using or abusing our individual powers and privileges.

I think that it is high time that we remembered that we have sworn to uphold and defend the Constitution. I think that it is high time that we remembered that the Constitution, as amended, speaks not only of the freedom of speech but also of trial by jury instead of trial by accusation.

Whether it be a criminal prosecution in court or a character prosecution in the Senate, there is little practical distinction when the life of a person has been ruined.

Those of us who shout the loudest about Americanism in making character assassinations are all too frequently those who, by our own words and acts, ignore some of the basic principles of Americanism:

The right to criticize;
The right to hold unpopular beliefs;
The right to protest;
The right of independent thought.

The exercise of these rights should not cost one single American citizen his reputation or his right to a livelihood nor should he be in danger of losing his reputation or livelihood merely because he happens to know someone who holds unpopular beliefs. Who of us doesn't? Otherwise none of us could call our souls our own. Otherwise thought control would have set in.

The American people are sick and tired of being afraid to speak their minds lest they be politically smeared as "Communists" or "Fascists" by their opponents. Freedom of speech is not what it used to be in America. It has been so abused by some that it is not exercised by others. . . .

As an American, I am shocked at the way Republicans and Democrats alike are playing directly into the Communist design of "confuse, divide, and conquer." As an American, I don't want a Democratic Administration "whitewash" or "cover-up" any more than I want a Republican smear or witch hunt.

As an American, I condemn a Republican "Fascist" just as much I condemn a Democratic "Communist." I condemn a Democrat "Fascist" just as much as I condemn a Republican "Communist." They are equally dangerous to you and me and to our country. As an American, I want to see our nation recapture the strength and unity it once had when we fought the enemy instead of ourselves.

It is with these thoughts that I have drafted what I call a "Declaration of Conscience." I am gratified that Senator Tobey, Senator Aiken, Senator Morse, Senator Ives, Senator Thye, and Senator Hendrickson have concurred in that declaration and have authorized me to announce their concurrence.

The declaration reads as follows:

1. *We are Republicans. But we are Americans first. It is as Americans that we express our concern with the growing confusion that threatens the security and stability of our country. Democrats and Republicans alike have contributed to that confusion.*
2. *The Democratic administration has initially created the confusion by its lack of effective leadership, by its contradictory grave warnings and optimistic assurances, by its complacency to the threat of communism here at home, by its oversensitiveness to rightful criticism, by its petty bitterness against its critics.*
3. *Certain elements of the Republican Party have materially added to this confusion in the hopes of riding the Republican party to victory through the selfish political exploitation of fear, bigotry, ignorance, and intolerance. There are enough mistakes of the Democrats for Republicans to criticize constructively without resorting to political smears.*
4. *To this extent, Democrats and Republicans alike have unwittingly, but undeniably, played directly into the Communist design of "confuse, divide and conquer."*
5. *It is high time that we stopped thinking politically as Republicans and Democrats about elections and started thinking patriotically as Americans about national security based on individual freedom. It is high time that we all stopped being tools and victims of totalitarian techniques—techniques that, if continued here unchecked, will surely end what we have come to cherish as the American way of life.*

SOURCE: 81st Congress, 2nd Session, Congressional Record 96 (June 1, 1950) 7894–5.

ANALYSIS

The short-lived peace following WWII was quickly replaced by a decades-long struggle between the United States and the Soviet Union as each raced to achieve global political, ideological, and atomic dominance. The Cold War had begun.

Senator Joseph McCarthy rose to power during this time by exploiting Americans' fears that Communists had infiltrated the government. He built upon preestablished negative stereotypes of Communists and nurtured an atmosphere of panic—among those who feared Communist infiltration and among those he accused of Communist affiliation.

McCarthy's four-year anti-Communist crusade was, in effect, the consummation of over a decade of efforts to prevent or expunge Communist subversion. The House Un-American Activities Committee was created in 1938 with the purpose of finding and investigating Communist threats to the United States The 1940 Smith Act criminalized written or spoken advocacy of overthrowing the government, thus eroding Constitutional protections for Communists. Truman's federal Loyalty Security Program of 1947 subjected every federal employee to loyalty investigations that specified membership in or association with the Communist Party as a disloyal activity. Similar state and local loyalty programs in the late 1940s followed suit.

SOURCE: Adkins, Judith. "These People Are Frightened to Death: Congressional Investigations and the Lavender Scare." *Prologue Magazine* 48, no. 2 (Summer 2016). National Archives. https://www.archives.gov/publications/prologue/2016/summer/lavender.html

Global events also contributed to McCarthy's rise to power. Following WWII, the Soviets wasted no time expanding their sphere of influence to include Poland, most of Eastern Europe, and East Germany, creating rising tension with the West. In 1946, British prime minister Winston Churchill referred to the division between Western governments and the Soviets as the "Iron Curtain," and in 1947, President Truman issued proclamations specifically calling for the containment of Communism (the Truman Doctrine). In August 1949, the Soviets shocked the United States by detonating the country's first atomic bomb, years ahead of U.S. government predictions. In a catastrophic loss a few months later, mainland China fell from the hands of U.S.-backed Chinese Nationalists under Chiang-Kai-shek to Chinese Communist leader Mao Zedong. Then, in mid-1950, the United States was again at war—this time fighting Soviet- and Chinese-backed Communists on the Korean peninsula.

It was at this historical moment that Joseph McCarthy, a young first-term senator from Wisconsin, rose to national prominence by claiming in a 1950 speech in Wheeling, West Virginia, that he believed the State Department was infiltrated with Communists. Although McCarthy provided no solid evidence to back his claims, never actually produced a complete list of names, and was subsequently inconsistent when alleging the number of supposed Communists within the State Department, he caught the attention of a frightened, war-weary American public unnerved by the idea of an internal Communist threat.

McCarthy exacerbated existing fears by insisting that all present or former Communists, even those who had joined the party in the 1930s and '40s in support of civil rights and economic reform, were connected to the Soviet Union and were thus a perpetual threat to

DID YOU KNOW?

In addition to targeting Communists, Joseph McCarthy also directed his ire toward homosexuals in government service. Playing on existing fears of homosexuality, McCarthy created a direct link between Communists and homosexuals, claiming in a Senate speech that homosexuals had "peculiar mental twists" that made them susceptible to Communism. One week later, ninety-one homosexual government employees were fired by the State Department. Officials justified the firing by declaring them to be "security risks."

This was not, however, the first instance of public or political discrimination against homosexuals. Along with greater awareness of homosexuality in America in the 1940s came fear and disdain. Being gay or lesbian carried a crushing social stigma; even the American Psychological Association in 1952 called homosexuality a "sociopathic personality disturbance." Few who identified as such were open about their sexuality, fearing the public and private repercussions.

Nevertheless, for nearly two decades, from the late 1940s through the late 1960s, thousands of individuals were singled out and fired from government jobs because of their sexuality. This era, known as the "Lavender Scare" was marked by government officials openly and actively working to rid the federal workforce of gays. Executive Order #10450 during the Eisenhower administration effectively legalized discrimination against homosexuals, banning gays and lesbians from government employment.

While McCarthy alone was not responsible for the Lavender Scare, his actions contributed to a long, repressive history of federal government discrimination against gay and lesbian individuals.

national security. After asking the now famous question, "Are you now or have you ever been a member of the Communist Party of the United Sates?" he typically subjected the accused to intense and often highly secretive congressional investigations.

Not all McCarthy's accusations were entirely unfounded. A small number of post-WWII cases in the United States and Canada exposed spy networks or agents working for the Soviet government. Just months after Senator McCarthy's 1950 Wheeling, West Virginia, speech, Julius Rosenberg was arrested for passing U.S. atomic secrets to the Soviets during WWII. He and his wife Ethel became the first American civilians executed for conspiracy to commit espionage. Although such spy cases were rare, they spooked the general public and added fuel to McCarthy's crusade. Much later, in the 1990s, declassified files would show there indeed were additional members of the U.S. government working as Soviet spies, although most had been dismissed by the time McCarthy began his quest.

McCarthy's initial targets were government officials, but soon, he began naming purported subversive Communists from all walks of life—journalists, artists, writers, poets, actors, educators, insurance providers, and even members of the military. He generally produced scant evidence and conducted most hearings for the accused behind closed doors, offering little or no chance for those targeted to publicly defend themselves. Nevertheless, he drew public support by infusing his crusade with patriotic overtones and contending that morality, Christianity, honesty, and decency drove his efforts to protect the country.

The greatest and perhaps most impactful aspect of Senator McCarthy's rise to power was his successful suppression of alternate voices and free speech. The McCarthy period produced some of the most flagrant violations of First Amendment protections in U.S. history. Those who challenged or questioned McCarthy were quickly added to a list of Communist traitors or sympathizers and targeted themselves. When the 1950 Tydings Committee Report concluded that McCarthy's allegations were false, for example, McCarthy responded by claiming that Communist traitors also sat on that committee. Inclusion on a McCarthy list was often enough to destroy a person's credibility and employment.

The sheer magnitude of voices suppressed by McCarthy produced an unchecked conformity. With the exception of Senator Margaret Chase Smith who spoke out immediately and consistently against McCarthy's tactics, most who distrusted McCarthy dared not speak up for fear of becoming the next victim.

McCarthy finally met his match in 1954 when he suggested during the Army-McCarthy congressional hearings that the Army was "coddling Communists." These hearings, among the first to be televised, offered the American public a chance to view McCarthy in action and recognize his scant evidence, use of bully tactics, and intimidation. They watched as the army's chief attorney responded to McCarthy's attacks with an impassioned plea, "Have you no sense of decency, sir, at long last?" And when the attorney called for an end to McCarthy's questions, viewers watched as the room burst into applause.

Soon after the Army-McCarthy hearings, the U.S. Senate denounced and censured McCarthy for "conduct unbecoming of a senator." After four years of accusations, interrogations, and hearings, McCarthy's reign of terror was over. During the McCarthy era 40,000 full-field investigations were conducted, and thousands of individuals' lives, jobs, and reputations were irreparably harmed. In spite of the remarkable scope of McCarthy's influence and power, his efforts failed to produce any indictments or convictions for espionage or treason and offered no evidence of massive Communist infiltration of government or civil agencies. McCarthy's actions did, however, leave a black mark on the history of free speech in the United States.

FURTHER READING

Bronner, Ethan. "Witching Hour; Rethinking McCarthyism, If Not McCarthy." *New York Times*. October 18, 1998. https://www.nytimes.com/1998/10/18/weekinreview/witching-hour-rethinking-mccarthyism-if-not-mccarthy.html

Shelton, Willard. "By Any Other Name, McCarthyism." *Nation* 173, no. 9 (1951): 166–67.

Shrecker, Ellen. "More Than Just a Man." PBS.org/American Experience. December 5, 2019. https://www.pbs.org/wgbh/americanexperience/features/mccarthy-more-than-just-a-man/

Stone, Geoffrey R. "Free Speech in the Age of McCarthy: A Cautionary Tale." *California Law Review* 93, no. 5 (2005):1387–412. https://chicagounbound.uchicago.edu/cgi/viewcontent.cgi?article=2961&context=journal_articles

Tye, Larry. *Demagogue: The Life and Long Shadow of Senator Joe McCarthy*. Boston: Houghton Mifflin Harcourt, 2020.

3

MOMENTOUS RULINGS AMID POLITICAL AND CULTURAL CHANGE (1950–1980)

- ***Document 21:*** Supreme Court's Majority Decision in *Roth v. United States*
- ***Date:*** Decided June 24, 1957
- ***Where:*** Supreme Court of the United States
- ***Significance:*** This Supreme Court decision redefined obscenity and established it as unprotected by the First Amendment. The judgment in this case replaced the formerly utilized Hicklin test of obscenity with a new determination based on community standards to determine if the dominant theme of a work appeals to prurient interest.

DOCUMENT

MR. JUSTICE BRENNAN delivered the opinion of the Court

The constitutionality of a criminal obscenity statute is the question in each of these cases. In *Roth,* the primary constitutional question is whether the federal obscenity statute violates the provision of the First Amendment that "Congress shall make no law . . . abridging the freedom of speech, or of the press. . . ." In *Alberts*, the primary constitutional question is whether the obscenity provisions of the California Penal Code invade the freedoms of speech and press as they may be incorporated in the liberty protected from state action by the Due Process Clause of the Fourteenth Amendment.

Other constitutional questions are: whether these statutes violate due process, because too vague to support conviction for crime; whether power to punish speech and press offensive to decency and morality is in the States alone, so that the federal obscenity statute violates the Ninth and Tenth Amendments (raised in *Roth*). . . .

The dispositive question is whether obscenity is utterance within the area of protected speech and press. Although this is the first time the question has been squarely presented to this Court, either under the First Amendment or under the Fourteenth Amendment, expressions found in numerous opinions indicate that this Court has always assumed that obscenity is not protected by the freedoms of speech and press. . . .

The guaranties of freedom of expression in effect in 10 of the 14 States which by 1792 had ratified the Constitution, gave no absolute protection for every utterance. Thirteen of the 14 States provided for the prosecution of libel, and all of those States made either blasphemy or profanity, or both, statutory crimes. As early as 1712, Massachusetts made it criminal to publish "any filthy, obscene, or profane song, pamphlet, libel or mock sermon" in imitation or mimicking of religious services. . . . Thus, profanity and obscenity were related offenses.

In light of this history, it is apparent that the unconditional phrasing of the First Amendment was not intended to protect every utterance. This phrasing did not prevent this Court from concluding that libelous utterances are not within the area of constitutionally protected speech. At the time of the adoption of the First Amendment, obscenity law was not as fully developed as libel law, but there is sufficiently contemporaneous evidence to show that obscenity, too, was outside the protection intended for speech and press. . . .

All ideas having even the slightest redeeming social importance—unorthodox ideas, controversial ideas, even ideas hateful to the prevailing climate of opinion—have the full protection of the guaranties, unless excludable because they encroach upon the limited area of more important interests. But implicit in the history of the First Amendment is the rejection of obscenity as utterly without redeeming social importance. . . .

We hold that obscenity is not within the area of constitutionally protected speech or press. . . .

However, sex and obscenity are not synonymous. Obscene material is material which deals with sex in a manner appealing to prurient interest. The portrayal of sex, *e. g.*, in art, literature and scientific works, is not itself sufficient reason to deny material the constitutional protection of freedom of speech and press. Sex, a great and mysterious motive force in human life, has indisputably been a subject of absorbing interest to mankind through the ages; it is one of the vital problems of human interest and public concern. As to all such problems, this Court said in *Thornhill v. Alabama*:

> "The freedom of speech and of the press guaranteed by the Constitution embraces at the least the liberty to discuss publicly and truthfully *all matters of public concern* without previous restraint or fear of subsequent punishment. . . . Freedom of discussion, if it would fulfill its historic function in this nation, must embrace *all issues about which information is needed or appropriate to enable the members of society to cope with the exigencies of their period.*" (Emphasis added.)

The fundamental freedoms of speech and press have contributed greatly to the development and well-being of our free society and are indispensable to its continued growth. Ceaseless vigilance is the watchword to prevent their erosion by Congress or by the States. The door barring federal and state intrusion into this area cannot be left ajar; it must be kept tightly closed and opened only the slightest crack necessary to prevent encroachment upon more important interests. It is therefore vital that the standards for judging obscenity safeguard the protection of freedom of speech and press for material which does not treat sex in a manner appealing to prurient interest. . . .

Both trial courts below sufficiently followed the proper standard. Both courts used the proper definition of obscenity. In addition, in the *Alberts* case, in ruling on a motion to dismiss, the trial judge indicated that, as the trier of facts, he was judging each item as a whole as it would affect the normal person, and in *Roth*, the trial judge instructed the jury as follows:

> ". . . The test is not whether it would arouse sexual desires or sexual impure thoughts in those comprising a particular segment of the community, the young, the immature or the highly prudish or would leave another segment, the scientific or highly educated or the so-called worldly-wise and sophisticated indifferent and unmoved. . . .

> "The test in each case is the effect of the book, picture or publication considered as a whole, not upon any particular class, but upon all those whom it is likely to reach. In other words, you determine its impact upon the average person in the community. The books, pictures and circulars must be judged as a whole, in their entire context, and you are not to consider detached or separate portions in reaching a conclusion. You judge the circulars, pictures and publications which have been put in evidence by present-day standards of the community. You may ask yourselves does it offend the common conscience of the community by present-day standards.
>
> "In this case, ladies and gentlemen of the jury, you and you alone are the exclusive judges of what the common conscience of the community is, and in determining that conscience you are to consider the community as a whole, young and old, educated and uneducated, the religious and the irreligious-men, women and children."

It is argued that the statutes do not provide reasonably ascertainable standards of guilt and therefore violate the constitutional requirements of due process. The federal obscenity statute makes punishable the mailing of material that is "obscene, lewd, lascivious, or filthy . . . or other publication of an indecent character." The California statute makes punishable, *inter alia*, the keeping for sale or advertising material that is "obscene or indecent." The thrust of the argument is that these words are not sufficiently precise because they do not mean the same thing to all people, all the time, everywhere.

Many decisions have recognized that these terms of obscenity statutes are not precise. This Court, however, has consistently held that lack of precision is not itself offensive to the requirements of due process. . . .

In summary, then, we hold that these statutes, applied according to the proper standard for judging obscenity, do not offend constitutional safeguards against convictions based upon protected material, or fail to give men in acting adequate notice of what is prohibited. . . .

The judgments are

Affirmed

SOURCE: Roth v. United States, 354 U.S. 476 (1956).

ANALYSIS

Although Supreme Court decisions dating back to the late 1800s had included obscenity under the broad category of unprotected speech, *Roth v. United States* was the first actual case in which the Supreme Court attempted to both clarify what constitutes obscenity and determine whether or not it was Constitutionally protected under the First Amendment. For sixty years, the court had avoided dealing with obscenity cases and constructing a standard by which to resolve them, leaving the lower courts to make such determinations. Finally, in 1957, the Supreme Court took up *Roth v. United States* along with *Alberts v. California*, a companion case also questioning the Constitutionality of an obscenity statute. Convictions were upheld in both cases, with the court determining that obscenity is not protected speech.

Samuel Roth was no stranger to the court system. For three decades he had faced a number of charges at the state level for distribution of material considered obscene. He was jailed multiple times for peddling smut, sensationalism and graphic pornography, including a three-year federal prison sentence in the late 1930s.

Roth's most famous offense began when he was arrested for sending what were deemed to be obscene books and advertising materials through the postal service. A jury in the Southern District of New York convicted him of violating a federal statute prohibiting the mailing of material that is "obscene, lewd, lascivious, or filthy . . . or other publication of an indecent character." The Second Circuit Court of Appeals upheld the conviction. Roth appealed to the Supreme Court, arguing that the federal law violated his First Amendment guarantee of freedom of expression. The Supreme Court disagreed, upholding the previous convictions and creating a new standard by which to define obscenity.

Prior to this ruling, courts had utilized an English standard known as the Hicklin Test to identify obscenities and support censorship efforts such as the Comstock Act. If material tended to "deprave and corrupt those whose minds are open to such immoral influence and into whose hands a publication of this sort may fall" it was considered obscene. Materials could be designated obscene based on the purported effect of isolated passages on the most susceptible audiences. Thus, small portions of a much larger text could result in the entire work being deemed obscene.

Subsequent cases progressively chipped away at the Hicklin Test by requiring new standards, including consideration of a work's prevailing theme or overall literary value instead of isolated passages. Justice Frankfurter wrote in his 1957 *Butler v. Michigan* opinion that application of the Hicklin standard to determine obscenity was equivalent to "burn[ing] the house to roast the pig."

With the *Roth* decision, however, the Hicklin Test was replaced with a new standard. Obscenity was now determined by "whether, to the average person, applying contemporary community standards, the dominant theme of the material, taken as a whole, appeals to the prurient interest." Justice Brennan's new test relied on an understanding of the prevailing theme of the material in question instead of isolated passages. It also shifted consideration of the work's impact from the most susceptible members of society to the "average person" who better reflected the "common conscience" or values of the entire community.

In his majority opinion, Justice Brennan emphasized judgment of a text should be based on its ideas, not just words or images. Even controversial or unpopular ideas, if housed within a work of any social value, are protected under the First Amendment. Brennan argued free exchange of such ideas is not only valuable but necessary to generate important political and social change. He felt only works containing ideas "utterly without redeeming social importance" remained constitutionally unprotected. Obscenity, as defined by the new Brennan standard, fell within this classification. However, this standard was still imprecise enough to prompt confusion and discussion regarding its application for another sixteen years.

Justices Douglas and Black dissented in the *Roth* case, arguing it is unconstitutional to censor materials or limit free expression simply because of the thoughts that may be invoked, as opposed to actions. They held that obscenity is protected by the First Amendment like any other form of speech.

In 1966 the Supreme Court attempted to clarify the *Roth* decision in its ruling for *Memoirs of a Woman of Pleasure v. Massachusetts*. This case concerned a book known as *Fanny Hill* that was said to be offensive and appealing to prurient interest. The Massachusetts Supreme Court had ruled that the manuscript was obscene, but a plurality of the Supreme Court reversed the ruling, partially based on its judgment that although the book appealed to a prurient interest in sex and violated contemporary community standards, it was not totally devoid of social worth. To be considered obscene, the court said, the book must be "utterly without any redeeming social value." The *Memoirs* ruling, as well as *Jacobellis v. Ohio*, refined the *Roth* test to some degree; however, the standard remained frustratingly ambiguous, even to the court. In 1969, meanwhile, the Supreme Court narrowly ruled in *Stanley v. Georgia* that private possession of obscene materials was not a crime because such possession was protected under the First and Fourteenth amendments.

In 1973, the *Memoirs* guidelines were significantly revised with a three-part obscenity test established in *Miller v. California*. The new standard maintained the *Roth* requirement that the average person, applying community standards, would determine if the overall message of a work appealed to the prurient interest. Second, instead of proving a work to be "utterly without redeeming social value," the *Miller* obscenity standard specified that the material as a whole would lack "serious literary, artistic, political or scientific value." Finally, to be obscene, a material must depict "in a patently offensive way, sexual conduct specifically defined by the applicable state law." Under *Miller*, a work not considered obscene in one locale might be deemed obscene in a population with more conservative views. This change gave judges, law enforcement agencies, and juries more discretion in deciding whether or not a material was obscene based on the standards of the local community. Although new considerations have continued to evolve with changing technologies and social landscapes, the core of the *Miller* test remains the prevailing standard in state and federal obscenity trials.

FURTHER READING

Calvert, Clay, and Robert D. Richards. "Stopping the Obscenity Madness 50 Years after Roth v. United States." *Texas Review of Entertainment & Sports Law* 9, no. 1 (2007): 1–38.

Engdahl, David E. "Requiem for Roth: Obscenity Doctrine Is Changing." *Michigan Law Review* 68, no. 2 (1969): 185–236. doi:10.2307/1287385

Kirk, Michael, and Peter J. Boyer. "An Overview of Past Pornography Rulings by the U.S. Supreme Court." In Frontline program: AMERICAN PORN. WGBH Boston. Aired February 7, 2002. https://www.pbs.org/wgbh/pages/frontline/shows/porn/prosecuting/overview.html

Strub, Whitney. *Obscenity Rules: Roth v. United States and the Long Struggle over Sexual Expression*. Lawrence, KS: University Press of Kansas, 2013.

- ***Document 22:*** Supreme Court's Majority Opinion in *New York Times Co. v. Sullivan*
- ***Date:*** Decided March 9, 1964
- ***Where:*** Supreme Court of the United States
- ***Significance:*** This Supreme Court libel case made clear that expression critical of public officials, even involving factual errors, is protected under the First Amendment because the constitution requires robust and uninhibited debate of public issues. The only exception to these protections is when the plaintiff provides clear and convincing evidence that critical statements are made with "actual malice." This ruling was a free speech victory for individuals and the press, granting both the liberty to openly criticize the government without fear of costly legal retribution.

DOCUMENT

MR. JUSTICE BRENNAN delivered the opinion of the Court

We are required in this case to determine for the first time the extent to which the constitutional protections for speech and press limit a State's power to award damages in a libel action brought by a public official against critics of his official conduct. . . .

Respondent's complaint alleged that he had been libeled by statements in a full-page advertisement that was carried in the New York Times on March 29, 1960. Entitled "Heed Their Rising Voices," the advertisement began by stating that "As the whole world knows by now, thousands of Southern Negro students are engaged in widespread nonviolent demonstrations in positive affirmation of the right to live in human dignity as guaranteed by the U.S. Constitution and the Bill of Rights." It went on to charge that "in their efforts to uphold these guarantees, they are being met by an unprecedented wave of terror by those who would deny and negate that document which the whole world looks upon as setting the pattern for modern freedom. . . ."

It is uncontroverted that some of the statements contained in the two paragraphs were not accurate descriptions of events which occurred in Montgomery. . . .

Under Alabama law as applied in this case, a publication is "libelous per se" if the words "tend to injure a person . . . in his reputation" or to "bring [him] into public contempt"; the trial court stated that the standard was met if the words are such as to "injure him in his public office, or impute misconduct to him in his office, or want of official integrity, or want of fidelity to a public trust. . . ." The jury must find that the words were published "of and concerning" the plaintiff, but where the plaintiff

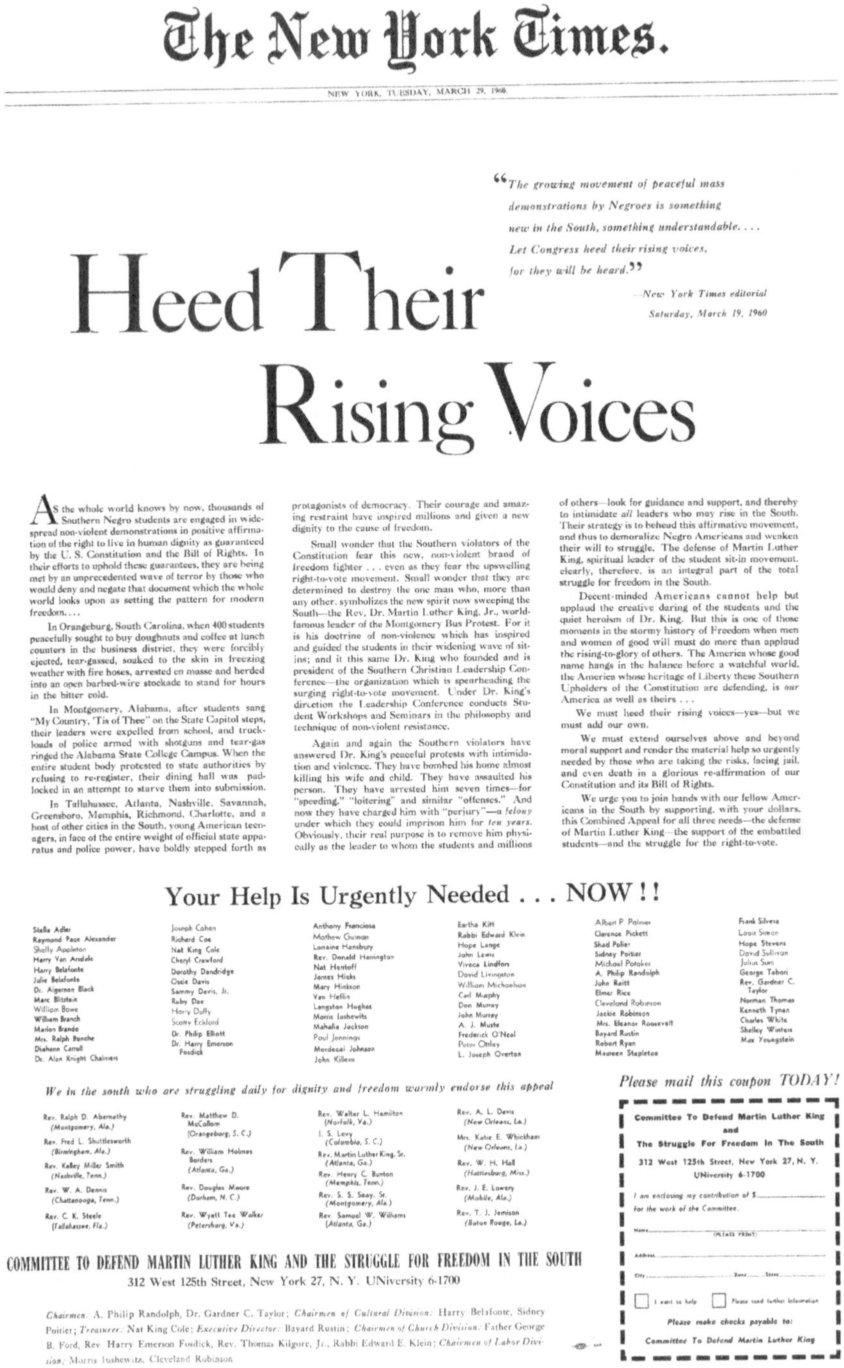

The New York Times.

NEW YORK, TUESDAY, MARCH 29, 1960.

"The growing movement of peaceful mass demonstrations by Negroes is something new in the South, something understandable. . . . Let Congress heed their rising voices, for they will be heard."

—New York Times editorial Saturday, March 19, 1960

Heed Their Rising Voices

As the whole world knows by now, thousands of Southern Negro students are engaged in widespread non-violent demonstrations in positive affirmation of the right to live in human dignity as guaranteed by the U. S. Constitution and the Bill of Rights. In their efforts to uphold these guarantees, they are being met by an unprecedented wave of terror by those who would deny and negate that document which the whole world looks upon as setting the pattern for modern freedom. . . .

In Orangeburg, South Carolina, when 400 students peacefully sought to buy doughnuts and coffee at lunch counters in the business district, they were forcibly ejected, tear-gassed, soaked to the skin in freezing weather with fire hoses, arrested en masse and herded into an open barbed-wire stockade to stand for hours in the bitter cold.

In Montgomery, Alabama, after students sang "My Country, 'Tis of Thee" on the State Capitol steps, their leaders were expelled from school, and truckloads of police armed with shotguns and tear-gas ringed the Alabama State College Campus. When the entire student body protested to state authorities by refusing to re-register, their dining hall was padlocked in an attempt to starve them into submission.

In Tallahassee, Atlanta, Nashville, Savannah, Greensboro, Memphis, Richmond, Charlotte, and a host of other cities in the South, young American teenagers, in face of the entire weight of official state apparatus and police power, have boldly stepped forth as protagonists of democracy. Their courage and amazing restraint have inspired millions and given a new dignity to the cause of freedom.

Small wonder that the Southern violators of the Constitution fear this new, non-violent brand of freedom fighter . . . even as they fear the upswelling right-to-vote movement. Small wonder that they are determined to destroy the one man who, more than any other, symbolizes the new spirit now sweeping the South—the Rev. Dr. Martin Luther King, Jr., world-famous leader of the Montgomery Bus Protest. For it is his doctrine of non-violence which has inspired and guided the students in their widening wave of sit-ins; and it this same Dr. King who founded and is president of the Southern Christian Leadership Conference—the organization which is spearheading the surging right-to-vote movement. Under Dr. King's direction the Leadership Conference conducts Student Workshops and Seminars in the philosophy and technique of non-violent resistance.

Again and again the Southern violators have answered Dr. King's peaceful protests with intimidation and violence. They have bombed his home almost killing his wife and child. They have assaulted his person. They have arrested him seven times—for "speeding," "loitering" and similar "offenses." And now they have charged him with "perjury"—a *felony* under which they could imprison him for *ten years.* Obviously, their real purpose is to remove him physically as the leader to whom the students and millions of others—look for guidance and support, and thereby to intimidate *all* leaders who may rise in the South. Their strategy is to behead this affirmative movement, and thus to demoralize Negro Americans and weaken their will to struggle. The defense of Martin Luther King, spiritual leader of the student sit-in movement, clearly, therefore, is an integral part of the total struggle for freedom in the South.

Decent-minded Americans cannot help but applaud the creative daring of the students and the quiet heroism of Dr. King. But this is one of those moments in the stormy history of Freedom when men and women of good will must do more than applaud the rising-to-glory of others. The America whose good name hangs in the balance before a watchful world, the America whose heritage of Liberty these Southern Upholders of the Constitution are defending, is *our* America as well as theirs . . .

We must heed their rising voices—yes—but we must add our own.

We must extend ourselves above and beyond moral support and render the material help so urgently needed by those who are taking the risks, facing jail, and even death in a glorious re-affirmation of our Constitution and its Bill of Rights.

We urge you to join hands with our fellow Americans in the South by supporting, with your dollars, this Combined Appeal for all three needs—the defense of Martin Luther King—the support of the embattled students—and the struggle for the right-to-vote.

Your Help Is Urgently Needed . . . NOW !!

Stella Adler
Raymond Pace Alexander
Shelly Appleton
Harry Van Arsdale
Harry Belafonte
Julie Belafonte
Dr. Algernon Black
Marc Blitztein
William Bowe
William Branch
Marlon Brando
Mrs. Ralph Bunche
Diahann Carroll
Dr. Alan Knight Chalmers

Joseph Cohen
Richard Coe
Nat King Cole
Cheryl Crawford
Dorothy Dandridge
Ossie Davis
Sammy Davis, Jr.
Ruby Dee
Harry Duffy
Scotty Eckford
Dr. Philip Elliott
Dr. Harry Emerson Fosdick

Anthony Franciosa
Mathew Guinan
Lorraine Hansbury
Rev. Donald Harrington
Nat Hentoff
James Hicks
Mary Hinkson
Van Heflin
Langston Hughes
Morris Iushewitz
Mahalia Jackson
Paul Jennings
Mordecai Johnson
John Killens

Eartha Kitt
Rabbi Edward Klein
Hope Lange
John Lewis
Viveca Lindfors
David Livingston
William Michaelson
Carl Murphy
Don Murray
John Murray
A. J. Muste
Frederick O'Neal
Peter Ottley
L. Joseph Overton

Albert P. Palmer
Clarence Pickett
Shad Polier
Sidney Poitier
Michael Potoker
A. Philip Randolph
John Raitt
Elmer Rice
Cleveland Robinson
Jackie Robinson
Mrs. Eleanor Roosevelt
Bayard Rustin
Robert Ryan
Maureen Stapleton

Frank Silvera
Louis Simon
Hope Stevens
David Sullivan
Julius Sum
George Tabori
Rev. Gardner C. Taylor
Norman Thomas
Kenneth Tynan
Charles White
Shelley Winters
Max Youngstein

We in the south who are struggling daily for dignity and freedom warmly endorse this appeal

Rev. Ralph D. Abernathy (*Montgomery, Ala.*)
Rev. Fred L. Shuttlesworth (*Birmingham, Ala.*)
Rev. Kelley Miller Smith (*Nashville, Tenn.*)
Rev. W. A. Dennis (*Chattanooga, Tenn.*)
Rev. C. K. Steele (*Tallahassee, Fla.*)

Rev. Matthew D. McCollom (*Orangeburg, S. C.*)
Rev. William Holmes Borders (*Atlanta, Ga.*)
Rev. Douglas Moore (*Durham, N. C.*)
Rev. Wyatt Tee Walker (*Petersburg, Va.*)

Rev. Walter L. Hamilton (*Norfolk, Va.*)
I. S. Levy (*Columbia, S. C.*)
Rev. Martin Luther King, Sr. (*Atlanta, Ga.*)
Rev. Henry C. Bunton (*Memphis, Tenn.*)
Rev. S. S. Seay, Sr. (*Montgomery, Ala.*)
Rev. Samuel W. Williams (*Atlanta, Ga.*)

Rev. A. L. Davis (*New Orleans, La.*)
Mrs. Katie E. Whickham (*New Orleans, La.*)
Rev. W. H. Hall (*Hattiesburg, Miss.*)
Rev. J. E. Lowery (*Mobile, Ala.*)
Rev. T. J. Jemison (*Baton Rouge, La.*)

COMMITTEE TO DEFEND MARTIN LUTHER KING AND THE STRUGGLE FOR FREEDOM IN THE SOUTH

312 West 125th Street, New York 27, N. Y. UNiversity 6-1700

Chairmen: A. Philip Randolph, Dr. Gardner C. Taylor; *Chairmen of Cultural Division:* Harry Belafonte, Sidney Poitier; *Treasurer:* Nat King Cole; *Executive Director:* Bayard Rustin; *Chairmen of Church Division:* Father George B. Ford, Rev. Harry Emerson Fosdick, Rev. Thomas Kilgore, Jr., Rabbi Edward E. Klein; *Chairmen of Labor Division:* Morris Iushewitz, Cleveland Robinson

Please mail this coupon TODAY!

Committee To Defend Martin Luther King
and
The Struggle For Freedom In The South
312 West 125th Street, New York 27, N. Y.
UNiversity 6-1700

I am enclosing my contribution of $________ for the work of the Committee.

Name ________ (PLEASE PRINT)

Address ________

City ________ Zone ____ State ________

☐ I want to help ☐ Please send further information

Please make checks payable to:

Committee To Defend Martin Luther King

is a public official his place in the governmental hierarchy is sufficient evidence to support a finding that his reputation has been affected by statements that reflect upon the agency of which he is in charge. Once "libel per se" has been established, the defendant has no defense as to stated facts unless he can persuade the jury that they were true in all their particulars. His privilege of "fair comment" for expressions of opinion depends on the truth of the facts upon which the comment is based. Unless he can discharge the burden of proving truth, general damages are presumed, and may be awarded without proof of pecuniary injury. A showing of actual malice is apparently a prerequisite to recovery of punitive damages, and the defendant may in any event forestall a punitive award by a retraction meeting the statutory requirements. Good motives and belief in truth do not negate an inference of malice, but are relevant only in mitigation of punitive damages if the jury chooses to accord them weight.

The question before us is whether this rule of liability, as applied to an action brought by a public official against critics of his official conduct, abridges the freedom of speech and of the press that is guaranteed by the First and Fourteenth Amendments. . . .

Thus we consider this case against the background of a profound national commitment to the principle that debate on public issues should be uninhibited, robust, and wide-open, and that it may well include vehement, caustic, and sometimes unpleasantly sharp attacks on government and public officials. The present advertisement, as an expression of grievance and protest on one of the major public issues of our time, would seem clearly to qualify for the constitutional protection. The question is whether it forfeits that protection by the falsity of some of its factual statements and by its alleged defamation of respondent.

Authoritative interpretations of the First Amendment guarantees have consistently refused to recognize an exception for any test of truth-whether administered by judges, juries, or administrative officials-and especially one that puts the burden of proving truth on the speaker. The constitutional protection does not turn upon "the truth, popularity, or social utility of the ideas and beliefs which are offered. . . ."

[E]rroneous statement is inevitable in free debate, and that it must be protected if the freedoms of expression are to have the "breathing space" that they "need . . . to survive . . ."

Injury to official reputation affords no more warrant for repressing speech that would otherwise be free than does factual error. . . . If judges are to be treated as "men of fortitude, able to thrive in a hardy climate," surely the same must be true of other government officials, such as elected city commissioners. Criticism of their official conduct does not lose its constitutional protection merely because it is effective criticism and hence diminishes their official reputations.

If neither factual error nor defamatory content suffices to remove the constitutional shield from criticism of official conduct, the combination of the two elements is no less inadequate. This is the lesson to be drawn from the great controversy over the Sedition Act of 1798 which first crystallized a national awareness of the central meaning of the First Amendment. . . . The Act allowed the defendant the defense of truth, and provided that the jury were to be judges both of the law and the facts. Despite these qualifications, the Act was vigorously condemned as unconstitutional in an attack joined in by Jefferson and Madison. . . .

Although the Sedition Act was never tested in this Court, the attack upon its validity has carried the day in the court of history. Fines levied in its prosecution were repaid by Act of Congress on the ground that it was unconstitutional. . . . Jefferson, as President, pardoned those who had been convicted and sentenced under the Act and remitted their fines . . . The invalidity of the Act has also been assumed by Justices of this Court. These views reflect a broad consensus that the Act, because of the restraint it imposed upon criticism of government and public officials, was inconsistent with the First Amendment. . . .

. . . Whether or not a newspaper can survive a succession of such judgments, the pall of fear and timidity imposed upon those who would give voice to public criticism is an atmosphere in which the First Amendment freedoms cannot survive. . . .

The state rule of law is not saved by its allowance of the defense of truth. . . . A rule compelling the critic of official conduct to guarantee the truth of all his factual assertions—and to do so on pain of libel judgments virtually unlimited in amount—leads to a comparable "self-censorship." Allowance of the defense of truth, with the burden of proving it on the defendant, does not mean that only false speech will be deterred. . . . Under such a rule, would-be critics of official conduct may be deterred from voicing their criticism, even though it is believed to be true and even though it is in fact true, because of doubt whether it can be proved in court or fear of the expense of having to do so. They tend to make only statements which "steer far wider of the unlawful zone." The rule thus dampens the vigor and limits the variety of public debate. It is inconsistent with the First and Fourteenth Amendments. . . .

We hold today that the Constitution delimits a State's power to award damages for libel in actions brought by public officials against critics of their official conduct. Since this is such an action, the rule requiring proof of actual malice is applicable. While Alabama law apparently requires proof of actual malice for an award of punitive damages, where general damages are concerned malice is "presumed." Such a presumption is inconsistent with the federal rule. . . . Since the trial judge did not instruct the jury to differentiate between general and punitive damages, it may be that the verdict was wholly an award of one or the other. But it is impossible to know, in view of the general verdict returned. Because of this uncertainty, the judgment must be reversed and the case remanded. . . .

Applying these standards, we consider that the proof presented to show actual malice lacks the convincing clarity which the constitutional standard demands, and hence that it would not constitutionally sustain the judgment for respondent under the proper rule of law. The case of the individual petitioners requires little discussion. Even assuming that they could constitutionally be found to have authorized the use of their names on the advertisement, there was no evidence whatever that they were aware of any erroneous statements or were in any way reckless in that regard. The judgment against them is thus without constitutional support. . . .

The judgment of the Supreme Court of Alabama is reversed and the case is remanded to that court for further proceedings not inconsistent with this opinion.

Reversed and remanded.

SOURCE: New York Times Co. v. Sullivan, 376 U.S. 254 (1963).

ANALYSIS

Montgomery, Alabama, is known as the birthplace of the civil rights movement in the United States. Many struggles, marches, and demonstrations that reshaped

America's understanding of equality and justice grew out of the city's segregationist history. Montgomery drew national attention for race-related conflicts numerous times during the 1950s and '60s, including the Rosa Parks–inspired bus boycott, the bombing of Martin Luther King Jr.'s home by segregationists, and mob attacks on "freedom riders" passing through the city.

In 1960, Montgomery was once again the epicenter of a critical racial issue—this time, involving a major libel lawsuit. On March 29, 1960, the *New York Times* ran an advertisement placed by the Committee to Defend Martin Luther King and the Struggle for Freedom in the South. The full-page advertisement described how authorities had responded with violence to peaceful student-led civil rights protests in the South. One section of the advertisement specifically described a group of students in Montgomery, Alabama, targeted by police for their civil rights actions. Well-known figures had signed on to the advertisement, including Eleanor Roosevelt, Jackie Robinson, Nat King Cole, Sammy Davis Jr., and twenty African American ministers from the South.

L.B. Sullivan, a city commissioner in Montgomery, sued the *New York Times* for libel, arguing that many facts in the ad were either exaggerated or false and that his reputation had been harmed as a result. Mistakes in the ad included: a description of the police "ringing" the Alabama State College campus when in fact they had just been deployed close to it, an inaccurate accounting of the number of times Martin Luther King had been arrested, and an error in naming which song student protesters had sung on the steps of the Alabama State Capitol. The mistakes were mostly minor, and importantly, the advertisement never mentioned Sullivan by name.

Sullivan countered that because it was his job as city commissioner to oversee the Montgomery police, criticisms of the law enforcement in the city directly implicated him and harmed his reputation. Alabama law was in Sullivan's favor, requiring only that he prove false statements had been made in the advertisement and that those statements had damaged his reputation. Lower court rulings in favor of Sullivan were upheld by the Alabama Supreme Court, and a jury awarded him damages in the amount of $500,000, an enormous sum in the early 1960s.

The New York Times Co. appealed the case to the Supreme Court, which unanimously reversed the Alabama Court ruling. In writing for the majority, Justice William J. Brennan Jr. stated that speech critical of elected officials is protected by the First Amendment. He elaborated "debate on public issues should be uninhibited, robust, and wide-open" even when such speech may include "vehement, caustic, and sometimes unpleasantly sharp attacks on government and public officials." Furthermore, damage to a public official's reputation as a result of effective criticism does not diminish the constitutional protection of that criticism or the right to speak freely about concerns regarding governmental conduct. Justice Brennan warned, "If liability can attach to political criticism because it damages the reputation of a public official as a public official, then no critical citizen can safely utter anything but faint praise about the government or its officials."

The justices acknowledged that factual mistakes are inevitable when making remarks critical of public policy but reasoned that freedom to denounce the actions of officials and express concern with public affairs was of more importance to a democracy than assurance that every detail of the criticism is factually correct. The burden of proving the absolute accuracy of every statement would result in self-censorship of those wishing to highlight an injustice or make an accusation; fear of costly legal actions and retribution would prevent the type of critiques necessary to hold public officials accountable for their actions.

Nevertheless, the court made clear that speech critical of government officials is not completely without limitations. Justices held that officials can still sue for damages if they provide clear and convincing proof that a false statement or unsubstantiated opinion was made with "actual malice" or "knowledge that it was false or with reckless disregard of whether it was false or not." However, this court ruling substantially changed the way libel law was adjudicated by removing the burden of proving truthfulness of the statement from the defendant and placing the burden of proof of actual malice on the official suing for libel.

In the case of *New York Times Co. v. Sullivan*, the Supreme Court not only found no evidence of actual malice on the part of the newspaper but also no evidence that the supposedly defamatory statements in any way implicated Mr. Sullivan or his official position. As an example, they pointed out some of the supposedly libelous statements made in the advertisement did not even involve the police and therefore would not have any connection to Mr. Sullivan.

In fact, in his concurrence, Justice Black pointed out there was scarcely any testimony given of actual damages suffered by Mr. Sullivan. Instead, he observed, the half-a-million-dollar verdict may have been a more direct result of hostility toward the "outside agitators."

This pivotal 1964 ruling was a giant free speech victory for newspapers and individuals alike. The decision effectively halted efforts by public officials to use costly libel judgments as a means of stifling the civil rights movement or putting newspapers out of business. A victory for Sullivan would have muzzled criticism of officials by inspiring fear among those who would otherwise protest. However, with the Supreme Court establishing that speech critical of public affairs or public officials is constitutionally protected, the civil rights movement took on new strength.

The *Times v. Sullivan* case established constitutional rules and standards that would thereafter be used more broadly to govern libel laws at all levels. On the fiftieth anniversary of the ruling, the *New York Times* called it "the clearest and most forceful defense of press freedom in American history" (2014).

FURTHER READING

Editorial Board. "The Uninhibited Press, 50 Years Later." *New York Times*. March 8, 2014. https://www.nytimes.com/2014/03/09/opinion/sunday/the-uninhibited-press-50-years-later.html

Moskowitz, Daniel B. "Drawing a Line on Libel." *American History* 54, no. 1 (2019): 22–23.

Pierce, Samuel R., Jr. "The Anatomy of an Historic Decision: New York Times Co. v. Sullivan," *North Carolina Law Review* 43, no. 2 (1965).

Savage, David G. "In New York Times Co. V. Sullivan, the Supreme Court Got It Right Then—And Now." *Georgia Law Review* 48, no. 3 (2014): 865–71.

Wermiel, Stephen. "*New York Times Co. v. Sullivan* (1964)." The First Amendment Encyclopedia. Middle Tennessee State University. https://www.mtsu.edu/first-amendment/article/186/new-york-times-co-v-sullivan

- *Document 23:* President Johnson's Statement upon Signing the Freedom of Information Act
- *Date:* July 4, 1966
- *Where:* Washington, DC
- *Significance:* This act, signed into law by President Lyndon B. Johnson, gave citizens the right to access information from the federal government that had previously been unreleased.

DOCUMENT

Statement by the President Upon Signing the "Freedom of Information Act."

July 04, 1966

THE MEASURE I sign today, S. 1160, revises section 3 of the Administrative Procedure Act to provide guidelines for the public availability of the records of Federal departments and agencies.

This legislation springs from one of our most essential principles: A democracy works best when the people have all the information that the security of the Nation permits. No one should be able to pull curtains of secrecy around decisions which can be revealed without injury to the public interest.

At the same time, the welfare of the Nation or the rights of individuals may require that some documents not be made available. As long as threats to peace exist, for example, there must be military secrets. A citizen must be able in confidence to complain to his Government and to provide information, just as he is—and should be—free to confide in the press without fear of reprisal or of being required to reveal or discuss his sources.

Fairness to individuals also requires that information accumulated in personnel files be protected from disclosure. Officials within Government must be able to communicate with one another fully and frankly without publicity. They cannot operate effectively if required to disclose information prematurely or to make public investigative files and internal instructions that guide them in arriving at their decisions.

I know that the sponsors of this bill recognize these important interests and intend to provide for both the need of the public for access to information and the need of Government to protect certain categories of information. Both are vital to the welfare of our people. Moreover, this bill in no way impairs the President's power under our Constitution to provide for confidentiality when the national interest so requires. There are some who have expressed concern that the language of this bill will be construed in such a way as to impair Government operations. I do not share this concern.

I have always believed that freedom of information is so vital that only the national security, not the desire of public officials or private citizens, should determine when it must be restricted.

I am hopeful that the needs I have mentioned can be served by a constructive approach to the wording and spirit and legislative history of this measure. I am instructing every official in this administration to cooperate to this end and to make information available to the full extent consistent with individual privacy and with the national interest.

I signed this measure with a deep sense of pride that the United States is an open society in which the people's right to know is cherished and guarded.

SOURCE: Lyndon B. Johnson. "Statement by the President Upon Signing the 'Freedom of Information Act.'" *Public Papers of the Presidents of the United States.* Lyndon B. Johnson: 1966, Book 2. Washington, DC: Government Printing Office, 1967, 699.

ANALYSIS

The mindset that citizens should have a right to access information pertaining to their government was evident in the colonies long before the formal founding of the United States. This ideal of accessibility formed one of the fundamental democratic principles that eventually shaped the new government. Efforts to publish newspapers and comment publicly on the actions and policies of authorities in the 1600s and early 1700s were bold and intentional repudiations of colonial authorities and the British monarchy, both of whom wished to keep the public uninformed (Foerstel 1999).

Throughout the nearly 250-year history of the United States, the public's right to know and the government's right to keep information private has proven to be a delicate balancing act. When the onus has fallen excessively to one side or the other, Congress and the Supreme Court have intervened to reconsider and redefine expectations, supporting a system that safeguards the necessary withholding of certain categories of data while still allowing citizens access to information that promotes government accountability.

Among the most important advances in public access to government information was passage of The Freedom of Information Act (FOIA) in 1966. However, the idea of granting the public greater access to official government documents took time to gain traction.

The push for greater public access began with John Moss, a first-term Congressman from California. Moss was elected to the U.S. House of Representatives in 1952, just as Joseph McCarthy was reaching the pinnacle of his anti-Communist crusade, using secret questioning and closed hearings to weed out suspected Communists (and homosexuals) in the government. The 1952 election also ushered in Dwight D. Eisenhower as president. Eisenhower did not like McCarthy but was hesitant to publicly oppose him. As McCarthy ramped up attacks on purported subversive Communists and homosexuals in the new administration, the Eisenhower administration fired several thousand government employees. When asked to provide records regarding the firings, Eisenhower refused.

Moss was disturbed by the actions of the administration and began focusing his congressional efforts on pushing for public access to federal documents and greater government transparency.

It took over ten years, three presidencies, and persistent efforts to prove important information was being withheld before Representative Moss was successful in passing open government legislation. Journalists supported the bill, but numerous government agencies lobbied against it. By 1966, Moss had convinced enough members of Congress the endeavor was worthy of passage. President Johnson was afraid of the bill's potential implications but ultimately determined it offered more benefits than challenges and signed it on July 4, 1966. He remarked he was proud that the legislation designated the United States as an "open society in which the people's right to know is cherished and guarded."

The Freedom of Information Act (FOIA) provides individuals or groups access to federal agency records, thus ensuring greater transparency in government and bolstering the right of the public to know what occurs within those agencies. According to the Department of Justice FOIA website, "The basic function of the Freedom of Information Act is to ensure informed citizens, vital to the functioning of a democratic society." Justice Thurgood Marshall noted FOIA is "needed to check against corruption and to hold the governors accountable to the governed" (*NLRB v. Robbins Tire & Rubber Co.*).

Anyone can make FOIA information requests from any of the executive branch agencies and departments of the U.S. government. There is no central office to take requests; each agency responds to the request directed to it. The law does not apply to records of Congress, the federal courts, the president and his immediate staff, and the vice president.

While broad in its coverage, there are exceptions to the type of information that must be disclosed through FOIA requests. The U.S. Department of State website lists nine categories of exemptions through which government agencies can legally withhold information:

1. classified information for national defense or foreign policy
2. internal personnel rules and practices
3. information that is exempt under other laws
4. trade secrets and confidential business information
5. inter-agency or intra-agency memoranda or letters that are protected by legal privileges
6. personnel and medical files
7. law enforcement records or information
8. information concerning bank supervision
9. geological and geophysical information

Additionally, there are exclusions within the law enforcement and national security categories.

If a request made through FOIA is denied or delayed, an appeal or lawsuit can be filed. Journalists have turned to the courts on numerous occasions to fight for the release of information from agencies who argue that withholding such information *is* a matter of national security. During the Obama administration, an average of 402 lawsuits were filed each year. Under the Trump administration, 860 were filed in 2018 alone.

FOIA requests have uncovered critical stories and exposed major abuses of government power. Examples include: documentation that officials had failed to complete current safety inspections for 17,000 bridges, evidence that Environmental Protection Agency officials knew paper mills were ejecting toxins into rivers, proof of wasteful government spending during Hurricane Katrina recovery efforts, verification that border officials intentionally undercounted border-crossing deaths, and evidence of prisoner abuse and torture by American troops in Guantanamo Bay, Afghanistan, and Iraq.

Since its passage in 1966, the FOIA has been amended seven times. The amended law now requires federal agencies to proactively post frequently requested records and other specific categories of information online for easy public access.

While concerns still arise regarding privacy, embarrassment of officials, and harmful repercussions from the release of government information, FOIA has overall been heralded as a great success. Senator Patrick Leahy remarked on FOIA's fiftieth anniversary, "Our democracy is built upon the premise that our government should not operate in secret. Fifty years ago, Congress confirmed this by passing the Freedom of Information Act, a landmark law which has brought sunshine into the halls of power and made the government more accountable to the people" (2016).

FURTHER READING

Finn, Mary. "Democracy in Crisis: The Man behind FOIA." *Baltimore Sun*. March 8, 2017. https://www.baltimoresun.com/citypaper/bcpnews-democracy-in-crisis-the-man-behind-foia-20170308-story.html

"Freedom of Information Act: Federal Agencies' Recent Implementation Efforts." 2020. *GAO Reports*, March, 6–28. https://www.gao.gov/assets/710/705284.pdf

Hudson, David L., Jr. "50 Years Later, Freedom of Information Act Still Chipping Away at Government's Secretive Culture." *ABA Journal* 102 no. 7 (July 2, 2016): 48–55.

Kwoka, Margaret B. "First-Person FOIA." *Yale Law Journal* 127, no. 8 (2018): 2204–69.

Lemov, Michael R. *People's Warrior: John Moss and the Fight for Freedom of Information and Consumer Rights*. Madison: Fairleigh Dickinson University Press, 2011.

U.S. Department of Justice. *The Freedom of Information Act*, 5 U.S.C. §552. Updated July 19, 2019. https://www.justice.gov/oip/freedom-information-act-5-usc-552

- ***Document 24:*** Supreme Court's Majority Decision in *Tinker v. Des Moines*
- ***Date:*** Decided February 24, 1969
- ***Where:*** Supreme Court of the United States
- ***Significance:*** This Supreme Court ruled that student nonverbal or symbolic speech is protected by the First Amendment, as long as such expression does not create disruption or invade the rights of other students. Additionally, the ruling emphasized that both students and teachers retain their First Amendment rights when they step onto school grounds.

DOCUMENT

MR. JUSTICE FORTAS delivered the opinion of the Court

. . .

I

The District Court recognized that the wearing of an armband for the purpose of expressing certain views is the type of symbolic act that is within the Free Speech Clause of the First Amendment. As we shall discuss, the wearing of armbands in the circumstances of this case was entirely divorced from actually or potentially disruptive conduct by those participating in it. It was closely akin to "pure speech" which, we have repeatedly held, is entitled to comprehensive protection under the First Amendment.

First Amendment rights, applied in light of the special characteristics of the school environment, are available to teachers and students. It can hardly be argued that either students or teachers shed their constitutional rights to freedom of speech or expression at the schoolhouse gate. This has been the unmistakable holding of this Court for almost 50 years. In *Meyer v. Nebraska* (1923), and *Bartels v. Iowa* (1923), this Court, in opinions by Mr. Justice McReynolds, held that the Due Process Clause of the Fourteenth Amendment prevents States from forbidding the teaching of a foreign language to young students. Statutes to this effect, the Court held, unconstitutionally interfere with the liberty of teacher, student, and parent. . . .

In *West Virginia v. Barnette, supra*, this Court held that under the First Amendment, the student in public school may not be compelled to salute the flag. Speaking through Mr. Justice Jackson, the Court said:

> "The Fourteenth Amendment, as now applied to the States, protects the citizen against the State itself and all of its creatures-Boards of Education not excepted. These have, of course, important, delicate, and highly discretionary functions, but none that they may not perform within the limits of the Bill of Rights. That they are educating the young for citizenship is reason for scrupulous protection of Constitutional freedoms of the individual, if we are not to strangle the free mind at its source and teach youth to discount important principles of our government as mere platitudes."

On the other hand, the Court has repeatedly emphasized the need for affirming the comprehensive authority of the States and of school officials, consistent with fundamental constitutional safeguards, to prescribe and control conduct in the schools. Our problem lies in the area where students in the exercise of First Amendment rights collide with the rules of the school authorities.

II

The problem posed by the present case does not relate to regulation of the length of skirts or the type of clothing, to hair style, or deportment. It does not concern aggressive, disruptive action or even group demonstrations. Our problem involves direct, primary First Amendment rights akin to "pure speech."

The school officials banned and sought to punish petitioners for a silent, passive expression of opinion, unaccompanied by any disorder or disturbance on the part of petitioners. There is here no evidence whatever of petitioners' interference, actual or nascent, with the schools' work or of collision with the rights of other students to be secure and to be let alone. Accordingly, this case does not concern speech or action that intrudes upon the work of the schools or the rights of other students.

Only a few of the 18,000 students in the school system wore the black armbands. Only five students were suspended for wearing them. There is no indication that the work of the schools or any class was disrupted. Outside the classrooms, a few students made hostile remarks to the children wearing armbands, but there were no threats or acts of violence on school premises.

The District Court concluded that the action of the school authorities was reasonable because it was based upon their fear of a disturbance from the wearing of the armbands. But, in our system, undifferentiated fear or apprehension of disturbance is not enough to overcome the right to freedom of expression. Any departure from absolute regimentation may cause trouble. Any variation from the majority's opinion may inspire fear. Any word spoken, in class, in the lunchroom, or on the campus, that deviates from the views of another person may start an argument or cause a disturbance. But our Constitution says we must take this risk, and our history says that it is this sort of hazardous freedom-this kind of openness-that is the basis of our national strength and of the independence and vigor of Americans who grow up and live in this relatively permissive, often disputatious, society.

In order for the State in the person of school officials to justify prohibition of a particular expression of opinion, it must be able to show that its action was caused by something more than a mere desire to avoid the discomfort and unpleasantness that always accompany an unpopular viewpoint. Certainly where there is no finding and no showing that engaging in the forbidden conduct would "materially and substantially interfere with the requirements of appropriate discipline in the operation of the school," the prohibition cannot be sustained. In the present case, the District Court made no such finding, and our independent examination of the record fails to yield evidence that the school authorities had reason to anticipate that the wearing of the armbands would substantially interfere with the work of the school or impinge upon the rights of other students. Even an official memorandum prepared after the suspension that listed the reasons for the ban on wearing the armbands made no reference to the anticipation of such disruption.

On the contrary, the action of the school authorities appears to have been based upon an urgent wish to avoid the controversy which might result from the expression, even by the silent symbol of armbands, of opposition to this Nation's part in the conflagration in Vietnam. It is revealing, in this respect, that the meeting at which the school principals decided to issue the contested regulation was called in response to a student's statement to the journalism teacher in one of the schools that he wanted to write an article on Vietnam and have it published in the school paper. (The student was dissuaded.)

It is also relevant that the school authorities did not purport to prohibit the wearing of all symbols of political or controversial significance. The record shows that students in some of the schools wore buttons relating to national political campaigns, and some even wore the Iron Cross, traditionally a symbol of Nazism. The order prohibiting the wearing of armbands did not extend to these. Instead, a particular symbol-black armbands worn to exhibit opposition to this Nation's involvement in Vietnam-was singled out for prohibition. Clearly, the prohibition of expression of one particular opinion, at least without evidence that it is necessary to avoid material and substantial interference with schoolwork or discipline, is not constitutionally permissible.

In our system, state-operated schools may not be enclaves of totalitarianism. School officials do not possess absolute authority over their students. Students in school as well as out of school are "persons" under our Constitution. They are possessed of fundamental rights which the State must respect, just as they themselves must respect their obligations to the State. In our system, students may not be regarded as closed-circuit recipients of only that which the State chooses to communicate. They may not be confined to the expression of those sentiments that are officially approved. In the absence of a specific showing of constitutionally valid reasons to regulate their speech, students are entitled to freedom of expression of their views. As Judge Gewin, speaking for the Fifth Circuit, said, school officials cannot suppress "expressions of feelings with which they do not wish to contend. . . ."

The principle of these cases is not confined to the supervised and ordained discussion which takes place in the classroom. The principal use to which the schools are dedicated is to accommodate students during prescribed hours for the purpose of certain types of activities. Among those activities is personal intercommunication among the students. This is not only an inevitable part of the process of attending school; it is also an important part of the educational process. A student's rights, therefore, do not embrace merely the classroom hours. When he is in the cafeteria, or on the playing field, or on the campus during the authorized hours, he may express his opinions, even on controversial subjects like the conflict in Vietnam, if he does so without "materially and substantially interfer[ing] with the requirements of appropriate discipline in the operation of the school" and without colliding with the rights of others. But conduct by the student, in class or out of it, which for any reason-whether it stems from time, place, or type of behavior-materially disrupts classwork or involves substantial disorder or invasion of the rights of others is, of course, not immunized by the constitutional guarantee of freedom of speech. . . .

As we have discussed, the record does not demonstrate any facts which might reasonably have led school authorities to forecast substantial disruption of or material interference with school activities, and no disturbances or disorders on the school premises in fact occurred. These petitioners merely went about their ordained rounds in school. Their deviation consisted only in wearing on their sleeve a band of black cloth, not more than two inches wide. They wore it to exhibit their disapproval of the Vietnam hostilities and their advocacy of a truce, to make their views known, and, by their example, to influence others to adopt them. They neither interrupted school activities nor sought to intrude in the school affairs or the lives of others. They caused discussion outside of the classrooms, but no interference with work and no disorder. In the circumstances, our Constitution does not permit officials of the State to deny their form of expression.

We express no opinion as to the form of relief which should be granted, this being a matter for the lower courts to determine. We reverse and remand for further proceedings consistent with this opinion.

Reversed and remanded.

SOURCE: Tinker v. Des Moines Independent Community School District, 393 U.S. 503 (1969).

ANALYSIS

This SCOTUS case stemmed from a 1965 incident involving three students in the Des Moines school district who wore black armbands to school to protest the Vietnam War and show sorrow for those on both sides who had died. School officials learned of the plan beforehand and adopted a policy requiring students wearing armbands to remove them or face suspension.

Those three students and a handful of others decided to wear the armbands anyway. Although some comments were made, little attention was paid overall. Nonetheless, the students (in three different schools) were suspended for wearing the bands. Their parents filed a complaint in U.S. District Court, but that court ruled that considering the possible disturbance the students may have caused, the schools' actions were reasonable. The court of appeals was divided, allowing the previous ruling to stand. The U.S. Supreme Court accepted the case.

At issue was whether or not the students had a constitutional right to protest by wearing the armbands in school. The schools had argued that they did not because wearing the bands could cause disruption, and it was the schools' right and duty to impose order and discipline. Many felt that as minors, students had fewer constitutional protections than adults and were obligated to respect and obey decisions made by school authorities.

The Supreme Court voted 7–2 to overturn the lower courts' rulings; justices affirmed that by prohibiting the armbands the school district had violated students' First Amendment Rights. Writing for the court, Justice Fortas expressed that the "symbolic speech" of the students wearing armbands "was closely akin to 'pure speech' which, we have repeatedly held, is entitled to comprehensive protection under the First Amendment."

The court's decision also established that students do not lose their full constitutional rights once they enter a school building. In what has become a widely quoted declaration, Justice Fortas continued, "It can hardly be argued that either students or teachers shed their constitutional rights to freedom of speech or expression at the schoolhouse gate." He continued, "In our system, state operated schools may not be enclaves of totalitarianism. School officials do not possess absolute authority over their students."

In response to the school's argument that authorities acted to prevent disruption, the court asserted schools cannot restrict student expression based on "an undifferentiated fear or apprehension of disturbance," nor may they prohibit expression based on a "mere desire to avoid the discomfort and unpleasantness that always accompany an unpopular viewpoint." Justice Fortas explained that any minority opinion can potentially create trouble, inspire fear, or result in a disturbance. However, he emphasized, "[O]ur Constitution says we must take this risk, and our history says that it is this sort of hazardous freedom-this kind of openness-that is the basis of our national strength and of the independence and vigor of Americans who grow up and live in this relatively permissive, often disputatious, society."

Furthermore, the court pointed out that the schools had restricted this specific political expression while allowing others. The administration admitted to allowing students to wear political buttons, religious symbols, and even Iron Crosses associated with Hitler's Third Reich. By banning armbands, the school was censoring one specific symbol expressing a particular political viewpoint, thus violating the students' First Amendment free speech rights.

However, the justices did acknowledge the need for schools to maintain order and enact discipline for misconduct. Therefore, they stated, speech may be regulated or prohibited when such expression would substantially interfere with learning and normal classroom behavior. With this caveat, the court delicately balanced the need for authorities to enact disciplinary measures with the rights of students to exercise First Amendment speech freedoms within school boundaries.

Justices Black and Harlan dissented, with Black writing a particularly passionate argument against the ruling:

> The truth is that a teacher of kindergarten, grammar school, or high school pupils no more carries into a school with him a complete right to freedom of speech and expression than an anti-Catholic or anti-Semite carries with him a complete freedom of speech and religion into a Catholic church or Jewish synagogue. Nor does a person carry with him into the United States Senate or House, or into the Supreme Court, or any other court, a complete constitutional right to go into those places contrary to their rules and speak his mind on any subject he pleases. It is a myth to say that any person has a constitutional right to say what he pleases, where he pleases, and when he pleases. Our Court has decided precisely the opposite. . . .
>
> It may be that the Nation has outworn the oldfashioned slogan that "children are to be seen not heard," but one may, I hope, be permitted to harbor the thought that taxpayers send children to school on the premise that at their age they need to learn, not teach. . . . This case, therefore, wholly without constitutional reasons in my judgment, subjects all the public schools in the country to the whims and caprices of their loudest-mouthed, but maybe not their brightest, students.

As the first Supreme Court case to address students' free speech rights, *Tinker* was a landmark decision that set the standard for free expression of students in schools. However, the scope of that freedom was limited by decisions in at least three subsequent Supreme Court Cases. In *Bethel School District No. 403 v.*

Fraser (1986), justices upheld the right of school authorities to discipline a student for delivering a speech full of sexual innuendos at a school assembly. Two years later in *Hazelwood School District v. Kuhlmeier*, the court ruled school authorities can restrict content in student newspapers without violating students' First Amendment rights as long as the newspapers are not established as public forums. In the decision, Justice White added that students' rights in a school setting are not equal to the rights of adults in other settings. This ruling effectively took the *Tinker* standard away for student journalists. Then, in 2007, the court ruled in *Morse v. Frederick* that First Amendment protections do not fully apply to certain types of student speech in school settings. In this case, school officials in Juneau, Alaska, had the right to suspend a student who displayed a banner promoting illegal drug use during a school-sponsored activity.

The advent of new technologies and social media has prompted new considerations of the *Tinker* test, particularly when technology-supported student speech takes place outside the school setting. Courts have generally ruled that such speech is punishable if a link can be drawn between the student's actions and the school, particularly if what the student says creates a disruption within the learning environment. This *Tinker* standard was applied to uphold punishment in cases involving online harassment of fellow students (*Kowalski v. Berkeley County Schools*, 2011), online harassment or intimidation of school staff via social media (*Bell v. Itawamba County School Board*, 2015), threats of school violence through instant messaging accounts (*Wynar v. Douglas County School District*, 2013), and use of blog sites to post racist and sexual messages about fellow students (*S.J.W. and S.W.W. v. Lee's Summit R-7 School District*, 2012). However, the 2015 District Court ruling for *Burge v. Colton School District* and the 2021 Supreme Court ruling for *Mahanoy Area School District v. B.L.*, upheld students' online free speech rights. The courts determined that schools cannot regulate or discipline harmful off-campus student behavior, including social media speech, if such behavior does not cause substantial disruption to the learning environment or present a safety threat.

FURTHER READING

Johnson, John W. *The Struggle for Student Rights: Tinker v. Des Moines and the 1960s*. Lawrence, KS: University Press of Kansas, 1997.

Moskowitz, Daniel B. "Schooled in Speech." *American History* 54, no. 4 (2019): 22–23.

Shackelford, Kelly. "Mary Beth and John Tinker and Tinker v. Des Moines: Opening the Schoolhouse Gates to First Amendment Freedom." *Journal of Supreme Court History* 39, no. 3 (2014): 372–85.

Tinker, Mary Beth, and John Tinker. "A Supreme Court Milestone for Students' Free Speech Rights." *Speak Freely (blog)*. *ACLU.org*. February 20, 2019. https://www.aclu.org/blog/free-speech/student-speech-and-privacy/supreme-court-milestone-students-free-speech-rights

Underwood, Julie. "Student Online Speech Rights On and Off Campus." *Phi Delta Kappan*, 98, no. 4 (2016): 76–77.

- ***Document 25:*** Supreme Court's Majority Opinion in *Brandenburg v. Ohio*
- ***Date:*** Decided June 9, 1969
- ***Where:*** Supreme Court of the United States
- ***Significance:*** This Supreme Court decision overruled *Whitney v. California* and discredited its "bad tendency" standard. In doing so, the court made the important distinction between mere advocacy and advocacy that incites criminal action. For speech to be prohibited, it must be "directed to inciting or producing imminent lawless action" and must be likely to produce that action.

DOCUMENT

PER CURIAM

The appellant, a leader of a Ku Klux Klan group, was convicted under the Ohio Criminal Syndicalism statute for "advocat[ing] . . . the duty, necessity, or propriety of crime, sabotage, violence, or unlawful methods of terrorism as a means of accomplishing industrial or political reform" and for "voluntarily assembl[ing] with any society, group, or assemblage of persons formed to teach or advocate the doctrines of criminal syndicalism." He was fined $1,000 and sentenced to one to 10 years' imprisonment. The appellant challenged the constitutionality of the criminal syndicalism statute under the First and Fourteenth Amendments to the United States Constitution. . .

. . . The Ohio Criminal Syndicalism Statute was enacted in 1919. From 1917 to 1920, identical or quite similar laws were adopted by 20 States and two territories. In 1927, this Court sustained the constitutionality of California's Criminal Syndicalism Act, the text of which is quite similar to that of the laws of Ohio. *Whitney v. California* (1927). The Court upheld the statute on the ground that, without more, "advocating" violent means to effect political and economic change involves such danger to the security of the State that the State may outlaw it. But *Whitney* has been thoroughly discredited by later decisions. These later decisions have fashioned the principle that the constitutional guarantees of free speech and free press do not permit a State to forbid or proscribe advocacy of the use of force or of law violation except where such advocacy is directed to inciting or producing imminent lawless action and is likely to incite or produce such action. As we said in *Noto v. United States* (1961), "the mere abstract teaching . . . of the moral propriety or even moral necessity for a resort to force and violence, is not the same as preparing a group for violent action and steeling it to such action."

A statute which fails to draw this distinction impermissibly intrudes upon the freedoms guaranteed by the First and Fourteenth Amendments. It sweeps within its condemnation speech which our Constitution has immunized from governmental control.

Measured by this test, Ohio's Criminal Syndicalism Act cannot be sustained. The Act punishes persons who "advocate or teach the duty, necessity, or propriety" of violence "as a means of accomplishing industrial or political reform"; or who publish or circulate or display any book or paper containing such advocacy; or who "justify" the commission of violent acts "with intent to exemplify, spread or advocate the propriety of the doctrines of criminal syndicalism"; or who "voluntarily assemble" with a group formed "to teach or advocate the doctrines of criminal syndicalism." Neither the indictment nor the trial judge's instructions to the jury in any way refined the statute's bald definition of the crime in terms of mere advocacy not distinguished from incitement to imminent lawless action.

Accordingly, we are here confronted with a statute which, by its own words and as applied, purports to punish mere advocacy and to forbid, on pain of criminal punishment, assembly with others merely to advocate the described type of action. Such a statute falls within the condemnation of the First and Fourteenth Amendments. The contrary teaching of *Whitney v. California*, supra, cannot be supported, and that decision is therefore overruled.

Reversed.

MR. JUSTICE BLACK, concurring.

I agree with the views expressed by MR. JUSTICE DOUGLAS in his concurring opinion in this case that the "clear and present danger" doctrine should have no place in the interpretation of the First Amendment. I join the Court's opinion, which, as I understand it, simply cites *Dennis v. United States* (1951), but does not indicate any agreement on the Court's part with the "clear and present danger" doctrine on which *Dennis* purported to rely.

MR. JUSTICE DOUGLAS, concurring.

While I join the opinion of the Court, I desire to enter a *caveat.*

The "clear and present danger" test was adumbrated by Mr. Justice Holmes in a case arising during World War I . . . Though I doubt if the "clear and present danger" test is congenial to the First Amendment in time of a declared war, I am certain it is not reconcilable with the First Amendment in days of peace.

The Court quite properly overrules *Whitney v. California* which involved advocacy of ideas which the majority of the Court deemed unsound and dangerous.

Mr. Justice Holmes, though never formally abandoning the "clear and present danger" test, moved closer to the First Amendment ideal when he said in dissent in *Gitlow v. New York*:

> "Every idea is an incitement. It offers itself for belief and if believed it is acted on unless some other belief outweighs it or some failure of energy stifles the movement at its birth. The only difference between the expression of an opinion and an incitement in the narrower sense is the speaker's enthusiasm for the result.

> Eloquence may set fire to reason. But whatever may be thought of the redundant discourse before us it had no chance of starting a present conflagration. If in the long run the beliefs expressed in proletarian dictatorship are destined to be accepted by the dominant forces of the community, the only meaning of free speech is that they should be given their chance and have their way."

We have never been faithful to the philosophy of that dissent. . . .

I see no place in the regime of the First Amendment for any "clear and present danger" test, whether strict and tight as some would make it, or free-wheeling as the Court in *Dennis* rephrased it.

When one reads the opinions closely and sees when and how the "clear and present danger" test has been applied, great misgivings are aroused. First, the threats were often loud but always puny and made serious only by judges so wedded to the status quo that critical analysis made them nervous. Second, the test was so twisted and perverted in *Dennis* as to make the trial of those teachers of Marxism an all-out political trial which was part and parcel of the cold war that has eroded substantial parts of the First Amendment.

Action is often a method of expression and within the protection of the First Amendment.

Suppose one tears up his own copy of the Constitution in eloquent protest to a decision of this Court. May he be indicted? . . .

The line between what is permissible and not subject to control and what may be made impermissible and subject to regulation is the line between ideas and overt acts.

The example usually given by those who would punish speech is the case of one who falsely shouts fire in a crowded theatre.

This is, however, a classic case where speech is brigaded with action. They are indeed inseparable and a prosecution can be launched for the overt acts actually caused. Apart from rare instances of that kind, speech is, I think, immune from prosecution. Certainly there is no constitutional line between advocacy of abstract ideas as in *Yates* and advocacy of political action as in *Scales*. The quality of advocacy turns on the depth of the conviction; and government has no power to invade that sanctuary of belief and conscience.

SOURCE: Brandenburg v. Ohio, 395 U.S. 444 (1968).

ANALYSIS

In *Brandenburg v. Ohio*, the Supreme Court was tasked with determining whether an Ohio law prohibiting dangerous or inflammatory speech was protected by the First Amendment. In doing so, they discarded previously used standards and established the imminent lawless action test. For speech advocating crime, violence, or the use of force to fall outside the protection of the First Amendment, it must be directed toward incitement of imminent criminal action, and it must be likely to produce that criminal action.

The case involved the Clarence Brandenburg, the leader of an Ohio Ku Klux Klan (KKK) group, who had organized a rally at a farm in Hamilton County and invited a local television announcer-reporter to the gathering. The reporter and a cameraman attended and filmed the events of the evening. Their recordings showed hooded figures carrying firearms, making derogatory statements about Negroes and Jews, and burning a wooden cross. During the rally, the KKK leader, dressed in Klan regalia but *not* carrying a weapon, made a speech declaring,

> "... We're not a revengent [sic] organization, but if our President, our Congress, our Supreme Court, continues to suppress the white, Caucasian race, it's possible that there might have to be some revengeance [sic] taken.
>
> We are marching on Congress July the Fourth, four hundred thousand strong. From there we are dividing into two groups, one group to march on St. Augustine, Florida, the other group to march into Mississippi. Thank you."
>
> He also stated in a similar speech, "Personally, I believe the nigger should be returned to Africa, the Jew returned to Israel."

Portions of the films from the rally were later broadcast on both local and national television networks.

Brandenburg was arrested and convicted under the Ohio Criminal Syndicalism statute, which prohibited "advocat[ing] the duty, necessity, or propriety of crime, sabotage, violence, or unlawful methods of terrorism as a means of accomplishing industrial or political reform" and "voluntarily assembl[ing] with any society, group, or assemblage of persons formed to teach or advocate the doctrines of criminal syndicalism." Brandenburg challenged the conviction, saying it was unconstitutional because it violated his First and Fourteenth Amendment rights, but Ohio courts were unsympathetic. Eventually, the Supreme Court reversed the conviction and, in the process, developed a new standard for determining when incendiary speech or advocacy extends beyond the protections normally afforded by the First Amendment.

The court's primary argument was that advocacy must be distinguished from action. The Ohio statute was unconstitutional, they said, because it did not recognize this distinction. Brandenburg had alluded to the possibility of violent action, but did not state specifics about when or how such action should take place, and did not actually inspire anyone to commit a crime in the immediate aftermath of the event. Additionally, no one was present at the rally except for the dozen or so Klansmen, plus the reporter and his cameraman, so the comments made by Brandenburg were unlikely to produce imminent lawless action.

By punishing mere advocacy, said the court, Ohio's law prohibited freedoms protected by the First and Fourteenth Amendments. Advocacy of violence or lawless action, as well as assembly with others to promote those ideas, cannot be criminalized *unless* the advocacy is directed toward inciting or producing imminent criminal action and is likely to incite or produce such action. Intent, imminence, and likelihood must all be present.

The ruling for *Brandenburg* was made *per curiam* (reflecting the views of the entire court). It ended a long history of reliance on the "bad tendency" standard applied to well-known cases such as *Abrams v. United States* (1919), *Gitlow v. New York* (1925), and *Whitney v. California* (1927). Separate but similar concurrences by Justices Black and Douglas in *Brandenburg* also affirmed that after fifty years, the "clear and present danger" test established in *Schenck* no longer had a place in First Amendment interpretations, although some scholars argue that the *Brandenburg* standard is just an evolved form or stronger version of the original test (Gilles 2010; Morrison 2014).

The *Brandenburg* decision ushered in an era of unprecedented free speech protection by the Supreme Court. From that point on, the court made it clear that subversive and hateful expression on its own, distasteful as it might be, is still guarded by the First Amendment. *Brandenburg's* imminent lawless action test has remained the primary criterion used by the court to determine the legality of dangerous or threatening speech. It's primary principle of protecting mere advocacy of force or violence was reiterated in the 1982 case *NAACP v. Claiborne Hardware Co.*, and the imminence standard was central to *Hess v. Indiana* (1973). Numerous cases with similar themes have also referenced *Brandenburg*, including *Texas v. Johnson* (1989), *R.A.V. v. St. Paul* (1992) and *Virginia v. Black* (2003).

DID YOU KNOW?

In the *R.A.V. v. St. Paul* symbolic speech case, a group of teenagers burned a cross on the lawn of a black family. One of the teenagers was subsequently charged with a misdemeanor under a St. Paul hate-crime ordinance. The bias-motivated city ordinance prohibited display of a symbol that "arouses anger, alarm, or resentment in others on the basis of race, color, creed, religion or gender." The Supreme Court was asked to determine whether that ordinance was unconstitutional because it was a content-based speech restriction.

The court unanimously ruled that the ordinance violated First Amendment's free speech clause because speech was restricted solely based on who was receiving the message. Although there are narrow categories of speech that can be regulated based on content (defamatory speech, for example), the Constitution does not allow laws that permit one point of view over another. Legal partiality toward a certain viewpoint is unconstitutional. The court illustrated this point by saying government does not have the right "to license one side of a debate to fight freestyle, while requiring the other to follow the Marquis of Queensbury Rules."

Relatively few cases involving advocacy of illegal action have come before the court since 1969. Recent scholarship has also raised questions about the adequacy of *Brandenburg* test standards to address contemporary challenges including: peaceful protests that erupt into violence, mediated incitement to violence including online messages, terrorist threats, violence accompanying polarizing speakers on college campuses, and application of the standard during a crisis (such as 9/11) or war to name a few. During the second impeachment trial of President Trump, *Brandenburg* standards were again cited this time in reference to incendiary messages by a sitting president. Application of the test to new contexts and unforeseen circumstances will ultimately determine the degree of its strength and longevity.

FURTHER READING

Calvert, Clay. "First Amendment Envelope Pushers: Revisiting the Incitement-to-Violence Test with Messrs. Brandenburg, Trump, & Spencer." *Connecticut Law Review* 51, no. 1 (2019): 411.

Gilles, Susan M. "Brandenburg v. State of Ohio: An Accidental, Too Easy, and Incomplete Landmark Case." *Capital University Law Review* 38 (2010): 517.

Guiora, Amos N. "Op-ed: In This Age of Internet Hate, It's Time to Revisit Limits of Free Speech." *Salt Lake Tribune*. December 4, 2016. https://archive.sltrib.com/article.php?id=4654643&itype=CMSID
Healy, Thomas. "Brandenburg in a Time of Terror." *Notre Dame Law Review* 84 (2008): 655.
Montgomery, Chris. "Can Brandenburg v. Ohio Survive the Internet and the Age of Terrorism?: The Secret Weakening of a Venerable Doctrine." *Ohio State Law Journal* 70, no. 1 (2009): 141.
Powe, Lucas A., Jr. "Brandenburg: Then and Now." *Texas Tech Law Review* 44 (2011): 69.

- ***Document 26:*** Speech Given by Ohio Governor Rhodes after Kent State Shootings
- ***Date:*** May 3, 1970
- ***Where:*** Governor's Office (Ohio)
- ***Significance:*** This speech by the Governor of Ohio was made in response to statewide campus protests, some of which had erupted into violence. One day prior, the mayor of Kent had declared a state of emergency and requested that the governor send National Guard troops to the Kent State campus to help quell the unrest. The next day, on May 4, members of the Ohio National Guard opened fire on the campus of Kent State, shooting thirteen unarmed students and killing four in what became known as the "Kent State Massacre."

DOCUMENT

Kent State University

Radio-TV Information

GOVERNOR RHODES SPEECH ON CAMPUS DISORDERS IN KENT, MAY 3, 1970

Now you know everybody here. This is—Robert Kopansky is the District Attorney for the Federal Government. You know the Mayor, Del Corso, Karamonte and Don Kane.

I want to sum this up and then you can ask questions of any of us. We have seen here at the City of Kent, especially, probably the most vicious form of campus-oriented violence yet perpetrated by dissident groups and their allies in the State of Ohio for this reason. Most of the dissident groups have operated within the campus. This has moved over where they have threatened and intimidated merchants and people of this community. Now it ceases to be a problem of the Colleges in Ohio. This, now, is the problem of the State of Ohio and I want to assure you that we're going to employ every force of law that we have under our authority not only to get to the bottom of the situation here at Kent—on the campus—in the city—and we have asked the complete cooperation of the District Attorney of the Federal Government because federal supplies were burned and destroyed in the ROTC building and these people, after we can find them—after a complete investigation—will be turned over to the Federal Government.

We have asked the County Prosecutor for a complete and comprehensive investigation. And there are some people now out on probation that—there has been a strong word to the fact that they have participated in this. Now we're going to put a stop to this for this reason.

The same group that we're dealing with here today—and there are three or four of them—they only have one thing in mind and that is to destroy higher education in Ohio. And if they continue this and continue what they're doing, they're going to reach their goal for the simple reason that you cannot continue to set fires to buildings that are worth $5 and $10 million dollars because you cannot get replacements from the Ohio General Assembly. And last night I think that we have seen all forms of violence—the worst. And when they start taking over communities, this is when we're going to use every part of the law enforcement agencies of Ohio to drive them out of Kent. We're going to make two recommendations to the Ohio General Assembly. Now we've had this at Miami in Oxford, Ohio. Also at Ohio State University and we had 32 police officers injured—and a couple very severe. We have the same groups going from one campus to the other and they use a university—state-supported by the tax payers of Ohio as a sanctuary-and in this they make definite plans of burning, destroying, and throwing rocks at police and at the National Guard and the Highway Patrol. We're asking the Legislature that any person throwing a rock, brick or stone at a law enforcement agency of Ohio—a sheriff, policeman, highway patrolman or National Guardsman becomes a felony and, secondly, we're going to ask for legislation that any person in the administrative side or as a student—if these people are convicted whether it is a misdemeanor or a felony for participating in a riot, they're automatically dismissed—there is no hearing, no recourse and they cannot enter another State University in the State of Ohio. We are going to eradicate the problem—we're not going to treat the symptoms. And as long as this continues, higher education in Ohio is in jeopardy and if they continue to give permissive consent, they will destroy higher education in this state.

I would like for us—we were very fortunate last night we had 700–700 National Guardsmen in this area on the truckers strike. Had they not been here there would have been 14 or 15 other burn-outs and I'm talking about buildings. And it was just through the good fortune of the other incident happening parallel with this one. And that we had here the County Prosecutor, the Mayor, the Chief of Police and the Fire Chief of every law enforcement agency here have been very cohesive in this and I want to congratulate all of them. They've done a great job—everybody here—the City Attorney—everybody here—the Judicial System, all of them have done a good job here but they're limited. There has to be some way of getting some subsidy for these people to fight and these people just move from one campus to the other and terrorize a community. They're worse than the "Brown Shirt" and the

Communist element and also the "night riders" in the Vigilantes. They're the worst type of people that we harbor in America. And I want to say that they're not going to take over the campus. And the campus now is going to be part of the County and the State of Ohio. There is no sanctuary for these people to burn buildings down of private citizens—of businesses in a community and then run into a sanctuary. It's over with in Ohio.

SOURCE: "Speech: Rhodes, James A." Kent State University Libraries. Special Collections and Archives, https://omeka.library.kent.edu/special-collections/items/show/6234. Used by permission of Kent State University Libraries. Special Collections & Archives.

- ***Document:*** Excerpts from the 1970 *Report of the President's Commission on Campus Unrest*
- ***Date:*** September 1970
- ***Where:*** Published in Washington, DC, U.S. Government Printing Office
- ***Significance:*** This report is the result of the President's Commission on Campus Unrest, tasked with uncovering the roots of the unrest that fueled campus protests around the country in 1970 and recommending a path forward. The commission spent three months directing a broad and detailed investigation. The final report, "Campus Unrest," stated that the various actions of students, universities, law enforcement officials, the government, and the administration all contributed to the turmoil on college campuses. However, the Committee reserved the largest share of culpability for President Nixon, whose policies they felt contributed to the national polarization and discontent that resulted in student protests.

DOCUMENT

PREFACE

To The American People

The crisis on American campuses has no parallel in the history of the nation. This crisis has roots in divisions of American society as deep as any since the Civil War. The divisions are reflected in violent acts and harsh rhetoric, and in the enmity of those Americans who see themselves as occupying opposing camps. Campus unrest reflects and increases a more profound crisis in the nation as a whole.

This crisis has two components: a crisis of violence and a crisis of understanding. We fear new violence and growing enmity.

Crisis of Violence

On the nation's campuses, and in their neighboring communities, the level of violence has been steadily rising. Students have been killed and injured; civil authorities have been killed and injured; bystanders have been killed and injured. Valuable public and private property and scholarly products have been burned.

Too many Americans have begun to justify violence as a means of effecting change or safeguarding traditions. Too many have forgotten the values and sense of shared humanity that unite us. Campus violence reflects this national condition.

Much of the nation is so polarized that on many campuses a major domestic conflict or an unpopular initiative in foreign policy could trigger further violent protest and, in its wake, counterviolence and repression.

The Constitution protects the freedom of all citizens to dissent and to engage in nonviolent protest. Dissent is a healthy sign of freedom and a protection against stagnation. But the right to dissent is not the right to resort to violence.

Equally, to respond to peaceful protest with repression and brutal tactics is dangerously unwise. It makes extremists of moderates, deepens the divisions in the nation, and increases the chances that future protest will be violent.

We believe it urgent that Americans of all convictions draw back from the brink. We must recognize even our bitter opponents as fellow Americans with rights upon which we cannot morally or legally encroach and as fellow human beings whom we must not club, stone, shoot, or bomb.

We utterly condemn violence. Students who bomb and burn are criminals. Police and National Guardsmen who needlessly shoot or assault students are criminals. All who applaud these criminal acts share in their evil. We must declare a national cease-fire.

There can be no more "trashing," no more rock-throwing, no more arson, no more bombing by protestors. No grievance, philosophy, or political idea can justify the destruction and killing we have witnessed. There can be no sanctuary or immunity from prosecution on the campus. If our society is to survive, criminal acts by students must be treated as such wherever they occur and whatever their purpose.

Crimes committed by one do not justify crimes committed by another. We condemn brutality and excessive force by officers and troops called to maintain order. The use of force by police is sometimes necessary and legal, but every unnecessary resort to violence is wrong, criminal, and feeds the hostility of the disaffected.

Our universities as centers of free inquiry are particularly vulnerable to violence. We condemn those groups which are openly seeking to destroy them.

We especially condemn bombing and political terrorism. The full resources of society must be employed to bring to justice those who commit terroristic acts. Anyone who aids or protects terrorists, on or off campus, must share the moral and legal responsibilities for the crimes they commit.

We find ominous and shocking reports that students are laying in supplies of weapons, and that others are preparing to take the law into their hands against protestors and minorities they dislike. There can be no place in our society for vigilantes, night riders, or militants who would bring destruction and death upon their opponents. No one serves the law by breaking it.

Violence must stop because it is wrong. It destroys human life and the products of human effort. It undermines the foundations of a just social order. No progress is possible in a society where lawlessness prevails.

Violence must stop because the sounds of violence drown out all words of reason. When students and officials resort to force and violence, no one can hear and the nation is denied a vital call to conscience. It must stop because no nation will long tolerate violence without repression. History offers grim proof that repression once started is almost impossible to contain.

Crisis of Understanding

Campus protest has been focused on three major questions: racial injustice, war, and the university itself.

The first issue is the unfulfilled promise of full justice and dignity for Blacks and other minorities. Blacks, like many others of different races and ethnic origins, are demanding today that the pledges of the Declaration of Independence and the Emancipation Proclamation be fulfilled now. Full social justice and dignity—an end to racism in all its human, social; and cultural forms—is a central demand of today's students—black, brown, and white.

A great majority of students and a majority of their elders oppose the Indochina war. Many believe it entirely immoral. And if the war is wrong, students insist, then so are all policies and practices that support it, from the draft to military research, from ROTC to recruiting for defense industry. This opposition has led to an ever-widening wave of student protests.

The shortcomings of the American university are the third target of student protest. The goals, values, administration, and curriculum of the modern university have been sharply criticized by many students. Students complain that their studies are irrelevant to the social problems that concern them. They want to shape their own personal and common lives, but find the university restrictive. They seek a community of companions and scholars, but find an impersonal multiversity. And they denounce the university's relationship to the war and to discriminatory racial practices.

Behind the student protest on these issues and the crisis of violence to which they have contributed lies the more basic crisis of understanding.

Americans have never shared a single culture, a single philosophy, or a single religion. But in most periods of our history, we have shared many common values, common sympathies, and a common dedication to a system of government which protects our diversity.

We are now in grave danger of losing what is common among us through growing intolerance of opposing views on issues and of diversity itself.

A "new" culture is emerging primarily among students. Membership is often manifested by differences in dress and life style. Most of its members have high ideals and great fears. They stress the need for humanity, equality, and the sacredness of life. They fear that nuclear war will make them the last generation in history. They see their elders as entrapped by materialism and competition, and as prisoners of outdated social forms. They believe their own country has lost its sense of human purpose. They see the Indochina war as an onslaught by a technological giant upon the peasant people of a small, harmless, and backward nation. The war is seen as draining resources from the urgent needs of social and racial justice. They argue that we are the first nation with sufficient resources to create not only decent lives for some, but a decent society for all, and that we are failing to do so. They feel they must remake America in its own image.

But among the members of this new student culture, there is a growing lack of tolerance, a growing insistence that their own views must govern, an impatience with the slow procedures of liberal democracy, a growing denial of the humanity and good will of those who urge patience and restraint, and particularly of those whose duty it is to enforce the law. A small number of students have turned to violence; an increasing number, not terrorists themselves, would not turn even arsonists and bombers over to law enforcement officials.

At the same time, many Americans have reacted to this emerging culture with an intolerance of their own. They reject not only that which is impatient, unrestrained, and intolerant in the new culture of the young, but even that which is good. Worse, they reject the individual members of the student culture themselves. Distinctive dress alone is enough to draw insult and abuse. Increasing numbers of citizens believe that students who dissent or protest—even those who protest peacefully—deserve to be treated harshly. Some even say that when dissenters are killed, they have brought death upon themselves. Less and less do students and the larger community seek to understand or respect the viewpoint and motivations of others.

If this trend continues, if this crisis of understanding endures, the very survival of the nation will be threatened. A nation driven to use the weapons of war upon its youth is a nation on the edge of chaos. A nation that has lost the allegiance of part of its youth is a nation that has lost part of its future. A nation whose young have become intolerant of diversity, intolerant of the rest of its citizenry, and intolerant of all traditional values simply because they are traditional has no generation worthy or capable of assuming leadership in the years to come.

*****

We urgently call for reconciliation. Tolerance and understanding on all sides must reemerge from the fundamental decency of Americans, from our shared aspirations as Americans, from our traditional tolerance of diversity, and from our common humanity. We must regain our compassion for one another and our mutual respect.

There is a deep continuity between all Americans, young and old, a continuity that is being obscured in our growing polarization. Most dissenting youth are striving toward the ultimate values and dreams of their elders and their forefathers. In all Americans there has always been latent respect for the idealism of the young. The whole object of a free government is to allow the nation to redefine its purposes in the light of new needs without sacrificing the accumulated wisdom of its living traditions. We cannot do this without each other.

Despite the differences among us, powerful values and sympathies unite us. The very motto of our nation calls for both unity and diversity: from many, one. Out of our divisions, we must now recreate understanding and respect for those different from ourselves.

Violence must end.

Understanding must be renewed.

All Americans must come to see each other not as symbols or stereotypes but as human beings.

Reconciliation must begin.

We share the impatience of those who call for change. We believe there is still time and opportunity to achieve change. We believe we can still fulfill our shared national commitment to peace, justice, decency, equality, and the celebration of human life.

We must start. All of us.

Our recommendations are directed toward this end. . . .

SOURCE: Report of the President's Commission on Campus Unrest. Washington, DC: Government Printing Office, 1970.

ANALYSIS

Free speech took on a lethal challenge with the killing of student protesters on college campuses in 1970. The events that led to what became known as the "Kent State massacre" and the "Jackson State killings" were products of years of protests and unrest over U.S. involvement in Vietnam. The American public wanted troops out of Asia, and they expected President Nixon to fulfill his 1968 campaign promise to end the war. However, on April 30, President Nixon unilaterally authorized the U.S. invasion of Cambodia, igniting new outrage.

College and university students and citizens across the country had been protesting U.S. involvement in Vietnam for years. By late April 1970 rumors of further military intervention had spread, and students were angry. On May 1, even before official news of the Cambodian invasion reached the public, hundreds of students at Kent State University in Ohio were protesting. That night violence and looting escalated, prompting the mayor of Kent to declare a state of emergency. The next day, amid rumors of further violence, the mayor asked the governor to send National Guard troops. Guardsmen arrived on the Kent State campus that evening to find the ROTC building on fire and confrontational protesters awaiting them.

On May 3, the governor reacted to events with an angry speech that classified student protesters as "dissident groups" and "the worst type of people that we harbor in America." He promised to stop further lawlessness and bring to justice those responsible.

What happened on May 4 is somewhat disputed, but what is known is that roughly 3,000 students and onlookers gathered in the campus commons area for a protest while 1,000 National Guard members looked on. When the speakers finished, the crowd refused to disperse. Some began harassing and throwing rocks at the Guardsmen, who responded by deploying tear gas. At one point as the guardsmen retreated from the crowd, twenty-nine soldiers turned and fired on the protesters. Seventy shots were fired in thirteen seconds, killing four students (two of whom were not protesters) and injuring nine others.

Immediately after the Kent State shootings, a nationwide student-led strike temporarily shut down many college and university campuses. Within two weeks, however, at Jackson State College in Mississippi, student protests similar to those at Kent State (and partially inspired by the shootings there) led to another fatal confrontation. Twelve students were wounded and two were killed when the Mississippi Highway and Safety Patrol opened fire on a crowd of demonstrators near a residence hall.

In the wake of the tragedies at Kent State University and Jackson State College, President Nixon, who had been criticized for statements lacking empathy for the students and their families, established the Commission on Campus Unrest to uncover the reasons behind unprecedented student unrest on college campuses. The Scranton Commission was tasked with assessing why breakdowns occurred in the process of otherwise orderly dissent, suggesting means though which legitimate conflicts might be resolved, and recommending ways to enhance and continue to protect academic freedom.

The Scranton Commission spent three months extensively studying campus unrest, student protests, the national student strike, and the responses of universities and law enforcement personnel to campus disorder.

The commission's final report, titled "Campus Unrest," was divided into two parts and released to the public on two separate dates. In the first report, the commission called the situation a "crisis" of both violence and understanding, and stated that what was happening on campuses reflected a "more profound crisis in the nation as a whole." Numerous factors were attributed to the unstable atmosphere that resulted in campus unrest, including unnecessary use of police force, aggressive student behavior, intolerance, and a youth culture that demanded their opinions be heard regarding social justice and political issues. The commission recognized that no singular group created or exacerbated the anger and distrust that led to violence. Instead, the commission made recommendations to students, universities, law enforcement, the government, and the president for proceeding in a manner conducive to promoting reconciliation and justice. The overall tone of the report, however, placed much of the blame for the violence and precipitating circumstances on the Nixon administration.

The second part of the report, released days later, specifically addressed the events at Kent State and Jackson State. Based on the commission's investigations, this section concluded that the killings of students at Kent State and Jackson State were "unnecessary, unwarranted, and inexcusable." While acknowledging the unlawfulness of radical protesters, the report seemed to generally support the free speech rights of student protesters.

However, in stark contrast to the Scranton Report, an official record of events of the Kent State shootings issued soon after told a different story. On October 16, 1970, a Special Grand Jury in Portage County, Ohio, released a report completely exonerating the members of the National Guard who had fired upon students. The Grand Jury classified the events leading up to the shooting as a "riot" and indicted twenty-five students and agitators. No mention was ever made of the four students who were killed and the nine others who were injured.

This report came as somewhat of a shock, considering the Scranton Report, FBI investigation, and other evidence all pointed to a different conclusion. Nevertheless, the official story had a significant effect on public sentiment. Blame for the tragedy largely fell on the students and victims. Hateful messages about victims and vilification of the protesters discouraged further student dissent.

Fifty years later, details have come to light that discredit the official version of events and more accurately describe what took place that day. For decades, however, public perceptions of the Kent State shootings were shaped by a report that coalesced the actions of peaceful protesters with those of violent agitators, thus condemning both and harming the institution of free speech in America.

The tragic events of 1970 have been memorialized in films, plays, books, photographs and songs like Neil Young's "Ohio," offering critical perspectives of how fear, violence, protest, and authority intersected to produce a dark stain on America's free speech history.

FURTHER READING

Cohen, Robert, and Michael Koncewicz. "'Tin Soldiers and Nixon's Coming:' The Shooting at Kent State and Jackson State at 50." *Nation*. May 5, 2020.

Lewis, Jerry M., and Thomas R. Hensley. "The May 4 Shootings at Kent State University: The Search for Historical Accuracy." *Ohio Council for the Social Studies Review* 34, no. 1 (Summer 1998): 9–21.

Means, Howard B. *67 Shots: Kent State and the End of American Innocence*. Boston, MA: Da Capo Press, 2016.

Mills, Emily, and Jennifer Pignolet. "Kent State Shootings: How Events of May 4, 1970 Influence Student Activism Today." *Akron Beacon Journal*. May 4, 2020. https://www.cincinnati.com/in-depth/news/history/2020/05/03/kent-state-shootings-how-events-may-4-1970-influence-student-activism-today-50-years/3061410001/

Whitaker, Bill. "The Big Chill: The Stifling Effect of the Official Response to the Kent State Killings." *Vietnam Generation* 2, no. 2 (1995): 147–54.

- ***Document 27:*** Morality in Media Cofounder Condemns the Final Report of the Commission on Obscenity and Pornography
- ***Date:*** September 1970
- ***Where:*** Report issued to the President and Congress of the United States, Washington, DC
- ***Significance:*** Rev. Morton Hill, co-founder of Morality in Media, was appointed in 1968 by President Lyndon Johnson to the President's Commission on Obscenity and Pornography. When the commission issued its final report, he was one of three members who dissented, citing strong objections to the report's findings and recommendations. Hill's lifelong commitment to protect society from the harms of pornography is reflected in his dissenting comments.

DOCUMENT

OVERVIEW

The Commission's majority report is a Magna Carta for the pornographer.

It is slanted and biased in favor of protecting the business of obscenity and pornography, which the Commission was mandated by the Congress to regulate.

The Commission leadership and majority recommend that most existing legal barriers between society and pornography be pulled down. In so doing, the Commission goes far beyond its mandate and assumes the role of counsel for the filth merchant—a role not assigned by the Congress of the United States. . . .

The conclusions and recommendations in the majority report will be found deeply offensive to Congress and to tens of millions of Americans. And what the American people do not know is that the scanty and manipulated evidence contained within this report is wholly inadequate to support the conclusions and sustain the recommendations. Thus, both conclusions and recommendations are, in our view, fraudulent.

What the American people have here for the two million dollars voted by Congress, and paid by the taxpayer, is a shoddy piece of scholarship that will be quoted ad nauseam by cultural polluters and their attorneys within society.

The fundamental "finding" on which the entire report is based is: that "empirical research" has come up with "no reliable evidence to indicate that exposure to explicit sexual materials plays a significant role in the causation of delinquent or criminal behavior among youth or adults."

The inference from this statement, i.e., pornography is harmless, is not only insupportable on the slanted evidence presented; it is preposterous. How isolate one factor and say it causes or does not cause criminal behavior? How determine that one book or one film caused one man to commit rape or murder? A man's entire life goes into one criminal act. No one factor can be said to have caused that act.

The Commission has deliberately and carefully avoided coming to grips with the basic underlying issue. The government interest in regulating pornography has always related primarily to the prevention of moral corruption and not to prevention of overt criminal acts and conduct, or the protection of persons from being shocked and/or offended.

The basic question is whether and to what extent society may establish and maintain certain moral standards. If it is conceded that society has a legitimate concern in maintaining moral standards, it follows logically that government has a legitimate interest in at least attempting to protect such standards against any source which threatens them.

The Commission report simply ignores this issue, and relegates government's interest to little more than a footnote—passing it off with the extremist cliché that it is "unwise" for government to attempt to legislate morality. Obscenity law in no way legislates individual morality, but provides protection for public morality. The Supreme Court itself has never denied society's interest in maintaining moral standards, but has instead ruled for the protection of the "social interest in order and morality."

The Commission report ignores another basic issue: the phrase "utterly without redeeming social value." This language has been propagandized by extremists and profit-seekers, and it is so propagandized in this report as being the law of the land. It is not the law of the land, since no Supreme Court ever voiced such an opinion, yet this erroneous concept has been built into the statutes of several states as a result of extremists asserting that it is a necessary "test" enunciated by the Supreme Court. This erroneous concept has led to a vast upsurge in the traffic in pornography in the past four years. The fact is, it is nothing more than an opinion of three judges, binding on no one, neither court nor legislature.

In sum, the conclusions and recommendations of the Commission majority represent the preconceived views of the Chairman and his appointed counsel that the Commission should arrive at those conclusions most compatible with the viewpoint of the American Civil Liberties Union. Both men singlemindedly steered the Commission to this objective.

In the interest of truth and understanding, it should be noted here that the policy of ACLU has been that obscenity is protected speech. Mr. Lockhart, the Chairman of the Commission, has long been a member of the American Civil Liberties Union. Mr. Bender, his general counsel, is an executive of the Philadelphia Civil Liberties Union.

The two million dollars voted by Congress have gone primarily to "scholars" who would return conclusions amenable to the extreme and minority views of Mr. Lockhart, Mr. Bender and the ACLU.

OUR POSITION

We stand in agreement with the Congress of the United States: the traffic in obscenity and pornography is a matter of national concern.

We believe that pornography has an eroding effect on society, on public morality, on respect for human worth, on attitudes toward family love, on culture.

We believe it is impossible, and totally unnecessary, to attempt to prove or disprove a cause-effect relationship between pornography and criminal behavior.

Sex education, recommended so strongly by the majority, is the panacea for those who advocate license in media. The report suggests sex education, with a plaint for the dearth of instructors and materials. It notes that three schools have used "hard-core pornography" in training potential instructors. The report does not answer the question that comes to mind immediately: Will these instructors not bring the hard-core pornography into the grammar schools? Many other questions are left unanswered: How assure that the instructor's moral or ethical code (or lack of same) will not be communicated to children? Shouldn't parents, not children, be the recipients of sex education courses?

Children cannot grow in love if they are trained with pornography. Pornography is loveless; it degrades the human being, reduces him to the level of animal. And if this Commission majority's recommendations are heeded, there will be a glut of pornography for teachers and children. . . .

SOURCE: United States Commission on Obscenity and Pornography. The Report. Washington, DC: Government Printing Office, 1970.

ANALYSIS

Morality in Media began as an interfaith clergy initiative in 1962 to protect children, and American culture in general, from the harms of pornography. Rev. Morton Hill, a priest in Upper Manhattan, initiated Operation Yorkville in response to a local parent's complaint that hard core pornography was circulating among sixth graders in a local grade school. Over the next six years, the group's efforts grew beyond New York City to surrounding states, and by 1968, the nonprofit, interfaith group Morality in Media (MiM) was founded to continue and expand upon original Operation Yorkville efforts.

The primary focus of MiM was elimination of pornography, sexual indecency, and sexual exploitation from media. In 1970, Rev. Hill was appointed to President Johnson's commission on obscenity and pornography. The report eventually released by the commission recommended repeal of laws restricting adult access to pornography, citing lack of evidence of its harms. Together, Rev. Hill and Charles H. Keating Jr. wrote a dissenting minority report rejecting the committee's conclusions and reiterating both the societal harm caused by pornographic material and the need for laws to restrict or criminalize obscenity. President Nixon and Congress joined Hill in renouncing the commission's report.

Morality in Media established the National Obscenity Law Center in 1973 and campaigned actively at all levels from local communities to Congress to raise awareness of sexual exploitation, educate about the harms of obscenity, and encourage enforcement of obscenity laws. The group's victories include a provision in the 1992 Cable Television Act, which allowed local cable operators to ban material they felt was indecent, enactment of the 1998 Child Online Protection Act, establishment of the permanent Child Exploitation and Obscenity Section in the Justice Department in 1987, and passage of the 1984 Child Protection Act (which MiM helped draft). MiM also sponsored wide-reaching campaigns such as the White Ribbon against Pornography Week, the *Dirty Dozen* list of leading porn facilitators, and the PORN HARMS National Awareness Campaign. Additionally, the *FCC v. Pacifica* Supreme Court indecency case was initiated by a member of MiM who was offended by a local radio broadcast of George Carlin's "Filthy Words" monologue.

In 2015, MiM changed its name to the National Center on Sexual Exploitation (NCOSE) "to better describe our scope and mission to expose the seamless connection between all forms of sexual exploitation." The organization now includes an international arm and a research institute. Legal efforts to shut down the porn industry and other sources of sexual exploitation continue through the NCOSE Law Center.

NCOSE's targets have not only been hardcore pornographers, producers, or broadcasters of obscenity. In more recent years NCOSE has been accused of using alarmist messages to gather support for campaigns that some consider an overreach or attack on free expression. One such campaign involved EBSCO, a database used by libraries and school libraries across the country to locate mainstream periodicals. Supporters of the campaign urged schools to cancel EBSCO subscriptions because they said unrestricted obscene and pornographic content was making its way into EBSCO search platforms, potentially exposing school children to the offensive content. EBSCO replied that it closely scrutinizes the content selected for databases, especially in schools, and that it works with school libraries to ensure that search platforms and content used there are age appropriate. EBSCO reminded accusers that no obscenity charges had ever been brought against the database. The American Library Association Office for Intellectual Freedom also pushed back against the campaign, stating it was not aware of a single report of "any minor seeking or finding illegal or even pornographic content through EBSCO" (LaRue 2017).

Such criticisms have not prevented NCOSE from continuing to try to prevent sexual exploitation and pornography in all its forms, including those found online. The organization has remained focused on combatting obscenity and upholding decency standards, in part by shaping tougher obscenity laws and pressuring the Justice Department to enforce obscenity laws already on the books.

Morality in Media's fight against pornography did not happen in isolation. Numerous anti-indecency groups were established and rose to prominence between the late 1960s and 1980s, in response to the relaxing of social and cultural norms regarding indecency. These groups also became very politically active, determined to push back against changes such as the increase of offensive content on the airwaves and more liberal Supreme Court interpretations of First Amendment freedoms. Four such examples are described below.

Charles H. Keating Jr., member of the President's Commission on Obscenity and Pornography, had already founded Citizens for Decent Literature in 1956. By the late 1960s, membership had reached 300 chapters across the country and included numerous senators and representatives. The organization primarily used legal channels to fight the spread of pornography but also initiated a documentary called "Perversion for Profit" that was widely shown throughout the country. The film created somewhat of a moral panic with allegations of the tremendous societal harms caused by pornography. In the 1980s, the group changed its name to Citizens for Decency through Law, which later disassociated with Keating and became the Children's Legal Foundation. Keating is perhaps remembered less for his anti-pornography crusade than for his infamous role in the Savings-and-Loan crisis of the 1980s and 1990s.

The National Federation for Decency was founded in 1977 by the Rev. Donald Wildmon, and states its mission as fostering "the biblical ethic of decency in American Society with the primary emphasis on television." The group was active in letter-writing campaigns protesting television violence, immorality, profanity, and vulgarity. In 1988, the organization was renamed the American Family Association (AFA). This group continues to direct some of its activism toward ensuring media integrity.

In February 1980, Wildmon worked with Jerry Falwell to found the Coalition for Better Television (CBTV). The coalition claimed to represent more than 1,300 organizations including the Moral Majority and the Eagle Forum. Citing the indecency and immorality of TV programming, the CBTV threatened boycotts of companies that advertised on prime-time television. When a dispute with Falwell led to the disbanding of the organization after just two years, Wildmon founded Christian Leaders for Responsible Television.

What began as a radio outreach by James Dobson in 1977 grew to become Focus on the Family, a remarkably influential American fundamentalist Christian organization promoting social conservative views on public policy. Dobson's doctorate in psychology established credibility within his family-centered ministry, which actively advocates for conservative positions on social issues. His organization uses broadcasts, podcasts, telecasts, films, websites, blogs, and radio drama programs to carry out its spiritual and political goals. Focus on the Family has been active in social campaigns to fight indecency, but the group's primary influence has been made through development of its own vast media networks advising parents on conservative Christian child-rearing and family issues. Although not a formal minister, Dobson was named the nation's most influential evangelical leader by the *New York Times* in 2005.

FURTHER READING

Bates, Stephen. "Father Hill and *Fanny Hill*: An Activist Group's Crusade to Remake Obscenity Law." *First Amendment Law Review* 8, no. 2 (2010): 217–82.

Krattenmaker, Thomas G., and Marjorie L. Esterow. "Censoring Indecent Cable Programs: The New Morality Meets the New Media." *Fordham Law Review* 51, no. 4 (1983): 606.

LaRue, James. "False Witness; Morality and Media and EBSCO." *Journal of Intellectual Freedom & Privacy* 2, no. 2 (2017): 13–19.

Morality in Media Inc. *Stranger in the House: Reclaiming the Decency Today's Media Has Abandoned*. New York: Morality in Media, 2000.

Schwalm, Steve. "Morality in Media." *Human Events*. September 27, 1996.

- ***Document 28:*** Amicus Brief Filed by ACLU for *New York Times Co. v. United States* (the Pentagon Papers Case)
- ***Date:*** Decided June 30, 1971
- ***Where:*** Supreme Court of the United States
- ***Significance:*** In one of the most famous freedom of the press cases in Supreme Court history, *New York Times v. U.S.*, the court ruled that Nixon administration efforts to block publication of what it considered classified information was a violation of the First Amendment. This amicus brief filed by the American Civil Liberties Union reminded the court of the importance of a free press and the dangers of government overreach resulting in censorship.

DOCUMENT

INTRODUCTION

The suits filed by the United States to enjoin publication of the Vietnam Papers by *The New York Times*, *The Washington Post*, and other newspapers are unprecedented in American history. We have been able to discover no case, and counsel for the parties have referred to none, in which the federal government has asked the courts to censor the publication of a newspaper. The effort to do so in this case-so far successfully-is a singular departure from a common understanding which exists between the government and the people, now breached for the first time in two hundred years. The central ingredient of that understanding is that the people have the right to know what their government is doing, whatever the effect on the reputation of officials or administrations. So long as the information relates to the conduct of government-no matter how embarrassing, deceitful or dishonest that conduct may be-the people have a right to know about it, and the press has a duty to publish it. The government's only duty is to stand aside. . . .

There are two additional points of importance. First, *The New York Times* and The *Washington Post* are not the only defending parties in this case. The readers of these newspapers and the general public, though not named in the caption of the case, are as much parties in interest as the nominal defendants. Indeed, their interest is *superior* to that of the newspapers because the latter are merely instruments for informing the public of day to day events without which they would be unable intelligently to fulfill their role as citizens interested in the welfare of the nation.

Second, the Court cannot overlook the subject matter of the documents which the government seeks to suppress. Those documents reveal how our country became involved in a war which is more controversial and divisive than any other governmental action of this century, and which cannot be matched by any event in American history with the exception of our Civil War. The country is torn over the Vietnam war. It has spawned violence, hatred and bitterness. It is on everyone's mind and everyone's lips. It has resulted in the deaths of tens upon tens of thousands of human beings-and its genesis, purposes, and effects are the subject of endless discussion.

Now, when it is learned that there are documents which might provide answers to some of those questions, which would allow the people to judge the men who generated the war, and which will give the people an opportunity to exercise their will in order to avert another such adventure-now the Government steps in to prevent the people from acquiring that information. . . .

The only legitimate claim of national security that can be advanced in this case is one made on behalf of the citizens of the United States. The right of the people to know, and the right of the press to be free, are the real interests of national security which are at stake in this case. The nation's security will be best insured by condemning the act of censorship here and by requiring that the First Amendment to the Constitution take precedence over all other claims. . . .

There should have been no stopping of the presses on the basis of the generalized allegations made by the Government in this litigation. Before a restraining order is granted which would prevent publication for even an hour the Government should be required to make *particularized* allegations of the relevant kind of harm to the national interest* that would ensue from publication and, in addition, make out a prima facie case to a District Judge *on the spot* that publication would in fact cause such harm. The Government has met neither of these requirements, and the course of litigation has shown that they could not have. It is therefore all the more unfortunate that the press and the people have endured two weeks of censorship of the important material involved in the Vietnam Papers.

SOURCE: Brief for the ACLU as Amicus Curiae, *New York Times Co. v. United States*, 403 U.S. 713, 1 (1971).

ANALYSIS

The Supreme Court case *New York Times v. United States* is considered by many legal scholars and media professionals to be one of the most important First Amendment decisions in U.S. history

The events behind this landmark 1971 case began four years prior, when Secretary of Defense Robert McNamara began to secretly investigate America's involvement in Vietnam. The study he commissioned was primarily compiled during the Johnson and Kennedy administrations and ended shortly after Nixon took office. The investigators' efforts resulted in a forty-seven-volume collection of highly classified documents revealing that the Truman, Eisenhower, Kennedy, and Johnson administrations had all knowingly deceived the public in regard to the nature and extent of U.S. involvement in Vietnam.

In March 1971, Daniel Ellsberg, one of the study's authors, covertly photocopied the 7,000-page report and eventually shared it with *New York Times* reporter Neil Sheehan. Sheehan and an entire team of reporters and editors meticulously reviewed the documents for three months before deciding to publish a series of articles about the secret report. The first two articles appeared as front-page stories on June 13. The Nixon administration was initially unconcerned about the public release of information regarding actions of previous administrations but quickly reconsidered and sued to stop publication of additional articles.

Initially, a federal court judge agreed national security was at stake and ordered the printing of the articles to stop. That injunction was eventually revoked. Meanwhile, however, Ellsberg had provided a copy of the Pentagon Papers to the *Washington Post*, which also began to make the documents public. The government pursued legal action against both newspapers, but appeals courts in New York and Washington could not agree on how to resolve the issue, so the case quickly made its way to the Supreme Court.

Understanding the immediacy of the issues at hand, the justices reached a decision just four days after hearing oral arguments. On June 30, 1971, the Supreme Court ruled 6–3 in favor of the two newspapers. The court's *per curiam* opinion held that the injunction prohibiting publication of the articles was unconstitutional because the government had not met the heavy burden of proof necessary to justify a prior restraint. "I am convinced that the Executive is correct with respect to some of the documents involved," Justice Stewart explained. "But I cannot say that disclosure of any of them will surely result in direct, immediate, and irreparable damage to our Nation or its people."

Justice Black went further, arguing that when the First Amendment was written, "The press was to serve the governed, not the governors. The Government's power to censor the press was abolished so that the press would remain forever free to censure the Government . . . Only a free and unrestrained press can effectively expose deception in government." He added, "To find that the President has 'inherent power' to halt the publication of news by resort to the courts would wipe out the First Amendment and destroy the fundamental liberty and security of the very people the Government hopes to make 'secure.'"

The injunctions were immediately lifted and the newspapers printed the remainder of the series about the Pentagon Papers. The information revealed in the Papers heightened the sentiments of a public already largely opposed to the war, but no national security issues ever arose from the study's publication. One government official later admitted there was no "trace of a threat to national security from the publication" (Altschuler 2009). Although the content of the papers did not affect President Nixon directly, the events surrounding this case indirectly contributed to his eventual impeachment and resignation. Angered by the leak and determined to put an end to perceived threats to his presidency, Nixon formed the White House Special Investigations Unit whose covert actions led to the Watergate scandal that ended his presidency.

This landmark case shaped the relationship between the U.S. government and its people, strengthening the principle that in a democratic society, citizens have a right to information concerning official actions carried out by their elected officials. Even more importantly, however, the case reshaped the relationship between the U.S. government and the press by fortifying the First Amendment right of media to provide information that enables the citizenry to not only better understand the government but also to hold it accountable—even when the reputations of public officials may be at stake.

FURTHER READING

Carroll, Maurine A. "New York Times Co. v. United States: Confrontation between Free Press and Presidential Power." *Loyola Law Review* 20 (1973): 140.

"In Praise of Leaks." 2018. *Time International (South Pacific Edition)* 191 (2): 42–43.

Lacy, Lee O. "The Case against WikiLeaks: The Pentagon Papers Reconsidered." *American Intelligence Journal* 30, no. 1 (2012): 129–33.

Liptak, Adam, and Veronica Majerol. "1971 The Pentagon Papers." *New York Times Upfront* 143, no. 10 (2011): 16–19.

Rudenstine, David. "The Pentagon Papers Case: Recovering Its Meaning Twenty Years Later." *Cardozo Law Review* 12 (1990): 1869.

Ungar, Sanford J. *The Papers & the Papers: An Account of the Legal and Political Battle over the Pentagon Papers*. New York: The Notable Trials Library, 1996.

- ***Document 29:*** Supreme Court Majority Opinion in *Miller v. California*
- ***Date:*** Decided June 21, 1973
- ***Where:*** Supreme Court of the United States

- ***Significance:*** This Supreme Court ruling established new standards for identifying obscenity and affirmed that obscenity is unprotected by the First Amendment. Justices established a three-prong standard, known as the Miller test, to determine if a work is obscene.

DOCUMENT

. . . MR. CHIEF JUSTICE BURGER delivered the opinion of the Court

This is one of a group of "obscenity-pornography" cases being reviewed by the Court in a re-examination of standards enunciated in earlier cases involving what Mr. Justice Harlan called "the intractable obscenity problem." . . .

I

This case involves the application of a State's criminal obscenity statute to a situation in which sexually explicit materials have been thrust by aggressive sales action upon unwilling recipients who had in no way indicated any desire to receive such materials. This Court has recognized that the States have a legitimate interest in prohibiting dissemination or exhibition of obscene material when the mode of dissemination carries with it a significant danger of offending the sensibilities of unwilling recipients or of exposure to juveniles. It is in this context that we are called on to define the standards which must be used to identify obscene material that a State may regulate without infringing on the First Amendment as applicable to the States through the Fourteenth Amendment. . . .

[I]t is useful for us to focus on two of the landmark cases in the somewhat tortured history of the Court's obscenity decisions. In *Roth v. United States* (1957), the Court sustained a conviction under a federal statute punishing the mailing of "obscene, lewd, lascivious or filthy . . ." materials. The key to that holding was the Court's rejection of the claim that obscene materials were protected by the First Amendment. . . .

Nine years later, in *Memoirs v. Massachusetts* (1966), the Court veered sharply away from the *Roth* concept and, with only three Justices in the plurality opinion, articulated a new test of obscenity. The plurality held that under the *Roth* definition

> "as elaborated in subsequent cases, three elements must coalesce: it must be established that (a) the dominant theme of the material taken as a whole appeals to a prurient interest in sex; (b) the material is patently offensive because it affronts contemporary community standards relating to the description or representation of sexual matters; and (c) the material is utterly without redeeming social value."

The sharpness of the break with *Roth*, represented by the third element of the *Memoirs* test and emphasized by MR. JUSTICE WHITE'S dissent was further underscored when the *Memoirs* plurality went on to state:

> "The Supreme Judicial Court erred in holding that a book need not be 'unqualifiedly worthless before it can be deemed obscene.' A book cannot be proscribed unless it is found to be *utterly* without redeeming social value" (emphasis in original).

While *Roth* presumed "obscenity" to be "utterly without redeeming social importance," *Memoirs* required that to prove obscenity it must be affirmatively established that the material is "*utterly* without redeeming social value." Thus, even as they repeated the words of *Roth*, the *Memoirs* plurality produced a drastically altered test that called on the prosecution to prove a negative, i.e., that the material was "utterly without redeeming social value"—a burden virtually impossible to discharge under our criminal standards of proof. Such considerations caused Mr. Justice Harlan to wonder if the "utterly without redeeming social value" test had any meaning at all.

Apart from the initial formulation in the *Roth* case, no majority of the Court has at any given time been able to agree on a standard to determine what constitutes obscene, pornographic material subject to regulation under the States' police power. We have seen "a variety of views among the members of the Court unmatched in any other course of constitutional adjudication." This is not remarkable, for in the area of freedom of speech and press the courts must always remain sensitive to any infringement on genuinely serious literary, artistic, political, or scientific expression. This is an area in which there are few eternal verities.

The case we now review was tried on the theory that the California Penal Code § 311 approximately incorporates the three-stage *Memoirs* test. But now the *Memoirs* test has been abandoned as unworkable by its author, and no Member of the Court today supports the *Memoirs* formulation.

II

This much has been categorically settled by the Court, that obscene material is unprotected by the First Amendment. We acknowledge, however, the inherent dangers of undertaking to regulate any form of expression. State statutes designed to regulate obscene materials must be carefully limited. As a result, we now confine the permissible scope of such regulation to works which depict or describe sexual conduct. That conduct must be specifically defined by the applicable state law, as written or authoritatively construed. A state offense must also be limited to works which, taken as a whole, appeal to the prurient interest in sex, which portray sexual conduct in a patently offensive way, and which, taken as a whole, do not have serious literary, artistic, political, or scientific value.

The basic guidelines for the trier of fact must be: (a) whether "the average person, applying contemporary community standards" would find that the work, taken as a whole, appeals to the prurient interest, (b) whether the work depicts or describes, in a patently offensive way, sexual conduct specifically defined by the applicable state law; and (c) whether the work, taken as a whole, lacks serious literary, artistic, political, or scientific value. We do not adopt as a constitutional standard the "*utterly* without redeeming social value" test of *Memoirs v. Massachusetts*; that concept has never commanded the adherence of more than three Justices at one time. If a state law that regulates obscene material is thus limited, as written or construed, the First Amendment values applicable to the States through the Fourteenth Amendment are adequately protected by the ultimate power of appellate courts to conduct an independent review of constitutional claims when necessary.

We emphasize that it is not our function to propose regulatory schemes for the States. That must await their concrete legislative efforts. It is possible, however, to give a few plain examples of what a state statute could define for regulation under part (b) of the standard announced in this opinion.:

(a) Patently offensive representations or descriptions of ultimate sexual acts, normal or perverted, actual or simulated.

(b) Patently offensive representations or descriptions of masturbation, excretory functions, and lewd exhibition of the genitals.

Sex and nudity may not be exploited without limit by films or pictures exhibited or sold in places of public accommodation any more than live sex and nudity can be exhibited or sold without limit in such public places. At a minimum, prurient, patently offensive depiction or description of sexual conduct must have serious literary, artistic, political, or scientific value to merit First Amendment protection. For example, medical books for the education of physicians and related personnel necessarily use graphic illustrations and descriptions of human anatomy. In resolving the inevitably sensitive questions of fact and law, we must continue to rely on the jury system, accompanied by the safeguards that judges, rules of evidence, presumption of innocence, and other protective features provide, as we do with rape, murder, and a host of other offenses against society and its individual members. . . .

It is certainly true that the absence, since *Roth*, of a single majority view of this Court as to proper standards for testing obscenity has placed a strain on both state and federal courts. But today, for the first time since *Roth* was decided in 1957, a majority of this Court has agreed on concrete guidelines to isolate "hard core" pornography from expression protected by the First Amendment. Now we may abandon the casual practice of *Redrup v. New York* (1967), and attempt to provide positive guidance to federal and state courts alike.

This may not be an easy road, free from difficulty. But no amount of "fatigue" should lead us to adopt a convenient "institutional" rationale—an absolutist, "anything goes" view of the First Amendment-because it will lighten our burdens. "Such an abnegation of judicial supervision in this field would be inconsistent with our duty to uphold the constitutional guarantees." . . .

III

Under a National Constitution, fundamental First Amendment limitations on the powers of the States do not vary from community to community, but this does not mean that there are, or should or can be, fixed, uniform national standards of precisely what appeals to the "prurient interest" or is "patently offensive." These are essentially questions of fact, and our Nation is simply too big and too diverse for this Court to reasonably expect that such standards could be articulated for all 50 States in a single formulation, even assuming the prerequisite consensus exists. When triers of fact are asked to decide whether "the average person, applying contemporary community standards" would consider certain materials "prurient," it would be unrealistic to require that the answer be based on some abstract formulation. The adversary system, with lay jurors as the usual ultimate factfinders in criminal prosecutions, has historically permitted triers of fact to draw on the standards of their community, guided always by limiting instructions on the law. To require a State to structure obscenity proceedings around evidence of a national "community standard" would be an exercise in futility. . . .

It is neither realistic nor constitutionally sound to read the First Amendment as requiring that the people of Maine or Mississippi accept public depiction of conduct found tolerable in Las Vegas, or New York City. People in different States vary in their tastes and attitudes, and this diversity is not to be strangled by the absolutism of imposed uniformity. . . .

The dissenting Justices sound the alarm of repression. But, in our view, to equate the free and robust exchange of ideas and political debate with commercial exploitation of obscene material demeans the grand conception of the First Amendment and its high purposes in the historic struggle for freedom. . . . The First Amendment protects works which, taken as a whole, have serious literary, artistic, political, or scientific value, regardless of whether the government or a majority of the people approve of the ideas these works represent. "The protection given speech and press was fashioned to assure unfettered interchange of *ideas* for the bringing about of political and social changes desired by the people," *Roth v. United States* (emphasis added). But the public portrayal of hard-core sexual conduct for its own sake, and for the ensuing commercial gain, is a different matter. . . .

In sum, we (a) reaffirm the *Roth* holding that obscene material is not protected by the First Amendment; (b) hold that such material can be regulated by the States, subject to the specific safeguards enunciated above, without a showing that the material is "*utterly* without redeeming social value"; and (c) hold that obscenity is to be determined by applying "contemporary community standards," not "national standards." The judgment of the Appellate Department of the Superior Court, Orange County, California, is vacated and the case remanded to that court for further proceedings not inconsistent with the First Amendment standards established by this opinion.

Vacated and remanded

SOURCE: Miller v. California, 413 U.S. 15 (1973).

ANALYSIS

The case of *Miller v. California* involved Marvin Miller, a California businessman whose mail-order company distributed pornographic materials. Miller sent out a graphic mass-mailing advertising the company's sexually explicit products and was arrested when recipients of the mailing complained to police. Miller was convicted under California's criminal obscenity laws prohibiting the mailing of unsolicited obscene materials. The state court of appeals upheld Miller's original conviction; he then appealed to the U.S. Supreme Court.

The Supreme Court considered Miller's suit the same day as another case involving obscenity statutes. In *Paris Adult Theatre I v. Slaton*, Georgia authorities sued to prevent two adult theaters in the town of Paris from showing allegedly obscene films. Theater owners argued that they had a right to show the films because their customers were willing adults.

In both cases, defendants argued that their right to mail or show obscene materials was protected by the First Amendment. Four years prior, the court had established in *Stanley v. Georgia* that private possession of obscene materials was not unlawful, but questions remained regarding the constitutional protection of the sale, distribution, or public showing of such materials.

In both cases, previous judgments were vacated and the cases were sent back to lower courts for reconsideration under new guidelines established by the court. These new guidelines, outlined in the court's opinion, changed the nature of the way courts would subsequently define obscenity. In practical terms, the court determined First Amendment protections did *not* extend to Miller because his advertisements exposed an unwilling general public to obscene materials. The court also rejected First Amendment arguments by the owners of the Paris theater, stating the right to privacy does not apply to films shown in a public venue, and the films in question constituted "hardcore pornography" which falls into the category of unprotected speech.

Thus, two critical elements arose from the court's consideration of these cases: a new definition of obscenity in *Miller* that built upon but revised the *Roth* standard and the determination in *Paris* that "patently offensive 'hard core' sexual conduct specifically defined by the regulating state law" is obscene and therefore is not protected by the First Amendment.

The court's conclusions emanated from the looming question of what exactly constitutes obscenity. Justices had previously attempted to establish a definition in *Roth v. United States* (1957). That ruling established a material is obscene if it is "utterly without redeeming social importance" and if "to the average person, applying contemporary community standards, the dominant theme of the material taken as a whole appeals to prurient interest."

The *Roth* definition of obscenity answered some questions, but raised many more. The notion of community standards was troublesome, particularly considering that standards in one community might be quite different from those in another. How can one precisely define what is accepted or rejected within a community, particularly if that community is large or diverse? Finding agreement on the definition of "prurient interest" also proved difficult. Two people could respond in very different ways to the same material, with some finding it artistic and others viewing it as obscene. The difficulty in establishing a firm definition of obscenity was encapsulated well in Justice Potter Stewart's renowned pronouncement in the 1964 *Jacobellis v. Ohio* ruling, "I know it when I see it."

The court then once again renegotiated its classification of obscenity and prurient interest in a 1966 case regarding one of English literature's first and most famous pornographic novels, *The Life and Adventures of Miss Fanny Hill.* The book had been banned in numerous countries since its publication in 1748, and it sparked the first obscenity trial in the United States in 1821. Nearly 150 years later, a divided Supreme Court ruled that although the novel was explicit, it was not obscene and therefore was protected by the First Amendment. According to the *Roth* test, for work to be considered obscene, it must be "utterly without redeeming social value." In a 6–3 ruling, justices explained they found the work did have *some* literary value and thus some social importance. However, the three dissenting justices interpreted the book as clearly pornographic. A more precise definition of obscenity was needed.

In the *Miller* decision, justices attempted to resolve this dilemma by establishing a three-tier standard to determine whether or not a material could be determined obscene. Justice Berger wrote in the court's opinion, "The basic guidelines for the trier of fact must be: (a) whether 'the average person, applying contemporary community standards' would find that the work, taken as a whole, appeals to the prurient interest. . . (b) whether the work depicts or describes, in a patently offensive way, sexual conduct specifically defined by the applicable state law; and (c) whether the work, taken as a whole, lacks serious literary, artistic, political, or scientific value." This revised criterion became known as the prurient interest, patently offensive, and SLAPS (serious, literary, artistic, political or scientific) test. While still imperfect in its ability to address all contextual situations or questions, this test remains the standard used by today's courts to determine whether or not speech or expression is obscene.

The new *Miller* test was also significant in that it rejected the necessity of a uniform national standard when determining if a work, taken as a whole, appeals to prurient interest or is patently offensive. Instead, justices allowed such identification to be made through application of local community standards. Justice Berger, referring to the populations of Maine, Mississippi, Las Vegas, and New York City, noted it would be unrealistic to think that individuals in these four distinct places would share the same views or interpretations of tolerable versus intolerable conduct.

FURTHER READING

Clor, Harry M. "Obscenity and the First Amendment: Round Three." *Loyola of Los Angeles Law Review*. 7 (1974): 207.

"Community Standards, Class Actions, and Obscenity under Miller v. California." 1975. *Harvard Law Review* 88, no. 8 (1975): 1838.

Hixson, Richard F. *Pornography and the Justices: The Supreme Court and the Intractable Obscenity Problem*. Carbondale: Southern Illinois University Press, 1996.

Miller, Beverly G. "Miller v. California: A Cold Shower for the First Amendment." *St. John's Law Review* 48 (1973): 568.

Waxman, Olivia B. "This Is What Americans Used to Consider Obscene." *Time*. June 1, 2016.

- ***Document 30:*** Supreme Court Ruling in *Federal Communications Commission v. Pacifica Foundation*
- ***Date:*** Decided July 3, 1978
- ***Where:*** Supreme Court of the United States
- ***Significance:*** This SCOTUS case established that government (through the Federal Communications Commission) did not violate the First Amendment by regulating the broadcasting of indecent speech. Furthermore, expression does not have to be obscene to be regulated; indecent speech transmitted through broadcast media can be treated as a special category in part because of the pervasive nature of such media and the probability of children's exposure to it.

DOCUMENT

. . . This case requires that we decide whether the Federal Communications Commission has any power to regulate a radio broadcast that is indecent but not obscene.

. . . Having granted the Commission's petition for certiorari, we must decide: (1) whether the scope of judicial review encompasses more than the Commission's determination that the monologue was indecent "as broadcast"; (2) whether the Commission's order was a form of censorship forbidden by § 326; (3) whether the broadcast was indecent within the meaning of § 1464; and (4) whether the order violates the First Amendment of the United States Constitution. . . .

II

The relevant statutory questions are whether the Commission's action is forbidden "censorship" . . . and whether speech that concededly is not obscene may be restricted as "indecent" . . .

Section 29 of the Radio Act of 1927 provided:

> "Nothing in this Act shall be understood or construed to give the licensing authority the power of censorship over the radio communications or signals transmitted by any radio station, and no regulation or condition shall be promulgated or fixed by the licensing authority which shall interfere with the right of free speech by means of radio communications. No person within the jurisdiction of the United States shall utter any obscene, indecent, or profane language by means of radio communication." 44 Stat. 1172.

The prohibition against censorship unequivocally denies the Commission any power to edit proposed broadcasts in advance and to excise material considered inappropriate for the airwaves. The prohibition, however, has never been construed to deny the Commission the power to review the content of completed broadcasts in the performance of its regulatory duties.

During the period between the original enactment of the provision in 1927 and its re-enactment in the Communications Act of 1934, the courts and the Federal Radio Commission held that the section deprived the Commission of the power to subject "broadcasting matter to scrutiny prior to its release," but they concluded that the Commission's "undoubted right" to take note of past program content when considering a licensee's renewal application "is not censorship."

Not only did the Federal Radio Commission so construe the statute prior to 1934; its successor, the Federal Communications Commission, has consistently interpreted the provision in the same way ever since. . . . Judge Wright forcefully pointed out that the Commission is not prevented from canceling the license of a broadcaster who persists in a course of improper programming. . . .

Entirely apart from the fact that the subsequent review of program content is not the sort of censorship at which the statute was directed, its history makes it perfectly clear that it was not intended to limit the Commission's power to regulate the broadcast of obscene, indecent, or profane language. . . .

We conclude, therefore, that § 326 does not limit the Commission's authority to impose sanctions on licensees who engage in obscene, indecent, or profane broadcasting.

III

The only other statutory question presented by this case is whether the afternoon broadcast of the "Filthy Words" monologue was indecent within the meaning of § 1464.13. . .

The Commission identified several words that referred to excretory or sexual activities or organs, stated that the repetitive, deliberate use of those words in an afternoon broadcast when children are in the audience was patently offensive, and held that the broadcast was indecent. Pacifica takes issue with the Commission's definition of indecency, but does not dispute the Commission's preliminary determination that each of the components of its definition was present. Specifically, Pacifica does not quarrel with the conclusion that this afternoon broadcast was patently offensive. Pacifica's claim that the broadcast was not indecent within the meaning of the statute rests entirely on the absence of prurient appeal.

The plain language of the statute does not support Pacifica's argument. The words "obscene, indecent, or profane" are written in the disjunctive, implying that each has a separate meaning. Prurient appeal is an element of the obscene, but the normal definition of "indecent" merely refers to nonconformance with accepted standards of morality.

Pacifica argues, however, that this Court has construed the term "indecent" in related statutes to mean "obscene," as that term was defined in *Miller v. California* . . .

Because neither our prior decisions nor the language or history of § 1464 supports the conclusion that prurient appeal is an essential component of indecent language, we reject Pacifica's construction of the statute. When that construction is put to one side, there is no basis for disagreeing with the Commission's conclusion that indecent language was used in this broadcast.

IV

Pacifica makes two constitutional attacks on the Commission's order. First, it argues that the Commission's construction of the statutory language broadly encompasses so much constitutionally protected speech that reversal is required even if Pacifica's broadcast of the "Filthy Words" monologue is not itself protected by the First Amendment. Second, Pacifica argues that inasmuch as the recording is not obscene, the Constitution forbids any abridgment of the right to broadcast it on the radio.

A

The first argument fails because our review is limited to the question whether the Commission has the authority to proscribe this particular broadcast. As the Commission itself emphasized, its order was "issued in a specific factual context." That approach is appropriate for courts as well as the Commission when regulation of indecency is at stake, for indecency is largely a function of context—it cannot be adequately judged in the abstract. . . .

It is true that the Commission's order may lead some broadcasters to censor themselves. At most, however, the Commission's definition of indecency will deter only the broadcasting of patently offensive references to excretory and sexual organs and activities. . . . Invalidating any rule on the basis of its hypothetical application to situations not before the Court is "strong medicine" to be applied "sparingly and only as a last resort." We decline to administer that medicine to preserve the vigor of patently offensive sexual and excretory speech.

B

When the issue is narrowed to the facts of this case, the question is whether the First Amendment denies government any power to restrict the public broadcast of indecent language in any circumstances. . . .

The words of the Carlin monologue are unquestionably "speech" within the meaning of the First Amendment. It is equally clear that the Commission's objections to the broadcast were based in part on its content. The order must therefore fall if, as Pacifica argues, the First Amendment prohibits all governmental regulation that depends on the content of speech. Our past cases demonstrate, however, that no such absolute rule is mandated by the Constitution. . . .

If there were any reason to believe that the Commission's characterization of the Carlin monologue as offensive could be traced to its political content—or even to the fact that it satirized contemporary attitudes about four-letter words—First Amendment protection might be required. But that is simply not this case. These words offend for the same reasons that obscenity offends. Their place in the hierarchy of First Amendment values was aptly sketched by Mr. Justice Murphy when he said: "[S]uch utterances are no essential part of any exposition of ideas, and are of such slight social value as a step to truth that any benefit that may be derived from them is clearly outweighed by the social interest in order and morality." *Chaplinsky v. New Hampshire*.

Although these words ordinarily lack literary, political, or scientific value, they are not entirely outside the protection of the First Amendment. Some uses of even the most offensive words are unquestionably protected. . . . It is a characteristic of speech such as this that both its capacity to offend and its "social value," to use Mr. Justice Murphy's term, vary with the circumstances. Words that are commonplace in one setting are shocking in another. . . .

In this case it is undisputed that the content of Pacifica's broadcast was "vulgar," "offensive," and "shocking." Because content of that character is not entitled to absolute constitutional protection under all circumstances, we must consider its context in order to determine whether the Commission's action was constitutionally permissible.

C

We have long recognized that each medium of expression presents special First Amendment problems. And of all forms of communication, it is broadcasting that has received the most limited First Amendment protection. Thus, although other speakers cannot be licensed except under laws that carefully define and narrow official discretion, a broadcaster may be deprived of his license and his forum if the Commission decides that such an action would serve "the public interest, convenience, and necessity." Similarly, although the First Amendment protects newspaper publishers from being required to print the replies of those whom they criticize, it affords no such protection to broadcasters; on the contrary, they must give free time to the victims of their criticism.

The reasons for these distinctions are complex, but two have relevance to the present case. First, the broadcast media have established a uniquely pervasive presence in the lives of all Americans. Patently offensive, indecent material presented over the airwaves confronts the citizen, not only in public, but also in the privacy of the home, where the individual's right to be left alone plainly outweighs the First Amendment rights of an intruder. Because the broadcast audience is constantly tuning in and out, prior warnings cannot completely protect the listener or viewer from unexpected program content. To say that one may avoid further offense by turning off the radio when he hears indecent language is like saying that the remedy for an assault is to run away after the first blow. One may hang up on an indecent phone call, but that option does not give the caller a constitutional immunity or avoid a harm that has already taken place.

Second, broadcasting is uniquely accessible to children, even those too young to read. Although Cohen's written message might have been incomprehensible to a first grader, Pacifica's broadcast could have enlarged a child's vocabulary in an instant. Other forms of offensive expression may be withheld from the young without restricting the expression at its source. Bookstores and motion picture theaters, for example, may be prohibited from making indecent material available to children. We held in *Ginsberg v. New York*, that the government's interest in the "well-being of its youth" and in supporting "parents' claim to authority in their own household" justified the regulation of otherwise protected expression. The ease with which children may obtain access to broadcast material, coupled with the concerns recognized in *Ginsberg* amply justify special treatment of indecent broadcasting.

It is appropriate, in conclusion, to emphasize the narrowness of our holding. This case does not involve a two-way radio conversation between a cab driver and a dispatcher, or a telecast of an Elizabethan comedy. We have not decided that an occasional expletive in either setting would justify any sanction or, indeed, that this broadcast would justify a criminal prosecution. The Commission's decision rested entirely on a nuisance rationale under which context is all-important. The concept requires consideration of a host of variables. The time of day was emphasized by the Commission. The content of the program in which the language is used will also affect the composition of the audience, and differences between radio, television, and perhaps closed-circuit transmissions, may also be relevant. As Mr. Justice Sutherland wrote, a "nuisance may be merely a right thing in the wrong place,—like a pig in the parlor instead of the barnyard." We simply hold that when the Commission finds that a pig has entered the parlor, the exercise of its regulatory power does not depend on proof that the pig is obscene.

The judgment of the Court of Appeals is reversed.

SOURCE: FCC v. Pacifica Foundation, 438 U.S. 726 (1977).

ANALYSIS

This SCOTUS case began on an October afternoon in 1973 when George Carlin's "Seven Filthy Words" monologue was broadcast on a New York radio station. Carlin's monologue, using satire as a means of commenting on societal attitudes toward language, contained numerous, repetitive offensive words and phrases.

A few weeks later, the Federal Communications Commission (FCC) received a letter of complaint from a motorist who had heard the broadcast while driving with his young son. The FCC forwarded the complaint to the radio station. The station owner, Pacifica Foundation, replied that listeners had been advised the program contained sensitive language that some might regard as offensive. Pacifica characterized Carlin as "a significant social satirist" who "like Twain and Sahl before him, examines the language of ordinary people . . . Carlin is not mouthing obscenities, he is merely using words to satirize as harmless and essentially silly our attitudes towards those words."

The FCC concluded that the language used in the broadcast was indecent and would be prohibited under an existing statute. Instead of forbidding indecent words altogether, the FCC recommended channeling programs like the George Carlin monologue to time slots when children were not likely to hear them. It issued a declaratory order stating the broadcast could have resulted in sanctions against Pacifica, but as an alternative, the FCC decided to associate the order with the station's license file to heighten the probability of sanctions if future complaints were received. The monologue, it said, was patently offensive rather than obscene,

DID YOU KNOW?

Another major Supreme Court case dealing with broadcasting rules was *Red Lion Broadcasting Co. v. Federal Communications Commission* (1969). The decision of the court upheld the fairness doctrine, a rule established by the Federal Communications Commission (FCC) in 1949 to ensure fair and balanced coverage of public issues discussed on any broadcast medium. The fairness doctrine required that opposing views of controversial issues be given equal air time to avoid political editorializing. Additionally, if the character, honesty, or integrity of a person or group was attacked on such a broadcast, the station was required to provide equal response time to those who had been criticized.

In this case, the Red Lion Broadcasting Company challenged the fairness doctrine by refusing to allow response time to an author criticized during a radio broadcast. The company argued the station's editorial discretion gave it the right to determine its broadcast content. Forcing the station to air responses to critical pieces, said the company, violated its constitutional rights.

A unanimous Supreme Court disagreed. Justices argued that because radio frequencies are scarce, the FCC grants licenses with the requirement and understanding that stations must also serve the public interest. The fairness doctrine served that public interest by trying to provide unbiased information that helped listeners better understand the issues at hand. This purpose, said the court, actually enhances First Amendment freedoms.

Nevertheless, citing First Amendment free speech restrictions on broadcast journalists, the FCC voted to abolish the fairness doctrine in 1987.

and should thus be regulated by principles of nuisance law, which attempts to channel behavior rather than prohibit it. The commission then highlighted why broadcast speech is treated differently than other types of expression and attempted to develop standards more clearly defining indecent speech.

Ultimately, applying such considerations (including the timing of the broadcast when children could be listening), the FCC found that the language in the monologue was indecent and thus prohibited by U.S. Code.

Pacifica Foundation argued that the FCC's actions amounted to censorship. Pacifica said it had a right to select programming for its stations, and any infringement of its programming decisions was a violation of the First Amendment. The Supreme Court was eventually tasked with considering multiple legal and constitutional aspects of the case.

First, the majority of the court upheld the FCC's authority to regulate broadcasting of indecent speech. The ruling referred to a section of the 1927 Radio Act (and the Communications Act of 1934) prohibiting transmission of "obscene, indecent, or profane language by means of radio communication." The Radio Act also forbade regulatory agencies from editing broadcasts in advance or preemptively removing offensive material from programming. However, the law did not prohibit licensing authorities from reviewing the content of previously aired broadcasts when carrying out regulatory duties or considering whether or not to renew a broadcaster's license.

The court was also tasked with determining whether the language in Carlin's monologue was rightly classified as indecent. Pacifica argued that it was not, because in spite of its offensive nature, it lacked prurient appeal. The justices in the majority rejected that argument, saying prurient appeal is an element of obscenity, but is not necessarily an essential component of indecent language. They concluded the language in the broadcast was indecent because it did not conform to society's accepted moral standards.

The court was also asked to consider whether the FCC had authority to regulate this particular broadcast, in response to Pacifica's assertions that: (1) FCC interpretation of its regulatory powers in this case would too broadly affect other types of constitutionally protected speech and (2) existing statutes allowed regulation only of obscenity, not indecent speech.

Justice Stevens acknowledged that the FCC's order may potentially cause other broadcasters to self-censor patently offensive language. However, invalidating a rule because of its hypothetical application to other speech, he wrote, would be "strong medicine" that should be applied "sparingly and only as a last resort." This was not the appropriate occasion to apply such strong medicine.

Second, the majority concluded indecent speech does not have to be obscene to be regulated. Justice Stevens pointed out that offensive speech often receives constitutional protection to ensure the free flow of ideas. However, he emphasized that context is important, writing, ". . . indecency is largely a function of context—it cannot be adequately judged in the abstract." In this case, the FCC's regulatory actions were based upon a nuisance rationale that considered the overall context of the programming including the timing (in the middle of the afternoon), content (indecent language was repeated), and the audience (children were much more likely to be listening at this time of day).

Finally, the majority court ruled the FCC's actions did not violate First Amendment freedoms, in part because broadcast media are held to a different standard than print media. There are a finite number of bandwidths on the spectrum, so broadcasters granted licenses to utilize the available frequencies are expected to serve the public interest in specific ways. For example, broadcasters must adhere to the fairness doctrine (*Red Lion Broadcasting Co. v. FCC*), which by its nature affords them less First Amendment protection than that enjoyed by the press.

Additionally, the majority cited the unique pervasiveness of broadcasts into the American home as a second reason for their limited First Amendment protections. Radio and television are primary news and information sources for most Americans. Justice Stevens noted: "[P]atently offensive, indecent material presented over the airwaves confronts the citizen, not only in public but also in the privacy of the home, where the individual's right to be left alone plainly outweighs the First Amendment rights of an intruder." Listeners tune in and out of radio broadcasts and could easily miss warnings about explicit material. Furthermore, wrote Stevens, even children too young to read can easily access broadcast media. The effect of indecent programming on these young audiences defies the established government interest in the well-being of the nation's youth.

The *FCC v. Pacifica* ruling was used as a model for broadcast indecency cases until 2004, when FCC chairman Michael Powell engaged in an aggressive campaign to crack down on isolated utterances of indecent speech ("fleeting expletives") and expand upon the list of impermissible indecent expressions. This effort was largely influenced by conservative religious organizations who sent massive numbers of

DID YOU KNOW?

After the *FCC v. Pacifica* decision in 1978 established that regulation of broadcast indecency did not violate the First Amendment, the Federal Communications Commission (FCC) generally enacted a "fleeting expletives" policy that overlooked the broadcast of an occasional vulgarity, but imposed sanctions on repeated broadcasts of obscene, indecent, or profane language. The commission examined the expletives in context to determine the extent of their offensive nature, but generally noted the distinction between isolated and repeated incidents when deciding if a violation of federal policy had occurred.

However, largely in response to the use of expletives by celebrities during award shows in 2002 and 2003, the FCC modified its indecency enforcement policy in 2004 and said that it could fine television stations even for isolated incidents of indecency during live broadcasts. Television stations cried foul, and Fox and other affected networks took the issue to court.

In *FCC v. Fox*, the Supreme Court unanimously ruled that the way the FCC's indecency policy had been applied was unconstitutionally vague. It added that the FCC had violated due process by not giving broadcasters advance notice that the "fleeting expletives" policy had been rescinded and that such instances would be subject to regulation. The court dismissed any fines the FCC had imposed. However, this decision did not address the constitutionality of the FCC's policy itself—only the way it had been applied and enforced.

complaints to the FCC through organized e-mail campaigns. The Supreme Court ruled in a 2012 case involving the Super Bowl XXXVIII Halftime show "wardrobe malfunction" that the FCC's new standards were vague.

Some stations responded by self-censoring to avoid potential sanctions. Meanwhile, new technologies such as the V-chip and parental controls allowed families to take censorship into their own hands. Political motivations, expanded individual controls over indecent programming in the home, and the development of new media not under FCC scrutiny have contributed to calls for reconsideration of the rationale behind the *FCC v. Pacifica* decision and its application to twenty-first-century broadcasting.

FURTHER READING

Gibeaut, John. "Fines, Fox, FCC . . . and Other F-words." *American Bar Association Journal* 94, no. 11 (2008): 28–29.

Lindvall, Alexander J. "Frankly My Dear, I Don't Give a-Darn—An Argument against Censoring Broadcast Media." *Arizona State University Sports & Entertainment Law Journal* 7 (2017): 153.

Marcus, Ann-Ellen. "Broadcasting Seven Dirty Words: FCC v. Pacifica Foundation." *Boston College Law Review* 20, no. 5 (1979): 975.

Powe, Lewis A., Jr. "Red Lion and Pacifica: Are They Relics." *Pepperdine Law Review* 36 (2008): 445.

Rosenfeld, Shelly. "An Indecent Proposal? What Clamping Down on Fleeting Expletives on the Airwaves Means for the TV Industry." *Texas Review of Entertainment & Sports Law* 12, no. 2 (2011): 225–38.

4

CULTURE WARS, STUDENT RIGHTS, AND CHALLENGES TO FREE SPEECH (1980–2000)

- ***Document 31:*** Supreme Court Decision in *Board of Education, Island Trees Union Free School District v. Pico*
- ***Date:*** Decided June 25, 1982
- ***Where:*** Supreme Court of the United States
- ***Significance:*** The court ruled that discretionary power of school boards to remove materials from a school library is not greater than the students' right to the exchange of ideas and expression protected by the First Amendment. This decision established that students have a qualified right of access to information from books already in place in their school libraries. However, the plurality opinion failed to create clear guidelines for future related cases because it did not establish specific guidelines for rightful removals.

DOCUMENT

. . . JUSTICE BRENNAN announced the judgment of the Court and delivered an opinion, . . .

The principal question presented is whether the First Amendment imposes limitations upon the exercise by a local school board of its discretion to remove library books from high school and junior high school libraries.

I

. . . In September 1975, petitioners Ahrens, Martin, and Hughes attended a conference sponsored by Parents of New York United (PONYU), a politically conservative organization of parents concerned about education legislation in the State of New York. At the conference these petitioners obtained lists of books described by Ahrens as "objectionable," and by Martin as "improper fare for school students" (The District Court noted, however, that petitioners "concede that the books are not obscene"). It was later determined that the High School library contained nine of the listed books, and that another listed book was in the Junior High School library. In February 1976, at a meeting with the Superintendent of Schools and the Principals of the High School and Junior High School, the Board gave an "unofficial direction" that the listed books be removed from the library shelves and delivered to the Board's offices, so that Board members could read them. When this directive was carried out, it became publicized, and the Board issued a press release justifying its action. It characterized the removed books as "anti-American, anti-Christian, anti-Sem[i]tic, and just plain filthy," and concluded that "[i]t is our duty, our moral obligation, to protect the children in our schools from this moral danger as surely as from physical and medical dangers."

A short time later, the Board appointed a "Book Review Committee," consisting of four Island Trees parents and four members of the Island Trees schools staff, to read the listed books and to recommend to the Board whether the books should be retained, taking into account the books' "educational suitability," "good taste," "relevance," and "appropriateness to age and grade level." In July, the Committee made its final report to the Board, recommending that five of the listed books be retained and that two others be removed from the school libraries. As for the remaining four books, the Committee could not agree on two, took no position on one, and recommended that the last book be made available to students only with parental approval. The Board substantially rejected the Committee's report later that month, deciding that only one book should be returned to the High School library without restriction, "that another should be made available subject to parental approval," but that the remaining nine books should "be removed from elementary and secondary libraries and [from] use in the curriculum." The Board gave no reasons for rejecting the recommendations of the Committee that it had appointed.

Respondents reacted to the Board's decision by bringing the present action under 42 U. S. C. § 1983 in the United States District Court for the Eastern District of New York. They alleged that petitioners had

> "ordered the removal of the books from school libraries and proscribed their use in the curriculum because particular passages in the books offended their social, political and moral tastes and not because the books, taken as a whole, were lacking in educational value." . . .

II

We emphasize at the outset the limited nature of the substantive question presented by the case before us. Our precedents have long recognized certain constitutional limits upon the power of the State to control even the curriculum and classroom. For example, *Meyer v. Nebraska* struck down a state law that forbade the teaching of modern foreign languages in public and private schools, and *Epperson v. Arkansas* declared unconstitutional a state law that prohibited the teaching of the Darwinian theory of evolution in any state-supported school. But the current action does not require us to re-enter this difficult terrain, which *Meyer* and *Epperson* traversed without apparent misgiving. For as this case is presented to us, it does not involve textbooks, or indeed any books that Island Trees students would be required to read. Respondents do not seek in this Court to impose limitations upon their school Board's discretion to prescribe the curricula of the Island Trees schools. On the contrary, the only books at issue in this case are library books, books that by their nature are optional rather than required reading. Our adjudication of the present case thus does not intrude into the classroom, or into the compulsory courses taught there. Furthermore, even as to library books, the action before us does not involve the acquisition of books. Respondents have not sought to compel their school Board to add to the school library shelves any books that students desire to read. Rather, the only action challenged in this case is the removal from school libraries of books originally placed there by the school authorities, or without objection from them. . . .

A

(1)

The Court has long recognized that local school boards have broad discretion in the management of school affairs. . . .

At the same time, however, we have necessarily recognized that the discretion of the States and local school boards in matters of education must be exercised in a manner that comports with the transcendent imperatives of the First Amendment. In *West Virginia Board of Education v. Barnette*, we held that under the First Amendment a student in a public school could not be compelled to salute the flag. . . . In sum, students do not "shed their constitutional rights to freedom of speech or expression at the schoolhouse gate," and therefore local school boards must discharge their "important, delicate, and highly discretionary functions" within the limits and constraints of the First Amendment.

Of course, courts should not "intervene in the resolution of conflicts which arise in the daily operation of school systems" unless "basic constitutional values" are "directly and sharply implicate[d]" in those conflicts. But we think that the First Amendment rights of students may be directly and sharply implicated by the removal of books from the shelves of a school library. . . . [W]e have recognized that "the State may not, consistently with the spirit of the First Amendment, contract the spectrum of available knowledge." In keeping with this principle, we have held that in a variety of contexts "the Constitution protects the right to receive information and ideas." This right is an inherent corollary of the rights of free speech and press that are explicitly guaranteed by the Constitution, in two senses. First, the right to receive ideas follows ineluctably from the sender's First Amendment right to send them: "The right of freedom of speech and press . . . embraces the right to distribute literature, and necessarily protects the right to receive it (*Martin v. City of Struthers*)." "The dissemination of ideas can accomplish nothing if otherwise willing addressees are not free to receive and consider them. It would be a barren marketplace of ideas that had only sellers and no buyers (*Lamont v. Postmaster General*)."

Petitioners emphasize the inculcative function of secondary education, and argue that they must be allowed unfettered discretion to "transmit community values" through the Island Trees schools. But that sweeping claim overlooks the unique role of the school library. It appears from the record that use of the Island Trees school libraries is completely voluntary on the part of students. Their selection of books from these libraries is entirely a matter of free choice; the libraries afford them an opportunity at self-education and individual enrichment that is wholly optional. Petitioners might well defend their claim of absolute discretion in matters of curriculum by reliance upon their duty to inculcate community values. But we think that petitioners' reliance upon that duty is misplaced where, as here, they attempt to extend their claim of absolute discretion beyond the compulsory environment of the classroom, into the school library and the regime of voluntary inquiry that there holds sway. . . .

. . . Petitioners rightly possess significant discretion to determine the content of their school libraries. But that discretion may not be exercised in a narrowly partisan or political manner. If a Democratic school board, motivated by party affiliation, ordered the removal of all books written by or in favor of Republicans, few would doubt that the order violated the constitutional rights of the students denied access to those books. The same conclusion would surely apply if an all-white school board, motivated by racial animus, decided to remove all books authored by blacks or advocating racial equality and integration. Our Constitution does not permit the official suppression of ideas. Thus whether petitioners' removal of books from their school libraries denied respondents their First Amendment rights depends upon the motivation behind petitioners' actions. If petitioners intended by their removal decision to deny respondents access to ideas with which petitioners disagreed, and if this intent was the decisive factor in petitioners' decision, then petitioners have exercised their discretion in violation of the Constitution. . . . On the other hand, respondents implicitly concede that an unconstitutional motivation would not be demonstrated if it were shown that petitioners had decided to remove the books at issue because those books were pervasively vulgar. And again, respondents concede that if it were demonstrated that the removal decision was based solely upon the "educational suitability" of the books in question, then their removal would be "perfectly permissible." In other words, in respondents' view such motivations, if decisive of petitioners' actions, would not carry the danger of an official suppression of ideas, and thus would not violate respondents' First Amendment rights. . . .

. . . Because we are concerned in this case with the suppression of ideas, our holding today affects only the discretion to remove books. In brief, we hold that local school boards may not remove books from school library shelves simply because they dislike the ideas contained in those books and seek by their removal to "prescribe what shall be orthodox in politics, nationalism, religion, or other matters of opinion." Such purposes stand inescapably condemned by our precedents.

SOURCE: Board of Education v. Pico, 457 U.S. 853 (1981).

ANALYSIS

This SCOTUS case involved the question of whether or not the First Amendment protects students' rights to access information and ideas in a school library. It was the first major Supreme Court case involving removal of materials from a school library.

In late 1975, three school board members of the Island Trees Union Free School District received a document containing excerpts from a list of books that a conservative parent group in the district found objectionable. The school board president and another member entered the high school library after hours and found nine of the books in the card catalog. Two more of the books were found at another school library in the district. By February of 1986 the board had asked the principals of the schools to remove the books in question, but the superintendent intervened and instead appointed a special committee of parents and teachers to review the books on the list. The recommendation of that committee was removal of two of the books, limited availability (with parental consent) of another, and return of the remaining books to the libraries. In spite of the committee's recommendation, the school board decided to remove nine books—eight from the high school library and one from the junior high library. The board called the books "anti-American, anti-Christian, anti-Semitic, and just plain filthy."

Five students filed suit against the district, saying their First Amendment rights had been violated with the decision to take the books from their school libraries. Lower courts disagreed with one another regarding the balance between a school board's discretionary power and students' right of access to information.

The Supreme Court also was not fully in agreement on the outcome of the case. Instead of a majority opinion, justices ruled in a 5–4 plurality (with seven separate opinions) that the board of education for the Island Trees Union Free School District acted unconstitutionally when it removed books from the two school libraries. The decision to take out the books was based on board members' personal objections to ideas in the texts instead of the educational value of the books or determination that the overall content of the books (obscenity, for example) was unprotected speech.

This restriction of students' access to multiple ideas and points of view was the constitutional issue that violated the First Amendment, said the court. In explaining the decision, Justice Brennan wrote, ". . . we have held that in a variety of contexts 'the Constitution protects the right to receive information and ideas.' This right is an inherent corollary of the rights of free speech and press that are explicitly guaranteed by the Constitution . . . The dissemination of ideas can accomplish nothing if otherwise willing addressees are not free to receive and consider them."

Applying this principle, the plurality reasoned that if the books were removed because they were obscene, extensively vulgar, or educationally unsuitable, the removal would not violate First Amendment principles. However, removing books because they contain ideas with which the school board disagrees was a violation of the school board's discretional authority. In this instance, the justices felt the school board had chosen to remove the books based on ideas in the texts that the board members found objectionable. The school board's decision was an overreach because it stemmed from an unconstitutional motivation to restrict ideas in conflict with their personal values and beliefs.

The justices explained why motivation for the removal of the books was the key factor in reaching their decision. The plurality argued that school boards do have broad discretion in how they choose to manage school affairs, but these "important, delicate, and highly discretionary functions" must be exercised within the limits of the First Amendment and not stem from either partisan or political beliefs. The court offered hypothetical

DID YOU KNOW?

The first lawsuit to challenge library censorship of online materials was a 1998 case in Virginia—*Mainstream Loudoun v. Board of Trustees of the Loudoun County Library*. Patrons of the Loudoun County Library charged that the library's choice to install filtering software violated their First Amendment rights by blocking access to constitutionally protected information on the internet. A district court judge ruled in their favor, determining that the 1982 Supreme Court decision in *Island Trees School District v. Pico* applied to public libraries as well. The judge felt the filtering software chosen by the library provided "inadequate standards for restricting access" and unconstitutionally prevented adults from acquiring web-based materials deemed unfit for children. As a less restrictive alternative, the judge suggested using filtering software only on computers for minors. Many libraries across the country, facing pressure to implement internet filtering software, chose this compromise—acknowledging the concerns of filtering advocates while honoring the constitutional freedoms of adult patrons. In 2000, the passage of the Child Internet Protection Act created additional filtering requirements for libraries that wished to receive federal funding.

examples of a Democratic school board choosing to remove books written by or in favor of Republicans or an all-white school board deciding to remove all books advocating integration or books by Black authors. In either case, the views of a few would greatly restrict the dissemination of ideas that promote other points of view. In order to become thoughtful, contributing members of society, students must have the opportunity to be exposed to multiple points of view and make decisions based on a variety of perspectives.

Justices also emphasized the role of the library as a unique site of voluntary inquiry and self-education. Students are not required to utilize materials from the library, but do so out of a desire to enrich their own learning and reading enjoyment. While school boards may have discretionary decision-making ability over the acquisition of new materials and the content of required curricula, the court felt it was an overreach of a school board's discretion to remove books from a school library where students voluntarily participate in an exchange of information and ideas that are paramount to their development as citizens.

The dissenting opinion was written by Chief Justice Burger, joined by Justices Rehnquist, Powell, and O'Connor. These justices felt the removal of books was well within the school board's authority and said that parents, teachers, and school boards—not judges—should be the authorities on discerning community standards of morality. Justice Rehnquist added that by their very nature school boards must make judgments based on the board members' "personal, social, political and moral views." Furthermore, the justices said, the materials that had been removed were available in other libraries and bookstores, so the students' right to read had not been violated.

These justices also disagreed that the formation of students as citizens depended upon materials outside the established curriculum. When deciding what information is necessary for instruction, public schools are naturally "inculcating fundamental values necessary to the maintenance of a democratic political system," they said. This role does not necessitate school access to additional information outside of what the school has already selected.

The court's narrow plurality opinion left many major issues and questions unanswered, inviting future legal challenges. One unresolved issue, for example, was how to establish a standard by which to evaluate justifiable motivations for withdrawal of a text. The plurality mentioned vulgarity, obscenity, and lack of educational value as valid reasons for removing books from school libraries, but it did not specify what other considerations, if any, might be constitutionally defensible. Thus, each future case involving school library materials must be judged individually—not by an established objective standard, but on the basis of the current court's interpretation of the motivating factors involved.

FURTHER READING

Dunn, Donald J. "Pico and Beyond: School Library Censorship Controversies." *Law Library Journal* 77 (1984): 435.

Kamhi, Michelle Marder. *Limiting What Students Shall Read: Books and Other Learning Materials in Our Public Schools: How They Are Selected and How They Are Removed: Summary Report on the Survey "Book and Materials Selection for School Libraries and Classrooms: Procedures, Challenges, and Responses."* Washington, DC: Association of American Publishers, 1981.

Nocera, Joseph. "The Big Book—Banning Brawl." *New Republic* 187, no. 11 (1982): 20–25.
Peltz, Richard J. "Pieces of Pico: Saving Intellectual Freedom in the Public School Library." *Brigham Young University Education & Law Journal* 2005, no. 2 (2005): 103–58.
Pherigo, Cherlyn. "Book Removal in Secondary Schools: A Violation of the First Amendment? Board of Education v. Pico." *Akron Law Review* 17, no. 3 (1984): 483–93.
Schultz, David and John R. Vile. "Board of Education v. Pico (1982)." In *The Encyclopedia of Civil Liberties in America*, 104–5. Armonk, NY: Routledge, 2005.

- ***Document 32:*** Excerpts from *New York v. Ferber* Supreme Court Ruling
- ***Date:*** Decided July 2, 1982
- ***Where:*** Supreme Court of the United States
- ***Significance:*** This unanimous SCOTUS decision established that child pornography is a category outside the protection of the First Amendment. States have a "compelling" interest in protecting children from the exploitation and abuse inherent in the making of such materials; therefore, state laws prohibiting the production and distribution of child pornography are constitutional. Furthermore, child pornography does not have to be classified as obscenity to be constitutionally unprotected.

DOCUMENT

JUSTICE WHITE delivered the opinion of the Court. . . .

I

. . . Like obscenity statutes, laws directed at the dissemination of child pornography run the risk of suppressing protected expression by allowing the hand of the censor to become unduly heavy. For the following reasons, however, we are persuaded that the States are entitled to greater leeway in the regulation of pornographic depictions of children.

First. It is evident beyond the need for elaboration that a State's interest in "safeguarding the physical and psychological well-being of a minor" is "compelling." "A democratic society rests, for its continuance, upon the healthy, well-rounded growth of young people into full maturity as citizens." Accordingly, we have sustained legislation aimed at protecting the physical and emotional well-being of youth even when the laws have operated in the sensitive area of constitutionally protected rights. In *Prince* v. *Massachusetts*, the Court held that a statute prohibiting use of a child to distribute literature on the street was valid notwithstanding the statute's effect on a First Amendment activity. In *Ginsberg v. New York*, we sustained a New York law protecting children from exposure to nonobscene literature. Most recently, we held that the Government's interest in the "well-being of its youth" justified special treatment of indecent broadcasting received by adults as well as children.

The prevention of sexual exploitation and abuse of children constitutes a government objective of surpassing importance. . . .

Second. The distribution of photographs and films depicting sexual activity by juveniles is intrinsically related to the sexual abuse of children in at least two ways. First, the materials produced are a permanent record of the children's participation and the harm to the child is exacerbated by their circulation. Second, the distribution network for child pornography must be closed if the production of material which requires the sexual exploitation of children is to be effectively controlled. Indeed, there is no serious contention that the legislature was unjustified in believing that it is difficult, if not impossible, to halt the exploitation of children by pursuing only those who produce the photographs and movies. While the production of pornographic materials is a low-profile, clandestine industry, the need to market the resulting products requires a visible apparatus of distribution. The most expeditious if not the only practical method of law enforcement may be to dry up the market for this material by imposing severe criminal penalties on persons selling, advertising, or otherwise promoting the product. Thirty-five States and Congress have concluded that restraints on the distribution of pornographic materials are required in order to effectively combat the problem, and there is a body of literature and testimony to support these legislative conclusions.

Respondent does not contend that the State is unjustified in pursuing those who distribute child pornography. Rather, he argues that it is enough for the State to prohibit the distribution of materials that are legally obscene under the *Miller* test. While some States may find that this approach properly accommodates its interests, it does not follow that the first Amendment prohibits a State from going further. The *Miller* standard, like all general definitions of what may be banned as obscene, does not reflect the State's particular and more compelling interest in prosecuting those who promote the sexual exploitation of children. Thus, the question under the *Miller* test of whether a work, taken as a whole, appeals to the prurient interest of the average person bears no connection to the issue of whether a child has been physically or psychologically harmed in the production of the work. Similarly, a sexually explicit depiction need not be "patently offensive" in order to have required the sexual exploitation of a child for its production. In addition, a work which, taken on the whole, contains serious literary, artistic, political, or scientific value may nevertheless embody the hardest core of child pornography. "It is irrelevant to the child [who has been abused] whether or not the material . . . has a literary, artistic, political or social value." We therefore cannot conclude that the *Miller* standard is a satisfactory solution to the child pornography problem.

Third. The advertising and selling of child pornography provide an economic motive for and are thus an integral part of the production of such materials, an activity illegal throughout the Nation. "It rarely has been suggested that the constitutional freedom for speech and press extends its immunity to speech or writing used as an integral part of conduct in violation of a valid criminal statute. . . ."

Fourth. The value of permitting live performances and photographic reproductions of children engaged in lewd sexual conduct is exceedingly modest, if not *de minimis*. We consider it unlikely that visual depictions of children performing sexual acts or lewdly exhibiting their genitals would often constitute an important and necessary part of a literary performance or scientific or educational work. As a state judge in this case observed, if it were necessary for literary or artistic value, a person over the statutory age who perhaps looked younger could be utilized. Simulation outside of the prohibition of the statute could provide another alternative. Nor is there any question here of censoring a particular literary theme or portrayal of sexual activity. The First Amendment interest is limited to that of rendering the portrayal somewhat more "realistic" by utilizing or photographing children.

Fifth. Recognizing and classifying child pornography as a category of material outside the protection of the First Amendment is not incompatible with our earlier decisions. "The question whether speech is, or is not, protected by the First Amendment often depends on the content of the speech." "[I]t is the content of [an] utterance that determines whether it is a protected epithet or an unprotected 'fighting comment.'" . . . Thus, it is not rare that a content-based classification of speech has been accepted because it may be appropriately generalized that within the confines of the given classification, the evil to be restricted so overwhelmingly outweighs the expressive interests, if any, at stake, that no process of case-by-case adjudication is required. When a definable class of material, such as that covered by § 263.15, bears so heavily and pervasively on the welfare of children engaged in its production, we think the balance of competing interests is clearly struck and that it is permissible to consider these materials as without the protection of the First Amendment.

C

There are, of course, limits on the category of child pornography which, like obscenity, is unprotected by the First Amendment. As with all legislation in this sensitive area, the conduct to be prohibited must be adequately defined by the applicable state law, as written or authoritatively construed. Here the nature of the harm to be combated requires that the state offense be limited to works that *visually* depict sexual conduct by children below a specified age. The category of "sexual conduct" proscribed must also be suitably limited and described.

The test for child pornography is separate from the obscenity standard enunciated in *Miller*, but may be compared to it for the purpose of clarity. The *Miller* formulation is adjusted in the following respects: A trier of fact need not find that the material appeals to the prurient interest of the average person; it is not required that sexual conduct portrayed be done so in a patently offensive manner; and the material at issue need not be considered as a whole. We note that the distribution of descriptions or other depictions of sexual conduct, not otherwise obscene, which do not involve live performance or photographic or other visual reproduction of live performances, retains First Amendment protection. As with obscenity laws, criminal responsibility may not be imposed without some element of scienter on the part of the defendant.

D

Section 263.15's prohibition incorporates a definition of sexual conduct that comports with the above-stated principles. The forbidden acts to be depicted are listed with sufficient precision and represent the kind of conduct that, if it were the theme of a work, could render it legally obscene: "actual or simulated sexual intercourse, deviate sexual intercourse, sexual bestiality, masturbation, sado-masochistic abuse, or lewd exhibition of the genitals." The term "lewd exhibition of the genitals" is not unknown in this area and, indeed, was given in *Miller* as an example of a permissible regulation. A performance is defined only to include live or visual depictions: "any play, motion picture, photograph or dance . . . [or] other visual representation exhibited before an audience." Section 263.15 expressly includes a scienter requirement.

We hold that § 263.15 sufficiently describes a category of material the production and distribution of which is not entitled to First Amendment protection. It is therefore clear that there is nothing unconstitutionally "underinclusive" about a statute that singles out this category of material for proscription. It also follows that the State is not barred by the First Amendment from prohibiting the distribution of unprotected materials produced outside the State.

III

It remains to address the claim that the New York statute is unconstitutionally overbroad because it would forbid the distribution of material with serious literary, scientific, or educational value or material which does not threaten the harms sought to be combated by the State. Respondent prevailed on that ground below, and it is to that issue that we now turn.

The New York Court of Appeals recognized that overbreadth scrutiny has been limited with respect to conduct-related regulation, but it did not apply the test enunciated in *Broadrick* because the challenged statute, in its view, was directed at "pure speech." The court went on to find that § 263.15 was fatally overbroad: "[T]he statute would prohibit the showing of any play or movie in which a child portrays a defined sexual act, real or simulated, in a nonobscene manner. It would also prohibit the sale, showing, or distributing of medical or educational materials containing photographs of such acts. Indeed, by its terms, the statute would prohibit those who oppose such portrayals from providing illustrations of what they oppose."

. . . [T]his Court is the final arbiter of whether the Federal Constitution necessitated the invalidation of a state law. It is only through this process of review that we may correct erroneous applications of the Constitution that err on the side of an overly broad reading of our doctrines and precedents, as well as state-court decisions giving the Constitution too little shrift. . . .

A

. . . The scope of the First Amendment overbreadth doctrine, like most exceptions to established principles, must be carefully tied to the circumstances in which facial invalidation of a statute is truly warranted. Because of the wide-reaching effects of striking down a statute on its face at the request of one whose own conduct may be punished despite the First Amendment, we have recognized that the overbreadth doctrine is "strong medicine" and have employed it with hesitation, and then "only as a last resort." We have, in consequence, insisted that the overbreadth involved be "substantial" before the statute involved will be invalidated on its face. . . .

B

. . . While the reach of the statute is directed at the hard core of child pornography, the Court of Appeals was understandably concerned that some protected expression, ranging from medical textbooks to pictorials in the National Geographic would fall prey to the statute. How often, if ever, it may be necessary to employ children to engage in conduct clearly within the reach of § 263.15 in order to produce educational, medical, or artistic works cannot be known with certainty. Yet we seriously doubt, and it has not been suggested, that these arguably impermissible applications of the statute amount to more than a tiny fraction of the materials within the statute's reach. Nor will we assume that the New York courts will widen the possibly invalid reach of the statute by giving an expansive construction to the proscription on "lewd exhibition[s] of the genitals." Under these circumstances, § 263.15 is "not substantially overbroad and . . . whatever overbreadth may exist should be cured through case-by-case analysis of the fact situations to which its sanctions, assertedly, may not be applied."

IV

Because § 263.15 is not substantially overbroad, it is unnecessary to consider its application to material that does not depict sexual conduct of a type that New York may restrict consistent with the First Amendment. As applied to Paul Ferber and to others who distribute similar material, the statute does not violate the First Amendment as applied to the States through the Fourteenth. The judgment of the New York Court of Appeals is reversed, and the case is remanded to that court for further proceedings not inconsistent with this opinion.

So ordered.

SOURCE: New York v. Ferber, 458 U.S. 747 (1981).

ANALYSIS

When bookstore owner Paul Ferber was arrested and convicted of distribution of materials involving the use of a child in a sexual performance, he challenged the ruling on the grounds that the materials were not obscene and therefore were protected by the First Amendment.

The Supreme Court unanimously ruled that child pornography is a category of speech unprotected by the First Amendment; therefore, state statutes prohibiting the production or distribution of such materials *are* constitutional. The court highlighted other categories of unprotected speech including obscenity, deceptive advertising, and speech advocating illegal action—all exempt from the First Amendment's shield because of the harm they cause to society. However, the *Ferber* ruling was a departure from that precedent. Child pornography was deemed exempt not because this type of expression harms society, but because it is the *result* of a societal harm to children (Colen 1983). Unlike the previous categories of unprotected speech, child pornography's impact on society (or its consumers) was never addressed by the court. Rather, the ruling was made based on the impact of child pornography on its victims.

Justice White, writing for the court, emphasized that states have a "compelling" interest in protecting the physical, emotional, and mental well-being of children. He cited numerous cases in which laws were sustained to protect children from exposure to indecent literature and broadcasts, even when those rulings challenged constitutional protections of such expression. The production of child pornography is unique, however, in that it involves illegal actions inherently harmful to the children being exploited. Justice White explained that the state's interest in preventing that type of exploitation and harm outweighs any interest in free expression. Therefore, even though child pornography does not fit the legal definition of obscenity, the objective of protecting the well-being of children is itself justification enough to exclude child pornography from First Amendment protections.

The *Ferber* decision also gave states permission to prohibit the sale and distribution of child pornography even if such materials are not deemed obscene under the *Miller* test. Standards established in *Miller v. California* considered a work obscene if "(a) the average person, applying contemporary community standards, would find that the work, taken as a whole, appeals to the prurient interest; [if] (b) the work depicts or describes, in a patently offensive way, sexual conduct specifically defined by the applicable state law; and [if] (c) the work, taken as a whole, lacks serious literary, artistic, political, or scientific value." Obscenity had been clearly ruled unprotected speech, but with this case the court determined for the first time what to do about speech that involved sexual exploitation of minors but was not necessarily obscene under the *Miller* standard.

The court's ruling placed protection of children above free speech, reflecting its paramount concern to prevent harm inflicted on children through production of these sexually explicit materials. By its very nature, child pornography offers visual evidence of criminal acts committed against children and inherent abuse of minors involved in the recorded acts. This harm occurs whether or not the finished product is "patently offensive" or has any semblance of value. Justice White, writing the court's opinion, quoted an advocate of protective laws saying, "It is irrelevant to the child [who has been abused] whether or not the material . . . has a literary, artistic, political or social value." Based on this new principle, the court felt the inherent harm and illegality involved in the production of child pornography made the *Miller* test irrelevant.

The justices went on to say that little, if any, literary, scientific or educational purpose is served by "live productions and photographic reproductions of children engaged in lewd sexual conduct." Any justifiable purpose that does exist could be fulfilled without live performances that exploit or abuse children.

The court also upheld the state's argument that the law under which Ferber was convicted was the least restrictive and most effective means of achieving the overarching goal of protecting children's welfare. The state believed eliminating economic incentive for the creation of child pornography would severely disrupt a market that both necessitates and promotes sexual mistreatment of children. By banning child porn products, the state hoped to prevent the harmful, illegal activities involved in creating them.

The court expanded on its *Ferber* ruling eight years later in *Osborne v. Ohio* by declaring the constitutionality of laws prohibiting not only production and distribution of child pornography but also the possession and viewing of such materials. The *Osborne* case differed from *Stanley v. Georgia* in that the pornography found in Osborne's private possession involved children, while that found in Stanley's possession did not. Again, the court reiterated that the state's interest in preventing abuse and exploitation of children outweighs free speech protections. This ruling, like many contemporary laws prohibiting possession of child porn (in addition to production and distribution), rely on the same principles of protecting children by disrupting or suspending the market that necessitates their abuse.

While *Ferber* established that state statutes prohibiting child pornography are constitutional, scholars point out that current laws may not adequately protect the victims of child pornography. Distribution of child porn robs victims of their privacy and perpetuates the abuse well beyond the date of the recorded incident. Children who are sexually exploited often feel violated well into adulthood, knowing that films, videos, and recordings of them are continually being downloaded or distributed by consumers of pornographic materials. Furthermore, inconsistencies between harsh federal punishments and comparatively lenient state consequences for child pornography–related offenses is problematic (Roos 2014), as are efforts to block online access to child pornography. These and other issues unaddressed by *Ferber* present new challenges as courts continue to deliberate the nature and impact of child pornography.

FURTHER READING

Colen, Joan S. "Child Pornography: Ban the Speech and Spare the Child?—New York v. Ferber." *DePaul Law Review* 32 (1983): 685.

Roos, Hanna. "Trading the Sexual Child: Child Pornography and the Commodification of Children in Society." *Texas Journal of Women & the Law* 23, no. 2 (2014): 131–56.

Schauer, Frederick. "Codifying the First Amendment: New York v. Ferber." *Supreme Court Review* 1982 (1982): 285–317.

Walker, Jesse. "The Blurry Boundaries of Child Porn." *Reason* 41, no. 3 (2009): 34–35.

Weinstein, James. "The Context and Content of New York v. Ferber." In *Refining Child Pornography Law: Crime, Language, and Social Consequences*, 19–56. Ann Arbor, MI: University of Michigan Press, 2016.

- ***Document 33:*** Excerpts from the Supreme Court Ruling in *Bethel School District No. 403 v. Fraser*
- ***Date:*** July 7, 1986
- ***Where:*** Supreme Court of the United States
- ***Significance:*** This ruling concerned a case in which a high school student, Matthew N. Fraser, was disciplined by his school for using disruptive and sexually explicit language during an address to a school assembly. It established that schools have the right to prohibit certain types of expression such as obscenity, profanity, vulgarity or other language inappropriate in the school setting. A school's decision to enact disciplinary measures in response to students' use of such speech does not violate students' First Amendment rights.

DOCUMENT

CHIEF JUSTICE BURGER delivered the opinion of the Court

We granted certiorari to decide whether the First Amendment prevents a school district from disciplining a high school student for giving a lewd speech at a school assembly. . . .

II

This Court acknowledged in *Tinker v. Des Moines Independent Community School Dist.* that students do not "shed their constitutional rights to freedom of speech or expression at the schoolhouse gate." The Court of Appeals read that case as precluding any discipline of Fraser for indecent speech and lewd conduct in the school assembly. That court appears to have proceeded on the theory that the use of lewd and obscene speech in order to make what the speaker considered to be a point in a nominating speech for a fellow student was essentially the same as the wearing of an armband in *Tinker* as a form of protest or the expression of a political position.

The marked distinction between the political "message" of the armbands in *Tinker* and the sexual content of respondent's speech in this case seems to have been given little weight by the Court of Appeals. In upholding the students' right to engage in a nondisruptive, passive expression of a political viewpoint in *Tinker*, this Court was careful to note that the case did "not concern speech or action that intrudes upon the work of the schools or the rights of other students."

It is against this background that we turn to consider the level of First Amendment protection accorded to Fraser's utterances and actions before an official high school assembly attended by 600 students.

III

The role and purpose of the American public school system was well described by two historians, who stated: "[P]ublic education must prepare pupils for citizenship in the Republic. . . . It must inculcate the habits and manners of civility as values in themselves conducive to happiness and as indispensable to the practice of self-government in the community and the nation." In *Ambach v. Norwick*, we echoed the essence of this statement of the objectives of public education as the "inculcat[ion of] fundamental values necessary to the maintenance of a democratic political system."

These fundamental values of "habits and manners of civility" essential to a democratic society must, of course, include tolerance of divergent political and religious views, even when the views expressed may be unpopular. But these "fundamental values" must also take into account consideration of the sensibilities of others, and, in the case of a school, the sensibilities of fellow students. The undoubted freedom to advocate unpopular and controversial views in schools and classrooms must be balanced against the society's countervailing interest in teaching students the boundaries of socially appropriate behavior. Even the most heated political discourse in a democratic society requires consideration for the personal sensibilities of the other participants and audiences.

In our Nation's legislative halls, where some of the most vigorous political debates in our society are carried on, there are rules prohibiting the use of expressions offensive to other participants in the debate. The Manual of Parliamentary Practice, drafted by Thomas Jefferson and adopted by the House of Representatives to govern the proceedings in that body, prohibits the use of "impertinent" speech during debate and likewise provides that "[n]o person is to use indecent language against the proceedings of the House." The Rules of Debate applicable in the Senate likewise provide that a Senator may be called to order for imputing improper motives to another Senator or for referring offensively to any state. . . . Can it be that what is proscribed in the halls of Congress is beyond the reach of school officials to regulate?

The First Amendment guarantees wide freedom in matters of adult public discourse. . . . It does not follow, however, that simply because the use of an offensive form of expression may not be prohibited to adults making what the speaker considers a political point, the same latitude must be permitted to children in a public school. In *New Jersey v. T.L.O.* we reaffirmed that the constitutional rights of students in public school are not automatically coextensive with the rights of adults in other settings. As cogently expressed by Judge Newman, "the First Amendment gives a high school student the classroom right to wear Tinker's armband, but not Cohen's jacket." . . .

Surely it is a highly appropriate function of public school education to prohibit the use of vulgar and offensive terms in public discourse. Indeed, the "fundamental values necessary to the maintenance of a democratic political system" disfavor the use of terms of debate highly offensive or highly threatening to others. Nothing in the Constitution prohibits the states from insisting that certain modes of expression are inappropriate and subject to sanctions. The inculcation of these values is truly the "work of the schools." The determination of what manner of speech in the classroom or in school assembly is inappropriate properly rests with the school board.

The process of educating our youth for citizenship in public schools is not confined to books, the curriculum, and the civics class; schools must teach by example the shared values of a civilized social order. Consciously or otherwise, teachers—and indeed the older students—demonstrate the appropriate form of civil discourse and political expression by their conduct and deportment in and out of class. Inescapably, like parents, they are role models. The schools, as instruments of the state, may determine that the essential lessons of civil, mature conduct cannot be conveyed in a school that tolerates lewd, indecent, or offensive speech and conduct such as that indulged in by this confused boy.

The pervasive sexual innuendo in Fraser's speech was plainly offensive to both teachers and students—indeed to any mature person. By glorifying male sexuality, and in its verbal content, the speech was acutely insulting to teenage girl students. The speech could well be seriously damaging to its less mature audience, many of whom were only 14 years old and on the threshold of awareness of human sexuality. Some students were reported as bewildered by the speech and the reaction of mimicry it provoked.

This Court's First Amendment jurisprudence has acknowledged limitations on the otherwise absolute interest of the speaker in reaching an unlimited audience where the speech is sexually explicit and the audience may include children. In *Ginsberg v. New York*, this Court upheld a New York statute banning the sale of sexually oriented material to minors, even though the material in question was entitled to First Amendment protection with respect to adults. And in addressing the question whether the First Amendment places any limit on the authority of public schools to remove books from a public school library, all Members of the Court, otherwise sharply divided, acknowledged that the school board has the authority to remove books that are vulgar. *Board of Education v. Pico*. These cases recognize the obvious concern on the part of parents, and school authorities acting *in loco parentis*, to protect children- especially in a captive audience-from exposure to sexually explicit, indecent, or lewd speech.

We have also recognized an interest in protecting minors from exposure to vulgar and offensive spoken language. In *FCC v. Pacifica Foundation*, we dealt with the power of the Federal Communications Commission to regulate a radio broadcast described as "indecent but not obscene." There the Court reviewed an administrative condemnation of the radio broadcast of a self-styled "humorist" who described his own performance as being in "the words you couldn't say on the public, ah, airwaves, um, the ones you definitely wouldn't say ever." The Commission concluded that "certain words depicted sexual and excretory activities in a patently offensive manner, [and] noted that they 'were broadcast at a time when children were undoubtedly in the audience.'" The Commission issued an order declaring that the radio station was guilty of broadcasting indecent language in violation of 18 U. S. C. § 1464. The Court of Appeals set aside the Commission's determination, and we reversed, reinstating the Commission's citation of the station. We concluded that the broadcast was properly considered "obscene, indecent, or profane" within the meaning of the statute. The plurality opinion went on to reject the radio station's assertion of a First Amendment right to broadcast vulgarity. . .

We hold that petitioner School District acted entirely within its permissible authority in imposing sanctions upon Fraser in response to his offensively lewd and indecent speech. Unlike the sanctions imposed on the students wearing armbands in *Tinker*, the penalties imposed in this case were unrelated to any political viewpoint. The First Amendment does not prevent the school officials from determining that to permit a vulgar and lewd speech such as respondent's would undermine the school's basic educational mission. A high school assembly or classroom is no place for a sexually explicit monologue directed towards an unsuspecting audience of teenage students. Accordingly, it was perfectly appropriate for the school to disassociate itself to make the point to the pupils that vulgar speech and lewd conduct is wholly inconsistent with the "fundamental values" of public school education. Justice Black, dissenting in *Tinker*, made a point that is especially relevant in this case:

> "I wish therefore, . . . to disclaim any purpose . . . to hold that the Federal Constitution compels the teachers, parents, and elected school officials to surrender control of the American public school system to public school students."

IV

Respondent contends that the circumstances of his suspension violated due process because he had no way of knowing that the delivery of the speech in question would subject him to disciplinary sanctions. This argument is wholly without merit. We have recognized that "maintaining security and order in the schools requires a certain degree of flexibility in school disciplinary procedures, and we have respected the value of preserving the informality of the student-teacher relationship." Given the school's need to be able to impose disciplinary sanctions for a wide range of unanticipated conduct disruptive of the educational process, the school disciplinary rules need not be as detailed as a criminal code which imposes criminal sanctions. Two days' suspension from school does not rise to the level of a penal sanction calling for the full panoply of procedural due process protections applicable to a criminal prosecution. The school disciplinary rule proscribing "obscene" language and the prespeech admonitions of teachers gave adequate warning to Fraser that his lewd speech could subject him to sanctions.

The judgment of the Court of Appeals for the Ninth Circuit is

Reversed

SOURCE: Bethel School Dist. No. 403 v. Fraser, 478 U.S. 675 (1985).

ANALYSIS

This case involved Matthew N. Fraser, a student who was disciplined for violating his high school's "disruptive-conduct" rule. Fraser gave a speech at a voluntary assembly in which he used metaphorical terms of a graphic and explicit sexual nature to describe a fellow student running for elected office. Fraser had been warned by teachers one day prior that the speech was inappropriate and that giving it could result in disciplinary action. Nevertheless, he gave the speech, which provoked responses varying from rowdy to incredulous to confused. One teacher reported needing to alter the content of the following day's class to discuss the speech with students.

The next day, the assistant principal informed Fraser he had violated school rules prohibiting conduct that interfered with the educational process. He was suspended for three days and informed he was removed from eligibility to speak at graduation.

The school district reviewed the disciplinary action and found it consistent with the district's grievance procedures. After two days of suspension, Fraser was allowed to return to school. He and his father subsequently filed a lawsuit alleging his free speech rights had been violated and sought injunctive relief and damages. The federal district court sided with Fraser, stating the school's disciplinary measures violated his First Amendment freedoms, the school district's disruptive conduct policy was vague and overbroad, and the removal of Fraser's name as a potential graduation speaker violated his Fourteenth Amendment right to due process. The ninth circuit court of appeals affirmed this judgment, likening Fraser's actions to that of students wearing armbands in *Tinker v. Des Moines Independent Community School District*.

The Supreme Court, however, reversed the lower court decisions, ruling 7–2 that school districts have a right to prohibit certain types of speech within the school setting and have the right to punish the use of prohibited speech.

Chief Justice Burger explained that although the *Tinker* case established that students do not "shed their constitutional rights to freedom of speech or expression at the schoolhouse gate," the students' speech in *Tinker* was passive pure political speech that did not intrude upon the learning environment. Fraser's presentation, however, involved direct, active, "vulgar" expression that was offensive to teachers and students and was inappropriate in a public school environment, particularly considering the younger ages of many members of the student body and the fact that the listeners were a captive audience.

The majority opinion emphasized the fact that schools are sites of preparation for citizenship. Student free speech in schools must be balanced against schools' responsibility for teaching civility and socially-appropriate behavior, essential components of self-government. Acting with civility requires tolerating divergent views, stated Justice Burger, but it also requires understanding how the content of a message may impact those who hear it. Fraser's speech provoked emotional responses from a student body made up of older students who laughed and mimicked the sexual behaviors he referenced, less mature younger students described by the justices as "on the threshold of awareness of human sexuality" who could have been psychologically harmed by the message, and teenage girls who may have been particularly insulted by Fraser's glorification of male sexuality.

The court's *Fraser* ruling was rooted in its history of limiting free expression when children could be exposed to vulgarities or obscenities. Justice Burger referenced arguments in the *Pacifica, Pico, and Ginsberg* cases that acknowledged the right of children to be protected from exposure to vulgar, sexually explicit, or offensive language.

DID YOU KNOW?

In the 2007 symbolic speech case *Morse v. Frederick*, the Supreme Court took up yet another issue involving student free speech. When the Olympic torch relay passed through Juneau, Alaska, ahead of the 2002 Winter Olympics, a local high school permitted students and staff to attend the relay as a school-sponsored event. As the torch passed by, student Joseph Frederick and a number of friends held up a banner reading "Bong Hits 4 Jesus." Interpreting the banner as a promotion of marijuana use, the principal instructed the students to take it down. All obeyed except Frederick, who was subsequently suspended for ten days because he had violated the school's policy prohibiting promotion of illegal drug use.

Frederick sued the principal for damages, claiming that his First Amendment rights had been violated. When the case finally made its way to the Supreme Court, Justices ruled 5–4 that the principal did *not* violate Frederick's First Amendment free speech rights by prohibiting a sign promoting illegal drug use at a school-sanctioned event. Justice Roberts wrote for the majority that even though students do have political free speech rights in school, those rights do not extend to the promotion of illegal activities in opposition to the school's mission of preventing such actions. When writing the majority opinion, Justice Roberts referenced the *Tinker, Hazelwood and Bethel* decisions to explain the court's rationale for limiting student speech in this instance.

Dissenting justices argued that free political speech is crucial for national debate of serious topics, but Justice Roberts pointed out that the banner was not meant to initiate political debate about drug use or possession. Rather, it was an attention-grabbing tactic that violated school policy; therefore, the principal was justified in punishing Frederick's actions.

The majority noted it is not possible to effectively teach lessons of civility and mature conduct in a school where "lewd, indecent, or offensive speech and conduct" are tolerated. Justices emphasized that the constitutional rights of students are not equal to those of adults. Given this distinction, school boards are tasked with determining what kinds of speech are inappropriate within the school setting. The court agreed with the school board that Fraser's speech and the ensuing reaction to it were not only inappropriate but also compromised the overall educational mission of the school. Therefore, the school district did not infringe upon Fraser's free speech or Fourteenth Amendment rights by enforcing disciplinary measures for his violation of established school guidelines.

Justice Burger also emphasized that even Congress has rules in place prohibiting "impertinent" speech and "indecent language." "Can it be," he stated, "that what is proscribed in the halls of Congress is beyond the reach of school officials to regulate?" On the contrary, the majority said parents, teachers, and elected school officials all have a role to play in teaching fundamental values in public schools, including the use of acceptable language within the school setting. Justice Burger wrote "[i]t is a highly appropriate function of public school education to prohibit the use of vulgar and offensive terms in public discourse."

In 1988, the court similarly limited student expression in *Hazelwood School District v. Kuhlmeier*. In this case, the court ruled a school principal did not violate students' First Amendment rights by removing articles of a controversial nature from the school newspaper because students were writing for a publication bearing the name of the school, not for themselves. Justices felt the principal had the right to censor content that could be harmful to the school or a portion of its students.

Critics argue the *Fraser* ruling did not provide specific enough parameters to guide subsequent decisions in student free speech cases (Hudson Jr. & Ferguson Jr. 2002; Plopper & McCool 2001). First, "vulgarity," "obscenity," and "disruption" are all subjective terms that can be interpreted very differently in divergent contexts. Second, narrow court readings of *Fraser* have evaluated only school-sponsored speech while broader court interpretations have been used to justify suppression of any vulgar or offensive student speech or ideas (such as messages on clothing). Strict censorship, say critics, does not encourage students to develop reasoned thinking or to practice engaging in civil discourse about contentious topics. Ultimately, they argue, this may be more harmful to democracy than permitting offensive words or ideas in the school setting (ibid).

FURTHER READING

Chmara, Theresa. "Do Minors Have First Amendment Rights in Schools?" *Knowledge Quest* 44, no. 1 (2015): 8–13.

Cordes, Mark W. "Making Sense of High School Speech after Morse v. Frederick." *William & Mary Bill of Rights Journal* 17 (2008): 657.

Hudson, David L., Jr. and John E. Ferguson Jr. "The Courts' Inconsistent Treatment of Bethel v. Fraser and the Curtailment of Student Rights." *John Marshall Law Review* 36 (2002): 181.

Marczely, Bernadette. "Student Freedom of Expression in the Wake of Hazelwood and Bethel." *Clearing House* 65, no. 5 (1992): 269–71.

Plopper, Bruce L., and Lauralee McCool. "The Impact of Fuzzy Logic on Student Press Law." *Journalism & Mass Communication Educator* 55, no. 4 (2001): 4–17.

- ***Document 34:*** Excerpts from the Supreme Court Decision in *Hustler Magazine, Inc. v. Falwell*
- ***Date:*** February 24, 1988
- ***Where:*** Supreme Court of the United States
- ***Significance:*** This unanimous Supreme Court decision protects the First Amendment right to publish parodies or facts that no reasonable person would regard as true, of public figures. The ruling held that public figures cannot sue for intentionally inflicted emotional distress from such representations unless they can prove a false statement was made with "actual malice."

DOCUMENT

CHIEF JUSTICE REHNQUIST delivered the opinion of the Court

. . . This case presents us with a novel question involving First Amendment limitations upon a State's authority to protect its citizens from the intentional infliction of emotional distress. We must decide whether a public figure may recover damages for emotional harm caused by the publication of an ad parody offensive to him, and doubtless gross and repugnant in the eyes of most. Respondent would have us find that a State's interest in protecting public figures from emotional distress is sufficient to deny First Amendment protection to speech that is patently offensive and is intended to inflict emotional injury, even when that speech could not reasonably have been interpreted as stating actual facts about the public figure involved. This we decline to do.

At the heart of the First Amendment is the recognition of the fundamental importance of the free flow of ideas and opinions on matters of public interest and concern. "[T]he freedom to speak one's mind is not only an aspect of individual liberty—and thus a good unto itself—but also is essential to the common quest for truth and the vitality of society as a whole." *Bose Corp. v. Consumers Union of United States, Inc.* (1984). We have therefore been particularly vigilant to ensure that individual expressions of ideas remain free from governmentally imposed sanctions. . . .

The sort of robust political debate encouraged by the First Amendment is bound to produce speech that is critical of those who hold public office or those public figures who are "intimately involved in the resolution of important public questions or, by reason of their fame, shape events in areas of concern to society at large." *Associated Press v. Walker*, decided with *Curtis Publishing Co. v. Butts* (1967) (Warren, C. J., concurring in result). Justice Frankfurter put it succinctly in *Baumgartner v. United States* (1944), when he said that "[o]ne of the prerogatives of American citizenship is the right to criticize public men and measures." Such criticism, inevitably, will not always be reasoned or moderate; public figures as well as public officials will be subject to "vehement, caustic, and sometimes unpleasantly sharp attacks," *New York Times*, supra, at 270. "[T]he candidate who vaunts his spotless record and sterling integrity cannot convincingly cry 'Foul!' when an opponent or an industrious reporter attempts to demonstrate the contrary." *Monitor Patriot Co. v. Roy* (1971).

Of course, this does not mean that any speech about a public figure is immune from sanction in the form of damages. Since *New York Times Co. v. Sullivan* (1964), we have consistently ruled that a public figure may hold a speaker liable for the damage to reputation caused by publication of a defamatory falsehood, but only if the statement was made "with knowledge that it was false or with reckless disregard of whether it was false or not." *Id.* False statements of fact are particularly valueless; they interfere with the truth-seeking function of the marketplace of ideas, and they cause damage to an individual's reputation that cannot easily be repaired by counterspeech, however persuasive or effective. See *Gertz*. But even though falsehoods have little value in and of themselves, they are "nevertheless inevitable in free debate," *id.*, and a rule that would impose strict liability on a publisher for false factual assertions would have an undoubted "chilling" effect on speech relating to public figures that does have constitutional value. "Freedoms of expression require "'breathing space.'" *Philadelphia Newspapers, Inc. v. Hepps* (1986) (quoting *New York Times*, supra, at 272). This breathing space is provided by a constitutional rule that allows public figures to recover for libel or defamation only when they can prove both that the statement was false and that the statement was made with the requisite level of culpability.

Respondent argues, however, that a different standard should apply in this case because here the State seeks to prevent not reputational damage, but the severe emotional distress suffered by the person who is the subject of an offensive publication. Cf. *Zacchini v. Scripps-Howard Broadcasting Co.* (1977) (ruling that the "actual malice" standard does not apply to the tort of appropriation of a right of publicity). In respondent's view, and in the view of the Court of Appeals, so long as the utterance was intended to inflict emotional distress, was outrageous, and did in fact inflict serious emotional distress, it is of no constitutional import whether the statement was a fact or an opinion, or whether it was true or false. It is the intent to cause injury that is the gravamen of the tort, and the State's interest in preventing emotional harm simply outweighs whatever interest a speaker may have in speech of this type.

Generally speaking the law does not regard the intent to inflict emotional distress as one which should receive much solicitude, and it is quite understandable that most if not all jurisdictions have chosen to make it civilly culpable where the conduct in question is sufficiently "outrageous." But in the world of debate about public affairs, many things done with motives that are less than admirable are protected by the First Amendment. In *Garrison v. Louisiana* (1964), we held that even when a speaker or writer is motivated by hatred or ill will his expression was protected by the First Amendment:

> "Debate on public issues will not be uninhibited if the speaker must run the risk that it will be proved in court that he spoke out of hatred; even if he did speak out of hatred, utterances honestly believed contribute to the free interchange of ideas and the ascertainment of truth." *Id.*, at 73.

Thus while such a bad motive may be deemed controlling for purposes of tort liability in other areas of the law, we think the First Amendment prohibits such a result in the area of public debate about public figures.

Were we to hold otherwise, there can be little doubt that political cartoonists and satirists would be subjected to damages awards without any showing that their work falsely defamed its subject. . . . The appeal of the political cartoon or caricature is often based on exploitation of unfortunate physical traits or politically embarrassing events—an exploitation often calculated to injure the feelings of the subject of the portrayal. The art of the cartoonist is often not reasoned or evenhanded, but slashing and one-sided. One cartoonist expressed the nature of the art in these words:

> "The political cartoon is a weapon of attack, of scorn and ridicule and satire; it is least effective when it tries to pat some politician on the back. It is usually as welcome as a bee sting and is always controversial in some quarters." Long, The Political Cartoon: Journalism's Strongest Weapon, The Quill 56, 57 (Nov. 1962).

Several famous examples of this type of intentionally injurious speech were drawn by Thomas Nast, probably the greatest American cartoonist to date, who was associated for many years during the post-Civil War era with Harper's Weekly. . . .

Despite their sometimes caustic nature, from the early cartoon portraying George Washington as an ass down to the present day, graphic depictions and satirical cartoons have played a prominent role in public and political debate. Nast's castigation of the Tweed Ring, Walt McDougall's characterization of Presidential candidate James G. Blaine's banquet with the millionaires at Delmonico's as "The Royal Feast of Belshazzar," and numerous other efforts have undoubtedly had an effect on the course and outcome of contemporaneous debate. Lincoln's tall, gangling posture, Teddy Roosevelt's glasses and teeth, and Franklin D. Roosevelt's jutting jaw and cigarette holder have been memorialized by political cartoons with an effect that could not have been obtained by the photographer or the portrait artist. From the viewpoint of history it is clear that our political discourse would have been considerably poorer without them.

Respondent contends, however, that the caricature in question here was so "outrageous" as to distinguish it from more traditional political cartoons. There is no doubt that the caricature of respondent and his mother published in Hustler is at best a distant cousin of the political cartoons described above, and a rather poor relation at that. If it were possible by laying down a principled standard to separate the one from the other, public discourse would probably suffer little or no harm. But we doubt that there is any such standard, and we are quite sure that the pejorative description "outrageous" does not supply one. "Outrageousness" in the area of political and social discourse has an inherent subjectiveness about it which would allow a jury to impose liability on the basis of the jurors' tastes or views, or perhaps on the basis of their dislike of a particular expression. An "outrageousness" standard thus runs afoul of our longstanding refusal to allow damages to be awarded because the speech in question may have an adverse emotional impact on the audience. See *NAACP v. Claiborne Hardware Co.* (1982) ("Speech does not lose its protected character . . . simply because it may embarrass others or coerce them into action"). And, as we stated in *FCC v. Pacifica Foundation* (1978):

> "[T]he fact that society may find speech offensive is not a sufficient reason for suppressing it. Indeed, if it is the speaker's opinion that gives offense, that consequence is a reason for according it constitutional protection. For it is a central tenet of the First Amendment that the government must remain neutral in the marketplace of ideas." *Id.*, at 745–746.

See also *Street v. New York* (1969) ("It is firmly settled that . . . the public expression of ideas may not be prohibited merely because the ideas are themselves offensive to some of their hearers").

Admittedly, these oft-repeated First Amendment principles, like other principles, are subject to limitations. We recognized in *Pacifica Foundation*, that speech that is "'vulgar,' 'offensive,' and 'shocking'" is "not entitled to absolute constitutional protection under all circumstances." In *Chaplinsky v. New Hampshire* (1942), we held that a State could lawfully punish an individual for the use of insulting "'fighting' words-those which by their very utterance inflict injury or tend to incite an immediate breach of the peace." *Id.* These limitations are but recognition of the observation in *Dun & Bradstreet, Inc. v. Greenmoss Builders, Inc.* (1985), that this Court has "long recognized that not all speech is of equal First Amendment importance." But the sort of expression involved in this case does not seem to us to be governed by any exception to the general First Amendment principles stated above.

We conclude that public figures and public officials may not recover for the tort of intentional infliction of emotional distress by reason of publications such as the one here at issue without showing in addition that the publication contains a false statement of fact which was made with "actual malice," i. e., with knowledge that the statement was false or with reckless disregard as to whether or not it was true. This is not merely a "blind application" of the *New York Times* standard, see *Time, Inc. v. Hill* (1967), it reflects our considered judgment that such a standard is necessary to give adequate "breathing space" to the freedoms protected by the First Amendment.

Here it is clear that respondent Falwell is a "public figure" for purposes of First Amendment law. The jury found against respondent on his libel claim when it decided that the Hustler ad parody could not "reasonably be understood as describing actual facts about [respondent] or actual events in which [he] participated." The Court of Appeals interpreted the jury's finding to be that the ad parody "was not reasonably believable," and in accordance with our custom we accept this finding. Respondent is thus relegated to his claim for damages awarded by the jury for the intentional infliction of emotional distress by "outrageous" conduct. But for reasons heretofore stated this claim cannot, consistently with the First Amendment, form a basis for the award of damages when the conduct in question is the publication of a caricature such as the ad parody involved here. The judgment of the Court of Appeals is accordingly

Reversed.

SOURCE: Hustler Magazine, Inc. v. Falwell, 485 U.S. 46 (1988).

ANALYSIS

The limits of the First Amendment were tested in the mid-1980s by a high-profile case involving two iconic figures of the time—the reverend Jerry Falwell, founder of the Moral Majority and Liberty University, and Larry Flynt, publisher of the monthly pornographic *Hustler* magazine.

In its November 1983 issue, *Hustler* published a parody advertisement featuring Falwell, a nationally recognized minister and conservative figure. The satirical ad was based on a real Italian Campari liqueur campaign that effectively used double entendre to sell its product by publishing interviews with various celebrities describing their "first time." *Hustler* played off this campaign, feigning an interview with Rev. Falwell in which he describes his "first time" as an incestuous, drunken rendezvous with his mother in an outhouse. *Hustler* placed a disclaimer at the bottom of the page identifying the "interview" as a parody and stating it was not meant to be taken seriously. Additionally, the ad was listed in the table of contents as "Fiction; Ad and Personality Parody."

Nevertheless, when the publication was brought to Falwell's attention, he sued the magazine for libel, invasion of privacy, and intentional infliction of emotional distress. A district court judge rejected Falwell's privacy claim, but sent the additional two claims to a jury. The jury ruled against Rev. Falwell on the libel claim, because the parody was not reasonably interpreted as a presentation of actual facts. However, the jury did find in Falwell's favor regarding the claim of infliction of emotional distress and awarded him damages of $150,000.00. This case was the first instance of a public figure using tort law to successfully seek damages for a distasteful and emotionally injurious publication.

A fourth circuit appeals court upheld the judgment, reasoning that Falwell's emotional distress claim was valid because the *Hustler* advertisement was sufficiently outrageous to prove it was written with the intention of causing emotional distress. However, the Supreme Court granted certiorari to determine whether, under the First and Fourteenth Amendments, it is constitutional to award damages to a public figure claiming emotional distress as the result of an offensive parody.

In what has been called one of the most important Supreme Court decisions of the past quarter century, a unanimous court ruled that public figures can only receive compensation for emotional distress if they can prove they were subject to false statements made with "actual malice." Justices agreed that above all, the First Amendment is based on the need to protect the free flow of ideas, particularly those regarding public interest and concern. Justice Rehnquist wrote for the court that "The State's interest in protecting public figures from emotional distress is not sufficient to deny First Amendment protection to speech that is patently offensive and is intended to inflict emotional injury when that speech could not reasonably have been interpreted as stating actual facts about the public figure involved."

This passage highlights the major points upon which the court's decision was based. First, demonstrating "actual malice" requires proving that a knowingly false statement was made about another person or that a harmful statement was made about someone with "reckless disregard" as to its veracity or falsity. Justices concluded the nature and content of the publication in question, specifically designated as a parody, did not suggest to the reader that actual facts were being stated about Falwell. It was not meant to be believed.

Second, Falwell argued that the publication depicting him was so "outrageous" in nature that it must be distinguished from normal political cartoons. Justices felt this classification of the parody as distinctively "outrageous" applied too broad and subjective a standard to political and public commentary. The view of what is outrageous and what is not could vary from jury to jury, thus offering no clear standard for what separates "outrageous" political and social discourse from that which is not. The fact that an expression causes offense is not alone sufficient justification for its suppression, as evidenced in *NAACP v. Claiborne Hardware Co.* (1982) and *Street v. New York* (1969).

That is not to say that all speech is entitled to First Amendment protection. Justices cited rulings in *FCC v. Pacifica Foundation* (1978) and *Chaplinsky v. New Hampshire* (1942) that provided examples of various types of speech outside the bounds of constitutional protection. However, they pointed out the *Hustler* publication did not fall under any of those unprotected free speech classifications. The "ad" in *Hustler* was offensive and vile but did not, for example, meet the legal standards of obscenity.

Additionally, justices pointed out that political satire, cartoons, and commentary are as old as the United States itself and have played an important role in debate and discussion of public matters. Political cartoons, by their very nature, often distort or exaggerate and have historically been considered a weapon of attack against those they depict. In spite of the fact that these historical cartoons were also often distasteful, offensive, and hurtful to those they portrayed, they nonetheless "have played a prominent role in public and political debate" and have retained constitutional protections for that reason.

Falwell's role as a public figure was also significant. Although Justice Rehnquist, writing for the court, acknowledged the depiction of Falwell was "doubtless gross and repugnant in the eyes of most," he stressed that preventing emotional distress among public figures is not more important than the First Amendment right to freely discuss and express opinions about social and political matters. Ordinary citizens who feel they have been emotionally harmed by a lewd or hurtful portrayal of themselves can seek damages under tort law. However, as a public figure involved with public and political issues, Falwell was not subject to that same protection, as tort liability does not apply to public debate about public figures. Without a higher standard of guilt for offensive commentary related to public issues, justices felt that political cartoonists, commentators, comedians, and others who use parody or satire to stimulate public discussion would all be forcibly silenced out of fear their viewpoints might cause offense.

Numerous critics decried the court's decision as an aberration of decency and an overreach in the protection of harmful expression. One scholar contended the *Hustler* parody was not actually speech because it failed to convey some sort of social idea, a requirement of constitutionally protected speech (Wright 1988). Even if it fell under consideration of First Amendment freedoms, Wright argued, the court should not have granted the parody such strong constitutional protection because it is clearly "low-value" speech that demonstrates little merit or purpose according to judicial consensus regarding high- and low-value expression (ibid).

The *Hustler* case attracted widespread attention because of the brazenly offensive nature of the content under consideration, but the court's ruling made history by establishing strong protections for speech and robust political debate. The justices' clarifications of First Amendment principles in *Hustler* have since been applied to more than twenty other Supreme Court decisions and hundreds of lower court discussions concerning various free speech issues (Gutterman 2013).

FURTHER READING

Gold, S.D. *Parody of Public Figures: Hustler Magazine v. Falwell.* New York: Cavendish Square Publishing, 2014.

Gutterman, Roy S. "Hustler v. Falwell: 25 Years of Protected Satire." *HuffPost.* April 30, 2013. https://www.huffpost.com/entry/hustler-v-falwell-25-year_b_2783713

Post, Robert C. "The Constitutional Concept of Public Discourse: Outrageous Opinion, Democratic Deliberation, and Hustler Magazine v. Falwell." *Harvard Law Review* 103, no. 3 (1990): 601–86.

Todd, Jeff. "Satire in Defamation Law: Toward a Critical Understanding." *Review of Litigation* 35, no. 1 (2016): 45–69.

Wright, George R. "Hustler Magazine v. Falwell and the Role of the First Amendment." *Cumberland Law Review* 19 (1988): 19–42.

DID YOU KNOW?

Twenty-three years after the Supreme Court ruled in favor of free speech in its *Hustler v. Falwell* decision, another very public case, *Snyder v. Phelps* (2011), forced examination of the degree to which the First Amendment protects offensive and hurtful expression.

The Kansas-based Westboro Baptist Church, founded by Pastor Fred Phelps, was known for its extremist views. Members of the church believed that God led the United States into war to punish the "evil nation" for its views on homosexuality, and any military deaths were simply a consequence of God's wrath. To promote this message, the Phelps family and other members of the church regularly picketed outside funerals of fallen military personnel.

In 2006, the group picketed the funeral of fallen marine Matthew Snyder, holding up signs with hateful statements such as "Thank God for Dead Soldiers," "God Hates Fags," and "You're Going to Hell." Snyder's father sued the group for a number of offenses, including intentional infliction of emotional distress, intrusion upon seclusion, and conspiracy to commit these torts.

In 2011, in an 8–1 decision, the Supreme Court upheld the right of Westboro church members to protest, even though their message was undoubtedly hurtful. Justice Roberts explained that because church members had protested peacefully on a public street about a matter of public concern, they were entitled to special protection under the First Amendment. He wrote "Such speech cannot be restricted simply because it is upsetting or arouses contempt."

In regard to the claim of intentional infliction of emotional distress, Justice Roberts referenced the court's *Hustler* decision, stating the definition of "outrageous" behavior was too subjective to apply to speech concerning public matters.

The court's emphasis on the importance of free speech preservation is encapsulated in Justice Roberts's written explanation:

> "Speech is powerful. It can stir people to action, move them to tears of both joy and sorrow, and—as it did here—inflict great pain. On the facts before us, we cannot react to that pain by punishing the speaker. As a Nation we have chosen a different course—to protect even hurtful speech on public issues to ensure that we do not stifle public debate."

Justice Alito dissented, writing that the statements and actions of Westboro members amounted to brutalizing Mr. Snyder and should not be constitutionally protected.

- ***Document 35:*** A Narrow Supreme Court Decision on Flag Burning in *Texas v. Johnson*
- ***Date:*** Decided June 21, 1989
- ***Where:*** Supreme Court of the United States
- ***Significance:*** In a narrow decision, the Supreme Court ruled that the burning of an American flag is a form of symbolic expression protected by the First Amendment, even though the action is highly offensive to those who see the flag as a unique, venerated national symbol. The ruling established that objectionability or unpopularity of an idea or message is not justification for its suppression; in fact, the court held that the First Amendment was written to guarantee such expression would not be stifled.

DOCUMENT

During the 1984 Republican National Convention in Dallas, Texas, respondent Johnson participated in a political demonstration to protest the policies of the Reagan administration and some Dallas-based corporations. After a march through the city streets, Johnson burned an American flag while protesters chanted. No one was physically injured or threatened with injury, although several witnesses were seriously offended by the flag burning. Johnson was convicted of desecration of a venerated object in violation of a Texas statute, and a State Court of Appeals affirmed. However, the Texas Court of Criminal Appeals reversed, holding that the State, consistent with the First Amendment, could not punish Johnson for burning the flag in these circumstances. The court first found that Johnson's burning of the flag was expressive conduct protected by the First Amendment. The court concluded that the State could not criminally sanction flag desecration in order to preserve the flag as a symbol of national unity. It also held that the statute did not meet the State's goal of preventing breaches of the peace, since it was not drawn narrowly enough to encompass only those flag burnings that would likely result in a serious disturbance, and since the flag burning in this case did not threaten such a reaction. Further, it stressed that another Texas statute prohibited breaches of the peace and could be used to prevent disturbances without punishing this flag desecration. . . .

JUSTICE BRENNAN delivered the opinion of the Court. . . .

II

Johnson was convicted of flag desecration for burning the flag rather than for uttering insulting words. This fact somewhat complicates our consideration of his conviction under the First Amendment. We must first determine whether Johnson's burning of the flag constituted expressive conduct, permitting him to invoke the First Amendment in challenging his conviction. If his conduct was expressive, we next decide whether the State's regulation is related to the suppression of free expression. If the State's regulation is not related to expression, then the less stringent standard we announced in *United States* v. *O'Brien* for regulations of noncommunicative conduct controls. If it is, then we are outside of *O'Brien's* test, and we must ask whether this interest justifies Johnson's conviction under a more demanding standard. A third possibility is that the State's asserted interest is simply not implicated on these facts, and in that event the interest drops out of the picture.

The First Amendment literally forbids the abridgment only of "speech," but we have long recognized that its protection does not end at the spoken or written word. While we have rejected "the view that an apparently limitless variety of conduct can be labeled 'speech' whenever the person engaging in the conduct intends thereby to express an idea," we have acknowledged that conduct may be "sufficiently imbued with elements of communication to fall within the scope of the First and Fourteenth Amendments."

In deciding whether particular conduct possesses sufficient communicative elements to bring the First Amendment into play, we have asked whether "[a]n intent to convey a particularized message was present, and [whether] the likelihood was great that the message would be understood by those who viewed it." Hence, we have recognized the expressive nature of students' wearing of black armbands to protest American military involvement in Vietnam, of a sit-in by blacks in a "whites only" area to protest segregation, of the wearing of American military uniforms in a dramatic presentation criticizing American involvement in Vietnam, and of picketing about a wide variety of causes.

Especially pertinent to this case are our decisions recognizing the communicative nature of conduct relating to flags. Attaching a peace sign to the flag, refusing to salute the flag, and displaying a red flag, we have held, all may find shelter under the First Amendment. . . .

We have not automatically concluded, however, that any action taken with respect to our flag is expressive. Instead, in characterizing such action for First Amendment purposes, we have considered the context in which it occurred. In *Spence*, for example, we emphasized that Spence's taping of a peace sign to his flag was "roughly simultaneous with and concededly triggered by the Cambodian incursion and the Kent State tragedy." The State of Washington had conceded, in fact, that Spence's conduct was a form of communication, and we stated that "the State's concession is inevitable on this record."

The State of Texas conceded for purposes of its oral argument in this case that Johnson's conduct was expressive conduct, and this concession seems to us as prudent as was Washington's in *Spence*. Johnson burned an American flag as part—indeed, as the culmination—of a political demonstration that coincided with the convening of the Republican Party and its renomination of Ronald Reagan for President. The expressive, overtly political nature of this conduct was both intentional and overwhelmingly apparent. At his trial, Johnson explained his reasons for burning the flag as follows: "The American Flag was burned as Ronald Reagan was being renominated as President. And a more powerful statement of symbolic speech, whether you agree with it or not, couldn't have been made at that time. . . ." In these circumstances, Johnson's burning of the flag was conduct "sufficiently imbued with elements of communication," to implicate the First Amendment.

III

The government generally has a freer hand in restricting expressive conduct than it has in restricting the written or spoken word. It may not, however, proscribe particular conduct *because* it has expressive elements. . . . It is, in short, not simply the verbal or nonverbal nature of the expression, but the governmental interest at stake, that helps to determine whether a restriction on that expression is valid. . . .

The State offers two separate interests to justify this conviction: preventing breaches of the peace and preserving the flag as a symbol of nationhood and national unity. We hold that the first interest is not implicated on this record and that the second is related to the suppression of expression.

A

Texas claims that its interest in preventing breaches of the peace justifies Johnson's conviction for flag desecration. However, no disturbance of the peace actually occurred or threatened to occur because of Johnson's burning of the flag. . . . The only evidence offered by the State at trial to show the reaction to Johnson's actions was the testimony of several persons who had been seriously offended by the flag burning.

The State's position, therefore, amounts to a claim that an audience that takes serious offense at particular expression is necessarily likely to disturb the peace and that the expression may be prohibited on this basis. Our precedents do not countenance such a presumption. On the contrary, they recognize that a principal "function of free speech under our system of government is to invite dispute. It may indeed best serve its high purpose when it induces a condition of unrest, creates dissatisfaction with conditions as they are, or even stirs people to anger." It would be odd indeed to conclude *both* that "if it is the speaker's opinion that gives offense, that consequence is a reason for according it constitutional protection," *and* that the government may ban the expression of certain disagreeable ideas on the unsupported presumption that their very disagreeableness will provoke violence.

Thus, we have not permitted the government to assume that every expression of a provocative idea will incite a riot, but have instead required careful consideration of the actual circumstances surrounding such expression, asking whether the expression "is directed to inciting or producing imminent lawless action and is likely to incite or produce such action." To accept Texas' arguments that it need only demonstrate "the potential for a breach of the peace," and that every flag burning necessarily possesses that potential, would be to eviscerate our holding in *Brandenburg*. This we decline to do.

Nor does Johnson's expressive conduct fall within that small class of "fighting words" that are "likely to provoke the average person to retaliation, and thereby cause a breach of the peace." No reasonable onlooker would have regarded Johnson's generalized expression of dissatisfaction with the policies of the Federal Government as a direct personal insult or an invitation to exchange fisticuffs.

We thus conclude that the State's interest in maintaining order is not implicated on these facts. The State need not worry that our holding will disable it from preserving the peace. We do not suggest that the First Amendment forbids a State to prevent "imminent lawless action." And, in fact, Texas already has a statute specifically prohibiting breaches of the peace, Tex. Penal Code Ann. §42.01 (1989), which tends to confirm that Texas need not punish this flag desecration in order to keep the peace.

B

The State also asserts an interest in preserving the flag as a symbol of nationhood and national unity. In *Spence*, we acknowledged that the government's interest in preserving the flag's special symbolic value "is directly related to expression in the context of activity" such as affixing a peace symbol to a flag. We are equally persuaded that this interest is related to expression in the case of Johnson's burning of the flag. The State, apparently, is concerned that such conduct will lead people to believe either that the flag does not stand for nationhood and national unity, but instead reflects other, less positive concepts, or that the concepts reflected in the flag do not in fact exist, that is, that we do not enjoy unity as a Nation. These concerns blossom only when a person's treatment of the flag communicates some message, and thus are related "to the suppression of free expression" within the meaning of *O'Brien*. We are thus outside of *O'Brien's* test altogether.

IV

It remains to consider whether the State's interest in preserving the flag as a symbol of nationhood and national unity justifies Johnson's conviction.

As in *Spence*, "[w]e are confronted with a case of prosecution for the expression of an idea through activity," and "[a]ccordingly, we must examine with particular care the interests advanced by [petitioner] to support its prosecution." Johnson was not, we add, prosecuted for the expression of just any idea; he was prosecuted for his expression of dissatisfaction with the policies of this country, expression situated at the core of our First Amendment values. . . .

Whether Johnson's treatment of the flag violated Texas law thus depended on the likely communicative impact of his expressive conduct. Our decision in *Boos v. Barry*, tells us that this restriction on Johnson's expression is content based. . . . In *Boos*, . . . we held that "[t]he emotive impact of speech on its audience is not a 'secondary effect'" unrelated to the content of the expression itself.

According to the principles announced in *Boos*, Johnson's political expression was restricted because of the content of the message he conveyed. We must therefore subject the State's asserted interest in preserving the special symbolic character of the flag to "the most exacting scrutiny."

Texas argues that its interest in preserving the flag as a symbol of nationhood and national unity survives this close analysis. . . . The State's argument is not that it has an interest simply in maintaining the flag as a symbol of *something*, no matter what it symbolizes; indeed, if that were the State's position, it would be difficult to see how that interest is endangered by highly symbolic conduct such as Johnson's. Rather, the State's claim is that it has an interest in preserving the flag as a symbol of *nationhood* and *national unity*, a symbol with a determinate range of meanings. According to Texas, if one physically treats the flag in a way that would tend to cast doubt on either the idea that nationhood and national unity are the flag's referents or that national unity actually exists, the message conveyed thereby is a harmful one and therefore may be prohibited.

If there is a bedrock principle underlying the First Amendment, it is that the government may not prohibit the expression of an idea simply because society finds the idea itself offensive or disagreeable.

We have not recognized an exception to this principle even where our flag has been involved. In *Street v. New York*, we held that a State may not criminally punish a person for uttering words critical of the flag. Rejecting the argument that the conviction could be sustained on the ground that Street had "failed to show the respect for our national symbol which may properly be demanded of every citizen," we concluded that "the constitutionally guaranteed 'freedom to be intellectually . . . diverse or even contrary,' and the 'right to differ as to things that touch the heart of the existing order,' encompass the freedom to express publicly one's opinions about our flag, including those opinions which are defiant or contemptuous." Nor may the government, we have held, compel conduct that would evince respect for the flag. . . .

In short, nothing in our precedents suggests that a State may foster its own view of the flag by prohibiting expressive conduct relating to it. To bring its argument outside our precedents, Texas attempts to convince us that even if its interest in preserving the flag's symbolic role does not allow it to prohibit words or some expressive conduct critical of the flag, it does permit it to forbid the outright destruction of the flag. The State's argument cannot depend here on the distinction between written or spoken words and nonverbal conduct. . . .

Texas' focus on the precise nature of Johnson's expression, moreover, misses the point of our prior decisions: their enduring lesson, that the government may not prohibit expression simply because it disagrees with its message, is not dependent on the particular mode in which one chooses to express an idea. If we were to hold that a State may forbid flag burning wherever it is likely to endanger the flag's symbolic role, but allow it wherever burning a flag promotes that role-as where, for example, a person ceremoniously burns a dirty flag-we would be saying that when it comes to impairing the flag's physical integrity, the flag itself may be used as "short cut from mind to mind"-only in one direction. We would be permitting a State to "prescribe what shall be orthodox" by saying that one may burn the flag to convey one's attitude toward it and its referents only if one does not endanger the flag's representation of nationhood and national unity. . . .

There is, moreover, no indication-either in the text of the Constitution or in our cases interpreting it-that a separate juridical category exists for the American flag alone. . . . We decline, therefore, to create for the flag an exception to the joust of principles protected by the First Amendment.

V

Johnson was convicted for engaging in expressive conduct. The State's interest in preventing breaches of the peace does not support his conviction because Johnson's conduct did not threaten to disturb the peace. Nor does the State's interest in preserving the flag as a symbol of nationhood and national unity justify his criminal conviction for engaging in political expression. The judgment of the Texas Court of Criminal Appeals is therefore

Affirmed.

SOURCE: Texas v. Johnson, 491 U.S. 397 (1989).

ANALYSIS

When Gregory Johnson burned a U.S. flag as part of a political demonstration during the 1984 Republican National Convention in Dallas, he was convicted of breaking a Texas law prohibiting desecration of a venerated object. However, this was not the first time a court had confronted mistreatment of the American flag, and Texas was not alone in enacting protective flag legislation.

By the end of the nineteenth century, support had grown for a national law protecting the U.S. flag from misuse. However, efforts to enact national legislation failed, so between 1897 and 1932 numerous individual states passed their own flag desecration statutes. Illinois, Pennsylvania, and South Dakota were the first states to pass such laws, but by 1932, all states had enacted some type of flag protection legislation. Most of these laws prohibited placing additional markings or symbols on the U.S. flag, using it for advertising, or otherwise defiling the national symbol. In 1907 (*Halter v. Nebraska*), the Supreme Court gave states the authority to uphold their flag desecration laws (in this case, barring commercial use of the flag on a beer label).

State flag desecration laws were essentially nationalized with Congress's passage of the Flag Protection Act of 1968, a direct response to public burning of the U.S. flag by Vietnam War protesters. Fines or imprisonment were imposed upon "[W]hoever knowingly mutilates, defaces, physically defiles, burns, maintains on the floor or ground, or tramples upon any flag of the United States." The 1968 Act was challenged numerous times, but lower courts always upheld its constitutionality, and the Supreme Court chose not to review the rulings.

In 1974, however, the Supreme Court took up an important flag case in *Spence v. Washington*. The court ruled that placing a peace sign made of removable tape on the face of an American flag was an example of symbolic speech, not defilement of the flag. The court's determination that use of the flag in an act of protest is protected expression was predictive of the court's ruling in *Texas v. Johnson* one decade later.

It was 1984 when Gregory Lee Johnson publicly burned the American flag to protest Reagan-era policies. Many who witnessed the burning were deeply offended by his actions, and under a Texas state law, Johnson was found guilty of desecrating a venerated object. A state court of appeals affirmed the conviction, but the Texas Court of Criminal Appeals reversed on the grounds that Johnson's actions constituted expressive conduct protected by the First Amendment. The Supreme Court agreed to hear the case to decide on the constitutionality of burning or otherwise desecrating the U.S. flag.

In June 1989, the court issued a narrow 5–4 decision in favor of Johnson, stating the Texas statute was inconsistent with the First Amendment. The entire court agreed that the flag is understood as a symbol that is communicative by its nature. However, the justices disagreed on whether the act of burning of the flag constituted use of the symbol for purposes of communication (nonverbal speech), or whether it was primarily an act of destruction of property—in this case, property deserving protection because of its unique value to the nation.

Justice Brennan, writing for the majority, held that the flag is one of many national symbols representing the United States. The government cannot require the public to revere those symbols, nor are states entitled to determine what type of conduct related to those symbols is or is not permissible. He referenced *West Virginia Board of Education v. Barnette* (1943), in which the court ruled that schoolchildren cannot be required to salute the flag. Brennan explained the same governmental limitations apply to *Johnson* because "nothing in our precedents suggests that a State may foster its own view of the flag by prohibiting expressive conduct relating to it."

The majority also rejected the argument that burning the flag would contribute to breaches of the peace and destroy the integrity of the flag's symbolic role as a national unifier. Justice Brennan pointed out that no breach of the peace resulted from Johnson's action, and people's disgust over the burning of the flag might actually strengthen public veneration of it as a sacred national symbol. Furthermore, he argued, "[I]f there is a bedrock principle underlying the First Amendment, it is that the Government may not prohibit the expression of an idea simply because society finds the idea itself offensive or disagreeable. . . . We do not consecrate the flag by punishing its desecration, for in doing so we dilute the freedom that this cherished emblem represents."

Justice Rehnquist's dissent countered that the flag is more than just a symbol. Rather, over 200 years of history has made it "the visible symbol embodying our Nation" that has produced "uniquely deep awe and respect" among the American people. Justice Stevens added the flag was such an important national asset that public desecration of it would tarnish its value. Dissenting justices felt the flag deserved special protection, with Justice Rehnquist writing, "I cannot agree that the First Amendment invalidates the Act of Congress, and the laws of 48 of the 50 States, which make criminal the public burning of the flag."

Reaction to the Supreme Court decision was emotional, particularly among those who felt the court had wrongly favored free speech over protection of a beloved national symbol. Within a month of the ruling, the House of Representatives had produced thirty-nine resolutions for a constitutional amendment prohibiting desecration of the U.S. flag. In October 1989, the Flag Protection Act was passed by Congress, and President Bush allowed it to become law without his signature. Within a year, the new law was challenged (*United States v. Eichman*) and found unconstitutional by the Supreme Court for the same reasons the Texas statute in the *Johnson* case was found unconstitutional.

Nearly every Congress convened since the *Eichman* decision in 1990 has attempted to gain a two-thirds vote to produce a constitutional amendment that would protect the integrity of the flag and outlaw its burning or desecration. None of these proposals to date has received the required votes in both the House and Senate.

FURTHER READING

Bezanson, Randall P. "The Burning Flag: The Medium and the Message (Texas v. Johnson, 491 U.S. 397 (1989))." In *How Free Can Speech Be?* 187–205. New York: New York University Press, 1998.

Constable, Marianne. "Flags, Words, Laws, and Things." In *Just Silences: The Limits and Possibilities of Modern Law*, 93–110. Princeton, NJ: Princeton University Press, 2005.
Goldstein, Robert Justin. *Flag Burning and Free Speech: The Case of Texas v. Johnson*. Lawrence, KS: University Press of Kansas, 2000.
Stone, Geoffrey R. "Flag Burning and the Constitution." *Iowa Law Review* 75 (1989): 111.
Warren, Earl, and Supreme Court of the United States. *U.S. Reports: United States v. O'Brien, 391 U.S. 367*. 1967. https://www.loc.gov/item/usrep391367/

- ***Document 36:*** Senators Condemn Using Federal Funds to Support "Abhorrent" Art
- ***Date:*** May 18, 1989
- ***Where:*** U.S. Congress (Senate floor)
- ***Significance:*** In 1989, anger over two controversial art exhibitions resulted in Congressional outrage and proposals to cut funding for the National Endowment for the Arts (NEA). Ensuing debates weighed the right of federal agencies to restrict funding for certain types of offensive or obscene artistic works against the right of artists to use federal grants to create works that, while controversial, might contribute to public discourse. This unresolved debate over public offense versus free expression in the art world continues as new, provocative pieces are introduced.

DOCUMENT

U.S. SENATE
Washington, DC, May 18, 1989

Mr. HUGH SOUTHERN, Acting Chairman, National Endowment for the Arts, Washington, DC.
DEAR MR. SOUTHERN:

We recently learned of the Endowment's support for a so-called "work of art" by Andres Serrano entitled "Piss Christ." We write to express our outrage and to suggest in the strongest terms that the procedures used by the Endowment to award and support artists be reformed.

The piece in question is a large and vivid photograph of Christ on a crucifix submerged in the artist's urine. This work is shocking, abhorrent and completely undeserving of any recognition whatsoever. Millions of taxpayers are rightfully incensed that their hard-earned dollars were used to honor and support Serrano's work.

There is a clear flaw in the procedures used to select art and artists deserving of taxpayers' support. That fact is evidenced by the Serrano work itself. Moreover, after the artist was selected and honored for his "contributions" to the field of art, his work was exhibited at government expense and with the imprimatur of the Endowment.

This matter does not involve freedom of artistic expression-it does involve the question whether American taxpayers should be forced to support such trash.

And finally, simply because the Endowment and the Southeastern Center for Contemporary Art did not have a direct hand in choosing Serrano's work, does not absolve either of responsibility. The fact that both the Endowment and the SECCA with taxpayer dollars promoted this work as part of the Awards in Visual Arts exhibition, is reason enough to be outraged.

We urge the Endowment to comprehensively review its procedures and determine what steps will be taken to prevent such abuses from recurring in the future.

We await your response.

Sincerely,

Alphonse D'Amato, Bob Kerrey, Warren B. Rudman, Rudy Boschwitz, Dennis DeConcini, Pete Wilson, Bob Dole, Chuck Grassley, James A. McClure, John Heinz, Wendell Ford, Howell Heflin, Harry Reid, Richard Shelby, John W. Warner, Larry Pressler, Conrad Burns, Tom Harkin, Trent Lott, Jesse Helms, John McCain, Arlen Specter, Steve Symms.

SOURCE: "Obscenity: Andres Serrano Controversy (1989): Correspondence 02" (1989). *Obscenity: Andres Serrano Controversy* (1989). Paper 4. http://digitalcommons.uri.edu/pell_neh_II_60/4http://digitalcommons.uri.edu/pell_neh_II_60/4

- ***Document:*** Letter from Harvey Lichtenstein, President and Executive Producer of the Brooklyn Academy of Music, Defending the National Endowment for the Arts
- ***Date:*** June 22, 1989
- ***Where:*** Sent to Senator William Armstrong of Colorado
- ***Significance:*** The letter written by Harvey Lichtenstein represents many such letters defending the National Endowment for the Arts and its process of selecting grant recipients. The letter clarifies the NEA's involvement in an exhibition featuring Andres Serrano's works and further bolsters both the purpose and historical achievements of the NEA. Lichtenstein also asserted that regardless of one's approval or disapproval of Serrano's artwork, censorship of artistic license is the greater threat to a free society.

DOCUMENT

June 22, 1989

Senator William L. Armstrong
Colorado
United States Senate
Washington, D.C. 20510

Dear Senator Armstrong:

> As you know, the National Endowment for the Arts sometimes grants funds to other agencies, which then make the specific choices. This sub-granting procedure recognizes the fact that in some instances there are other entities which are better able to achieve the objectives of a specific program, hence the sub-granting. This is true of grants to states and regions, and other organizations with more specialized knowledge in the field. It remains a very small part of the grant process at the N.E.A., but is, I believe, an important option.

Andres Serrano was not awarded an N.E.A. grant, rather he was awarded a fellowship of $15,000 by the Southeastern Center for Contemporary Art in Winston Salem, N.C., in 1987. The N.E.A. had granted the Southeastern Center $15,000 to support its fellowship program, but the N.E.A. was not involved in the choice of the fellowship recipients.

My information is that the Southeastern Center for Contemporary Art is a reputable organization; that its track record substantiated to the N.E.A. Panel and Council its worthiness to be awarded the grant for the purposes specified.

I disagree with the Senator's assessment of the N.E.A. in this instance, but I hope that the Senator can agree with me that the record of the N.E.A. is quite extraordinary in keeping favoritism and amateurism at arms length, by its use of the peer panel system. Whatever one thinks of the Serrano work, the record of the N.E.A. in awarding hundreds of thousands of grants, has been exemplary. On the basis of the N.E.A.'s sterling record of arts' support in the United States over the past years, I believe that the views expressed in your letter are unwarranted. And I would strongly support the sub-granting procedure as a useful and valuable option in some selected situations, the Serrano affair notwithstanding.

What I find disturbing is the problem of censorship. When you say "Piss Christ is a travesty; it is not art," whose judgment is that? Is one allowed a different opinion? The history of civilization is full of instances of artists being castigated and indeed suffering severe calumny because of their work. Indeed, the martyrdom of scientists, philosophers, and theologians, as well as artists, fill our history books. Was not Jesus Christ vilified and martyred for his beliefs, which offended officialdom at the time?

Let us be fair about it. The N.E.A.'s record of impartiality and good judgment is written large through the years of its existence. It has served American artists and arts institutions with great distinction. That is not to say that I haven't disagreed, sometimes vehemently, with the Council's decisions; nor do I think that there have not been errors in judgment. But the process has been painstakingly fair and aboveboard; no influence peddling, no skimming, and no empire building. It is about as clean and as responsive a government agency as I could imagine.

I do not believe that the Endowment has committed any error in this case. In making the grant to the Southeastern Center for Contemporary Art, it was acting with due process and in a proper manner. I would hope that we would all be more concerned with creeping censorship and threats to artistic freedom, which are the true issues in this situation, and which are the real threats to a free society.

Most respectfully,
Harvey Lichtenstein

SOURCE: Lichtenstein, Harvey, "Obscenity: Andres Serrano Controversy (1989): Correspondence 01" (1989). *Obscenity: Andres Serrano Controversy* (1989). Paper 9. https://digitalcommons.uri.edu/cgi/viewcontent.cgi?article=1017&context=pell_neh_II_59

ANALYSIS

Support of free expression through the arts is another First Amendment protection that sets the United States apart from many other nations. However, even as one of the most speech-protected societies in the world, the United States has a long history of suppressing or censoring controversial art at local, state, or federal levels. Protests of visual artwork have often focused on nudity or sexual themes, although works addressing race and power have also challenged accepted societal norms and led to suppression of provocative pieces and performances.

The issue of government funding for the arts was brought into focus during the culture wars of the 1980s and 1990s. Much of the debate centered around the use of taxpayer money to fund National Endowment for the Arts (NEA) grants that supported controversial or provocative art. In reality, only a tiny fraction of grants awarded during the NEA's fifty-five-year history have resulted in any sort of controversy. Nevertheless, the few controversies that arose impacted the organization's influence and its congressional support.

Congress established the National Endowment for the Arts (NEA) in 1965 to stimulate artistic participation by Americans and to provide funding opportunities that help inspire artists to pursue their creative endeavors. Through this independent government agency, Congress hoped to promote art education, emphasize the country's cultural heritage, and ensure that all communities in the United States had equal access to the arts. NEA grants supported visual art, performances, exhibitions, festivals, educational programs, and artist residencies, as well as arts education in schools across the United States.

In 1989, however, the NEA became a lightning rod of controversy when civic leaders and legislators rose up against a handful of contentious exhibitions that had ties to NEA funding. Two exhibits in particular were criticized: a photograph by Andres Serrano and a retrospective of the late Robert Mapplethorpe.

Although most of Serrano's work caused no disapproval, anger arose over a single photograph of a crucifix dipped in a plexiglass tank containing the artist's urine. When the photograph was named by the Southeastern Center for Contemporary

Arts as one of ten "Awards in the Visual Arts" winners, backlash ensued. Donald Wildmon of the conservative American Family Association called the work "anti-Christian bigotry" and demanded public funding be retracted from the NEA. Numerous senators joined the protest, including Orrin Hatch and Jesse Helms, who said disgustedly, "Serrano is not an artist. He is a jerk." In a letter to the NEA, these senators called the artwork "trash" and decried the use of taxpayer dollars to support Serrano's work.

Serrano defended his art, expressing concern with modern society's idolatry and misuse of Christian icons. He wrote, "I am neither a blasphemer nor 'anti-Christian,' as some have called me, and I stand by my work as an artist and as a Christian." He continued, "Where the photograph has ignited spirited debate, that has been a good thing. Perhaps it reminds some people to question what we unthinkingly fetishize (and thereby often minimize) in lieu of pondering seriously what the crucifix actually symbolizes: the unimaginably torturous death of Christ, the Son of God" (2015).

Soon after the Serrano controversy, similar furor arose over a traveling exhibit of selected Robert Mapplethorpe photographs titled *The Perfect Moment*. Mapplethorpe was well known for his striking, often sensual, black-and-white photographs. Although much of the *Perfect Moment* exhibition consisted of portraits and flowers, seven of the 175 photographs depicted overt sexual acts or provocative homoerotic images. The American Family Association, private citizens, and numerous members of Congress publicly condemned the exhibition as pornographic and demanded its cancellation. Under intense pressure, the Corcoran Gallery of Art in Washington, DC, canceled the exhibit. In Cincinnati, the art director of the Contemporary Arts Center was criminally charged with obscenity for allowing the exhibition to take place—the first time a U.S. museum had been charged with such a crime. The director was later acquitted.

The Mapplethorpe protests added fuel to the already heated debate about public funding of controversial art. As a result of the uproar, the NEA budget was cut by the amount of funding received by Serrano and Mapplethorpe, and Congress amended the NEA's 1990 reauthorization bill to ensure "artistic excellence and artistic merit are the criteria by which [grant] applications are judged, taking into consideration general standards of decency and respect for the diverse beliefs and values of the American public." Congress also made clear obscenity was not protected speech and would not receive federal funding.

Prior to this congressional amendment, four performance artists had applied for NEA grants. Their applications were initially approved by an NEA advisory committee but later rejected upon the recommendation of the National Council for the Arts. The artists and the National Association of Artists' Organizations filed suit—first, based on First Amendment and statutory claims, and later, based on the claim that amendments made to the NEA grant selection process were unconstitutionally vague and discriminatory. Lower courts ruled in favor of the artists, but in 1998, the Supreme Court ruled 8–1 in *NEA v. Finley* that the amended NEA grant guidelines were neither impermissibly vague nor discriminatory. The court said Congress enjoys broad discretion in appropriating federal tax dollars, and the new criteria for awarding NEA grants do not further hamper what is already a subjective process.

The *Finley* ruling largely settled the debate over federal funding of the arts, but state and local struggles ensued. These included a 1999 effort by New York

City mayor Rudy Giuliani to end the city's financial support of the Brooklyn Museum of Art over a controversial art exhibit. The city was ordered by a judge to restore funding to the museum. Two years later, after taking offense to a photograph on exhibit portraying Jesus as a naked black woman, Mayor Giuliani created a "decency panel" to evaluate the morality of publicly funded art. The panel was immediately denounced by numerous artists, scholars, and politicians.

Although courts have largely protected artistic freedom of expression under the First Amendment, opponents of publicly supported programs still argue that taxpayer money should not fund controversial art. Artists counter that the purpose and value of art is often to provoke and inspire new ways of thinking. In 2020, the NEA was allotted $162.5 million, or roughly 0.003 percent of the federal budget.

FURTHER READING

Devlin, Gary E. "NEA v. Finley: Explicating the Rocky Relationship between the Government and the Arts." *Pepperdine Law Review* 27 (1999): 345.

Howard, Marcus E. "U.S. Has Funded Artists and Intellectuals for Half a Century, But It's a Perennial Fight." *Los Angeles Times*. October 2, 2015. https://www.latimes.com/nation/la-na-arts-humanities-endowments-20151002-story.html

Kovner, Victor A., Edward J. Davis, and Anke E. Steinecke. "NYC Mayor Giuliani Loses Round One in Battle Against the First Amendment." *Comm. Law.* 17 (1999): 3.

National Coalition against Censorship. "Art and Culture Censorship Timeline." February 10, 2011. https://ncac.org/resource/art-and-culture-censorship-timeline

Schindler, Steve, and Katie Wilson-Milne. "Art, Censorship, and the First Amendment." *The Art Law Podcast*. July 2, 2018. http://artlawpodcast.com/2018/07/02/art-censorship-and-the-first-amendment/

Walker, Michael Wingfield. "Artistic Freedom v. Censorship: The Aftermath of the NEA's New Funding Restrictions." *Washington University Law Review* 71, no. 3 (1993): 937–56.

- ***Document 37:*** Congressional Hearing on "Violent Video Games: What Parents Need to Know"
- ***Date:*** December 9, 1993
- ***Where:*** U.S. Congress, Washington, DC
- ***Significance:*** A series of congressional hearings in late 1993 and early 1994 addressed lawmakers' concerns about increasingly violent and sexual content of video games marketed to children. The eventual result of these hearings and proposed legislation ("Video Game Rating Act of 1994") was establishment of the Entertainment Software Ratings Board (ESRB), an effort by the video game industry to self-regulate to avoid additional government oversight.

DOCUMENT

. . . Statement of Hon. Joseph I. Lieberman, a U.S. Senator from the state of Connecticut

. . . Every day, the news brings more and more images of random violence, torture, and sexual aggression right into our living rooms—just this week, the dreadful story of the young girl abducted from a slumber party in her own home and then found killed; a man on a commuter train begins coldly and methodically to fire away at innocents on their way home, killing five people and injuring many others.

Violence and violent images permeate more and more aspects of our lives, and I think it is time to draw the line. I know that one place parents want us to draw the line is with violence in video games. The fact is that a new generation of video games crosses that line, containing the most horrible depictions of graphic violence and sex, including particularly violence against women. Like the Grinch who stole Christmas, these violent video games threaten to rob this particular holiday season of a spirit of goodwill. Instead of enriching a child's mind, these games teach a child to enjoy inflicting torture.

For those who have not seen these so-called games before, I want to show you what we are talking about. What you are about to see are scenes from two of the most violent new video games. First, we have "Mortal Kombat," which is a martial arts contest involving digitized characters. We are going to show two versions of the game.

In the first segment, which is Sega's version, blood splatters from the contestants' heads. When a player wins, the so-called death sequence begins. The game narrator instructs the player to, and I quote, "finish" his opponent. The player may then choose a method of murder ranging from ripping the heart out to pulling off the head of the opponent with spinal cord attached. The second version, made by Nintendo, leaves out the blood and decapitation, but as you will see, it is still a violent game. . . .

The second game is "Night Trap," which is a game set in a sorority house. The object is to keep hooded men from hanging the young woman from a hook or drilling her neck with a tool designed to drain her blood. "Night Trap" uses actual actors and achieves an unprecedented level of realism. What is particularly troubling about the scene in this film that we have an extract of is a graphic depiction of the violence against women, with strong overtones of sexual violence. I find this segment deeply offensive, and believe that it simply should be taken off the market. . . .

Today, just a short while ago, I gather that some members of the video game industry announced their intention to create a voluntary rating or warning label system. I am pleased that the video game business, by this action, has shown that it recognizes that there is a problem here. A credible rating system will help parents determine which games are appropriate for children of different ages, and that is exactly what our proposed legislation contemplates.

But I must say here that creating a rating system is, in my opinion, the very least the video game industry can do, not the best they can do. It would be far better for America's parents and children if the industry simply kept the worst violence and sex out of their games.

Now, I have three major concerns as the industry develops a rating system. First, there are questions about the system itself. Who will do the rating? Will all manufacturers participate? How many age-specific ratings will there be? Will the industry spend money to inform parents about the meanings of the ratings?

Second, a rating system must not be perverted into a cynical marketing ploy to attract children to more violent games. A rating system without some industry self-regulation may put us just where we don't want to be. We must not allow the industry to trumpet a violent rating as a selling point.

Third, the industry must work to enforce whatever rating system it creates. It should consider licensing agreements and contracts which specify that ratings will be clearly visible in any advertising and understandable by parents and consumers. Distributors, including video rental stores or toy stores, should face some kind of incentives or, in fact, penalties from manufacturers if they sell or rent to children below the minimum ages in the ratings.

Because of these concerns, Senator Kohl and I are certainly going to proceed with our legislative proposal. Since we believe that our announcing the intention to introduce this bill has helped us get this far, going forward with the legislation is the best insurance that we get as far as we can in resolving this problem.

Now, let me stress that a rating system will only be as strong as the weakest link in the distribution system, from manufacturer to advertiser to retailer, and the industry, I think, must make sure that all those links are strong. I want to note here for the record that we contacted several of the biggest toy stores— Toys "R" Us and KayBee, among others; I believe Walmart also—to invite them to join us today, but they failed to respond and I am disappointed by that decision. They, too, have a responsibility to cooperate in creating a credible system to keep adult games out of the hands of children. Without their cooperation, no rating or warning label system can work.

Even if all of these concerns with a rating system are addressed, the video game industry, in my opinion, will not have done as much as it should do to avoid creating more violence in our already too violent society. The rating system must not be a fig leaf for the industry to hide behind. They must also accept their responsibility to control themselves and simply stop producing the worst of this junk.

Now, the industry is blessed with some of the most exciting technology existing today. Millions are being spent to gain the interest of our children in that technology, but when they gain that interest, I think the industry also accepts a responsibility. As Bob Keeshan, who is Captain Kangaroo, said last week, the industry has a responsibility to nurture healthy children and a healthy society, or at least, I would add, not to undermine the attempts by parents to nurture healthy children.

The video game industry has not lived up to its responsibility to America's parents and children. I hope they will do so in the coming months, at least by developing a credible and enforceable rating system, and at best by taking the worst games, or the worst parts of those games, off the market.

Bob Keeshan made another excellent point last week when he said that children don't need violence to be entertained. His show proved that for over 30 years. As the father of a 5-year-old, I couldn't agree more, but I am not naive. I know that all the public outcry and Congressional interest may not stop the flood of violent video games. For this reason, we need to make sure that parents have the information they need to establish a healthy environment for their kids, and that parents use their power as consumers to convince the video industry to regulate itself. If the violence and sex doesn't come out of the games, parents should be able to keep the games out of their homes. . . .

SOURCE: United States. Congress. Senate. Committee on the Judiciary. Subcommittee on Juvenile Justice, United States. Congress. Senate. Committee on Governmental Affairs. Subcommittee on Regulation and Government Information. *Rating video games: a parent's guide to games: Joint Hearings before the Subcommittee on Juvenile Justice of the Committee on the Judiciary and the Subcommittee on Regulation and Government Information of the Committee on Governmental Affairs, United States Senate, One Hundred Third Congress, first session . . . December 9, 1993, March 4, and July 29, 1994.* Washington: Government Printing Office, 1995.

ANALYSIS

The early 1990s were characterized by heightened public concern about violence in the United States, including murders and gang-related crimes committed by teenagers. Some of the rhetoric was fueled by the idea that increasing brutality in entertainment—particularly video games—was contributing to violent behavior in the real world. Beginning in December 1993, Senators Joseph Lieberman and Herb Kohl cosponsored a series of congressional hearings to address increasingly violent content in video games. The first of these hearings specifically addressed the content of two popular but controversial video games: "Night Trap" and "Mortal Kombat."

Critics of the games cited the violent nature of the story lines and sexual aggression toward women as inappropriate, even for older children. "Mortal Kombat" was accused of glorifying violence by giving players options of killing opponents by ripping their hearts out or removing their heads and spines. Lieberman chided game developers for teaching children to "enjoy inflicting the most gruesome forms of cruelty imaginable." Even Captain Kangaroo (Bob Keeshan) spoke out against the violent games, saying greed had driven development of the inappropriate material (Associated Press 1993).

"Night Trap" was also the focus of the December 9 hearing that included testimony from child psychologists, education experts, and gaming industry leaders. Senator Lieberman, despite never having played the game, showed clips of a screaming teenager being captured and attacked as evidence of the game's violence. Game creators defended "Night Trap," arguing the object is to save, not harm the women characters. They insisted the vampire-like attackers were meant to be so fantastical and unrealistic that their violence would seem unreproducible.

Lieberman countered, "[I]nstead of enriching a child's mind, these games teach a child to enjoy inflicting torture." Other witnesses agreed; Senator Dorgan called it a "sick, disgusting video game," adding, "it is child abuse in my judgment." Howard Lincoln, the senior VP of Nintendo even testified, saying, "I want to state that 'Night Trap' will never appear on a Nintendo system. Obviously, it would not pass our guidelines. This game . . . which promotes violence against women, simply has no place in our society."

Senator Lieberman stated although he would prefer to see violent video games banned, they are shielded under the First Amendment. However, he and other advocates pushed for protections to limit children's exposure to games with violent, mature themes. As the hearings drew to a close, Senator Kohl addressed video game industry representatives, saying, "I hope you walk away from here with one thought. If you don't do something about this, we will." Industry leaders left with the threat of government regulation looming.

When the hearings were completed, Senator Lieberman introduced legislation to create a rating commission responsible for reviewing and ranking the content of video games. Before legislation could be passed, however, industry leaders announced their own plans to self-regulate by establishing a unified content rating system through formation of the Entertainment Software Ratings Board (ESRB). Prior to this, Sega had created its own ratings system in hopes of quelling concerns about video game content, but other corporations had not followed suit. Now, review of the gaming industry would be standardized, with the ESRB assigning age and content ratings to video games to more accurately depict their substance and assist parents and consumers in making informed purchasing decisions.

The ESRB's rating system consisted of five categories: C = early childhood, K-A = kids to adults, T = teens, M = mature audiences, and A = adults only. That original system has since been modified to reflect more specific age categories: E = Everyone, E 10+ = ages 10 and up, T = Teen (age 13+), M = generally for ages 17 and up, AO = Adults Only (ages 18+), and a new category of RP = Rating Pending.

The ESRB ratings system also added nuanced descriptors to certain categories to help consumers better understand the nature of violence or themes in the games. ERSB's efforts have been largely credited with blocking children's direct access to violent video games, although critics lament that many kids still find ways to acquire games they could not otherwise purchase on their own. Gaming advocates say the rating system works and contend that the most effective way to ensure ongoing regulation is through support of industry efforts, not restrictive legislation.

The 1993 hearings and proposed "Video Game Rating Act" legislation also affected the gaming industry in other, more direct ways. Following the 1993 Senate hearings, "Night Trap" was dropped from distribution by Toys "R" Us and FAO Schwarz, and Sega subsequently withdrew the video game from distribution. However, modified versions of the game were later returned to store shelves, and an updated, remastered version of "Night Trap" was re-released on the twenty-fifth anniversary of the game's original debut.

Although many consider "Night Trap" and "Mortal Kombat" tame and somewhat boring by contemporary standards, the original games garnered a huge following—especially after stirring controversy within the halls of Congress.

Concerns about the effects of violent video games have arisen repeatedly since the original 1993 hearings. In the wake of national tragedies involving gun violence, numerous lawsuits have been filed by parents and citizens who blame the influence of brutal video games on school shooters and other perpetrators of violence. Most of these lawsuits, however, have been dismissed for various reasons.

State and national legislatures have also passed laws to restrict access to violent games, but the majority of those have since been declared unconstitutional. Regulatory efforts were further hindered in 2011 when the Supreme Court struck down a California law banning the sale of violent video games to children without a parent's permission (*Brown v. Entertainment Merchants Association*).

Although more than two decades of research has largely discredited the purported connections between video games and violence, the games that sparked controversy in the early 1990s nevertheless made their mark on history. Now considered nostalgic remnants of the industry's early years, the most profound legacy of creations like "Night Trap" and "Mortal Kombat" is that they drove the creation of the ESRB and the modern video game rating system.

FURTHER READING

Crabtree, Steve. "Grand Theft of Innocence? Teens and Video Games." *Gallup Poll Tuesday Briefing*. September 1, 2003.

"Entertainment Software Rating Board (ESRB)." *Congressional Digest* 84, no. 2 (2005): 56–58.

Hsu, Tiffany. "When Mortal Kombat Came under Congressional Scrutiny." *New York Times*. March 8, 2018.

Kenyota, Gregory. "Thinking of the Children: The Failure of Violent Video Game Laws." *Fordham Intellectual Property Media & Entertainment Law Journal* 18 (2007): 785.

Laczniak, Russell N., Les Carlson, Doug Walker, and E. Deanne Brocato. "Parental Restrictive Mediation and Children's Violent Video Game Play: The Effectiveness of the Entertainment Software Rating Board (ESRB) Rating System." *Journal of Public Policy & Marketing* 36, no. 1 (2017): 70–78.

National Coalition against Censorship. "A Timeline of Video Game Controversies." October 31, 2010. https://ncac.org/resource/a-timeline-of-video-game-controversies

---

- ***Document 38:*** *Cyberporn and Children: The Scope of the Problem, the State of the Technology, and the Need for Congressional Action*—U.S. Senate Hearings Discussing Senate Bill 892, Later Amended and Passed as the Communications Decency Act (Title V of the Telecommunications Act of 1996)
- ***Date:*** First hearing held July 24, 1995 (Communications Decency Act became law February 8, 1996)
- ***Where:*** U.S. Congress, Washington, DC
- ***Significance:*** This was one of numerous Senate hearings held to discuss the issue of children's access to indecent material over the internet, a technology then still in its infancy. The Senate bill discussed in this hearing was later amended and passed as the Communications Decency Act of 1996. It was Congress's first attempt to regulate minors' access to pornography and indecent materials over the internet. The Supreme Court later struck down the "indecent transmission" and "patently offensive display" provisions of the Act in *Reno v. American Civil Liberties Union* (1997), declaring they unconstitutionally abridged First Amendment freedom of speech protections.

DOCUMENT

Senator GRASSLEY [presiding]. Good afternoon, everybody. At the outset, I want to welcome everyone to the first ever congressional hearing on the topic of pornography in cyberspace. This issue is one of the more important and difficult issues facing Congress today. I have introduced the Protecting Children from Computer Pornography Act of 1995 which targets this problem, I think in a reasonable and disciplined way.

Fundamentally, the controversy this committee faces today is about how much protection we are willing to extend to children. Sadly, this has become a dangerous country in which to raise a family. Certainly there is far more for parents to worry about now than when I was a child or, more recently, a parent raising kids.

Playgrounds have become hunting grounds for child molesters. Schools have become places where drugs are rampant. Teenage pregnancy is on the rise. Just look at the recent polls. Teenage drug use is way up, and teen pregnancy rates are at near epidemic proportions.

Until very recently, parents could breathe a little easier in their own homes. After all, the home is supposed to be safe and is supposed to be a barrier between your children and the dark forces which seek to corrupt and destroy our youth. But enter the Internet and other computer networks. Suddenly, now not even the home is safe. Now the dark forces which were once stopped by the front door have found their way into the home through personal computers. Something needs to be done. . . .

Giving Federal prosecutors a tool to use to punish those who would prey on America's children is a good step in the right direction. My bill is that tool. I also believe that the computer communications industry has a role to play as well. I believe that efforts to create software programs to try to block some sexually explicit content on computers are commendable. In fact, in substitute language that I have circulated to committee members, I have included a 2-year report-back provision, requiring the Justice Department to report to Congress on technological innovations which might warrant the alteration or repeal of my legislation.

But at least for now I do not believe that technology is the entire answer either, and I do not accept the notion that parents should have the sole responsibility to spend their hard-earned money to ensure that cyberporn does not flood into their homes through their personal computers.

If you were to follow that reasoning, parents should pay then protection money to third persons so that drug pushers would not sell drugs to their children. Now, that is upside down logic and contrary to the way that we have always done things in this country.

Those elements in the computer communications industry which choose to provide sexually explicit material should bear the responsibility and the cost of preventing children from accessing sexually explicit material. That is what my bill does. It uses criminal sanctions to punish those in the computer communications industry who knowingly transmit indecent pornography to children or who willfully aid and abet such activity.

My bill is perfectly reasonable, and virtually every State in the Nation has had laws on the books against selling or displaying certain types of pornography to children for decades. Now that the problem of children's exposure to pornographic materials has taken on a significant interstate character, it is time for Congress to get into the act. . . .

To my knowledge, there is only one comprehensive study dealing with the overall issue of pornography and cyberspace, and after criticism, that study is under review, as it should be. But today we are not even focusing on this general issue. The specific issue we are dealing with today involves knowingly or willfully transmitting indecent pornographic material to children. And that is it. Very simply, that is it.

What adults want to receive or take part in with other adults is not the focus of this hearing. Opponents of my legislation will try to downplay the problems, saying that there is only anecdotal evidence. Well, our first panel of witnesses who have been victimized will reflect the problem in real human terms and highlight the need to address the problem effectively.

Now, in order to clarify what my bill does, I would point my colleagues to this chart that I have prepared. As the chart shows, my bill creates criminal liability in two very narrow circumstances. Under the Protection of Children from Computer Pornography Act, it is unlawful for computer system operators to knowingly transmit indecent material to a child. That is under scenario 1. Second, my bill makes it unlawful for computer system operators to willfully permit their system to be used as a conduit for indecent communications intended for children. That is it—simple, clear, and reasonable. . . .

OPENING STATEMENT OF ON. PATRICK J. LEAHY, A U.S. SENATOR FROM THE STATE OF VERMONT

Senator LEAHY. Thank you, Mr. Chairman.

Mr. Chairman, interestingly enough, this is, as you already said, the first congressional hearing held on the issue of regulating indecent and obscene material on the Internet. In fact, when the problem of children's access to objectionable online material first came up for a vote, when the Senate passed a version of the Exon-Coats Communications Decency Act on June 14, [1995] remarkably the Senate acted without the benefit of hearings or anything approaching the thorough examination of the matter that you have set out. . . .

It is especially interesting because most of the Senators who voted would not have the foggiest idea how to get on the Internet in the first place. They do not use it. They do not have any idea of how to get on to it. They would have to have their staffs show them how to do it. . . . They voted in large part based on inflammatory stories about pornography on the Internet, like the study by Mr. Rimm. Incidentally, he was supposed to be here, but got disinvited once a number of people brought out the fact that the study, which was treated as gospel on the Senate floor, was a little bit less than gospel. And I would expect any time now to see Time Magazine, for example, which did a cover story based on it too, point out that even great media can be conned.

But these issues of child pornography are valid issues and ought to be talked about, and you are to be commended for having the hearing because of that. They are issues that concern me. We have all these issues interconnected here: the future of the Internet, the best way for parents to control their children's access to the Internet and to protect against inappropriate and offensive materials; and the appropriate role of law enforcement.

I am a parent. I have raised three children. I spent nearly a decade in law enforcement. I think I have a pretty good idea of how to differentiate between what the responsibility of law enforcement is and what the responsibility of parents is. We sometimes have this attitude that the Government should take over for the parents. I think parents ought to carry some of that basic responsibility. . . .

We hear a lot about the free market in this Congress and trying to give it a chance to work. Well, we are finding that software entrepreneurs and the vibrant forces of the free market are providing tools that can empower parents to restrict their children's access to offensive material and address the problem of online pornography by empowering parents and not the Government to screen children's computer activities. . . .

All of us may wonder what magazines, books, or anything else our children buy. We do not know how to check that out, but we can check on the computer exactly where they have been and what they have looked at. Other commercially available products limit children's access to "chat rooms" where they might be solicited. They limit children's ability to receive pornographic pictures through electronic mail that we could not limit otherwise in the print press media. Other products, as I said, allow parents to monitor their children's usage of the Internet: where have you been, who have you rung up, what chat group have you looked at.

Interested organizations like the Christian Coalition or Mothers Against Drunk Driving could provide parents that use blocking technology with lists of sites, and these lists of sites that they consider inappropriate could be programmed in, and the kids could not log on to them.

But, if instead of giving parents the tools to police their kids, you rely on government regulation, I think you stifle the Internet. The Internet has grown as well as it has and as dramatically and amazingly because it has not had the Government second-guessing every move. When you talk about communication technology, the worst thing in the world is to invite government regulation, which always slows up advances, always slows up advances in computer and communication technology. The Internet has been growing at an exponential rate with new uses for devices daily. Overly restrictive bans against indecency on the Internet will prove not only unconstitutional, but will hamper the growth of this communication medium. . . .

Imposing the same government regulation applied to broadcasters to the Internet, I think it is inappropriate. Anyone with a computer and a modem can send something out on the Internet. But unlike a broadcaster, if you want to listen to it, you have got to seek out the information. You have got to download it. And a parent can stop a child from downloading it if they want. But that parent acting through the Government should not be able to stop you or me or others from downloading it if we want to.

Any legislative approach has to take into consideration online users' privacy and free speech interests. If we grant too much power to online providers to screen for indecent material, then public discourse and online content in cyberspace would be controlled by the providers and not by the users. We want our laws to encourage and not discourage online providers from creating a safe environment for children, but we do not want to say "do not let the children on the Internet altogether." If they are liable for any exposure of indecent material to children, people under the age of 18 are just going to be shut out of the technology, relegated by the Government to sanitized "kids-only" services that contain only a fraction of the entire Internet. It is sort of like locking kids out of whole sections of libraries.

What are we going to do if we discourage the Project Gutenberg from placing online the works of not only Charles Dickens but Geoffrey Chaucer or D.H. Lawrence for fear of prosecution because somebody somewhere might find something in there indecent?

Basically I will sum up with this, Mr. Chairman: Parents know their children better than any government official. I did not want the Government telling my children, especially when they were younger, what they could read or write or see. I want that ability. As a parent, I believe I am in the best position to know the sort of online material to which children might be exposed. . . .

SOURCE: U.S. Congress. Senate Committee on the Judiciary. *Cyberporn and Children: The Scope of the Problem, the State of the Technology, and the Need for Congressional Action. Hearing on S.892, a Bill To Amend Section 1464 of Title 18, United States Code, To Punish Transmission by Computer of Indecent Material to Minors, before the Committee on the Judiciary, United States Senate.* July 24, 1995. 104th Cong., 1st sess., 1995. Serial No. J-104–36.

ANALYSIS

Although the building blocks of the modern internet were developed in the late 1960s, it was not until August of 1991 that a Swiss computer programmer created the World Wide Web. This means of sending information through interconnected networks accessible to anyone around the world revolutionized not only communication but modern society in general. However, little attention was paid to the internet's global debut; it took years for the public to fully grasp and embrace the immense interconnectedness and limitless possibilities made possible by the new technology.

By 1996, the internet had begun to take hold. Although still in its infancy, the web was used by both children and adults for research, entertainment, and communication purposes. The capacity to access limitless sources of knowledge and connect virtually with other online users created unprecedented opportunities, but also stirred concerns about potential dangers. Public leaders became increasingly worried about children being harmed through exposure to indecent or obscene internet content.

In February 1995 Senator Exon of Nebraska and Senator Gordon of Washington proposed legislation that would hold new forms of telecommunications to the same standards of decency that had been developed for telephone use. The proposal—the Communications Decency Act (CDA)—included provisions to punish the transmission of indecent and obscene materials available to children on the internet and over cable television. The bill was Congress's first attempt to regulate content of these two new media forms. In statements to Congress, Senator Exon expressed his desire to "protect the sanctuary of the home from uninvited indecencies" and "provide much needed protection for children."

DID YOU KNOW?

Although the Rimm study garnered a great deal of attention, not all of it was favorable. Fellow researchers quickly pointed out inherent discrepancies in Rimm's research. A Georgetown University law professor described one aspect of the flawed methodology this way: "Rimm's conclusion is the precise methodological equivalent to the following: (a) restricting a study of printed pornography to magazines located in the 'adult' area of a bookstore, (b) finding that 83.5% of the reader submissions during a one-week period were to magazines that contained 'pornographic' material, and concluding (c) that 83.5% of all reader submissions to all magazines are pornographic" (Post 1995).

In addition to methodological problems, the Rimm study apparently was not subject to the normal peer review process and was similar enough to a Canadian study of Internet pornography that Rimm was accused of plagiarism. His alma mater, Carnegie Mellon, launched an ethics inquiry into his work. Finally, both private correspondence and an unpublished work by Rimm titled "The Pornographer's Handbook: How to Exploit Women, Dupe Men & Make Lots of Money" suggest that Rimm may not have been the neutral researcher he professed to be (Cannon 1996; Kanaley 1995).

Rimm had originally been asked to testify at the July 26, 1995, Senate hearing concerning Internet pornography, but his invitation was revoked after the validity of his research came into question.

On June 15, 1995, the Senate voted 81-18 to add a revised version of the Communications Decency Act to its version of the larger telecommunications bill. The overwhelming support for the act was based partly on the shocking conclusions of a widely publicized study by Marty Rimm, announced while Congress was discussing the proposed legislation. Rimm's study, featured on the cover of *Time* magazine, involved a massive survey of pornographic images on the web. The findings indicated pornography was rampant and easily accessible on the internet, with Rimm concluding "83.5% of all images posted on the Usenet are pornographic." This seemed to provide evidence that the World Wide Web had a dark and dangerous side in need of supervision and restrictions.

The Senate was also influenced by Senator Exon's presentation of a "Blue Book" of pornography. As a means of demonstrating the "filth" children might encounter on the web, Senator Exon asked a friend to download a collection of internet pornography, which was then compiled into a binder and made available on the Senate floor. Graphic examples in the "Blue Book" bolstered Senate support for the CDA.

Roughly one month following the Senate's inclusion of the CDA into the telecommunications bill, the first hearing was held to discuss the nature and content of the proposed legislation. By this time, the validity of the Rimm study was being scrutinized and additional questions had arisen about implications of restricting information transmission on the internet. Witnesses testified both to the urgency of legislation protecting a burgeoning new technology and to the moral imperative of protecting children from internet-based harms. The hearings provoked critical discussions about how internet connectivity would affect homes, businesses, and society in general.

With amendments made to the original legislation, the Communications Decency Act (Title V of the Telecommunications Act) was signed into law by President Clinton on February 8, 1996. The CDA was challenged almost immediately, and questions regarding the legality of its anti-obscenity provisions were accepted for consideration by the Supreme Court in *Reno v. American Civil Liberties Union*. Numerous organizations publicly opposed the law; the U.S. Chamber of Commerce argued the CDA's ill-defined standards "presented a threat to the country's ability to compete globally in an age of new communications."

On June 26, 1997, the Supreme Court ruled in a landmark decision that CDA provisions regarding "indecent transmission" and "patently offensive display" of materials were vague and overly broad and therefore unconstitutional. The heart of the CDA had been struck down. The court's ruling not only affirmed the internet as a medium of speech to which First Amendment protections apply but also established that citizen use of the internet deserves the highest level of First Amendment protections.

Justice Stevens wrote for the majority, "It is true that we have repeatedly recognized the governmental interest in protecting children from harmful materials. But that interest does not justify an unnecessarily broad suppression of speech addressed to adults." In *Sable*, he noted, the court said restricting speech would be like "burn[ing] the house to roast the pig." A broader restriction of expression under the CDA, he argued, "threatens to torch a large segment of the Internet community."

While the Supreme Court ruled that most of the CDA was unconstitutional, it upheld the obscenity provisions. Another provision left intact was Section 230, originally included in the legislation to protect interactive computer service providers and users from liability for third-party postings. Lawmakers wished to encourage and protect the free flow of information, so they included Section 230 to shield internet service providers and platforms from lawsuits resulting from defamatory or harmful third-party content. (Original content authors can still be sued.) Section 230 also included a "Good Samaritan" provision allowing those companies, acting in good faith, to moderate harmful content. The tech industry argued for this provision, saying the sheer volume of third-party content would make it impossible to preview every posting to determine malicious or harmful impact. Without it, sites would have to widely censor questionable content to protect themselves, thus squelching freedom of expression. Social media platforms have also affirmed the importance of Section 230; companies like Twitter and Facebook say they cannot prescreen user messages because message content is not visible until posted.

In 2020, President Trump threatened to repeal Section 230, arguing Section 230 allows platforms to censor conservative voices without repercussions. Instead, he issued an Executive Order limiting some of its protections. Democrats have also called for its repeal, saying tech companies are not doing enough to curb the spread of false information and hate speech over online platforms. Tech companies say the removal of Section 230 protections would completely upend the current function of the internet. It is unclear if or how Congress will choose to handle the controversy.

DID YOU KNOW?

The heart of Section 230 of the Communications Decency Act (CDA) reads: **"No provider or user of an interactive computer service shall be treated as the publisher or speaker of any information provided by another information content provider."**

This provision helped transform a fledgling internet into a trillion-dollar industry and cornerstone of modern life. However, it has come under attack for allowing the proliferation of harmful or false information with few incentives for tech companies to intervene and regulate it themselves. Experts point out that algorithms used by platforms like Facebook actually amplify inflammatory content because it garners attention and increases profits. Internet platforms have also been chastised for presenting credible news alongside unsubstantiated information from unreliable sources, creating a false equivalence that sews confusion and distrust among media consumers. Public leaders attribute misleading web-based information to setbacks in public health, race relations, voter registration and elections, and a host of other social issues.

Critics say industry self-regulation under the "Good Samaritan" clause has been largely nonexistent or ineffective, and as a result "the worst impulses of humanity continue to thrive" (McNamee 2020). Courts, however, have repeatedly affirmed that Section 230 shields internet websites and platforms from legal responsibility, even when they have been used as conduits of hate speech, white supremacy, terrorism, libel, and sex trafficking or prostitution. Under Section 230 of the CDA, the internet still enjoys some of the most rigorous First Amendment protections of any communication medium.

FURTHER READING

Cannon, Robert. "The Legislative History of Senator Exon's Communications Decency Act: Regulating Barbarians on the Information Superhighway." *Federal Communications Law Journal* 49, no. 1, Article 3 (1996): 51.

Gillette, Felix. "How We Got into This Mess." *Bloomberg Businessweek*, no. 4625 (August 2019): 50–55.

Halverson, Haley. "Ending Immunity of Internet-Facilitated Commercial Sexual Exploitation through Amending the Communications Decency Act." *Journal of Internet Law* 21, no. 12 (2018): 3–18.

Machado, Leslie Paul. "Immunity under § 230 of the Communications Decency Act of 1996: A Short Primer." *Journal of Internet Law* 10, no. 3 (2006): 3–11.

McNamee, Roger. "Facebook Cannot Fix Itself." *Time* 195, no. 22 (2020): 20–21.

"Section 230 as First Amendment Rule." *Harvard Law Review* 131, no. 7 (2018): 2027–48.

Schorr, Joanna. "Malicious Content on the Internet: Narrowing Immunity under the Communications Decency Act." *St. John's Law Review* 87, no. 2/3 (2013): 733–62.

5

THE FIRST AMENDMENT IN THE POST-9/11 ERA (2001–2015)

- ***Document 39:*** "On Opposing the USA PATRIOT Act" by Senator Russell Feingold of Wisconsin
- ***Date:*** October 12, 2001
- ***Where:*** *Associated Press* Managing Editors Conference, Milwaukee Art Museum, Milwaukee, Wisconsin
- ***Significance:*** In the aftermath of the terrorist attacks on Sept. 11, 2001, Congress passed the PATRIOT Act to aid in the identification of potential terrorists and deter future attacks. The act granted federal officials sweeping powers to investigate potential terrorist threats, but many civil rights groups asserted that it accomplished these goals by restricting or altering numerous First Amendment freedoms. Nevertheless, under pressure to act quickly, Congress overwhelmingly approved the legislation. The only senator to vote against the act was Russell Feingold of Wisconsin.

DOCUMENT

. . . There have been periods in our nation's history when civil liberties have taken a back seat to what appeared at the time to be the legitimate exigencies of war. Our national consciousness still bears the stain and the scars of those events: The Alien and Sedition Acts, the suspension of habeas corpus during the Civil War, the internment of Japanese-Americans, German-Americans, and Italian-Americans during World War II, the blacklisting of supposed communist sympathizers during the McCarthy era, and the surveillance and harassment of antiwar protesters, including Dr. Martin Luther King Jr., during the Vietnam War. We must not allow these pieces of our past to become prologue. . . .

As it seeks to combat terrorism, the Justice Department is making extraordinary use of its power to arrest and detain individuals, jailing hundreds of people on immigration violations and arresting more than a dozen "material witnesses" not charged with any crime. Although the government has used these authorities before, it has not done so on such a broad scale. Judging from government announcements, the government has not brought any criminal charges related to the attacks with regard to the overwhelming majority of these detainees. . . .

Even as America addresses the demanding security challenges before us, we must strive mightily also to guard our values and basic rights. We must guard against racism and ethnic discrimination against people of Arab and South Asian origin and those who are Muslim.

We who don't have Arabic names or don't wear turbans or headscarves may not feel the weight of these times as much as Americans from the Middle East and South Asia do. But as the great jurist Learned Hand said in a speech in New York's Central

Park during World War II: "[T]he spirit of liberty is the spirit which seeks to understand the minds of other men and women; the spirit of liberty is the spirit which weighs their interests alongside its own without bias. . . ."

Was it not at least partially bias, however, when passengers on a Northwest Airlines flight in Minneapolis three weeks ago insisted that Northwest remove from the plane three Arab men who had cleared security?

Of course, given the enormous anxiety and fears generated by the events of September 11th, it would not have been difficult to anticipate some of these reactions, both by our government and some of our people. And, of course, there is no doubt that if we lived in a police state, it would be easier to catch terrorists. If we lived in a country that allowed the police to search your home at any time for any reason; if we lived in a country that allowed the government to open your mail, eavesdrop on your phone conversations, or intercept your email communications; if we lived in a country that allowed the government to hold people in jail indefinitely based on what they write or think, or based on mere suspicion that they are up to no good, then the government would no doubt discover and arrest more terrorists.

But that probably would not be a country in which we would want to live. That would not be a country for which we could, in good conscience, ask our young people to fight and die. In short, that would not be America.

Preserving our freedom is the reason that we are now engaged in this new war on terrorism. We will lose that war without firing a shot if we sacrifice the liberties of the American people. . . .

. . . Let me take a moment to discuss some of the shortcomings of the bill that we passed in the Senate very late Thursday night, by a vote of 96–1. And I guess you know by now who the "one" was.

First, the bill contains some very significant changes in criminal procedure that will apply to every federal criminal investigation in this country, not just those involving terrorism. One provision would greatly expand the circumstances in which law enforcement agencies can search homes and offices without notifying the owner prior to the search. The longstanding practice under the Fourth Amendment of serving a warrant prior to executing a search could be easily avoided in virtually every case because the government would simply have to show that it has "reasonable cause to believe" that providing notice "may" "seriously jeopardize an investigation." This is a significant infringement on personal liberty.

Notice is a key element of Fourth Amendment protections. It allows a person to point out mistakes in a warrant and make sure that a search is limited to the terms of a warrant. Just think about the possibility of the police showing up at your door with a warrant to search your house. You look at the warrant and say, "yes, that's my address, but the name on the warrant isn't me." And the police realize a mistake has been made and go away. If you're not home, and the police have received permission to do a "sneak and peak" search, they can come in your house, look around, and leave, and may never have to tell you.

Another very troubling provision has to do with the effort to combat computer crime. The bill allows law enforcement to monitor a computer with the permission of its owner or operator, without the need to get a warrant or show probable cause. That's fine in the case of a so called "denial of service attack" or plain old computer hacking. A computer owner should be able to give the police permission to monitor communications coming from what amounts to a trespasser on the computer.

As drafted in the Senate bill, however, the provision might permit an employer to give permission to the police to monitor the emails of an employee who has used her computer at work to shop for Christmas gifts. Or someone who uses a computer at a library or at school and happens to go to a gambling or pornography site in violation of the Internet use policies of the library or the university might also be subjected to government surveillance—without probable cause and without any time limit.

I am also very troubled by the broad expansion of government power under the Foreign Intelligence Surveillance Act, known as FISA. When Congress passed FISA in 1978 it granted to the executive branch the power to conduct surveillance in foreign intelligence investigations without meeting the rigorous probable cause standard under the Fourth Amendment that is required for criminal investigations. There is a lower threshold for obtaining a wiretap order from the FISA court because the FBI is not investigating a crime, it is investigating foreign intelligence activities. The law currently requires that intelligence gathering be the primary purpose of the investigation in order for this lower standard to apply.

The bill that passed the Senate last night changes that requirement. If it becomes law, and there is every reason to believe with a Senate vote of 96–1 that it will, the government will only have to show that intelligence is a "significant purpose" of the investigation. Even if the *primary* purpose is a criminal investigation, the heightened protections of the Fourth Amendment won't apply.

It seems obvious that with this lower standard, the FBI will try to use FISA as much as it can. And of course, with terrorism investigations that won't be difficult because the terrorists are apparently sponsored or at least supported by foreign governments.

But the significance of the breakdown of the distinction between intelligence and criminal investigations becomes apparent when you see the other expansions of government power under FISA in this bill. One provision that troubles me a great deal is a provision that permits the government under FISA to compel the production of records from any business regarding any person if that information is sought in connection with an investigation of terrorism or espionage.

Now we're not talking here about travel records pertaining to a terrorist suspect, which we all can see can be highly relevant to an investigation of a terrorist plot. FISA already gives the FBI the power to get airline, train, hotel, car rental and other records of a suspect.

But under the Senate bill, the government can compel the disclosure of anyone—perhaps someone who worked with, or lived next door to, or went to school with, or sat on an airplane with, or has been seen in the company of, or whose phone number was called by the target of the investigation.

And under this new provisions *all* business records can be compelled, including those containing sensitive personal information like medical records from hospitals or doctors, or educational records, or records of what books someone has taken out of the library. This is an enormous expansion of authority, under a law that provides only minimal judicial supervision.

Under this provision, the government can apparently go on a fishing expedition and collect information on virtually anyone. All it has to allege in order to get an order for these records from the court is that the information is sought for an investigation of international terrorism or clandestine intelligence gathering. That's it. On that minimal showing in an ex parte application to a secret court, with no showing even that the information is *relevant* to the investigation, the government can lawfully compel a doctor or hospital to release medical records, or a library to release circulation records. This is a truly breathtaking expansion of police power. . . .

Let me turn to a final area of real concern about this legislation because I think it brings us full circle to the cautions I expressed on the day after the attacks. There are two very troubling provisions dealing with our immigration laws in this bill.

First, the Administration's original proposal would have granted the Attorney General extraordinary powers to detain immigrants indefinitely, including legal permanent residents. . . .

The second provision in the bill that deeply troubles me allows the detention and deportation of people engaging in innocent associational activity. But the Senate bill would allow for the detention and deportation of individuals who provide lawful assistance to groups that are not even designated by the Secretary of State as terrorist organizations, but instead have engaged in vaguely defined "terrorist activity" sometime in the past. To avoid deportation, the immigrant is required to prove a negative: that he or she did not know, and should not have known, that the assistance would further terrorist activity.

This language creates a very real risk that truly innocent individuals could be deported for innocent associations with humanitarian or political groups that the government later chooses to regard as terrorist organizations. Groups that might fit this definition could include Operation Rescue, Greenpeace, and even the Northern Alliance fighting the Taliban in northern Afghanistan. This provision amounts to "guilt by association," which I believe violates the First Amendment.

And speaking of the First Amendment, under this bill, a lawful permanent resident who makes a controversial speech that the government deems to be supportive of terrorism might be barred from returning to his or her family after taking a trip abroad. . . .

We must grant law enforcement the tools that it needs to stop this terrible threat. But we must give them only those extraordinary tools that they need and that relate specifically to the task at hand. . . .

Protecting the safety of the American people is a solemn duty of the Congress; we must work tirelessly to prevent more tragedies like the devastating attacks of September 11th. We must prevent more children from losing their mothers, more wives from losing their husbands, and more firefighters from losing their brave and heroic colleagues. But the Congress will fulfill its duty only when it protects *both* the American people and the freedoms at the foundation of American society. So let us preserve our heritage of basic rights. Let us practice that liberty. And let us fight to maintain that freedom that we call America.

SOURCE: Feingold, Russell. "On Opposing the U.S.A. PATRIOT Act." Address given to the *Associated Press* Managing Editors Conference in Milwaukee, WI. October 12, 2001. http://www.archipelago.org/vol6-2/feingold.htm

- ***Document:*** Testimony of Attorney General John Ashcroft to the Senate Committee on the Judiciary on the PATRIOT Act
- ***Date:*** December 6, 2001
- ***Where:*** Washington, DC
- ***Significance:*** In an effort to bolster support for the U.S.A. PATRIOT Act and the administration's policies after 9/11, Attorney General John Ashcroft testified before a Senate Committee that Americans who criticize or question PATRIOT Act policies actually aid the efforts of terrorists.

DOCUMENT

Testimony of Attorney General John Ashcroft

Senate Committee on the Judiciary

(NOTE: THE ATTORNEY GENERAL OFTEN DEVIATES FROM PREPARED REMARKS)

December 6, 2001

. . . On the morning of September 11, as the United States came under attack, I was in an airplane with several members of the Justice Department en route to Milwaukee, in the skies over the Great Lakes. By the time we could return to Washington, thousands of people had been murdered at the World Trade Center. 189 were dead at the Pentagon. Forty-four had crashed to the ground in Pennsylvania. From that moment, at the command of the President of the United States, I began to mobilize the resources of the Department of Justice toward one single, over-arching and over-riding objective: to save innocent lives from further acts of terrorism.

America's campaign to save innocent lives from terrorists is now 87 days old. It has brought me back to this committee to report to you in accordance with Congress's oversight role. I welcome this opportunity to clarify for you and the American people how the Justice Department is working to protect American lives while preserving American liberties.

Since those first terrible hours of September 11, America has faced a choice that is as stark as the images that linger of that morning. One option is to call September 11 a fluke, to believe it could never happen again, and to live in a dream world that requires us to do nothing differently. The other option is to fight back, to summon all our strength and all our resources and devote ourselves to better ways to identify, disrupt and dismantle terrorist networks.

Under the leadership of President Bush, America has made the choice to fight terrorism—not just for ourselves but for all civilized people. Since September 11, through dozens of warnings to law enforcement, a deliberate campaign of terrorist disruption, tighter security around potential targets, and a preventative campaign of arrest and detention of lawbreakers, America has grown stronger—and safer—in the face of terrorism. . . .

The terrorist enemy that threatens civilization today is unlike any we have ever known. It slaughters thousands of innocents—a crime of war and a crime against humanity. It seeks weapons of mass destruction and threatens their use against America. No one should doubt the intent, nor the depth, of its consuming, destructive hatred.

Terrorist operatives infiltrate our communities—plotting, planning and waiting to kill again. They enjoy the benefits of our free society even as they commit themselves to our destruction. They exploit our openness—not randomly or haphazardly—but by deliberate, premeditated design.

This is a seized al Qaeda training manual—a "how-to" guide for terrorists—that instructs enemy operatives in the art of killing in a free society. Prosecutors first made this manual public in the trial of the al Qaeda terrorists who bombed U.S. embassies in Africa. We are posting several al Qaeda lessons from this manual on our website today so Americans can know our enemy.

In this manual, al Qaeda terrorists are told how to use America's freedom as a weapon against us. They are instructed to use the benefits of a free press—newspapers, magazines and broadcasts—to stalk and kill their victims. They are instructed to exploit our judicial process for the success of their operations. Captured terrorists are taught to anticipate a series of questions from authorities and, in each response, to lie—to lie about who they are, to lie about what they are doing and to lie about who they know in order for the operation to achieve its objective. Imprisoned terrorists are instructed to concoct stories of torture and mistreatment at the hands of our officials. They are directed to take advantage of any contact with the outside world to, quote, "communicate with brothers outside prison and exchange information that may be helpful to them in their work. The importance of mastering the art of hiding messages is self-evident here."

Mr. Chairman and members of the committee, we are at war with an enemy who abuses individual rights as it abuses jet airliners: as weapons with which to kill Americans. We have responded by redefining the mission of the Department of Justice. Defending our nation and its citizens against terrorist attacks is now our first and overriding priority.

We have launched the largest, most comprehensive criminal investigation in world history to identify the killers of September 11 and to prevent further terrorist attacks. Four thousand FBI agents are engaged with their international counterparts in an unprecedented worldwide effort to detect, disrupt and dismantle terrorist organizations. . . .

We have sought and received additional tools from Congress. Already, we have begun to utilize many of these tools. Within hours of passage of the USA PATRIOT Act, we made use of its provisions to begin enhanced information sharing between the law-enforcement and intelligence communities. We have used the provisions allowing nationwide search warrants for e-mail and subpoenas for payment information. And we have used the Act to place those who access the Internet through cable companies on the same footing as everyone else.

Just yesterday, at my request, the State Department designated 39 entities as terrorist organizations pursuant to the USA PATRIOT Act.

We have waged a deliberate campaign of arrest and detention to remove suspected terrorists who violate the law from our streets. Currently, we have brought criminal charges against 110 individuals, of whom 60 are in federal custody. The INS has detained 563 individuals on immigration violations.

We have investigated more than 250 incidents of retaliatory violence and threats against Arab Americans, Muslim Americans, Sikh Americans and South Asian Americans. . . .

. . . The Department of Justice has sought to prevent terrorism with reason, careful balance and excruciating attention to detail. Some of our critics, I regret to say, have shown less affection for detail. Their bold declarations of so-called fact have quickly dissolved, upon inspection, into vague conjecture. Charges of "kangaroo courts" and "shredding the Constitution" give new meaning to the term, "the fog of war."

Since lives and liberties depend upon clarity, not obfuscation, and reason, not hyperbole, let me take this opportunity today to be clear: Each action taken by the Department of Justice, as well as the war crimes commissions considered by the President and the Department of Defense, is carefully drawn to target a narrow class of individuals—terrorists. Our legal powers are targeted at terrorists. Our investigation is focused on terrorists. Our prevention strategy targets the terrorist threat. . . .

We need honest, reasoned debate; not fearmongering. To those who pit Americans against immigrants, and citizens against non-citizens; to those who scare peace-loving people with phantoms of lost liberty; my message is this: Your tactics only aid terrorists—for they erode our national unity and diminish our resolve. They give ammunition to America's enemies, and pause to America's friends. They encourage people of good will to remain silent in the face of evil.

Our efforts have been carefully crafted to avoid infringing on constitutional rights while saving American lives. We have engaged in a deliberate campaign of arrest and detention of law breakers. All persons being detained have the right to contact their lawyers and their families. Out of respect for their privacy, and concern for saving lives, we will not publicize the names of those detained.

We have the authority to monitor the conversations of 16 of the 158,000 federal inmates and their attorneys because we suspect that these communications are facilitating acts of terrorism. Each prisoner has been told in advance his conversations will be monitored. None of the information that is protected by attorney-client privilege may be used for prosecution. Information will only be used to stop impending terrorist acts and save American lives.

We have asked a very limited number of individuals—visitors to our country holding passports from countries with active Al Qaeda operations—to speak voluntarily to law enforcement. We are forcing them to do nothing. We are merely asking them to do the right thing: to willingly disclose information they may have of terrorist threats to the lives and safety of all people in the United States.

Throughout all our activities since September 11, we have kept Congress informed of our continuing efforts to protect the American people. Beginning with a classified briefing by Director Mueller and me on the very evening of September 11, the Justice Department has briefed members of the House, the Senate and their staffs on more than 100 occasions. . . .

The advice I give to the President, whether in his role as Commander-in-Chief or in any other capacity, is privileged and confidential. I cannot and will not divulge the contents, the context, or even the existence of such advice to anyone—including Congress—unless the President instructs me to do so. I cannot and will not divulge information, nor do I believe that anyone here would wish me to divulge information, that will damage the national security of the United States, the safety of its citizens or our efforts to ensure the same in an ongoing investigation.

As Attorney General, it is my responsibility—at the direction of the President—to exercise those core executive powers the Constitution so designates. The law enforcement initiatives undertaken by the Department of Justice, those individuals we arrest, detain or seek to interview, fall under these core executive powers. In addition, the President's authority to establish war-crimes commissions arises out of his power as Commander in Chief. For centuries, Congress has recognized this authority and the Supreme Court has never held that any Congress may limit it.

In accordance with over two hundred years of historical and legal precedent, the executive branch is now exercising its core Constitutional powers in the interest of saving the lives of Americans. I trust that Congress will respect the proper limits of Executive Branch consultation that I am duty-bound to uphold. I trust, as well, that Congress will respect this President's authority to wage war on terrorism and defend our nation and its citizens with all the power vested in him by the Constitution and entrusted to him by the American people.

SOURCE: U.S. Congress, Senate, Committee on the Judiciary. *Testimony of Attorney General John Ashcroft.* 107th Cong., December 6, 2001. https://www.justice.gov/archive/ag/testimony/2001/1206transcriptsenatejudiciarycommittee.htm

ANALYSIS

The September 11, 2001, terrorist attacks on U.S. soil forever changed the soul of America. Coordinated assaults orchestrated by al-Qaeda leader Osama bin Laden claimed 2,977 innocent lives, stripped the country of its relative sense of safety and security, and crushed the long-held belief that the United States could isolate itself from foreign disputes and threats.

But the damage inflicted upon America did not end on 9/11. In the aftermath of the terrorist attacks, the U.S. government restricted or abolished numerous personal freedoms in an effort to strengthen national security and prevent further attacks. That shift toward an erosion of certain civil liberties reshaped the country's character and sense of identity in many ways over the next two decades.

Americans were caught off guard by the events of September 11. By hijacking and intentionally crashing four large airplanes, suicide bombers from the Middle East and Egypt had carried out the deadliest foreign attack ever on U.S. soil. The death toll was even higher than the number of fatalities from the Japanese attack on Pearl Harbor during WWII. The 9/11 attacks produced unprecedented physical and emotional devastation among the American people. In addition, an ever-present fear of additional threats fueled a widespread sense of vulnerability and helplessness among Americans now caught up in a war with an unknown enemy.

Then, just weeks after the September 11 atrocities, the country watched in horror as another crisis unfolded. An unknown individual unleashed biological warfare on an already grief-stricken country by sending anthrax-laced letters to major media corporations and prominent members of Congress. In total, seventeen individuals who came into contact with contaminated letters fell ill, and five more died. These biological attacks exacerbated the nation's sense of panic.

Americans wanted evidence that the U.S. government was vigorously working to protect the country from additional harm. Therefore, when the Uniting and

Strengthening America by Providing Appropriate Tools Required to Intercept and Obstruct Terrorism Act (the USA PATRIOT Act) was proposed in Congress, the 342-page legislation was passed quickly by overwhelming majorities in the House and Senate. Attorney General John Ashcroft had urged Congress to pass the new law without delay, testifying on September 24 that "The American people do not have the luxury of unlimited time in erecting the necessary defenses to future terrorist acts." In spite of the fact that there had been no public debate of the bill, a sense of urgency among lawmakers prevailed; in the Senate, only one "no" vote was cast. The PATRIOT Act was signed into law by President George W. Bush on October 26, 2001, forty-five days after the 9/11 attacks.

Many provisions of the PATRIOT Act were designed to update or modify existing laws to enhance national security. For example, the act updated electronic surveillance regulations written before the widespread use of computers and the development of the internet. It also strengthened airport security practices, mandated rigorous oversight of potential biological/chemical weapons, increased intelligence-sharing among government agencies, and fortified money laundering laws to prevent funds from reaching terrorist organizations.

Although these measures offered a worried nation a stronger sense of collective security, civil libertarians contended that many of the PATRIOT Act's other provisions constituted a direct assault on individual liberties. The act, they said, destroyed checks and balances by giving government and law enforcement excessive investigative authority and permission to use covert methods of obtaining information.

Critics also cited other specific concerns with the new law, including: expanded government surveillance powers, expanded ability to conduct secret searches, unprecedented intelligence-sharing, weakened privacy protections, increased capacity to deport noncitizens without due process, potentially broad interpretations regarding the new federal crime of "domestic terrorism," mandatory detention of suspected terrorists, inflated executive powers, and weakened judicial oversight of many PATRIOT Act provisions.

Concerns about the act, however, were largely drowned out by the patriotic fervor that erupted after 9/11. Initially, a spirit of solidarity arose among citizens around the world, united against the common enemy of terrorism. In the United States, this initial sense of unity morphed into an extreme nationalism that pervaded everyday life, from the ubiquitous display of American flags to the serving of "freedom fries" and "freedom toast." In November, President Bush called on foreign nations for support, saying, "[Y]ou're either with us or you're against us in the fight against terror." Many Americans, however, regarded his message as a domestic warning as well. Consequently, they viewed any disapproval of government policy as disloyalty. A fissure began to grow between supporters of the Bush administration and individuals who dared question administrative methods used to fight the war on terror.

Attorney General John Ashcroft cultivated patriotism by encouraging Americans to set aside personal liberties for the sake of national security. In his testimony to the Senate Committee on the Judiciary in December 2001, Ashcroft underscored the need for expanded government powers to secure the nation. He stated, "[T]o those who scare peace-loving people with phantoms of lost liberty; my message is this: Your tactics only aid terrorists—for they erode our national unity and diminish our resolve. They give ammunition to America's enemies, and pause to America's friends."

Ashcroft's statement caused an outcry among Americans who saw it as a justification for stifling dissent. His implication that disagreement with federal policies was akin to aiding the enemy was interpreted by many as a major threat to freedom of speech. Questioning policy was necessary, they said, to exposing the secretive nature of "anti-terrorism" policies that allowed the administration to operate with nearly unchecked power.

But a new dynamic had come into play in the post-9/11 U.S. landscape. The number of hate crimes against foreign nationals grew, and anti-Muslim sentiment was widespread. Acts of violence against innocent foreigners increased. Such acts were largely condemned, but fear of the unknown and unfamiliar perpetuated a sense of "othering" that made minorities the target of bigotry in many communities.

The gap between supporters and critics of Bush administration policies widened as the war on terror continued for months, and then years. Americans who supported expanded government power over civil liberties often believed the drastic measures were necessary for the country's safety and stability. They saw no room for doubt or opposition, and the administration affirmed their singular commitment. The resulting pushback against "anti-American" sentiment muffled legitimate conversation about potential overreach of government power; those who questioned the legitimacy of government policies were labeled "soft" on terrorism or unpatriotic.

Numerous lawsuits challenging the legitimacy of the PATRIOT Act have been filed since its passage in 2001. Some provisions of the act have been ruled unconstitutional, while others were upheld. Congress has periodically reviewed the act, allowing the "sunsetting" process to eliminate some portions of the law while rewriting and reauthorizing others. In 2015 a reformed, retitled PATRIOT Act (now called "The USA Freedom Act") was signed into law by President Obama.

FURTHER READING

Abdolian, Lisa Finnegan, and Harold Takooshian. "The USA Patriot Act: Civil Liberties, the Media, and Public Opinion." *Fordham Urban Law Journal* 30, no. 4 (2002): 1429.

Doyle, Charles. "The USA PATRIOT Act: A Legal Analysis." Library of Congress. Washington, DC: Congressional Research Service, 2002. https://apps.dtic.mil/dtic/tr/fulltext/u2/a467389.pdf

Evans, Jennifer C. "Hijacking Civil Liberties: The USA Patriot Act of 2001." *Loyola University Chicago Law Journal* 33, no. 4 (2002): 933.

Lind, Dara. "Everyone's Heard of the Patriot Act. Here's What It Actually Does." *Vox*, June 2, 2015. https://www.vox.com/2015/6/2/8701499/patriot-act-explain

Raab, Christopher P. "Fighting Terrorism in an Electronic Age: Does the Patriot Act Unduly Compromise Our Civil Liberties?" *Duke Law & Technology Review* 4, no. 1 (2006): 1–21.

U.S. Department of State Archive. "The Global War on Terrorism: The First 100 Days." Information released online from January 20, 2001, to January 20, 2009. https://2001-2009.state.gov/s/ct/rls/wh/6947.htm

- ***Document 40:*** Editorial Cartoon by Ann Telnaes Titled *Adulterer?*
- ***Date:*** December 12, 2001
- ***Where:*** United States
- ***Significance:*** This editorial cartoon depicts two Puritan women, one of whom wears an "A" on her chest. When asked if she wears the letter because she was accused of adultery, she responds, "Anti-American. I questioned the Administration's policies." The labeled woman in the cartoon represents the sentiment of Americans who felt unable to speak critically of the government after 9/11 because of negative social and political repercussions that would ensue.

DOCUMENT

SOURCE: Telnaes, Ann, Artist, and Nathaniel Hawthorne. *Adulterer?/Ann Telnaes.* United States, 2001. Photograph. Library of Congress. Reprinted with permission of the artist.

ANALYSIS

The terrorist attacks of September 11, 2001, were a source of unimagined pain for the United States. Never before had the country faced attacks from foreigners on its own soil, and never before had so many American civilians been killed in such an unthinkable manner—not by traditional bombs or firearms, but through the hijacking and subsequent detonation of passenger-filled airplanes.

The attacks on 9/11 stunned the entire world, which was quick to offer displays of support and solidarity. Americans also turned to one another for strength, comfort, and a sense of unity. The weeks following the attack were marked by record blood donations, candlelight vigils promoting a spirit of hope and unity, prolific public displays of American flags, and donations collected for victims' families and rescue workers. A strong sense of national identity was born from the heinous attacks, and patriotism swelled as a nation searched deeply within itself for both resolution and healing.

The government's response to 9/11 was swift and far-reaching. One week after the attacks, Congress passed the Authorization for Use of Military Force (AUMF) bill, which gave the president authority to respond to the terrorist attacks with military force. Within a month, Congress had also approved the Uniting and Strengthening America by Providing Appropriate Tools Required to Intercept and Obstruct Terrorism Act (USA-PATRIOT Act). The PATRIOT Act gave federal law enforcement and government agencies expanded search and surveillance powers that would better enable them to strengthen national security. However, many of the law's provisions, such as allowing authorities to spy on citizens and search homes without a warrant, ignited concerns about erosion of civil liberties and privacy. Courts eventually ruled specific aspects of the law illegal.

Nevertheless, the Bush administration's "War on Terror" offered a sense of protection to the American people. The president initiated numerous policies and directives to fortify national security, including creation of the Department of Homeland Security (DHS), development of various military and intelligence measures, and (unbeknown to most) formation of a highly secretive "terrorism industrial complex" in which more than 850,000 individuals were granted "top secret" security clearance (Priest & Arkin 2013). The combination of patriotic fervor, desire for national unity, and a need for protection offered an ideal context for public support of expanded government surveillance and authority. His decision to invade Afghanistan and, later, declare war on Iraq, also initially enjoyed broad popular support from the American public.

However, the country's security-driven, hyperpatriotic environment also made it difficult for individuals to speak out when they disagreed with the direction of the government's response. Widespread popular support of federal strategies bolstered an underlying sentiment that any form of questioning or dissent was unpatriotic, even Anti-American. The president reinforced this notion. In a joint session of Congress, President Bush made a global appeal for support, saying to foreign leaders, "Either you are with us, or you are with the terrorists" (2011). That dichotomy was often repeated in his addresses to the American people and to foreign leaders. The president's declaration left no room for doubt or reflection, but instead demanded support and unwavering trust in the decisions of American leadership.

What emerged from this context was a form of self-censorship that stifled opposition voices, even from within Congress. For example, the AUMF bill authorizing use of military force was passed unanimously in the Senate and with only one "no" vote in the House. Lone dissenter Rep. Barbara Lee later told reporters that other legislators had indicated they shared her concerns about giving the president a blank check for use of military force but feared the repercussions of standing up to the Bush administration (Snow & Taylor 2006).

Post 9/11 censorship found its way into social expression as well. For a time, the entertainment industry modified television and movie projects to remove images of the Twin Towers; the National Football League issued an advisory asking announcers not use words like "blitz," "bomb," or "draft" in their descriptions of plays; Gary Trudeau self-censored by withholding a series of previously completed Doonesbury cartoons critical of the president; and major U.S. television networks willingly agreed to self-censor images or videos of known terrorists at the request of U.S. National Security Advisor Condoleezza Rice (Mitchell 2003).

Media and music industries also self-censored in an attempt to avoid inflammatory images or references to the events of 9/11. Within days of the attacks, a program director for Clear Channel Radio sent its member stations nationwide a list of 150 "questionable" or possibly "inappropriate" songs that stations were encouraged to pull from airplay (Garofalo 2013). The extensive list included all songs by Rage against the Machine, John Lenin's "Imagine," and Metallica's "Seek and Destroy" (ibid). Civil libertarians quickly denounced the list as an attack against freedom of expression.

But patriotic-driven censorship was a powerful force, particularly for those who spoke out against post-9/11 policies. Even popular bands were not immune.

In 2003, on the eve of the U.S. invasion of Iraq, Dixie Chicks band member Natalie Maines told an audience in London, "Just so you know, we're on the good side with y'all. We do not want this war, this violence. And we're ashamed the President of the United States is from Texas." The backlash was almost immediate. Country radio stations stopped playing the band's songs, radio giant Cumulus banned their music from 250 of its stations, concertgoers boycotted the group's American tour, and protesters publicly destroyed their albums.

Numerous lawmakers pushed back against censorship of the band, saying the growth of corporate media conglomerates enabled large broadcasting networks to set the public agenda. Senator John McCain testified at a Senate Commerce Committee hearing, "If someone else offends you, and you decide to censor those people, my friend, the erosion of our First Amendment is in progress" (Sanders 2003).

In spite of the public furor surrounding Maines's political statement, the Dixie Chicks stood by their principles and went on to win numerous awards for their music, including GRAMMYS in 2006 for both an album and a single that addressed the retaliation they experienced for expressing their political views.

Nearly twenty years after 9/11, socially driven free speech challenges remain, although they are not exclusively based on national security concerns. Instead, political polarization and racial strife, reinforced greatly through social media, have impaired the nation's ability to overcome major challenges through free exchange of ideas and civil dialogue.

FURTHER READING

American Civil Liberties Union. "Freedom under Fire: Dissent in Post-9/11 America." ACLU. May 2003. https://www.aclu.org/files/FilesPDFs/dissent_report.pdf

Cooper, Gloria. "The Censors: New Patterns in Opinion Control." *Columbia Journalism Review* 43, no. 2 (2004): 58–60.

Garofalo, Reebee. "Pop Goes to War, 2001–2004: US Popular Music after 9/11." In *Music in the Post-9/11 World*. Hoboken, NJ: Taylor and Francis, 2013: 3–26. http://www.123library.org/book_details/?id=113539

Marlette, Doug. "Freedom of Speech and the Editorial Cartoon." *Nieman Reports*. Winter 2004. https://niemanreports.org/articles/freedom-of-speech-and-the-editorial-cartoon/

Moftah, Lora. "Charlie Hebdo Cartoons: Political Cartoonists Debate Free Speech after Attack." *International Business Times*, January 8, 2015. https://www.ibtimes.com/charlie-hebdo-cartoons-political-cartoonists-debate-free-speech-after-attack-1778040

Priest, Dana, and William M. Arkin. *Top Secret America: The Rise of the New American Security State*. New York: Little, Brown and Company, 2013.

- ***Document 41:*** *Ashcroft v. Free Speech Coalition* Supreme Court Decision
- ***Date:*** Decided April 16, 2002
- ***Where:*** Supreme Court of the United States
- ***Significance:*** The history of online child pornography legislation in the United States was largely shaped by Supreme Court decisions like *Ashcroft v. Free Speech Coalition*. Many laws designed to protect children, like the Child Pornography Prevention Act at issue in this case, were struck down for being overbroad and unconstitutional. As Congress addressed potential dangers accompanying the development of the internet, lawmakers sought to maintain the delicate balance between protecting children from online harm and preserving First Amendment speech protections. Over the past forty years, that challenge has been met through the enactment of laws outlawing child pornography and establishment of the internet as a domain deserving of First Amendment protections.

DOCUMENT

JUSTICE KENNEDY delivered the opinion of the Court

We consider in this case whether the Child Pornography Prevention Act of 1996 (CPPA), 18 U. S. C. § 2251 *et seq.*, abridges the freedom of speech. The CPPA extends the federal prohibition against child pornography to sexually explicit images that appear to depict minors but were produced without using any real children. The statute prohibits, in specific circumstances, possessing or distributing these images, which may be created by using adults who look like minors or by using computer imaging. The new technology, according to Congress, makes it possible to create realistic images of children who do not exist. . . .

By prohibiting child pornography that does not depict an actual child, the statute goes beyond *New York v. Ferber,* which distinguished child pornography from other sexually explicit speech because of the State's interest in protecting the children exploited by the production process. As a general rule, pornography can be banned only if obscene, but under *Ferber,* pornography showing minors can be proscribed whether or not the images are obscene under the definition set forth in *Miller* v. *California*. *Ferber* recognized that "[t]he *Miller* standard, like all general definitions of what may be banned as obscene, does not reflect the State's particular and more compelling interest in prosecuting those who promote the sexual exploitation of children."

While we have not had occasion to consider the question, we may assume that the apparent age of persons engaged in sexual conduct is relevant to whether a depiction offends community standards. Pictures of young children engaged in certain acts might be obscene where similar depictions of adults, or perhaps even older adolescents, would not. The CPPA, however, is not directed at speech that is obscene; Congress has proscribed those materials through a separate statute. Like the law in *Ferber,* the CPPA seeks to reach beyond obscenity, and it makes no attempt to conform to the *Miller* standard. For instance, the statute would reach visual depictions, such as movies, even if they have redeeming social value.

The principal question to be resolved, then, is whether the CPPA is constitutional where it proscribes a significant universe of speech that is neither obscene under *Miller* nor child pornography under *Ferber*.

I

Before 1996, Congress defined child pornography as the type of depictions at issue in *Ferber,* images made using actual minors. The CPPA retains that prohibition . . . and adds three other prohibited categories of speech, of which the first, and the third, are at issue in this case. Section 2256(8)(B) prohibits "any visual depiction, including any photograph, film, video, picture, or computer or computer-generated image or picture," that "is, or appears to be, of a minor engaging in sexually explicit conduct." The prohibition on "any visual depiction" does not depend at all on how the image is produced. The section captures a range of depictions, sometimes called "virtual child pornography," which include computer-generated images, as well as images produced by more traditional means. For instance, the literal terms of the statute embrace a Renaissance painting depicting a scene from classical mythology, a "picture" that "appears to be, of a minor engaging in sexually explicit conduct." The statute also prohibits Hollywood movies, filmed without any child actors, if a jury believes an actor "appears to be" a minor engaging in "actual or simulated . . . sexual intercourse."

These images do not involve, let alone harm, any children in the production process; but Congress decided the materials threaten children in other, less direct, ways. Pedophiles might use the materials to encourage children to participate in sexual activity. . . . Furthermore, pedophiles might "whet their own sexual appetites" with the pornographic images, "thereby increasing the creation and distribution of child pornography and the sexual abuse and exploitation of actual children." Under these rationales, harm flows from the content of the images, not from the means of their production. In addition, Congress identified another problem created by computer-generated images: Their existence can make it harder to prosecute pornographers who do use real minors. As imaging technology improves, Congress found, it becomes more difficult to prove that a particular picture was produced using actual children. To ensure that defendants possessing child pornography using real minors cannot evade prosecution, Congress extended the ban to virtual child pornography. . . .

Respondents do challenge § 2256(8)(D). Like the text of the "appears to be" provision, the sweep of this provision is quite broad. Section 2256(8)(D) defines child pornography to include any sexually explicit image that was "advertised, promoted, presented, described, or distributed in such a manner that conveys the impression" it depicts "a minor engaging in sexually explicit conduct." One Committee Report identified the provision as directed at sexually explicit images pandered as child pornography . . . The statute is not so limited in its reach, however, as it punishes even those possessors who took no part in pandering. Once a work has been described as child pornography, the taint remains on the speech in the hands of subsequent possessors, making possession unlawful even though the content otherwise would not be objectionable.

Fearing that the CPPA threatened the activities of its members, respondent Free Speech Coalition and others challenged the statute in the United States District Court for the Northern District of California. The Coalition, a California trade association for the adult-entertainment industry, alleged that its members did not use minors in their sexually explicit works, but they believed some of these materials might fall within the CPPA's expanded definition of child pornography. The other respondents are Bold Type, Inc., the publisher of a book advocating the nudist lifestyle; Jim Gingerich, a painter of nudes; and Ron Raffaelli, a photographer specializing in erotic images. Respondents alleged that the "appears to be" and "conveys the impression" provisions are overbroad and vague, chilling them from producing works protected by the First Amendment. The District Court disagreed and granted summary judgment to the Government. The court dismissed the overbreadth claim because it was "highly unlikely" that any "adaptations of sexual works like 'Romeo and Juliet,' . . . will be treated as 'criminal contraband.'" . . .

II

The First Amendment commands, "Congress shall make no law . . . abridging the freedom of speech." The government may violate this mandate in many ways, but a law imposing criminal penalties on protected speech is a stark example of speech suppression. The CPPA's penalties are indeed severe. A first offender may be imprisoned for 15 years. A repeat offender faces a prison sentence of not less than

5 years and not more than 30 years in prison. While even minor punishments can chill protected speech, this case provides a textbook example of why we permit facial challenges to statutes that burden expression. With these severe penalties in force, few legitimate movie producers or book publishers, or few other speakers in any capacity, would risk distributing images in or near the uncertain reach of this law. The Constitution gives significant protection from overbroad laws that chill speech within the First Amendment's vast and privileged sphere. Under this principle, the CPPA is unconstitutional on its face if it prohibits a substantial amount of protected expression. . . .

Congress may pass valid laws to protect children from abuse, and it has. The prospect of crime, however, by itself does not justify laws suppressing protected speech. . . . It is also well established that speech may not be prohibited because it concerns subjects offending our sensibilities. . . .

As a general principle, the First Amendment bars the government from dictating what we see or read or speak or hear. The freedom of speech has its limits; it does not embrace certain categories of speech, including defamation, incitement, obscenity, and pornography produced with real children. While these categories may be prohibited without violating the First Amendment, none of them includes the speech prohibited by the CPPA. In his dissent from the opinion of the Court of Appeals, Judge Ferguson recognized this to be the law and proposed that virtual child pornography should be regarded as an additional category of unprotected speech. It would be necessary for us to take this step to uphold the statute.

As we have noted, the CPPA is much more than a supplement to the existing federal prohibition on obscenity. Under *Miller* v. *California* the Government must prove that the work, taken as a whole, appeals to the prurient interest, is patently offensive in light of community standards, and lacks serious literary, artistic, political, or scientific value. The CPPA, however, extends to images that appear to depict a minor engaging in sexually explicit activity without regard to the *Miller* requirements. The materials need not appeal to the prurient interest. Any depiction of sexually explicit activity, no matter how it is presented, is proscribed. The CPPA applies to a picture in a psychology manual, as well as a movie depicting the horrors of sexual abuse. It is not necessary, moreover, that the image be patently offensive. Pictures of what appear to be 17-year-olds engaging in sexually explicit activity do not in every case contravene community standards.

The CPPA prohibits speech despite its serious literary, artistic, political, or scientific value. The statute proscribes the visual depiction of an idea—that of teenagers engaging in sexual activity—that is a fact of modern society and has been a theme in art and literature throughout the ages. Under the CPPA, images are prohibited so long as the persons appear to be under 18 years of age. This is higher than the legal age for marriage in many States, as well as the age at which persons may consent to sexual relations. It is, of course, undeniable that some youths engage in sexual activity before the legal age, either on their own inclination or because they are victims of sexual abuse. . . .

Our society, like other cultures, has empathy and enduring fascination with the lives and destinies of the young. Art and literature express the vital interest we all have in the formative years we ourselves once knew, when wounds can be so grievous, disappointment so profound, and mistaken choices so tragic, but when moral acts and self-fulfillment are still in reach. Whether or not the films we mention violate the CPPA, they explore themes within the wide sweep of the statute's prohibitions. If these films, or hundreds of others of lesser note that explore those subjects, contain a single graphic depiction of sexual activity within the statutory definition, the possessor of the film would be subject to severe punishment without inquiry into the work's redeeming value. This is inconsistent with an essential First Amendment rule: The artistic merit of a work does not depend on the presence of a single explicit scene. Under *Miller,* the First Amendment requires that redeeming value be judged by considering the work as a whole. . . .

In contrast to the speech in *Ferber,* speech that itself is the record of sexual abuse, the CPPA prohibits speech that records no crime and creates no victims by its production. Virtual child pornography is not "intrinsically related" to the sexual abuse of children, as were the materials in *Ferber.* While the Government asserts that the images can lead to actual instances of child abuse, the causal link is contingent and indirect. The harm does not necessarily follow from the speech, but depends upon some unquantified potential for subsequent criminal acts. . . .

IV

Respondents challenge § 2256(8)(D) as well. This provision bans depictions of sexually explicit conduct that are "advertised, promoted, presented, described, or distributed in such a manner that conveys the impression that the material is or contains a visual depiction of a minor engaging in sexually explicit conduct." The parties treat the section as nearly identical to the provision prohibiting materials that appear to be child pornography. In the Government's view, the difference between the two is that "the 'conveys the impression' provision requires the jury to assess the material at issue in light of the manner in which it is promoted." The Government's assumption, however, is that the determination would still depend principally upon the content of the prohibited work.

We disagree with this view. The CPPA prohibits sexually explicit materials that "conve[y] the impression" they depict minors. While that phrase may sound like the "appears to be" prohibition in § 2256(8)(B), it requires little judgment about the content of the image. Under § 2256(8)(D), the work must be sexually explicit, but otherwise the content is irrelevant. Even if a film contains no sexually explicit scenes involving minors, it could be treated as child pornography if the title and trailers convey the impression that the scenes would be found in the movie. The determination turns on how the speech is presented, not on what is depicted. While the legislative findings address at length the problems posed by materials that look like child pornography, they are silent on the evils posed by images simply pandered that way. . . .

Section 2256(8)(D), however, prohibits a substantial amount of speech that falls outside *Ginzburg's* rationale. Materials falling within the proscription are tainted and unlawful in the hands of all who receive it, though they bear no responsibility for how it was marketed, sold, or described. The statute, furthermore, does not require that the context be part of an effort at "commercial exploitation." As a consequence, the CPPA does more than prohibit pandering. It prohibits possession of material described, or pandered, as child pornography by someone earlier in the distribution chain. The provision prohibits a sexually explicit film containing no youthful actors, just because it is placed in a box suggesting a prohibited movie. Possession is a crime even when the possessor knows the movie was mislabeled. The First Amendment requires a more precise restriction. For this reason, § 2256(8)(D) is substantially overbroad and in violation of the First Amendment.

V

For the reasons we have set forth, the prohibitions of §§2256(8)(B) and 2256(8)(D) are overbroad and unconstitutional. Having reached this conclusion, we need not address respondents' further contention that the provisions are unconstitutional because of vague statutory language. The judgment of the Court of Appeals is affirmed.

It is so ordered.

SOURCE: Ashcroft v. Free Speech Coalition, 535 U.S. 234 (2001).

ANALYSIS

Although the Communications Decency Act (CDA) was one of Congress's most notable attempts to prohibit transmission of obscene or indecent materials to minors through cable or internet, general congressional efforts to protect children from sexual exploitation dated back much further. The first nationwide law criminalizing child pornography was the Protection of Children against Sexual Exploitation Act, passed in 1977. This law punished anyone who performed sexually explicit conduct against a minor. In 1988, Congress addressed the development of online child pornography through the Child Protection and Obscenity Enforcement Act, which prohibited computerized transportation, distribution and receipt of child pornography, and required producers of sexually explicit materials to prove that individuals depicted in their materials were eighteen years of age or older. The Child Protection Restoration and Penalties Enhancement Act, passed in 1990, criminalized the knowing possession of child pornography. All three of these laws have withstood legal challenges with their basic tenants intact.

Ensuing legislation with similar intentions, however, met a different fate. In September 1996, Congress attempted to expand the definition and reach of child pornography with the Child Pornography Prevention Act (CPPA). This legislation was prompted by technological production of virtual images nearly indistinguishable from real children and pornographic presentation of adults who looked like kids. The law prohibited "any visual depiction, including any photograph, film, video, picture, or computer-generated image or picture" that "is, or appears to be, of a minor engaging in sexually explicit conduct." It also prohibited the advertising, promotion, presentation, description or distribution of any sexually explicit image that "conveys the impression" of depicting "a minor engaging in sexually explicit conduct." Under CPPA, even drawings or computer-generated depictions of what appeared to be child pornography were subject to criminal sanctions because proponents felt even virtual sexual exploitation of children would feed the appetites of pedophiles and encourage illegal activity.

Key sections of the CPPA were struck down by the Supreme Court as overbroad and unconstitutional in *Ashcroft v. Free Speech Coalition* (2002). Justices said the CPPA did not meet the standards of the Miller test, so it could not be seen as a prohibition of obscenity. It could not be supported by *New York v. Ferber* because pornography involving virtual images of children shows no evidence of a crime committed against minors. Additionally, the CPPA proscribed forms of expression that were legal for adults under the assumption that doing so would prevent crimes against children. However, the court pointed out that mere tendency of speech to promote illegal activity is not sufficient grounds for censorship; a direct relationship must be shown between speech and action. Justice Kennedy's majority opinion established that no precedents or aspects of First Amendment law support the limitations that the CPPA's disputed provisions placed on freedom of speech.

Next came the landmark *Reno v. American Civil Liberties Union* Supreme Court decision in 1997, which deemed major aspects of the Communications Decency Act (CDA) unconstitutional only a year and a half after its passage. (See previous entry for more information on the CDA). This ruling was an additional major blow to advocates of internet child protection laws.

Lawmakers, however, did not give up. In October 1998, Congress passed the Child Online Protection Act (COPA) as a direct response to the *Reno* decision. COPA was written more narrowly in an attempt to correct the constitutional deficiencies of the CDA cited by the court. The law criminalized knowingly posting communications "harmful to minors" on the worldwide web "for commercial purposes." Contemporary community standards were applied to define material "harmful to minors" (a narrower classification than the CDA's "indecency" provision). COPA also included an affirmative "good faith" defense to protect honest attempts to restrict access of harmful material to minors and a requirement for age-verification tools such as credit cards, debit accounts, and so on to be used by adults wanting to access such materials.

In spite of attempts by COPA's authors to avoid First Amendment violations, critics felt the law was still an overreach that would stifle free expression on the web. In fact, COPA never actually went into effect because its constitutionality was immediately challenged in court by the ACLU. By 2002, the case had made its way to the Supreme Court (*Ashcroft v. American Civil Liberties Union*). Justices expressed concerns about the legality and impact of applying local community standards to the internet. In his concurrence, Justice Breyer wrote, "[T]o read the statute as adopting the community standards of every locality in the United States would provide the most puritan of communities with a heckler's veto affecting the rest of the Nation." The court remanded the case to lower courts for reconsideration.

In 2004 *Ashcroft v. American Civil Liberties Union* once again came before the Supreme Court, which then ruled that COPA, like its predecessor, was unconstitutionally overbroad. The court's decision emphasized that COPA did not use the least restrictive means to protect children from harmful material. Not only would implementation of blocking and filtering software be less restrictive than COPA restrictions, majority justices said, but the software would also potentially be more effective because its reach is international, unlike COPA regulations.

Successful legislative efforts include passage of the Children's Internet Protection Act (CIPA) in 2000, which required libraries to install filtering technology on internet-connected computers as a prerequisite for certain types of federal funding. The filters could be disabled by librarians if adults requested access for research or other legal purposes. This law, too, was challenged by numerous groups, including the American Civil Liberties Union and the American Library Association (ALA). Librarians complained that filtering software was not sophisticated enough to accurately identify "harmful" or "obscene" content based on keywords or phrases. As a result, it often overblocked legitimate websites providing information on subjects like AIDS, breast cancer, and sex education.

In spite of these concerns, the Supreme Court upheld the constitutionality of CIPA, arguing this filtering is hardly different from the normal filtering process librarians use when selecting materials. Justices added that libraries can simply refuse federal funding if they do not wish to install the filtering software. CIPA was updated by the Federal Communications Commission in 2011 with new requirements for educating minors about appropriate online behavior, including cyberbullying and use of chat rooms.

One of Congress's most significant efforts in the fight against child exploitation was signed into law by President George W. Bush in April 2003. The Prosecutorial Remedies and Other Tools to End the Exploitation of Children Today (PROTECT) Act rectified the unconstitutional aspects of the CPPA. This extensive law, among other things, criminalized pandering and solicitation of child pornography of any type, including computer-generated child pornography. These PROTECT Act provisions were upheld by the Supreme Court in *United States v. Williams* (2008).

FURTHER READING

Batch, Kristen R., Trina Magi, and Michelle Luhtala. "Filtering beyond CIPA: Consequences of and Alternatives to Overfiltering in Schools." *Knowledge Quest* 44, no. 1 (2015): 60–66.

Holland, Bill. "Online Child Protection Act Opposed." *Billboard* 111, no. 4 (1999): 6.

McCarthy, Martha. "The Continuing Saga of Internet Censorship: The Child Online Protection Act." *Brigham Young University Education & Law Journal*, no. 2 (2005): 83–101.

Mota, Sue Ann. "The US Supreme Court Addresses the Child Pornography Prevention Act and Child Online Protection Act in Ashcroft v. Free Speech Coalition and Ashcroft v. American Civil Liberties Union." *Federal Communications Law Journal* 55 (2002): 85.

Sanchez, Barbara A. "United States v. American Library Association: The Choice between Cash and Constitutional Rights." *Akron Law Review* 38 (2005): 463.

Steinberg, Stacey. "Changing Faces: Morphed Child Pornography Images and the First Amendment." *Emory Law Journal* 68, no. 5 (2019): 909–38.

Wu, Felix. "United States v. American Library Ass'n: The Children's Internet Protection Act, Library Filtering, and Institutional Roles." *Berkeley Technology Law Journal* 19, no. 1 (2004): 555–83.

- ***Document 42:*** Arkansas District Court Strikes Down *Harry Potter* Book Banning in *Counts v. Cedarville School District*
- ***Date:*** Decided April 22, 2003
- ***Where:*** U.S. District Court for the Western District of Arkansas, Ft. Smith Division
- ***Significance:*** This district court case involving the popular Harry Potter series established once again that Constitutional rights apply to school libraries. The court ruling affirmed that materials cannot be removed or restricted in school libraries based on a desire to suppress the ideas contained within them or based on concerns the books will promote disobedience or disrespect. Restricting access without actual evidence of disruption caused by the books constitutes suppression of ideas in violation of students' First Amendment rights.

DOCUMENT

Memorandum Opinion

HENDREN, District Judge.

. . . 1. Plaintiffs, Billy Ray Counts, Individually, in his official capacity as a Library committee member, and Mary Nell Counts, both as parents of Dakota Counts . . . brought suit pursuant to 42 U.S.C. § 1983, alleging that their rights under the First and Fourteenth Amendments to the United States Constitution were being abridged by the decision of the defendant, Cedarville School District, to restrict the access of students, including Dakota Counts, to certain books in defendant's library. . . .

Defendant denies that any constitutional rights have been violated by its actions and argues affirmatively that the matter should be dismissed because the plaintiffs lack standing to bring their claims. . . .

3. The Court will first address defendant's motion to dismiss for lack of standing, given that it touches on the jurisdiction of the Court to resolve the substantive issues in this case. . . .

The Court is persuaded that Dakota Counts has alleged sufficient injury to give her standing to pursue her claims in this case. The right to read a book is an aspect of the right to receive information and ideas, an "inherent corollary of the rights of free speech and press that are explicitly guaranteed by the Constitution." *Board of Education v. Pico* (1982). The Supreme Court in *Pico* recognized that a school library is an "environment especially appropriate for the recognition of the First Amendment rights of students."

The loss of First Amendment rights, even minimally, is injurious. . . .

In the case at bar, it is suggested in plaintiffs' Complaint that Dakota's rights are burdened because the books in question are "stigmatized," with resulting "stigmatization" of those who choose to read them . . . In addition, should Dakota want to review a passage in one of the books while at school, she cannot simply walk into the library and do so. . . .

The Court finds that these burdens, albeit relatively small, constitute a sufficient allegation of an actual concrete and particularized invasion of a legally protected interest to establish Dakota's standing to bring this suit. . . .

The fact that Dakota has access to the books at home does not undermine this decision. The Supreme Court has held that "one is not to have the exercise of his liberty of expression in appropriate places abridged on the plea that it may be exercised in some other place." *Reno v. American Civil Liberties Union* (1997) (citing *Schneider v. State* (1939)). . . .

The motion to dismiss will, therefore, be denied. . .

4. Having concluded that plaintiffs have standing to bring a claim of constitutional violation on behalf of Dakota Counts, the Court now turns to the issue of whether summary judgment in their favor is appropriate. . . .
5. . . . From the plaintiffs' uncontested submission—and from other facts appearing in the briefs and evidentiary documents which cannot be considered seriously disputed—the following significant undisputed facts are made to appear:

* In November, 2001, Angie Haney (the mother of a child enrolled in the Cedarville School District) and her pastor, Mark Hodges (who is on the Cedarville School Board) became concerned that a series of books known as the Harry Potter books were in general circulation in the school libraries at Cedarville.
* Hodges and Cedarville School Superintendent Dave Smith contacted Estella Roberts, Cedarville High School librarian, about the matter. Roberts told Hodges and Smith that under school policy, they would need to complete a form—called a Reconsideration Request Form—to bring about any change in the status of the Harry Potter books.
* Hodges gave the blank Reconsideration Request Form to Haney, who completed it and returned it to the defendant. On the form, Haney asked that one of the Harry Potter books, *Harry Potter And The Sorcerer's Stone*, be withdrawn from all students.
* After receiving the Reconsideration Request Form, and pursuant to its stated policies, the defendant formed a Library Committee to consider the matter. The Library Committee consisted of five representatives from the high school, five from the middle school, and five from the elementary school. The five people from each school were the principal, the librarian, a teacher, a student, and the parent of a student from that school.
* The Library Committee reviewed *Harry Potter And The Sorcerer's Stone*, and voted unanimously in favor of keeping the book in circulation without any restrictions.
* After receiving the recommendation of the Library Committee, Roberts made a presentation about the matter to the Cedarville School Board. Defendant's board then voted 3–2 to restrict access not only to *Harry*

Potter And The Sorcerer's Stone, but also to the other three books in the Harry Potter series. Members of defendant's board voting to restrict access were Mark Hodges, Jerry Shelly, and Gary Koonce. . .

* The Board members voting in favor of restricted access did not do so because of concerns about profanity, sexuality, obscenity, or perversion in the books, nor out of any concern that reading the books had actually led to disruption in the schools. Only one of the three had even read *Harry Potter And The Sorcerer's Stone*, and none of them had read the other three books in the series.

* As a result of the vote of defendant's board, Cedarville High School Principal Glennis Cook issued a memo stating that all Harry Potter books were to be removed from defendant's library shelves and placed "where they are highly visible, yet not accessible to the students unless they are checking them out." To check out the books, a student must have "a signed permission statement from their parent/legal guardian." Hodges, Shelly and Koonce intended this directive to be a restriction on access to the books.

* Plaintiffs Billy Ray Counts and Mary Nell Counts sued on behalf of their minor child Dakota Counts, a Cedarville student, alleging that the restrictions placed on the Harry Potter books violate her First Amendment rights to freedom of speech and to receive information. Billy Ray Counts also alleged an individual claim in his official capacity as a member of the Cedarville School District Library Committee.

* Dakota has already read three of the Harry Potter books, owns the fourth, and has written permission from her parents to check the books out of the school library.

6. Given these undisputed facts, the following issue is presented: Does a school board's decision—to restrict access to library books only to those with parental permission—infringe upon the First Amendment rights of a student who has such permission? Before the Court can decide this issue on a motion for summary judgment, it must first determine if there is any genuine issue of material fact in dispute concerning whether Dakota's rights are so infringed.

Both this issue and the Court's determination of it must be addressed and decided in light of Supreme Court precedent calling for "the most exacting scrutiny [of] regulations that suppress, disadvantage, or impose differential burdens upon speech because of its content." *Turner Broadcasting System, Inc. v. FCC* (1994).

7. In support of their assertion that summary judgment is appropriate, plaintiffs rely on *Sund v. City of Wichita Falls* (N.D. Texas 2000), holding that removing a children's book to the adult section of a public library constituted restriction on access because children searching for the book in the designated children's areas would be unable to locate it and browsers risked never discovering the book at all. . . . the stigmatizing effect of having to have parental permission to check out a book constitutes a restriction on access. Further, the fact that Dakota cannot simply go in the library, take the books off the shelf and thumb through them—perhaps to refresh her mind about a favorite passage—without going through the permission and check-out process is a restriction on

her access. Thus, unless it is shown that such restrictions are justified, they amount to impermissible infringements of First Amendment rights.

8. Having concluded that a burden on Dakota's right of access exists, the Court must consider whether the restrictions are justified by some exigency of the educational environment in the Cedarville School District.

Hodges, Shelly and Koonce testified by deposition that their vote to restrict access to the Harry Potter books was based on (a) their concern that the books might promote disobedience and disrespect for authority, and (b) the fact that the books deal with "witchcraft" and "the occult." The Court will examine these positions seriatim.

(a) The first asserted justification for the restriction appears to be the shared concern among Hodges, Shelly and Koonce that the Harry Potter books might promote disobedience and disrespect for authority. The constitutional soundness of such a restriction depends on whether there is any evidence to support application of a very narrow exception to the First Amendment rights of primary and secondary public school students. While such students do not shed their constitutional rights at the schoolhouse gate, in First Amendment cases the Supreme Court has recognized a very limited restriction where "necessary to avoid material and substantial interference with school-work or discipline." *Tinker v. Des Moines Independent Community School District* (1969).

The Court in *Tinker* was careful to emphasize how limited this restriction is, and to stress the importance of freedom of speech in the education of America's youth:

> In our system, state-operated schools may not be enclaves of totalitarianism. School officials do not possess absolute authority over their students. Students in school as well as out of school are 'persons' under our Constitution. They are possessed of fundamental rights which the State must respect, just as they themselves must respect their obligations to the State. In our system, students may not be regarded as closed-circuit recipients of only that which the State chooses to communicate. They may not be confined to the expression of those sentiments that are officially approved. In the absence of a specific showing of constitutionally valid reasons to regulate their speech, students are entitled to freedom of expression of their views.

Tinker also quoted with approval from *Keyishian v. Board of Regents* (1967), as follows:

> The vigilant protection of constitutional freedoms is nowhere more vital than in the community of American schools. The classroom is peculiarly the "marketplace of ideas." The Nation's future depends upon leaders trained through wide exposure to that robust exchange of ideas which discovers truth "out of a multitude of tongues, (rather) than through any kind of authoritative selection."

Thus, while it is recognized that Boards of Education "have important, delicate, and highly discretionary functions," it is also recognized that there are "none that they may not perform within the limits of the Bill of Rights. That they are educating the young for citizenship is reason for scrupulous protection of Constitutional freedoms of the individual, if we are not to strangle the free mind at its source and teach youth to discount important principles of our government as mere platitudes." *Tinker, id.*

Turning to the evidence which might support defendant's contention that the restrictions in question are "necessary to avoid material and substantial interference with schoolwork or discipline," the Court finds the following relevant testimony in the depositions of Hodges, Shelly and Koonce:

- * Hodges (the only one of the three who had actually read an entire Harry Potter book) testified that the books are "going to create problems in the school," and "could create . . . anarchy." However he did not know of any behavioral problems that had been created by the series, and he admitted that his vote to restrict access was "a preventative measure at that school to prevent any signs that will come up like Columbine and Jonesboro."
- * Shelly (who had not read any of the books) testified that books teaching that sometimes rules need to be disobeyed should not be allowed in the school library.
- * Koonce (who had not read any of the books in full but "just kind of read here and there" in the first book of the series) testified that he believed it "could" lead kids into juvenile delinquency, but that he was motivated not by what the students were doing, only by what they "might do later."

There is no evidence that any of the three Board members was aware of any actual disobedience or disrespect that had flowed from a reading of the Harry Potter books. Their concerns are, therefore, speculative. Such speculative apprehensions of possible disturbance are not sufficient to justify the extreme sanction of restricting the free exercise of First Amendment rights in a public school library. . . .

(b) The second asserted justification for the restriction is the shared concerns of Hodges, Shelly and Koonce that the Harry Potter books deal with "witchcraft" and "the occult". The Court notes that all three men appear to strongly disapprove of "witchcraft" and "the occult."

This second asserted basis for restricting access to the books is, in the Court's view, no more persuasive than was the first. . . .

Along with the freedom of expression considerations which apply when witchcraft and the occult are viewed simply as ideas to which students have a right to choose to be exposed, another First Amendment consideration comes into play. The proof before the Court shows that Hodges, Shelly and Koonce admittedly want to restrict access to the books because of their shared belief that the books promote a particular religion, e.g.:

- * Hodges testified that witchcraft is a religion and that he objected to a book which would expose Cedarville students to the "witchcraft religion."

* Shelly testified that he objected to the books because they "teach witchcraft"—but that if the books "promoted Christianity" he would not object to them.
* Koonce testified that the books "teach about witchcraft," and that witchcraft is a religion.

Regardless of the personal distaste with which these individuals regard "witchcraft," it is not properly within their power and authority as members of defendant's school board to prevent the students at Cedarville from reading about it. As the Supreme Court said in *Pico, supra,*

> "[o]ur Constitution does not permit the official suppression of ideas. Thus whether petitioners' removal of books from their school libraries denied respondents their First Amendment rights depends upon the motivation behind petitioners' actions. If petitioners intended by their removal decision to deny respondents access to ideas with which petitioners disagreed, and if this intent was the decisive factor in petitioners' decision, the petitioners have exercised their discretion in violation of the Constitution. . . . In brief, we hold that local school boards may not remove books from school library shelves simply because they dislike the ideas contained in those books and seek by their removal to prescribe what shall be orthodox in politics, nationalism, religion, or other matters of opinion."

The Court, therefore, finds no merit in the second asserted justification for the restrictions in question.

9. There is no evidence shown to the Court which might reasonably have led defendant's Board members "to forecast substantial disruption of or material interference with school activities" if students were to be allowed unfettered access to the Harry Potter books (as would be required to bring them within the narrow *Tinker* restriction), nor can the defendant permissibly restrict access on the basis of the ideas expressed therein—whether religious or secular. . . .

Accordingly . . . when the evidence is viewed in the light most favorable to the defendant, the conclusion is inevitable that defendant removed the books from its library shelves for reasons not authorized by the Constitution.

There being no genuine issue of material fact in dispute as to these matters, the Court finds that Dakota Counts' First Amendment rights are being infringed by defendant's decision to restrict access to the Harry Potter books to those students whose parents sign a permission slip allowing them to check out the books. Summary judgment in her favor will therefore be granted. . . .

IT IS SO ORDERED.

SOURCE: Counts v. Cedarville School District, 295 F. Supp. 2d 996 (W.D. Ark. 2003).

ANALYSIS

The banning or censorship of controversial books in the United States is less a singular event than a series of challenges to First Amendment freedom of expression that has affected nearly every generation of Americans. In fact, book banning is the most prevalent form of censorship in the United States (Webb 2009). Books written for children and youth are challenged more frequently than any other literary genre, often because books involving sensitive topics are said to be inappropriate or unsuited for impressionable young minds.

As societal norms have shifted over the past two and a half centuries, so have the categories of banned and restricted books. One of the first well-known books to be banned in the United States was *Uncle Tom's Cabin* by Harriet Beecher Stowe. Published in 1852, the book was forbidden in parts of the South because of its antislavery themes; it was challenged elsewhere for its vulgar language, racial stereotypes, or use of the word "nigger." Nevertheless, the book made a tremendous social impact on readers through its antislavery themes. Abraham Lincoln, when meeting Harriet Beecher Stowe, reportedly said, "So this is the little lady who made this big war" (Baldassarro 2011). The only book in the nineteenth century to sell more copies than *Uncle Tom's Cabin* was the Bible (ibid).

Many other wildly popular books have also been banned because of their treatment of racial or social issues or use of harsh language. Such arguments were used to support censorship of books now considered classics, including Nathaniel Hawthorne's *The Scarlet Letter* (1850), Mark Twain's *Huckleberry Finn* (1884), Joseph Conrad's *Heart of Darkness* (1902), and Margaret Mitchell's *Gone with the Wind* (1936), one of the bestselling books in American history. Additional books challenged for racial, social, or political themes include *To Kill a Mockingbird* by Harper Lee (1960), *Autobiography of Malcom X* (1965) and *Bury My Heart at Wounded Knee* by Dee Brown (1970), *The Color Purple* by Alice Walker (1982), and *Beloved* by Toni Morrison (1987), to name a few.

Sexually related content has also driven scores of book censorship efforts in the United States. In fact, prior to the 1970s, obscenity and explicit sexuality were the primary cause for challenges or bans on books (Webb 2009). The first erotic novel written in English, John Cleland's *Memoirs of a Woman of Pleasure* (also known as *Fanny Hill*), was published in 1748 and 1749 but banned in the UK and the United States until the midtwentieth century. Other well-known books banned for sexual content or obscenity (and sometimes other concerns as well) include *Lady Chatterly's Lover* by D.H. Lawrence (1950s in the United States), *Ulysses* by James Joyce (1930s in the United States), *Lolita* by Vladimir Nabokov (1955), *Slaughterhouse V* by Kurt Vonnegut (1969), and *I Know Why the Caged Bird Sings* by Maya Angelou (1969).

While the previous examples were rejected for their treatment of heterosexual relationships, themes of same-sex relationships or nontraditional families have also prompted censorship efforts. Nancy Garden's 1982 young adult novel *Annie on My Mind* was both burned and banned, and removal of the book from Kansas City school libraries even sparked a 1993 U.S. federal court case. Children's book *And Tango Makes Three* by Peter Parnell and Justin Richardson (2005) was the most frequently challenged book from 2006 to 2008 and second most challenged in 2009 (Chamberlain 2010). The book is based on the true story of two male penguins in the Central Park Zoo who care for an orphaned egg and raise a female chick together. Efforts to withdraw the book from school and public libraries were led by critics who felt the story of two male parents taught acceptance of homosexuality. Most public efforts to remove the book failed.

Profanity has also been used as a justification for banning or challenging books. Use of profane language, particularly when in combination with sexual content or controversial political themes, has made ripe targets of many celebrated works including *The Grapes of Wrath* by John Steinbeck (1939). Steinbeck's use of raw language, combined with sexual overtones and discussion of political and social themes, made his grim portrayal of "Dust Bowl migrants" during the Great Depression one of the most controversial books of the twentieth century. Although the bestseller is now considered a classic, *The Grapes of Wrath* was banned, challenged, and burned in multiple parts of the United States following its publication (Neary 2008). *The Catcher in the Rye* by J.D. Salinger (1951) was censored for similar reasons.

Disrespect and bad behavior are additional themes that have prompted book bans and challenges. The *Junie B. Jones* series by Barbara Park, greatly loved by lower elementary–aged children who relate to the everyday struggles of Junie B., has been criticized by parents and teachers for the main character's poor grammar and language, "bratty" attitude and disrespect for authority, and poor decision-making. Barbara Park, who wrote the series as a lighthearted look at life from the perspective of a young child, was on the top ten list of challenged authors in 2004 (Grossman 2007). Dav Pilkey's *Captain Underpants* series has been challenged for similar reasons; the main character shows disrespect, engages in pranks and other bad behavior, and uses offensive language (references to undergarments). In 2012, the *Captain Underpants* series beat out *Fifty Shades of Grey* for the #1 spot on the list of most banned books in America (Engel 2013).

However, in recent history, few books have been as challenged or censored as the Harry Potter series by J.K. Rowling. According to the American Library Association (ALA), *Harry Potter* books were the #1 most challenged/banned books from 2000 to 2009, and were #7 on the list of most frequently challenged books from 1990 to 2000.

The widespread popularity of the Harry Potter series has resulted in a near ubiquitous presence of the books in school and public libraries. The fantastical tales about a young wizard attending Hogwarts School of Witchcraft and Wizardry became a cultural phenomenon and inspired voracious reading appetites among multiple generations of global fans. However, *Harry Potter* also attracted critics who tried to restrict or remove the books from libraries, citing disrespectful or dangerous themes. Some rejected the stories on the grounds that they promote disobedience to authorities or themes contrary to family unity; others, notably Christian groups, argued that the books promote themes of death, magic, Satanism, and witchcraft.

By 2006, the Harry Potter series topped the list of the most challenged books of the twenty-first century (Clark & Morales 2006), but that did not harm the stories' popularity. By 2018, more than 500 million copies of the books had been sold, making Harry Potter the best-selling book series in the world (Shisia 2018). Nearly two decades after the release of the first book, Harry Potter remains as popular as ever.

Although critics continue to advocate censorship of the books, most efforts—including legal ones—have been unsuccessful. As noted in the *Island Trees School District v. Pico* and *Counts v. Cedarville School District* rulings, it is a violation of the First Amendment to restrict access to books based on mere disapproval of the ideas contained within them. Students, too, have a constitutional right to engage in a marketplace of ideas within their schools.

FURTHER READING

Doyle, Robert P. *Banned Books: Defending Our Freedom to Read*. Chicago, IL: American Library Association, 2017.

Foerstel, Herbert N. *Banned in the USA: A Reference Guide to Book Censorship in Schools and Public Libraries*. Westport, CT: Greenwood Publishing Group, 2002.

"Frequently Challenged Books." American Library Association Office for Intellectual Freedom. March 26, 2013. http://www.ala.org/advocacy/bbooks/frequentlychallengedbooks

Jarvis, Zeke. *Silenced in the Library: Banned Books in America*. Santa Barbara, CA: Greenwood, 2017.

Knapp, Nancy Flanagan. "In Defense of Harry Potter: An Apologia." *School Libraries Worldwide* 9 (2003): 78–91.

Meadors, Brian. *Harry Potter and the Cedarville Censors: Inside the Precedent-Setting Defeat of an Arkansas Book Ban*. Jefferson, NC: McFarland, 2019.

Scales, Pat. "What Makes a Good Banned Book?" *Horn Book Magazine* 85, no. 5 (2009): 533–36.

- ***Document 43:*** Testimony of James E. Hansen on Science Censorship to Committee on Oversight and Government Reform
- ***Date:*** March 19, 2007
- ***Where:*** Capitol Hill, Washington, DC
- ***Significance:*** Scientist Dr. James E. Hansen testified in 2007 that the results of scientific studies at NASA were being censored, modified, or purposely manipulated by government and special interest groups for their own political purposes. Dr. Hansen also raised concerns about the withholding of congressional funding for projects not in line with the administration's political views. Dr. Hansen's concerns were not unique; suppression of scientific information has become increasingly worrisome to many who warn that global warming, infectious diseases, and other major challenges pose grave threats to the planet and its inhabitants.

DOCUMENT

1. MY EXPERIENCE

A. White House Approval and Editing of Congressional Testimony

During the past 25 years I have noticed an increase in the degree of political interference with scientific testimony to Congress. My first testimony was to a United States House of Representatives hearing organized by Representative Al Gore in early 1982. I do not recall whether White House approval of that testimony was required, but in any case there were no objections to the content of that testimony.

I testified to the United States Senate about climate change at least three times in the period 1984–1988. These testimonies required approval by the White House Office of Management and Budget (OMB). I did not have direct contact with people in OMB, rather NASA Headquarters (usually the NASA Office of Legislative Affairs) was an intermediary between the scientist (me) and OMB. In one case I strongly objected to changes that OMB made to my testimony, because I felt that the changes substantially altered the conclusions of our research and served to reduce concern about possible human-made climate change.

In this case the NASA intermediary in the Office of Legislative Affairs volunteered the information that I had the right to testify as a private citizen and present my testimony with the wording that I preferred. I took advantage of that right, testifying as a private citizen, and never felt any repercussions for doing so.

In 1989, after climate change had become of greater public and political concern, the constraints on communication via congressional testimony became stricter, at least in my experience. When I submitted written testimony to NASA Headquarters in 1989 for presentation to a Senate Committee chaired by Senator Gore, my secretary was instructed by NASA Headquarters to send the original typescript to NASA Headquarters so that they could insert several changes that were required by the White House OMB. When I was informed of this I was angered, intercepted the typescript, and insisted that any changes had to be made in my office. . . . but three changes that OMB required were unacceptable to me. Unlike the case earlier in the 1980s, I was told by NASA Headquarters that I needed to accept the changes or not testify. I agreed to accept the changes, but I then sent a fax to Senator Gore requesting that he ask me during the hearing about those specific statements, because I wanted to make clear that they were the opinion of the White House OMB, not my opinion. (This exchange was briefly shown in the documentary "An Inconvenient Truth".)

Review and editing of scientific testimony by the White House OMB seems to now be an accepted practice. . . . It seems to me that this raises constitutional questions, because it is my understanding that the Constitution provides the power of the purse strings to Congress, not the Executive Branch of our government. . . .

B. Communication Constraints by NASA Office of Public Affairs

The Office of Public Affairs in science agencies such as NASA exists for the purpose of helping communicate scientific results to the public. During my career I have noticed an increasing politicization of Public Affairs at the Headquarters level, with a notable effect on communication from scientists to the public. I refer not to the professionals in the Public Affairs offices at the NASA science centers, but to Public Affairs at NASA Headquarters, which is in charge overall and is generally headed by a political appointee. Interference with communication of science to the public has been greater during the current Administration than at any time in my career. . . .

The effect of the filtering of climate change science during the current Administration has been to make the reality of climate change less certain than the facts indicate and to reduce concern about the relation of climate change to human-made greenhouse gas emissions. For example, one of my staff members submitted a story based on his paper that found the ocean was less effective at removing human-made CO2 than had previously been estimated. Public Affairs decided that this story should not be provided to the media. Another staff member had to attend a 'practice' press conference, in which he was asked whether anything could be done to stem accelerating loss of sea ice. When he suggested "we could reduce emissions of greenhouse gases" he was told sternly "that's unacceptable!", with the explanation that scientists are not allowed to say anything that relates to policy.

An important example of political interference with the public's right to know has occurred with press releases relating to global warming science that have gone from NASA Headquarters to the White House for review, approval or disapproval, and editing. . . .

Communication constraints by NASA Headquarters Public Affairs came to light in December 2005, after some of the instructions by Headquarters Public Affairs were written down in memos and e-mails. This occurred shortly after my "Keeling" talk at the American Geophysical Union meeting in San Francisco and the release within a week thereafter of our (GISS, Goddard Institute for Space Studies) analysis of global temperature, which showed record global temperature in 2005. NASA Headquarters Public Affairs was furious about the media attention, their anger being sparked by a call from the White House objecting to the publicity on global warming. The consternation, expressed during several three-way telecons between Headquarters-GSFC/Greenbelt-GISS/New York, was described by a participant as a "shit-storm". The upshot was a new explicit set of constraints on me, including requirement that any media interviews be approved beforehand and that Headquarters have the "right of first refusal" on all interviews, that I provide my calendar of all planned talks and meetings, and that I obtain prior approval for every posting on the GISS web site.

These orders were delivered orally, as usual, as was a threat of "dire consequences" if I did not comply. However, a new young political appointee at Public Affairs, apparently was not well-schooled in the rules and left a paper trail, including a description of a specific instance in which Public Affairs barred me from speaking to NPR, offering the Associate Administrator in my stead. . . . The paper trail that he left showed that the problem starts at the top, the decision to bar me from speaking with NPR being made "on the ninth floor" of Headquarters.

It became clear that the new constraints on my communications were going to be a real impediment when I was forced to take down from our web site our routine posting of updated global temperature analysis. At that time I decided to write down the constraints that I had been placed under and to inform the media. An article appeared in the New York Times by Andy Revkin, who had the courage to go with a story that had a limited paper trail. To NASA's credit, the Administrator promptly issued an unequivocal statement in support of scientific openness.

However, in no way has the impact of deception of the public about climate change been undone by NASA's forthright decision in favor of scientific openness. There remains a vast gap between what is understood about global warming, by the relevant scientific community, and what is known about global warming by those who need to know, the public and policy-makers. . . .

C. Executive Control of Purse Strings

The American Revolution launched the radical proposition that the commonest of man should have a vote of equal weight to that of the richest, most powerful citizen. Our forefathers devised a remarkable Constitution, with checks and balances, to guard against the return of despotic governance and subversion of the democratic principle for the sake of the powerful few with special interests. They were well aware of the difficulties that would be faced, however, placing their hopes in the presumption of an educated informed citizenry, an honestly informed public. . . .

Yet Franklin, Jefferson and the other revolutionaries must be distraught by recent tendencies in America, specifically increasing power of special interests in our government, concerted efforts to deceive the public, and arbitrary actions of government executives that arise from increasing concentration of authority in a unitary executive, in defiance of the aims of our Constitution's framers. These tendencies have dramatic impact on the global warming story. . . .

When the administration announced its fiscal 2007 budget, NASA science was listed as having typical changes of 1 percent or so. However, Earth Science Research and Analysis actually had a staggering reduction of about 20 percent from the 2006 budget that Congress had passed. How could that be accomplished? Simple enough: reduce the 2006 research budget retroactively by 20 percent! One-third of the way into fiscal year 2006, NASA Earth Science was told to go figure out how to live with a 20-percent loss of the current year's funds.

The Earth Science budget was further tightened in 2007 and is almost a going-out-of-business budget. . . .

Bizarrely, this is happening just when NASA data are yielding spectacular and startling results. Two small satellites that measure the Earth's gravitational field with remarkable precision found that the mass of Greenland is now decreasing by about 150 cubic kilometers of ice per year and West Antarctica by a similar amount. The area on the ice sheets with summer melting has increased markedly, major ice streams (portions of the ice sheet moving most rapidly toward the ocean and discharging icebergs) have increased doubled [sic] in flow speed, and the area in the Arctic Ocean with summer sea ice has decreased 20 percent in the last 25 years.

One way to avoid bad news: stop the measurements! Only hitch: the first line of the NASA mission is "to understand and protect our home planet." Maybe that can be changed to ". . . protect special interests' backside."

I should say that the mission statement used to read "to understand and protect our home planet." That part has been deleted—a shocking loss to me, as I had been using that phrase to justify speaking out about the dangers of global warming. . . .

3. PRACTICAL IMPACT OF POLITICAL INTERFERENCE WITH CLIMATE CHANGE SCIENCE

A. Communication of Climate Change Threat

There is little doubt that the Administration's downplaying of evidence about global warming has had some effect on public perception of the climate change issue. The impact is to confuse the public about the reality of global warming, and about whether that warming can be reliably attributed to human-made greenhouse gases.

However, I believe that the gap between scientific understanding of climate change and public knowledge about the status of that understanding probably is due more to the impact of special interests on public discourse, especially fossil fuel special interests, rather than political interference with climate change science.

I have no knowledge of whether special interests have had a role in political interference with climate change science. Nevertheless, it is my personal opinion that the most fundamental government reform that could be taken to address climate change and government accountability in general would be effective campaign finance reform. . . .

4. ISSUES AND QUESTIONS RAISED

A. Propriety of Filtering Congressional Testimony

What is the basis, what is the rationale, by which Congress allows the Administration to filter, edit and alter scientific testimony of government scientists delivered to Congress? Is this behavior a right that is granted to the Executive branch by the Constitution or authorized by other official instruments?

Presumably there is basis for this practice or it would not be tolerated. However, based on my experiences, discussed in part above, it seems to me that the practice is detrimental to the functioning of our democracy. The taxpayers foot the bill for most of the research by government and academic scientists. Thus the public should not be denied the full benefit of knowledge that derives from that research. . . .

C. Executive Control of the Purse Strings

When I came to NASA 40 years ago as a 25 year old post-doc . . . I did not get any sense that NASA was working for the White House. There has been a huge change between then and now.

The Executive branch seems to be exercising greater control in the functioning of our government, in ways that our forefathers probably did not imagine and almost certainly would not approve. This includes White House control of testimony to Congress, White House control of information that scientists provide to the public through Public Affairs, and most decidedly through control of the purse strings.

Control of the purse strings is the most powerful of the tools in the hands of the Executive branch. It has a tremendous effect on information that is provided to Congress and to the public. You may think that a government scientist can easily exercise his right of free speech, to speak as a private citizen as I am today. But how many will do so, when the power of the purse strings is held by the Executive branch? You may think that there are plenty of government scientists who are confident of their ability to get a job elsewhere or would not mind being sent off to pasture. But it is not so simple as that. With the purse strings the Executive branch holds hostage your "children", your science programs, and your colleagues' livelihood. It is not easy to face your colleagues when they feel that you are damaging their support.

5. SUMMARY IMPLICATIONS OF CLIMATE CHANGE SCIENCE

. . . B. Impact of Political Interference on Quality of Decision Making

Political interference in transmittal of information about climate change science to the public has deleterious effects on the quality of decision making. Science cannot make decisions for the public. The public and policy makers must consider all factors in making decisions and setting policy. But these other factors should not influence the science itself or the presentation of science to the public.

One consequence of political interference is that the public is not yet well-informed about the nature and scale of actions that will be needed to address climate change. This is important because it will take time for the public and their policy makers to thoughtfully consider these matters. . . .

C. Recommendations to Policy-Makers. . .

. . . 5. Congress needs to address the following threats to American democracy: (1) the public's right to unfiltered information, including congressional testimony free of political interference, and Public Affairs (public information) offices that are staffed by professionals not by political appointees, (2) the absence of effective campaign finance reform.

As long as these threats to democracy are not addressed it will be difficult to deal with human-made climate change successfully. The Committee on Government Oversight and Reform seems an appropriate place to raise these issues.

SOURCE: United States Congress. House of Representatives. Committee on Oversight and Government Reform. "Political Interference with Government Climate Change Science." United States House of Representatives, 110th Congress, 1st Session. March 19, 2007. Washington, DC: Government Printing Office.

- ***Document:*** Statement Issued by Presidents of National Academy of Sciences and National Academy of Medicine: "NAS and NAM Presidents Alarmed by Political Interference in Science amid Pandemic"
- ***Date:*** September 24, 2020
- ***Where:*** Washington, DC
- ***Significance:*** In this remarkable statement, leaders of both the National Academy of Sciences and the National Academy of Medicine charged that the work of the nation's top scientists during the COVID-19 pandemic was being hampered by political interference from the Trump administration.

DOCUMENT

As advisers to the nation on all matters of science, medicine, and public health, we are compelled to underscore the value of science-based decision-making at all levels of government. Our nation is at a critical time in the course of the COVID-19 pandemic with important decisions ahead of us, especially concerning the efficacy and safety of vaccines. Policymaking must be informed by the best available evidence without it being distorted, concealed, or otherwise deliberately miscommunicated. We find ongoing reports and incidents of the politicization of science, particularly the overriding of evidence and advice from public health officials and derision of government scientists, to be alarming. It undermines the credibility of public health agencies and the public's confidence in them when we need it most.

Ending the pandemic will require decision-making that is not only based on science but also sufficiently transparent to ensure public trust in, and adherence to, sound public-health instructions. Any efforts to discredit the best science and scientists threaten the health and welfare of us all.

Marcia McNutt
President, National Academy of Sciences
Victor J. Dzau
President, National Academy of Medicine

SOURCE: National Academies of Science and Medicine. "NAS and NAM Presidents Alarmed by Political Interference in Science amid Pandemic." Statement. September 24, 2020. https://www.nationalacademies.org/news/2020/09/nas-and-nam-presidents-alarmed-by-political-interference-in-science-amid-pandemic

ANALYSIS

Science denial is not new. Some of the world's greatest scientists were ignored, persecuted, or killed for critical findings rejected by their contemporaries, that we now know to be true. However, effects of science denial over the past half century have become much more far-reaching. The line between scientific truth and falsehood has been blurred by the instant, unlimited dissemination of misleading and false information via new technologies. This distortion has been intensified by large-scale corporate and government-led efforts to suppress or discredit scientific findings to further specific economic or political goals.

The nation's founding fathers believed that effective functioning of a democratic government depended on the ability of individuals to engage in robust, free dialogue, interchange of ideas, and expression of opposing viewpoints. However, in the case of numerous science-denial campaigns, this interpersonal dialogue has succumbed to divisive political narratives, sometimes driven by special interests, that purposely promote distrust in science in order to further political or economic agendas.

One of the most impactful corporate disinformation campaigns in U.S. history involved the tobacco industry, which spent decades suppressing scientific evidence and using dishonest tactics to convince consumers tobacco products were not dangerous. These efforts were initiated in spite of, and largely because of, overwhelming scientific evidence linking smoking to cancer. In addition to denying health risks associated with the use of tobacco products, the tobacco industry intentionally manipulated nicotine content in its products to increase the likelihood of addiction. It then marketed what it implied were "safe" products to consumers, including women and children (Bero 2003; Carpenter et al. 2005).

Although science had drawn the link between tobacco use and cancer for years, it took a warning in the Surgeon General's 1964 Report to change public opinion about the risks of smoking. In response, companies began producing "low tar" or "light" cigarettes, advertised as less harmful than regular cigarettes. Cigarette companies manufactured these as "healthier" cigarettes in terms of lung cancer risk

(Pollay 2001), and in 1976, tobacco industry consultant Dr. Gio Gori claimed on national news that a person could smoke up to two packs of reduced-tar cigarettes each day with only a minimal risk of developing cancer (*ABC Evening News*, 1976). However, the scientific community came to a much different conclusion; non-industry-sponsored studies overwhelmingly showed that low-tar cigarettes were no less dangerous than regular cigarettes (Rigotti & Tindle 2004). In fact, smokers of the "light" or "low tar" cigarettes were found to be at greater risk of developing certain types of lung cancer (Ohio 2017). Tobacco companies tried to discredit the findings; battles between scientists and the tobacco industry are still being waged in court.

Corporate involvement was once again clearly visible in disinformation campaigns designed to promote denial of global warming and climate change. In 2015, the Union of Concerned Scientists published the "Climate Deception Dossiers," internal memos from the fossil fuel industry that showed evidence of numerous decades-long campaigns by the world's largest fossil fuel companies to manufacture doubt about scientific data. The documents show these companies deceived the public about the effects of carbon emissions and climate change, even when they knew the evidence supporting climate change was sound. Among the chief goals of the campaign were 1) shaping climate policy by suppressing scientific studies warning about the effects of climate change and 2) blocking the Kyoto Treaty and other carbon-reducing efforts that would have a negative financial impact on the petroleum industry.

Although James Hansen's testimony regarding manipulation of scientific data occurred during the George W. Bush administration, the Trump administration has also found itself at odds with the scientific community over denial of scientific evidence. President Trump and his cabinet have been criticized for appointing climate skeptics and petroleum industry leaders to key cabinet positions, deleting climate change information from federal websites, and refusing to acknowledge the implications of climate change in spite of overwhelming empirical evidence that it has contributed to the intensification of storms, hurricanes, droughts, wildfires, and other weather-related phenomena (Tirrell et al. 2020).

Discrediting of science by government leaders and disinformation campaigns also impacted the U.S. response to the global COVID-19 pandemic. As coronavirus infections spread around the world in early 2020, a global consortium of scientists worked frantically to identify how the virus was transmitted and develop a vaccine. Based on the scientific evidence available at the time, the World Health Organization (WHO) recommended countries implement large-scale public health measures such as aggressive detection, testing, treatment, isolation, and contact tracing (Winsor 2020).

The Trump administration's pandemic response often contradicted WHO recommendations. The president repeatedly diminished the severity of the crisis, derided social distancing measures, politicized mask-wearing, discouraged state efforts to close schools or businesses, and appointed White House Coronavirus Task Force members with little or no public health or infectious disease experience. Trump also renounced the advice of national health experts, including the CDC and members of his own coronavirus task force.

Recordings of personal interviews, released in September 2020, revealed that President Trump understood the severity of the coronavirus early on during the pandemic (Pelley 2020). Nevertheless, he downplayed its danger, demanding a full

DID YOU KNOW?

Science Denial in the Trump Administration

In the face of scientific research and recommendations during the global pandemic of 2019–2020, the Trump administration became a leading source of science denial. As COVID-19 related infections and deaths grew throughout the United States, the Trump administration repeatedly and adamantly contradicted scientific evidence about the nature, spread, and severity of the virus. Instead of following public health officials' recommendations, President Trump insisted the virus was not severe and that "one day . . . like a miracle, it will disappear" (Milman 2020).

When scientists determined social distancing and widespread use of masks would help prevent spread of COVID-19, President Trump disparaged reporters and public figures who wore masks and required neither masks nor distancing at his large campaign rallies. The president also disseminated unverified, potentially dangerous information regarding COVID-19 treatments, speculating about ingestion of disinfectants or the internal use of ultraviolet light to kill the virus inside the body (*CBS*, April 24), and promoting use of unproven drugs like hydroxychloroquine to prevent infection (Clark 2020; Solender 2020). President Trump muted the voices of coronavirus task force members whose public health messages did not align with his opinions and appointed new task force members with little or no public health or infectious disease expertise (Perez 2020). He also repeatedly contradicted the work and recommendations of Centers for Disease Control (CDC) officials and downplayed the agency's role in responding to the pandemic (Sonmez 2020).

President Trump's denial of climate change has also put his administration at odds with the scientific community. During a visit to fire-ravaged California, the president told one official concerned about the impact of climate change on the fires, "It'll start getting cooler, you just watch." The official answered, "I wish science agreed with you," to which the president smiled and replied, "I don't think science knows, actually" (*BBC* 2020).

In September 2020, President Trump handpicked a known climate skeptic, David Legates, for a top position in the National Oceanic and Atmospheric Administration (NOAA). The selection of Legates drew an outcry from the scientific community, who pointed out that he is both a climatologist who spent much of his career casting doubt on climate change research and a member of the Heartland Institute, a think tank that has worked to influence American opinions about climate change by labeling scientific evidence as untrustworthy (Hersher 2020).

President Trump also created a stir with NOAA in 2019 when he admonished NOAA officials for correcting his inaccurate description of Hurricane Dorian's path. The president demanded that NOAA back up his version of the storm's trajectory, even though the information was erroneous (Madhani 2020).

reopening of the country. Trump justified his response by saying he did not want to create panic (Pelley, 2020).

Critics argue that individuals can be prosecuted for providing false or misleading information on tax forms, applications, or other official documents, or for neglecting to disclose information about assets, criminal records, or previous names to offer a few examples. Lying to the government constitutes perjury. Why, then, should corporations or government entities not be held to the same standard of truth-telling when scientific research is involved?

The answer is complicated in part by tactics employed by disinformation campaigns that are not technically illegal, but rely on questionable maneuvers to spread false narratives or create doubt in the scientific process. Some examples include censoring or invalidating peer-reviewed, approved research; presenting industry-funded counterfeit studies as valid investigations; creating front groups said to be independent that are actually linked to specific advocacy groups or think tanks; threatening, intimidating, or harassing scientists; influencing policy by positioning industry leaders in key government positions; and rejecting findings that do not meet a standard of absolute certainty (Jacques Dunlap & Freeman, 2008; Morgan 2018).

Whether the issue concerns tobacco use, climate change, or a global pandemic, the looming constitutional question is whether or not a business, corporation, or government should be held liable for suppressing scientific evidence or deliberately spreading false narratives that directly impact the American public. To date, no single judicial ruling has effectively answered that question.

FURTHER READING

Farkas, Johan, and Jannick Schou. *Post-Truth, Fake News and Democracy: Mapping the Politics of Falsehood*. New York: Routledge, 2020.

Lewandowsky, Stephan, Klaus Oberauer, and Gilles E. Gignac. "NASA Faked the Moon Landing—Therefore, (Climate) Science is a Hoax: An Anatomy of the Motivated Rejection of Science." *Psychological Science* 24, no. 5 (2013): 622–33.

Prasad, Ajnesh. "Denying Anthropogenic Climate Change: Or, How Our Rejection of Objective Reality Gave Intellectual Legitimacy to Fake News." *Sociological Forum*, 34 (2019): 1217–34.

Sutton, Robbie M., Aino Petterson, and Bastiaan T. Rutjens. "Post-Truth, Anti-truth, and Can't-Handle-the-Truth: How Responses to Science Are Shaped by Concerns about Its Impact." *Belief Systems and the Perception of Reality*. New York: Routledge Taylor & Francis Group, 2019.

Tucker, William C. "Deceitful Tongues: Is Climate Change Denial a Crime?" *Ecology Law Quarterly* 39, no. 3 (2012): 831–94.

U.S. Congress. Senate. Committee on Energy and Natural Resources. "Greenhouse Effect and Global Climate Change: Hearings before the Committee on Energy and Natural Resources." United States Senate, One Hundredth Congress, First Session. Washington: U.S. G.P.O., 1988.

DID YOU KNOW?

The demand for impossible certainties has been a critical component of numerous science denial campaigns, particularly those refuting scientific evidence about climate change. Efforts to create doubt about the credibility of the scientific community have often been based on examples of past research that have since been revised or discredited. However, this line of reasoning fails to acknowledge that the scientific process itself is not based on absolute truths, but on discovery. Science demands an ongoing quest for new evidence, information, and breakthroughs that can lead to new, deeper interpretations and understandings of the world and its processes. The idea that scientific research must demonstrate absolute certainty in order to be credible would eliminate centuries of seminal discoveries that, although not completely accurate, were foundational to our modern understanding of genetics, germs, the environment, and countless other topics.

As an example, scientific research and studies have proven handwashing helps eliminate germs that can cause illness. Handwashing does not prevent sickness 100 percent of the time, because some illnesses are genetic in nature, and sometimes people get sick through other types of exposure (inhalation of viruses or microbes, etc.). Regardless, the link between handwashing and disease prevention is clearly established and accepted by most people who understand that even though sickness can occur in spite of frequent handwashing, the scientific evidence is still sound and trustworthy.

- ***Document 44:*** President Obama Calls for Increased Openness and Transparency in Government
- ***Date:*** January 21, 2009
- ***Where:*** The White House
- ***Significance:*** One of the first things President Obama did when he took office was issue a memorandum to top federal officials outlining his plans to create a more open and transparent government. The memorandum emphasized that transparency, public participation, and collaboration between citizens and government officials are essential to achieve this goal.

DOCUMENT

January 21, 2009

Memorandum for the Heads of Executive Departments and Agencies

SUBJECT: Transparency and Open Government

My Administration is committed to creating an unprecedented level of openness in Government. We will work together to ensure the public trust and establish a system of transparency, public participation, and collaboration. Openness will strengthen our democracy and promote efficiency and effectiveness in Government.

Government should be transparent. Transparency promotes accountability and provides information for citizens about what their Government is doing. Information maintained by the Federal Government is a national asset. My Administration will take appropriate action, consistent with law and policy, to disclose information rapidly in forms that the public can readily find and use. Executive departments and agencies should harness new technologies to put information about their operations and decisions online and readily available to the public. Executive departments and agencies should also solicit public feedback to identify information of greatest use to the public.

Government should be participatory. Public engagement enhances the Government's effectiveness and improves the quality of its decisions. Knowledge is widely dispersed in society, and public officials benefit from having access to that dispersed knowledge. Executive departments and agencies should offer Americans increased opportunities to participate in policymaking and to provide their Government with the benefits of their collective expertise and information. Executive departments and agencies should also solicit public input on how we can increase and improve opportunities for public participation in Government.

Government should be collaborative. Collaboration actively engages Americans in the work of their Government. Executive departments and agencies should use innovative tools, methods, and systems to cooperate among themselves, across all levels of Government, and with nonprofit organizations, businesses, and individuals in the private sector. Executive departments and agencies should solicit public feedback to assess and improve their level of collaboration and to identify new opportunities for cooperation.

I direct the Chief Technology Officer, in coordination with the Director of the Office of Management and Budget (OMB) and the Administrator of General Services, to coordinate the development by appropriate executive departments and agencies, within 120 days, of recommendations for an Open Government Directive, to be issued by the Director of OMB, that instructs executive departments and agencies to take specific actions implementing the principles set forth in this memorandum. The independent agencies should comply with the Open Government Directive.

This memorandum is not intended to, and does not, create any right or benefit, substantive or procedural, enforceable at law or in equity by a party against the United States, its departments, agencies, or entities, its officers, employees, or agents, or any other person.

This memorandum shall be published in the *Federal Register*.

BARACK OBAMA

SOURCE: Obama, Barack. "Transparency and Open Government." The White House. January 21, 2009. https://obamawhitehouse.archives.gov/the-press-office/transparency-and-open-government

- ***Document:*** Letter from Journalists to President Obama Accusing His Administration of Straying from Its Vows of Government Transparency
- ***Date:*** July 8, 2014
- ***Where:*** Letter sent to White House
- ***Significance:*** This letter to President Obama, signed by the leaders of thirty-eight professional journalism and information-gathering groups, criticized his administration's lack of openness, especially in light of his promise at the outset of his presidency to make government more transparent.

DOCUMENT

President Barack Obama

The White House
Washington, D.C
July 8, 2014
Mr. President,

You recently expressed concern that frustration in the country is breeding cynicism about democratic government. You need look no further than your own administration for a major source of that frustration—politically driven suppression of news and information about federal agencies. We call on you to take a stand to stop the spin and let the sunshine in.

Over the past two decades, public agencies have increasingly prohibited staff from communicating with journalists unless they go through public affairs offices or through political appointees. This trend has been especially pronounced in the federal government. We consider these restrictions a form of censorship—an attempt to control what the public is allowed to see and hear.

The stifling of free expression is happening despite your pledge on your first day in office to bring "a new era of openness" to federal government—and the subsequent executive orders and directives which were supposed to bring such openness about.

Recent research has indicated the problem is getting worse throughout the nation, particularly at the federal level. Journalists are reporting that most federal agencies prohibit their employees from communicating with the press unless the bosses have public relations staffers sitting in on the conversations. Contact is often blocked completely. When public affairs officers speak, even about routine public matters, they often do so confidentially in spite of having the title "spokesperson." Reporters seeking interviews are expected to seek permission, often providing questions in advance. Delays can stretch for days, longer than most deadlines allow. Public affairs officers might send their own written responses of slick non-answers. Agencies hold on-background press conferences with unnamed officials, on a not-for-attribution basis.

In many cases, this is clearly being done to control what information journalists—and the audience they serve—have access to. A survey found 40 percent of public affairs officers admitted they blocked certain reporters because they did not like what they wrote.

Some argue that controlling media access is needed to ensure information going out is correct. But when journalists cannot interview agency staff, or can only do so under surveillance, it undermines public understanding of, and trust in, government. This is not a "press vs. government" issue. This is about fostering a strong democracy where people have the information they need to self-govern and trust in its governmental institutions.

It has not always been this way. In prior years, reporters walked the halls of agencies and called staff people at will. Only in the past two administrations have media access controls been tightened at most agencies. Under this administration, even non-defense agencies have asserted in writing their power to prohibit contact with journalists without surveillance. Meanwhile, agency personnel are free to speak to others—lobbyists, special-interest representatives, people with money—without these controls and without public oversight.

Here are some recent examples:

- The New York Times ran a story last December on the soon-to-be implemented ICD-10 medical coding system, a massive change for the health care system that will affect the whole public. But the Centers for Medicare and Medicaid Services (CMS), one of the federal agencies in charge of ICD-10, wouldn't allow staff to talk to the reporter.
- A reporter with Investigative Post, an online news organization in New York, asked three times without success over the span of six weeks to have someone at EPA answer questions about the agency's actions regarding the city of Buffalo's alleged mishandling of "universal waste" and hazardous waste.
- A journalist with Reuters spent more than a month trying to get EPA's public affairs office to approve him talking with an agency scientist about the effects of climate change. The public affairs officer did not respond to him after his initial request, nor did her supervisor, until the frustrated journalist went over their heads and contacted EPA's chief of staff.

The undersigned organizations ask that you seek an end to this restraint on communication in federal agencies. We ask that you issue a clear directive telling federal employees they're not only free to answer questions from reporters and the public, but actually encouraged to do so. We believe that is one of the most important things you can do for the nation now, before the policies become even more entrenched.

We also ask you provide an avenue through which any incidents of this suppression of communication may be reported and corrected. Create an ombudsman to monitor and enforce your stated goal of restoring transparency to government and giving the public the unvarnished truth about its workings. That will go a long way toward dispelling Americans' frustration and cynicism before it further poisons our democracy.

Further ***examples*** on the issue are provided as well as other ***resources***.

Sincerely,

David Cuillier
President
Society of Professional Journalists

Beth Parke
Executive Director
Society of Environmental Journalists
. . . (includes 36 additional signatories from various professional associations)

SOURCE: Society of Professional Journalists. "Letter Urges President Obama to Be More Transparent." July 8, 2014. https://www.spj.org/news.asp?ref=1253. Used by permission of the Society of Professional Journalists.

ANALYSIS

Barack Obama pledged during his presidential campaign that he would work to create a more transparent, open, and trustworthy government. To this end, on his first day in office, President Obama issued a memorandum to the heads of executive departments and agencies, reinforcing that he was "committed to creating an unprecedented level of openness in Government" and outlining how that goal could be achieved (January 21, 2009). The memorandum aimed to make government more accessible and reliable in the eyes of the public by reducing influence from special interests, tracking government spending, and improving means for the public to access government information.

An official Open Government Directive from President Obama was released eleven months later in December 2009. The document emphasized that transparency, participation, and collaboration were essential to establishing a more open government. Additionally, the directive provided agencies with established deadlines for specific initiatives such as publishing government information online, improving the quality of government information, working cooperatively to create a culture of open government, and creating a policy framework for open government (Orszag 2009).

President Obama took additional steps to achieve his goals of government transparency. For instance, he opened White House visitor logs to the public so citizens would know who had direct access to the administration, and he revoked an executive order from President George W. Bush that had further restricted access to the records of former U.S. presidents. Obama also issued his own executive orders, leading to the declassification of a huge backlog of federal documents.

Expanding federal records availability through the Freedom of Information Act (FOIA) was another Obama administration goal. In January 2009, the president stated in a memorandum "In the face of doubt, openness prevails. The Government should not keep information confidential merely because public officials might be embarrassed by disclosure, because errors and failures might be revealed, or because of speculative or abstract fears" (Obama 2009). In 2016, President Obama signed the "FOIA Improvement Act," widening access to official documents.

In spite of these efforts to bridge the gap between the public and its government by creating greater openness and transparency, five years into his presidency, Obama was being roundly criticized for betraying his original pledge and failing to institute the open government he had promised. In 2016, more than thirty-six journalism and open government leaders united to pen a collective letter to the president, denouncing constrictive practices within the administration that prevented them from obtaining and delivering important information to the American public. Signatories of the letter pointed out that in contrast to President Obama's promises to be the most transparent president in history, he directed an administration in which officials and federal employees repeatedly restricted and suppressed requested information. They called on the president to restore journalists' access to important information by encouraging unrestricted communications with federal employees, creating a system to report violations of his directive, and monitoring progress toward established goals.

Others went further, accusing the Obama administration of not only failing to be transparent but of purposely concealing information through official policies and actions, such as rescinding an existing regulation requiring federal officials to comply with FOIA (Burnett 2016). An *Associated Press* analysis showed record numbers of FOIA requests that were censored or denied during Obama's presidency (Bridis 2017). And during Obama's presidency, the government prosecuted more leaks under the 1917 Espionage Act than all preceding administrations combined (ARTICLE 19 et al. 2018). The Committee to Protect Journalists issued a blistering assessment of the administration's secrecy and aggressive prosecution of whistleblowers and leakers. *New York Times* public editor Margaret Sullivan commented, "It's turning out to be the administration of unprecedented secrecy and unprecedented attacks on a free press" (Downie Jr. & Rafsky 2013).

Not all agreed, however, with the harsh assessment. While acknowledging Obama failed to meet all his stated goals, Steven Aftergood, director of the Federation of American Scientists Project on Government Secrecy, gave the administration credit for major achievements made. "If this was not the most transparent administration in history," he said, "then which administration was?" (White 2017).

The transparency of Obama's successor, President Donald Trump, has also been called into question, to the extent that it partially defined his presidency. In spite of his assertions of being the most transparent president in history (Jacobson 2019), his record has drawn repeated criticism from journalists, government watchdog groups, and other information-seeking organizations for misrepresenting or concealing important data. Experts cite President Trump's refusal to release information made public during previous administrations including personal tax records, White House visitor logs, and unfiltered information about general health or medical visits. Concealment of health-related information became an issue of worldwide concern when the president contracted COVID-19 in October 2020 and refused or sidestepped repeated requests for information regarding date of infection, type and severity of symptoms, nature of test results, and possible contacts—all questions related to his capacity to fulfill his duties as commander-in-chief (Kreiter 2020).

Analysts also point to President Trump's handling of the coronavirus pandemic. Trump repeatedly downplayed its severity, telling Americans it was completely under control and would disappear quickly. As late as September, he said the virus "affects virtually nobody," contradicting all available scientific data. The president also routinely eschewed CDC recommendations to wear masks, engage in social distancing, and participate in contact tracing. Even after contracting the virus, the president continued to minimize the pandemic, telling Americans "Don't let it [coronavirus] dominate you. Don't be afraid of it" in spite of the United States having the highest death toll in the world at that time (Bendix & Gould 2020).

Oversight groups have raised concerns that precedents set by the Trump administration could have far-reaching effects for future administrations and for the American public (Bublé 2020). Withholding information was common practice under the Trump administration, they say, and included actions like concealment of documents related to investigations of the administration, blocking congressional testimony, concealment of illegal or inhumane policies against migrants being held in U.S. detention centers, defiance of reporting and declassification requirements outlined in the 2020 National Defense Authorization Act, and removal of data and information (particularly related to climate change) from government websites, to name a few (Tringali & Kinsella 2020; Cortez 2019; Ellington 2019; U.S. Commission 2019; Schoenberger 2018).

Access to government documents and information also became more complicated and costly under the Trump administration. In 2017, 78 percent of requests for documents under FOIA were denied, or the files were said to be censored. This contributed to a record 1,448 lawsuits filed in 2019 on behalf of individuals or agencies unsatisfied with what they received after filing FOIA requests (compared to 456 in 2001) (Bublé 2020).

Analysts point out that in some regards, President Trump was uniquely transparent because he communicated directly with the American public through Twitter. However, watchdog groups counter that this type of information-sharing was neither formal nor data-driven, was often inaccurate, and did not inform the public about the administration's actions in a way that promoted or ensured accountability (Jacobson 2019).

FURTHER READING

Bublé, Courtney. "Transparency in the Trump Era." *Government Executive*. March 10, 2020. https://www.govexec.com/management/2020/03/transparency-trump-era/163574/

Dawe, Sharon S., and Natalie Helbig. "Information Strategies for Open Government: Challenges and Prospects for Deriving Public Value from Government Transparency." In *International Conference on Electronic Government*, 50–60. Berlin, Heidelberg: Springer, 2010.

Metcalfe, Daniel J. "The History of Government Transparency." In *Research Handbook on Transparency*. United Kingdom: Edward Elgar Publishing, 2014.

Orszag, Peter R. "Open Government Directive: Memorandum for the Heads of Executive Departments and Agencies." White House. December 8, 2009. https://obamawhitehouse.archives.gov/open/documents/open-government-directive

Roberts, Alasdair. *Blacked Out: Government Secrecy in the Information Age*. Cambridge University Press, 2006.

Wasike, Ben. "FOI in Transition: A Comparative Analysis of the Freedom of Information Act Performance between the Obama and Trump Administrations." *Government Information Quarterly* 37, no. 2 (2020).

- ***Document 45:*** Obama White House Press Reaction to Wikileaks Release of Classified Documents
- ***Date:*** November 28, 2010
- ***Where:*** White House, Washington, DC
- ***Significance:*** The release of classified State Department documents through the Wikileaks website was condemned by the Obama Administration and denounced as a threat to foreign policy. The White House subsequently called on each department or agency to review its security practices and ensure classified information would not again be breached and publicly disclosed.

DOCUMENT

The White House

Office of the Press Secretary
For Immediate Release
November 28, 2010
Statement by the Press Secretary

We anticipate the release of what are claimed to be several hundred thousand classified State Department cables on Sunday night that detail private diplomatic discussions with foreign governments. By its very nature, field reporting to Washington is candid and often incomplete information. It is not an expression of policy, nor does it always shape final policy decisions. Nevertheless, these cables could compromise private discussions with foreign governments and opposition leaders, and when the substance of private conversations is printed on the front pages of newspapers across the world, it can deeply impact not only US foreign policy interests, but those of our allies and friends around the world. To be clear—such disclosures put at risk our diplomats, intelligence professionals, and people around the world who come to the United States for assistance in promoting democracy and open government. These documents also may include named individuals who in many cases live and work under oppressive regimes and who are trying to create more open and free societies. President Obama supports responsible, accountable, and open government at home and around the world, but this reckless and dangerous action runs counter to that goal. By releasing stolen and classified documents, Wikileaks has put at risk not only the cause of human rights but also the lives and work of these individuals. We condemn in the strongest terms the unauthorized disclosure of classified documents and sensitive national security information.

SOURCE: Office of the Press Secretary. "Statement by the Press Secretary." The White House, November 28, 2010. https://obamawhitehouse.archives.gov/the-press-office/2010/11/28/statement-press-secretary

ANALYSIS

Following the terrorist attacks of September 11, 2001, the U.S. government was on high alert, actively searching for additional threats to the nation's safety. Some of the more troubling subsequent breaches of security, however, did not involve terrorists, bombs, or airplanes. They came in the form of leaked government documents disseminated quickly and widely through the internet, raising new questions about the balance between the public's right to be informed of government activities and the government's right to withhold information from the public for the sake of national security.

The First Amendment generally protects the publication of sensitive or classified information obtained legally. However, the constitutionality of acquiring or distributing such information without authorization is much more ambiguous. In spite of the fact that government officials often refer to unauthorized disclosure of classified information as illegal, no single statute makes it a crime. Rather, a series of laws and considerations determine the legality or illegality of such disclosure based on factors like the intention of the person supplying the leak, the identity of the recipient, the nature of the information disclosed, and the manner and extent to which the leak is shared.

In the post 9/11 context, a number of major leaks involving government documents begged the question of who can be held responsible when confidential information is disclosed without authorization. Historically, prosecutions have been reserved for government employees who breached their obligations to protect classified information. These leakers were usually charged with violating one or more sections of the century-old Espionage Act or similar statutes that prohibit dissemination of national defense information.

However, such charges can be problematic because the Espionage Act does not specifically define what constitutes a matter of national security. Whistleblowers have often challenged government prosecutorial attempts, saying authorities targeted them not because they actually disclosed matters of national security, but because the information they revealed was embarrassing or unflattering to government officials.

While government employees are most often prosecuted for leaking classified data, anyone can be charged for removal and/or retention of classified materials. Receipt of classified documents by foreign governments is also prohibited under existing laws. However, those who publish classified information have remained relatively shielded from punishment. The historic function of a free press in a democratic society has largely protected newspapers, internet sites, and other information-sharing platforms from legal ramifications for publishing such materials. The Supreme Court reinforced this in its 1971 "Pentagon Papers" decision (*New York Times Co. v. United States*). As of 2017, the government had never successfully prosecuted a traditional news organization for publishing information obtained through a leak.

Two of the largest leaks in recent U.S. history involved the posting of classified documents on the WikiLeaks website. The first involved U.S. army intelligence analyst Chelsea Manning (then Bradley Manning) who in 2009 began to covertly copy and share with WikiLeaks more than 250,000 U.S. State Department diplomatic cables, videos, and other documents. The leaks revealed sensitive information about topics including U.S. intelligence and counterintelligence, nuclear disarmament, and the War on Terror. Among the documents was a video showing U.S. troops in Iraq killing unarmed civilians. Manning was convicted of multiple espionage-related charges in 2013 and sentenced to thirty-five years in prison. Her sentence was commuted in 2017 by President Obama.

Manning's leaks, however, would have been impossible without the cooperation of WikiLeaks and its founder, Julian Assange. The Australian internet activist was known for encouraging hackers to breach classified systems and share private government documents. His publication of top-secret documents on the WikiLeaks website exposed a technological national security vulnerability that had never before been challenged so broadly and directly. Like whistleblowers who leaked *The Pentagon Papers* to publicly expose decisions made by the Nixon administration, Assange alleges that he also disclosed classified government documents for the public's benefit. However, while Nixon-era whistleblowers relied on the press to circulate classified information, Assange benefitted from the rapid and direct reach of internet technology to publish massive numbers of documents on a global platform.

In 2019, authorities sought to extradite Assange from the UK to the United States to face seventeen Espionage Act charges and one additional charge related to his role in conspiring with Manning and others to acquire and leak classified documents. This is the first time the Espionage Act has been used to indict a publisher. Journalists, citing the need to conspire with sources on a regular basis as part of their job, fear an Assange conviction would set a dangerous precedent for the press.

Assange was granted asylum by the Ecuadorian embassy in London but was later arrested by British authorities for jumping bail in 2012. If extradited to the United States and convicted of all charges, he faces up to 175 years in prison.

In 2013, another major national security breach occurred when Edward Snowden, a former contractor for the National Security Administration (NSA), leaked a trove of top secret documents to the *Washington Post* and the *Guardian* newspapers. The documents disclosed a secret NSA program that gathered metadata on millions of Americans through telephone surveillance. Top NSA officials had repeatedly insisted that they were not spying on Americans until the Snowden documents proved otherwise.

Snowden fled first to Hong Kong and then to Russia to avoid prosecution under the Espionage Act. He was granted asylum in Russia in 2014 and remained there as of September 2020 on residency permit extensions.

Meanwhile, in September 2020, the U.S. Court of Appeals for the Ninth Circuit ruled that the NSA's telephony metadata program was illegal; by collecting phone records of millions of individuals, the agency had greatly exceeded its congressionally granted authority and thus violated the Foreign Intelligence Surveillance Act. The court also hinted the program may have unconstitutionally violated the Fourth Amendment but declined to rule on that issue. If the lower court's decision is appealed, it is likely that the Supreme Court will address this constitutionality question.

Although the appeals court ruling did not directly involve Snowden, he viewed it as a vindication of his decision to expose the secret program through leaked documents. Prominent members of Congress agreed. Representative Matt Gaetz and Senator Rand Paul argued, for example, that Snowden should be pardoned because his whistleblower actions revealed critical abuses of government power that were of greater importance to the country than his violation of the law. Others disagree; numerous U.S. officials have called for Snowden's extradition and prosecution as a traitor whose actions undermined U.S. intelligence capabilities. As of January 2021, Snowden's legal fate remained uncertain.

Although retrieval and disclosure of classified information has been generally considered outside the bounds of the First Amendment, publication of the information has more often been regarded as protected speech. As courts ultimately decide the constitutionality of this unique application of press freedom, they will have to balance national security threats with the public interest to determine who might best be served, or harmed, by the release of classified information.

FURTHER READING

Altschuler, Bruce E. "Is the Pentagon Papers Case Relevant in the Age of WikiLeaks?" *Political Science Quarterly (Wiley-Blackwell)* 130, no. 3 (2015): 401–23.

Greenberg, Andy. "Is WikiLeaks a Media Organization? The First Amendment Doesn't Care." *Forbes*. April 22, 2011. https://www.forbes.com/sites/andygreenberg/2011/04/21/is-wikileaks-a-media-organization-the-first-amendment-doesnt-care/#3e372b5310e0

Grier, Peter. "WikiLeaks: Would First Amendment Protect Julian Assange?" *Christian Science Monitor*. December 3, 2010. https://www.csmonitor.com/USA/2010/1203/WikiLeaks-Would-First-Amendment-protect-Julian-Assange

Stone, Geoffrey R. "Wikileaks and the First Amendment." *Federal Communications Law Journal* 64 (2011): 477.

U.S. Library of Congress. Congressional Research Service. *Criminal Prohibitions on Leaks and Other Disclosures of Classified Defense Information*, by Stephen P. Mulligan and Jennifer K. Elsea. R41404. March 7, 2017.

- ***Document 46:*** Excerpts from *Citizens United v. Federal Election Commission* Supreme Court Decision
- ***Date:*** January 21, 2010

- ***Where:*** Supreme Court of the United States
- ***Significance:*** This 5–4 Supreme Court ruling granted corporations and labor unions the same First Amendment free speech rights as individuals, including the right to spend money on political communication as a form of free speech. This decision overturned existing restrictions that had prohibited corporations and unions from making independent expenditures for electioneering communications. The decision led to a dramatic increase in political spending by industry groups, major corporations, labor unions, and other politically powerful special interests.

DOCUMENT

. . . The First Amendment provides that "Congress shall make no law . . . abridging the freedom of speech." Laws enacted to control or suppress speech may operate at different points in the speech process. The following are just a few examples of restrictions that have been attempted at different stages of the speech process—all laws found to be invalid: restrictions requiring a permit at the outset, *Watchtower Bible & Tract Soc. of N.Y., Inc.* v. *Village of Stratton* (2002); imposing a burden by impounding proceeds on receipts or royalties, *Simon & Schuster, Inc.* v. *Members of N.Y. State Crime Victims Bd.* (1991); seeking to exact a cost after the speech occurs, *New York Times Co.* v. *Sullivan* (1964); and subjecting the speaker to criminal penalties, *Brandenburg* v. *Ohio* (1969) *(per curiam)*.

The law before us is an outright ban, backed by criminal sanctions. Section 441b makes it a felony for all corporations—including nonprofit advocacy corporations—either to expressly advocate the election or defeat of candidates or to broadcast electioneering communications within 30 days of a primary election and 60 days of a general election. Thus, the following acts would all be felonies under §441b: The Sierra Club runs an ad, within the crucial phase of 60 days before the general election, that exhorts the public to disapprove of a Congressman who favors logging in national forests; the National Rifle Association publishes a book urging the public to vote for the challenger because the incumbent U. S. Senator supports a handgun ban; and the American Civil Liberties Union creates a Web site telling the public to vote for a Presidential candidate in light of that candidate's defense of free speech. These prohibitions are classic examples of censorship. . . .

Section 441b's prohibition on corporate independent expenditures is thus a ban on speech. As a "restriction on the amount of money a person or group can spend on political communication during a campaign," that statute "necessarily reduces the quantity of expression by restricting the number of issues discussed, the depth of their exploration, and the size of the audience reached." *Buckley* v. *Valeo* (1976) *(per curiam)*. Were the Court to uphold these restrictions, the Government could repress speech by silencing certain voices at any of the various points in the speech process.

See *McConnell*, *supra*, at 251 (opinion of Scalia, J.) (Government could repress speech by "attacking all levels of the production and dissemination of ideas," for "effective public communication requires the speaker to make use of the services of others"). If §441b applied to individuals, no one would believe that it is merely a time, place, or manner restriction on speech. Its purpose and effect are to silence entities whose voices the Government deems to be suspect.

Speech is an essential mechanism of democracy, for it is the means to hold officials accountable to the people. See *Buckley*, *supra*, at 14–15 ("In a republic where the people are sovereign, the ability of the citizenry to make informed choices among candidates for office is essential"). The right of citizens to inquire, to hear, to speak, and to use information to reach consensus is a precondition to enlightened self-government and a necessary means to protect it. The First Amendment "'has its fullest and most urgent application' to speech uttered during a campaign for political office." . . .

For these reasons, political speech must prevail against laws that would suppress it, whether by design or inadvertence. Laws that burden political speech are "subject to strict scrutiny," which requires the Government to prove that the restriction "furthers a compelling interest and is narrowly tailored to achieve that interest." *WRTL*, 551 U. S., at 464 (opinion of Roberts, C. J.). While it might be maintained that political speech simply cannot be banned or restricted as a categorical matter, see *Simon & Schuster*, 502 U. S., at 124 (Kennedy, J., concurring in judgment), the quoted language from *WRTL* provides a sufficient framework for protecting the relevant First Amendment interests in this case. We shall employ it here.

Premised on mistrust of governmental power, the First Amendment stands against attempts to disfavor certain subjects or viewpoints. See, *e.g.*, *United States* v. *Playboy Entertainment Group, Inc.*, (2000) (striking down content-based restriction). Prohibited, too, are restrictions distinguishing among different speakers, allowing speech by some but not others. See *First Nat. Bank of Boston* v. *Bellotti*, (1978). As instruments to censor, these categories are interrelated: Speech restrictions based on the identity of the speaker are all too often simply a means to control content.

Quite apart from the purpose or effect of regulating content, moreover, the Government may commit a constitutional wrong when by law it identifies certain preferred speakers. By taking the right to speak from some and giving it to others, the Government deprives the disadvantaged person or class of the right to use speech to strive to establish worth, standing, and respect for the speaker's voice. The Government may not by these means deprive the public of the right and privilege to determine for itself what speech and speakers are worthy of consideration. The First Amendment protects speech and speaker, and the ideas that flow from each.

The Court has upheld a narrow class of speech restrictions that operate to the disadvantage of certain persons, but these rulings were based on an interest in allowing governmental entities to perform their functions. . . . The corporate independent expenditures at issue in this case, however, would not interfere with governmental functions, so these cases are inapposite. These precedents stand only for the proposition that there are certain governmental functions that cannot operate without some restrictions on particular kinds of speech. By contrast, it is inherent in the nature of the political process that voters must be free to obtain information from diverse sources in order to determine how to cast their votes. At least before *Austin*, the Court had not allowed the exclusion of a class of speakers from the general public dialogue.

We find no basis for the proposition that, in the context of political speech, the Government may impose restrictions on certain disfavored speakers. Both history and logic lead us to this conclusion.

SOURCE: Citizens United v. Federal Election Commission, 558 U.S.310 (2010)

ANALYSIS

Citizens United v. Federal Election Commission was, at the time, considered one of the most influential Supreme Court First Amendment decisions in decades. This narrow 5–4 decision paved the way for corporations and labor unions to play a much larger role in elections by granting them the same First Amendment rights as individuals, thus allowing them to influence political campaigns through funding of campaign communications.

For much of the twentieth century, campaign funding by corporations, unions, and federal employees was limited under various campaign finance laws including the Tillman Act (1907) and Taft-Hartley Act (1947). In 1971, Congress passed more stringent regulations under the Federal Elections Campaign Act (FECA). This act required campaign finance transparency through public reporting of funding sources and emphasized balance by limiting individual and group political campaign contributions. Amendments to FECA in 1974 led to creation of the Federal Elections Commission (FEC), an independent regulatory agency charged with enforcing federal campaign finance law.

Initially, the FEC attempted to place caps on campaign spending, but these limitations were struck down as unconstitutional by the Supreme Court in *Buckley v. Valeo* (1976). The court argued that for both individuals and groups, independent spending is a First Amendment free speech right that cannot be restricted. The *Buckley* decision established financial support of a candidate or political party as a form of protected speech. Then in 1978 the Supreme Court ruled 5–4 in *First National Bank of Boston v. Bellotti* that attempting to influence the outcome of an election is a free speech right afforded to corporations as well as individuals.

However, in *Austin v. Michigan State Chamber of Commerce* (1990), the court upheld a Michigan law that prohibited corporations from using general treasury money to support or oppose a candidate in a state election. The court argued that use of general funds could result in excessive political influence, given the numerous legal advantages enjoyed by these companies. Additionally, the court said, corporations were still free to participate politically through the expenditure of segregated funds.

In 2002, Congress amended the 1971 Federal Election Campaign Act by passing the Bipartisan Campaign Reform Act (BCRA). Also known as the McCain-Feingold Act, BCRA regulated campaign financing and limited the scope and nature of political campaign contributions that could be made by corporations and labor unions. BCRA was passed in part to eliminate the use of "soft money" (unlimited contributions to a political party or political action committee) to fund political advertising for or against a particular candidate. The Supreme Court upheld most provisions of BCRA when it was challenged in *McConnell v. Federal Election Commission* (2003).

The vast majority of campaign finance laws established to balance citizens' interests with corporate and union interests were upended in 2010, however, by the Supreme Court's ruling in *Citizens United v Federal Election Commission*. The case arose from the desire of the nonprofit group Citizens United to circulate a movie it had made that was critical of presidential candidate Hillary Clinton. The group challenged BCRA restrictions affecting the distribution and promotion of the movie. Its primary argument against regulations focused on campaign finance laws that prohibited corporations or unions from spending general funds on "electioneering communications"—publicly distributed broadcast, cable, or satellite communications referring to a federal candidate that appear within thirty days of a primary or sixty days of a general election. It also challenged rules requiring disclosure of funding sources.

In a 5–4 decision, a sharply divided Supreme Court ruled that BCRA's provisions banning use of corporate general treasury funds for political advocacy or electioneering communications violates First Amendment freedom of speech. This decision overruled *Austin* and established political spending as a form of protected free speech, thus giving companies permission to finance communications that were politically based. The court did not, however, overturn the BCRA's disclaimer and disclosure requirements, nor did it overturn the ban on direct contributions to political candidates.

The *Citizens* ruling gave unions and corporations the same First Amendment speech rights as individuals, with Justice Anthony Kennedy noting "the First Amendment does not allow political speech restrictions based on a speaker's corporate identity." Justice Kennedy rejected the government's anti-corruption justification for restricting corporate and union political participation, noting in the majority opinion that he could find no solid basis for such an argument and that political expression should be among the most protected forms of speech.

Citizens United significantly impacted corporate involvement in politics in the United States by granting corporations greater power and ability to influence messaging. With restrictions on political speech and political spending essentially removed, corporations are now free to spend unlimited amounts of "soft money" on ads and other political communications intended to indirectly help a particular campaign. (Direct contributions to candidates are still prohibited.)

Those who viewed the court's decision as a advancing a positive public policy laud the ruling as a victory for free speech. They commend the removal of restrictions on corporate and union political spending, saying existing regulations were unduly prohibitive and failed to give adequate voice to corporate concerns. Those opposing the ruling, however, contend that political donations from individuals are no match for the big money and the resulting political influence of large corporations. They argue allowing corporations to spend large sums on political advertising weakens the role of individual Americans in the political process. Considering the court's argument that political spending is a form of speech, they maintain the *Citizens* ruling grants far greater speech to the wealthy than the poor.

Analysts also point out that just two months after the *Citizens United* decision, the court made another major ruling in *SpeechNow.org v. FEC* that eliminated individual contribution limits. This decision led to the rise and influence of super political action committees (PACs) that have given wealthy individuals an even more disproportionate influence over elections at all levels.

A Brennan Center for Justice report found that in 2014, for example, outside groups outspent the candidates in 80 percent of the competitive races, and almost 60 percent of the $1 billion spent in federal elections that year was given by just 195 individuals and their spouses (Vandewalker 2015). Furthermore, as outside contributions to political advocacy have grown, so have "dark money" contributions from nonprofits that are not required to disclose where their funding comes from.

Federal efforts to overturn *Citizens* with a constitutional amendment have so far been unsuccessful, but numerous states have modified their own campaign finance laws in response to the landmark decision.

FURTHER READING

Ahmad, Samar. "Unmasking Democracy: How Corporate Influence Is Eroding Democratic Governance." *Harvard International Review* 41, no. 2 (2020): 54–57.

Dunbar, John. "The 'Citizens United' Decision and Why It Matters." Center for Public Integrity. May 10, 2018. https://publicintegrity.org/politics/the-citizens-united-decision-and-why-it-matters/

Hansen, Wendy L., Michael S. Rocca, and Brittany Leigh Ortiz. "The Effects of Citizens United on Corporate Spending in the 2012 Presidential Election." *Journal of Politics* 77, no. 2 (2015): 535–45.

Lau, Tim. "Citizens United Explained." Brennan Center for Justice. December 12, 2019. https://www.brennancenter.org/our-work/research-reports/citizens-united-explained

Torchinsky, Jason, and Ezra Reese. "State Legislative Responses to Citizens United: Five Years Later." *Syracuse Law Review* 66 (2016): 273.

Tribe, Laurence H. "Dividing Citizens United: The Case v. The Controversy." *Constitutional Commentary* 30, no. 2 (2015): 463–94.

- ***Document 47:*** Syllabus from Supreme Court Case *Elonis v. United States*
- ***Date:*** June 1, 2015
- ***Where:*** Supreme Court of the United States
- ***Significance:*** In this SCOTUS case addressing the nature of "true threats," justices overturned the interpretations of lower courts and ruled the defendant's conviction under the federal threats statute could not be based on a reasonable person's interpretation of violent messages he posted to Facebook. By basing their opinion on statutory requirements rather than First Amendment considerations, justices failed to establish exactly what degree of intent to threaten others is necessary to establish criminal wrongdoing. As a result, the category of "true threats" as unprotected speech under the First Amendment remains largely undefined.

DOCUMENT

Syllabus

ELONIS v. UNITED STATES

CERTIORARI TO THE UNITED STATES COURT OF APPEALS FOR THE THIRD CIRCUIT

No. 13–983. Argued December 1, 2014—Decided June 1, 2015

After his wife left him, petitioner Anthony Douglas Elonis, under the pseudonym "Tone Dougie," used the social networking Web site Facebook to post self-styled rap lyrics containing graphically violent language and imagery concerning his wife, co-workers, a kindergarten class, and state and federal law enforcement. These posts were often interspersed with disclaimers that the lyrics were "fictitious" and not intended to depict real persons, and with statements that Elonis was exercising his First Amendment rights. Many who knew him saw his posts as threatening, however, including his boss, who fired him for threatening co-workers, and his wife, who sought and was granted a state court protection-from-abuse order against him.

When Elonis's former employer informed the Federal Bureau of Investigation of the posts, the agency began monitoring Elonis's Facebook activity and eventually arrested him. He was charged with five counts of violating 18 U. S. C. §875 (c), which makes it a federal crime to transmit in interstate commerce "any communication containing any threat . . . to injure the person of another." At trial, Elonis requested a jury instruction that the Government was required to prove that he intended to communicate a "true threat." Instead, the District Court told the jury that Elonis could be found guilty if a reasonable person would foresee that his statements would be interpreted as a threat. Elonis was convicted on four of the five counts and renewed his jury instruction challenge on appeal. The Third Circuit affirmed, holding that Section 875 (c) requires only the intent to communicate words that the defendant understands, and that a reasonable person would view as a threat.

Held: The Third Circuit's instruction, requiring only negligence with respect to the communication of a threat, is not sufficient to support a conviction under Section 87 (c). Pp. 7–17.

(a) Section 875(c) does not indicate whether the defendant must intend that the communication contain a threat, and the parties can show no indication of a particular mental state requirement in the statute's text. Elonis claims that the word "threat," by definition, conveys the intent to inflict harm. But common definitions of "threat" speak to what the statement conveys—not to the author's mental state. The Government argues that the express "intent to extort" requirements in neighboring Sections 875(b) and (d) should preclude courts from implying an unexpressed "intent to threaten" requirement in Section 875(c). The most that can be concluded from such a comparison, however, is that Congress did not mean to confine Section 875(c) to crimes of extortion, not that it meant to exclude a mental state requirement. Pp. 7–9.

(b) The Court does not regard "mere omission from a criminal enactment of any mention of criminal intent" as dispensing with such a requirement. *Morissette v. United States.* This rule of construction reflects the basic principle that "wrongdoing must be conscious to be criminal," and that a defendant must be "blameworthy in mind" before he can be found guilty. *Id.* The "general rule" is that a guilty mind is "a necessary element in the indictment and proof of every crime." *United States v. Balint.* Thus, criminal statutes are generally interpreted "to include broadly applicable scienter requirements, even where the statute . . . does not contain them." *United States v. X-Citement Video, Inc.* This does not mean that a defendant must know that his conduct is illegal, but a defendant must have knowledge of "the facts that make his conduct fit the definition of the offense." *Staples v. United States.* Federal criminal statutes that are silent on the required mental state should be read to include "only that mens rea which is necessary to separate" wrongful from innocent conduct. *Carter v. United States.* In some cases, a general requirement that a defendant act knowingly is sufficient, but where such a requirement "would fail to protect the innocent actor," the statute "would need to be read to require . . . specific intent." *Ibid.*

(c) The "presumption in favor of a scienter requirement should apply to each of the statutory elements that criminalize otherwise innocent conduct." *X-Citement Video.* In the context of Section 875 (c), that requires proof that a communication was transmitted and that it contained a threat. And because "the crucial element separating legal innocence from wrongful conduct," *id.* is the threatening nature of the communication, the mental state requirement must apply to the fact that the communication contains a threat. Elonis's conviction was premised solely on how his posts would be viewed by a reasonable person, a standard feature of civil liability in tort law inconsistent with the conventional criminal conduct requirement of "awareness of some wrongdoing," *Staples.* This Court "ha[s] long been reluctant to infer that a negligence standard was intended in criminal statutes." *Rogers v. United States* (Marshall, J., concurring). And the Government fails to show that the instructions in this case required more than a mental state of negligence. *Hamling v. United States.* Section 875(c)'s mental state requirement is satisfied if the defendant transmits a communication for the purpose of issuing a threat or with knowledge that the communication will be viewed as a threat. The Court declines to address whether a mental state of recklessness would also suffice. Given the disposition here, it is unnecessary to consider any First Amendment issues. Pp. 13–17.

730 F. 3d. 321, reversed and remanded.

ROBERTS, C. J., delivered the opinion of the Court, in which SCALIA, KENNEDY, GINSBURG, BREYER, SOTOMAYOR, and KAGAN, JJ., joined. ALITO, J., filed an opinion concurring in part and dissenting in part. THOMAS, J., filed a dissenting opinion.

SOURCE: Elonis v. United States. 575 U.S. ____ (2015).

ANALYSIS

"True threats" constitute one of the few classes of unprotected speech under the First Amendment. While general threats are often protected under free speech doctrines, "true threats" are punishable because of the danger they pose and the likelihood that the threats will be carried out. However, distinguishing between hyperbole, frustrated rants, artistic expression, and true threats has proven challenging. Courts adjudicating true threats cases try to balance the right to protection from threat of violence with the right to engage in free expression.

The *Elonis* case hinges on the question of whether messages sent over the internet that would be considered threatening by a "reasonable person" constitute an unprotected true threat or whether subjective proof of intent to threaten is required before the messages can be considered a violation of the law.

Anthony Douglas Elonis posted numerous violent messages on Facebook under the pseudonym "Tone Dougie" after his wife of seven years left him. His messages, styled to resemble rap lyrics, were often accompanied by disclaimers stating they were not intended to depict real individuals and that Elonis was using his First Amendment rights to express himself.

Elonis's Facebook messages first drew attention when he posted a picture from a Halloween party at the amusement park where he worked. In the picture, captioned "I wish," he held a knife to the throat of a coworker. When the chief of park security saw the post, he fired Elonis, who then responded with additional messages indicating he still had access to the facility's keys and insinuating the facility could not be secured from "a man as mad as me." He was indicted for threatening employees and customers of the amusement park.

Elonis wrote additional disturbing posts directed toward his estranged wife, expressing his desire to kill her and describing in detail how her murder could be carried out. Even after she sought a Protection from Abuse order, Elonis continued publishing explicit messages on Facebook that described lethal actions toward his estranged wife and also toward law enforcement and local elementary schools. In spite of FBI investigations and monitoring of his posts, Elonis persisted, writing scenarios about engaging in heinous school shootings, desiring to slit an FBI agent's throat, and setting off a bomb if arrested.

At this point, federal prosecutors intervened. Elonis was arrested and charged with five counts of violating 18 U.S.C. Section 875(c), the federal statute that forbids interstate communication of any threat to kidnap or injure another person. The indictment was based on posts directed toward his ex-wife, local police, local elementary schools, and the FBI agent.

In district court, Elonis argued that the indictment should be dismissed based on the Supreme Court's *Virginia v. Black* (2003) decision, the first case in which the court established that a "true threat" required proof of subjective intention to threaten others. Elonis argued that it was not his intention to threaten anyone and therefore he did not violate the federal interstate communication statute. His motion to dismiss was denied. The district court referred to a third circuit precedent that the communication of a threat required only negligence to be considered criminal; proof of intent to threaten was not required.

Elonis then used the same argument in a jury instruction request, saying the government should explain to the jury that subjective intent is required to establish a "true threat." His request was once again denied, and the jury was instead instructed that a conviction could be based on a reasonable person's interpretation of Elonis's posts as threats. The jury found at least two of the counts against him were "true threats," and Elonis was convicted and sentenced to nearly four years in jail and three years of supervised release.

Elonis appealed to the Third Circuit Court of Appeals, saying the jury should have been instructed that a conviction required proof that he intended to make a true threat. A verdict not based on such proof, he said, violated his right to free speech. However, the third circuit affirmed the jury's decision, stating most courts relied upon an objective standard consideration when interpreting the federal threat statute. The fact that Elonis intentionally wrote the posts and that a reasonable person would consider them a threat was sufficient to warrant a conviction.

However, the Supreme Court did not share this view and granted certiorari (review of a lower court decision) to determine what standard of intent is necessary for an expression to constitute a "true threat."

The Supreme Court reversed and remanded the district court's decision based on what it considered an erroneous jury instruction. Chief Justice Roberts wrote for the majority that the "reasonable person" objective standard was not consistent with other requirements for criminal conduct, which necessitate an awareness of wrongdoing (mens rea). He applied the criminal law principle that in order for wrongdoing to be criminal, the person committing the crime must be aware that he or she is involved in wrongdoing. Although the statute under which Elonis was convicted required only transmission of a threat and interpretation as such by a reasonable person, Roberts reasoned that consideration of the "mental state of the author" must still be applied. He stated the requirement for intent or knowledge of wrongdoing is a principle broadly applied to criminal statutes, even when not explicitly stated in the statutes themselves.

Justice Roberts further explained the "reasonable person interpretation" standard applied by the third circuit was equivalent to civil liability in tort law. Under §875 (c), conduct is deemed either innocent or wrongful based on "the threatening nature of the communication," but determining that communication is threatening requires proof the defendant understands it as such. Without such proof, the standard for criminal liability is simple negligence. In other words, under the objective "reasonable person" standard, there is great risk that accidental conduct could be misinterpreted as criminal wrongdoing. For that reason, knowledge and intent to communicate a threat are essential (Federal 2015).

The court chose not to rule on the First Amendment question of whether or not 18 U.S.C. § 875 (c) violated Elonis's right to engage in free speech and instead reversed and remanded the decision leading to his conviction on statutory grounds. While lower courts had routinely interpreted § 875 (c) by applying the "true threats" doctrine from cases such as *Watts v. United States* and *Virginia v. Black* the court in *Elonis* neglected to apply these precedents. Instead, the majority focused on standards and statutory principles of intent in determining that a valid conviction for violation of § 875 (c) must involve proof of Elonis's intent to threaten others.

Perhaps most consequential was that the court's decision in this case did not resolve the constitutional question of what constitutes a "true threat." It also offered lower courts little indication of how to determine what mental state or degree of intent (mens rea) is required to distinguish innocent communication from a "true threat." In his partial dissention, Justice Alito argued that recklessness is a sufficient requirement, but said in this context, the lyrics written by Elonis were not likely to be interpreted as probable actions. Justice Thomas reasoned that proof of general intent to threaten was enough to merit punishment (in agreement with the interpretations of nine circuit courts). He felt Elonis's words alone met the objective standard for a true threat.

Because of the Supreme Court's lack of definitive guidance, however, circuit courts have varied widely in their interpretations of intent (mens rea) requirements. Some apply objective standards, others apply subjective standards, and some rely on both to determine whether a message is mere intimidation, or a constitutionally unprotected "true threat" (Best 2015).

FURTHER READING

"Before the Court in Elonis v. United States." *Supreme Court Debates* 18, no. 1 (2015): 32–35.

Best, Alison J. "Elonis v. United States: The Need to Uphold Individual Rights to Free Speech while Protecting Victims of Online True Threats." *Maryland Law Review* 75 (2015): 1127.

"Federal Threats Statute—Mens Rea and the First Amendment—Elonis v. United States." *Harvard Law Review* 129, no. 1 (2015): 331–40.

Hudson, David L., Jr. "When Do Rants Exceed First Amendment Boundaries and Become True Threats?" *ABA Journal*, August 24, 2018. https://www.abajournal.com/magazine/article/threatening_words_courts_protected_speech

Quek, Jing Xun. "Elonis v. United States: The Next Twelve Years." *Berkeley Technology Law Journal* 31, no. 2 (2016): 1109–36.

- ***Document 48:*** Foundation for Individual Rights in Education (FIRE) President Greg Lukianoff Decries Free Speech Restrictions on College Campuses
- ***Date:*** June 2, 2015
- ***Where:*** U.S. House of Representatives Committee on the Judiciary, Subcommittee on the Constitution and Civil Justice

- ***Significance:*** In this Congressional testimony, FIRE president and chief executive officer Greg Lukianoff outlines specific challenges to free speech on the nation's public colleges and university campuses and makes recommendations on how these restrictions might be addressed through policy revisions and Congressional intervention.

DOCUMENT

INTRODUCTION

The Supreme Court of the United States has identified America's colleges and universities as "vital centers for the Nation's intellectual life," but the reality today is that many of these institutions severely restrict free speech and open debate.

Speech codes—policies prohibiting student and faculty speech that would, outside the bounds of campus, be protected by the First Amendment—have repeatedly been struck down by federal and state courts. Yet they persist, even in the very jurisdictions where they have been ruled unconstitutional. The majority of American colleges and universities maintain speech codes.

The First Amendment prohibits the government—including governmental entities such as state universities—from restricting freedom of speech. Generally, if a state law would be declared unconstitutional for violating the First Amendment, a similar regulation at a state college or university is likewise unconstitutional. Despite the overwhelming weight of legal authority against college speech codes, the majority of institutions—including some of those that have been successfully sued over speech restrictions—still maintain and enforce unconstitutional policies.

Speech codes are almost never identified as such by the many colleges and universities that impose and enforce them. Instead, speech codes come in many forms, often with innocuous—sounding titles: "free speech zone" policies that limit student or faculty expression to small, remote areas of campus; email policies that ban "offensive" communication; civility policies that mandate politeness on pain of punishment; and—most commonly—overbroad, vague harassment policies that rely on subjective, amorphous definitions and thus restrict vast swaths of protected speech.

The effect of decades of speech codes in higher education is now sadly apparent in the attitudes of today's students towards speech with which they disagree. Increasingly, students are seizing the initiative from administrators by leading their own campaigns for censorship. Having been taught to fear freedom of speech, too many of today's students instead seek freedom from speech. This troubling, illiberal phenomenon has many manifestations: student-led campaigns to "disinvite" outside speakers who hold minority, contrarian, unpopular views; demands that literature dealing with mature content be accompanied by "trigger warnings"; and the demand for colleges to be "safe places" free from emotional harm.

Faculty free speech rights are also at risk. FIRE frequently defends professors who have been threatened with disciplinary action or punished for expressing unpopular views. The speech rights of faculty at public institutions have been particularly imperiled by confusion over the applicability, in the collegiate setting, of the Supreme Court's decision in *Garcetti v. Ceballos*—where the Court held that speech by public employees made pursuant to their official duties receives no First Amendment protection. With some appellate courts finding an academic freedom exception to *Garcetti* and others refusing to do so, faculty members are increasingly uncertain as to whether they may face retaliation for speech made in the context of their roles as public academics. This threat to academic freedom affects not only faculty members, but also students and American society more generally.

Although free speech on campus is imperiled in all of the ways described above, this testimony will focus on the three areas that Congress is uniquely positioned to help: (1) overly broad harassment policies, (2) impermissibly restrictive "free speech zone" policies, and (3) threats to academic freedom. If Congress were to address these three areas, college campuses might again begin to honor and fulfill their role as "the marketplace of ideas."

I. Harassment Policies

Federal anti-discrimination law requires colleges and universities receiving federal funding—virtually all institutions, both public and private—to prohibit discriminatory harassment on campus. Simultaneously, public universities are required by the First Amendment to honor students' freedom of speech. While private institutions of higher education are not bound by the First Amendment, those that explicitly promise free speech must honor that commitment.

Actual harassment is not protected by the First Amendment. The Supreme Court of the United States has set forth a clear definition of discriminatory harassment in the educational setting, a definition carefully tailored to fulfill public schools' twin obligations to respect free speech and prevent harassment. In *Davis v. Monroe County Board of Education* (1999), the Supreme Court defined student-on-student harassment in the educational context as targeted, unwelcome discriminatory conduct that is "so severe, pervasive, and objectively offensive, and that so undermines and detracts from the victims' educational experience, that the victim-students are effectively denied equal access to an institution's resources and opportunities." Public colleges and universities are legally obligated to maintain policies and practices aimed at preventing this type of genuine harassment from happening on their campuses while also honoring student and faculty First Amendment rights.

The *Davis* definition's utility in the educational setting is widely acknowledged. . . .

Unfortunately, institutions often inappropriately cite obligations under federal anti-discrimination laws to investigate and punish protected speech that is unequivocally not harassment. . . .

These misguided policies contribute to a climate of chilled speech on campuses across the nation—an effect apparent in the statistical data, which indicate that many students are reluctant to engage in open and robust debate in school. . . .

When students learn that saying the "wrong" thing can get them in trouble, they react predictably, interacting only with people with whom they already agree and otherwise keeping their opinions about important topics to themselves. The result is a group polarization that follows graduates into the real world. As the sociologist Diana C. Mutz discovered in her 2006 book *Hearing the Other Side: Deliberative versus Participatory Democracy*, those with the highest levels of education have the lowest exposure to people with conflicting points of view, while those who have not graduated from high school can claim the most diverse discussion partners. In other words, people with the highest levels of education are most likely to live in the tightest echo chambers. Of course, it should be the opposite: A good education ought to teach students to seek out the opinions of intelligent people with whom they disagree, in order to prevent the problem of "confirmation bias."

Despite the Supreme Court's clear guidance, far too many universities continue to maintain harassment policies that fall far short of the Court's *Davis* standard and prohibit or threaten speech protected by the First Amendment—or, in the case of private universities, speech protected by the school's own promises. . . .

We ask that Congress recall the *Davis* Court's concerns for First Amendment rights. The dissenting opinion in *Davis*, authored by Justice Anthony Kennedy, warned of "campus speech codes that, in the name of preventing a hostile educational environment, may infringe students' First Amendment rights." Kennedy noted that "a student's claim that the school should remedy a sexually hostile environment will conflict with the alleged harasser's claim that his speech, even if offensive, is protected by the First Amendment." In response, Justice Sandra Day O'Connor's majority opinion in *Davis* was very careful to "acknowledge that school administrators shoulder substantial burdens as a result of legal constraints on their disciplinary authority." Speaking precisely to Kennedy's concerns, O'Connor reassured the dissenting justices that it would be "entirely reasonable for a school to refrain from a form of disciplinary action that would expose it to constitutional or statutory claims." The majority's careful, exacting standard was purposefully designed to impose what O'Connor characterized as "very real limitations" on liability, in part as recognition of the importance of protecting campus speech rights. The *Davis* standard is stringent because the First Amendment requires it to be.

Overly broad and vague harassment and bullying policies benefit no one. Colleges risk lawsuits by chilling or punishing protected speech, while students learn the wrong lesson about their expressive rights, concluding that self-censorship is safer than risking discipline for speaking their mind. Thankfully, the fix is simple: Congress should require universities to implement anti-discriminatory harassment policies that precisely track the Supreme Court's *Davis* standard. By simply incorporating a definition carefully crafted by the Supreme Court, such a requirement could end decades of confusion and abuse of harassment policies on campus and eliminate what has historically been the most common form of unconstitutional speech code. Precisely defining peer-on-peer harassment as no more or less than the requirements of *Davis* will ensure that institutions have the ability to meet both their legal and moral obligations to maintain campus environments free from discriminatory harassment while protecting free speech. . . .

II. Free Speech Zones

Far too many universities have "free speech zones," which limit rallies, demonstrations, distribution of literature, petition circulation, and speeches to small and/or out-of-the-way parts of campus. Many also require students to inform university administrators that they intend to engage in expressive activity, even requiring that the university give permission for such activities. . . .

Such prior restraints are generally inconsistent with the First Amendment. Universities may enact reasonable, narrowly tailored "time, place, and manner" restrictions that prevent demonstrations and speeches from unduly interfering with the educational process. They may not, however, regulate speakers and demonstrations on the basis of content or viewpoint, nor may they maintain regulations that burden substantially more speech than is necessary to prevent material disruption to the functioning of the institution. Restricting student speech to tiny free speech zones diminishes the quality of debate and discussion on campus by preventing expression from reaching its target audience.

The threat to student and faculty speech presented [by] free speech zones is often exacerbated by burdensome requirements. Sometimes students are required to obtain signatures from multiple officials, a process that can take days or weeks depending on the bureaucratic process, to even use a free speech zone. In contrast, much campus speech involves spontaneous responses to recent or still-unfolding circumstances. Requiring students to remain silent until a university administrator has completed paperwork may interfere with the demonstrators' message by rendering it untimely and ineffective. (For instance, such policies would have prevented students from gathering for candlelight vigils on the evening of the Boston Marathon attack in memory of the victims.) Furthermore, these permitting requirements often become mechanisms for viewpoint discrimination, as university administrators may waive or expedite requirements for non-controversial events but insist on observing the procedures for a more contentious event. In short, the permitting regulations that often accompany free speech zones are an invitation for administrative abuse.

These free speech quarantines persist despite a string of defeats in court. . . .

The continued maintenance of free speech zones is detrimental to all campus community members. Institutions risk losing lawsuits; students risk punishment for protected speech and learn the wrong lesson about their expressive rights, concluding that speaking their minds is not worth the punishment. Establishing that outdoor areas on public campuses are traditional public forums will ensure that our public universities continue to be a traditional space for debate aptly and memorably recognized by the Supreme Court as "peculiarly the 'marketplace of ideas.'"

When Congress reauthorizes the Higher Education Act, it should include a provision that would guarantee that public campuses are once again places where expressive activity may flourish, subject only to reasonable, content- and viewpoint-neutral time, place, and manner restrictions.

III. Garcetti and Faculty Speech

. . . the Supreme Court placed academic freedom in our nation's public colleges and universities in jeopardy when it held that that a public employee's speech made pursuant to official duties is not protected by the First Amendment in *Garcetti v. Ceballos* (2006). The Court acknowledged that its decision "may have important ramifications for academic freedom," but declined to decide whether an exception for the academic setting was warranted. 547 U.S. at 425 ("We need not, and for that reason do not, decide whether the analysis we conduct today would apply in the same manner to a case involving speech related to scholarship or teaching.").

The Court's *Garcetti* decision has created considerable confusion at universities and in the lower courts. . . .

By leaving unanswered the question of whether an academic freedom exception applies to public employee speech doctrine following *Garcetti*, the Supreme Court's decision threatens academic freedom and free speech. Congress should statutorily protect academic freedom by making clear that there is an exception to *Garcetti* for academics.

CONCLUSION

The recommendations suggested by FIRE are intended to advance the cause of student and faculty rights at our nation's public institutions of higher education so that our colleges and universities might fulfill their promise by serving as engines for innovation and true marketplaces of ideas.

SOURCE: U.S. Congress. House. Committee on the Judiciary, Subcommittee on the Constitution and Civil Justice. First Amendment Protections on Public College and University Campuses. Written Testimony of Greg Lukianoff. 114th Cong., 1st sess., June 2, 2015. Washington, DC: Government Printing Office, 2015.

ANALYSIS

The 1960s and 1970s in the United States were decades marked by fervent activism on college and university campuses. Students led protests, sit-ins, rallies, demonstrations, and even riots to protest government policies and demand social change. Their participation made a historical impact, as the nation's attention was drawn to their causes during pivotal periods like the 1960s Civil Rights Movement protests and tragic events such as the 1970 Kent State shootings.

Campus activism during the twenty-first century, however, shifted greatly in focus and tone as student free speech became a major issue and source of controversy.

As public colleges and universities became more diverse during the post-1970s era, incidences of racist, homophobic, and sexually offensive speech increased. Many campuses reacted by implementing regulations or codes that prohibited hateful or discriminatory speech. These codes were meant to promote tolerance and diversity and protect minority populations from hate speech or otherwise harmful, demeaning, or offensive expression (Aichinger & Vile 2017).

Although intended to create a safe and protective campus environment for all students, such codes also had the effect of marginalizing some students who felt they could not express honest opinions and views without violating official policy. Free speech advocates also became concerned about the establishment of "safe zones" on campus where offensive or hurtful expression was prohibited, "free speech zones" that limited demonstrations and other expressive activities to specific (often small) areas of the campus, and the use of "trigger warnings" to signal potentially upsetting content.

What emerged was a contentious environment on many American campuses marked by backlash against what numerous conservative groups felt were restrictive speech codes and policies in public institutions. Many colleges and universities saw a surge in complaints, protests, and counter-protests related to students' rights to freely speak throughout the campus, and not just in designated zones. Some student activists, like their predecessors, addressed social problems as they fought for free expression. Protests over race-related issues, for example, attracted national attention and forced major changes at the University of Michigan, University of Missouri, and Evergreen State College in Olympia, Washington.

Existing tensions over free speech were magnified as controversial speakers invited to various institutions were either disinvited because of their viewpoints or were effectively drowned out by protesters when they did come to campus to speak. Leading conservatives expressed outrage over two examples in particular. In a 2017 incident at Middlebury College, conservative speaker Charles Murray and a liberal campus professor serving as a respondent were shouted down, physically surrounded and jostled by angry protesters, and then harassed once inside the car sent to escort them away from the scene. That same year at the University of California, Berkeley, violence erupted just hours before the scheduled speech of right-wing commentator Milo Yiannopoulos, resulting in destruction of property, injuries, and vandalism. Organizers were forced to cancel the speech due to the chaos, which university officials blamed on "150 masked agitators who came onto campus and interrupted an otherwise non-violent protest."

Aside from the alarming violence, among the greatest concerns of First Amendment scholars and advocates is that excessive protections against offensive speech are turning college campuses into echo chambers as opposed to robust marketplaces of ideas. Many worry that campuses suffer from a decline in viewpoint diversity, and students are inadequately prepared to engage with critical ideas and viewpoints when they enter society. They point to deep political divisions within the American populace as a major challenge students will need to navigate and overcome as they engage with fellow citizens.

The American Civil Liberties Union (ACLU) and numerous First Amendment scholars have responded to campus free speech battles by promoting counter-speech instead of regulation. These groups maintain that with the exception of threatening speech or expression that creates a pervasively hostile environment, the best answer to hate-filled or biased speech is more speech, not less. Articulating alternate viewpoints through counter-protests, articles, and other democratic forms of expression, they argue, goes much further to suppress hateful viewpoints than campus censorship, regulations, or codes. "Real social change," says the ACLU, "comes from hard work to address the underlying causes of inequality and bigotry, not from purified discourse."

In place of restrictive speech codes and policies, more than seventy-five U.S. institutions have chosen to adopt a University of Chicago faculty-penned piece known as the "Chicago Statement" or a substantially similar document. The Chicago Statement emphasizes responsible debate and dialogue and affirms the obligation of the entire campus community to maintain a "climate of mutual respect" (FIRE 2020). Advocates praise the statement's communicative approach as preferable to measures that stifle free and open discussion of ideas.

While numerous public university campuses have taken proactive measures to ensure their policies do not inhibit students' constitutional freedom of expression rights, federal powers have also offered support. Democrats and Republicans both defended free speech policies during a 2017 congressional hearing on college campus free speech challenges (Friedersdorf 2017). In March 2019, President Trump issued an executive order intended to ensure free speech on public college and university campuses by threatening to withhold billions of dollars of federal research funding for noncompliant schools. In August 2020, multiple U.S. senators built upon the president's executive order by introducing the Campus Free Speech Restoration Act, which established distinct regulations to ensure free expression at public and private institutions.

Additionally, courts considering the constitutionality of campus speech codes and regulations have frequently ruled in favor of free expression. The first federal court ruling on campus speech was *Doe v. University of* Michigan (1993). In this case, a District Court struck down a University of Michigan hate speech policy, saying it was unconstitutionally vague, overbroad, and promoted viewpoint discrimination. The court held that "in the university setting . . . the free and unfettered interplay of competing views is essential to the institution's educational mission" and emphasized that "While the Court is sympathetic to the University's obligation to ensure equal educational opportunities for all of its students, such efforts must not be at the expense of free speech." Subsequent courts have frequently relied on the *Doe* rationale when ruling on speech code cases. For example, in November 2020, a Fifth Circuit Court of Appeals ruled that a lawsuit initiated by a group of University of Texas, Austin, students challenging campus speech codes that prohibited "biased, offensive, or harassing" writing or speech could proceed in federal court (Anderson 2020).

The Supreme Court has yet to issue a ruling clarifying the constitutionality of campus policies limiting free speech.

FURTHER READING

Ben-Porath, Sigal R. *Free Speech on Campus*. Philadelphia: University of Pennsylvania Press, 2017.

Chemerinsky, Erwin, and Howard Gillman. *Free Speech on Campus*. New Haven, CT: Yale University Press, 2017.

Moskowitz, P.E. *The Case against Free Speech: The First Amendment, Fascism, and the Future of Dissent*. New York: Bold Type Books, 2019.

Stone, Geoffrey R., Marianne Bertrand, Angela Olinto, Mark Siegler, David A. Strauss, Kenneth W. Warren, and Amanda Woodward. "Report of the Committee on Freedom of Expression." University of Chicago, 2015. https://provost.uchicago.edu/sites/default/files/documents/reports/FOECommitteeReport.pdf

Strossen, Nadine. "Don't Silence Graduation Speakers: Fight Hate Speech with More Speech." *USA Today*. May 1, 2018. https://www.usatoday.com/story/opinion/2018/05/01/censorship-hate-speech-freedom-first-amendment-column/564868002/

6

FREEDOM OF THE PRESS AND CENSORSHIP DURING THE TRUMP YEARS (2016–2021)

- *Document 49:* The Committee to Protect Journalists Calls Trump "a Threat to Press Freedom"
- *Date:* October 13, 2016
- *Where:* CPJ Headquarters, New York, NY
- *Significance:* This statement, issued before the 2016 presidential election by the Committee to Protect Journalists, lists numerous ways in which candidate Donald Trump's opposition to the media undermined the role of the press and threatened the work and safety of journalists. The statement warns that a Trump presidency would be a threat to press freedom.

DOCUMENT

CPJ chairman says Trump is threat to press freedom

New York, October 13, 2016—The chairman of the board of the Committee to Protect Journalists, Sandra Mims Rowe, issued the following statement on behalf of the organization:

> Guaranteeing the free flow of information to citizens through a robust, independent press is essential to American democracy. For more than 200 years this founding principle has protected journalists in the United States and inspired those around the world, including brave journalists facing violence, censorship, and government repression.

Donald Trump, through his words and actions as a candidate for president of the United States, has consistently betrayed First Amendment values. On October 6, CPJ's board of directors passed a resolution declaring Trump an unprecedented threat to the rights of journalists and to CPJ's ability to advocate for press freedom around the world.

Since the beginning of his candidacy, Trump has insulted and vilified the press and has made his opposition to the media a centerpiece of his campaign. Trump has routinely labeled the press as "dishonest" and "scum" and singled out individual news organizations and journalists.

He has mocked a disabled *New York Times* journalist and called an ABC News reporter a "sleaze" in a press conference. He expelled Univision anchor Jorge Ramos from a campaign press conference because he asked an "impertinent" question, and has publicly demeaned other journalists.

Trump has refused to condemn attacks on journalists by his supporters. His campaign has also systematically denied press credentials to outlets that have covered him critically, including *The Washington Post*, *BuzzFeed*, *Politico*, *The Huffington Post*, *The Daily Beast*, Univision, and *The Des Moines Register*.

Throughout his campaign, Trump has routinely made vague proposals to limit basic elements of press and internet freedom. At a rally in February, Trump declared that if elected president he would "open up our libel laws so when they write purposely negative and horrible and false articles, we can sue them and win lots of money." In September, Trump tweeted, "My lawyers want to sue the failing @nytimes so badly for irresponsible intent. I said no (for now), but they are watching. Really disgusting."

While some have suggested that these statements are rhetorical, we take Trump at his word. His intent and his disregard for the constitutional free press principle are clear.

A Trump presidency would represent a threat to press freedom in the United States, but the consequences for the rights of journalists around the world could be far more serious. Any failure of the United States to uphold its own standards emboldens dictators and despots to restrict the media in their own countries. This appears to be of no concern to Trump, who indicated that he has no inclination to challenge governments on press freedom and the treatment of journalists.

When MSNBC's Joe Scarborough asked him in December if his admiration of Russian President Vladimir Putin was at all tempered by the country's history of critical journalists being murdered, his response was: "He's running his country, and at least he's a leader, unlike what we have in this country . . . Well, I think that our country does plenty of killing, too."

Through his words and actions, Trump has consistently demonstrated a contempt for the role of the press beyond offering publicity to him and advancing his interests.

For this reason CPJ is taking the unprecedented step of speaking out now. This is not about picking sides in an election. This is recognizing that a Trump presidency represents a threat to press freedom unknown in modern history.

We call on Trump to ensure that journalists are able to cover his campaign and his rallies without interference or impediment; to condemn threats against journalists made by his supporters; and to ensure that his statements and actions in the balance of this campaign are consistent with America's First Amendment tradition.

CPJ is a nonpartisan advocacy organization that does not take a position on this or any election. At the same time, we cannot be silent when we believe the conduct of the campaign does damage to America's standing on free press issues around the world, and to CPJ's ability to protect global press freedom.

We hold all candidates and political leaders to the same standard. In 2013, CPJ published a critical report on President Obama's press freedom record. No matter who is elected president, CPJ will hold the administration accountable for the highest standards at home and for strong advocacy for the rights of journalists around the world.

SOURCE: Mims Rowe, Sandra. "CPJ Chairman Says Trump Is Threat to Press Freedom." Committee to Protect Journalists. October 13, 2016. https://cpj.org/2016/10/cpj-chairman-says-trump-is-threat-to-press-freedom/

- ***Document:*** Selected Tweets from President Donald J. Trump's Twitter Account
- ***Date:*** February 17, 2017, May 9, 2018, April 5, 2019, August 20, 2019, and May 3, 2020
- ***Where:*** Twitter

- ***Significance:*** These tweets by President Trump state his belief, often repeated at rallies and public events, that media are the enemy of the people. His tweets and comments typically reference "fake news media," "fake news," or "fake and corrupt media" and often portray media as "the enemy." President Trump's constant delegitimization of the free press and criticism of factual reporting has, according to numerous First Amendment experts, imperiled the future of America's democracy.

DOCUMENT

Feb. 17, 2017 *3:48 PM*	The FAKE NEWS media (failing @nytimes, @NBCNews, @ABC, @CBS, @CNN) is not my enemy, it is the enemy of the American People! Retweets: 43.9K Likes: 138.4K *Source:* https://twitter.com/realdonaldtrump/status/832708293516632065
May 9, 2018 *6:38 AM*	The Fake News is working overtime. Just reported that, despite the tremendous success we are having with the economy & all things else, 91% of the Network News about me is negative (Fake). Why do we work so hard in working with the media when it is corrupt? Take away credentials? Retweets: 21.9K Likes: 101.8K *Source:* https://twitter.com/realDonaldTrump/status/994179864436596736
April 5, 2019 *12:41 PM*	The press is doing everything within their power to fight the magnificence of the phrase, MAKE AMERICA GREAT AGAIN! They can't stand the fact that this Administration has done more than virtually any other Administration in its first 2yrs. They are truly the ENEMY OF THE PEOPLE! Retweets: 24.7K Likes: 106.3K *Source:* https://twitter.com/realdonaldtrump/status/1114221533461790721
August 20, 2019 *8:26 AM*	The Fake and Corrupt Media is sooo bad for our Country, the Enemy of the People! Retweets: 10.7K Likes: 43.4K *Source:* https://twitter.com/realDonaldTrump/status/1163804496939692033
May 3, 2020 *6:57 AM*	The Fake News doesn't show real polls. Lamestream Media is totally CORRUPT, the Enemy of the People! Retweets: 15.2K Likes: 60.5K *Source:* https://twitter.com/realDonaldTrump/status/1256915740432760835

SOURCE: Donald Trump Twitter account: Donald J. Trump@realDonaldTrump

ANALYSIS

It is not uncommon for presidents to have contentious relationships with media. Numerous presidents have feuded with journalists over what they perceive as unfavorable treatment or invasion of personal privacy. Thomas Jefferson, often regarded as a fierce defender of the free press, was so angered by political bias and personal slurs in press reports that he later said "Nothing can now be believed which is seen in a newspaper" (1807). Authorities in Abraham Lincoln's administration silenced opposition to the Civil War by closing newspaper offices, jailing journalists, and destroying printed materials. Although Lincoln did not officially direct such actions, he also made little effort to prevent or punish them (Holzer 2015). During World War I, President Woodrow Wilson tried unsuccessfully to censor the press in the name of public safety and later launched his own government propaganda campaign to control messaging (Daly 2017). President Nixon, angered by the press's role in breaking the Watergate scandal that ended his presidency, formulated the "Opponents List and Political Enemies Project," which targeted numerous members of the press (Nixon Library n.d.).

President Trump, however, established a bellicose approach to traditional media that was unique in many regards. For instance, his disdain for well-established media sources was on display long before he took office. While campaigning for president, he frequently lambasted traditional mainstream media, barred access to his campaign to journalists he did not like, and ridiculed media professionals—even to the point of mocking a disabled reporter (*Snopes* 2016).

Attempts by President Trump to delegitimize traditional journalism became so ubiquitous that they will likely be remembered as one of the defining factors of his political career. His combative relationship with traditional news media was also unique in that it developed during a digital age that allowed the president instant, direct, and inexpensive access to a global audience. Through the use of social media, he could bypass the press entirely. His ability to speak directly to his base via Twitter endeared him to supporters and provided a type of echo chamber of positive feedback that reinforced his messaging about the dishonesty of mainstream media.

Donald Trump's public statements of disgust for the press, journalists, and other media professionals increased in number, frequency, and intensity after he moved into the Oval Office. In post-inauguration tweets, President Trump frequently asserted that media were "fake" or "corrupt" at the same time he decried their "negative" reporting—suggesting that any negative coverage must be fake. He simultaneously praised *Fox News* for its coverage, using examples like its high inauguration ratings and his own willingness to be interviewed on *Fox News* programs as a sign of the network's integrity and success.

Some media scholars contend it was ironically Trump's self-proclaimed "running war with the media" (Trump, January 21, 2017) that gave him the press coverage and exposure he desired. As a master of media spectacle, he was able to create and present a persona that captivated the attention of both media and the public (Kellner 2016). His constant degradation of traditional media sources was the topic of nonstop commentary and analysis. While he seemingly eschewed mainstream media in favor of communicating with the public through tweets, he was well aware that his rhetoric, in addition to appealing to certain members of his base, earned him free coverage and air time. Others contend that when he chose to engage with media, President Trump exploited journalistic practices such as norms of objectivity that behoove journalists to treat presidential comments as newsworthy, even when untrue or outlandish (Feldstein 2017). If media pointed out such dishonesty, President Trump simply reverted to the well-worn message adopted by his base that mainstream media cannot be trusted (ibid).

President Trump's public comments also framed the work of journalists as diametrically opposed to the patriotism and moral values of his supporters. At a rally in Phoenix, Arizona, on August 22, 2017, President Trump described media professionals as unpatriotic and deceitful, saying, "for the most part, honestly, these are really, really dishonest people. And they're bad people. And I really think they don't like our country. I really believe that."

He continued by asking the crowd:

> "You know the thing I don't understand? You would think they'd want to make our country great again, and I honestly believe they don't. I honestly believe it. If you want to discover the source of the division in our country, look no further than the fake news and the crooked media, which would rather get ratings and clicks than tell the truth." (Trump 2017)

President Trump attempted to weaken media protections during his presidency by threatening to change libel laws so he could more easily sue the press for defamation. However, federal libel laws do not exist. This issue is controlled exclusively at the state level, and states have followed Supreme Court precedents establishing strong First Amendment protections for most forms of criticism of public officials.

Aside from President Trump's anti-media rhetoric, the most worrisome aspects of eroded free press protections may well be cumulative effects of changes that began during previous presidencies, but were exacerbated during and after the Trump presidency. Even prior to Trump's election, traditional media markets were exhibiting financial fragility due to market changes and new technologies affecting the nature of news delivery (Jones & West 2017). Deterioration of trust between media professionals and government officials has made information-gathering more difficult (ibid). Police, border agents, security officials (including the president's own), and even public citizens have become increasingly hostile and aggressive toward journalists, particularly during protests, rallies, and reporting of public controversies (ARTICLE 19 2018; First 2020). Media partisanship has increased over recent decades as conservatives have grown increasingly distrustful of mainstream media they feel do not fairly represent their views (Alberta 2018). And the overall confidence of the American public in news media has declined significantly. A 2018 Knight-Gallup survey report released in 2018 found public confidence in media was at an all-time low; a Pew survey that year showed 52 percent of respondents reporting "not too much" or "no confidence at all" in the news media (Dastagir 2019).

Collectively, these changes have led to the cumulative weakening and potential collapse of political, economic, and social structures (including public goodwill, financial strength of media institutions, judicial support, and political tradition) that have reinforced the role of the free press as a fourth pillar of democracy (Jones & West 2017). The danger of such a shift is that continued erosion of institutions that have protected the free press for over 200 years will destabilize the system in its entirety, irreparably injuring the nation's democracy in the process (ibid). Attacks on the press have survived multiple administrations hostile to its mission, but whether or not an increasingly adverse environment will damage news media's ability to act as an effective Fourth Estate remains to be seen.

FURTHER READING

Jones, RonNell Anderson, and Sonja R. West. "The Fragility of the Free American Press." *Northwestern University Law Review* 112, no. 3 (2017): 567–95.

Kalb, Marvin. *Enemy of the People: Trump's War on the Press, the New McCarthyism, and the Threat to American Democracy*. Washington, DC: Brookings Institution Press, 2018.

Karel, Thomas. *The Presidents vs. the Press: The Endless Battle between the White House and the Media—from the Founding Fathers to Fake News*. New York: Dutton, 2020.

Lamer, Wiebke. "Promoting the People's Surrogate: The Case for Press Freedom as a Distinct Human Right." *Journal of Human Rights* 15 (3): 361–82.

PR Newswire. "U.S. Press Freedom Leaders Implore Law Enforcement Agencies across America to Halt Alarming Pattern of Attacks on Journalists." *PR Newswire US*, September 16, 2020. https://www.prnewswire.com/news-releases/us-press-freedom-leaders-implore-law-enforcement-agencies-across-america-to-halt-alarming-pattern-of-attacks-on-journalists-301132530.html

Zick, Timothy. *The First Amendment in the Trump Era*. New York: Oxford University Press, 2019.

- ***Document 50:*** Summary of "Allow States and Victims to Fight Online Sex Trafficking Act of 2017"
- ***Date:*** Signed into law on April 11, 2018
- ***Where:*** U.S. Congress, White House
- ***Significance:*** This legislation eliminated provisions of Section 230 of the Communications Decency Act (1996) that had provided legal immunity to websites facilitating various aspects of sex trafficking or promoting unlawful prostitution.

DOCUMENT

Summary (authored by CRS)
Public Law No: 115–164 (04/11/2018)
Allow States and Victims to Fight Online Sex Trafficking Act of 2017

(Sec. 2) This bill expresses the sense of Congress that section 230 of the Communications Act of 1934 was not intended to provide legal protection to websites that unlawfully promote and facilitate prostitution and websites that facilitate traffickers in advertising the sale of unlawful sex acts with sex trafficking victims. Section 230 limits the legal liability of interactive computer service providers or users for content they publish that was created by others.

(Sec. 3) The bill amends the federal criminal code to add a new section that imposes penalties—a fine, a prison term of up to 10 years, or both—on a person who, using a facility or means of interstate or foreign commerce, owns, manages, or operates an interactive computer service (or attempts or conspires to do so) to promote or facilitate the prostitution of another person.

Additionally, it establishes enhanced penalties—a fine, a prison term of up to 25 years, or both—for a person who commits the offense in one of the following aggravating circumstances: (1) promotes or facilitates the prostitution of five or more persons, or (2) acts with reckless disregard that such conduct contributes to sex trafficking.

A person injured by an aggravated offense may recover damages and attorneys' fees in a federal civil action.

A court must order mandatory restitution, in addition to other criminal or civil penalties, for an aggravated offense in which a person acts with reckless disregard that such conduct contributes to sex trafficking.

A defendant may assert, as an affirmative defense, that the promotion or facilitation of prostitution is legal in the jurisdiction where it was targeted.

(Sec. 4) The bill amends the Communications Act of 1934 to declare that section 230 does not limit: (1) a federal civil claim for conduct that constitutes sex trafficking, (2) a federal criminal charge for conduct that constitutes sex trafficking, or (3) a state criminal charge for conduct that promotes or facilitates prostitution in violation of this bill.

The amendments apply regardless of whether alleged conduct occurs before, on, or after this bill's enactment.

(Sec. 5) The bill amends the federal criminal code to define a phrase related to the prohibition on sex trafficking. Currently, it is a crime to knowingly benefit from participation in a venture that engages in sex trafficking. This bill defines "participation in a venture" to mean knowingly assisting, supporting, or facilitating a sex trafficking violation.

(Sec. 6) A state may file a federal civil action to enforce federal sex trafficking violations.

(Sec. 7) This section states that this bill does not limit federal or state civil actions or criminal prosecutions that are not preempted by section 230 of the Communications Act of 1934.

(Sec. 8) The Government Accountability Office must report to Congress on information related to damages and mandatory restitution for aggravated offenses under this bill.

SOURCE: U.S. Congress, House, *Allow States and Victims to Fight Online Sex Trafficking Act of 2017*, H.R. 1865.115th Cong. *https://www.congress.gov/bill/115th-congress/house-bill/1865*

ANALYSIS

The Fight Online Sex Trafficking Act (FOSTA), also known as FOSTA-SESTA to attribute the bill's Senate name of Stop Enabling Sex Traffickers Act of 2017, was passed by Congress in 2017 and signed into law on April 11, 2018. The legislation amended the safe harbor provision of the Communications Decency Act of 1996 (catalogued as Section 230 of the Communications Act of 1934) that had previously provided legal immunity to content service providers for information posted on their sites by users. The FOSTA legislation removed protections for websites that "unlawfully promote and facilitate prostitution and websites that facilitate traffickers in advertising the sale of unlawful sex acts with sex trafficking victims."

The passage of FOSTA was billed as an effort to fight sex trafficking and to protect its potential victims, particularly underage individuals. The principal target of the legislation was Backpage, a prominent classified ads website. Backpage primarily made its profits from an "adult ads" section that in 2013 brought in more than 80 percent of all sex advertising revenues (U.S. Congress 2017). A Senate subcommittee investigation found that Backpage, which at one point edited 70–80 percent of its adult ads to "sanitize" them and conceal their true nature, was complicit in knowingly facilitating prostitution and child trafficking (ibid). Backpage voluntarily shut down its online prostitution ads in January 2017 (Matula 2020), and other websites eventually followed suit out of concern they, too, could be held liable for ads placed on their platforms that might be used for prostitution-related purposes. Craigslist, for example, shuttered its entire personals section roughly one month after FOSTA went into effect.

The passage of FOSTA was largely hailed as an important step toward crippling the sex trafficking industry by removing its ability to advertise online. The law provided justice for girls and women who had been trafficked on the website and later tried unsuccessfully to sue Backpage; almost all their lawsuits had been dismissed because of the website's protection under Section 230 (Riviera et al. 2017). However, practical ramifications of the new law were not altogether positive—even for those fighting to end the sex trafficking industry. Lois Lee, founder of a nonprofit that works to rescue child sex trafficking victims, called Backpage a critical investigative tool that vice detectives and agents in the field rely upon to locate and recover missing children (ibid). Without the online presence of Backpage, law enforcement officials find it much more difficult to successfully pursue investigations of trafficked children (Burnitis 2019).

Others who spoke out against the passage of FOSTA included civil liberties advocates, open internet proponents, social advocates who argued sex work would be pushed further underground, and scholars who felt the suppression of internet free speech was a dangerous by-product of the well-intended law. Advocates for tech companies also complained the weakening of Section 230 would lead to censorship of the internet (Burnitis 2019).

The greatest impacts of FOSTA, however, were felt by adult sex workers themselves. According to the results of a survey administered after FOSTA's passage, many sex workers felt harmed by the law because the language did not differentiate between sex trafficking victims and those who choose willingly to engage in consensual sex work (Peterson, Robinson & Shih 2019). After advertising sites like Backpage were shut down, sex workers no longer had the means to screen potential clients before seeing them, therefore leading to an increase in the number of violent clients. Additionally, these workers reported loss of income attributed to fewer places to advertise their services, riskier behaviors because they were forced to do things outside their comfort zones in order to make ends meet, and a rise in the number of predators or would-be pimps who recognized and preyed on the workers' desperation (ibid).

Because FOSTA prohibited use of the internet for any activity promoting or facilitating sex work, it also stripped consensual sex workers of an important social resource. Through internet communities, these workers had shared health information, lists of potentially dangerous clients, and other safety practices (Matula 2020). After passage of the new law, they could no longer use the internet as a tool to communicate with one another about such issues (Chapman-Schmidt 2019). They also were forced back onto the street, a more dangerous place to solicit business than from the comfort of their homes (Burnitis 2019).

Some researchers argue that the difficulties sex workers faced as a result of FOSTA were not by-products of the legislation, but part of its intended effect (Chapman-Schmidt 2019). Legal discourse in the United States refers to "sex trafficking" as "the traffic in sex," which includes all forms of sex work. Even consensual adult sex work legally falls under this definition. FOSTA simply reflected general discourse about sex work that failed to differentiate between voluntary engagement and involuntary trafficking of an individual for sexual exploitation, thus serving as a form of epistemic violence against sex workers (ibid). Chapman-Schmidt argues that to adequately address problems inherent in both categories, it is critical to differentiate "sex trafficking" from "human trafficking for sexual exploitation."

In March 2020, a bill similar to FOSTA was introduced in the U.S. Senate. The "Eliminating Abuse and Rampant Neglect of Interactive Technology" (EARN IT) Act, intended to address continued online exploitation of children, would further weaken protections currently in place under Section 230. The legislation proposes a National Commission on Online Child Sexual Exploitation Prevention that would determine the proper steps companies must take to prevent online child exploitation. Advocates say the legislation is necessary to keep children safe; critics say it is an overreach of government authority and a threat to user privacy and encryption practices (Paul 2020). As of March 2021, no further action had been taken on the bill.

FURTHER READING

Burnitis, Caitlyn. "Facing the Future with FOSTA: Examining the Allow States and Victims to Fight Online Sex Trafficking Act of 2017." *University of Miami Race & Social Justice Law Review.* 10 (2019): 139.

Chapman-Schmidt, Ben. "'Sex Trafficking' as Epistemic Violence." *Anti-Trafficking Review* 12 (2019): 172–87.

Donovan, Elizabeth M. "Fight Online Sex Trafficking Act and Stop Enabling Sex Traffickers Act: A Shield for Jane Doe." *Connecticut Law Review* 52 (2020): 85.

Peterson, Meghan, Bella Robinson, and Elena Shih. "The New Virtual Crackdown on Sex Workers' Rights: Perspectives from the United States." *Anti-Trafficking Review* 12 (2019): 189–93.

Pike, George H. "The End of Social Media Immunity?" *Information Today* 35, no. 4 (2018): 19.

U.S. Congress. Senate. Permanent Subcommittee on Investigations. Committee on Homeland Security and Governmental Affairs. *Backpage.com's Knowing Facilitation of Online Sex Trafficking: Staff Report. 115th Cong., 1st sess., January 10, 2017.* https://www.hsgac.senate.gov/imo/media/doc/Backpage%20Report%202017.01.10%20FINAL.pdf

- ***Document 51:*** Statement in Support of Freedom of the Press from Eighty Organizations "Committed to the First Amendment"
- ***Date:*** March 2, 2017
- ***Where:*** The statement published by each of the signatories
- ***Significance:*** A coalition of eighty organizations published this statement, defending and underscoring the importance of freedom of the press in the United States. The statement was issued as a response to attacks and false statements made during the first year of the Trump administration that undermined the credibility and integrity of the media. Signatories to the statement include both journalistic and non-journalistic groups.

DOCUMENT

Statement in Support of Freedom of the Press

"In the First Amendment the Founding Fathers gave the free press the protection it must have to fulfill its essential role in our democracy. The press was to serve the governed, not the governors. The Government's power to censor the press was abolished so that the press would remain forever free to censure the government." Supreme Court Justice Hugo Black

As organizations committed to the First Amendment right of freedom of speech and the press, we are alarmed by the efforts of the President and his administration to demonize and marginalize the media and to undermine their ability to inform the public about official actions and policies.

Such efforts include the President's refusal to answer questions posed by a reporter from CNN because the President asserts it promotes "fake news"; charges that the media "manipulated" images of the inauguration; false accusations that the media has covered up terrorist attacks; and repeated claims that the media is "failing" and "dishonest." All of this recently culminated in the President calling the New York *Times*, CBS, CNN, ABC, and NBC News "the enemy of the American People!" and in the exclusion of representatives of various media outlets from a press briefing. In these and other examples, the President and his designees have attempted to villainize and discredit the press for any reporting he dislikes. However, the job of the press is not to please the President but to inform the public, a function that is essential to democracy.

The expressions of disdain for the press and its role in democracy by federal officials send a signal to state and local officials. In the aftermath of an election season that witnessed outright intimidation of journalists in communities around the country, there is a compelling need for highly placed federal officials to acknowledge the crucial role of a free press under our Constitution and the responsibility of government officials at all levels to respect it. In one chilling example, multiple individuals who identified themselves as journalists were arrested, detained, and charged with felonies while simply doing their job: reporting on Inauguration Day protests in Washington, D.C. Those arrests were made by local police and pursued by the U.S. Attorney's Office, both of which displayed an alarming lack of concern for fundamental constitutional rights. The fact that those charges have since been dropped suggests that the arrests were unwarranted and highlights the need for our nation's leaders to set national policy that unequivocally supports a free and independent press and the public's right to know.

Our Constitution enshrines the press as an independent watchdog and bulwark against tyranny and official misconduct. Its function is to monitor and report on the actions of public officials so that the public can hold them accountable. The effort to delegitimize the press undermines democracy, and officials who challenge the value of an independent press or question its legitimacy betray the country's most cherished values and undercut one of its most significant strengths.

The First Amendment protects the right to protest, dissent, and petition government for a redress of grievances, but these rights cannot be exercised without a free press that provides information to the public. Together, these rights represent *the* constitutionally sanctioned method for the public to oppose government policies and activities and to seek change. The wisdom of this system can be seen in parts of the world where such a right does not exist, or is not honored, and violent opposition is the only available avenue to express opposition or remedy injustice.

We condemn in the strongest possible terms all efforts by elected and appointed officials to penalize, delegitimize, or intimidate members of the press.

March 2, 2017

Endorsed by:

Alliance for Community Media
Alliance for Media Arts + Culture
American Association of Law Libraries. . . *(Total of 80 signatories)*

SOURCE: National Press Foundation et al. "NPF Joins Effort to Support Freedom of Press: Statement in Support of Freedom of the Press." March 2, 2017. https://nationalpress.org/newsfeed/npf-joins-effort-to-support-freedom-of-press/

ANALYSIS

The term "fourth estate" was first used in early-nineteenth-century England to refer to the role of the free press as a safeguard against government wrongdoing or tyranny (Tréguer 2016). By publishing parliamentary debates and reporting on activities of government leaders, the press was seen as a fourth branch of government that protected against abuse of power.

The phrase "fourth estate" evolved in tandem with media technology, and now describes the ways media—in all its forms—serves as both informant and watchdog of the government. Although not a distinct component of the political system, media are nonetheless recognized as vastly influential in providing oversight of these three branches (or estates) that make up America's democratic system. The freedom of news organizations to interpret, analyze, and inform the public about activities of elected leaders is among the most prized and protected staples of a free, democratic society.

Attacks on media, therefore, undermine a critical pillar of democracy—an institution that serves as a sentinel to guard against abuse of power and as a conduit through which citizens and their government are connected.

The role of media as the fourth estate has been called into question throughout U.S. history by presidents who felt the press wielded too much power or misused its power. Even George Washington complained that falsehoods and misrepresentations spread by the press chipped away at his confidence and reputation (Holzer 2020). However, media were also responsible for exposing conditions in Chicago's meatpacking plants, uncovering the Watergate scandal, broadcasting the Army-McCarthy hearings that led to Senator McCarthy's downfall, revealing warrantless wiretapping by the National Security Agency after 9/11, and detailing abuse of Guantanamo Bay prisoners, to name a few examples.

Attacks on media by government officials, therefore, are often viewed as attacks on the very institution that promotes the accountability of government leaders and gives voice and power to the people. Anti-media discourse in the United States since 2016 has been largely fueled by Donald Trump, whose criticism of media drew red flags even before he was elected to office. In 2016, the Committee to Protect Journalists (CPJ) issued a report warning of potential challenges of a Trump presidency based on his already prolific attacks on the press. In 2017, a coalition of eighty organizations signed a "Statement in Support of Freedom of the Press" condemning federal officials' delegitimization and intimidation of the press. A follow-up CPJ report in 2020 documented additional evidence of Trump administration officials undercutting the reputation and validity of the mainstream media and traditional journalistic investigation through false claims, the spread of conspiracy theories, and direct attempts to undermine the role of media as the fourth pillar of democracy.

Analysts suggest Donald Trump's disparaging of mainstream media was part of a political strategy to discredit the integrity of traditional journalism. They point to his success attracting followers and energizing base supporters by circumventing traditional media and communicating directly through tweets, which he often used to comment about the dishonesty of mainstream news outlets. Additionally, President Trump discontinued daily White House news briefings, limited reporters' access to the White House, and even suspended the press credentials of reporters from various news organizations (Ingram 2019; Rhodan 2018). He berated specific network news outlets as "fake" or "dishonest," alleging their negative coverage of him was "unfair." Conversely, the president extolled the work of journalists who portrayed him positively and regularly appeared on his preferred network, *Fox News*.

Veteran journalist Leslie Stahl recounted that during a conversation with President Trump in 2018, she asked why he kept hammering at the media. He responded, "You know why I do it? I do it to discredit you and demean you all, so that, when you write negative stories about me, no one will believe you" (CPJ 2020).

President Trump frequently used violent or militaristic messages to depict mainstream media. In 2017, he posted a video to Twitter depicting him as a wrestler beating up his opponent, whose head was covered by the *CNN* logo (Newsy 2017). He also often referred to "fake media" as "the enemy of the people."

Supporters reacted to the President's ill will toward media with attacks of their own: reporters at Trump political rallies were at times berated, booed, and physically accosted; certain journalists covering the president received death threats and had to hire security guards; and pipe bombs were sent to the headquarters of at least one major news outlet (CPJ 2020).

Politicians have added their own inflammatory statements to the president's rhetoric. Rep. Devin Nunes of California defended the president, saying his actions expose bias in the mainstream media. "We should not be talking to the mainstream media," he stated. "They are assassins" (Clark 2020, February 7).

However, not all members of Congress have supported President Trump's approach to media. In August 2018, the U.S. Senate unanimously passed a resolution reaffirming and supporting the vital role of the free press in America's democracy. The resolution recounted the importance of the free press throughout U.S. history and reiterated that the press is not beholden to those in power. Quoting Supreme Court Justice Hugo Black, the document stated "The Government's power to censor the press was abolished so that the press would remain forever free to censure the Government." Authors noted that "tyrannical and authoritarian governments and leaders throughout history have sought to undermine, censor, suppress, and control the press to advance their undemocratic goals and actions" (U.S. Congress Senate 2018).

The Senate resolution did not explicitly refer to President Trump, but clearly referred to his rhetoric about the press. The document affirmed "that the press is not the enemy of the people" and condemned "the attacks on the institution of the free press and . . . efforts to systematically undermine the credibility of the press as an attack on the democratic institutions of the United States."

On the same day this Senate resolution was passed, the *Boston Globe* initiated an effort among 300+ newspapers across the country to run editorials defending freedom of the press. The coordinated effort was a direct response to President Trump's frequent attacks on the media. The *Globe* encouraged participating newspapers to stand up against the "dirty war against the free press" (Reiss 2018). Marjorie Pritchard, deputy managing editor of the *Globe's* opinion page, said, "I hope it would educate readers to realize that an attack on the First Amendment is unacceptable. We are a free and independent press; it is one of the most sacred principles enshrined in the Constitution" (ibid).

DID YOU KNOW?

In January 2015, a series of terrorist attacks rocked France. The spate of violence began when the offices of *Charlie Hebdo*, a satirical weekly newspaper in Paris, were overrun by two gunmen who killed eleven journalists and injured many more. Over the next few days, related assaults claimed the lives of six more individuals.

The gruesome attacks were organized by radical Islamic terrorists angry over *Charlie Hebdo's* decision to reprint cartoons from a Danish newspaper that showed a visual depiction of the Prophet Muhammad, something strictly forbidden by the Islamic faith. *Charlie Hebdo* was no stranger to such attacks; the magazine's editorial offices had been firebombed in 2011 by radicals angry about what they felt was incitement of hatred against Muslims.

In spite of the attacks, *Charlie Hebdo* stood behind its decision to print the cartoons, defending its right to free expression. The French government did not condone the depictions but agreed that the publication has a right to choose its content.

However, in recent years, the *Charlie Hebdo* attacks have inspired additional terrorist incidents in France and elsewhere, including the beheading of a French schoolteacher in November 2020. Although the acts of violence took place outside U.S. borders, implications of these attacks on free speech have been felt in the United States and around the world. As editors make difficult decisions regarding content, they must constantly weigh the right to free expression against the reality of horrific violence that has at times been directed toward defenders of that right.

Media professionals continue to respond to hateful rhetoric by underscoring the role of the press to inform the public, expose wrongdoing, and hold leaders accountable. Margaret Talev, president of the White House Correspondents' Association, emphasized "A free press must be able to report on the good, the bad, the momentous and the mundane, without fear or favor. And a president preventing a free and independent press from covering the workings of our republic would be an unconscionable assault on the First Amendment" (Fabian 2018).

FURTHER READING

Committee to Protect Journalists (CPJ). "The Trump Administration and the Media." Report issued by CPJ. April 16, 2020. https://cpj.org/reports/2020/04/trump-media-attacks-credibility-leaks/

Dutton, William H. "The Fifth Estate Emerging through the Network of Networks." *Prometheus* 27 (1): 1–15.

Frontline. "The Press's Role as a Watchdog on Government." PBS February 27, 2007. https://www.pbs.org/wgbh/pages/frontline/newswar/tags/watchdog.html

Jones, Dylon. "The State of the Fourth Estate: A Media Lawyer and a Journalist Discuss Social Media, 'Fake News' and the First Amendment." *Louisville Magazine* 69, no. 1: 32–34.

Shea, J.P. "The Role of the Media in a Democratic Society." Speaking Notes by Dr. Shea, NATO Spokesman, for NATO Seminar. July 2–3, 1998. https://www.nato.int/docu/speech/1998/s980702c.htm

U.S. Congress Senate. "A Resolution Reaffirming the Vital and Indispensable Role the Free Press Serves." 115th Cong., 2nd sess., August 16, 2018. https://www.congress.gov/bill/115th-congress/senate-resolution/607/tex

---

- ***Document 52:*** Selected Tweets of President Trump Regarding the NFL National Anthem Controversy
- ***Date:*** Selected dates from 2017 to 2020
- ***Where:*** Twitter
- ***Significance:*** NFL quarterback Colin Kaepernick's decision to kneel during the national anthem in protest of police brutality and systemic racism sparked a national debate about the treatment of people of color in the United States. While many applauded the silent protest and the conversations that followed, critics felt the act was disrespectful to the flag and the country. Calls by President Trump and others to prohibit these protests evoked debate about the First Amendment's treatment of national symbols and citizens' right to protest.

DOCUMENT

DONALD J. TRUMP—Selected tweets from 2017 to 2020

Sept. 23, 2017 1:11 PM, 1:18 PM	If a player wants the privilege of making millions of dollars in the NFL, or other leagues, he or she should not be allowed to disrespect. . . . . . . our Great American Flag (or Country) and should stand for the National Anthem. If not, YOU'RE FIRED. Find something else to do! Retweets: 37.3 K / 32.9 K Likes: 155.5 K / 135.8 K Source: https://twitter.com/realDonaldTrump/status/911654184918880260 https://twitter.com/realDonaldTrump/status/911655987857281024
Sept. 25, 2017 6:39 AM	The issue of kneeling has nothing to do with race. It is about respect for our Country, Flag and National Anthem. NFL must respect this! Retweets: 44.7 K Likes: 176.2 K Source: https://twitter.com/realDonaldTrump/status/912280282224525312
Sept. 26, 2017 5:28 AM	Ratings for NFL football are way down except before game starts, when people tune in to see whether or not our country will be disrespected! Retweets: 14.3K Likes: 75.7K Source: https://twitter.com/realDonaldTrump/status/912624892239077376
Sept. 26, 2017 5:35 AM	The booing at the NFL football game last night, when the entire Dallas team dropped to its knees, was loudest I have ever heard. Great anger. Retweets: 17.2K Likes: 94.8K Source: https://twitter.com/realDonaldTrump/status/912626731357540353
Nov. 28, 2017 6:45 AM	At least 24 players kneeling this weekend at NFL stadiums that are now having a very hard time filling up. The American public is fed up with the disrespect the NFL is paying to our Country, our Flag and our National Anthem. Weak and out of control! Retweets: 15.8 K Likes: 85 K Source: https://twitter.com/realDonaldTrump/status/935489831005810688

June 4, 2018 9:55 PM	The Philadelphia Eagles Football Team was invited to the White House. Unfortunately, only a small number of players decided to come, and we canceled the event. Staying in the Locker Room for the playing of our National Anthem is as disrespectful to our country as kneeling. Sorry! Retweets: 20.3K Likes: 100.4 K Source: https://twitter.com/realDonaldTrump/status/1003832766511894528
July 20, 2018 5:17 PM	The NFL National Anthem Debate is alive and well again—can't believe it! Isn't it in contract that players must stand at attention, hand on heart? The $40,000,000 Commissioner must now make a stand. First time kneeling, out for game. Second time kneeling, out for season/no pay! Retweets: 23.9 K Likes: 108.6 K Source: https://twitter.com/realDonaldTrump/status/1020432499082702849
August 10, 2018 7:32 AM	. . . . . Be happy, be cool! A football game, that fans are paying soooo much money to watch and enjoy, is no place to protest. Most of that money goes to the players anyway. Find another way to protest. Stand proudly for your National Anthem or be Suspended Without Pay! Retweets: 27.6 K Likes: 148.3 K Source: https://twitter.com/realDonaldTrump/status/1027895506809364480
June 5, 2020 3:08 PM	. . . We should be standing up straight and tall, ideally with a salute, or a hand on heart. There are other things you can protest, but not our Great American Flag—NO KNEELING! Retweets: 39.9K Likes: 201.8K Source: https://twitter.com/realDonaldTrump/status/1268998143733051394

SOURCE: Donald J. Trump Twitter account: Donald J. Trump@realDonaldTrump

---

- ***Document:*** Excerpt from *The Congressional Record* "Kneeling in Recognition of the Glory of Our Nation"
- ***Date:*** September 26, 2017
- ***Where:*** *The Congressional Record* (U.S. House of Representatives)

- ***Significance:*** This speech, given on the floor of the U.S. House of Representatives by Rep. Sheila Jackson Lee of Texas, emphasizes her belief that taking a knee to protest unjust systems does not demonstrate disrespect for the flag. Rather, she sees it as an act of respect toward that symbol and the freedoms it represents, including the ability to speak freely and call attention to the need for justice for all Americans.

DOCUMENT

Kneeling in Recognition of the Glory of Our Nation

. . . Ms. JACKSON LEE. Mr. Speaker, last evening, I took to kneeling on this floor in recognition, first of all, of the glory of this Nation, the pride that I have in representing the Nation in faraway places as a Member of Congress, and visiting heads of states, and visiting with the people of other countries who have such an admiration for the purity of our freedom.

I also take great pride in Texas being a State that is home to any number of military bases and reservists and Active Duty and veterans. We interact all the time. Our military liaison in my office is a veteran of the Iraq and Afghan wars.

There is no lacking in sense of pride, and not one of us remembers missing the national anthem and the Pledge of Allegiance as children growing up in our daily activities as we went to school. But I also have come to understand what those symbols mean. They are not just cloth or music. They, in fact, represent ideals and values, and many people interpret them in different ways.

I abhor spitting or burning or destroying of the flag. I have not done any of those. Colin Kaepernick's kneeling in the early months past was no disrespect of his love of this country, but a recognition that people were hurting and people were losing their lives, and we needed to reform systems of justice to be able to respond to the grieving mothers who lost children, in many instances—I would say all the instances—that we can recall of the recent 2 years, unnecessarily.

It did not mean that we did not have, again, the greatest respect for our men and women in blue. I will take no backseat to my honoring them, fighting for them, working alongside them during Hurricane Harvey, thanking them for the first responders and enormous work they did, working alongside them as we rescued a group of individuals in a church who have fled for their lives during Hurricane Harvey.

We must understand each other as people, and it is unfortunate that the Commander in Chief has taken to a distraction that wants to peel away our unity and report in the news: They like it, don't they? He is really, working for his base.

I don't know anything about a base. I know about Americans. I see them all the time, and they don't look like me. They disagree with me. They have different opinions. I still respect that opinion, but I do believe that we can all come together.

That knee was in respect of Colin and the young men who have now successfully taken to their knees, and the owners. . . .

I rise today to say that I remain on bended knee in spirit with all of those young men. I look forward to working with the NFL and all the sports as we explain that these young men are vital parts of the community. Thank you to J.J. Watt and the Texans and all of those who have contributed.

SOURCE: Representative Sheila Jackson Lee, speaking about *Kneeling in Recognition of the Glory of Our Nation*, 115th Cong., 1st sess., *Congressional Record* (September 26, 2017): H 7494.

ANALYSIS

In 2016, a silent act by a well-known U.S. football player sparked a national movement that called attention to systemic racism, discrimination, and police misconduct. In the process, the movement also generated impassioned debate about the degree to which free speech protections apply to athletes who make political statements while representing their teams and leagues.

The gesture that captured the country's attention was made during the third preseason game of 2016, when San Francisco 49ers quarterback Colin Kaepernick sat down on the bench during the playing of the national anthem. He repeated this action at subsequent games, eventually choosing to kneel during the anthem instead of sitting so as to not disrespect the flag and members of the armed forces (Rollins 2018). When questioned about his actions, Kaepernick made clear that his purpose was to protest police brutality and systemic racism. He said, "I am not going to stand up to show pride in a flag for a country that oppresses black people and people of color. To me, this is bigger than football and it would be selfish on my part to look the other way. There are bodies in the street and people getting paid leave and getting away with murder" (Wyche 2016). He added, "I am not looking for approval. I have to stand up for people that are oppressed. . . . If they take football away, my endorsements from me, I know that I stood up for what is right" (ibid).

Numerous players joined in the protests over subsequent months and years. Soon, entire teams were kneeling or remaining in locker rooms during the national anthem to draw attention to racial injustices. The movement grew beyond the NFL to include players in little leagues, high school, and college football.

DID YOU KNOW?

Although Kaepernick is best known for his silent protests during football games, his advocacy has extended far beyond the field. In 2016, Kaepernick donated $1 million to charities working in oppressed communities and encouraged other celebrities to donate as well. His own charity, the Colin Kaepernick Foundation, continues to contribute money and time to education and social activism efforts, including free "Know Your Rights" camps for young people. In 2020, Kaepernick pledged $100,000 for a COVID relief fund (Kozlowski 2020).

And in spite of the backlash he received for his protests, Kaepernick has also been recognized positively for the stand he has taken. His teammates in 2016 voted to name him the recipient of the Len Eshmont Award, given to the 49er who "best exemplifies the inspirational and courageous play of Len Eshmont, an original member of the 1946 49ers team" (Wagoner 2016). Kaepernick was named recipient of the 2017 Sports Illustrated Muhammad Ali Legacy Award and in 2018 was chosen as a face of Nike's thirtieth anniversary "Just Do It" campaign. The advertisement featuring him won an Emmy for outstanding commercial. Also in 2018, Kaepernick received Amnesty International's most prestigious honor, the Ambassador of Conscience award. Both Kaepernick and Dr. Anthony Fauci were honored as 2020 Robert F. Kennedy Human Rights Ripple of Hope award laureates. In October 2020, the University of Nevada named Kaepernick one of six members of its 2020 Hall of Fame Class. His advocacy and activism continue to inspire other celebrities to become involved in social justice efforts.

Athletes in baseball, basketball, soccer, and other sports were also inspired to kneel in solidarity (Gaydos 2018).

Kaepernick's silent protests soon swelled into a deafening national debate about whether or not he should be allowed, both contractually and ethically, to refuse to stand for the national anthem. While many praised Kaepernick for using his platform to draw attention to important social issues, others roundly criticized his manner of protesting as disrespectful to the flag, the military, and the country. Media commentators inflamed tensions by repeatedly framing the issue as a dispute over kneeling, not social injustice—focusing on Kaepernick's method of protesting rather than the message behind it (Boykoff & Carrington 2020; Coombs et al. 2019).

Among the more vocal critics of the NFL protests was President Trump, who repeatedly tweeted, retweeted, and spoke about the need for the NFL to put a stop to the kneeling. During a 2017 speech in Alabama, President Trump said to the crowd, "Wouldn't you love to see one of these NFL owners, when somebody disrespects our flag, to say, 'Get that son of a bitch off the field right now. Out! He's fired. He's fired!'" (Graham 2017).

Protesters also faced major pushback from NFL corporate leadership. Initially, after Kaepernick announced his reasons for protesting, the NFL issued a statement saying it recognized Kaepernick's right as a citizen to not stand during the anthem (Wyche 2016). However, after the 2016 season, he was let go by the 49ers and has remained unsigned since that time. In May 2018, Kaepernick and former teammate Eric Reid, who protested alongside his friend, filed grievance claims against the NFL for colluding to ban them from playing in the league. A year and a half later, the parties settled the case out of court.

Many assumed Kaepernick's activism was a violation of NFL policy, but it was not. Although one portion of the NFL game operations manual describes *how* players are to stand at attention during the national anthem, it does not expressly require them to *do* so (Lindholm 2017). As public pressure grew to discipline Kaepernick and racial tensions mounted throughout the United States, the NFL sought compromise with a new policy requiring all players on the field to stand for the national anthem, but allowing those who chose to remain in the locker room to do so without penalty. President Trump declared the policy change a good move, but added "You have to stand proudly for the national anthem, or you shouldn't be playing, you shouldn't be there. Maybe you shouldn't be in the country" (Gaydos 2018). Shortly after the new policy was announced, the NFL Players Association filed a grievance, and the policy was suspended (Draper & Belson 2019).

The NFL's failure to impose its anthem policy was due in part to contractual and working conditions agreements within the league that acknowledged players' rights to free expression up to the point at which such expression threatens "an increase of injury to the NFL, team owners, and the public interest" (McGinty 2017). Determining the boundaries of what constitutes "injury" remains a major challenge for NFL leadership.

Overall, negative consequences for Kaepernick and other protesters were the result of public and political pressure, not legal challenges. Any mandate requiring someone to rise for the anthem could be called into question on free speech grounds. The Supreme Court has ruled on numerous occasions that acts involving national symbols are not exceptions to the First Amendment right of free expression. Among the most well-known cases involving treatment of national symbols was *Texas v.*

Johnson (1989) in which the Supreme Court upheld the right of an individual to burn the American flag without legal repercussions. Additional landmark decisions protecting other forms of symbolic speech include *United States v. O'Brien* (1968), *Tinker v. Des Moines* (1969), and *R.A.V. v. St. Paul* (1992).

By 2020, support for the silent protests had expanded, with the majority of Americans indicating that kneeling during the anthem is an acceptable form of protest (de Pinto 2020). In June 2020, amid nationwide protests following George Floyd's death at the hands of a Minneapolis police officer, NFL Commissioner Roger Goodall made a video in which he acknowledged kneeling for the anthem was not about disrespecting the flag. He said, "We, the NFL, admit we were wrong for not listening to NFL players earlier and encourage all to speak out and peacefully protest. We, the NFL, believe Black Lives Matter. . . . I personally protest with you and want to be part of the much-needed change in this country" (NFL 2020).

Nevertheless, tensions persist. As of October 2020, Kaepernick remained unsigned, and Reid, who successfully played two years for the Carolina Panthers, was released after year one of a three-year extension. Nationally, protests over racial injustice continue as additional abuses occur. At the close of 2020 and beginning of 2021, silent, peaceful protest actions by athletes during the playing of the National Anthem continued at sporting events in a range of professional, college, and amateur sports.

FURTHER READING

Hunter, Richard J., Jr. and John H. Shannon. "'Taking a Knee for the Constitution': The Kaepernick and Reid Grievances May Be Settled but Do They Nevertheless Raise Important Constitutional Questions?" *Journal of Education and Social Policy* 6, no. 4 (December 2019): 86–100.

Jones, Mike. "Opinion: Four Years after Colin Kaepernick Began His Protests, Sports Figures' Voices Are Growing Louder—Because They Have No Choice." *USA Today*. August 27, 2020. https://www.usatoday.com/story/sports/nfl/columnist/mike-jones/2020/08/26/colin-kaepernick-nfl-protest-anthem-kneeling-police-brutality-racial-injustice/5637412002/

Kaepernick, Colin. Acceptance Speech after Being Named Amnesty International's 2018 Ambassador of Conscience. April 21, 2018. https://www.amnesty.nl/content/uploads/2018/04/Colin-Kaepernicks-Speech-Ambassador-of-Conscience-Final.pdf?x66178

Lindholm, Johan. "From Carlos to Kaepernick and Beyond: Athletes' Right to Freedom of Expression." *International Sports Law Journal* 17 (2017): 1–3.

McNeal, Laura Rene. "From Hoodies to Kneeling during the National Anthem: The Colin Kaepernick Effect and Its Implications for K–12 Sports." *Louisiana Law Review* 78 (2017): 145.

Murtha, Ryan. "'The Highest Form of Patriotism:' Toward an Understanding of First Amendment Precedents and NFL Protests." *Journal of Emerging Sport Studies* 1, no. 1 (2018): 6.

- ***Document 53:*** "Truth and Democracy" by Senator Jeff Flake of Arizona
- ***Date:*** January 17, 2018
- ***Where:*** Senate floor, Washington, DC

- ***Significance:*** This speech by Republican Senator Jeff Flake of Arizona rebukes President Trump's attacks on the news media and on truth. The senator likens President Trump's behavior to that of dictators and authoritarians and calls his disregard for truth an assault on the country's democratic institutions. Senator Flake warns that for democracy to remain strong, truth cannot be compromised for the sake of politics.

DOCUMENT

Mr. FLAKE. Mr. President, near the beginning of the document that made us free, our Declaration of Independence, Thomas Jefferson wrote: "We hold these truths to be self-evident." So from our very beginnings, our freedom has been predicated on truth. The Founders were visionary in this regard, understanding well that good faith and shared facts between the governed and the government would be the very basis of this ongoing idea of America.

As the distinguished former Member of this body, Daniel Patrick Moynihan of New York, famously said, "Everyone is entitled to his own opinion, but not his own facts." During this past year, I am alarmed to say, Senator Moynihan's proposition has likely been tested more severely than at any time in our history. It is for that reason that I rise today to talk about the truth and the truth's relationship to democracy, for without truth and a principled fidelity to truth and to shared facts, our democracy will not last.

Mr. President, 2017 was a year which saw the truth—objective, empirical, evidence-based truth—more battered and abused than at any time in the history of our country, at the hands of the most powerful figure in our government. It was a year which saw the White House enshrine "alternative facts" into the American lexicon as justification for what used to be simply called old-fashioned falsehoods. It was a year in which an unrelenting daily assault on the constitutionally protected free press was launched by the same White House, an assault that is as unprecedented as it is unwarranted.

"The enemy of the people" was what the President of the United States called the free press in 2017. It is a testament to the condition of our democracy that our own President uses words infamously spoken by Joseph Stalin to describe his enemies. It bears noting that so fraught with malice was the phrase "enemy of the people" that even Nikita Khrushchev forbade its use, telling the Soviet Communist Party that the phrase had been introduced by Stalin for the purpose of "annihilating such individuals" who disagreed with the supreme leader. This alone should be the source of great shame for us in this body—especially for those of us in the President's party—for they are shameful, repulsive statements.

And, of course, the President has it precisely backward—despotism is the enemy of the people. The free press is the despot's enemy, which makes the free press the guardian of democracy. When a figure in power reflexively calls any press that doesn't suit him "fake news," it is that person who should be the figure of suspicion, not the press.

I dare say that anyone who has the privilege and awesome responsibility to serve in this Chamber knows that these reflexive slurs of "fake news" are dubious at best. Those of us who travel overseas, especially to war zones and other troubled areas all around the globe, encounter members of U.S.-based media who risk their lives and sometimes lose their lives reporting on the truth. To dismiss their work as "fake news" is an affront to their commitment and their sacrifice. According to the International Federation of Journalists, 80 journalists were killed in 2017. A new report from the Committee to Protect Journalists documents that the number of journalists imprisoned around the world has reached 262, which is a new record. This total includes 21 reporters who are being held on "false news" charges.

So powerful is the Presidency that the damage done by the sustained attack on the truth will not be confined to this President's time in office. Here in America, we do not pay obeisance to the powerful. In fact, we question the powerful most ardently. To do so is our birthright and a requirement of our citizenship. And so we know well that, no matter how powerful, no President will ever have dominion over objective reality. No politician will ever tell us what the truth is and what it is not.

And anyone who presumes to try to attack or manipulate the press for his own purposes should be made to realize his mistake and be held to account. That is our job here. That is just as Madison, Hamilton, and Jay would have it.

Of course, a major difference between politicians and the free press is that the free press usually corrects itself when it has made a mistake. Politicians don't.

No longer can we compound attacks on truth with our silent acquiescence. No longer can we turn a blind eye or a deaf ear to those assaults on our institutions.

An American President who cannot take criticism, who must constantly deflect and distort and distract, who must find someone else to blame, is charting a very dangerous path. And a Congress that fails to act as a check on the President adds to that danger.

Now we are told via Twitter that today the President intends to announce his choice for the "most corrupt and dishonest" media awards. It beggars belief that an American President would engage in such a spectacle, but here we are.

So 2018 must be the year in which the truth takes a stand against power that would weaken it. In this effort, the choice is quite simple, and in this effort, the truth needs as many allies as possible. Together, my colleagues, we are powerful. Together, we have it within us to turn back these attacks, to right these wrongs, repair this damage, restore reverence for our institutions, and prevent further moral vandalism. Together, united in this purpose to do our jobs under the Constitution, without regard to party or party loyalty, let us resolve to be allies of the truth and not partners in its destruction.

It is not my purpose here to inventory all the official untruths of the past year, but a brief survey is in order. Some untruths are trivial, such as the bizarre contention regarding the crowd size at last year's inaugural, but many untruths are not at all trivial, such as the seminal untruth of the President's political career—the oft-repeated conspiracy about the birthplace of President Obama. Also not trivial are the equally pernicious fantasies about rigged elections and massive voter fraud, which are as destructive as they are inaccurate; to the effort to undermine confidence in the

Federal courts, Federal law enforcement, the intelligence community, and the free press; to perhaps the most vexing untruth of all—the supposed "hoax" at the heart of Special Counsel Robert Mueller's Russia investigation.

To be very clear, to call the Russian matter a "hoax," as the President has done so many times, is a falsehood. We know that the attacks orchestrated by the Russian Government during the election were real. They constituted a grave threat to both American sovereignty and to our national security. It is in the interest of every American to get to the bottom of this matter, wherever the investigation leads.

Ignoring or denying the truth about hostile Russian intentions toward the United States leaves us vulnerable to future attacks. We are told by our intelligence agencies that these attacks are ongoing. Yet it has recently been reported that there has not been a single Cabinet-level meeting regarding Russian interference and how to defend America against these attacks—not one. What might seem like a casual and routine untruth—so casual and routine that it has now become the white noise of Washington—is, in fact, a serious lapse in the defense of our country.

Let us be clear. The impulses underlying the dissemination of such untruths are not benign. They have the effect of eroding trust in our vital institutions and conditioning the public to no longer trust them. The destructive effect of this kind of behavior on our democracy cannot be overstated.

Every word that a President utters projects American values around the world. The values of free expression and reverence for the free press have been our global hallmark, for it is our ability to freely air the truth that keeps our government honest and keeps the people free. Between the mighty and the modest, truth is a great leveler. So respect for freedom of the press has always been one of our most important exports.

But a recent report published in our free press should raise an alarm. I will read from the story: "In February, Syrian President Bashar Assad brushed off an Amnesty International report that some 13,000 people had been killed at one of his military prisons by saying, 'You can forge anything these days,' we are living in a fake news era."

In the Philippines, President Rodrigo Duterte has complained of being "demonized" by "fake news." Last month, the report continues, with our President "laughing by his side" Duterte called reporters "spies."

In July, Venezuelan President Nicolas Maduro complained to the Russian propaganda outlet that the world media had "spread lots of false versions, lots of lies" about his country, adding: "This is what we call 'fake news' today, isn't it?"

There are more.

A state official in Myanmar recently said: "There is no such thing as Rohingya. It is fake news."

He was referring to the persecuted ethnic group.

Leaders in Singapore, a country known for restricting free speech, have promised "fake news" legislation in the next year—and on and on and on.

This feedback loop is disgraceful. Not only has the past year seen an American President borrow despotic language to refer to the free press, but it seems he has now, in turn, inspired dictators and authoritarians with his own language. That is reprehensible.

We are not in a "fake news" era, as Bashar Assad said. Rather, we are in an era in which the authoritarian impulse is reasserting itself to challenge free people and free societies everywhere.

In our own country, from the trivial to the truly dangerous, it is the range and regularity of the untruths we see that should be the cause for profound alarm and spur to action. Add to that the by now predictable habit of calling true things false and false things true, and we have a recipe for disaster.

George Orwell warned: "The further a society drifts from the truth, the more it will hate those who speak it."

Any of us who have spent time in public life have endured news coverage we felt was jaded or unfair, but in our positions, to employ even idle threats, to use laws or regulations to stifle criticism is corrosive to our democratic institutions. Simply put, it is the press's obligation to uncover the truth about power. It is the people's right to criticize their government, and it is our job to take it.

What is the goal of laying siege to the truth? In his spurring speech on the 20th anniversary of the Voice of America, President John F. Kennedy was eloquent in the answer to that question. He said: "We are not afraid to entrust the American people with unpleasant facts, foreign ideas, alien philosophies, and competitive values. For a nation that is afraid to let its people judge the truth and falsehood in an open market is a nation afraid of its people."

The question of why the truth is now under such assault may be for historians to determine, but for those who cherish American constitutional democracy, what matters is the effect on America and her people and her standing in an increasingly unstable world, made all the more unstable by these very fabrications. What matters is the daily disassembling of our democratic institutions.

We are a mature democracy. It is past time to stop excusing or ignoring or, worse, endorsing these attacks on the truth. For if we compromise the truth for the sake of our politics, we are lost. . . .

SOURCE: Truth and Democracy speech. Sen. Jeff Flake (AZ). 115th Cong., 2nd sess., *Congressional Record* January 17, 2018. S215–217. https://www.congress.gov/115/crec/2018/01/17/CREC-2018-01-17-pt1-PgS215-4.pdf

DID YOU KNOW?

The spread of information (true or false) throughout early history was primarily verbal in nature. This changed drastically with the development of Gutenberg's printing press in 1493, which made news widely accessible to the literate and those with the means to afford books and newspapers. Greater accessibility also meant greater opportunity for the spread of false information. One notable example was the Great Moon Hoax of 1835, when the *New York Sun* published multiple articles claiming discovery of an alien civilization on the moon (Borel 2017). Yellow journalism of the 1890s was also rife with disinformation, as newspapers competed to attract readers by generating ever more sensational headlines and exaggerated news stories.

The development of radio and television in the twentieth century greatly expanded the reach of mass media, as literacy was no longer a requirement to easily access news. The new media forms gave rise to the development of satirical news, sometimes confused with factual news by undiscerning audiences. Even radio dramas inadvertently perpetuated "fake news" as with the example of the infamous 1938 radio adaptation of H.G. Wells's *War of the Worlds*. The broadcast produced nationwide hysteria as listeners who had not heard the introduction to the program mistook fake news bulletins of a Martian invasion for actual news reports.

Propaganda—ideas or information spread purposely to promote an agenda or manipulate beliefs—was also widely distributed through radio, television, and printed materials during World Wars I and II to encourage public support of war efforts. Ironically, propaganda was also one of Hitler's most effective tools in building support among German citizenry for the persecution of Jews during WWII (Herzstein 1978).

In the late twentieth century, the internet revolutionized communication by providing low-cost, highly accessible means of distributing and consuming messages on a global scale. Content creators became their own publishers, opening the door to extensive distribution of information mimicking real news but lacking journalistic accuracy or credibility (Lazer et al. 2018). Traditional news sources that had always enjoyed high degrees of public trust found themselves competing with independent news sources that at times promoted false or misleading narratives.

ANALYSIS

"Fake news" is, paradoxically, an old concept and a new phenomenon. Disinformation wars were waged in the ancient Roman Empire and canards circulated in seventeenth-century France to influence public opinion and understanding (Kaminska 2017; Burkhardt 2017).

While the purposeful spread of falsehoods prior to the twentieth century was somewhat restricted by geographical and communicative limitations, modern misinformation campaigns are much broader and more influential, thanks to the hyperconnectivity of new communication technologies. The pervasiveness of modern disinformation campaigns, their role in modern politics, and the resulting impact of public distrust in news media have made "fake news" both a common household phrase (*Collins Dictionaries* named it the 2017 word of the year) and a particularly troubling contemporary issue. The World Economic Forum even listed "massive digital misinformation" as one of the biggest threats to society (2013).

What, exactly, is "fake news"? There is no universally accepted definition, and the meaning of the phrase has evolved along with its varied usage. "Fake news," broadly defined, is untrue information presented as fact. It is "frequently used to describe a political story which is seen as damaging to an agency, entity, or person" (*Merriam-Webster* n.d.). However, the phrase can encompass a wide range of information disorders including misinformation (false or misleading in nature), disinformation (false information purposely shared in order to deceive), propaganda, hoaxes, and satire. Depending on context, each can fall under the umbrella of "fake news."

Further complicating a universal understanding of the phrase is a relatively new characterization of what constitutes "fake news." Although the concept was born over a century ago (ibid), modern use of the term emerged during the 2016 presidential election campaign. Hillary Clinton was the first to incorporate the expression "fake news" in a speech, but Donald Trump quickly co-opted and popularized the phrase—employing it to disparage and discredit sources of news with which he disagreed (Wendling 2018; Stelter 2018). During his first year in office, President Trump used the word "fake" more than 400 times, often describing "fake news," "fake polls," "fake media," and "fake stories" (Stelter 2018). Analysts point out that under the Trump administration, "fake news" was used as a political weapon—not only to discredit journalists and media sources that reported unfavorable news about President Trump, but also to support or perpetuate conspiracy theories and the President's own false claims (van der Linden et al. 2020; Ross & Rivers 2018). A July 2020 *Fact Checker* analysis reported that President Trump made 20,055 false or misleading claims since taking office (Fact Checker 2020).

The destructive nature of fake news and misinformation has become one of modern society's greatest challenges. Mitigating its influence is problematic; a Yale study found that the more people were exposed to a false message, the more they believed it (Pennycook, Cannon & Rand 2018). Amid proposals for reducing its influence, however, two persistent questions arise—to what degree is false speech protected under the Constitution? Under the First Amendment, can free speech coexist with patently false or misleading speech?

Not always, according to specific historical laws and court decisions. Punishment for false speech against the U.S. government was instituted as early as 1798 with the Alien and Sedition Acts. Twentieth-century Supreme Court rulings established false advertising and certain types of defamation as unprotected by the First Amendment. False reporting of a crime or false statements made under oath are also punishable acts.

Aside from a few narrow categories, however, the Supreme Court has predominantly ruled that even false speech should be protected and allowed to enter the marketplace of ideas, where justices felt true speech would prevail. In *NAACP v. Button* (1963) and *The New York Times v. Sullivan* (1964), the court established that the government must maintain narrow parameters in defining and regulating unprotected speech if the First Amendment is to have the "breathing space" necessary for free expression of ideas. In *United States v. Alvarez* (2012), the court again shielded false speech from criminal punishment.

However, more recent sophisticated disinformation campaigns have given rise to a new level of concern about the effects of purposely disseminated falsehoods on American democracy (Lee 2019). One study estimated that during a specific time period prior to the 2016 presidential election, one in four Americans visited fake news sites and that fact checks almost never reached consumers of fake news (Guess, Nyhan & Reifler 2018). Both foreign and domestic fake news sources were found to have influenced voters in the 2016 presidential race, possibly affecting the election's outcome (Allcott & Gentzkow 2017). Fake news impacted voter choices in the 2018 midterm elections (West 2018), and the FBI warned of foreign disinformation campaigns intended to affect the outcome of the 2020 elections Winter 2019). Disinformation, conspiracy theories, and belief in "fake news" were all catalysts for the January 6, 2021, attack on the U.S. Capitol.

DID YOU KNOW?

Social media platforms such as Facebook and Twitter have become the primary conduits for disinformation spread in the twenty-first century. Deceptive messaging is easily propagated on social media platforms for a number of reasons: there is little or no recourse for circulation of false information; media consumers often struggle to distinguish between real news and false narratives on social media; and advertising revenue incentivizes the circulation of content that attracts the most attention, often leading to content emphasizing sensationalism over truth (Burkhardt 2017). Additionally, algorithms built into social media sites strengthen existing bias by constantly suggesting additional content similar to that of users' established preferences, thereby reinforcing preexisting beliefs (Borel 2017). Furthermore, bots (non-human, automated accounts) easily perpetuate fake news by searching, liking, and sharing information with unlimited numbers of users (Lazer et al. 2018).

Perhaps, most importantly, social media platforms provide important spaces of belonging for users with homogeneous views (Wardle & Derakhshan 2017). Through social media, an individual's relationship with information becomes publicly defined through "likes," "dislikes," preferences, and membership in online social groups. This emotionally driven aspect of social media use, combined with heightened political polarization in recent years, has decreased the likelihood that users will consider alternate viewpoints and has increased the likelihood that fake news content will be validated and further spread (Lazer et al. 2018).

Additionally, terrorists have successfully used social media in recent years to jeopardize America's national security through circulation of dangerous propaganda (Bergen 2016).

Fake news, both as a reality and as a political weapon, also played a major role in domestic political and social battles during the Trump presidency. From providing inaccurate information about hurricane Dorian's trajectory to insisting the 2020 election was stolen, President Trump's repeated falsehoods and denouncements of mainstream media heightened both incivility and partisan polarization surrounding major social, political, and ecological events (Nithyanad, Schaffner & Gill 2017). The impacts of fake news on public health were also dire (Naeem, Bhatti & Khan 2020), particularly during the first year of the COVID-19 pandemic when President Trump was the source of false and potentially dangerous information (Holmes 2020; Yamey & Gonsalves 2020).

Such examples have led to calls for stricter measures to stop the spread of false news. Experts warn that continuous dissemination of falsehoods will ultimately hurt the marketplace of ideas by sowing chaos and confusion within it (Napoli 2018).

However, responses have been mixed at best. Globally, the number of fact-checking organizations has risen from 96 in 2016 to 290 in 2020 (Stencel & Luther 2020), offering the public some measure of recourse against false claims. But efforts to fact-check or flag/ban false statements on social media platforms, the primary channels through which fake news is spread, have been insufficient, allowing false narratives to persist (Social 2020; Burkhardt 2017). Activists have called for harsher laws, but legislators are hesitant to impose government regulations on media because of censorship concerns that such attempts would raise.

Concerned politicians have suggested repealing Section 230 of the Communications Decency Act: Republicans allege the sites are biased against conservative voices, and Democrats argue tech companies do not go far enough in moderating hate messages and other harmful speech on their platforms. In October 2020, the Federal Communications Commission (FCC) chairman Ajit Pai initiated an official FCC rulemaking proceeding to clarify the application of Section 230 to social media companies, saying he believes the agency has the legal authority to regulate these companies (Spangler 2020).

Adequate solutions to problems caused by fake news will necessitate varied approaches, including media literacy campaigns, greater social media accountability, and a combination of judicial and legal efforts to punish harmful false speech.

FURTHER READING

Allcott, Hunt, and Matthew Gentzkow. "Social Media and Fake News in the 2016 Election." *Journal of Economic Perspectives* 31, no. 2 (2017): 211–36.

Burkhardt, Joanna M. *Combating Fake News in the Digital Age*. Chicago: American Library Association (2017).

Farkas, Johan, and Jannick Schou. *Post-Truth, Fake News and Democracy: Mapping the Politics of Falsehood*. New York: Routledge, 2020.

Gorbach, Julien. "Not Your Grandpa's Hoax: A Comparative History of Fake News." *American Journalism* 35, no. 2 (2018): 236–49.

Graves, Lucas. *Deciding What's True: The Rise of Political Fact-Checking in American Journalism*. New York: Columbia University Press, 2016.

Napoli, Philip M. "What If More Speech Is No Longer the Solution: First Amendment Theory Meets Fake News and the Filter Bubble." *Federal Communications Law Journal* 70 (2018): 55.

- ***Document 54:*** Statement by Senator Feinstein at Congressional Hearing on "Facebook, Social Media Privacy, and the Use and Abuse of Data"
- ***Date:*** April 10, 2018
- ***Where:*** U.S. Senate Committee on the Judiciary and U.S. Senate Committee on Commerce, Science, and Transportation
- ***Significance:*** This statement by Senator Feinstein outlines serious problems that have arisen with Facebook and other social media platforms, including breaches of user privacy, unauthorized

collection of data about consumers of the products, and manipulation of personal information for purposes of election interference. Senator Feinstein also asks how Facebook will work to ensure this platform will not be used to compromise the integrity of future elections and suggests that if social media companies are unable to make these assurances, Congress may need to take regulatory action.

DOCUMENT

Prepared Statement by Senator Dianne Feinstein of California
Ranking Member, Senate Judiciary Committee
Joint hearing of the Senate Judiciary Committee and Senate Commerce Committee
Facebook, Social Media Privacy, and the Use and Abuse of Data
April 10, 2018

. . . What we have learned over the past few months is alarming. We have seen how foreign actors are abusing social media platforms, like Facebook, to interfere in elections and taking millions of Americans' personal information without their knowledge to manipulate public opinion and target individual voters.

Specifically, on February 16th, Special Counsel Mueller issued an indictment against the Russia-based Internet Research Agency and thirteen of its employees for "interference operations targeting the United States."

Through this thirty-seven page indictment, we learned that the IRA ran a coordinated campaign through 470 Facebook accounts and pages. The campaign included ads and false information to create discord and harm Secretary Clinton's campaign—and the content was seen by an estimated 157 million Americans.

A month later, on March 17th, news broke that Cambridge Analytica exploited the personal information of approximately 50 million Facebook users without their knowledge or permission.

And last week we learned that number was even higher—87 million Facebook users who had their private information taken without their consent. [Facebook, April 4, 2018]

Specifically, using a personality quiz he created, Professor Aleksandr Kogan collected the personal information of 300,000 Facebook users, and then collected data on millions of their "friends."

It appears the information collected included everything these individuals had on their Facebook pages—and, according to some reports, even included private direct messages between users.

Prof. Kogan is said to have taken data from over 70 million Americans. It has also been reported that he sold this data to Cambridge Analytica for $800,000.

If accurate, that means Cambridge Analytica paid less than one penny ($0.009) for each person's private information.

Cambridge Analytica then took this data and created a "psychological warfare tool" to influence U.S. elections. In fact, CEO Alexander Nix, declared that Cambridge Analytica "ran all the digital campaign, the television campaign and [its] data informed all the strategy" for the Trump campaign.

The reporting has also speculated that Cambridge Analytica worked with the Internet Research Agency to help Russia identify which American voters to target with its propaganda.

I am concerned that press reports indicate Facebook learned about this breach back in 2015, but appears to have not taken significant steps to address it until this year.

Today's hearing is the first step toward learning how this happened, who knew about these tactics, what can be done to prevent this in the future, and what else we can do to protect individual privacy and the integrity of our elections.

This hearing takes on a significance with the testimony of this CEO. It is important that he take the initiative and outline specific steps his company will take to regulate and control its platforms so that this cannot happen again.

Hopefully private industry will reform and monitor its practices to prevent manipulation of elections and violations of individual privacy. But if they won't, Congress will have to do it for them.

This is a critical time to take real action and remedy a bad situation. Thank you.

SOURCE: U.S. Congress. Senate. Committee on the Judiciary and Committee on Commerce, Science, and Transportation. *Facebook, Social Media Privacy, and the Use and Abuse of Data.* 115th Cong., 2nd sess., 2018. https://www.judiciary.senate.gov/imo/media/doc/04-10-18%20Feinstein%20Statement.pdf

ANALYSIS

The birth of social media introduced new global platforms for voicing opinions, creating connections, and acquiring information. However, major controversies including the discovery of personal data privacy breaches and use of social media to spread disinformation have tested the limits of free speech and prompted new considerations of the moral and ethical responsibilities of social media companies.

Hate speech and disinformation, for example, are technically protected under the First Amendment, but some argue the ramifications of their unimpeded spread on social media are too dangerous to ignore. Advocates have pushed for tech companies to take on a greater role in monitoring content on their platforms and enacting policies that prohibit harmful messages.

Others insist that content monitoring on social media platforms amounts to censorship and should not be allowed to impede free speech. They argue it is dangerous to trust private companies to determine which voices are heard in what is now one of the largest global spheres for idea and information exchange. Compared to democratic governments that have legal and judicial structures in place to protect expression, these large for-profit companies are more capable of restricting speech and less accountable for their oversight and decisions about what is truthful or acceptable expression (Keller 2019). Even Facebook CEO Mark Zuckerberg stated at one point it is not the role of private companies to be "arbiters of truth" (McCarthy 2020).

In reality, however, the spread of disinformation through social media has caused serious problems, adding to social and political unrest (Tucker et al. 2018) and posing dangers to public health (Wang et al. 2019). Researchers have found that fake news also spreads more rapidly and easily than real news (Moravec, Minas & Dennis 2018), creating real world consequences when users believe propaganda over truth. False stories about protests, politicians, vaccines, voting information, school shootings, and conspiracy theories like "Pizzagate" and "QAnon" have elicited harmful, violent, and sometimes deadly responses (Winter 2020).

A growing number of politicians have insisted that it is the responsibility of social media companies like Facebook to more closely monitor content and censor speech that is ultimately harmful to society. Members of both political parties have issued calls for regulation, although their reasons for wanting such restrictions are not necessarily mutual. While Democrats have primarily voiced concern about Facebook's role in election interference, its lack of accountability for hate speech, and its function as a conduit of disinformation, members of the GOP have expressed frustration over what they allege is Facebook's censorship of conservative news and voices (Allyn 2020).

Many social media companies have tried to demonstrate accountability by implementing hate and harassment policies that prohibit specific types of content on their platforms. But efforts to block, flag, or delete content that violates rules have frequently been met with accusations of bias or censorship. President Trump, for instance, was furious when Facebook and Twitter censored a number of his posts and tweets that violated the companies' policies. Some were blocked (or flagged) because they glorified violence (Hern 2020), others because they contained false information, including "misleading and potentially harmful information related to COVID-19" (Baker-Jordan 2020; Wong & Mihelcik 2020). And when Facebook and Twitter both censored a news story alleging wrongdoing by presidential candidate Joe Biden's son in October 2020, angry Senate Republicans announced they would subpoena the heads of both companies to testify about what they felt was election interference (Rodrigo 2020).

Pushback from both citizens and government leaders unhappy with the nature of social media companies' efforts to moderate content has placed legislators in the awkward position of determining the degree to which free speech can or should be protected—even when it causes harm. When is the danger to society great enough to warrant regulatory measures?

The First Amendment protects speech from *government* punishment or censorship; however, that protection does not apply to private organizations. Companies like Facebook and Twitter are free to regulate content as they see fit. Nevertheless, lawmakers face increasing public demands to hold such organizations accountable when the free speech they restrict or permit causes harm or is alleged to be shaped by political considerations. This delicate intersection of state and private interests requires careful consideration of if or when private management of free expression becomes so threatening to society that government intervention is warranted.

Facebook CEO Mark Zuckerberg was first called to testify before Congress in March 2018, just after the Cambridge Analytica data and privacy breach was exposed. This breach involved the collection of personal user data of 87 million Facebook users by a third party, who then shared it with a political consulting firm without users' consent. Zuckerberg took responsibility for the data breach and acknowledged Facebook had also been the conduit for a Russian disinformation campaign during the 2016 election. He promised to implement a number of measures to ensure users' privacy would be protected, and he outlined steps the company would take to try to locate and moderate hateful or false content.

Two years later, Facebook's data deals with some of the world's largest technology companies were under criminal investigation, and lawmakers were more frustrated than ever over the lack of accountability among this and other social media giants. In addition to making questionable progress toward protecting data, Congress was alarmed by the way Facebook and other social media companies handled free speech considerations when regulating content. These combined harms inspired a sense of urgency in Congress to break up Big Tech and regulate social media platforms.

During a summer 2020 House Judiciary Antitrust Subcommittee Hearing, Chairman Cicilline suggested Facebook had grown too large for the company to effectively contain false or deadly content. "There's no competition forcing you to police your own platform," he told Zuckerberg. "Allowing this misinformation to spread can lead to violence. And frankly, I believe it strikes at the very heart of American democracy" (U.S. Congress, House, July 29, 2020).

Similar sentiments and pleas for reform have come from within Big Tech itself. In May 2019, Facebook cofounder Chris Hughes called for a breakup of the company, cautioning that CEO Mark Zuckerberg's unchecked power must be held accountable by the government. Tim Kendall, former Facebook executive, called the current business model of social media companies "a threat to democracy" in need of reform and regulation (Social 2020). Kendall warned "[E]xtreme outcomes are the logical end conclusion if there is no action on social media reform during the increasing destabilization of civil society" (Flood 2020).

In May 2020, the same month Facebook launched an international oversight board to review online content (Hawkinson 2020), President Trump signed an executive order initiating the process of removing legal protections for Big Tech under Section 230 of the Communications Decency Act (Kelly 2020). In October of that year, the Federal Communications Commission said it would move forward with rulemaking to clarify the meaning of Section 230, effectively seeking to regulate social media platforms. That same month at a House Judiciary Hearing, Democrats and Republicans united in rare bipartisan support for strengthened antitrust laws intended to rein in Big Tech.

Congress's eventual regulatory decisions will not only shape the future of Big Tech, but some would argue, the future of American democracy.

FURTHER READING

Hawkinson, Katie. "Facebook Appoints International Oversight Board to Regulate Online Posts, Raising Questions of Censorship and Free Speech." Free Speech Project. August 30, 2020. https://freespeechproject.georgetown.edu/tracker-entries/facebook-appoints-international-oversight-board-to-regulate-online-posts-raising-questions-of-censorship-and-free-speech/

Hooker, Matthew P. "Censorship, Free Speech & Facebook: Applying the First Amendment to Social Media Platforms via the Public Function Exception." *Washington Journal of Law, Technology & Arts* 15 (2019): 36.

Isaak, Jim, and Mina J. Hanna. "User Data Privacy: Facebook, Cambridge Analytica, and Privacy Protection." *Computer* 51, no. 8 (2018): 56–59.

Keller, Daphne. "Facebook Restricts Speech by Popular Demand." *Atlantic*. September 22, 2019. https://www.theatlantic.com/ideas/archive/2019/09/facebook-restricts-free-speech-popular-demand/598462/

Rozsa, Matthew. "Both the GOP and the Democrats Want to Break Up Big Tech. Could It Really Happen?" *Salon*. October 20, 2020. https://www.salon.com/2020/10/20/both-the-gop-and-the-democrats-want-to-break-up-big-tech-could-it-really-happen/

U.S. Congress House. "Committee on Oversight and Reform: Subcommittee on Civil Rights and Civil Liberties Briefing." *First Amendment Violations at Black Lives Matter Protests*. 116th Cong., 2nd Sess., June 20, 2020. https://oversight.house.gov/legislation/briefings/select-subcommittee-briefing-on-first-amendment-violations-at-black-lives

U.S. Congress House. "Committee on the Judiciary, Subcommittee on Antitrust, Commercial, and Administrative Law." *Online Platforms and Market Power, Part 6. Examining the Dominance of Amazon, Apple, Facebook, and Google*. 116th Cong., 2nd Sess., July 29, 2020.

U.S. Congress Senate. "Committee on the Judiciary, Zuckerberg Responses To Judiciary Committee Questions for the Record." *Facebook, Social Media Privacy, and the Use and Abuse of Data*. 115th Cong., 2nd Sess., 2018. https://www.judiciary.senate.gov/imo/media/doc/Zuckerberg%20Responses%20to%20Judiciary%20Committee%20QFRs.pdf

---

- ***Document 55:*** Amicus Brief Written by First Amendment Scholars and Media Law Scholars for *Gilmore v. Jones*
- ***Date:*** June 19, 2018
- ***Where:*** Filed in U.S. District Court for the Western District of Virginia
- ***Significance:*** On March 13, 2018, Brennan Gilmore filed a defamation lawsuit against Alex Jones and related associates for issuing patently false statements and conspiracy theories about Gilmore that resulted in harassment and threats against him. This amicus brief, written by First Amendment and media law scholars, urged the court to reject a motion by Jones to dismiss this case.

DOCUMENT

Brief of First Amendment and Media Law Scholars

I. INTEREST OF AMICI

As amici curiae, the signatories to this brief urge the Court to reject the instant Motions to Dismiss and to allow this suit to proceed. Each signatory is a distinguished professor of constitutional and/or media law, with expertise and interest in application of the First Amendment. They file this brief in order to share their perspective on the twin considerations of protection of speech and protection of reputation that are implicated in this case. Ultimately, they urge the Court that the First Amendment does not counsel dismissal of this suit. Further, they urge the Court to consider the detrimental effects that dismissal of this case would have on witnesses who seek to come forward with facts others deem inconvenient

II. INTRODUCTION

On August 12, 2017, in Charlottesville, Virginia, Brennan Gilmore witnessed James Alex Fields, Jr., a neo-Nazi, deliberately drive into a crowd of peaceful protestors, killing Heather Heyer and injuring many others. After hearing that media outlets were suggesting that the attack was an accident or an act of self-defense, Mr. Gilmore shared his account of the attack with the public via Twitter. In response to Mr. Gilmore's eyewitness account, Defendants targeted Mr. Gilmore with publications alleging false and absurd conspiracy theories implicating Mr. Gilmore in the planning of the attack. As a direct result of these statements, Mr. Gilmore has been subject to threats and harassment.

The Defendants' publications, written with the intention of destroying Mr. Gilmore's reputation for the benefit of their own political agenda, are not protected by the First Amendment. While "some false statements are inevitable if there is to be open and vigorous expression of views in public and private conversation," *United States v. Alvarez* (2012), the Supreme Court has never endorsed the view that knowingly false statements causing direct, legally cognizable harm to another should be protected. The law of defamation serves to anchor public discourse in truth and protect our system of freedom of expression from knowing or malicious lies about an individual. Indeed, defamation has always involved two interests—protection of speech on the one hand and protection of reputation on the other.

Reputation is "a concept at the root of any decent system of ordered liberty" and it should not be treated lightly here. *Rosenblatt v. Baer* (1966) (Stewart, J., concurring). To do so would be to grant an undue privilege to untrue statements of facts, maliciously made. And it would do so at the expense of a private individual who stepped forward with newsworthy information in the wake of a troubling event. This would set a dangerous precedent. Further, it is unwarranted by the law. The statements made by the Defendants were defamatory. Mr. Gilmore is not a public figure but, even if he were, he has properly pleaded actual malice. The Motions to Dismiss should be rejected.

III. ARGUMENT

A. Protection of reputation is an important societal interest

The protections afforded to speech under the First Amendment have been much expounded upon. Content-based restrictions on speech are presumed invalid, save for a few "historic and traditional categories of expression," including defamation. *Alvarez*. Indeed, defamation law creates and enforces social boundaries about what speech is and is not acceptable. It "exists not merely to validate the dignitary interests of individual plaintiffs" but also "helps to make meaningful discourse possible," and "gives society a means for announcing that certain speech has crossed the bounds of propriety.". . . Lyrissa Barnett Lidsky, Silencing John Doe: Defamation & Discourse in Cyberspace, 49 *Duke L.J.* 855, 885–86 (2000) (citing Robert C. Post, Constitutional Domains (1995); Robert C. Post, The Social Foundations of Defamation Law: Reputation and the Constitution, 74 Cal. L. Rev. 691, 713 (1986)). Nor is it a recent innovation—defamation is a feature of ancient laws dating back at least to the ecclesiastical courts of the Middle Ages.

Defamation law seeks to protect both public and private figures from malicious lies, which debase our entire system of free expression. To do this, defamation law deems certain types of speech beyond the pale—when it comes to public figures, this includes speech uttered with reckless disregard for the truth. For private figures, the law places even more speech beyond the pale—and there are sound reasons behind this, including the fact that private figures do not have the same means and ability to disseminate their own side of the story. . . .

Without defamation law, the ordinary citizen would be left unsure of who and what can be trusted, and those subject to knowing or malicious untruths left without recourse. The press would likewise be impoverished by this state. . . . Defamation and libel law thus protect legitimate fact-based journalists, who seek to present true information to the public.

Libel and defamation law further serve the interests of the press—and the public—by protecting individuals like the Plaintiff who are injected into public debate. Mr. Gilmore was not a public figure prior to the events in Charlottesville. . . . [H]e was a private citizen who happened to capture something newsworthy—footage of James Alex Fields Jr. deliberately driving his car into a crowd of peaceful protestors—and who then felt comfortable coming forward with that footage.

That footage was deemed newsworthy by many news outlets, many of whom welcomed the chance to interview Mr. Gilmore himself. Had Mr. Gilmore known that he could be defamed with no recourse for sharing his footage, he would have had a powerful incentive to stay quiet, depriving the press and the public of an eyewitness account of an important event. Defamation law allows individuals thrust into the public light redress should untruths be spread, and thus encourages them to come forward.

Protection of speech under the First Amendment is a priority of the first order. But in the field of defamation law, it is not and cannot be the only priority. Protection of reputation is an important social good in and of itself. And in a case, such as this, where a private citizen steps forward with information of great public import, that individual's reputation should not be lightly cast aside. It should be valued as, in Justice Stewart's words, "at the root of any decent system of ordered liberty."

B. There is no constitutional value in knowing or malicious false statements of fact

The false statements of fact that were made about Mr. Gilmore were numerous. Defendants said, variously:

- Mr. Gilmore had links to the Central Intelligence Agency ("CIA") and "various other black ops kind of actors."
- That Mr. Gilmore had foreknowledge the events in Charlottesville were going to happen.
- That Mr. Gilmore was a "deep state shill."
- That Mr. Gilmore had links to George Soros or was even in his pay.
- That Mr. Gilmore had links to the campaigns of Hillary Clinton and Barack Obama.
- That Mr. Gilmore colluded to remove his name from the State Department website.

And the statements, taken together, connoted an even bigger falsehood: that Mr. Gilmore was a CIA agent who participated in planning the attack in Charlottesville. Mr. Gilmore has been harmed by these verifiably false statements of fact in ways that were eminently predictable.

Readership of the Defendants' publications, for instance, shared his parents' address online and sent him threatening and harassing messages. As a direct result of Defendant's statements, Mr. Gilmore has been subject to hate mail, death threats, hacking attempts, and harassment. He was even physically accosted in the street. His career as a Foreign Service Officer has been compromised; he has lost potential partners and clients in his most recent business venture; and his social and romantic relationships have been polluted by the content that comes up in a Google search of Mr. Gilmore's name.

One way in which courts can distinguish between protected speech and speech that is unduly damaging to reputation is by examining the truth of the statements at issue. False speech does not serve the public interest the way that true speech does. And indeed, "there is no constitutional value in false statements of fact. Neither the intentional lie nor the careless error materially advances society's interest in 'uninhibited, robust, and wide-open' debate on public issues.'" . . . Nor can Defendants excuse themselves from making false statements on the basis that it is merely "connotation" or "opinion." A statement that contains a "provably false factual connotation" is actionable. . . . And opinion itself is no defense—as the Supreme Court has recognized, "expressions of 'opinion' may often imply an assertion of objective fact." . . .

Likewise, despite the claims of Defendants, repetition is not a defense. . . .

The Defendants' attempt to parse their words to avoid the clear connotations of them should not be allowed. Not only are the ultimate implications of their words clear—that Mr. Gilmore participated in planning the Charlottesville attacks—they contain numerous explicit falsehoods that are equally damaging to Mr. Gilmore (for example, assertions that he, a State Department official, is connected to the CIA). Ruling for Defendants in this case would set a dangerous precedent. It would allow unscrupulous news organizations to couch their language as "opinion" and to mask their meaning with implication and insinuation, leaving readers clear as to the message but avoiding all liability for defamatory remarks. This should not be allowed and, in fact, is not allowed. Courts have rejected attempts, like that by the Defendants, to avoid liability through insinuation.

In sum, the statements at issue in this case have all the hallmarks of unprotected speech. There is no social value in permitting the falsehoods that have harmed Mr. Gilmore's reputation and career to stand. The Defendants' arguments to the contrary should be rejected. . . .

C. Mr. Gilmore is not a public figure . . .

. . . Mr. Gilmore's actions should be viewed not as an attempt to influence but rather as an attempt to inform. Indeed, Mr. Gilmore's conduct is exactly the type of conduct that the law should encourage. If an eyewitness to events knew he could be deemed a public figure merely by coming forward and stating what he knew, there would be a powerful disincentive to refrain from coming forward at all. Mr. Gilmore behaved precisely as we would hope one in his position would behave—he shared footage and an eyewitness account in order to inform his fellow citizens about a newsworthy event he happened to witness. That should not be deemed sufficient to transmute a private figure into a public one; nor should it be considered an attempt to influence the outcome of the controversy at hand. Certainly it should not be deemed sufficient to rule that Mr. Gilmore attempted to influence events at the motion to dismiss stage of the lawsuit. . . .

D. Mr. Gilmore has properly pleaded actual malice

Even if this Court finds that Mr. Gilmore is a limited purpose public figure, Mr. Gilmore has established that the statements in question were made with actual malice. The Supreme Court has made clear that "neither lies nor false communications serve the ends of the First Amendment," and that the actual malice standard represents the line between false Statements about public figures that are protected and those that are not. As noted, the false statements made by Defendants are numerous and—in point of fact—absurd. Mr. Gilmore has met his burden to plead that they were made with actual malice.

Actual malice "requires at a minimum that the statements were made with reckless disregard for the truth," . . . such that the defendant "in fact entertained serious doubts as to the truth of his publication," . . . and that there were "obvious reasons to doubt the veracity of the informant or the accuracy of his reports." Nor are professions of good faith sufficient, as the Court found in *St. Amant* . . .

By presenting evidence that Defendants twisted true facts about Mr. Gilmore's employment history with false, unverified assertions for which defendants had ample reason to doubt the veracity, Mr. Gilmore has presented a plausible inference that the Defendants entertained serious doubts as to the truth of the statements and implications published in their articles. . . . Here, at the motion to dismiss stage, this Court must "accept as true all of the allegations contained in a complaint," . . ., and find that Mr. Gilmore has met his burden to establish actual malice. To find otherwise would be to countenance a shocking departure from journalistic standards which resulted in putting forth allegations so absurd that only a "reckless man would have put them in circulation." This court should reject such an outcome.

IV. CONCLUSION

This Court should reject the Motions to Dismiss filed by each Defendant and allow this suit to proceed.

SOURCE: Brief for First Amendment Scholars & Media Law Scholars as Amici Curiae Supporting Defendants, at page 1299, *Gilmore v. Jones*, 370 F.Supp.3d 630 (W.D. Va. 2019) (No. 18–00017).

ANALYSIS

Should false speech be protected as free speech under the First Amendment? Do First Amendment protections apply when false or defamatory statements cause injury or harm to another? These questions lie at the heart of a lawsuit involving the victims of false messaging promoted by far-right wing radio host Alex Jones.

During a Unite the Right rally in Charlottesville, Virginia, in August 2017, a neo-Nazi drove a vehicle into a crowd of peaceful counter-protesters, injuring dozens and killing Heather Heyer. Fellow counter-protester Brennan Gilmore was near the scene of the attack when it occurred and captured the incident on video. Gilmore shared his video with local police and later posted his eyewitness account on Twitter to disprove false rumors about the events of that day.

Gilmore subsequently became a target of Alex Jones, a syndicated radio host known for promoting conspiracy theories on his daily four-hour program. Jones also shared personal political views on his *Infowars.com* and *Prisonplanet.tv* websites and on his YouTube channel.

Jones perpetuated a defamatory conspiracy theory involving Gilmore alleging, among other things, that Gilmore was a "deep state shill" with links to the CIA who had previous knowledge the events in Charlottesville would happen because he was working with other political operatives. This conspiracy theory spread quickly on the internet, and Jones's followers responded by publicly distributing the home address of Gilmore's parents and sending threatening and harassing messages, hate mail, and death threats to Gilmore himself. Gilmore sought police protection due to additional harassment and a physical attack. He also experienced hacking attempts and damage to both his professional and personal life because of the false statements and character misrepresentations made by Jones. Gilmore sued Alex Jones, Infowars, and other parties responsible for proliferating the false conspiracy theories, citing defamation and intentional infliction of emotional distress they had caused.

Although this case has not yet come to trial, previous defamation rulings grant some indication of the extent to which Jones may or may not enjoy constitutional protection.

Free speech of individuals has historically been protected under the First Amendment—even when such speech is unwelcome or unpopular. There are, however, exceptions—particularly when the potential to cause harm to another is at stake. Justice Holmes's "clear and present danger" doctrine in *Schenck v. United States* established that the First Amendment does not protect someone who falsely yells "fire!" in a crowded theater. This principle was later replaced by the "imminent lawless action" test in *Brandenburg v. Ohio*, which excluded from protection speech likely to cause imminent violation of the law. Supreme Court rulings have also established that child pornography, obscenity, and fighting words fall outside the bounds of First Amendment protection, in part, because of the harm they cause (as in child pornography) or because of their propensity to cause harm.

An additional category of unprotected speech involves defamation, or harmful misrepresentations of fact concerning another individual. Defamation can take on two forms: libel (written statements or oral remarks that include a transcript) or slander (oral remarks). Libel was actually one of the earliest categories of unprotected speech in the United States, as libel laws were used in the American colonies to impose criminal penalties on those who criticized the king of England, colonial leaders, or the church (Hudson Jr. 2020).

Defamation laws are state laws that can vary from one state to another, but at times, higher courts have ruled on issues concerning the nature and application of such laws. In 1964, the Supreme Court ruled in *New York Times Co. v. Sullivan* that libel law must "be measured by standards that satisfy the First Amendment." The court's decision applied, for the first time, constitutional considerations to the question of the legality of false speech. The ruling established that those who issue false statements about public officials can only be held liable if they acted with "actual malice." The court emphasized that errors are inevitable in free debate, and erroneous statements "must be protected if the freedoms of expressions are to have the 'breathing space' that they 'need to survive.'" The court wished to safeguard the public's ability to criticize public officials and their

DID YOU KNOW?

In a separate but related case, Alex Jones was sued for defamation by the parents of a six-year-old who was killed in 2012 in the mass shooting at Sandy Hook Elementary School in Newtown, Connecticut. This was one of many cases brought against him by parents of the victims who say they suffered additional threats and distress as a result of Jones's conspiracy theories about Sandy Hook.

Twenty first-graders and six school staff members were shot and killed on December 14, 2012, by a lone gunman who entered Sandy Hook Elementary School. After the incident, Jones repeatedly either suggested or contended on his radio show and websites that the mass shooting was a hoax, carried out by actors who opposed the Second Amendment. Some of his listeners or readers responded by harassing the parents of the Sandy Hook victims, even sending death threats.

In their lawsuits, the parents alleged that Jones had acted with actual malice and reckless disregard for the truth in making defamatory statements about the victims and their families. They cited the enormous psychological pain caused by ridicule, contempt, and attack from those believing Jones's conspiracy theory (Maxouris & Joseph 2019). Jones initially insisted that he was justified in spreading the hoax theory but later acknowledged the shooting was real and said he suffered a form of psychosis when he made the allegations (Jones 2019).

In 2018, major social media platforms such as Apple, Facebook, You Tube, and Spotify banned Alex Jones and removed content associated with him because he had violated their hate speech policies (Tobias 2018). By late 2020, he had been assessed nearly $150,000 in legal fees related to preliminary motions; the two major lawsuits against him had not yet gone to trial (Tilove 2020).

actions, thus defending the Constitution's protection of free speech regarding conduct of public officials. The court later extended this rule to include public figures.

Whether concerning libel or slander, however, defamation lawsuits offer individuals the opportunity to protect or defend themselves against false information that would harm their reputations. Justice Potter Stewart explained in *Rosenblatt v. Baer* (1966) that a defamation offense "reflects no more than our basic concept of the essential dignity and worth of every human being—a concept at the root of any decent system of ordered liberty."

Justices were also wary of the threat of defamation suits being used to intimidate individuals who would otherwise come forward with important information about a matter of public concern. In an effort to prevent this type of restriction on free speech, many states have passed anti-SLAPP (Strategic Lawsuit against Public Participation) laws as a way of avoiding meritless lawsuits.

In *Gertz v. Robert Welch, Inc.* (1974), the Supreme Court distinguished how the law protected private figures differently than public figures in defamation cases. Private individuals initiating a defamation lawsuit do not need to prove actual malice on the part of the defendant, only negligence or fault. Evidence of actual malice *is* required, however, if the plaintiff is a public official, public figure, or limited-purpose public figure (someone who chooses to prominently engage in a public controversy in order to affect its outcome) or if the plaintiff wishes to collect punitive damages. The *Gertz* case also clarified that *Sullivan* standards should apply when a statement concerns a matter of public importance.

This distinction between public versus private individuals was important in the case of *Gilmore v. Jones*. The defendants filed motions to dismiss the lawsuit against them on various grounds, including the argument that Gilmore was a public figure, and therefore, his defamation claim was invalid. In an amicus brief to the court, however, scholars argued that Gilmore is not a public figure, and even if he were, he met the burden of proving actual malice. They also argued there is no constitutional value in false statements, and protection of reputation is an important societal interest.

A district court judge eventually found Gilmore to be a limited-purpose public figure whose defamation claims were indeed valid because the evidence he provided proved actual malice on the part of the defendants.

Jones was banned from major social media platforms in 2018, and as of October 2020, he was facing multiple defamation lawsuits stemming from his promotion of harmful conspiracy theories on his radio program and websites. The outcomes of these cases will likely have enormous implications for future application of defamation law.

FURTHER READING

Leader, Alyssa R. "A SLAPP in the Face of Free Speech: Protecting Survivors' Rights to Speak Up in the Me Too Era." *First Amendment Law Review* 17 (2018): 441.

Lux, Anthony. "Spread of False Information Causes Dangers, Says Sunstein." *Harvard Law Today*. December 12, 2008. https://today.law.harvard.edu/spread-of-false-information-causes-dangers-says-sunstein/

McNamara, Lawrence. *Reputation and Defamation*. New York: Oxford University Press, 2007.

Sellnow, Timothy L., Adam Parrish, and Lauren Semenas. "From Hoax as Crisis to Crisis as Hoax: Fake News and Information Disorder as Disruptions to the Discourse of Renewal." *Journal of International Crisis and Risk Communication Research* 2, no. 1 (2019): 6.

Williamson, Elizabeth. "Truth in a Post-Truth Era: Sandy Hook Families Sue Alex Jones, Conspiracy Theorist." *New York Times*. 2018.

Wydra, Elizabeth B., Brianne J. Gorod, Ashwin Phatak, Andrew Charles Mendrala, and Aderson Bellegarde Francois. "Gilmore v. Jones, et al." Court Brief. Constitutional Accountability Center. n.d. https://www.theusconstitution.org/litigation/gilmore-v-jones-et-al/

- ***Document 56:*** Lawsuit Filed by Black Lives Matter (BLM) Activists against the Iowa State Patrol
- ***Date:*** October 5, 2020
- ***Where:*** United States District Court, Southern District of Iowa, Central Division
- ***Significance:*** This lawsuit, involving BLM protesters banned from the Iowa Capitol grounds after an altercation with police and state patrol, alleged the officers violated protesters' First Amendment free speech and freedom of assembly rights. Activists argued that prohibiting them from protesting in the area where they are most likely to encounter and affect decisions of lawmakers is a clear violation of their constitutional rights and retaliation for expressing a message with which authorities disagreed.

DOCUMENT

Docket No. 20–306

CIVIL RIGHTS COMPLAINT FOR DECLARATORY AND PRELIMINARY AND PERMANENT INJUNCTIVE RELIEF, AND DAMAGES AND DEMAND FOR A JURY TRIAL

INTRODUCTION

1. Plaintiffs are among a group of 17 supporters of the Black Lives Matter movement who on July 1, 2020 were banned by the Iowa State Patrol from the State of Iowa Capitol and the Iowa Capitol Complex grounds—in some cases for six months, until January 1, 2020, and in others for one year, until July 1, 2021.
2. Iowa State Patrol officers banned all the Plaintiffs verbally following their participation in a protest organized by the Des Moines Black

Liberation Movement ("Des Moines BLM") and arrests at the State Capitol on July 1, 2020. Subsequently, some of the Plaintiffs were also given written bans through letters mailed by the Iowa State Patrol to their homes.

3. The First Amendment to the United States Constitution protects "the freedom of speech, or of the press; or the right of the people peaceably to assemble, and to petition the government for a redress of grievances." It is the solemn duty of law enforcement and of state administrative agencies to faithfully uphold and protect the Constitutional rights of residents of this country. More than any other law enforcement group in the State, this duty must be most faithfully fulfilled by Division 16 of the Iowa State Patrol. Division 16 is responsible for law enforcement at the Iowa State Capitol and the surrounding Iowa Capitol Complex grounds where Iowans routinely and freely go to petition the Legislature and the Governor. The Iowa State Capitol and Iowa Capitol Complex, where Plaintiffs may no longer exercise any protected First Amendment expression until at least January 1, 2021 and in some cases until July 1, 2021, include many important and traditional public fora.
4. Plaintiffs challenge the Defendant's stunning misuse of power to retaliate against them for exercising their protected free speech, institute a prior restraint on their future protected expression, and disrupt the right of people to speak, peaceably to assemble, and petition the government for redress of grievances. The bans likewise unconstitutionally interfere with the Plaintiffs' fundamental freedom of movement. Additionally, Plaintiffs challenge the bans as violating due process by failing to provide them constitutionally sufficient notice and an opportunity to be heard to contest the bans.
5. In this action, as further supported by a separate, contemporaneous motion, Plaintiffs seek a preliminary injunction to immediately stop the enforcement of Defendants' unconstitutional ban from all Iowa Capitol Complex grounds. Plaintiffs wish to return to the Iowa Capitol Complex grounds as soon as possible to exercise their protected constitutional rights once more. In addition to the preliminary injunction, Plaintiffs seek declaratory and permanent injunctive relief, damages, and attorney's fees. . . .

STATEMENT OF FACTS

21. Black Americans and other people of color have long experienced disproportionate use of force and other abuses by law enforcement officers. Black Americans are disproportionately arrested for offenses committed at the same rates by Black and white people. They also make up a disproportionately high percentage of people confined in America's jails and prisons.

22. In Iowa, these racial disparities are among the worst in the country. A Black person in Iowa is seven times more likely to be arrested for drugs than a white person, although the two groups use at equal rates. This is the fifth-worst disparity in the country. While only three percent of Iowans are Black, twenty-six percent of prison inmates in Iowa are Black. A Black person in Iowa is 11 times more likely to be incarcerated than a white person. This is the third-worst disparity in the country.
23. On May 25, 2020, George Floyd, a 46-year old Black man, was killed by Minneapolis, Minnesota police officer Derek Chauvin. The nation watched cell phone video footage that spread quickly across traditional and social media of Derek Chauvin cruelly and senselessly pressing his knee into Mr. Floyd's neck, obstructing his breathing for nearly 9 [sic] minutes. Spontaneous protests emerged and grew across the country, including in Des Moines, Iowa, to voice outrage and despair at police violence against Black people, and to call for dramatic change to policing in America.
24. In the days that followed, organizations and individuals supporting the Black Lives Matter movement in Des Moines organized demonstrations, vigils, and protests calling for police reform and racial justice more broadly. The vast majority of protests and protesters were peaceful.
25. Des Moines BLM emerged early as the leader of the Black Lives Matter movement in Des Moines. Des Moines BLM's protests were well-organized, and expressly non-violent.
26. The activism of Des Moines BLM has been a catalyst to drive important reforms in Des Moines and in the State of Iowa, including the adoption of a city ordinance banning racial profiling, state legislation prohibiting law enforcement from using chokeholds in many circumstances, and the adoption of an executive order restoring voting rights to most people convicted of felony offenses.
27. Many of the protests organized by Des Moines BLM and others were held at the Iowa State Capitol, where protesters could reach an audience of both state and local policymakers, including legislators, the Governor, and local police.
28. On July 1, 2020, Des Moines BLM organized a day-time protest at the State Capitol to end lifetime disenfranchisement of Iowans with felony convictions. As was the case with a daytime protest held at the Capitol the day before, clergy and families, including children, attended, and protesters did not expect or desire to experience a confrontation with local or state police.
29. Des Moines Police Department officers came to the protest with warrants to arrest individuals they suspected of engaging in damage of a police vehicle at a prior protest held at a HyVee store. As they pulled those individuals out of the crowd of lawfully-protesting Des Moines BLM supporters in order to arrest them, police offered no explanation of their actions, causing alarm and confusion among the crowd of protesters.

30. In the chaos, Des Moines Police Department officers arrested over 17 protesters in addition to the people that they arrived up with warrants to arrest. None of the Plaintiffs were arrested for the prior Hy-Vee protest.
31. Once they were arrested, Iowa State Patrol officers, including Defendants Trooper Pearston and Trooper John Doe #1, verbally banned all 17 protesters from the Iowa Capitol Complex. Both officers were on duty and wearing their Iowa State Patrol uniforms, and spoke to the Plaintiffs with apparent authority on behalf of the State of Iowa, Department of Public Safety while the Plaintiffs were being held in the custody of the Des Moines Police Department. Some Plaintiffs were banned for six months, until January 1, 2021. Others were banned for one year, until July 1, 2021. They were all told if they were found on the premises of the Iowa Capitol Complex they would be arrested or cited and referred for prosecution for criminal trespass.
32. Two weeks later, some of the group of 17, but not all, received an additional written ban from the Iowa Capitol Complex for six months until January 1, 2021. This letter was signed by Iowa State Patrol Sergeant Tyson Underwood on the official State of Iowa letterhead of Stephan K. Bayens, Commissioner of the Iowa Department of Public Safety.
33. The identical written letters provided that the basis of the ban was "your actions and/or behavior towards citizen(s) and/or employee(s) of the State of Iowa on July 1st, 2020". The letter purported that the bans were "pursuant to Section 716.8(1) of the Iowa Code". The letter stated that entry "upon any portion of the property known as 1007 East Grand Avenue, Des Moines, IA 50319 including yards, parking areas, state owned streets and sidewalks, and all state owned facilities within the Capitol Complex grounds" "will be reported to law enforcement for criminal prosecution."
34. The Iowa Capitol Complex is a huge area taking up approximately 24 city blocks. . .
35. There is no statutory authority for such a ban. Iowa Code section 716.8(1), cited in the letter, actually just sets out that the penalty imposed on a person who "knowingly trespasses upon the property of another" is a simple misdemeanor punishable with a fine, and allowing officers to arrest the person so charged. It does not purport to authorize state patrol officers to enforce a six month or one-year prior restraint on individuals' exercise of core First Amendment rights and freedoms on the State Capitol Complex based on their (here, alleged and un-convicted) behavior.
36. Plaintiffs were given no prior notice or opportunity to be heard to contest the bans. If the Iowa State Patrol undertook any fact-finding prior to banning Plaintiffs from the Iowa Capitol Complex, they did so in secret without notice to the Plaintiffs or opportunity for Plaintiffs to be heard.
37. Nor did the bans result from any judicial process of any kind.
38. There is also no process to appeal the bans available to Plaintiffs.
39. As a result of the bans imposed by Iowa State Patrol, Plaintiffs have already been kept from organizing and participating in protests and other

constitutionally protected and lawful activities at the Capitol. They will continue to be blocked from engaging in these activities for the duration of the bans. . . .

CLAIMS FOR RELIEF

81. All individually named Defendants have acted, are acting, and threaten to act with apparent authority and under color of state law to deprive Plaintiffs of their constitutional rights. . . .

Injunctive Relief

84. Plaintiffs are entitled to an injunction. Plaintiffs will suffer irreparable injury under the real and immediate threat of enforcement of the challenged bans. Plaintiffs have no plain, adequate, or speedy remedy at law. Plaintiffs are refraining from constitutionally protected activities solely for fear of arrest, citation, and/or prosecution if they violate the bans.

Damages

85. Plaintiffs are entitled to damages for the violations of their constitutional rights which they have already endured as a result of the bans.

CAUSES OF ACTION

Count I:

42 U.S.C. § 1983—Violation of Civil Rights Provided Under the First Amendment, Fifth, and Fourteenth Amendments—Prior Restraint

. . . 87. Defendants' six-month and one-year bans from the Iowa Capitol Complex came without any required judicial procedural safeguards or exception for the wide variety of protected First Amendment activities necessarily implicated, including the rights of free speech, assembly, and the right to petition their government for redress of grievances. As such, each ban is an odious and constitutionally intolerable prior restraint of those rights under the First, Fifth, and Fourteenth Amendments.

88. This prior restraint is made all the worse by the fact that it limits free speech on what are traditional public fora—indeed, the State Capitol and

surrounding public spaces are perhaps our state government's *most important traditional* public fora for Iowans to gather and express their speech where it may be heard best by an audience of elected state government officials. Other areas included in the premises of the ban are designated public fora and nonpublic fora, where the ban also fails any conceivable level of scrutiny. . . .

Count II:

42 U.S.C. § 1983—Violation of Civil Rights Provided Under the First and Fourteenth Amendments—Speech. . .

91. A total ban necessarily prohibits all expressive activity, including core political speech, on the traditional public fora and designated public fora within the premises of the State Capitol Complex, including many of its green spaces, paved terraces, streets, and sidewalks. The ban's complete prohibition of all expressive activity is not a reasonable time, place, manner restriction; nor is it narrowly drawn. The total prohibition on all speech by the Plaintiffs on the State Capitol Complex not only fails all applicable levels of scrutiny; it is a per se violation of the Plaintiffs First Amendment rights to free speech. . . .

Count III:

42 U.S.C. § 1983—Violation of Civil Rights Provided Under the First and Fourteenth Amendments—Assembly. . .

94. It is indisputable that Defendants' bans, which prohibit Plaintiffs from entering the Iowa Capitol Complex premises for any reason under threat of citation or arrest for criminal trespass, reasonably chills Plaintiffs in engaging in the right to peacefully assemble there, including all the traditional and designated public fora contained therein, and violates their rights under the First and Fourteenth Amendments. . . .

Count IV:

42 U.S.C. § 1983—Violation of Civil Rights Provided Under the First and Fourteenth Amendments—Petition Government for Redress of Grievances. . .

97. Defendants' bans violate Plaintiffs' rights to petition their state government for redress of grievances by prohibiting their presence altogether at the locus

of that government, where the Governor and other executive branch officials, as well as members of the legislature, meet to engage in their elected duties, including hearing from their constituents. As such, the bans violate the Plaintiffs' rights under the First and Fourteenth Amendments. . . .

Count VII:

42 U.S.C. § 1983—Violation of Civil Rights Provided Under the First Amendment—First Amendment Retaliation. . .

106. Defendants' six-month and one-year bans from the Iowa Capitol Complex was in retaliation for Plaintiffs' prior constitutionally-protected speech, violating the Plaintiffs' rights under the First and Fourteenth Amendments to the U.S. Constitution to be free from retaliation for exercising their constitutional rights. . . .

Prayer for Relief

108. Plaintiffs respectfully request that the Court grant the following relief:

a. Issue an injunction ordering Defendants, their subordinates, agents, employees, and all others acting in concert with them to rescind the Iowa Capitol Complex bans described herein;
b. Issue an injunction ordering Defendants, their subordinates, agents, employees, and all others acting in concert with them to cease all enforcement of the bans, including the threatened arrest and/or citation for criminal trespass;
c. Enter a judgment declaring the bans unlawful under the First, Fifth, Ninth, and Fourteenth Amendments to the United States Constitution;
d. Order Defendants to pay Plaintiffs compensatory and punitive damages for the deprivations of Plaintiffs' rights under the First, Fifth, Ninth, and Fourteenth Amendments to the United States Constitution which have already occurred, in an amount to be determined at trial;
e. Award Plaintiffs reasonable attorney's fees and costs; and
f. Grant any other such relief as this Court may deem just and proper.

JURY DEMAND

109. Plaintiff demands a trial by jury of all issues triable pursuant to Rule 38 of the Federal Rules of Civil Procedure. Dated this 5th day of October, 2020. . . .

SOURCE: *Johnson et al. v. Bayens et al.*, S.D. Iowa, Case 4:20-cv-00306-RGE-CFB Document 1, Filed 10/05/20, Docket No. 20–306.

ANALYSIS

In 2013, unarmed teenager Trayvon Martin was shot and killed by George Zimmerman, a neighborhood watch coordinator in a Sanford, Florida, gated community, where Martin was visiting relatives. The following year, Zimmerman was cleared of all charges in Martin's death. In an emotional reaction to Zimmerman's acquittal, activist Alicia Garza of California wrote on her Facebook post: "I continue to be surprised at how little Black lives matter." She felt the jury's verdict and public celebrations of Zimmerman's legal victory were a painful reflection of "anti-Black racism that permeates our society" (Garza 2014).

Within months, Garza and friends Patrisse Cullors and Opal Tometi turned their frustration into action, transforming the phrase "Black Lives Matter" into a globally recognized Twitter hashtag, a national movement, and a call to action (Garza 2014). They described Black Lives Matter (BLM) as "an ideological and political intervention in a world where Black lives are systematically and intentionally targeted for demise" (Garza 2014). At the heart of their campaign was a call for police and other authorities to treat Black people fairly.

Over the ensuing six years, Black Lives Matter grew from localized efforts to call attention to racial injustices into a powerful force for systemic change. By 2020, millions of individuals around the world had been inspired by the BLM movement to march or advocate for Blacks or minorities to be treated with dignity and justice. Although the Zimmerman acquittal initiated the BLM movement, subsequent police violence toward Black people soon gave the campaign a sense of urgency.

In 2014, New York resident Eric Garner died when police put him in a prohibited chokehold while arresting him for illegally selling cigarettes. Garner's repeated statement "I can't breathe" became a rallying cry for BLM protesters. A month later in Ferguson, Missouri, eighteen-year-old unarmed Michael Brown was shot and killed during an altercation with a white police officer who said he fired in self-defense. In both cases, the officers were found not guilty. Activists responded by forming localized BLM groups that held protests in cities across the country.

The deaths of Freddie Gray, Walter Scott, Philandro Castile, and numerous other Black individuals at the hands of the police drove ever greater numbers of protesters to the streets with demands for justice and systemic change. In 2016 alone, more than one hundred BLM protests were held in the United States.

Public support for BLM grew as the movement captured media attention and gained backing from celebrities like LeBron James and Colin Kaepernick. Protests erupted in size and intensity however, after Breonna Taylor (Louisville, Kentucky) and George Floyd (Minneapolis, Minnesota) were killed at the hands of the police in 2020. Global demands for police reform followed circulation of a bystander's video that showed an officer pressing his knee into Floyd's neck for more than nine minutes as a gasping Floyd repeatedly pleaded, "I can't breathe," before losing consciousness. By June 2020, a poll of Americans found 67 percent supported the BLM movement (Fisher 2020).

However, as BLM became stronger and more influential, various groups began to challenge the legitimacy and rights of protesters. Counter-narratives such as "Blue Lives Matter" (a reference to police officers) and "All Lives Matter" emerged as opposition voices, which BLM organizers saw as delegitimizing the historical discrimination against Blacks. Conservative politicians critical of the movement labeled BLM as a "Marxist organization" made up of dangerous radicals (Kertscher 2020).

President Trump was among the most vocal critics of BLM, calling participants "anarchists, not protesters" and "thugs" and suggesting their right to free expression should be shut down in the name of "law and order" (September 8, 2020). Under the Trump administration, the FBI classified "Black Identity Extremism" as a domestic terror threat (Llorente 2017). According to *Newsweek*, leaked documents show that by 2018, the FBI had labeled "black identity extremists" a bigger threat to national security than foreign terrorist organizations such as Al Qaeda (Fearnow 2019).

Conflicts between officials critical of the movement and BLM participants have at times led to claims of censorship and free speech violations. In July 2020 in Iowa, after altercations and violence broke out at the Capitol between BLM protesters, police, and state patrol officers, seventeen protesters received a combination of verbal and written warnings not to return to the Capitol or Capitol complex grounds for six months to a year BLM activists responded with a lawsuit, accusing the Iowa State Patrol of violating their First Amendment rights to gather and protest in that public space. They claimed the action was taken in retaliation for the message they were promoting. In August 2021, the state agreed to withdraw all bans and pay a financial settlement to the protesters named in the lawsuit.

In other instances, protesters have cited law enforcement using violence to stifle their peaceful protests and assembly. Police have been documented using rubber bullets and tear gas to dispel activists, in one case deploying a chemical irritant against legal protesters gathered in Lafayette Square near the White House (Behrmann & Fritze 2020). Unjustified arrests and brutal police tactics drove lawsuits in Seattle, Portland, Chicago, New York, Los Angeles, DC, and other U.S. cities (Court & *Associated Press* 2020; Gandel 2020). In some cities, journalists and protesters testified that they were shoved, arrested, and their phones were confiscated when police saw them recording violent police responses (U.S. Congress House, 2020). Confrontations between BLM activists and counter-protesters or white supremacy groups in some cities further escalated tensions, leading to physical violence and deaths (*CBS*, September 4, 2020). One activist was killed when a man drove his car into a peaceful BLM crowd (*Associated Press*, July 6, 2020).

While the vast majority of BLM protests across the United States were peaceful (Hauck et al. 2020), some were marred by violence and chaos, necessitating vigorous law enforcement responses. Police said their reactions were justified when confronting protesters throwing projectiles, blocking streets or highways, or engaging in other unlawful behavior that threatened the safety of officers and the public (Williams 2020). BLM was blamed for inspiring widespread violence and chaos, including rioting and looting, during nationwide protests sparked by the death of George Floyd. Critics of the protests placed the blame for this unrest squarely on BLM and other "extremist" groups, while reporters and other observers said much of the looting and rioting was carried out by smaller subsets of lawbreakers taking advantage of the confusion on the streets. Regardless, these incidents of violent criminal behavior were met with aggressive police responses and military intervention. In eleven states, National Guard soldiers were sent in to help restore order (VOA 2020). Additionally, officials in many cities responded by imposing curfews or restrictions on mass gatherings (Kirk 2020).

The controversy over such violence and its societal roots has created deep divisions in the United States between those who view BLM protesters as the problem and those who view racial injustice as a primary concern. Despite the controversy, BLM has succeeded in forcing issues of racial equity to the forefront of a national debate. In 2020, *Time* magazine named the three BLM founders in its list of the one hundred most influential people in the United States (Fulton 2020).

FURTHER READING

Bradley, Brendan. "Everything Wrong with the Black Lives Matter Movement." *Hill*. December 6, 2016. https://thehill.com/blogs/pundits-blog/civil-rights/309140-everything-wrong-with-the-black-lives-matter-movement

Lebron, Christopher J. *The Making of Black Lives Matter: A Brief History of an Idea*. New York: Oxford University Press, 2017.

Rickford, Russell. "Black Lives Matter: Toward a Modern Practice of Mass Struggle." *New Labor Forum* 25, no. 1 (2016): 34–42. Los Angeles, CA: SAGE Publications.

Szetela, Adam. "Black Lives Matter at Five: Limits and Possibilities." *Ethnic and Racial Studies* 43, no. 8 (2020): 1358–83.

U.S. Congress House. "Committee on Oversight and Reform: Subcommittee on Civil Rights and Civil Liberties Briefing." *First Amendment Violations at Black Lives Matter Protests*. 116th Cong., 2nd Sess., June 20, 2020. https://oversight.house.gov/legislation/briefings/select-subcommittee-briefing-on-first-amendment-violations-at-black-lives

CHRONOLOGY

1215	The *Magna Carta* is agreed to by King John of England. Written to address abuses of power in England, its content offered foundational principles later used in the crafting of formative governing documents in the United States, including the Declaration of Independence and the Bill of Rights.
1735	A "not guilty" verdict in the John Peter Zenger trial influences opinion about how seditious libel and freedom of the press should be legally addressed. Free speech principles established in this case later lead to legal protections for the press in the Constitution, Bill of Rights, and the 1798 Sedition Act.
1776	Virginia's House of Burgesses passes the Virginia Declaration of Rights, which included inherent rights and civil liberties later influential in the development of the U.S. Constitution and the Bill of Rights.
1787	Delegates to the first Constitutional Convention in Philadelphia begin drafting the U.S. Constitution in May 1787. The completed Constitution is signed September 17 and sent to the states for ratification.
1788	Federalist Paper No. 84, one of eighty-five essays urging ratification of the Constitution, is published by Alexander Hamilton under the pseudonym Publius. In it, Hamilton urges preserving the liberty of the press.
June 21, 1788	The U.S. Constitution is officially adopted when New Hampshire becomes the ninth state to ratify it. Today, it remains the world's oldest functioning constitution.
1789	During the first Congress, James Madison proposes a Bill of Rights to accompany the Constitution.
December 15, 1791	The Bill of Rights, which includes ten out of the original twelve proposed amendments, is ratified. These first ten amendments to the Constitution guarantee individual rights and freedoms that are among the most cherished liberties in the United States of America.

1798	The Alien and Sedition Acts are passed. The Sedition Act prohibits false or defamatory utterance or writing about the government or any writing intended to "stir up sedition within the United States." The Kentucky and Virginia Resolutions, drafted by Thomas Jefferson and James Madison, challenged the acts' constitutionality and inspired one of the first in-depth debates about First Amendment freedoms.
1801	All convicted of crimes under the Sedition Act are pardoned by the newly elected president Thomas Jefferson, and the act is allowed to expire.
1821	The Supreme Court makes its first definitive reference to the First Amendment rights of free speech and the free press in *Anderson v. Dunn*.
1859	John Stuart Mill's influential essay *On Liberty* is published. This British philosopher's essay presents long-standing, powerful arguments defending freedom of speech.
1861–1865	Free speech is tested during the Civil War. Critics charge that restrictions on civil liberties imposed by army generals, President Lincoln, and other authorities are unconstitutional.
1868	The Fourteenth Amendment of the U.S. Constitution is ratified, addressing the rights of citizens and equal protection under the law.
1873	In support of the efforts of crusader Anthony Comstock, Congress passes the Comstock Act, prohibiting the trade and circulation of obscene literature. The U.S. Post Office is granted extensive censorship authority over materials considered lewd and obscene.
1902	The Free Speech League is formed. This is the first U.S. organization to broadly defend free speech, regardless of the viewpoint. The league later represents well-known figures like Emma Goldman and Margaret Sanger.
1917 and 1918	Congress passes the Espionage Act and Sedition Act, respectively, after the United States enters WWI. The acts prohibit individuals from obtaining and circulating information related to national security but are written broadly enough to be used to stifle wartime dissent.
1919	Justice Oliver Wendell Holmes establishes the "clear and present danger test" in *Schenck v. United States*, the first major free speech case taken up by the U.S. Supreme Court.
1919	The "clear and present danger test" is used to uphold the conviction of Socialist Eugene Debs under the Espionage Act.
1919	Justice Holmes pens a dissent in the landmark *Abrams v. United States* Supreme Court case arguing for greater protection of expression and free trade of ideas. Starting with this dissent, the court begins to shift its views on free expression and First Amendment liberties.

1919	The First Red Scare begins. In 1920, U.S. Attorney General A. Mitchell Palmer restricts civil liberties in the name of protecting the country from communism.
1920	The American Civil Liberties Union is founded to defend Americans' freedoms and constitutional rights.
1925	In *Gitlow v. New York*, the Supreme Court rules that First Amendment free speech protections apply also to states through the Fourteenth Amendment's due process clause.
1927	Judge Louis D. Brandeis's powerful defense of free speech in his concurring opinion for *Whitney v. California* influences the court's subsequent approach to First Amendment freedoms.
1930	The Motion Picture Production Code is adopted as the first of many attempts in Hollywood to self-regulate the content of films and avoid government censorship.
1931	*Stromberg v. California* is the first Supreme Court case recognizing that free expression can be symbolic or nonverbal in nature.
1931	In *Near v. Minnesota*, the Supreme Court cites the First Amendment in ruling that prior restraint of publications is an unconstitutional form of censorship.
1934	Congress passes the Communications Act of 1934, the foundation of modern U.S. communication policy.
1936	The Supreme Court bolsters the free press by ruling that Louisiana's effort to impose distinct taxes on large newspapers is unconstitutional in *Grosjean v. American Press Co.*
1940	In *Thornhill v. Alabama*, the Supreme Court defends freedom of speech and the press by rejecting Alabama's anti-picketing and loitering law.
1940	The Alien Registration Act (Smith Act) restricts free speech by criminalizing advocacy of the use of force or violence to overthrow the U.S. government.
1940	In *Minersville School District v. Gobitis*, the Supreme Court rules that states can require children to recite the Pledge of Allegiance in public schools.
1941	President Franklin D. Roosevelt establishes the Office of Censorship.
1941	Zechariah Chafee Jr., First Amendment scholar and author of *Freedom of Speech* (1920), publishes *Freedom of Speech in the United States*.
1942	The Supreme Court establishes "fighting words" as unprotected speech in *Chaplinsky v. New Hampshire*.
1943	The Supreme Court overturns its *Minersville v. Gobitis* ruling in *West Virginia State Board of Education v. Barnette*.
1949	The Federal Communications Commission establishes the Fairness Doctrine for broadcast media.

1949	The Supreme Court alters its "fighting words" doctrine in *Terminiello v. Chicago*.
1950	President Truman vetoes the Internal Security Act (McCarran Act), saying it stifles freedom of expression. Congress overrides his veto and passes the act, stoking domestic anti-Communist fervor.
1950	Senator Joseph McCarthy delivers his "Enemies from Within" Speech, ushering in the country's second Red Scare.
1951	In *Dennis v. United States*, the Supreme Court deems the 1940 Smith Act constitutional by upholding the convictions of twelve American Communists originally sentenced under the act.
1952	The Supreme Court determines in *Burstyn v. Wilson* that First Amendment protections also extend to motion pictures.
1954	The U.S. Senate censures and denounces Senator Joseph McCarthy after the Army-McCarthy hearings, ending his anti-Communist crusade.
1957	The Supreme Court redefines obscenity and deems it unprotected by the First Amendment in *Roth v. United States*.
1964	The *New York Times v. Sullivan* Supreme Court ruling reinforces First Amendment protections of speech critical of public officials and establishes principles of modern libel law.
1966	President Lyndon B. Johnson signs the Freedom of Information Act.
1966	The Supreme Court revises its definition of obscenity in *Memoirs v. Massachusetts*.
1966	The Supreme Court overturns a murder conviction in *Sheppard v. Maxwell* due to excessive publicity and media presence in the courtroom and recognizes the legitimacy of gag orders.
1968	In *United States v. O'Brien*, the Supreme Court upholds the conviction of David Paul O'Brien for publicly destroying draft cards, rejecting his argument that burning the documents constitutes protected "symbolic speech."
1968	In *Pickering v. Board of Education*, the Supreme Court establishes that public employees enjoy First Amendment rights to speak out about matters of public concern.
1968	The Federal Flag Protection Act is passed.
1969	The Supreme Court rules in *Stanley v. Georgia* that while distribution of obscene materials is a criminal act, private possession and viewing of obscene materials in one's own home is protected under the First and Fourteenth Amendments.
1969	The Supreme Court establishes in *Tinker v. Des Moines Independent Community School District* that students do not lose their First Amendment rights when they enter a school building; censorship of nondisruptive student expression is unconstitutional.
1969	In *Brandenburg v. Ohio*, the Supreme Court outlines the punishable standard for advocacy of illegal conduct; inflammatory speech can be punished only when the speech is intended to incite imminent lawless action and when it is likely to incite or produce such action.

1969 In *Red Lion Broadcasting Co. v. the Federal Communication Commission*, the Supreme Court rules that the FCC's Fairness Doctrine does not violate the First Amendment.

1970 Members of the Ohio National Guard fire on student protesters at Kent State University, resulting in the "Kent State Massacre."

1970 The National Commission on Obscenity and Pornography releases its report, which is soundly rejected by President Nixon.

1971 In *Cohen v. California*, the Supreme Court determines that offensive speech and profanity are protected by the First Amendment.

1971 The landmark Supreme Court decision in *New York Times Co. v. United States* (the Pentagon Papers case) protects the free press from prior restraint efforts by the government and reiterates the importance of a free press.

1972 The Supreme Court rules in *Lloyd Corp., Ltd. v. Tanner* that a citizen's right to expression under the First Amendment does not extend to private property.

1973 The Supreme Court establishes a three-part test (the Miller Test) for identifying obscenity in *Miller v. California*.

1973 In *Paris Adult Theater I v. Slaton*, the Supreme Court preserves the right of states to prohibit obscene exhibitions or displays, even when access is limited to adults.

1974 The Supreme Court rules in *Miami Herald Publishing Co. v. Tornillo* that newspaper editors have the right to choose what they print and are not required to provide reply space to political candidates after criticizing them.

1978 In *Federal Communications Commission v. Pacifica Foundation*, the Supreme Court upholds the power of the FCC to regulate (but not completely censor) indecency in broadcast media.

1978 The Supreme Court rules in *First National Bank of Boston et al. v. Bellotti* that corporations, just like individuals, enjoy free speech rights allowing them to make certain types of political contributions.

1980 The Supreme Court's ruling in *Central Hudson Gas & Electric Corp. v. Public Service Commission of New York* establishes a four-part test to determine regulation of commercial speech by the states.

1980 The Supreme Court establishes the public and press's First and Fourteenth Amendment rights to attend criminal proceedings in *Richmond Newspapers, Inc., v. Virginia*.

1982 The Supreme Court deems child pornography unprotected by the First Amendment in *New York v. Ferber*.

1982 In *Board of Education, Island Trees v. Pico*, the Supreme Court prohibits the removal of books from school libraries by officials who disagree with the ideas they contain.

1982 The Supreme Court rules that states cannot prohibit peaceful political activity such as boycotts in *NAACP v. Claiborne Hardware*.

1983 In *Connick v. Myers*, the Supreme Court clarifies First Amendment rights of public employees in the workplace.

1985	The U.S. Senate holds a special hearing on proposals to add warning labels to sexually explicit popular music or "porn rock." The hearing features testimony from representatives of the activist group Parents Media Resource Center-PMRC, which wanted the music industry to adopt a voluntary rating system such as the one used for motion pictures, as well as well-known rock musicians who characterized the proposal as censorship.
1986	In *Bethel School District v. Frasier*, the Supreme Court grants public schools the right to regulate lewd or disruptive student speech.
1988	The Supreme Court's *Hazelwood School District v. Kuhlmeier* decision makes regulation of school-sponsored speech permissible.
1988	The Supreme Court's ruling in *Hustler Magazine v. Falwell* requires that public figures show actual malice in order to collect damages for emotional distress.
1989	The Supreme Court rules that flag burning is protected under the First Amendment in *Texas v. Johnson*.
1989	Congress passes the Flag Protection Act.
1990	The Flag Protection Act is invalidated by the Supreme Court in *United States v. Eichman*.
1991	The Supreme Court overturns New York's Son of Sam law in *Simon & Schuster, Inc. v. Members of the New York State Crime Victims Board*.
1992	The Supreme Court rules that a Minnesota hate speech ordinance violates the First Amendment in *R.A.V. v. City of St. Paul*.
1996	In an attempt to regulate internet pornography, Congress passes the Communications Decency Act as part of the Telecommunications Act.
1996	Congress passes the Child Pornography Prevention Act (CPPA).
1997	In *Reno v. ACLU*, the Supreme Court declares key provisions of the Communications Decency Act unconstitutional.
1998	Congress passes the Child Online Protection Act (COPA).
1998	In *National Endowment for the Arts v. Finley*, the Supreme Court permits the government to establish community standards as a consideration for the funding of art projects.
2000	Congress passes the Children's Internet Protection Act (CIPA).
2001	Congress adopts the USA PATRIOT Act after the 9/11 attacks. This act restricts numerous First Amendment freedoms in the name of national security.
2002	In *Ashcroft v. Free Speech Coalition*, the Supreme Court struck down central provisions of the 1996 CPPA.
2003	In *Virginia v. Black*, the Supreme Court rules a state law prohibiting cross burning constitutional, because some of the burnings constitute true threats.
2003	In *United States v. American Library Association*, the Supreme Court ties installation of filtering software to federal funding for public libraries and schools, upholding CIPA.

2003 In *McConnell v. Federal Election Commission*, the Supreme Court upholds a ban on soft money contributions passed as part of a 2002 campaign reform bill.

2004 In *Ashcroft v. ACLU II*, the Supreme Court rules that the 1998 COPA Act is overly broad and that filtering software would be a less restrictive alternative.

2004 A Super Bowl Halftime performance involving partial nudity led to network fines and legal battles with the FCC over purported violations of the indecency provision of the Communications Act.

2007 In *Morse v. Frederick*, the Supreme Court upholds the right of schools to limit or punish student expression advocating illegal drug use.

2010 In *Citizens United v. Federal Election Commission*, the Supreme Court invalidates Campaign Reform Act provisions prohibiting corporations from using general treasury funds for political advertising. Supporters consider the decision a free speech victory.

2010 Whistleblower Chelsea Manning releases thousands of classified government documents on WikiLeaks. Advocates of transparency and free speech praise her actions.

2011 Protesters' right to demonstrate at military funerals is upheld in *Snyder v. Phelps*.

2011 The Supreme Court classifies video games as expression protected by the First Amendment in *Brown v. Entertainment Merchants Association*.

2013 Edward Snowden leaks thousands of National Security Administration documents.

2013 The acquittal of George Zimmerman in the shooting death of unarmed Black teenager Trayvon Martin inspires national protests and leads to the founding of the Black Lives Matter (BLM) movement.

2015 Free speech challenges arise on college and university campuses throughout the United States.

2017 "Fake news," a phrase regularly employed by the Trump administration, becomes a social concern and weaponized political phrase.

2017 NFL player Colin Kaepernick kneels during the national anthem to protest police brutality and systemic racism, sparking national debates about the treatment of people of color and the right of athletes to exercise free speech on the field.

2018 Congress considers regulation of Big Tech as it examines societal consequences of social-media fueled falsehoods protected under the First Amendment.

2018 Congress passes the "Allow States and Victims to Fight Online Sex Trafficking Act of 2017," stripping immunity from websites facilitating sex trafficking or unlawful prostitution.

2020 Nationwide protests against police brutality and racism erupt after the killing of George Floyd by Minneapolis police officer Derek

Chauvin is captured on video. Free speech concerns are raised as a result of both the violent nature of the protests in some cases, and the violent responses of law enforcement to peaceful protests in others.

2021 A rioting mob of Trump supporters storm the United States Capitol to stop Congress from fulfilling its Constitutional duty to validate Democratic nominee Joe Biden's Electoral College victory in the November 2020 presidential election. The attack on the Capitol results in five deaths, hundreds of arrests, and the largest criminal investigation in U.S. history.

2021 Free speech becomes a central element in former president Donald Trump's impeachment defense, and a key defense in his role in the January 6 attack on the U.S. Capitol.

BIBLIOGRAPHY

ABC Evening News. UCSF Industry Documents Library. "DEF-0657.MPG" Video. November 5, 1976. https://www.industrydocuments.ucsf.edu/tobacco/docs/#id=lqgl0191

Abdolian, Lisa Finnegan, and Harold Takooshian. "The USA Patriot Act: Civil Liberties, the Media, and Public Opinion." *Fordham Urban Law Journal* 30, no. 4 (2002): 1429.

Abrams, Douglas E. "Justice Jackson and the Second Flag-Salute Case: Reason and Passion in Opinion-Writing." *Journal of Supreme Court History* 36, no. 1 (2011): 30–47.

ACLUVA. "On Hate Speech: The Westboro Baptist Church, Campuses, and Nazis in Virginia." ACLU Virginia. March 24, 2011. https://acluva.org/en/news/hate-speech-westboro-baptist-church-campuses-and-nazis-virginia

Adler, Amy. "The Thirty-Ninth Annual Edward G. Donley Memorial Lectures: The Art of Censorship." *West Virginia Law Review* 103 (2000): 205.

Ahmad, Samar. "Unmasking Democracy: How Corporate Influence Is Eroding Democratic Governance." *Harvard International Review* 41, no. 2 (2020): 54–57.

Aichinger, Alex. "Campus Speech Codes." *The First Amendment Encyclopedia*. Middle Tennessee State University, 2009 (updated in June 2017, updated by John R. Vile). https://mtsu.edu/first-amendment/article/991/campus-speech-codes

Alberta, Tim. "The Deep Roots of Trump's War on the Press." *Politico Magazine*. April 26, 2018. https://www.politico.com/magazine/story/2018/04/26/the-deep-roots-trumps-war-on-the-press-218105

Allcott, Hunt, and Matthew Gentzkow. "Social Media and Fake News in the 2016 Election." *Journal of Economic Perspectives* 31, no. 2 (2017): 211–36.

Allyn, Bobby. "Facebook Keeps Data Secret, Letting Conservative Bias Claims Persist." October 5, 2020. https://www.npr.org/2020/10/05/918520692/facebook-keeps-data-secret-letting-conservative-bias-claims-persist

Altschuler, Bruce E. "Is the Pentagon Papers Case Relevant in the Age of WikiLeaks?" *Political Science Quarterly (Wiley-Blackwell)* 130, no. 3 (2015): 401–23.

Altschuler, Bruce. "Pentagon Papers." *The First Amendment Encyclopedia*. Middle Tennessee State University, 2009. https://mtsu.edu/first-amendment/article/873/pentagon-papers

Alumkal, Antony. *Paranoid Science: The Christian Right's War on Reality*. New York University Press, 2019.

American Civil Liberties Union. "Freedom under Fire: Dissent in Post-9/11 America." ACLU.org. May 2003. https://www.aclu.org/files/FilesPDFs/dissent_report.pdf

American Civil Liberties Union. "How the USA-Patriot Act Expands Law Enforcement 'Sneak and Peek' Warrants." ACLU.org. n.d. https://www.aclu.org/other/how-usa-patriot-act-expands-law-enforcement-sneak-and-peek-warrants

American Civil Liberties Union. "Myths and Realities about the PATRIOT Act." ACLU.org. n.d. https://www.aclu.org/other/myths-and-realities-about-patriot-act

American Civil Liberties Union. "Speech on Campus." ACLU.org. n.d. https://www.aclu.org/other/speech-campus

American Civil Liberties Union. "Surveillance under the USA/PATRIOT Act." ACLU.org. n.d. https://www.aclu.org/other/surveillance-under-usapatriot-act

Anastaplo, George. *Reflections on Freedom of Speech and the First Amendment*. Lexington, KY: University Press of Kentucky, 2007.

Anderson, Greta. "Federal Appeals Court: Free Speech May Be Chilled at UT Austin." *Inside Higher Ed*. October 30, 2020. https://insidehighered.com/quicktakes/2020/10/30/federal-appeals-court-free-speech-may-be-chilled-ut-austin

ARTICLE 19, Committee to Protect Journalists, Index on Censorship, IFEX, International Press Institute, and Reporters without Borders. "Press Freedom under Threat: International Press Freedom Mission to the United States." May 2018. https://www.article19.org/wp-content/uploads/2018/05/Press-Freedom-Under-Threat-International-Press-Freedom-Mission-to-the-United-States.pdf

Aryanfard, Ojan. "National Security." The First Amendment Encyclopedia. Middle Tennessee State University. https://www.mtsu.edu/first-amendment/article/1134/national-security

Associated Press. "Summer Taylor, Protestor Killed in Seattle, Honored for 'Standing up for Black Lives.'" July 6, 2020. https://www.theguardian.com/us-news/2020/jul/06/summer-taylor-death-seattle-protest

Baker-Jordan, Skylar. "Why Twitter and Facebook Blocking Trump's Posts Could Actually Help Him Stay in the White House." *The Independent*. August 6, 2020. https://www.independent.co.uk/voices/trump-twitter-ban-post-facebook-coronavirus-video-covid-2020-election-a9658236.html

Baldassarro, R. Wolf. *Banned Books Awareness: "Uncle Tom's Cabin" by Harriet Beecher Stowe*. Deep Forest Productions. March 6, 2011. http://bbark.deepforestproductions.com/column/2011/03/06/banned-book-awareness-uncle-toms-cabin-harriet-beecher-stowe/

Barstow, David T. "The Freedom of Information Act and the Press: Obstruction or Transparency?" *Social Research* 77, no. 3 (Fall 2010): 805–10.

BBCnews. "US West Coast Fires: I Don't Think Science Knows about Climate, Says Trump." *BBC News*. September 15, 2020. https://www.bbc.com/news/world-us-canada-54144651

Behrmann, Savannah, and John Fritze. "Tear Gas vs. Pepper Spray: Debate over Methods Used to Clear Lafayette Square Turns Political." *USA Today*. June 3, 2020. https://www.usatoday.com/story/news/politics/2020/06/03/floyd-protests-tear-gas-used-clear-park-trumps-walk/3128855001/

Bendix, Aria and Skye Gould. "How the US Coronavirus Outbreak Compares to Other Countries in 11 Charts." *Businessinsider.com*. October 26, 2020. https://www.businessinsider.com/how-us-coronavirus-outbreak-compares-to-other-countries-charts-2020-10

Bennett, John T. "Trump Reacts to Woodward Tapes by Admitting He May Have Underplayed Coronavirus Danger to 'Avoid Panic.'" *Independent*. September 9, 2020. https://www.independent.co.uk/news/world/americas/us-election/woodward-tapes-trump-press-conference-today-coronavirus-b421204.html

Ben-Porath, Sigal R. *Free Speech on Campus*. Philadelphia: University of Pennsylvania Press, 2017.

Benson, Thomas W. *Writing JFK: Presidential Rhetoric and the Press in the Bay of Pigs Crisis*. College Station, TX: Texas A & M University Press, 2004.

Bergen, Peter. "ISIS Online: Countering Terrorist Radicalization & Recruitment on the Internet & Social Media." Testimony for U.S. Senate Committee on Homeland Security, Permanent Subcommittee on Investigations. July 6, 2016. https://www.hsgac.senate.gov/imo/media/doc/Bergen%20Testimony_PSI%202016-07-06.pdf

Berkeley Library. "Emma Goldman and Free Speech." The Emma Goldman Papers. University of California, Berkeley. https://www.lib.berkeley.edu/goldman/MeetEmmaGoldman/emmagoldmanandfreespeech.html

Bero, Lisa. "Implications of the Tobacco Industry Documents for Public Health and Policy." *Annual Review of Public Health* 24, no. 1 (2003): 267–88.

Best, Alison J. "Elonis v. United States: The Need to Uphold Individual Rights to Free Speech while Protecting Victims of Online True Threats." *Maryland Law Review* 75 (2015): 1127.

Bezanson, Randall P. "The Burning Flag: The Medium and the Message (Texas v. Johnson, 491 U.S. 397 (1989))." In *How Free Can Speech Be?* 187–205. New York: New York University Press, 1998.

Bill of Rights Institute. "Free Speech or "Safe" Speech?" https://billofrightsinstitute.org/educate/educator-resources/lessons-pladns/debating-free-speech-on-campus/.

Black, Gregory. "Hollywood Censored: The Production Code Administration and the Hollywood Film Industry, 1930–1940." *Film History* 3, no. 3 (1989): 167–89.

Blanchard, Margaret, and John Semonche. "Anthony Comstock and His Adversaries: The Mixed Legacy of This Battle for Free Speech." *Communication Law and Policy* 11, no. 3 (2006): 317–66. doi:10.1207/s15326926clp1103_2

Blasi, Vincent. "The First Amendment and the Ideal of Civic Courage: The Brandeis Opinion in Whitney v. California." *William & Mary Law Review* 29, no. 4 (1988): 653–97.

Borel, Brooke. "Fact-Checking Won't Save Us from Fake News." *FiveThirtyEight*. January 4, 2017.

Boston, Rob. "By Order of the Court: The Supreme Court on School Prayer." *Church & State* 72, no. 3 (2019): N.PAG.

Boykoff, Jules, and Ben Carrington. "Sporting Dissent: Colin Kaepernick, NFL Activism, and Media Framing Contests." *International Review for the Sociology of Sport* 55, no. 7 (November 2020): 829–49. doi:10.1177/1012690219861594

Bridis, Ted. "In Obama's Final Year, U.S. Spent $36 Million in FOIA Lawsuits." Associated Press. https://www.pbs.org/newshour/nation/obamas-final-year-u-s-spent-36-million-foia-lawsuits

Bronner, Ethan. "Witching Hour; Rethinking McCarthyism, If Not McCarthy." *New York Times*. October 18, 1998. https://www.nytimes.com/1998/10/18/weekinreview/witching-hour-rethinking-mccarthyism-if-not-mccarthy.html

Bruce, Erik. "Dangerous World, Dangerous Liberties: Aspects of the Smith Act Prosecutions." *American Communist History* 13, no. 1 (2014): 25–38.

Bublé, Courtney. "Transparency in the Trump Era." *Government Executive*. March 10, 2020. https://www.govexec.com/management/2020/03/transparency-trump-era/163574/

Burkhardt, Joanna M. *Combating Fake News in the Digital Age*. Chicago: American Library Association, 2017.

Burnett, H. Sterling. "So Much for Obama's Pledge to Transparency." *Forbes*. March 2, 2016. https://www.forbes.com/sites/realspin/2016/03/02/so-much-for-obamas-pledge-to-transparency/#19a96b496cf9

Burnitis, Caitlyn. "Facing the Future with FOSTA: Examining the Allow States and Victims to Fight Online Sex Trafficking Act of 2017." *University of Miami Race & Social Justice Law Review* 10 (2019): 139.

Burns, Ken, and Lynn Novick. "The War: Communication: News and Censorship." (excerpts from film). PBS.org. September 23, 2007. http://www.pbs.org/thewar/at_home_communication_news_censorship.htm

Bush, George W. "Address Before a Joint Session of the Congress of the United States: Response to the Terrorist Attacks of September 11." September 20, 2001. Online by Gerhard Peters and John T. Woolley, The American Presidency Project. https://www.presidency.ucsb.edu/node/213749

Byron, Elizabeth Todd. "A Progressive Mind: Louis D. Brandeis and the Origins of Free Speech." *Touro Law Review* 33, no. 1 (2017): 195–210.

Caine, Burton. "The Trouble with Fighting Words: Chaplinsky v. New Hampshire Is a Threat to First Amendment Values and Should Be Overruled." *Marquette Law Review* 88 (2004): 441.

Calvert, Clay. "First Amendment Envelope Pushers: Revisiting the Incitement-to-Violence Test with Messrs. Brandenburg, Trump, & Spencer." *Connecticut Law Review* 51, no. 1 (2019): 411.

Campbell, Douglas. "Reexamining the Origins of the Adoption of the ALA's Library Bill of Rights." *Library Trends* 63, no. 1 (2014): 42–56.

Cannon, Robert. "The Legislative History of Senator Exon's Communications Decency Act: Regulating Barbarians on the Information Superhighway." *Federal Communications Law Journal* 49, no. 1, Article 3 (1996): 51.

Carnovsky, Leon. "Clear and Present Danger." *ALA Bulletin* 47, no. 10 (1953): 467–70. www.jstor.org/stable/25694089

Carpenter, Carrie Murray, Geoffrey Ferris Wayne, and Gregory N. Connolly. "Designing Cigarettes for Women: New Findings from the Tobacco Industry Documents." *Addiction* 100, no. 6 (2005): 837–51.

Carroll, Thomas F. "Freedom of Speech and of the Press in War Time: The Espionage Act." *Michigan Law Review* 17, no. 8 (1919): 621–65. doi:10.2307/1277922

CBS News. "Donald Trump's Conversations with Bob Woodward about Coronavirus, Black Lives Matter, and Nuclear War." *60 Minutes*. September 13, 2020. https://www.cbsnews.com/news/donald-trump-bob-woodward-rage-60-minutes-2020-09-13/

CBS News. "Suspect in Killing of Right-Wing Protester Fatally Shot during Arrest." *CBS News*. September 4, 2020. https://www.cbsnews.com/news/michael-reinoehl-suspect-portland-shooting-killed-federal-task-force/

CBS News. "Trump Speculates about Injecting Disinfectants to Treat COVID-19." *CBS News*. April 24, 2020. https://www.cbsnews.com/news/coronavirus-trump-injecting-disinfectant-covid-19/

Chamberlain, Katherine. "Spotlight on Censorship—And Tango Makes Three." American Library Association Intellectual Freedom Blog. September 30, 2010. https://www.oif.ala.org/oif/?p=1541

Chapman-Schmidt, Ben. "'Sex Trafficking' as Epistemic Violence." *Anti-Trafficking Review* 12 (2019): 172–87.

Chastagner, Claude. "The Parents' Music Resource Center: From Information to Censorship." *Popular Music* 18, no. 2 (1999): 179–92.

Chemerinsky, Erwin, and Howard Gillman. *Free Speech on Campus*. New Haven, CT: Yale University Press, 2017.

Clark, Chrissy. "Devin Nunes Says Trump's Most Important Accomplishment Is Outing Hostile Media." *The Federalist*. February 7, 2020. https://thefederalist.com/2020/02/07/devin-nunes-says-trumps-most-important-accomplishment-is-outing-hostile-media/

Clark, Dartunorro. "Trump Suggests 'Injection' of Disinfectant to Beat Coronavirus and 'Clean' the Lungs." *NBCnews.com*. April 23, 2020. https://www.nbcnews.com/politics/donald-trump/trump-suggests-injection-disinfectant-beat-coronavirus-clean-lungs-n1191216

Clark, Laura, and Macey Morales. "Harry Potter Tops List of Most Challenged Books of 21st Century." *American Library Association*. September 21, 2006. http://www.ala.org/news/news/pressreleases2006/september2006/harrypottermostchallenge

Cohen, Robert, and Michael Koncewicz. "'Tin Soldiers and Nixon's Coming:' The Shooting at Kent State and Jackson State at 50." *Nation*. May 5, 2020.

Colen, Joan S. "Child Pornography: Ban the Speech and Spare the Child?—New York v. Ferber." *DePaul Law Review* 32 (1983): 685.

Collins, Ronald K.L., and David M. Skover. "Curious Concurrence: Justice Brandeis's Vote in Whitney v. California." *Supreme Court Review* 2005, no. 1 (2005): 333–97.

Committee to Protect Journalists (CPJ). "The Trump Administration and the Media." Report issued by CPJ. April 16, 2020. https://cpj.org/reports/2020/04/trump-media-attacks-credibility-leaks/

"Community Standards, Class Actions, and Obscenity under Miller v. California." *Harvard Law Review* 88, no. 8 (1975): 1838.

Constable, Marianne. "Flags, Words, Laws, and Things." In *Just Silences: The Limits and Possibilities of Modern Law*, 93–110. Princeton, NJ: Princeton University Press, 2005.

Constitutional Rights Foundation. "The Alien and Sedition Acts: Defining American Freedom." Constitutional Rights Foundation. n.d. http://www.crf-usa.org/america-responds-to-terrorism/the-alien-and-sedition-acts.html

Coombs, Danielle Sarver, Cheryl Ann Lambert, David Cassilo, and Zachary Humphries. "Flag on the Play: Colin Kaepernick and the Protest Paradigm." *Howard Journal of Communications* 31, no. 4 (2019): 317–36.

Cooper, Gloria. "The Censors: New Patterns in Opinion Control." *Columbia Journalism Review* 43, no. 2 (2004): 58–60.

Cordes, Mark W. "Making Sense of High School Speech after Morse v. Frederick." *William & Mary Bill of Rights Journal* 17 (2008): 657.

Cortez, Nathan. "Information Mischief under the Trump Administration." *Chi.-Kent L. Rev.* 94 (2019): 315.

Court, Andrew and Associated Press. "Sixty BLM Protesters File Lawsuit against Chicago Police Claiming They Were Subjected to 'Brutal and Violent' Treatment During Demonstrations over Death of George Floyd." *Mail Online*. November 19, 2020. https://www.dailymail.co.uk/news/article-8967553/Protesters-sue-Chicago-Police-brutal-violent-tactics.html

Daly, Christopher B. "How Woodrow Wilson's Propaganda Machine Changed American Journalism." *Smithsonian Magazine*. April 28, 2017. https://www.smithsonianmag.com/history/how-woodrow-wilsons-propaganda-machine-changed-american-journalism-180963082/

Dastagir, Allia E. "Trust No One? Americans Lack Faith in the Government, the Media, and Each Other, Survey Finds." *USA Today*. July 23, 2019. https://www.usatoday.com/story/news/nation/2019/07/23/pew-study-american-trust-declines-government-media-and-each-other/1798963001/

Davis, Angela J. "Racial Profiling Post 9/11—Still a Bad Idea." *Brennan Center for Justice*. November 5, 2002. https://www.brennancenter.org/our-work/research-reports/racial-profiling-post-911-still-bad-idea

De Pinto, Jennifer. "Most View Kneeling during Anthem as Acceptable Form of Protest—CBS News Poll." *CBS News*. July 29, 2020. https://www.cbsnews.com/news/kneeling-athletes-anthem-opinion-poll-28-07-2020/

Devlin, Gary E. "NEA v. Finley: Explicating the Rocky Relationship between the Government and the Arts." *Pepperdine Law Review* 27 (1999): 345.

Dierenfield, Bruce J. *The Battle over School Prayer: How Engel v. Vitale Changed America*. Lawrence, KS: University Press of Kansas, 2007.

DiMarco, Scott, and Mansfield University of Pennsylvania. "I Banned a Book to Make People Notice the Problem." *Time*. October 7, 2015. https://time.com/4059646/banned-books-why/

Donovan, Elizabeth M. "Fight Online Sex Trafficking Act and Stop Enabling Sex Traffickers Act: A Shield for Jane Doe." *Connecticut Law Review* 52 (2020): 85.

Downie, Leonard, Jr., and Sara Rafsky. "The Obama Administration and the Press: Leak Investigations and Surveillance in Post-9/11 America." Committee to Protect Journalists. October 10, 2013. https://cpj.org/reports/2013/10/obama-and-the-press-us-leaks-surveillance-post-911/

Doyle, Charles. "The USA PATRIOT Act: A Legal Analysis." Library of Congress. Washington, DC: Congressional Research Service, 2002.

Doyle, Robert P. *Banned Books: Defending Our Freedom to Read*. Chicago, IL: American Library Association, 2017.

Draper, Kevin and Ken Belson. "Colin Kaepernick and the N.F.L. Settle Collusion Case." *New York Times*. February 15, 2019. https://www.nytimes.com/2019/02/15/sports/nfl-colin-kaepernick.html

Dueholm, James. "Lincoln's Suspension of the Writ of Habeas Corpus: An Historical and Constitutional Analysis." *Journal of the Abraham Lincoln Association* 29, no. 2 (Summer 2008): 47–66. http://hdl.handle.net/2027/spo.2629860.0029.205

Dunbar, John. "The 'Citizens United' Decision and Why It Matters." Center for Public Integrity. May 10, 2018. https://publicintegrity.org/politics/the-citizens-united-decision-and-why-it-matters/

Eastland, Terry, ed. *Freedom of Expression in the Supreme Court: The Defining Cases*. Lanham, MD: Rowman & Littlefield Publishers, 2000.

Electronic Privacy Information Center. "USA Patriot Act." EPIC.org. n.d. https://epic.org/privacy/terrorism/usapatriot/#

Ellington, Thomas C. "Transparency under Trump: Policy and Prospects." *Public Integrity* 21, no. 2 (2019): 127–40.

Embassy of the United States. *Freedom of Expression in the United States*. U.S. Department of State, Bureau of International Information Programs. April 2013.

Engdahl, David E. "Requiem for Roth: Obscenity Doctrine Is Changing." *Michigan Law Review* 68, no. 2 (1969): 185–236. doi:10.2307/1287385

Engel, Jeffrey A. *The Four Freedoms: Franklin D. Roosevelt and the Evolution of an American Idea*. New York: Oxford University Press, 2016.

Engel, Pamela. "Why 'Captain Underpants' Is the Most Banned Book in America." *Business Insider*. September 26, 2013. https://www.businessinsider.com/why-captain-underpants-is-the-most-banned-book-in-america-2013-9

Evans, Jennifer C. "Hijacking Civil Liberties: The USA Patriot Act of 2001." *Loyola University Chicago Law Journal* 33, no. 4 (2002): 933.

Fabian, Jordan. "White House 'Committed to a Free Press,' Says Sanders." *The Hill*. May 19, 2018. https://thehill.com/homenews/administration/386979-sanders-says white-house-committed-to-a-free-press

Fact Checker. "In 1,267 Days, President Trump Has Made 20,055 False or Misleading Claims." *Washington Post*. July 9, 2020. https://www.washingtonpost.com/graphics/politics/trump-claims-database/

Farkas, Johan, and Jannick Schou. *Post-Truth, Fake News and Democracy: Mapping the Politics of Falsehood*. New York: Routledge, 2020.

Fearnow, Benjamin. "FBI Ranks 'Black Identity Extremists' Bigger Threat than Al Qaeda, White Supremacists: Leaked Documents." *Newsweek*. August 8, 2019. https://www.newsweek.com/fbi-leak-black-identity-extremist-threat-1453362

Federal Communication Commission. "The FCC and Freedom of Speech." Consumer Guide. FCC Consumer and Governmental Affairs Bureau. Reviewed December 30, 2019. https://www.fcc.gov/sites/default/files/the_fcc_and_freedom_of_speech.pdf

"Federal Threats Statute—Mens Rea and the First Amendment—Elonis v. United States." *Harvard Law Review* 129, no. 1 (2015): 331–40.

Feinberg, Lotte E. "Managing the Freedom of Information Act and Federal Information Policy." *Public Administration Review* 46, no. 6 (1986): 615–21.

Feldstein, Mark. "The Jungle-Warfare Theory of Trump." *Politico Magazine*. May/June 2017. https://www.politico.com/magazine/story/2017/04/28/the-jungle-warfare-theory-of-trump-215045/

Finn, Mary. "Democracy in Crisis: The Man behind FOIA." *Baltimore Sun*. March 8, 2017. https://www.baltimoresun.com/citypaper/bcpnews-democracy-in-crisis-the-man-behind-foia-20170308-story.html

First Amendment Watch. "Trump Supporter Attacks Reporter Ahead of Trump Rally in Minnesota." *First Amendment Watch*, New York University. October 2, 2020. https://firstamendmentwatch.org/trump-supporter-attacks-reporter-ahead-of-trump-rally-in-minnesota/

Fischer, Susanna Frederick. "Does the Child Online Protection Act Violate the First Amendment?" *2003–2004 Preview U.S. Supreme Court Cases*, no. 5 (2004): 289–95.

Fiset, Louis. "Return to Sender: U.S. Censorship of Enemy Alien Mail in World War II." Prologue 33, no. 1 (2001). *National Archives*. https://www.archives.gov/publications/prologue/2001/spring/mail-censorship-in-world-war-two-1.html

Fisher, Deborah. 2020. "Black Lives Matter." The First Amendment Encyclopedia. Middle Tennessee State University. https://mtsu.edu/first-amendment/article/1512/black-lives-matter

Flood, Brian. "Ex-Facebook Honcho Tim Kendall Says Big Tech Is a 'Threat to Democracy,' Calls for Social Media Reform." *Foxnews.com*. October 13, 2020.

Foerstel, Herbert N. *Banned in the USA: A Reference Guide to Book Censorship in Schools and Public Libraries*. Westport, CT: Greenwood Publishing Group, 2002.

Foerstel, Herbert N. *Freedom of Information and the Right to Know: The Origins and Applications of the Freedom of Information Act*. Westport, CT: Greenwood Press, 1999.

Foundation for Individual Rights in Education (FIRE). "Chaplinsky v. New Hampshire." Oyez. https://www.thefire.org/first-amendment-library/decision/chaplinsky-v-new-hampshire/

Foundation for Individual Rights in Education (FIRE). "Chicago Statement: University and Faculty Body Support." FIRE. July 14, 2020. https://www.thefire.org/chicago-statement-university-and-faculty-body-support/

Foundation for Individual Rights in Education (FIRE). "Model Federal Campus Anti-Harassment Act of 2017." FIRE. April 5, 2017. https://www.thefire.org/model-federal-campus-anti-harassment-act-of-2017/

"Frequently Challenged Books." American Library Association Office for Intellectual Freedom. March 26, 2013. http://www.ala.org/advocacy/bbooks/frequentlychallengedbooks

Friedersdorf, Conor. "Congress Finds Consensus on Free Speech on Campus." *Atlantic*. August 1, 2017. https://www.theatlantic.com/politics/archive/2017/08/highlights-from-a-congressional-hearing-on-campus-speech/535515/

Frontline. "The Press's Role as a Watchdog on Government." PBS. February 27, 2007. https://www.pbs.org/wgbh/pages/frontline/newswar/tags/watchdog.html

Fulton, Sybrina. "The 100 Most Influential People of 2020: Black Lives Matter Founders Alicia Garza, Patrisse Cullors, and Opal Tometi." *Time Magazine*. September 22, 2020. https://time.com/collection/100-most-influential-people-2020/5888228/black-lives-matter-founders/

Garofalo, Reebee. "Pop Goes to War, 2001–2004: US Popular Music after 9/11." *Music in the Post-9/11 World* (2013): 3–26.

Garza, Alicia. "A Herstory of the #BlackLivesMatter Movement." *The Feminist Wire*. October 7, 2014. https://thefeministwire.com/2014/10/blacklivesmatter-2/

Gaydos, Ryan. "Trump Supports NFL's Decision on National Anthem Policy." *Fox News*. May 24, 2018. https://www.foxnews.com/politics/trump-supports-nfls-decision-on-national-anthem-policy

Geelhart, Chris. "Censoring the Weather during WWII." National Weather Service. n.d. https://vlab.ncep.noaa.gov/web/nws-heritage/-/censoring-the-weather

Gibeaut, John. "Fines, Fox, FCC . . . and Other F-words." *American Bar Association Journal* 94, no. 11 (2008): 28–29.

Gilfoyle, Timothy J. *City of Eros: New York City, Prostitution, and the Commercialization of Sex, 1790–1920*. New York: W. W. Norton, 1992.

Gilles, Susan M. "Brandenburg v. State of Ohio: An Accidental, Too Easy, and Incomplete Landmark Case." *Capital University Law Review* 38 (2010): 517.

Glanville, Jo. "Leaks, Hacks and Science." *New Scientist* 212 (2841): 34. doi:10.1016/S0262-4079(11)62966-7

Gold, S.D. *Parody of Public Figures: Hustler Magazine v. Falwell*. New York: Cavendish Square Publishing, 2014.

Goldman, Emma. "United States v. Emma Goldman: Address to the Jury by Emma Goldman." July 9, 1917. The Emma Goldman Papers. Berkeley Library, University of California. https://www.lib.berkeley.edu/goldman/Features/unitedstatesvsemmagoldman.html

Goldstein, Robert Justin. *Flag Burning and Free Speech: The Case of Texas v. Johnson*. Lawrence, KS: University Press of Kansas, 2000.

Gould, Gretchen Brooke. "Obscenity and Pornography: A Historical Look at the American Library Association, the Commission on Obscenity and Pornography, and the Supreme Court." *Electronic Theses and Dissertations*. 201. 2010. https://scholarworks.uni.edu/etd/201

Graham, Bryan Armen. "Donald Trump Blasts NFL Anthem Protesters: 'Get That Son of a Bitch Off the Field.'" *The Guardian.com*. September 23, 2017. https://www.theguardian.com/sport/2017/sep/22/donald-trump-nfl-national-anthem-protests

Graham, Fred P. "Broad Attack on Attempts to Regulate Sex Morals." *New York Times*. July 12, 1970.

Grasso, Marco. "Oily Politics: A Critical Assessment of the Oil and Gas Industry's Contribution to Climate Change." *Energy Research & Social Science* 50 (2019): 106–15.

Greenberg, Andy. "Is WikiLeaks A Media Organization? The First Amendment Doesn't Care." *Forbes*. April 22, 2011. https://www.forbes.com/sites/andygreenberg/2011/04/21/is-wikileaks-a-media-organization-the-first-amendment-doesnt-care/#3e372b5310e0

Grier, Peter. "WikiLeaks: Would First Amendment Protect Julian Assange?" *Christian Science Monitor*. December 3, 2010. https://www.csmonitor.com/USA/2010/1203/WikiLeaks-Would-First-Amendment-protect-Julian-Assange

Grossman, Anna Jane. "Is Junie B. Jones Talking Trash?" *New York Times*. July 26, 2007. https://www.nytimes.com/2007/07/26/fashion/26junie.html

Guess, Andrew, Brendan Nyhan, and Jason Reifler. "Selective Exposure to Misinformation: Evidence from the Consumption of Fake News during the 2016 US Presidential Campaign." *European Research Council* 9, no. 3 (2018): 4.

Gutterman, Roy S. "Hustler v. Falwell: 25 Years of Protected Satire." *HuffPost*. April 30, 2013. https://www.huffpost.com/entry/hustler-v-falwell-25-year_b_2783713

Halverson, Haley. "Ending Immunity of Internet-Facilitated Commercial Sexual Exploitation through Amending the Communications Decency Act." *Journal of Internet Law* 21, no. 12 (2018): 3–18.

Hauck, Grace, Trevor Hughes, Omar Abdel-Baqui, Ricardo Torres, and Hayes Gardner. "'A Fanciful Reality': Trump Claims Black Lives Matter Protesters Are Violent, But the Majority Are Peaceful." *USA Today*. October 25, 2020. https://www.usatoday.com/in-depth/news/nation/2020/10/24/trump-claims-blm-protests-violent-but-majority-peaceful/3640564001/

Hawkinson, Katie. "Facebook Appoints International Oversight Board to Regulate Online Posts, Raising Questions of Censorship and Free Speech." Free Speech Project. August 30, 2020. https://freespeechproject.georgetown.edu/tracker-entries/facebook-appoints-international-oversight-board-to-regulate-online-posts-raising-questions-of-censorship-and-free-speech/

Healy, Thomas. "Brandenburg in a Time of Terror." *Notre Dame Law Review* 84 (2008): 655.

Healy, Thomas. *The Great Dissent: How Oliver Wendell Holmes Changed His Mind—and Changed the History of Free Speech in America*. New York: Metropolitan Books, 2013.

Heins, Marjorie. *Not in Front of the Children: "Indecency," Censorship, and the Innocence of Youth*. New Brunswick, NJ: Rutgers University Press, 2007.

Heins, Marjorie. *Sex, Sin, and Blasphemy: A Guide to America's Censorship Wars*. New York: New Press, 1998.

Herbeck, Dale. "Chaplinsky v. New Hampshire." In *Free Speech on Trial: Communication Perspectives on Landmark Supreme Court Decisions*. Tuscaloosa, AL: University of Alabama Press, 2003.

Hern, Alex. "Twitter Hides Donald Trump Tweet for 'Glorifying Violence.'" *Guardian*. May 29, 2020. https://www.theguardian.com/technology/2020/may/29/twitter-hides-donald-trump-tweet-glorifying-violence

Hersher, Stephanie. "Longtime Climate Science Denier Hired at NOAA." NPR.org. September 12, 2020. https://www.npr.org/2020/09/12/912301325/longtime-climate-science-denier-hired-at-noaa

Herzstein, Robert Edwin. *The War That Hitler Won: Goebbels and the Nazi Media Campaign*. New York: Paragon House Publishers, 1978.

Hibbitts, Chynna Breann. "To Kneel or Not to Kneel: A Balancing Act of First Amendment Rights." *Kentucky Law Journal*. Blog Post. October 8, 2018.

History.com Editors. "Freedom of Information Act." History. August 21, 2018. https://www.history.com/topics/1960s/freedom-of-information-act

Hixson, Richard F. *Pornography and the Justices: The Supreme Court and the Intractable Obscenity Problem*. Carbondale: Southern Illinois University Press, 1996.

Holmes, Oliver. "What Donald Trump Has Said about Covid-19–A Recap." *The Guardian*. October 2, 2020. https://www.theguardian.com/us-news/2020/oct/02/what-donald-trump-has-said-about-covid-19-a-recap

Holzer, Harold. *Lincoln and the Power of the Press: The War for Public Opinion*. New York: Simon & Schuster, 2015.

Holzer, Harold. *The Presidents vs. the Press*. New York: Dutton, 2020.

Hooker, Matthew P. "Censorship, Free Speech & Facebook: Applying the First Amendment to Social Media Platforms via the Public Function Exception." *Washington Journal of Law, Technology & Arts* 15 (2019): 36.

Horowitz, Helen Lefkowitz. "Victoria Woodhull, Anthony Comstock, and Conflict over Sex in the United States in the 1870s." *Journal of American History* 87, no. 2 (2000): 403–34. doi:10.2307/2568758

Howard, Marcus E. "U.S. Has Funded Artists and Intellectuals for Half a Century, But It's a Perennial Fight." *Los Angeles Times*. October 2, 2015. https://www.latimes.com/nation/la-na-arts-humanities-endowments-20151002-story.html

Hudson, David L., Jr. "Can Anti-Profanity Laws and the Fighting Words Doctrine Be Squared with the First Amendment?" ABA Journal 104, no. 4 (2018): 1.

Hudson, David L., Jr. "Libel and Slander. The First Amendment Encyclopedia." Middle Tennessee State University. May 14, 2020. https://mtsu.edu/first-amendment/article/997/libel-and-slander

Hudson, David L., Jr. "When Do Rants Exceed First Amendment Boundaries and Become True Threats?" *ABA Journal*, August 24, 2018. https://www.abajournal.com/magazine/article/threatening_words_courts_protected_speech

Hudson, David L., Jr. and John E. Ferguson Jr. "The Courts' Inconsistent Treatment of Bethel v. Fraser and the Curtailment of Student Rights." *John Marshall Law Review* 36 (2002): 181.

Hunter, Richard J., Jr. and John H. Shannon. "'Taking a Knee for the Constitution': The Kaepernick and Reid Grievances May be Settled but Do They Nevertheless Raise Important Constitutional Questions?" *Journal of Education and Social Policy* 6, no. 4 (December 2019): 86–100.

Hutchinson, Bill. "Turning Point: Black Lives Matter Organizers Say Right-Wing Backlash Was Expected as Movement Grew." *ABC News*. October 25, 2020. https://abcnews.go.com/US/turning-point-black-lives-matter-organizers-wing-backlash/story?id=72863444

Ingram, Matthew. "White House Revokes Press Passes for Dozens of Journalists." *Columbia Journalism Review*. May 9, 2019. https://www.cjr.org/the_media_today/white-house-press-passes.php

"In Praise of Leaks." 2018. *Time International (South Pacific Edition)* 191 (2): 42–43.

Irons, Peter H. "'Fighting Fair': Zechariah Chafee, Jr., the Department of Justice, and the 'Trial at the Harvard Club.'" *Harvard Law Review* 94, no. 6 (1981): 1205–36. doi:10.2307/1340754

Isaak, Jim, and Mina J. Hanna. "User Data Privacy: Facebook, Cambridge Analytica, and Privacy Protection." *Computer* 51, no. 8 (2018): 56–59.

Jacobson, Louis. "Is Donald Trump the Most Transparent President Ever? No." Politifact. June 4, 2019. https://www.politifact.com/factchecks/2019/jun/04/donald-trump/trump-administration-most-transparent-ever-no/

Jacques, Peter J., Riley E. Dunlap, and Mark Freeman. "The Organization of Denial: Conservative Think Tanks and Environmental Skepticism." *Environmental Politics* 17, no. 3 (2008): 349–85.

Jarvis, Zeke. *Silenced in the Library: Banned Books in America*. Santa Barbara, CA: Greenwood, 2017.

Jones, Alex. "Sandy Hook Elementary School Shooting." *Encyclopedia Britannica. YouTube video of testimony*. March 29, 2019. https://www.youtube.com/watch?v=R8ioAYjkLRI&feature=emb_logo

Jones, Dylon. "The State of the Fourth Estate: A Media Lawyer and a Journalist Discuss Social Media, 'Fake News' and the First Amendment." *Louisville Magazine* 69, no. 1 (2018): 32–34.

Jones, RonNell Anderson, and Sonja R. West. "The Fragility of the Free American Press." *Northwestern University Law Review* 112, no. 3 (2017): 567–95.

Jones, Sarah E. "Unanswered Prayers?" *Church & State* 67, no. 3 (2014): 6–8.

Kalb, Marvin. *Enemy of the People: Trump's War on the Press, the New McCarthyism, and the Threat to American Democracy*. Washington, DC: Brookings Institution Press, 2018.

Kaminska, Izabella. "A Lesson in Fake News from the Info-wars of Ancient Rome." *Financial Times*. January 17, 2017. https://www.ft.com/content/aaf2bb08-dca2-11e6-86ac-f253db7791c6

Kanaley, Reid. August 1, 1995. "Report on Pornography Draws Fire on the Internet." *The Baltimore Sun*. https://www.baltimoresun.com/news/bs-xpm-1995-08-01-1995213154-story.html

Kaplan, Rebecca. "Former CIA Deputy Director: NSA 'Is Not Spying on Americans.'" *Face the Nation*. December 22, 2013. https://www.cbsnews.com/news/former-cia-deputy-director-nsa-is-not-spying-on-americans/

Katz, Al. "Privacy and Pornography: Stanley v. Georgia." *Supreme Court Review* 1969 (1969): 203–17.

Keller, Daphne. "Facebook Restricts Speech by Popular Demand." *Atlantic*. September 22, 2019. https://www.theatlantic.com/ideas/archive/2019/09/facebook-restricts-free-speech-popular-demand/598462/

Kellner, Douglas. *American Nightmare: Donald Trump, Media Spectacle, and Authoritarian Populism*. Rotterdam: Sense Publishers, 2016.

Kelly, Makena. "FCC Will Move to Regulate Social Media after Censorship Outcry." *Theverge.com*. October 15, 2020. https://www.theverge.com/2020/10/15/21518097/fcc-social-media-censorship-moderation-ajit-pai-section-230-nypost-biden

Kertscher, Tom. "Is Black Lives Matter a Marxist Movement?" *Politifact*. The Poynter Institute. July 21, 2020. https://www.politifact.com/article/2020/jul/21/black-lives-matter-marxist-movement/

Kim, Jonathan. "Habeas Corpus." Legal Information Institute. June 2017. https://www.law.cornell.edu/wex/habeas_corpus

Kirk, Bryan. "Curfews Imposed in 42 Cities across 24 States as Protesters Clash with Police." *Newsweek*. June 1, 2020. https://www.newsweek.com/curfews-imposed-42-cities-across-24-states-protesters-clash-police-1507801

Kirk, Michael, and Peter J. Boyer. "An Overview of Past Pornography Rulings by the U.S. Supreme Court." In Frontline program: "American Porn." WGBH Boston. Aired February 7, 2002. https://www.pbs.org/wgbh/pages/frontline/shows/porn/prosecuting/overview.html

Knapp, Nancy Flanagan. "In Defense of Harry Potter: An Apologia." *School Libraries Worldwide* 9 (2003): 78–91.

Knight Foundation. "10 Reasons Why American Trust in the Media Is At an All-Time Low." January 15, 2018. https://medium.com/trust-media-and-democracy/10-reasons-why-americans-dont-trust-the-media-d0630c125b9e

Knight Foundation. "American Views: Trust, Media, and Democracy." Gallup/Knight Foundation Survey, 2018. https://knightfoundation.org/wp-content/uploads/2019/06/KnightFoundation_AmericansViews_Client_Report_010917_Final_Updated.pdf

Kosseff, Jeff. *The Twenty-Six Words That Created the Internet*. Cornell University Press, 2019.

Kozlowski, Joe. "How Much Money Has Colin Kaepernick Donated to Charity over the Years?" *Sportscasting.com*. June 3, 2020. https://www.sportscasting.com/how-much-money-has-colin-kaepernick-donated-to-charity-over-the-years/

Kreiter, Marcy. "Trump's Medical Condition: What We Know and Don't Know about His Status Amid Confusion over Privacy." *International Business Times*. October 5, 2020. https://www.ibtimes.com/trumps-medical-condition-what-we-know-dont-know-about-his-status-amid-confusion-over-3057143

Kwoka, Margaret B. "First-Person FOIA." *Yale Law Journal* 127, no. 8 (2018): 2204–69.

Lain, Corinna Barrett. "God, Civic Virtue, and the American Way: Reconstructing Engel." Stanford Law Review 67, no. 3 (2015): 479–555.

Latts, Adam. "Our Schools, Our Country: American Evangelicals, Public Schools, and the Supreme Court Decisions of 1962 and 1963." *Journal of Religious History* 36, no. 3 (2012): 319–34.

Lau, Tim. "Citizens United Explained." Brennan Center for Justice. December 12, 2019. https://www.brennancenter.org/our-work/research-reports/citizens-united-explained

Lazer, David, Matthew Baum, Yochai Benkler, Adam Berinsky, Kelly Greenhill, Filippo Menczer Miriam Metzger, Brendan Nyhan, Gordon Pennycook, David Rothschild, Michael Schudson, Steven Sloman, C. Sunstein, Emily Thorson, Duncan Wattsand Jonathan Zittrain. "The Science of Fake News." *Science* 359, no. 6380 (2018): 1094–6.

Leahy, Patrick. "Keynote Address, National Archives and Records Administration." March 14, 2016. https://www.leahy.senate.gov/imo/media/doc/2016%20FOIA%200301116%20PJL%20Nara%20Speech%20draft%20final.pdf

Lee, Terry. "The Global Rise of 'Fake News' and the Threat to Democratic Elections in the USA." *Public Administration and Policy: An Asia-Pacific Journal* 22, no. 1 (2019): 15–24.

Lemov, Michael R. *People's Warrior: John Moss and the Fight for Freedom of Information and Consumer Rights*. Madison: Fairleigh Dickinson University Press, 2011.

Lewandowsky, Stephan, Klaus Oberauer, and Gilles E. Gignac. "NASA Faked the Moon Landing—Therefore, (Climate) Science is a Hoax: An Anatomy of the Motivated Rejection of Science." *Psychological Science* 24, no. 5 (2013): 622–33.

Lind, Dara. "Everyone's Heard of the Patriot Act. Here's What It Actually Does." *Vox*, June 2, 2015. https://www.vox.com/2015/6/2/8701499/patriot-act-explain

Lindholm, Johan. "From Carlos to Kaepernick and Beyond: Athletes' Right to Freedom of Expression." *International Sports Law Journal* 17 (2017): 1–3.

Lindvall, Alexander J. "Frankly My Dear, I Don't Give a-Darn—An Argument against Censoring Broadcast Media." *Arizona State University Sports & Entertainment Law Journal* 7 (2017): 153.

Llorente, Elizabeth. "FBI Cites Black Extremists as New Domestic Terrorist Threat." *Fox News*. October 14, 2017. https://www.foxnews.com/us/fbi-cites-black-extremists-as-new-domestic-terrorist-threat

Lockhart, William B. "The Findings and Recommendations of the Commission on Obscenity and Pornography: A Case Study of the Role of Social Science in Formulating Public Policy." *Oklahoma Law Review* 24 (1971): 209.

Lynskey, Bill. "'I Shall Speak in Philadelphia': Emma Goldman and the Free Speech League." *Pennsylvania Magazine of History and Biography* 133, no. 2 (2009): 167–202. www.jstor.org/stable/40543455

Madhani, Aamer. "'Sharpiegate' Hurricane Report Is Being Blocked, Commerce Department Inspector General Says." Associated Press. July 2, 2020. https://www.chicagotribune.com/nation-world/ct-nw-trump-sharpie-hurricane-dorian-20200702-knityezjq-jaenpy3p6ycbomhqy-story.html

Mannheimer, Michael J. "The Fighting Words Doctrine." *Columbia Law Review* 93, no. 6 (1993): 1527–71.

Marantz, Andrew. "Free Speech Is Killing Us." *New York Times*. October 4, 2019. https://www.nytimes.com/2019/10/04/opinion/sunday/free-speech-social-media-violence.html

Marcus, Ann-Ellen. "Broadcasting Seven Dirty Words: FCC v. Pacifica Foundation." *Boston College Law Review* 20, no. 5 (1979): 975.

Marcus, Robert D., and Anthony Marcus, eds. "The Army-McCarthy Hearings, 1954." In *On Trial: American History through Court Proceedings and Hearings*, 136–51. Vol. II. St. James, NY: Brandywine Press, 1998.

Marczely, Bernadette. "Student Freedom of Expression in the Wake of Hazelwood and Bethel." *Clearing House* 65, no. 5 (1992): 269–71.

Marlette, Doug. "Freedom of Speech and the Editorial Cartoon." *Nieman Reports*. Winter 2004. https://niemanreports.org/articles/freedom-of-speech-and-the-editorial-cartoon/

Matula, Charles. "Any Safe Harbor in a Storm: SESTA-FOSTA and the Future of § 230 of the Communications Decency Act." *Duke Law & Technology Review* 18, no. 1 (2020): 353–68.

Maxouris, Christina, and Elizabeth Joseph. "Alex Jones Says 'Form of Psychosis' Made Him Believe Events Like Sandy Hook Massacre Were Staged." *CNN*. April 1, 2019. https://www.cnn.com/2019/03/30/us/alex-jones-psychosis-sandy-hook/index.html

McCarthy, Tom. "Zuckerberg Says Facebook Won't Be 'Arbiters of Truth' after Trump Threat." *theguardian.com*. May 28, 2020. https://www.theguardian.com/technology/2020/may/28/zuckerberg-facebook-police-online-speech-trump

McChesney, Robert Waterman. *Telecommunications, Mass Media, and Democracy: The Battle for the Control of U.S. Broadcasting, 1928–1935*. New York: Oxford University Press, 1994.

McGinty, Ryan J. "Fourth & Inches: Marking the Line of Athletes' Free Speech." (A Colin Kaepernick Inspired Discussion). *Pace. Intell. Prop. Sports & Ent. L.F.* 8, no. 1 (2017): 39. https://digitalcommons.pace.edu/pipself/vol8/iss1/3

McNamee, Roger. "Facebook Cannot Fix Itself." *Time* 195, no. 22 (2020): 20–21.

Meadors, Brian. *Harry Potter and the Cedarville Censors: Inside the Precedent-Setting Defeat of an Arkansas Book Ban*. Jefferson, NC: McFarland, 2019.

Means, Howard B. *67 Shots: Kent State and the End of American Innocence*. Boston, MA: Da Capo Press, 2016.

Merriam-Webster Dictionary. "The Real Story of 'Fake News.'" n.d. https://www.merriam-webster.com/words-at-play/the-real-story-of-fake-news

Miller, Beverly G. "Miller v. California: A Cold Shower for the First Amendment." *St. John's Law Review* 48 (1973): 568.

Milman, Oliver. "Seven of Donald Trump's Most Misleading Coronavirus Claims." The Guardian.com. March 31, 2020. https://www.theguardian.com/us-news/2020/mar/28/trump-coronavirus-misleading-claims

Mitchell, Gordon R. "American Itsesensuuri: A Typology of Self-Censorship in the 'War on Terror.'" *Proceedings of the Fifth ISSA Conference on Argumentation* (2003): 767–72.

Moftah, Lora. "Charlie Hebdo Cartoons: Political Cartoonists Debate Free Speech after Attack." *International Business Times*. January 8, 2015. https://www.ibtimes.com/charlie-hebdo-cartoons-political-cartoonists-debate-free-speech-after-attack-1778040

Moran, Jordan. "Nixon and the Pentagon Papers." Miller Center, University of Virginia. n.d. https://millercenter.org/the-presidency/educational-resources/first-domino-nixon-and-the-pentagon-papers

Moravec, Patricia, Randall Minas, and Alan R. Dennis. "Fake News on Social Media: People Believe What They Want to Believe When It Makes No Sense At All." *Kelley School of Business Research Paper* (2018): 18–87. https://ssrn.com/abstract=3269541

Morgan, Susan. "Fake News, Disinformation, Manipulation and Online Tactics to Undermine Democracy." *Journal of Cyber Policy* 3, no. 1 (2018): 39–43.

Morrison, Steven R. "The System of Modern Criminal Conspiracy." *Catholic University Law Review* 63, no. 2 (2014): 371.

Moskowitz, Daniel B. "Drawing a Line on Libel." *American History* 54, no. 1 (2019): 22–23.

Moskowitz, Daniel B. "Praying for Clarity." *American History* 52, no. 2 (2017): 26–27.

Murray, Robert K. *Red Scare: A Study in National Hysteria, 1919–1920*. Westport, CT: Greenwood Press, 1980.

Murtha, Ryan. "'The Highest Form of Patriotism': Toward an Understanding of First Amendment Precedents and NFL Protests." *Journal of Emerging Sport Studies* 1, no. 1 (2018): 6.

Naeem, Salman Bin, Rubina Bhatti, and Aqsa Khan. "An Exploration of How Fake News is Taking Over Social Media and Putting Public Health at Risk." *Health Information & Libraries Journal* (2020).

Napoli, Philip M. "What If More Speech Is No Longer the Solution? First Amendment Theory Meets Fake News and the Filter Bubble." *Federal Communications Law Journal* 70 (2018): 55.

National Coalition against Censorship. "Art and Culture Censorship Timeline." February 10, 2011. https://ncac.org/resource/art-and-culture-censorship-timeline

National Coalition against Censorship. "A Timeline of Video Game Controversies." October 31, 2010. https://ncac.org/resource/a-timeline-of-video-game-controversies

National Coalition against Censorship. "National Endowment for the Arts: Controversies in Free Speech." https://ncac.org/resource/national-endowment-for-the-arts-controversies-in-free-speech

Neary, Lynn. "'Grapes of Wrath' and the Politics of Book Burning." *National Public Radio*. September 30, 2008. https://www.npr.org/templates/story/story.php?storyId=95190615

Newsy.com. "Trump Tweets GIF of Himself Tackling 'CNN.'" *YouTube.com*. July 2, 2017. https://youtu.be/bDZNNtyc46k

NFL [@NFL.com]. Roger Goodell video statement about anthem protests. *Twitter.com*. June 5, 2020. https://twitter.com/NFL/status/1269034074552721408

Nithyanand, Rishab, Brian Schaffner, and Phillipa Gill. "Online Political Discourse in the Trump Era." *arXiv preprint arXiv:1711.05303* (2017).

Nixon, Richard. "Enemies List." Nixon Presidential Library. n.d. https://www.nixonlibrary.gov/media/31483

"No Self Censorship." *Time* 77, no. 21 (1961): 48.

"Note: Section 230 as First Amendment Rule." *Harvard Law Review* 131, no. 7 (2018): 2027–48.

Obama, Barack. "Freedom of Information Act." Memorandum for the Heads of Executive Departments and Agencies. *The White House*. January 21, 2009. https://obamawhitehouse.archives.gov/the-press-office/freedom-information-act

Ohio State University Wexner Medical Center. "Rise in Lung Adenocarcinoma Linked to 'Light' Cigarette Use: Researchers Urge Food and Drug Administration to Take Immediate Action, Possibly Banning Use of Ventilation Holes on Cigarettes." *ScienceDaily*. May 22, 2017. www.sciencedaily.com/releases/2017/05/170522080802.htm

O'Neill, Robert. *Free Speech in the College Community*. Bloomington: Indiana University Press, 1997.

Pappas, Stephanie. "The History of Pornography No More Prudish Than the Present." *Live Science*. October 11, 2010. https://www.livescience.com/8748-history-pornography-prudish-present.html

Paul, Kari. "Online Privacy Experts Sound Alarm as US Senate Bill Sparks Surveillance Fears." *The Guardian*. July 2, 2020. https://www.theguardian.com/technology/2020/jul/02/earn-it-act-online-privacy-surveillance

Pennycook, Gordon, Tyrone D. Cannon, and David G. Rand. "Prior Exposure Increases Perceived Accuracy of Fake News." *Journal of Experimental Psychology: General* 147, no. 12 (2018): 1865.

Perez, Matt. "Who Is Dr. Scott Atlas? Trump's New Covid Health Adviser Seen as Counter to Fauci and Birx." *Forbes*. August 12, 2020. https://www.forbes.com/sites/mattperez/2020/08/12/who-is-dr-scott-atlas-trumps-new-covid-health-adviser-seen-as-counter-to-fauci-and-birx/#4d24c56e20a4

Peterson, Meghan, Bella Robinson, and Elena Shih. "The New Virtual Crackdown on Sex Workers' Rights: Perspectives from the United States." *Anti-Trafficking Review* 12 (2019): 189–93.

Pike, George H. "The End of Social Media Immunity?" *Information Today* 35, no. 4 (2018): 19.

Pollay, Richard W. and Timothy Dewhirst. "Marketing Cigarettes with Low Machine-Measured Yields." *Smoking and Tobacco Control Monograph* 13 (2001): 199–233.

Post, David G. "A Preliminary Discussion of Methodological Peculiarities in the Rimm Study of Pornography on the 'Information Superhighway.'" June 28, 1995. (Post to a newsgroup.) http://www.mit.edu/activities/safe/writings/pornography/cmu-study/critique-by-post

Post, Robert C. "The Constitutional Concept of Public Discourse: Outrageous Opinion, Democratic Deliberation, and Hustler Magazine v. Falwell." *Harvard Law Review* 103, no. 3 (1990): 601–86.

Powe, Lewis A., Jr. "Red Lion and Pacifica: Are They Relics." *Pepperdine Law Review* 36 (2008): 445.

Priest, Dana, and William M. Arkin. *Top Secret America: The Rise of the New American Security State*. New York: Little, Brown and Company, 2013.

Quek, Jing Xun. "Elonis v. United States: The Next Twelve Years." *Berkeley Technology Law Journal* 31, no. 2 (2016): 1109–36.

Quigley, Margaret. "The Mapplethorpe Censorship Controversy." Political Research Associates. May 1, 1991. https://www.politicalresearch.org/1991/05/01/mapplethorpe-censorship-controversy

Raab, Christopher P. "Fighting Terrorism in an Electronic Age: Does the Patriot Act Unduly Compromise Our Civil Liberties?" *Duke Law & Technology Review* 4, no. 1 (2006): 1–21.

Ragan, Fred D. "Justice Oliver Wendell Holmes, Jr., Zechariah Chafee, Jr., and the Clear and Present Danger Test for Free Speech: The First Year, 1919." *Journal of American History* 58, no. 1 (1971): 24–45. doi:10.2307/1890079

Ramos, Mitzi. "Flag Protection Acts of 1968 and 1989." The First Amendment Encyclopedia. Middle Tennessee State University. https://www.mtsu.edu/first-amendment/article/1079/flag-protection-acts-of-1968-and-1989

Reiss, Jaclyn. "More than 300 Newspapers Join Globe Effort on Freedom of the Press Editorials." *Boston Globe*. August 15, 2018. https://www.bostonglobe.com/metro/2018/08/14/newspapers-join-globe-effort-freedom-press-editorials/yvvZ0yepu8j1lJ3G3qYbSJ/story.html

Rhodan, Maya. "Trump is Threatening to Take Away 'Reporters' Credentials. He Told TIME He Wouldn't Do That." *TIME.com*. May 9, 2018. https://time.com/5270968/donald-trump-reporters-credentials-media/

Riggs, Robert E. "Miller v. California Revisited: An Empirical Note." *BYU Law Review* (1981): 247.

Rigotti, Nancy A., and Hilary A. Tindle. "The Fallacy of 'Light' Cigarettes." *BMJ* 328, no. 7440 (2004): E278–E279. doi:10.1136/bmj.328.7440.E278

Rimm, Marty. "Marketing Pornography on the Information Superhighway: A Survey of 917,410 Images, Descriptions, Short Stories, and Animations Downloaded 8.5 Million Times by Consumers in Over 2000 Cities in Forty Countries, Provinces, and Territories." *Georgetown Law Journal* 83 (1995): 1849–934.

Riviera, Gloria, Jackie Jesko, Sally Hawkins, and Jenna Millman. "Emotional Senate Hearing Finds Backpage.com Complicit in Underage Sex Trafficking as Victim's Families Testify." *ABCNews*. January 13, 2017. https://abcnews.go.com/US/emotional-senate-hearing-finds-backpage-complicit-underage-sex/story?id=44762342

Rodrigo, Chris Mills. "Republicans on Senate Panel Subpoena Facebook, Twitter CEOs." *The Hill*. October 22, 2020. https://thehill.com/policy/technology/522220-republicans-on-senate-panel-subpoena-facebook-twitter-ceos

Rollins, Khadrice. "Why Do NFL Players Kneel during the National Anthem?" *Sports Illustrated*. May 23, 2018. https://www.si.com/nfl/2018/05/23/why-do-players-kneel-during-national-anthem

Roos, Hanna. "Trading the Sexual Child: Child Pornography and the Commodification of Children in Society." *Texas Journal of Women & the Law* 23, no. 2 (2014): 131–56.

Rosenfeld, Shelly. "An Indecent Proposal? What Clamping Down on Fleeting Expletives on the Airwaves Means for the TV Industry." *Texas Review of Entertainment & Sports Law* 12, no. 2 (2011): 225–38.

Ross, Andrew S., and Damian J. Rivers. "Discursive Deflection: Accusation of 'Fake News' and the Spread of Mis- and Disinformation in the Tweets of President Trump." *Social Media + Society* 4, no. 2 (2018): 1–12. https://journals.sagepub.com/doi/pdf/10.1177/2056305118776010

Rozsa, Matthew. "Both the GOP and the Democrats Want to Break Up Big Tech. Could It Really Happen?" *Salon*. October 20, 2020. https://www.salon.com/2020/10/20/both-the-gop-and-the-democrats-want-to-break-up-big-tech-could-it-really-happen/

Russomanno, Joseph. *Speaking Our Minds: Conversations with the People behind Landmark First Amendment Cases*. Mahwah, NJ: Lawrence Erlbaum Associates, 2002.

Samples, John. "Fighting Words and Free Speech." CATO Institute. June 25, 2018. https://www.cato.org/blog/fighting-words-free-speech

Sanders, Edmund. "Senators Scold Radio Chain for Tuning Out Dixie Chicks." *Los Angeles Times*. July 9, 2003. https://www.latimes.com/archives/la-xpm-2003-jul-09-fi-cumulus9-story.html

Scales, Pat. "What Makes a Good Banned Book?" *Horn Book Magazine* 85, no. 5 (2009): 533–36.

Schauer, Frederick. "Codifying the First Amendment: New York v. Ferber." *Supreme Court Review* 1982 (1982): 285–317.

Scheiber, Harry N. *The Wilson Administration and Civil Liberties, 1917–1921*. Ithaca, NY: Cornell University Press, 1960.

Schindler, Steve, and Katie Wilson-Milne. "Art, Censorship, and the First Amendment." *The Art Law Podcast*. July 2, 2018. http://artlawpodcast.com/2018/07/02/art-censorship-and-the-first-amendment/

Schlafly, Phyllis. "The Morality of First Amendment Jurisprudence." *Harvard Journal of Law & Public Policy* 31, no. 1 (2008): 95.

Schoenberger, Nicole. "Access to Information in the Age of Trump." *Emerging Library & Information Perspectives* 1 (2018): 6–33.

Schorr, Joanna. "Malicious Content on the Internet: Narrowing Immunity under the Communications Decency Act." *St. John's Law Review* 87, no. 2/3 (2013): 733–62.

Schultz, David, and John R. Vile. *The Encyclopedia of Civil Liberties in America*. Hoboken: Taylor and Francis, 2015.

Segers, Grace and Kathryn Watson. "Trump Admitted to Woodward He Downplayed Coronavirus Threat in Early Days of Outbreak." *CBS News*. September 10, 2020. https://www.cbsnews.com/news/trump-woodward-book-claims-downplayed-covid-19-threat/

Serrano, Andres. "Protecting Freedom of Expression, from Piss Christ to Charlie Hebdo." *Creative Time Reports*. January 30, 2015. https://creativetimereports.org/2015/01/30/free-speech-piss-christ-charlie-hebdo-andres-serrano/

S.G.F. "The Suspension of Habeas Corpus during the War of the Rebellion." *Political Science Quarterly* 3, no. 3 (1888): 454–88. doi:10.2307/2139053

Sharma, Iona, and Zhou Sicheng. "Obscenity and the First Amendment." Cornell University Law School. 2010. https://courses2.cit.cornell.edu/sociallaw/student_projects/ObscenityFirstAmendment.htm

Shea, J.P. "The Role of the Media in a Democratic Society." Speaking notes by Dr. Shea, NATO Spokesman, for NATO Seminar. July 2–3, 1998. https://www.nato.int/docu/speech/1998/s980702c.htm

Shepley, Nick. *The Palmer Raids and the Red Scare: 1918–1920: Justice and Liberty for All*. 2nd ed. Explaining Modern History, 3. Luton: Andrews UK, 2011.

Shisia, Maureen. "The Best Selling Book Series in the World." *World Atlas*. May 25, 2018. https://www.worldatlas.com/articles/best-selling-book-series.html

Simon, Roger. "There's No Good Excuse for Horrifying Video Game." *Baltimore Sun*. December 10, 1993. https://www.baltimoresun.com/news/bs-xpm-1993-12-10-1993344011-story.html

Smith, Stephen A. "Schenck v. United States and Abrams v. United States." In *Free Speech on Trial: Communication Perspectives on Landmark Supreme Court Decisions*. Tuscaloosa, AL: University of Alabama Press, 2003.

Snopes Staff. "Donald Trump Criticized for Mocking Disabled Reporter." *Snopes*. July 28, 2016. https://www.snopes.com/news/2016/07/28/donald-trump-criticized-for-mocking-disabled-reporter/

Snow, Nancy, and Philip M. Taylor. "The Revival of the Propaganda State: US Propaganda at Home and Abroad since 9/11." *International Communication Gazette* 68, no. 5–6 (2006): 389–407.

Social Dilemma. Directed by Jeff Orlowski. Netflix, 2020.

Solender, Andrew. "All the Times Trump Has Promoted Hydroxychloroquine." *Forbes*. May 22, 2020. https://www.forbes.com/sites/andrewsolender/2020/05/22/all-the-times-trump-promoted-hydroxychloroquine/#1a74d8214643

Sonmez, Felicia. "Trump Aide Raises Tension with CDC after Criticizing Health Agency Publicly." *msn.com*. May 18, 2020. https://www.msn.com/en-us/news/us/trump-aide-raises-tension-with-cdc-after-criticizing-health-agency-publicly/ar-BB14dKsR

Sostaric, Katarina. "ACLU Lawsuit Accuses Iowa State Patrol of Violating BLM Protesters' Free Speech Rights." *Iowa Public Radio*. October 5, 2020. https://www.iowapublicradio.org/race/2020-10-05/aclu-lawsuit-accuses-iowa-state-patrol-of-violating-blm-protesters-free-speech-rights

Southwick, Thomas P. "Presidential Commission Gives Report on Campuses." *Harvard Crimson*. September 28, 1970. https://www.thecrimson.com/article/1970/9/28/presidential-commission-gives-report-on-campuses/

Spangler, Todd. "FCC Chief Warns Social Media Firms That They Don't Have Right to 'Special Immunity.'" *Variety*. October 15, 2020.

Spears, Victoria Prussen. "The Warren Court Protects the Private Possession of Obscene Matter: *Stanley v. Georgia*." *Privacy and Data Security Law Journal*. March 2009. https://www.meyerowitzcommunications.com/pdf/warren-court.pdf

Stelter, Brian. "Trump Averages a 'Fake' Insult Every Day. Really. We Counted." *CNN Business*. January 17, 2018. https://money.cnn.com/2018/01/17/media/president-trump-fake-news-count/index.html

Stencel, Mark and Joel Luther. "Annual Census Finds Nealy 300 Fact-Checking Projects Around the World." *Duke Reporters' Lab*. June 22, 2020. https://reporterslab.org/annual-census-finds-nearly-300-fact-checking-projects-around-the-world/

Sternberg, Sarah. "The Child Pornography Prevention Act of 1996 and the First Amendment: Virtual Antitheses." *Fordham Law Review* 69 (2000): 2783.

Stone, Geoffrey R. "Flag Burning and the Constitution." *Iowa Law Review* 75 (1989): 111.

Stone, Geoffrey R. "Wikileaks and the First Amendment." *Federal Communications Law Journal* 64 (2011): 477.

Stone, Geoffrey R., and David A. Strauss. *Democracy and Equality: The Enduring Constitutional Vision of the Warren Court*. New York: Oxford University Press, 2020.

Strossen, Nadine. "Don't Silence Graduation Speakers: Fight Hate Speech with More Speech." *USA Today*. May 1, 2018. https://www.usatoday.com/story/opinion/2018/05/01/censorship-hate-speech-freedom-first-amendment-column/564868002/

Strub, Whitney. *Obscenity Rules: Roth v. United States and the Long Struggle over Sexual Expression*. Lawrence, KS: University Press of Kansas, 2013.

Sweeney, Michael S. "Censorship Missionaries of World War II." *Journalism History* 27, no 1 (2001): 4–13.

Tilove, Jonathan. "Alex Jones Must Pay Legal Fees for 'Frivolous' Sandy Hook Appeal." *Statesman*. March 26, 2020. https://www.statesman.com/news/20200326/alex-jones-must-pay-legal-fees-for-rsquofrivolousrsquo-sandy-hook-appeal

Tirrell, Chris, Laura Senier, Sara Ann Wylie, Cole Alder, Grace Poudrier, Jesse DiValli, Marcy Beck, Eric Nost, Rob Brackett, and Gretchen Gehrke. "Learning in Crisis: Training Students to Monitor and Address Irresponsible Knowledge Construction by US Federal Agencies under Trump." *Engaging Science, Technology, and Society* 6 (2020): 81–93.

Tobias, Manuela. "Why Infowars' Alex Jones Was Banned from Apple, Facebook, Youtube and Spotify." Politifact: The Poynter Institute. August 7, 2018. https://www.politifact.com/article/2018/aug/07/why-infowars-alex-jones-was-banned-apple-facebook-/

Todd, Jeff. "Satire in Defamation Law: Toward a Critical Understanding." *Review of Litigation* 35, no. 1 (2016): 45–69.

Tréguer, Pascal, "Meaning and Origin of 'The Fourth Estate.'" *Word Histories Blog*. August 9, 2016. https://wordhistories.net/2016/08/09/the-fourth-estate/

Tringali, Izabela and Kinsella, Martha. "Forced Sterilization Accusations at ICE Facility Fit with Trump's Poor Treatment of Migrants." Brennan Center for Justice. September 18, 2020. https://www.brennancenter.org/our-work/analysis-opinion/forced-sterilization-accusations-ice-facility-fit-trumps-poor-treatment

Trump, Donald J. Remarks at a "Make America Great Again" Rally in Phoenix, Arizona. Online by Gerhard Peters and John T. Woolley, The American Presidency Project. August 22, 2017. https://www.presidency.ucsb.edu/node/331393

Trump, Donald J. Remarks at the Central Intelligence Agency in Langley, Virginia. Online by Gerhard Peters and John T. Woolley, The American Presidency Project. January 21, 2017. https://www.presidency.ucsb.edu/node/323537

Tuchman, Claudia. "Does Privacy Have Four Walls-Salvaging Stanley v. Georgia." *Columbia Law Review* 94 (1994): 2267.

Tucker, Joshua A., Andrew Guess, Pablo Barberá, Cristian Vaccari, Alexandra Siegel, Sergey Sanovich, Denis Stukal, and Brendan Nyhan. "Social Media, Political Polarization, and Political Disinformation: A Review of the Scientific Literature." Hewlett Foundation. March 19, 2018. https://eprints.lse.ac.uk/87402/1/Social-Media-Political-Polarization-and-Political-Disinformation-Literature-Review.pdf

Tucker, William C. "Deceitful Tongues: Is Climate Change Denial a Crime?" *Ecology Law Quarterly* 39, no. 3 (2012): 831–94.

Tye, Larry. *Demagogue: The Life and Long Shadow of Senator Joe McCarthy*. Boston: Houghton Mifflin Harcourt, 2020.

Union of Concerned Scientists. "The Climate Deception Dossiers." June 29, 2015. https://ucsusa.org/resources/climate-deception-dossiers

Union of Concerned Scientists. "The Disinformation Playbook." May 18, 2018. https://www.ucsusa.org/resources/disinformation-playbook

University of Minnesota. "Evolution of Radio Broadcasting." In *Understanding Media and Culture: An Introduction to Mass Communication*. https://open.lib.umn.edu/mediaandculture/chapter/7-2-evolution-of-radio-broadcasting/

U.S. Commission on Civil Rights. "Trauma at the Border: The Human Cost of Inhumane Immigration Policies." Briefing Report. October 2019. https://www.usccr.gov/pubs/2019/10-24-Trauma-at-the-Border.pdf

U.S. Commission on Obscenity and Pornography. *The Report*. Washington, DC: Government Printing Office, 1970.

U.S. Congress House. Committee on Oversight and Reform: Subcommittee on Civil Rights and Civil Liberties Briefing. *First Amendment Violations at Black Lives Matter Protests*. 116th Cong., 2nd Sess., June 20, 2020. https://oversight.house.gov/legislation/briefings/select-subcommittee-briefing-on-first-amendment-violations-at-black-lives

U.S. Library of Congress. Congressional Research Service. Flag Protection: A Brief History and Summary of Recent Supreme Court Decisions and Proposed Constitutional Amendments, by John R. Luckey. CRS 95–709.

U.S. Senate. Permanent Subcommittee on Investigations. Committee on Homeland Security and Governmental Affairs. Backpage.com's Knowing Facilitation of Online Sex Trafficking: Staff Report. 115th Cong., 1st Sess., January 10, 2017. https://www.hsgac.senate.gov/imo/media/doc/Backpage%20Report%202017.01.10%20FINAL.pdf

U.S. Senate. "A Declaration of Conscience." Senate Historical Office. June 1, 1950. https://www.cop.senate.gov/artandhistory/history/minute/A_Declaration_of_Conscience.htm

van der Linden, Sander, Costas Panagopoulos, and Jon Roozenbeek. "You Are Fake News: Political Bias in Perceptions of Fake News." *Media, Culture & Society* 42, no. 3 (2020): 460–70.

Vandewalker, Ian and Eric Petry. "Election Spending 2014: Outside Spending in Senate Races Since 'Citizens United.'" Brennan Center for Justice. December 1, 2015.

https://www.brennancenter.org/our-work/research-reports/election-spending-2014-outside-spending-senate-races-citizens-united

"Video Game Violence." *C-SPAN*. December 9, 1993. https://www.c-span.org/video/?52848-1/video-game-violence

VOA News. "National Guard Called up in 11 States to Handle Protests." *Voice of America News*. May 31, 2020. https://www.voanews.com/usa/national-guard-called-11-states-handle-protests

Wagoner, Nick. "Colin Kaepernick Wins 49ers' Award for 'Inspirational, Courageous Play.'" *ESPN.com*. December 30, 2016. https://www.espn.com/nfl/story/_/id/18379314/colin-kaepernick-san-francisco-49ers-voted-teammates-winner-len-eshmont-award

Walker, Jesse. "The Blurry Boundaries of Child Porn." *Reason* 41, no. 3 (2009): 34–35.

Walker, Michael Wingfield. "Artistic Freedom v. Censorship: The Aftermath of the NEA's New Funding Restrictions." *Washington University Law Review* 71, no. 3 (1993): 937–56.

Wang, Yuxi, Martin McKee, Aleksandra Torbica, and David Stuckler. "Systematic Literature Review on the Spread of Health-Related Misinformation on Social Media." *Social Science & Medicine* 240 (2019): 112552.

Wardle, Claire and Hossein Derakhshan. "How Did the News Go 'Fake?' When the Media Went Social." *The Guardian*. November 10, 2017. https://www.theguardian.com/commentisfree/2017/nov/10/fake-news-social-media-current-affairs-approval

Wasike, Ben. "FOI in Transition: A Comparative Analysis of the Freedom of Information Act Performance between the Obama and Trump Administrations." *Government Information Quarterly* 37, no. 2 (2020): 101443.

Waxman, Olivia B. "This Is What Americans Used to Consider Obscene." *Time*. June 21, 2016. https://time.com/4373765/history-obscenity-united-states-films-miller-ulysses-roth/

Webb, Susan L. "Book Banning." The First Amendment Encyclopedia. Middle Tennessee State University. https://mtsu.edu/first-amendment/article/986/book-banning

Weber, Jennifer L. *Copperheads: The Rise and Fall of Lincoln's Opponents in the North*. Oxford: Oxford University Press, 2008.

Weinstein, James. "The Context and Content of New York v. Ferber." In *Refining Child Pornography Law: Crime, Language, and Social Consequences*, 19–56. University of Michigan Press, 2016.

Weinstein, James. "An Overview of American Free Speech Doctrine and Its Application to Extreme Speech." In *Extreme Speech and Democracy*. Oxford University Press, 2009.

Wendling, Mike. "The (Almost) Complete History of 'Fake News.'" *BBC News*. January 22, 2018. https://www.bbc.com/news/blogs-trending-42724320

Whitaker, Bill. "The Big Chill: The Stifling Effect of the Official Response to the Kent State Killings." *Vietnam Generation* 2, no. 2 (1995): 147–54.

White, Lee. "How Transparent Was the Obama Administration?" Perspectives on History: The American Historical Association. February 1, 2017. https://www.historians.org/publications-and-directories/perspectives-on-history/february-2017/how-transparent-was-the-obama-administration

"Why Freedom of Speech?" *New Republic*. June 1, 1927. 34.

Wike, Richard. "Americans More Tolerant of Offensive Speech Than Others in the World." Pew Research Center Fact Tank. October 12, 2016. https://www.pewresearch.org/fact-tank/2016/10/12/americans-more-tolerant-of-offensive-speech-than-others-in-the-world/

Williams, Pete. "Supreme Court Sends Louisiana Black Lives Matter Lawsuit Back for Another Round." *NBC News*. November 2, 2020. https://www.nbcnews.com/news/us-news/supreme-court-sends-louisiana-black-lives-matter-lawsuit-back-another-n1245758

Williamson, Elizabeth. "Truth in a Post-Truth Era: Sandy Hook Families Sue Alex Jones, Conspiracy Theorist." *New York Times*. 2018.

Winsor, Morgan. "Timeline: WHO's Response to the Coronavirus Pandemic and the Ensuing Controversy." *ABC News*. August 15, 2020. https://abcnews.go.com/Health/timeline-response-coronavirus-pandemic-ensuing-controversy/story?id=71690767

Winter, Jana. "Exclusive: FBI Document Warns Conspiracy Theories Are a New Domestic Terrorism Threat." *Yahoo!News*. August 1, 2019. https://news.yahoo.com/fbi-documents-conspiracy-theories-terrorism-160000507.html

Wirin, A.L., and Samuel Rosenwein. "The Smith Act Score." *Nation* 180, no. 9 (1955): 177–80.

Wong, Queenie and Carrie Mihalcik. "Facebook, Twitter Block Trump Post for Spreading COVID-19 Misinformation." *cnet.com*. October 6, 2020. https://www.cnet.com/news/facebook-twitter-block-trump-post-for-spreading-covid-19-misinformation/

Wood, Mary. "McCarthy Era Offers Cautionary Tale for Post-9/11 America, Stone Says." University of Virginia School of Law, News and Media. April 15, 2004. https://www.law.virginia.edu/news/2004_spr/mccarthy.htm

World Economic Forum. "Digital Wildfires in a Hyperconnected World." WEF Report 2013. http://reports.weforum.org/global-risks-2013/risk-case-1/digital-wildfires-in-a-hyperconnected-world/

Wright, George R. "Hustler Magazine v. Falwell and the Role of the First Amendment." *Cumberland Law Review* 19 (1988): 19–42.

Wyche, Steve. "Colin Kaepernick Explains Why He Sat during National Anthem." *NFL Media*. August 27, 2016. https://www.nfl.com/news/colin-kaepernick-explains-why-he-sat-during-national-anthem-0ap3000000691077

Zick, Timothy. *The First Amendment in the Trump Era*. New York: Oxford University Press, 2019.

INDEX

ABOUT THE AUTHOR

CARI LEE SKOGBERG EASTMAN, PhD, is an independent communication scholar specializing in border and immigration issues. She is also the author of *Immigration: Examining the Facts* (ABC-CLIO, 2017) and *Shaping the Immigration Debate: Contending Civil Societies on the US-Mexico Border* (2012).